FOUNDATION PRESS

CRIMINAL LAW STORIES

Edited By

DONNA COKER

University of Miami
School of Law

and

ROBERT WEISBERG

Stanford Law School

FOUNDATION PRESS
2013

THOMSON REUTERS

© 2013 By THOMSON REUTERS/FOUNDATION PRESS

      1 New York Plaza, 34th Floor

      New York, NY 10004

      Phone Toll Free 1–877–888–1330

      Fax 646–424–5201

      foundation–press.com

Printed in the United States of America

ISBN 978–1–59941–439–3

Mat #40682961

ACKNOWLEDGEMENTS

We thank first the contributors to this volume, whose careful attention to nuance and detail has brought to life the "back stories" collected here. We are grateful, too, for their unflagging patience and good humor through the extended period of time it took to bring this book to press.

Thanks as well to Paul Caron, creator of the Law Stories series, and the Foundation Press team, especially John Bloomquist, for making the book possible.

Tara Lora deserves a medal for her extraordinary administrative support. We are also grateful to Julia Glick who drew on her newspaper past to provide invaluable editing work, and to Meghan Paraschak, who provided invaluable research assistance for the volume.

Donna wishes to thank her co-editor, Bob Weisberg, whose insight, broad expertise, generosity, and unflappable disposition have been invaluable in making this volume a reality. She is grateful to Deans Dennis Lynch and Patricia White for their support. She owes a special debt of gratitude to Tom Dukowitz for his steadfast encouragement.

Bob wishes to thank his co-editor, Donna Coker, for her energy and imagination in widening the circle of authors and subjects, and for possessing that rare combination of grace and relentlessness required to successfully bring such diverse scholars together.

Miami, Florida
and Stanford, California
October 2012

CRIMINAL LAW STORIES

	Page
Introduction	1

Donna Coker & Robert Weisberg

Chapter One:

The Story of *Keller:* The Irrelevance of the Legality
Principle in American Criminal Law   23

Markus D. Dubber

Chapter Two:

The Story of *Robinson*: From Revolutionary
Constitutional Doctrine to Modest Ban on Status
Crimes   47

Erik Luna

Chapter Three:

The Story of *Staples* and the Innocent Machine Gun
Owner: The Good, the Bad and the Dangerous   85

Joseph E. Kennedy

Chapter Four:

The Story of *Berry*: When Hot Blood Cools   129

Susan D. Rozelle

Chapter Five:

"The Look in His Eyes": The Story of *Rusk* and Rape
Reform   171

Jeannie Suk

Chapter Six:

The Story of *Wanrow*: The Reasonable Woman and the
Law of Self–Defense   213

Donna Coker & Lindsay C. Harrison

Page

Chapter Seven:

    The Story of *Clark*: The Incredible Shrinking Insanity
Defense   263

    Janine Young Kim

Chapter Eight:

    The Story of *Jacobson*: Catching Criminals or Creating
Crime?   299

    Gabriel J. Chin

Chapter Nine:

    The Story of *Rizzo*: The Shifting Landscape of
Attempt   329

    Robert Weisberg

Chapter Ten:

    The Story of *Tally*: Judge Tally and the Problem of the
Superfluous Accomplice   373

    Leo Katz

Chapter Eleven:

    The Story of *Rahman*: Religious Advocacy at the
Intersection of Crime and Free Speech   399

    Mario L. Barnes

Chapter Twelve:

    The Story of *Ewing:* Three Strikes Laws and the
Limits of the Eighth Amendment Proportionality
Review   427

    Sara Sun Beale

Biographies of Contributing Authors   465

FOUNDATION PRESS

CRIMINAL LAW STORIES

Introduction

Donna Coker & Robert Weisberg

Beginning law students sometimes have somewhat skewed expectations about the field broadly known as criminal law. Like most people, they have been inundated with literary and media depictions of the criminal justice system, and the most dramatic of such depictions tend to involve police investigations or criminal trials. Thus, it is criminal *procedure* that they are most familiar with, and when they take the course in *substantive* criminal law—in many schools a required first-year course—their reaction is often that it is far more abstract and conceptual than the "real" world of criminal justice they have seen all their lives in popular imagery. This may be even more true for students who actually plan to practice criminal law. For these students, the cases may feel removed from the social and political issues that attract them to the practice—justice for victims, racial fairness, and limitations on state power, for example.

Criminal Law Stories is an effort to bridge this gap between expectations and the realities of criminal justice. Substantive criminal law is an area especially suitable for a "law stories" book precisely because the factual background and social context of its cases offer the most compelling of human dramas, and because in few fields of law is the human drama in the backstory so directly relevant to the legal issues in the cases. In addition, criminal law stories offer compelling examples of the importance of narrative and cultural framing.[1] We are accustomed to recognizing that litigators do well to present jurors with a clear "story"—a compelling narrative of events and individual motivations, but narrative frames are no less important at every other stage of criminal justice decision making. Prosecutors enjoy significant discretion in determining what charges to bring, what plea deals to offer, or whether to even bring charges at all. In making those decisions, prosecutors are likely to be influenced by and subsequently invoke a narrative that weaves the facts into a consistent persuasive story. The prosecutor's

---

1. As Jonathan Simon notes in describing judicial use of narrative, "The study of case law that consumes American Criminal Law classes is all about how judges use somewhat different techniques to bring facts and law together through the manipulation of culture, such as the ensemble of narratives that provide categories of meaning available in a particular historically specific society." Jonathan Simon, *Teaching Criminal Law in An Era of Governing Through Crime*, 48 St. Louis U. L.J. 1313, 1334 (2004).

narrative may reflect a larger narrative—a cultural frame in which an individual crime becomes part of a larger social phenomenon[2] or it may reflect a "stock story,"[3] a culturally resonant narrative that reflects common social understandings. Prosecutors and defense counsel are not the only ones to use stories. Law reform activists, legislators, judges, and occasionally even the defendant him or herself, similarly attempt to exploit cultural frames.[4] Many of the stories collected in this volume highlight these framing choices and the limits to those choices created by culture and law.

The stories told here reflect three major legal movements that have dramatically influenced the shape of today's criminal law as well as the social understanding of crime. The first movement is one that is essen-

---

2. *See* Kay L. Levine, *The Intimacy Discount: Prosecutorial Discretion, Privacy, and Equality in the Statutory Rape Caseload*, 55 Emory L.J. 691 (2006) (California prosecutors developed typologies to determine which statutory rape cases deserved to be prosecuted, distinguishing between those perpetrators they identified as "predators" versus those identified as partners in intimate relationships.) Narrative is no less important for cases that result in a plea bargain, in which "[d]efense counsel makes normative arguments as to why the prosecutor should come down on the charges, and the prosecutor makes similar arguments as to why the defense should settle for the charges on the table. Those arguments will appeal to fairness or to consequences—those ancient and abstract ideas of retribution and utility...." Donald A. Dripps, *On Cases, Casebooks, and the Real World of Criminal Justice: A Brief Response to Anders Walker*, 7 Ohio St. J. Crim. L. 257, 259–59 (2009).

3. See Gerald P. Lopez, *Lay Lawyering*, 32 UCLA L. Rev. 1, 3 (1984) ("To solve a problem through persuasion of another, we ... must understand and manipulate the stock stories the other person uses in order to tell a plausible and compelling story....") Social cognition research underscores the importance of largely unconscious heuristics in the interpretations that individuals give to events. *See, e.g.,* Dan M. Kahan, David A. Hoffman, and Donald Braman, *Whose Eyes Are You Going to Believe? Scott v. Harris and the Perils of Cognitive Illiberalism* (individual determinations of risk are subject to "value-motivated cognition," the "tendency ... to resolve factual ambiguities in a manner that generates conclusions congenial to self-defining values"). The expression of bias—notably racial, gender, and class, in the development of "stock stories" is explored by a number of scholars. *See, e.g.,* Katheryn K. Russell, *The Color of Crime: Racial Hoaxes, White Fear, Black Protectionism, Police Harassment, and Other Microaggressions* (1998). As the cases of exoneration demonstrate, individuals can become so wedded to a particular narrative that they cling to it in the face of contrary facts. Barry Scheck, Peter Neufeld, & Jim Dwyer, *Actual Innocence: When Justice Goes Wrong and How to Make It Right* (2001). For a discussion of the ways in which law shapes individual narratives (and identity) as well as society, *see* Guyora Binder and Robert Weisberg, *Cultural Criticism of Law*, 49 Stan. L. Rev. 1149 (1997).

4. The alleged victim often has less opportunity to frame a story. With the exception of Susan Rozelle's description of Rachel Pessah (*The Story of* Berry), there is very little of the victim's story in this volume. Their silence in this volume is not unique. Despite the advent of "victim impact statements" and other efforts to "give voice to victims," victims often continue to feel misunderstood and not "heard." See generally, Susan L. Miller, *After the Crime: the Power of Restorative Justice Dialogues Between Victims and Violent Offenders* (2011).

tially internal to the law—the doctrinal evolution from the common law to contemporary codification associated with the rise of the Model Penal Code. The evolution has been an effort to transform the somewhat loose language and broad moralistic definitions of common law crimes into a more technical and coordinated scheme of criminal law elements. These elements are rooted in rational social policy and rely on calibrated enumerations of cognitive states that serve as proxies for moral culpability. The stages of this transition are captured, for example, in *The Story of* Rizzo, depicting the movement in the area of attempt law from the common law to MPC paradigms. In addition, the strong but often fitful effort to refine our taxonomy of mental states and to determine the proper criteria for culpability is captured in *The Story of* Staples.

But equally pervasive have been movements that change legal doctrine from the outside. One has been the "tough on crime" phenomenon of the last few decades, of which the "victim's rights" movement is sometimes understood to be a part.[5] By "tough on crime" we refer to a combination of legislative changes and law enforcement priorities that include increasingly long prison sentences and mandatory minimums, "three strikes" legislation that ratchets up punishment for recidivists, increasing resort to criminal punishment for a broad range of social ills,[6] and aggressive drug enforcement policies largely focused on racial minority neighborhoods.[7] As a result of these policies, the U.S. inmate population has experienced a staggering six-fold increase since the 1970s.[8] With more than two million people behind bars, the U.S. incarceration rate is higher than that of any other country.[9] Another five million individuals

---

5. The phenomenon has been variously described by its critics as "The Culture of Control," "The Carceral State," "Governing through Crime," "The New Jim Crow," and "Prison Nation." *See* David Garland, *The Culture of Control: Crime and Social Order in a Contemporary Society* (2001); Marie Gottschalk, *The Prison and the Gallows: The Politics of Mass Incarceration* (2005); Jonathan Simon, *Governing Through Crime: How the War on Crime Transformed American Democracy and Created a Culture of Fear* (2007); Michelle Alexander, *The New Jim Crow: Mass Incarceration in the Age of Colorblindness (2010)*; Beth E. Richie, *Arrested Justice: Black Women, Violence, and America's Prison Nation (2012)*.

6. *See, e.g.,* Simon, *id.* at 21–22 ("[T]he importance the state has assigned to crime nudges out other kinds of opportunities that a different hierarchy of public problems might produce—*e.g.,* a government obsessed with governing by educating would produce all kinds of incentives to define various people as efficient or deficient in education, capable or incapable, and so on.")

7. *See, e.g.,* Tracey L. Meares, *Norms, Legitimacy and Law Enforcement*, 79 Or. L. Rev. 391 (2000); Jeffrey Fagan, *et al., Reciprocal Effects of Crime and Incarceration in New York City Neighborhoods*, 30 Fordham Urban L.J. 1551 (2003).

8. Marie Gottschalk, *The Past, Present, and Future of Mass Incarceration in the United States*, 10(3) Criminology & Public Policy 483 (2011).

9. Roy Walmsley, *World Prison Population List*, International Centre for Prison Studies (9th edition 2011). The U.S. prison population rate of 743 per 100,000 is highest

are on probation, parole, or some other form of state supervision.[10] Incarceration rates are marked by shocking racial disparities: African American men are imprisoned at a rate seven times that of white men; African American women are imprisoned at a rate nearly three times that of white women.[11] Though African Americans make up about 13% of the U.S. population, they are nearly 40% of male prisoners and 25% of female prisoners.[12] Despite social science evidence that a significant amount of this disparity is the result of differential enforcement and racial bias rather than differential offending, the Supreme Court has rejected claims that racially disparate outcomes violate Constitutional guarantees of equal protection.[13]

The impact of this move to more punitiveness in the definition and interpretation of criminal doctrines is reflected in a number of the cases described in this volume: *The Story of* Clark (insanity defense), *The Story of* Rahman (conspiracy), and *The Story of* Ewing ("three strikes" legislation and the Eighth Amendment).

The third major influence on criminal law evident in this collection is the feminist movement of the 1970s, particularly in the areas of law that address "gendered violence." The influence of feminist analysis and activism on changes in law and social consciousness is apparent in *The Story of* Rusk (rape), *The Story of* Berry (heat of passion), and *The Story of* Wanrow (self-defense). Together, these chapters illustrate the significant efforts of feminists to expose the male lens through which concepts such as "reasonableness" were constructed, an effort that became part of a larger change in criminal law doctrine to understand "reasonableness" in more individualized terms, with more attention to the specific cultural context within which the accused's behavior arose.[14]

---

among the 218 independent countries and dependent territories included in the study, followed by Rwanda (595), Russia (568), Georgia (547), U.S. Virgin Islands (539), and Seychelles (507). *Id.* at 1. There are several limitations to the study: data from seven countries was not available for comparison; the data represented numbers ranging from the end of 2008 through the beginning of 2011; for the most part, only incarceration that occurred under the authority of the prison administration was included. Using a different methodology and focused only on data from one year, the DOJ reported a U.S. incarceration rate of 500 per 100,000 for the year 2010. *See* Paul Guerino, Paige M. Harrison, and William J. Sabol, *Prisoners in 2010*, U.S. Dep't of Justice, OJP, BJS, NCJ 236096 (Dec. 2011) at 1.

    10. *See,* Gottschalk, *supra* note 8 at 489.

    11. *See,* Guerino, *et al.*, *supra* note 9 at 7.

    12. *See, id.* at 26.

    13. *See generally*, Donna Coker, *Addressing the Real World of Racial Injustice in the Criminal Justice System*, 93 J. Crim. L. & Criminol. 827 (2003).

    14. Despite significant changes in doctrine, several scholars argue that these changes are incomplete and that the paradigm for "reasonableness" continues to be white,

There remains one final reason that substantive criminal law is a particularly good fit for a "law stories" collection: it is hard to imagine a field of law whose study would benefit more from the "humanizing" effects of rich storytelling. Popular culture is replete with stories of the pain suffered by violent crime victims and their loved ones. Less familiar are the human consequences of involvement in the criminal justice system for the accused and their loved ones. Those convicted of crime are frequently understood in popular culture to be the "incorrigibles"—some even say that the dominant metaphor for today's criminal justice system is that of "waste management."[15] By providing a human dimension to these stories, many of the stories place the most important morality questions in deeply personal human terms.

* * *

In a sense, the challenge of substantive criminal law is straightforward. Any society will have some consensus about what actions are either so immoral or so risky or so destructive as to merit criminal prohibition. But at what level of generality should legislatures write prohibitions, when these punishment-worthy actions are so varied and unpredictable? If a legislature could anticipate every specific example of such action it could write a code listing them. But this is a ludicrously quixotic idea. Any such enumeration would be both insanely long and woefully underinclusive, and would invite creative efforts to engage in conduct that falls in the cracks among items on the list. Conversely, a legislature could enact a simple code making it a crime "to commit any act that causes or threatens harm to society, unless the person can present a plausible excuse or justification for the act" and allow the court (or jury) to determine the proper punishment "upon consideration of all relevant factors." But such a law would surely run afoul of the Constitution on the void-for-vagueness principle, which holds that a law violates due process if it is so vague as to deny the populace clear notice of what behavior is forbidden and if it invites arbitrary or prejudiced enforcement and interpretation by the officials to whom it grants power.[16]

Instead, a criminal code that purports to be based on democratic ideals must strike a balance with mid-level generalizations about punishable behavior. It must strive to describe human actions in categories that are sufficiently specific so as to give fair warning and curb government excess, while remaining flexible enough to capture all the nuances of action and motivation with which humans operate. And those generaliza-

---

heterosexual, and male. *See, e.g.,* Cynthia Lee, *Murder and the Reasonable Man: Passion and Fear in the Criminal Courtroom* (2003).

   15.   Simon, *supra* note 5 at 142.

   16.   *See* Chicago v. Morales, 527 U.S. 41 (1999).

tions must be framed within an overall structure that establishes general criteria for the acts and mental states that constitute the key elements of crime. Such a code must group certain types of offenses into coherent clusters, like homicide and theft. It must develop principles of attribution, such as attempt and complicity, determining when to hold persons liable for offenses for which they are not the direct or successful perpetrators. And of course it may provide for affirmative defenses—justification and excuse—that negate liability for a wide variety of these crimes.

But any overall structure of criminal prohibitions requires some foundational principles, and some of the cases examined in this volume are about very individualized stories that happen to provoke questions about these principles. One can sum up these foundational principles as follows: Punishment can only be imposed for a past, voluntary act, specified by statute. This meta-statement then breaks down into several key components. There can be no punishment for mere thought, however malevolent. There can be no punishment to prevent an act that is merely a matter of contemplation. The predicate for punishment must be an action, as opposed to a status or condition.[17] The act must be the result of actual volition, not the appearance of an act due to some mere reflex. To avoid the bar on ex post facto laws, the act must have been designated as criminal in advance, normally by a law expressed in a statute, and, to respect the void-for-vagueness doctrine, that law must achieve at least a minimal level of clarity.[18]

Markus Dubber's essay on *Commonwealth v. Keller*[19] might be described as a foundational critique of this foundation. *Keller* deals with one of the key components of the foundation, the so-called "rule of legality." This rule dictates that the law condemning the act must be in a statute, not merely common law judicial doctrine. There are many cases asserting that principle, but Dubber picks a case that stands out for going the other way—authorizing common law crime definition by common law evolution. Like so many important criminal cases, it arises in tragic and obscure circumstances that just happen to expose a legal problem demanding resolution by appellate courts. A desperate woman is suspected of killing her child, but the cause of death is too unclear to

---

17. On the other hand, there can be punishment for an omission to act where action is required by some legal duty. *See* Jones v. United States, 308 F.2d 307 (1962) (duty can arise from an express requirement in a statute, certain preexisting status or familial relationships, or certain contractual or voluntarily assumed duties to protect another).

18. We can add to these criteria a requirement that the actual or threatened harm of the act be one that lies within the constitutional power of the state to prevent. *See* Lawrence v. Texas, 539 U.S. 558 (2003) (right of privacy immunizes from punishment consensual sexual activity between adults).

19. 35 Pa. D. & C.2d 615 (1964).

prove murder, so the prosecution clutches at another charge—"indecent disposition of a corpse." The court assumes it has authority to wield its judicial artistry to infer a customary basis for this charge, drawing on cases from other states and from religious and cultural traditions.

The issue of whether judges can define crimes is usually posed as a question of separation or allocation of powers. But in Dubber's view, *Keller* reaches farther back into our jurisprudence to establish the rationale for how *any* organ of the state can claim authority to impose criminal punishment. He traces the rationale to that venerable phrase "the police power," the general authority of all governments to secure the peace. Dubber explains that this power lies in the *pater familias* status of the sovereign under monarchal law, a principle that was incorporated into American law without careful consideration of how it translated into a non-monarchal democracy. Dubber then reviews the principle of legality, along with such related matters as the ex post facto principle (the only one of these explicitly in the Constitution whereby a person cannot be punished for an act if the law condemning it comes after the act, the void for vagueness principle, and such related notions as the rule of lenity) by which ambiguous laws should be construed against the government. Dubber argues that these supposedly sacred principles are not rooted in any coherent principle defining the power of the state to punish under the modern democratic ideal of the self-governing individual. Instead, he argues, these restrictions simply reflect discretionary decisions in American jurisprudence to limit the frighteningly broad police power, and he therefore finds fascinating cases like *Keller* where the power of common law crime definition is upheld. Although, as he notes, Pennsylvania ultimately joined the modern chorus of jurisdictions forbidding such common law crime definition, the case is a stern reminder of how the police power remains the great underlying principle of criminal law generally, and even though these limitations purport to replace it with a rule of law, that rule of law remains a set of discretionary principles that lie at the heart of our system of broad police power.

The requirement that punishable conduct be voluntary would seem to be uncontroversial, especially in the constitutionally attractive form of rejecting punishment for status or condition. Yet as Erik Luna shows with the famous case of *Robinson v. California*,[20] defining voluntariness has been a stubborn challenge for our legal system. In *Robinson*, the Court rebuffed California's effort to punish someone for being a drug addict, because to do so is to punish him for what he is, not for what he has done. Robinson offers powerful moral rhetoric—as Justice Stewart famously said, "[e]ven one day in prison would be a cruel and unusual

---

20. 370 U.S. 660 (1962).

punishment for the 'crime' of having a common cold."[21] But the complex
narrative of Lawrence Robinson illustrates the difficulty of separating a
person's state of being from his actions when the two are causally
intertwined. Lawrence Robinson used narcotics a fair amount, but it
took some broad inferences to say he was an addict and in turn, some
might argue that he took drugs *because* he was an addict. Some thought
the California statute was just a jurisdictional device to help convict
people for *using* drugs when it was hard to establish the time and place
of any actual ingestion. But the case soon crystallized some deep questions in American law.

First, *Robinson* was a landmark in the long American debate about
whether, and how, to punish "morals crimes" that might not be harmful, at least to anyone other than the person charged. Second, the case
indirectly raised broad civil liberty concerns, because going after drug
addicts may have been a pretext for going after unruly and threateningly
antisocial figures. That concern was especially salient at a time when the
old-fashioned vagrancy laws were losing force, in part because they were
being struck down as void for vagueness. Further, of course, Robinson's
appeal raised a general concern about how much we allow scientific
explanations of diseases and involuntary conditions to challenge the
criminal law's presumptions about free will. Finally, when Robinson
framed his claim under the Eighth Amendment, he invited the Court to
make a rare foray into invoking the Constitution to control substantive
criminal definitions by the states, as opposed to the more common
application to criminal procedures. On all of these counts, when Robinson won in the Supreme Court there were predictions that the decision
would prove to be a very dramatic precedent. It would allow far more
illness-based excuses for crime and would represent a greater move
toward constitutional constraints on criminal law making. But as Luna
shows, having stepped up to or just over some major brinks, the Court
immediately pulled back. In the follow-up case of *Powell v. Texas*,[22] the
Court seemed to allow punishment of almost any observable behavior
that could arguably be described as voluntary conduct, even if that
conduct seemed to be entailed by a condition or disease. As such,
Robinson stands as a case where the Court frightened itself into drawing
a sharp line between legislative and constitutional power over the
definition of crimes, and made clear that if there was to be a close
scientific scrutiny of the voluntariness of behavior, that was a matter for
legislation, not grand deontological principle.

Paralleling the much-declaimed act requirement is the principle that
there can be no crime without a mens rea—some evil state of mind. As
with the act requirement, this is an important and meaningful principle,
so long as it is not expected to translate into any simple rule or formula.

---

21. *Id.* at 667.

22. 392 U.S. 514 (1968).

Common law courts required there be some culpable mental state that accompanied or animated the harmful act, but they were notoriously unsystematic about how to define and identify the exact nature of that mental state. For centuries Anglo–American law spoke of two levels of mens rea, called specific and general intent, but the definitions of those terms were never very settled, and even when crimes were set by legislatures, many statutes used evocative but imprecise common law terms like "willfully." At the far end of this historical spectrum, the Model Penal Code insisted on the need to assign carefully defined and calibrated mental states, not just to a crime in its entirety, but to each material element of the crime—including any act, result, or circumstance, and it enumerated the mental states as purpose, knowledge, recklessness, and negligence.[23] But most jurisdictions are still caught somewhere in between the old common law and the high-tech MPC. Legislatures still pass laws that are silent, ambiguous, or vague in their required mental states, in part because the question of what mental state to assign is so fraught with moral, cultural, and various utilitarian questions. Those quandaries are well illustrated in federal criminal law, as told in Joseph Kennedy's recounting of the *Staples* case. The charge in *Staples v. United States*[24] lay right in the vortex of all these issues. Harold Staples was indicted under a statute that forbade possession of a machine gun, but Congress not only failed to provide a precise definition of such a gun, it gave courts and prosecutors no guidance at all on the mental state required.

Although the mens rea dilemma is often put as a choice between "strict liability" and criminal intent, the dilemma is rarely so starkly binary. Virtually no court would read this statute as punishing someone who was handed a box and told it contained a violin if it turned out to contain a machine gun instead. But if we require mens rea, of what level, and about what? Was it enough that the nature of the object put Staples on notice that the gun might be classified as a machine gun? Did the prosecution have to show that Staples knew it was so classified? That he would not have wanted the gun unless it was truly a machine gun? And what if Staples knew it was a machine gun but sincerely believed there was no law against possessing it, thus raising the classic problem of ignorance of law versus ignorance of fact. Courts facing statutes like this struggle with these questions, and they have relied on some general criteria, as *Staples* illustrates. In construing federal statutes, the Court has roughly delineated crimes into so-called *malum in se* or traditional crimes, where a high degree of culpability is required, and *malum prohibitum* or public welfare crimes, where the inherent danger necessi-

---

23. *See* Model Penal Code and Commentaries, sections 2.02–2.04 (1985).

24. 511 U.S. 600 (1994).

tates a lower mens rea.[25] But these distinctions and criteria are very slippery, and the Court often finds itself worrying over just how inherently dangerous a type of conduct is, whether its inherent danger necessarily puts the actor on notice of the harm, whether heedlessness of that danger is itself a moral flaw, and whether the severity of the penalty attached to a crime signals what the mens rea should be. Moreover, as with the dispute over gun control that lies in the background of *Staples*, social and cultural perceptions of the legitimacy of the conduct at issue bear on whether it carries with it some indicium of moral violation. The *Staples* Court's compromise solution well illustrates the perennial challenges of mens rea analysis by court and implicitly, mens rea definition by legislatures.

Criminal Law Stories then turns to some specific criminal laws, because the general principles of the criminal law are best illustrated in their nuances in the context of particular types of criminal conduct. Two of the classic areas are homicide and rape.

Homicide is of course the most serious of crimes, but it is also at first glance the simplest analytically. Because its key element is simply causing a death, all the analytic action is on the side of mens rea. But no crime has a more complex menu of mens rea calibrations to offer than homicide. Although we distinguish murder from manslaughter by the criterion of "malice aforethought," that term tells us little. Traditionally, a crime is first-degree and potentially capital murder if it is done intentionally and with that enhanced kind of intent called premeditation. Otherwise a homicide can be murder if it is committed with unpremeditated intent or very gross recklessness, and anything less in terms of ordinary recklessness or negligence is a species of involuntary manslaughter. The controversial felony murder rule allows for the possibility of even a negligent homicide becoming murder if it is caused in the course of committing a dangerous felony, such as robbery, rape, or burglary. But felony murder is not the only oddity of homicide mens rea. Perhaps the subtlest is the category of heat of passion or "adequate provocation," that while not a full defense, can mitigate an otherwise intentional murder to voluntary manslaughter and thereby remove the component of "malice." No doctrine is so morally and psychologically controversial, and as rooted in such historical specific conditions and values, as heat of passion. And as Susan Rozelle shows, a modern case of domestic violence like *People v. Berry*,[26] can exhibit deep roots in our cultural history. At its origins, this mitigation principle applied only in fairly well-defined categories, including a provocative assault, but most notoriously where an angry husband found his wife in the act of adultery

---

25.   Morissette v. United States, 342 U.S. 246 (1952).

26.   18 Cal. 3d 509 (1976).

and killed her or her paramour. This latter may strike readers as an embarrassing moral anachronism,[27] but one arguable virtue of the common law is that by relying on fixed categories, it limited the provocation doctrine so as not to mitigate too many homicides simply because the defendant claimed some right to feel anger or outrage.

Those fixed categories have now come to fade away. Voluntary manslaughter law has changed in recent decades and thereby manifested one of the larger, key themes in criminal law. Criminal law, like other fields, relies heavily on the notion of the reasonable person. The figure of the reasonable person had once been an abstraction or some bland demographic average. Early courts addressed the question whether the reasonable person encompassed an adult standard, or whether when the defendant was a juvenile the jury should instead be instructed to take age into consideration in determining whether his conduct was reasonable. Later critics noted that the purported generic reasonableness standard, in fact, frequently incorporated a "male" and "white" standard. A trend emerged in the area of manslaughter as elsewhere to understand reasonableness in more specific cultural contexts, and with special attention to identify factors like gender and particular social situations. A major challenge in this evolution of the reasonable person in criminal law has been to "contextualize" the reasonable person without turning the objective test of reasonableness into a pure measure of subjective feeling. The bizarre narrative of sex and violence contained in Berry is a remarkable test of these issues.

On the one hand, Albert Berry very slowly developed an animus against his wife and, after assaulting her twice before, ultimately carried out a homicidal plan by strangling her. On the other hand, he acted in a fit of outrage over provocative remarks she made to him, his passion culminating when she began screaming. The trial judge denied him a voluntary manslaughter instruction, ruling that his twenty hour wait before killing Rachel was sufficient cooling off to preclude heat of passion. He was convicted of murder. Had the judge taken a noble step toward ensuring that women received the equal protection of homicide law? Or had the judge been overly rigid and psychologically obtuse in not allowing Berry a chance to persuade the jury that a reasonable person in his situation would have been provoked? Equally controversial, was the decision of the trial judge to allow extensive testimony by a psychiatrist who asserted that the decedent, a woman he had never met, had been motivated by her own suicidal desires to so torture the defendant with

---

27. Victoria Nourse's study of Model Penal Code jurisdictions, however, found that the "provocation" engendered by a female partner's sexual infidelity remains powerful in modern MPC jurisdictions, and that the meaning of provocation under the more liberal MPC definition has frequently included cases where the decedent's only provocative act was to leave a relationship with the defendant. Victoria Nourse, *Passion's Progress: Modern Law Reform and the Provocation Defense,* 106 Yale L.J. 1331(1997).

talk of her adultery as to cause him to kill her. When the California Supreme Court held that Berry was entitled to a voluntary manslaughter instruction, was this a social advance recognizing the complexity of human motivation? Or did the Court invite all manner of illicit human motivation to mitigate intentional murder and invite junk psychiatric science to excuse people for their meretricious emotions? The more flexible "contextual" *Berry* doctrine, paralleled by the MPC's own rule for heat-of-passion manslaughter,[28] may represent the enhanced psychological sophistication of American law, but it may also reflect the moral cost of such sophistication.

Homicide law compels us because of the complexity with which it examines the thinking and feeling of the individual defendant. With greater prosecutorial willingness to charge "acquaintance rapes," rape law has now become similarly compelling when it confronts us with the mutual perceptions and feelings of two people. As we turn to rape law, there is an ironic link back to the *Berry* case, because one of the controversial aspects of that case was whether Berry's defense was to put his female victim on trial—the very concern that has traditionally plagued rape trials.

Rape might be defined, with superficial confidence, as sexual intercourse without the consent of one of the parties. But perhaps no term in criminal law has been subject to greater doctrinal distortions and vagaries as "consent" in the context of a rape charge. The stock story of modern rape law would run as follows: Well into the twentieth century the term "consent" was something of a misnomer. By long tradition, there could be no rape conviction unless the complainant offered up the "utmost resistance"—and that meant risking her life to save her honor. Anything less than a risk of death in resistance was presumed to mean the woman had "consented" to sex. Other rules compounded the difficulty of proving rape, including the right of the defendant to delve into the sexual history of the complainant and the requirement that the complainant have made an immediate report of the attack to be credible. Especially as the feminist movement arose in the 1960s and 1970s, things changed by statute, judicial decision, and social attitude. The utmost resistance requirement was redefined to something called "reasonable resistance." Before long, in some jurisdictions any reference to "resistance" disappeared, with laws only requiring that there be "force" or simply phrasing rape in terms of absence of consent or even lack of affirmative expression of consent.

---

28. MPC section 210.3 (murder reduced to manslaughter if "committed under the influence of extreme mental or emotional disturbance for which there is reasonable explanation or excuse," and "reasonableness . . . shall be determined from the viewpoint of a person in the actor's situation under the circumstances as he believes them to be").

By that time, most discussion of rape doctrine came to focus on so called "date rape" or "acquaintance rape" cases where consent was often a very nuanced issue on the facts of particular cases. *State v. Rusk*[29] is one of the great transitional cases of this kind. In these cases, an acquaintance—often a new acquaintance—of the complainant has intercourse with her under circumstances that he characterizes as at worst aggressive seduction, followed by her retroactive remorse and contrived claim of rape. The complainant in turn characterizes the encounter as forcible rape, with her avoiding physical resistance out of fear of greater harm. Tied up in these cases as well is the developing social science evidence both as to what degree of resistance a truly nonconsenting woman would offer and what it is safe for her to offer. As Jeannie Suk describes it, the credibility of the conflicting stories in *Rusk* is mirrored in the case's tortured movement through the trial and appellate courts. When the rape conviction was finally affirmed, we saw a key step toward the modern rape law, so much more complainant- and prosecution-friendly than the old law. But because these subtleties of mutual expression and perception are so complex, it is inevitable that the case turns not so much on formal doctrinal language and jury instructions as on the very old-fashioned notion that appellate courts should defer to jury fact-finding. In any event, the deep moral and cultural divisions about the distinction between "seduction" and "rape" persist, as courts claim authority to understand the natural or reasonable responses of women to sexual threat in weighing the evidentiary value of those responses to the determination of force or non-consent.

Despite the outcome of the case, a great number of the state's appellate judges thought Rusk had not been proved a rapist, as illustrated by the somewhat infamous statement of one dissenter with regard to what he expects of a woman:

> She may not simply say, "I was really scared," and thereby transform consent or mere unwillingness into submission by force. These words do not transform a seducer into a rapist. She must follow the natural instinct of every proud female to resist, by more than mere words, the violation of her person by a stranger or an unwelcomed friend. She must make it plain that she regards such sexual acts as abhorrent and repugnant to her natural sense of pride.[30]

Modern rape law has diminished the respectability, but hardly has erased the influence, of such an attitude.

Self-defense is perhaps the paradigm of justification defenses. Moreover, in recent decades the paradigm situations for deeper examination of the doctrines of self-defense have been the so-called battered wives' or

29. 424 A.2d 720 (Md. 1981).

30. *Id.* at 733.

battered women's cases. The case of a woman using violence to protect herself from domestic abuse has been the key test case for refining our understanding of when a defendant's fear of imminent death or serious bodily injury is reasonable. As with voluntary manslaughter, the challenge has been to guide juries to view the perceptions of fatal threat in the context of gender and the relational situation, without resort to dangerous stereotyping, and without converting the desirable objectivity of reasonableness into a test of pure subjectivity. Under classic doctrine, if a person sincerely but unreasonably believes that killing someone is necessary to save herself from a fatal threat, then the outcome should be so-called imperfect self-defense and hence voluntary manslaughter, not the complete exoneration that true self-defense supplies. As depicted by Donna Coker, the saga of *State v. Wanrow*[31] became the iconic case of this kind. Yet ironically, it is not a battered women's case. Yvonne Wanrow was surely hoping to protect herself from the man she killed. She was equally engaged in the related act of defense of others—her children—in the face of a threat by a man who she believed had molested her neighbor's child and had threatened to molest her own son. The man was not her spouse or partner, nor had he ever assaulted her. But the issue in the case was the same core issue at the heart of the battered women's cases: Whether she was entitled to a jury instruction alerting the jury to take into account her gendered experience. In Wanrow's case this included her experience as a woman, one who had reason from her personal and social experience not to trust the police to protect her, and one who had no training in using her fists to defend herself from a much larger male attacker. Wanrow's defense counsel argued that she received an unfair trial because the court's instruction encouraged the jury to view her actions from the standpoint of a man facing another man of equal strength.

Wanrow's appellate victory spurred future successful claims of battered women that they too should get a contextual instruction. Post-*Wanrow* claimants also won the right to introduce expert psychological evidence to educate juries on what were rational responses to threats when made by an abusive spouse in the context of a battering relationship.[32] *Wanrow*, then, led us to the dramatically new understanding of self-defense, and of the situational nature of reasonableness, that are now staples of a criminal law course.

Recall that one of the foundational principles of the act requirement in criminal law is that there can be no punishment for mere thought.

---

31. 559 P.2d 548 (1977).

32. United States v. Ibn–Tamas, 407 A.2d 626 (D.C. Ct. App. 1979). Wanrow herself was partly denied this benefit. The appellate court held that she was not entitled to expert testimony on the question of how her background in Native American culture also influenced her response to the threat.

But of course that principle hardly requires that every crime result in harm. Although possible or intended harm would seem to underlie most criminal legislation, many laws punish "harmless" crimes—not just in the sense of morals crimes where social harm is philosophically controversial, but in the cluster of inchoate crimes that includes attempt, conspiracy and solicitation, but also of course such deceptively inchoate crimes as possession and drunk-driving.

Wanrow illustrates how a combination of statutory law, statutory interpretation, and a touch of common law evolution can alter and expand justification defenses in light of changes in our psychological and social understanding of human perception. It also, at least indirectly, led to the vindication of scientific, indeed social-scientific, expertise in helping jurors understand those perceptions. As related by Janine Kim's account of *Clark v. Arizona*,[33] Eric Clark's experience with the insanity defense was just the opposite in a number of ways. Clark killed a police officer, apparently believing that the officer came from another planet. Clark was not seeking to justify his crime—he was seeking to excuse it. If self-defense is the paradigm justification defense, insanity is the paradigm excuse. Of course, no social good came from Clark's killing of a police officer; he conceded it was a criminal act, but one for which he argued he was not responsible. Further, whereas Wanrow's triumph was one under evolving state law, Clark's defeat in the Supreme Court was in terms of constitutional law. And in that regard, it was no surprise. At its core, the *Clark* decision simply ratifies that as with other areas of criminal law, the federal Constitution imposes few constraints on the substantive side. But the ups and downs of Clark's legal story illustrate the larger vagaries of the insanity defense as it now arises in state law. The story epitomizes the historical struggle our system has faced in dealing with the relationship between insanity and conventional mens rea, and the role we are willing to allow psychiatric expertise to play in criminal law.

The state conceded that Clark suffered from paranoid schizophrenia, the illness that most often "qualifies" someone for a not guilty by reason of insanity ("NGI") verdict. But the criteria for an NGI verdict have a tortured history. Once there was the *M'Naghten* rule, limiting the insanity defense to cases where the criminal did not know the nature or the wrongfulness of his act. Then in the mid–20th century many jurisdictions made their laws more lenient. Some allowed for insanity acquittals where the crime was the product of severe mental illness. Others softened *M'Naghten* by allowing the defense where even if the defendant "knew" the wrongfulness of his act he did not fully "appreciate it." Then after John Hinckley's attempted assassination of Ronald Reagan in 1981, the pendulum swung back to *M'Naghten*, and in states like

---

33. 548 U.S. 735 (2006).

Arizona even farther. Arizona abolished the cognitive prong of *M'Naght-en*, and Clark, believing that this change weakened his legitimate insanity defense, asked the Supreme Court to conclude that at least the traditional, severe *M'Naghten* test was part of our fundamental liberties protected by the federal constitution.

This the Court would not do, in effect holding that there is no constitutional right to an insanity defense. But Arizona had done something else—subtler and equally significant. Over the years many defendants had tried an end-run around the tough restrictions and burden of proof of insanity by introducing expert psychiatric testimony to rebut the prosecution's case that the defendant exhibited the required mens rea. So if Eric Clark thought the police officer was a Martian and also suffered from other agonizing delusions, he could not even form the intent required for murder. This alternative approach could even have constitutional status, were we to view this use of psychiatric expert evidence as part of the due process right to proof beyond a reasonable doubt. But the Supreme Court also found no constitutional fault in this Arizona restriction, at least in disallowing expert testimony on the issue if the testimony was based on expert opinion and not direct clinical observation. While the *Clark* opinion can be read as yet another case of constitutional non-intervention into substantive criminal law, it also serves to illustrate more fundamental doubts about what psychiatric science can teach us and more conceptually whether it is possible for someone to intend a criminal result and yet not be psychologically responsible for it.

One more affirmative defense, entrapment, falls into a unique category. It is at best an excuse—not a justification—but unlike other affirmative defenses it sits on the border between substantive criminal law and criminal procedure. This unusual character is due to the source of the defense—the fact that it was the police who arguably caused the crime. Indeed, in one of its formulations entrapment is sometimes viewed as a doctrine of procedure: Under the so-called "objective" test, if the criminal conduct resulted from police action that on its own terms is outrageously unfair, then even if the defendant committed the bad act with the requisite mens rea, there was no crime. But the objective test is actually the minority rule in America, and the reason may be that its procedural rationale is shaky. This is because when the police set up a sting, or otherwise try to induce someone to commit a crime, they are not crossing any Fourth or Fifth Amendment threshold that would require anything like probable cause.

So instead, the majority rule is the so-called "subjective" test, which fits more comfortably into substantive criminal law because it is a subtle kind of mens rea doctrine. That subtlety is well illustrated in Gabriel Chin's retelling of the almost poignant story of *Jacobson v. United*

States,[34] the case of a quiet, otherwise law-abiding fellow who succumbed to a postal authority sting. Even though Jacobson exhibited the required mens rea of clear intent or knowledge that he was examining child pornography—Jacobson claimed he had not been "predisposed" to do so until the government induced in him this state of mind.

Was Jacobson a low-life pervert who simply took advantage of a prurient opportunity the government provided him? Was he an innocent, if eccentric person, goaded into committing a crime he was otherwise not likely to ever commit? Does it matter that his earlier interest in certain pornographic material—before the government goaded him—would strike most as immorally prurient, though it was not yet technically a federal crime? Do we evaluate the defendant's proclivity for criminal behavior from the first moment that the government communicates with him, or only starting at the point that a clear act of inducement to a specific crime occurs? Is there a kind of estoppel principle where, as here, the government not only goads a person into doing the act but also pummels him with propaganda about why that act should be legal under the First Amendment? More broadly, are aggressive law enforcement tactics examples of the government actually *creating* crime? The surprising Supreme Court decision in *Jacobson* allowing the entrapment defense—and making it good as a matter of law in some cases and not just something to be argued to the jury—makes entrapment one of the most intriguing of criminal law doctrines.

The areas of attempt, complicity, and conspiracy deal with different problems, but at their common core is a question about causation: What happens if the defendant intends or risks a criminal harm but cannot be proved to have caused it—when can we still assign liability to her? Analytically the simplest area is attempt, where by definition the feared harm does not occur. Recall that one of the foundational principles of the act requirement is that there can be no punishment for merely contemplating harm, but that principle nonetheless allows punishment for attempt, so long as some modicum of action occurs. The common law produced a wide variety of tests for how much action is sufficient to go from mere "preparation" to attempt. In evaluating which of these rules works best, one might first ask what role the required action plays. Does overt action itself, even if it fails to reach the object, cause real harm, perhaps by stirring social fear? Or is the point that an action can establish punishable attempt when it comes so close to the last act, possibly as the last or penultimate step, so that as a matter of probability, we can be confident that the actor would have continued to the end had he not been thwarted by some exogenous force? Or is the heart of the matter still the bad intent itself, with the act requirement serving

---

34.   503 U.S. 540 (1992).

simply to confirm our inference of the defendant's intent to do the target crime?

Robert Weisberg recounts the entertaining story of one of the classics in this area, *People v. Rizzo*.[35] This case is a comic narrative of blunders by a gang of low-lifes who drove around the Bronx in 1927, futilely searching for their victim, a payroll delivery man, only to be interrupted by the police before they found their target. *Rizzo* represents one of the more conservative versions of attempt law, reversing the conviction because the would-be robbers simply did not get close enough to success. But *Rizzo* did not spell out a very convincing rationale for this result, other than the need for line-drawing at the point of direct encounter with the victim. In later decades, courts and the drafters of the MPC moved the preparation/attempt line to an earlier stage of a criminal effort. With its requirement of a "substantial step," the MPC tilts the law more in the direction of a mens rea-based approach where the act requirement is there to corroborate the bad intent.[36] *Rizzo* teaches another lesson as well: In cases where the final harm does not occur because of early intervention, the ability of the state to prove the bad intent may depend on separate bodies of procedural law that enhance police investigation. *Rizzo* thereby introduces us to the full panoply of legal issues raise by attempt doctrine.

Perhaps no area of criminal law suffers from such a conundrum or mystery at its very heart as accomplice liability. In any crime where causation of some result is explicitly or implicitly a key element, the multiplicity of actors creates a major problem of what Leo Katz, in his chapter on the famous *State v. Tally* case,[37] calls one of overdetermination. Often the action of one, or fewer than all, of the participants in a crime can be sufficient to achieve the desired result. If so, there is a logic by which each one can say he played no causal role deserving punishment, because the crime would have occurred without him anyway. This is a perverse logic because even were this claim allowed on empirical grounds, the result is intolerable—all parties would be immune from liability. (Of course often the defendant's argument is unconvincing on empirical grounds because his conduct was the last necessary decisive contribution.) The challenge in such cases is that some actors encourage other actors toward a criminal goal without themselves engaging in any act beyond the expression of encouragement. In response, the law generally follows the common instinct to require a much weaker chain of causation when the thing caused is a volitional act by another human being than is true when the harm is the result of unintended physical

---

35.   246 N.Y. 334 (1927).

36.   MPC section 5.01.

37.   15 So. 722 (Ala. 1894).

forces. Of course, as noted below, sometimes we get around this problem by defining the crime of conspiracy, and then the very act of agreeing to commit a future crime becomes the harm itself. But the amazing story of Judge Tally shows that many complicity cases cannot be conspiracy cases, because the accomplice at issue, here the malevolent judge himself, may have helped cause the death of the victim but he never communicated his aid or desire to aid to the ultimate killers. He never formed the "agreement" that conspiracy requires.

Tally, perhaps the most famous accomplice in the criminal law canon, learned that family members were trying to vindicate the honor of a female relative by killing a man who had an affair with her, and when the judge heard that a warning telegram was sent to the target, the judge found a way to intercept the warning. The actual *Tally* opinion is itself a literary marvel. Technically a hearing on the judge's impeachment and not a criminal case per se, it is also long and elegant enough to be read as a Victorian era novella, rendered in exquisitely complex sentences and obsessive detail. Katz offers a side literary perspective on the case through discovery of rich newspaper accounts in which local folk looked at the controversial figure of the judge in sympathetic ways. But as Katz shows, the heart of the case is the famous passage in which the court says:

> If the aid in homicide can be shown to have put the deceased at a disadvantage, to have deprived him of a single chance of life which but for it he would have had, he who furnishes such aid is guilty, though it cannot be known or shown that the dead man, in the absence thereof, would have availed himself of that chance; ... so where he who facilitates murder even by so much as destroying a single chance of life the assailed might otherwise have had, he thereby supplements the efforts of the perpetrator....[38]

Thus, and in a way hugely influential on future American law, the law solves the conundrum of complicity law through a kind of reverse burden of proof. So long as the possibility of causal contribution cannot be categorically negated, the case is allowed to go forward. The defendant may be offered the collateral protection of a higher mens rea requirement than would be required of a single person crime, but, in the end, the law finds a conceptual means—or rationalization, to avoid letting the would-be accomplice get off simply because it cannot be shown that his aid was necessary to the criminal outcome.

Then we turn to conspiracy. The notion of making an independent and serious crime out of an unexecuted agreement to commit a crime, without even any action close to what would constitute an attempt, has always been controversial. Indeed, conspiracy is a rare example of a

---

38. *Id.* at 739.

venerable criminal law that some think should not be a law at all.[39] The
Model Penal Code drafters were themselves skeptical.[40] They included
conspiracy only begrudgingly, treating it as an inchoate crime equivalent
in severity to attempt, and eschewing such prosecution-friendly extensions as the *Pinkerton*[41] rule by which each conspirator is liable for any
collateral crime committed by any co-conspirator in foreseeable furtherance of the object crime. By contrast, the most extensive version of
conspiracy law is that of the federal criminal system. Federal prosecutors
enjoy the power to prosecute great numbers of barely related parties,
often people engaged in separate criminal objects that are arguably
mutually reinforcing or have enabling effects, and to extend vicarious co-
conspirator liability as far as possible.[42] As told by Mario Barnes, the case
of *United States v. Rahman*[43] is a striking, and for many, disturbing,
example of the reach of federal conspiracy law. Sheikh Omar Abdel–
Rahman, of course, was charged with instigating the earlier (1993)
bombing of the World Trade Center. After Sept. 11, 2001, much of the
federal government's focus on terrorism has involved legal doctrines that
go well beyond domestic criminal law, such as the law of war or the
designation of people as enemy combatants. But the *Rahman* case shows
how terrorism crimes can still fit within regular federal law, especially as
augmented by the key other statute used against Rahman—the old
seditious conspiracy law.[44] As Barnes shows, seditious conspiracy—to
wage war against or seek to overthrow the government—may seem like
an exotic version of regular conspiracy law. Yet it also epitomizes the key
aspects and most controversial aspects of regular conspiracy law. Moreover, seditious conspiracy captures some of the core concepts of conspiracy going back to the law's medieval origins. Conspiracy has always been
associated with the somewhat paranoid notion that the mere fact of
secretive agreement itself threatens the public order. Even more troubling, since "agreement" is often simply a form of verbal communication, expressions of persuasion and encouragement can become criminal,
thereby posing a risk of interference with free speech. And when that
encouragement takes the form of religious indoctrination, the freedom of

---

39. See Philip Johnson, *The Unnecessary Crime of Conspiracy*, 61 Calif. L. Rev. 1137
(1973).

40. MPC section 5.03.

41. Pinkerton v. United States, 328 U.S. 640 (1946).

42. Federal law also permits a person to be convicted of both a conspiracy to commit
a crime and the successful object crime. Callanan v. United States, 364 U.S. 587 (1961).
That result is permitted by the Double Jeopardy clause, because technically neither crime
is as lesser-included offense of the other. Blockburger v. United States, 284 U.S. 299
(1932). The MPC and most states decline to exploit the space provided by the *Blockburger*
rule.

43. 189 F.3d 88 (2d. Cir. 1999).

44. 18 U.S.C. § 2384 (2011).

religion part of the First Amendment is implicated as well. So the *Rahman* case, and the affirmance of the conviction, is a great illustration of how a maximal conspiracy law can work, and also a troubling example of how the act of agreement may be hard to distinguish from protected expression and belief.

Criminal Law Stories closes with sentencing. Because the question of how much to punish first requires us to consider *why* we punish, this subject could have opened the volume. But it is a fitting finale because it reminds us of the powerful social and political vectors that animate all of criminal law. The provision of the Constitution most conducive to limiting the power of the state to define crime and punishment is of course the Eighth Amendment's "cruel and unusual punishments" clause. And the Supreme Court has made much use of that clause in one area—capital punishment. As treated in the companion volume *Death Penalty Stories*,[45] the Court has invoked the Eighth Amendment not only to impose strict procedural requirements on the issuance of a death sentence, but to draw strict boundaries about what crimes and what criminals can be subject to the death penalty. Thus, capital punishment is now forbidden for any nonhomicide crime,[46] and for defendants who are mentally retarded[47] or are under 18 years of age when they kill.[48] But while that Eighth Amendment jurisprudence has been extended slightly to the penalty of life without the possibility of parole ("LWOP"),[49] the Court has been reluctant to deploy the Constitution to draw any lines when the issue is a term of years of imprisonment. Proportionality review for prison sentences would seem to require some settled under-standing of why we punish, as well as some metric, whether abstract or empirical, against which to test the fairness of any particular penalty. On the former question, the Court has chosen to leave it to the legislatures to determine whether retributive principles or such utilitari-an goals as incapacitation, deterrence, or rehabilitation, should motivate and help measure punishment. On the latter question, the "unusual" term in the Eighth Amendment calls us, as in the death penalty cases, to be alert to anomalous outliers within a state's penal code or as between states for similar crimes.

As Sara Sun Beale shows in *Ewing v. California*,[50] the Court offers a tour of the purposes of criminal punishment. But that tour will normally

---

45. *Death Penalty Stories* (John Blume & Jordan Steiker, eds. 2009).

46. Kennedy v. Louisiana, 554 U.S. 407 (2008).

47. Atkins v. Virginia, 536 U.S. 304 (2002).

48. Roper v. Simmons, 543 U.S. 551 (2005).

49. The Supreme Court ruled most recently in *Miller v. Alabama* that statutes that required mandatory life without parole for juvenile defendants violated the Eighth Amendment. Miller v. Alabama, 132 S.Ct. 2455 (2012).

50. 538 U.S. 11 (2003).

come to a dead end for Eighth Amendment claimants. As recounted by Beale, the Court has essentially adopted an eclectically deferential standard of review: So long as there is *some* defensible basis for a particular penalty, and so long as it is not "grossly disproportionate" to the crime or criminal, it will be up to the legislature to draw the sentencing line. *Ewing* was the ultimate test of this defense, because the California Three Strikes law under review is arguably the most draconian sentencing scheme in the nation outside LWOP and the death penalty. Under that law, while arguably the first two crimes must be serious or dangerous felonies, almost any felony can count as the third strike, and under the oddities of California law, even a small act of larceny can sometimes be aggravated to a felony and then, as a third strike, lead to a twenty-five years to life sentence.

Ewing illustrates American sentencing from at least two distinct perspectives. On the one hand it shows how the philosophers' categories of punishment often get deployed in law through very visceral expressions of popular will. As Beale shows us, opponents of the draconian turn in American sentencing view the case of Gary Ewing as the story of a minor criminal who essentially got sent away for life because he stole a few hundred dollars of golf equipment. But Beale tells the parallel story of a turn in American social attitudes. When California's voters enacted a Three-Strikes law by popular initiative, they were declaring that some criminals had proven themselves so resistant to criminal law norms that they were beyond rehabilitation and no longer susceptible to deterrence. Many viewed the law as exacting a retributive penalty because of the seriousness of Ewing's recalcitrance, but it makes more sense to view the law as incapacitative. Under that view, each new crime in effect magnifies the severity of the previous one so that the whole is much greater than the sum of its parts. In effect, the law expressed the view that accumulated data about the personal character of a defendant retrospectively aggravates the culpability of his past acts. By declining to rule Ewing's sentence unconstitutional, the Supreme Court made it plain that relief from the most draconian effects of the "tough on crime" agenda rests in the democratic process.

1

Markus D. Dubber

The Story of *Keller:* The Irrelevance of the Legality Principle in American Criminal Law

Commonwealth v. Keller[1] is not a famous leading case, but it should be. It raises important questions about the foundation of the state's power to punish through criminal law. These questions generally do not receive much attention in American criminal law teaching, nor have they received much attention in American legal and political discourse in general.

More specifically, *Keller's* irrelevance is symptomatic of the unfortunate irrelevance of the principle of legality in American criminal law. Rather than being regarded and employed as a fundamental principle of legitimacy of state penal power, the principle of legality is poorly understood as a disconnected aggregate of maxims, rules, and guidelines—preferably cited in lawyers' Latin phrases of uncertain formulation and meaning ("nullum crimen sine lege" and "nullum crimen, nulla poena sine lege"—"no crime without law" and "no crime, no punishment without law"—being two popular variations). It thereby joins other groundless, anachronistic, and ill-examined bedrocks of American criminal law passed down from a mystical and timeless time before time in the history of the English Common Law, most notably actus reus and mens rea, or their combination as "actus non facit reum nisi mens sit rea".[2]

---

1. 35 Pa. D. & C.2d 615 (1964).

2. Ironically, the common Latinness of the two (or three) maxims masks different origins. The *nullum crimen* maxim (along with several other variations) is generally attributed to P.J.A. Feuerbach, an early nineteenth-century Bavarian criminal law scholar, judge, and codifier. Markus D. Dubber & Mark Kelman, *American Criminal Law: Cases, Statutes, and Comments* 106–07 (2d ed. 2009). The origin of the actus reus maxim is less

Commonwealth v. Keller affirms, and then exercises, judges' power to recognize new common law crimes (here "indecent disposition of a dead body"). That this short-yet-rambling 1964 opinion by a Pennsylvania trial judge should thereby provide the most searching analysis, however brief, of the state's—and not merely the judiciary's—power to punish through criminal law is both ironic and significant. It is significant because it indicates the lack of interest this fundamental question has attracted in American legal and political discourse. The state's power to punish was taken for granted by the Founding Generation. Considerable effort was expended on the question of *who* should exercise this awesome power, both among different branches of a single government (the legislature vs. the judiciary and, more recently, the executive) and among different governments (states vs. federal). Yet no one bothered to address the primary, substantive and non-institutional, question of what could possibly justify the state's, any state's, use of penal violence against its own citizens, of whom, by whom, and for whom it was constituted.

Keller is ostensibly concerned only with the question of who gets to punish through criminal law—judges or (only) legislators. But the case also offers a glimpse of the preliminary, and both unasked and unanswered question of *why* any state actor—judge, legislator, administrator[3] —gets to punish through criminal law in a modern democratic state grounded in the (literally) revolutionary ideal of the self-governing person who, in the political realm, appears as the citizen.

The passage in *Keller* that addresses the foundation of the state's power to punish through criminal law is short and easy to miss. (In fact, it tends to be omitted from casebook excerpts of the case.) It consists almost entirely of a quotation from an 1881 Pennsylvania case, often cited as a key case on the doctrine of (judge-made) common law misdemeanors, which in turn consists almost entirely of a quotation from the fourth volume of Blackstone's *Commentaries* (first published in 1769):

> The landmark case in this Commonwealth which enounces the principle of preserving common law offenses is Commonwealth v. McHale, 97 Pa. 397. After analyzing and determining that common law crimes are preserved, Mr. Justice Paxton, at page 408, asks the question, "What is a common-law offense?"

---

certain, but also more ancient, and may trace itself back to St. Augustine. Thomas A. Gowan, *Toward an Experimental Definition of Criminal Mind*, in *Philosophical Essays in Honor of Edgar Arthur Singer, Jr.* 163 (Francis Palmer Clarke, *et al.* eds., 1942).

3. Given that judicial criminal lawmaking has sunk into desuetude, the executive branch today arguably represents a more significant challenge to the legislative monopoly on criminal lawmaking than does the judiciary. *See, e.g.*, Gerard E. Lynch, *The Sentencing Guidelines as a Not–So–Model Penal Code*, 7 Fed. Sent. Rep. 112 (1994); Mistretta v. United States, 488 U.S. 361 (1989).

"The highest authority upon this point is Blackstone. In chap. 13, of vol. 4, of Sharswood's edition, it is thus defined: 'The last species of offenses which especially affect the Commonwealth are those against the public police or economy. By the public police and economy I mean the due regulation and domestic order of the kingdom, whereby the individuals of the state, like members of a well-governed family, are bound to conform their general behavior to the rules of propriety, good neighborhood and good manners, and to be decent, industrious and inoffensive in their respective stations. This head of offenses must therefore be very miscellaneous, as it comprises all such crimes as especially affect public society, and are not comprehended under any of the four preceding series. These amount some of them to felony, and other to misdemeanors only.' "[4]

The bulk of this paper will be devoted to unpacking this short but remarkable passage. Its subtly rich language grounds a twentieth-century American state trial judge's power to create new criminal offenses in a passage from a nineteenth-century American state supreme court's judgment, which in turn quotes a passage from a distinctly pre-revolutionary eighteenth-century English treatise on "The Laws of England" that affirms the English king's power to maintain the "public police or economy" of "the kingdom," composed of individuals conceptualized as "members of a well-governed family," all this in a passage that concerns itself with state (i.e., royal) power in general, rather than addressing judicial power in particular.

In all its haphazard brevity and lack of depth or serious engagement, this passage from *Keller* points to, and illustrates, a conception of the state's power to punish through criminal law that has driven, without serious reflection or critique, American legal and political discourse since the Founding Era. That conception is the *police power* model, which regards the state's power to punish as an obvious incident of the state's power to police, which in turn is regarded as firmly rooted in the very notion of state sovereignty itself, and therefore ultimately beyond question and scrutiny.

The police power model, however, is best understood in contrast to a radically different conception of the state's power to punish, the *law power* model, which regards the object of punishment as a person capable of self-government, or autonomy, rather than as a member of a well-governed, or not-so well-governed family or household, in need of management and, occasionally, penal discipline. This model, unlike the police power model, attempts to legitimate state punishment in light of the

---

4. 35 Pa. D. & C.2d at 624 (quoting Commonwealth v. McHale, 97 Pa. 397, 408 (1881) (quoting 4 William Blackstone, *Commentaries on the Laws of England* 162 (1769))).

principles of a modern liberal democracy (and of the historical ideals of the American Revolution).[5]

If it is properly understood as addressing the question of why (or whether) to punish—and not merely that of who (or how)—the "principle of legality" is a principle of law, or lawfulness. As such it plays a central role in the law power model of state punishment. But, if so, it has no place in the police power model of state punishment, the dominant model of American penality since the Founding Generation, which simply adopted—and in fact interpreted expansively, as we will see—the patriarchal English conception of state punishment as managing and disciplining "the kingdom" (now relabeled "the people") as a householder would govern his household, or a father his family.

The Keller *Opinion*

Violet Keller was estranged from her husband and lived with their four-year-old son and her boyfriend, Roy Schaeffer.[6] In March of 1963, she secretly gave birth in the bathroom of her apartment. When she went to the hospital later that day, staff notified the District Attorney's office; a consensual search of her bathroom turned up a box containing the corpse of a baby girl.

In June of the same year, Keller was tried for murder before a jury in Lebanon, Pennsylvania, a "small, working-class city located on the fringe of Pennsylvania's Amish country."[7] The trial judge, G. Thomas Gates, however, directed a not guilty verdict on the ground that the prosecution had failed to prove the cause of death; the expert pathologist could not rule out the possibility that the baby had been stillborn.[8] Keller returned to her job at the local telephone company.

---

5. For more extended discussions of the police power and law power models, see Markus D. Dubber, *The Police Power: Patriarchy and the Foundations of American Government* (2005); Markus D. Dubber, *The New Police Science and the Police Power Model of the Criminal Process*, in *The New Police Science: The Police Power in Domestic and International Governance* 107 (Markus D. Dubber & Mariana Valverde eds., 2006).

6. *See generally* Edna J. Carmean, *Nine Men on the Bench: A Story of the 52nd Judicial District of Pennsylvania, 1894–1994*, 201–03 (1994); *see also Myerstown Woman Pleads Not Guilty*, Reading Eagle, Sept. 7, 1963.

7. *Town Unruffled over Transsexual*, Reading Eagle (Lebanon, Pa.), Nov. 18, 1998, at B7.

8. By 1963, Gates had been on the bench for three years, after a brief but successful career as a local lawyer following his military service. A graduate of Brown University and Boston University Law School, he remained on the bench for thirty years, from 1960 until 1990. He taught various law related courses at local colleges, was an adjunct faculty member in the moot court program at Dickinson Law School, and published *A History of Hangings for Homicide in Lebanon County* (1972), as well as an essay ("A Judge Views Psychology") in *Psychology and Professional Practice: The Interface of Psychology and the Law* 147 (Francis R.J. Fields & Rudy J. Horwitz, eds., 1982). Gates was thirty-six years old

Shortly thereafter, her landlord cleaned out the basement and, in the part accessible from Keller's kitchen, found a box filled with infant bones. Keller explained that she secretly had given birth to a stillborn baby girl in April of 1962.

In December of 1963, Keller was tried, and convicted, again before Judge Gates,[9] on one count of adultery (about which, more later on) and two counts of the common law misdemeanor of "indecent disposition of a dead body." She was sentenced to five to twenty-three months in the county jail and a $100 fine, with a suspended sentence on the adultery charge.

The trial court's opinion, handed down in August of 1964, addresses the question whether indecent disposition of a dead body "is a crime cognizable under the laws of the Commonwealth of Pennsylvania." The court concludes that it is, denying the defendant's motions in arrest of judgment and for a new trial.

In his decision, the trial judge searches in vain for a statutory offense of indecent disposition of a dead body. Attempts to find cases defining such an offense, either in Pennsylvania or in any other American jurisdiction, are also unsuccessful. The judge does hit upon two cases, one from Maine, the other from Arkansas, that he finds relevant. The indictment in the Maine case (from 1939), *Bradbury*, alleged that the defendant

> with force and arms, unlawfully and indecently did take the human body of one Harriet P. Bradbury, and then and there indecently and unlawfully put and place said body in a certain furnace, and then and there did dispose of and destroy the said body of the said Harriet P. Bradbury by burning the same in said furnace, the great indecency of Christian burial, in evil example to all others in like case offending, against the peace of said State and contrary to the laws of the same.[10]

---

when the governor appointed him to serve out the two years remaining in the ten-year term of his predecessor, who had resigned for health reasons. The appointment apparently was "popular with both Republicans and Democrats," Gates having been a star athlete at Lebanon High and known for his "unlimited personality and charm." *Id.* at 188. (He was elected for the first of three ten-year terms in November 1961.) One of his obituaries, along with offering praise of his judicial compassion and wisdom, remarked that "[i]t is hard, almost, to assume a properly mournful countenance at the passing of a man whose name evokes so many fond and funny memories, brings such quick smiles." *Remembered with a Smile*, Lebanon Daily News, Nov. 26, 2001.

9. With a population of between 90,000 and 95,000, Lebanon County remained a one-judge judicial district until 1968. The population increased from 90,853 in 1960 to 130,506 (est.) in 2009; by last count, in 2008, it was 96% white and heavily German (in the 2000 Census, 41.3% of inhabitants reported German ancestry, the second largest category, at 9.1%, being "United States or American," closely followed by "Irish" at 8.8%).

10. State v. Bradbury, 9 A.2d 657 (Me. 1939).

The defendant in the Arkansas case (1949), *Baker*, was charged, more succinctly, with "treating a dead body indecently." Canna Baker had propped up the disguised corpse of a dead tenant, displaying it in various poses to passers-by long enough to cash his monthly welfare check.[11] For good measure, the *Keller* trial judge proceeds to list "evidence that there existed a standard of decency and respect for the dead and their resting places" from since the beginning of time, including the Bible, "the renowned pyramids of Egypt," "American Indian lore," the "Code of Justinian," and "the tomb of William Shakespeare," in a tour de force of broad, if not also deep, erudition that may be seen as reflective of the judge's varied extra-judicial ambitions and interests, scholarly, authorial, and even thespian,[12] as well as the socially conservative character of the community he served for three decades as President Judge in the Court of Common Pleas.[13]

Much could be said about the judge's discussion of the Maine and Arkansas cases, none of which—as he acknowledges—is on all fours with the case before him. Even more could be said about his romp through human history. In particular, as we will see shortly, his invocation of cultural norms as the foundation for penal sanctions, both in form and in substance, goes to the legitimacy of morals offenses in general, and

---

11. For a detailed discussion of *Baker*, see Paul H. Robinson, *Criminal Law Case Studies* (3d ed. 2006).

12. On Gates as scholar and author, see *supra* note 8. (In the collection to which he contributed the essay "A Judge Views Psychology," he identifies himself as, among other things, a "member of the American Association of University Professors.") On Gates as thespian, see Leonard W. Boasberg, *"The Blue–Eyed Six": From Greed to the Gallows One Escaped Death*, Phila. Inquirer, Aug. 20, 1995, at F01 (review of a play based on a case discussed in Gates's *A History of Hangings for Homicide in Lebanon County* (1972), in which Gates plays the reporter/narrator).

13. Some thirty-five years after Keller's "indecent disposition" conviction, an article in the local newspaper still described Lebanon as a "conservative community of porch-front rowhouses and street-corner diners, where coal-carrying trains stop local traffic as they travel through the heart of downtown." *Town Unruffled over Transsexual*, Reading Eagle (Lebanon, Pa.), Nov. 18, 1998, at B7. The article concerned the case of Raul Valentin, a young transsexual who pursued his federal civil rights case under 42 U.S.C. § 1983 against Judge Gates all the way to the U.S. Supreme Court. According to the article, Valentin in the summer of 1987 had been sentenced to thirty days in jail for disorderly conduct following an altercation at a local swimming pool, where Valentin had appeared wearing a bikini. After his release, Gates ordered him to leave town and never to come back, at the risk of having other charges brought against him and being sent to prison. *Id.*; *see also Supreme Court Upholds Banishment of Transsexual*, Chi. Trib., Nov. 16, 1998, at C2; Brief of Appellant Raul Valentin, Valentin v. Gates 162 F.3d 1153 (3d Cir. 1998) (No. 97–7481). The federal district court dismissed the case on the ground of absolute judicial immunity; the Third Circuit affirmed without an opinion; and the Supreme Court denied certiorari. *See* Valentin V. Gates, 162 F.3d 1153 (3d Cir.), *cert. denied,* 525 U.S. 1002 (1998); *see also* Brief on Behalf of Appellees Senior Judge G. Thomas Gates and Catherine M. Coyle, Valentin v. Gates, 162 F.3d 1153 (3d Cir. 1998) (No. 97-7481).

not merely that of criminal lawmaking from the bench. What interests me here, though, is not the application of the definition of common law misdemeanor, but the definition itself—along with the fact that the judge in *Keller* thought such a definition necessary, apart from the obvious fact that the Pennsylvania Supreme Court had supplied one a century before, in *McHale*.

Keller differs from other twentieth-century common law crime cases because it goes beyond merely asserting the courts' longstanding authority, or even obligation, to define common law crimes as necessary. *Baker*, the 1949 Arkansas case, skirts the issue by simply asserting that "treating a dead body indecently" is a common law crime, after all, so that no invention, but merely discovery, was necessary.[14] *Bradbury*, ten years older, contents itself with marveling at the ever evolving nature of the common law, whose flexibility is uniquely suited to adjust to new situations (or, in the case at hand, not-so-new situations having to do with the disposal of corpses). The *Bradbury* court observes that the common law is always a step ahead of (or just a short step behind) the devious inventions of the likewise ever evolving criminal mind (even if, again, in *Bradbury* itself, the criminal—and possibly not quite sound—mind was that of an old man who, when asked about his sister's whereabouts "took down the crank used for shaking down the furnace, turned over the grates, shovelled out the ashes and said: 'If you want to see her, there she is' "). These musings in *Bradbury* are then amplified with a gratuitous—and unexplored though well-known—quotation from Holmes's *Common Law*, to the effect that law ought to "correspond with the actual feelings and demands of the community, whether right or wrong."

Similarly, the notorious English common law crime case, *Shaw v. Director of Public Prosecutions*,[15] decided shortly before, but not mentioned in *Keller*, does not go beyond insisting that (English) judges have a "duty as servants and guardians of the common law" and that: "Whatever is contrary, *bonos mores et decorum*, the principles of our law prohibit, and the King's court, as the general censor and guardian of the public manners, is bound to restrain and punish." At best, the House of Lords here can be taken to rely implicitly on the theory of common law misdemeanors set out in *Keller*: namely the power of English *common law* to recognize new crimes stems from their nature as royal courts, which presumably derive their authority from the King's now familiar power to discipline his subjects in the name of maintaining the "public

---

14. Baker v. State, 223 S.W.2d 809 (Ark. 1949).

15. Shaw v. DPP, [1962] AC 220 (H.L.). Shaw had published a "Ladies' Directory" of prostitutes' names and addresses and was convicted not only of various statutory offenses but also of "conspiracy to corrupt public morals" for having conspired with the prostitutes "to debauch and corrupt the morals of youth and other subjects of the Queen."

police." *Keller*, in this reading, identifies the state (royal) power the exercise of which by (royal) judges *Shaw* merely asserts—the power to police.

The Police Power and Common Law Misdemeanors

To appreciate the significance of the passage from Blackstone's *Commentaries* quoted in *Keller* (and *McHale*), it is important to recognize three things. First, the power to police was traditionally regarded in American legal and political discourse as the broadest, most flexible, and least limitable powers of government. Second, the power to police has repeatedly been cited as the basis of the state's power to punish through criminal law.[16] And third, the Blackstone passage was frequently quoted by American courts and commentators as a definition of the power to police.[17]

Keller, then, in what appears to be an unremarkable reference to a nineteenth-century Pennsylvania case on the doctrine of common law misdemeanors, in fact put its finger on the widely acknowledged source of American criminal law, if not on the essence of American state power in general. For its immediate objective, namely to answer the seemingly simple question "What is a common law crime?" this passage proves too much, to put it mildly. Rather than highlighting the nature of *judicial* criminal lawmaking, it identifies the source of *all* criminal lawmaking.

This apparent weakness, however, in fact is *Keller's* great strength, insofar as it shifts attention from the secondary, institutional, question of who wields the power to punish through criminal law to the primary, substantive, question of *whether*, and if so, *why* the state legitimately could violate the very rights to person and property of those it legitimately exists to protect. This question is significant, and demands an answer, or at least a sustained attempt at an answer, in and of itself. Incidentally, the answer to it may well suggest an answer to the more limited, and subsidiary question at issue in *Keller*, namely the question of who should, or may, exercise this most awesome state power in general, or in a particular case.

It is not surprising that *Keller*, in 1964, makes no effort to directly take on a question as fundamental as the legitimacy of state punishment through criminal law. The surprise is that it takes the answer to the question for granted, in the case of a question that has never been asked with the appropriate urgency. More surprising, or at least noteworthy, is

---

16. *See, e.g.,* Foucha v. Louisiana, 504 U.S. 71, 80 (1992); Wayne R. LaFave & Austin W. Scott, Jr. *Substantive Criminal Law* § 2.10 (2d ed. 1986); Clarence E. Laylin & Alonzo H. Tuttle, *Due Process and Punishment*, 20 Mich. L. Rev. 614, 622 (1922); Sutton v. New Jersey, 244 U.S. 258 (1917).

17. *See* Dubber, *The Police Power, supra* note 5, chs. 2, 3.

the failure of the Founding Generation, some two centuries before, to tackle this question, or even to recognize its crucial importance for its comprehensive project of legal-political reform. *Keller* thus both gestures at the fundamental challenge of legitimating the state's power to punish through criminal law and, at the same time, highlights the failure to meet, or even to frame, that challenge in American legal and political discourse.

Without a comprehensive reconception of criminal law *as law*, rather than as an unexamined and unchallenged exercise of the ultimately patriarchal power to police, American criminal law remains without principled foundation. It rests uneasily and uncritically on empty lawyers' Latin maxims that are thought, or rather vaguely felt, to emanate from a Whiggish lawyers' history of the common law of crime as an ever widening and thickening web of precedents held together by various "golden threads."[18] Among these golden threads are *nullum crimen sine lege* (at issue in *Keller*) and *actus non facit reum nisi mens sit rea*. In the police power model, these supposed principles, or requirements, are in fact maxims or guidelines that the state, in the end, is free to mold and even to ignore entirely if it sees fit under the circumstances.

The principle of legality, in particular, is not a *principle* in the first place, nor is it a principle of *legality*; it is a maxim of police power—or, yet more precisely, it is not even a single maxim, but a collection of unconnected maxims, including "no common law crimes," "void-for-vagueness," "lenity," "strict construction," "ex post facto," etc.

But before we return to *Keller* and the principle of legality, we need to take a closer look at the origins and contours of the American police power model glimpsed through *Keller's* overbroad answer to the apparently narrow and straightforward question, "What is a common law crime?"

State Punishment as Sovereign Police

The most noteworthy feature of the Founding Generation's revision of the foundation of state punishment through criminal law was its absence. On the continent, and even in England, the radical critique of state power that the Enlightenment produced, was as a matter of course, a series of fundamental reconceptions of state punishment, from Beccaria in Italy (and, in his footsteps, Bentham in England and Voltaire in France) to Kant and Hegel (and, less comprehensive but more immediately influential, P.J.A. Feuerbach) in Germany. After all, what was the point of challenging existing structures and traditions of state power in light of the invention, or discovery, of the right-bearing (or at least pleasure-and-pain feeling), rational and autonomous, individual, the per-

---

18. See, most explicitly and notoriously, Woolmington v. DPP, [1935] AC 462.

son, without taking a good hard look at the most intrusive and therefore troubling exercise of state power against that individual—the threat, imposition, and infliction of punishment, through imprisonment, expropriation, beating, maiming, and killing in the name of the state?

One would have thought that the American Founding Generation would have felt a particular urge to challenge the state's depriving, in the name of punishment, its constituents of the very rights it existed to preserve: the right to life, to liberty, to property, and even the pursuit of happiness. Instead, the thinkers and doers of the Founding Era focused on taxation without representation, i.e., taxation in violation of their right to self-government as persons endowed with the capacity for autonomy. By contrast, the far more obvious and grievous violation of that right, and the far more obvious and grievous interference with that capacity, in the form of punishment—threatened, imposed, and inflicted—was not thought to raise basic questions of legitimacy.

The state's power to punish through criminal law, instead, was simply taken for granted; in fact, it was so taken for granted that the English model of state punishment was left undisturbed and unexamined—in substance and, largely, even in form. The sole exception was an occasional relabeling, using a global though occasionally imperfect, find-and-replace command. The relabeling changed references to, say, the "King's peace" for the "public peace," the "peace of the commonwealth," or the "peace of the state," reflecting the more general, but similarly straightforward, substitution of "the King" as sovereign with "the people," without, however, challenging the underlying conception of sovereignty itself.

Punishment remained an aspect of the power to police, which in turn remained central to the very notion of sovereignty, having been transferred from the person of the King to the amorphous construct of "the people" (or "the commonwealth," "the state," "the public" and so on). The offense of treason, for instance, remained unchanged. It retained the definition, word for word, of the English Treason Act of 1351, with the one obvious exception of eliminating the clause having to do with the death of the King—reference to whom had fallen victim to the above-mentioned find-and-replace procedure.[19] The definition of the police power, like that of treason, was simply lifted from its English source. In fact, so obvious and unworthy of attention was the matter of defining the sovereign's power to police that Blackstone's definition—in one example of incomplete finding-and-replacing—was simply adopted lock, stock, and barrel, with no effort to update royal references. The police

---

19. *See* Markus D. Dubber, *The State as Victim: Treason and the Paradox of American Criminal Law*, in *Offences Against the State* (Mordechai Kremnitzer & Khalid Ghanayim, eds., forthcoming 2012).

power was the King's power, as "pater-familias of the nation" to govern "the individuals of the state, like members of a well-governed family" and to maintain "the public police and economy," thereby attending to "the due regulation and domestic order of the kingdom"[20] in Blackstone's England of 1769. And it remained so, verbatim, in the new United States, after the Revolution—in fact, as *Keller* illustrates, well into the twentieth century.

It is stunning that American legal and political discourse would simply swallow the deeply patriarchal, hierarchical, and monarchical English concept of police power whole. That power, by its nature, was discretionary, flexible, and in the end, unlimitable, as American courts and commentators pointed out again and again. They waxed positively poetic about a power that "is and must be from its very nature, incapable of any very exact definition or limitation."[21]

The career of the police power in American constitutional law is a worthwhile subject by itself, even apart from its role as the source of the power to punish, which concerns us in particular.[22] Throughout, its essential connection to the very notion of sovereignty and sovereign power remained constant; as a result, it served as the site for many of the basic struggles in the American constitutional system, including that between the states and the federal government and among the branches of government, notably between the judiciary and the legislature (and, to a lesser extent, the executive).

So central was the police power to the concept of sovereignty that the entire federalist system rests on the fiction that the states retained the power to police while that power was denied to the federal government. By, at the same time, insisting on the police power as an essential ingredient of sovereignty and denying it to the federal government, the federal system is built on the paradox of establishing a national sovereign state without sovereignty. It is no surprise, then, that a de facto federal police power arose despite the continued insistence on its de jure absence: By 1904, it had become "impossible to deny that the federal government exercises a considerable police power of its own."[23]

---

20. Blackstone, *supra* note 4, at 162.

21. Slaughter–House Cases, 83 U.S. 36, 49 (1873).

22. *See generally* Dubber, *The Police Power*, *supra* note 5; William J. Novak, *The People's Welfare: Law and Regulation in Nineteenth–Century America* (1996).

23. Ernst Freund, *The Police Power: Public Policy and Constitutional Rights* 63 (1904). Of course there is also the denial of the existence of a federal "state" altogether, requiring carefully replacing references to "state" with references to "government." No one doubts the federal "government's" sovereignty in any number of other contexts, including the government, or self-government, of Indian tribes. *See, e.g.*, United States v. Lara, 541 U.S. 193 (2004).

This arrangement has allowed the steady, and eventually enormous, expansion of the federal state in the name of other officially recognized federal powers, notably the power to regulate interstate commerce. This trend is only very rarely interrupted by the insistence that the *de jure* exercise of some recognized federal power or another (such as the commerce power) amounts to a *de facto* exercise of a supposedly non-existent federal police power.[24] At any rate, even these—occasional— reminders of the federalist police power arrangement do nothing to challenge the notion of the *limitlessness* of the power to police; on the contrary, they rely on it, since it is this unchallenged characteristic of the police power that, if exercised by the federal government, threatens state sovereignty.

That essential limitlessness of the police power, springing from its intimate connection to the concept of sovereignty, also animates its role as a site of interbranch relations and occasionally conflicts. The police power, in general, functioned as an "idiom of apologetics" in constitutional discourse, with courts hesitating to interfere with the exercise of the police power by the legislature (as well as de facto, if not de jure, by the executive, which instead relied on such stand-ins as "executive privilege" or "presidential prerogative").[25] *Lochner v. New York*,[26] where the U.S. Supreme Court overturned an ostensible exercise of (state) police power, is regarded as a shocking outlier in American constitutional history, an embarrassing instance of judicial overreach and (conservative) disrespect for an exercise of the state's police power by a (progressive) legislature.[27]

The police power's role in conflicts among governments (the states and the federal government), and among branches within a government (judiciary vs. legislative vs. executive[28]), both illustrates and obscures its significance in the American constitutional regime. It is important to recognize that the police power is an incident of the power of the sovereign itself, not a power of some particular states or sovereigns, nor, for that matter, is it a power of one state branch rather than another. As a power of the state per se, it can be wielded by any and all state

---

24. *See, e.g.,* United States v. Lopez, 514 U.S. 549 (1995).

25. Walton H. Hamilton & Carlton C. Rodee, *Police Power*, in 12 *Encyclopedia of the Social Sciences* 190 (Edwin R A Seligman & Alvin Johnson eds., 1933).

26. 198 U.S. 45 (1905).

27. The literature on *Lochner* is enormous and growing. For a useful (revisionist) account of the case and its significance, see Howard Gillman, *The Constitution Besieged: The Rise and Demise of Lochner Era Police Powers Jurisprudence* (1993).

28. While judicial interference with legislative exercises of the police power (à la *Lochner*) tend to get all the attention, legislative interference with the executive's exercise of the police power (dubbed privilege or prerogative) should not be overlooked. In each case, the challenged branch insists on being the exclusive, or ultimate, holder of the power.

officials, no matter how loudly some states, or some branches within the state apparatus, may insist on their exclusive, or even superior, power to police.

Therefore, to talk about the police power, is to talk about the possibility—or rather the impossibility—of the limitation, definition, or legitimacy of the very phenomenon of state power. The questions of who, or what, is best suited to exercise that power in a particular case is of secondary importance. Those are the more mundane questions of institutional competence that exercised the Legal Process School dominant in American law in the 1950s, a school of thought that proceeded from an assumed, if only implicit, consensus about the primary, substantive, issue of legitimacy.[29]

This fundamental substantive issue is obscured in American constitutional discourse in general, which simply takes the police power and its essential connection to sovereignty for granted; it is likewise ignored, and therefore remains unaddressed, in American penal discourse, which after all simply takes the power to punish to be a manifestation of the power to police. And so, the same debates about the who, rather than the why, play themselves out at the level of the power to punish.

Part of the general federalist police power compromise was the strict prohibition of federal common law crimes, i.e., of judge-made federal criminal law.[30] This prohibition was aimed at preventing the federal government from using its judiciary to evade the denial of a federal police power or, put another way, to limit the denial of a federal police power to the federal *legislature*. The federal judiciary eventually came to exercise the same de facto police power as the federal legislature, if only through the co-creative interpretation of deliberately broad criminal statutes as partners in the fight against federal crime.[31]

The issue in *Keller*—courts' power to recognize new crimes, and common law misdemeanors in particular—likewise reflects, at a less abstract level, the question of which branch of government should, or may, exercise the police power. But as *Keller*, if unintentionally, makes clear by citing Blackstone's definition of the state's (or rather the King's) power to police in general, and as the House of Lords in *Shaw* emphasizes by insisting on its common law power as the King's court to wield

---

29. *See generally* Henry Melvin Hart & Albert M Sacks, *The Legal Process: Basic Problems in the Making and Application of Law* (William N. Eskridge, Jr. & Philip P. Frickey eds., 1994).

30. *See* Hudson v. Goodwin, 11 U.S. 32 (1812).

31. Wayne R. LaFave, *Substantive Criminal Law* § 2.1 (2d ed. 2003); Ben Rosenberg, *The Growth of Federal Criminal Common Law*, 29 Am. J. Crim. L. 193 (2002); *see* United States v. Maze, 414 U.S. 395, 405–06 (1974) (Burger, C.J., dissenting) (federal mail fraud statute).

the patriarchal power to police, the judiciary's power to recognize common law misdemeanors is not a self-standing doctrine, but merely one aspect of the state's foundational power to punish. The assignment of authority to wield that power to a particular state official, or branch, or institution, is not only a secondary issue, but also a matter of discretion, rather than of principle. As an incident of the essentially discretionary, unlimitable, and indefinable police power, the state can determine who is best suited to exercise it in a particular circumstance. Any constraints on this determination are self-imposed by the state; they are matters of efficacy, competence, or perhaps prudence, rather than of legitimacy.

Note, in light of the fact that American law tends to frame legitimacy critiques in constitutional terms, that there has never been a successful, or even a serious—or (perhaps) *any*—constitutional challenge to the judiciary's common law crime-making power. Many American (and English) courts continue to enjoy this power, even though they generally decline to exercise it or, more to the point, they simply have no occasion to exercise it given the proliferation of legislative and executive criminal laws and "regulations." When American legislatures, through criminal codes, explicitly restrict criminal law to legislative codes or at least statutes (criminal and others, not to mention administrative regulations), they do so not on account of some fundamental principle, or constitutional norm. Rather, they do so without fanfare and in passing, as confirming a state of affairs in which the courts' practice of making criminal law has fallen into desuetude, as part of a kind of gentleman's agreement.[32] Indeed, this is a tacit agreement which is liable to be revoked, or amended, at any time, as the House of Lords made clear in *Shaw*, a case that is significant not so much for the exercise of the courts' power to make criminal law as for the insistence on the courts' discretion, and even the duty, to exercise it when appropriate.

Here, then, is the trouble with the legality principle in a police power regime: It is the *principle* which is thought to place constraints of *legality* on the assignment of the power to punish to one state branch or another. But, as we have seen, under a penal system that regards the

---

32. The relevant provision in the Pennsylvania Crimes Code, modeled closely on the American Law Institute's Model Penal Code and adopted some years after *Keller*, did not prompt any legislative debate, nor comment from the drafting commission, other than the lapidary remark that "[a] code cannot truly be a 'criminal code' if it leaves undefined areas of criminality; such a code would unfairly deny notice of illegality." Gen. Assemb. of the Commonwealth of Pa., Joint State Gov't Comm'n, Proposed Crimes Code for Pennsylvania, Assemb. Doc. No. 219, at 20–21 (1967), *available at* http://jsg.legis.state.pa.us/publications. cfm?JSPU_PUBLN_ID=219. The bill's sponsors on the floor, however, did mention in passing that the bill as a whole had the support of the state's trial judges. Pa. Senate, S.B. 455, Legislative Journal–Senate, at 1696, 1698 (Sen. Hill) (Sept. 25, 1972). I am happy to acknowledge the kind assistance of Diana Sacks and David Hostetter, Joint State Government Commission, Harrisburg, Pennsylvania.

power to punish as an instance of the power to police, there can be no such *principles* in general, nor principles of *legality* (or lawness) in particular. At best, the principle of legality is a maxim of police, rather than a principle of law, a self-imposed and self-policed guideline that the state might adopt, or follow, in furtherance of the "due regulation and domestic order of the kingdom."

The Principle of Legality as a Bundle of Maxims

The legality principle, or *nullum crimen sine lege* (or *nullum crimen nulla poena sine lege*), as we noted before, is thought to consist of not only one maxim, "no common law crimes," but of a bundle of maxims—including "void-for-vagueness," "lenity," "strict construction," and "ex post facto"—that are either unconnected, or whose connectedness at least is not considered worth exploring, or particularly interesting.[33] The very fact that *nullum crimen* functions more as a loose label, or a convenient organizing device akin to a "miscellaneous" file, already hints that it hardly qualifies as a "principle," and certainly not one that can claim fundamental status in general, and derivation from some more basic account of "legality" in particular. It is unclear what sort of "legality" is at stake, or, more precisely, just what the "lex" is without which *crimen* (or *poena*) is said to be impossible (or perhaps illegitimate). The point here is not the indeterminacy of the concepts involved, but the absence of even the beginning of an account of how that indeterminacy might be resolved.

Feuerbach did attempt to provide such an account, one based on his idiosyncratic theory of punishment that combined retributive and consequentialist components in a way that anticipated the mixed theories of punishment associated with Hart and Rawls by some 150 years.[34] In fact, in his *Textbook of Common Criminal Law in Germany*, he distinguished between three principles, which he thought were interrelated:[35]

> I.   Every infliction of punishment requires a criminal statute. (*Nulla poena sine lege*. [No punishment without law.]) Because only the statutory threat of harm justifies the concept and the legal possibility of a punishment.

---

33. Fuller perhaps would have said that these maxims are not aspects of some principle of legality, or the rule of law, but guidelines of "managerial direction." *See* Lon L. Fuller, *The Morality of Law* 207 (rev. ed. 1969).

34. On Feuerbach, see Paul J.A. Ritter von Feuerbach, *The Foundations of Criminal Law and the Nullum Crimen Principle*, 5 J. Int'l Crim. J. 1005 (2007). Feuerbach (1775–1833) was the father of the important philosopher Ludwig Feuerbach (1804–72), and a colorful figure in his own right.

35. Paul Johann Anselm von Feuerbach, *Textbook of Common Criminal Law in Germany* (1st ed. 1801).

II. The infliction of punishment presumes the existence of the conduct threatened with harm. (*Nulla poena sine crimine.* [No punishment without crime.]) Because only the statute connects the threatened punishment to the act as a legally necessary precondition.

III. The act subject to the statutory threat of punishment (the statutory precondition) presumes the statutory punishment. (*Nullum crimen sine poena legali.* [No crime without legal punishment.]) Because the statute connects the specific violation of the law to the harm [of punishment] as a necessary legal consequence.

Needless to say, citations of *nullum crimen* in American criminal law make no reference to Feuerbach's broader account of punishment, or *nullum crimen*'s place within it. Again, the point is not that Feuerbach's account is particularly compelling or that it deserves attention for its own sake, but that American criminal law has developed nothing in its place. Even if we imagine the principle of legality as a single norm, rather than as a grab bag for disconnected norms, it is not, for instance, grounded, as one might think, in "the rule of law" nor in its early American version of the insistence on "a government of laws, and not of men."[36] Nor is it connected to the fundamental principle of self-government that has driven the liberal democratic rhetoric of American legal and political discourse since the Founding Era. As a "principle," what we call the legality principle has no content; some other label, perhaps "a collection of maxims for good governance," would serve the same organizing function, if with less pathos.

If we leave aside the label and consider the individual norms collected under it, we find prudential guidelines, rather than a single legitimating principle or set of principles. We already have seen the free-floating flexibility of the "no common law crimes" maxim at issue in *Keller.* The "rule of lenity" and its indeterminately close sibling the "rule of strict construction" do not generally—occasional hints of constitutional status notwithstanding—even pretend to principle status and are honored mostly in their breach (if it is possible to breach a prudential guideline), with courts invoking or ignoring them willy-nilly.

Their constitutional cousin, the doctrine of "void-for-vagueness," is of indeterminate constitutional status.[37] The void-for-vagueness doctrine

---

36. Mass. Const., Part The First, art. XXX (1780).

37. For a recent representative statement of the void-for-vagueness doctrine, which is recited with remarkably little variation (and apparent) attention in case after case, see Chicago v. Morales, 527 U.S. 41, 56 (1999): "Vagueness may invalidate a criminal law for either of two independent reasons. First, it may fail to provide the kind of notice that will enable ordinary people to understand what conduct it prohibits; second, it may authorize and even encourage arbitrary and discriminatory enforcement."

is itself astonishingly vague, beginning with its very name, with no effort being devoted to account for the voidness—rather than the unconstitutionality or illegality or illegitimacy—that may result from its application. Its two-pronged test has no substantive content: The first prong, having to do with notice, is routinely ignored on the (implicit) prudential ground that any meaningful notice requirement would cut a wide swath of voidness through modern criminal law; the second prong is concerned with process, rather than substance, and vaguely and flexibly considers whether the statute under scrutiny provides state actors, notably law enforcement personnel, with meaningful guidance in the exercise in their generally unfettered discretion.

Consider that, from the perspective of the police power model, vagueness is not a problem, but an opportunity. Vague criminal statutes supply state officials with the necessary flexibility to identify and eliminate offensive behavior that, thanks to the ingenuity of the criminal mind or the lack of ingenuity of the legislative mind, might not fall under more specifically framed criminal statutes. Prime examples of purposely vague criminal statutes include the Racketeer Influenced and Corrupt Organizations Act (RICO), which explicitly provides that it "seek[s] the eradication of organized crime" and to that end "shall be liberally construed,"[38] and the federal mail fraud law, which has drawn praise from the judiciary as "a stopgap device to deal on a temporary basis with [a 'new' fraud], until particularized legislation can be developed and passed to deal directly with the evil."[39]

The ex post facto norm obviously enjoys constitutional status—given that it appears in the federal constitution itself. It is clear that no criminal statute could threaten punishment for conduct that occurred prior to its enactment. Still, it is remarkable both how flexible the apparently clear federal constitutional provision that "No ... ex post facto Law shall be passed" has turned out to be in the American legal regime, and the penal legal regime in particular, and how rootless the criminal ex post facto norm has remained, despite—or perhaps also because of—its constitutional source.

It did not bode well for the clarity of the *ex post facto* norm (another Latinism), that the U.S. Supreme Court almost immediately decided that the Constitution did not in fact mean that "No ... ex post facto Law shall be passed," but rather that it prohibited only retroactive criminal (not civil) statutes (not judicial decisions, as the U.S. Supreme Court recently made clear in *Rogers v. Tennessee*[40]) that either (1) criminalize

---

38. Pub. L. No. 91–452, §§ 1, 904, 84 Stat. 922 (1970).

39. United States v. Maze, 414 U.S. 395, 405 (1974) (Burger, C.J., dissenting).

40. 532 U.S. 451 (2001) (retroactivity of judicial abolition of year-and-a-day rule in homicide).

previously noncriminal conduct, (2) increase the seriousness of an existing criminal offense (e.g., from misdemeanor to felony), (3) increase the
punishment for an existing criminal offense, or (4) diminish the evidentiary requirements for conviction of an existing criminal offense.[41] Since
then, the ex post facto norm, in its drastically reduced form, has been
interpreted and applied with the same flexibility that characterizes the
other prudential maxims collected under the *nullum crimen* label, most
notably through the distinction between criminal and civil state action.
The most notorious recent example here is the exemption of sweeping
and highly intrusive registration, notification, and indefinite detention
regimes for various dangerous offenders (thought to be even more
abnormally dangerous than the normal abnormally dangerous offender[42])
from the ex post facto prohibition.[43]

The malleability of the apparently firm constitutional prohibition of
"ex post facto Law" may be related to the failure to ground this norm in
anything other than the constitutional text. It may be the only *nullum
crimen* maxim that appears in the federal constitution, but it nonetheless remains just as disconnected from the principle of legality—or any
other account of the nature and limits of state action in general and
state punishment in particular. The prohibition did not attract much
attention during the Founding Era, or during the Constitutional Con-
vention, and was, at any rate, not regarded as a revolutionary innovation
in light of new principles of American government; instead it was simply
lifted from English sources, including Blackstone's *Commentaries*.[44]

The ex post facto prohibition shares this story of origin with the
clause in the Bill of Rights that would appear to be most directly
concerned with the state's power to punish through criminal law, the
Eighth Amendment prohibition of inflicting cruel and unusual punishments.[45] That provision, too, did not spring from any consideration of the
legitimacy challenge faced by state punishment in a republican democracy ostensibly grounded in the ideals of autonomy and equality. Instead,
the prohibition was copied without debate from a provision in the very
English, and decidedly pre-revolutionary and pre-republican, Bill of
Rights of 1689 (which itself derived from the Magna Carta of 1215).[46] In

---

41. Calder v. Bull, 3 U.S. 386, 390 (1798).

42. On abnormal dangerousness as the touchstone of criminal liability, notably under
the Model Penal Code, see *infra* text accompanying note 53.

43. Kansas v. Hendricks, 521 U.S. 346 (1997).

44. 1 William Blackstone, *Commentaries on the Laws of England*, intro. § 2 (Of the
Nature of Laws in General) (1765).

45. *See generally* Anthony F. Granucci, *"Nor Cruel and Unusual Punishments
Inflicted": The Original Meaning*, 57 Calif. L. Rev. 839 (1969).

46. *Compare* U.S. Const. amend. VIII ("Excessive bail shall not be required, nor
excessive fines imposed, nor cruel and unusual punishments inflicted"), *with* The English

fact, the very formulation of the prohibition parallels maxims long familiar from limitations on the disciplinary authority of householders; cruel and unusual measures were taken as evidence of the sort of malignant, malicious, and wantonly arbitrary character that marked a householder as unfit for his governing post.[47]

The principle of legality, or *nullum crimen*, and the various and sundry prudential maxims collected under its head, thus are not alone in lacking a foundation in the new and distinctly American conception of law that drew legitimacy from the self-government of equals, rather than manifesting the essential distinction between king as ruler and *his* subject as ruled. The Eighth Amendment was not seen as addressing a new republican legitimacy challenge to the state's power to punish through criminal law.[48]

The lack of interest in the *nullum crimen* norm, and the Cruel and Unusual Punishment prohibition, reflects the lack of interest in the foundations of state punishment through criminal law in general. Another lawyer Latinism, *actus non facit reum nisi mens sit rea*—which combines the supposed bedrocks of American criminal law, actus reus and mens rea—is likewise best understood as a police maxim, rather than as a legal principle. It is a maxim copied without critical analysis from the same English penal regime that regarded crime as an offense against "the King's peace" and an affront against his sovereignty. With the King as the ultimate victim of crime, even homicide *se defendendo* was at best excusable, and therefore pardonable, rather than justified as a matter of right; after all, since any homicide deprived the King of one of his subjects, it should be up to the King to decide, in his merciful discretion, whether or not to excuse the offense.[49] This maxim saw the harm of maiming as partially depriving the King of a human resource to

---

Bill of Rights: An Act Declaring the Rights and Liberties of the Subject and Settling the Succession of the Crown (1689) ("That excessive bail ought not to be required, nor excessive fines imposed, nor cruel and unusual punishments inflicted"), *and* Magna Carta ch. 20 (1215) ("A freeman shall not be amerced for a slight offense, except in accordance with the degree of the offense; and for a grave offense he shall be amerced in accordance with the gravity of the offense, yet saving always his livelihood, and a merchant in the same way, saving his merchandise, and a villein shall be amerced in the same way, saving his wainage; if they fall into our mercy.").

47. *See* Dubber, *The Police Power*, *supra* note 5, at 6, 31, 39–41.

48. In fact, the Eighth Amendment itself played at best a modest role in even the constitutional, never mind the systematic, scrutiny of American criminal law. *Robinson v. California*, 370 U.S. 660 (1962), here is the late, rare, and awkward exception, quickly contained in *Powell v. Texas*, 392 U.S. 514 (1968). *See generally* Markus D. Dubber, *Toward a Constitutional Law of Crime and Punishment*, 55 Hastings L.J. 509 (2004) (Eighth Amendment as source of constitutional constraints on the substantive law of crime and punishment).

49. *See* Blackstone, *supra* note 4, at 182.

use as he saw fit (notably in wartime),[50] and it thereby signified the sentiments that by the late eighteenth century had produced the Bloody Code that threatened roughly two hundred offenses with death. As such, *actus non facit reum nisi mens sit rea* would, one might think, have been ripe for a fundamental reconsideration; that reconsideration never occurred. So actus reus remained as an undermotivated appendage to mens rea, serving merely as evidence of mens rea, rather than fulfilling some other, independent, function.

Mens rea, however, was a symptom of character, or more precisely of status, that identified the offender as malicious or, literally, base or mean. It would therefore be susceptible to penal discipline at the hands of the King as *pater familias*, or state householder (*parens patriae*), who may, in his discretion, decide to exercise his disciplinary power to assert the sovereignty offended by his malicious subject's criminal act.[51] It was the mens rea that marked an act as offensive, as a disturbance of the King's peace, and therefore a challenge to his authority and ability to maintain that peace. Note, however, that the discretionary penal power of the householder extends to both the exercise and the non-exercise in a particular case; since crime was an offense against the King's sovereignty, it was up to the King, acting through his officials, both to diagnose the offensiveness of the conduct (or, in the extreme case of high treason, of the "compassed" conduct) and to respond to the offense as he saw fit. English criminal law, copied with surprisingly superficial relabeling in the new republic, does not recognize the procedural principle of compulsory prosecution, or the legality principle (*Legalitätsprinzip*), adopted after considerable debate in the German criminal procedure code of 1877, which is designed to eliminate, or at least to constrain, the discretion *not* to exercise the state's penal power (as exercised by law enforcement officials, including police officers and prosecutors).[52]

This conception of mens rea and penal discretion persists in American criminal law to this day. Take, for instance, the most ambitious effort to codify, though not to legitimate, American criminal law—the American Law Institute's Model Penal and Correctional Code of 1962. The Model Code similarly regards mens rea as an indicium of that characteristic which triggers the state's power to punish, though that characteristic is no longer malice or meanness, but a similarly amorphous "criminal dangerousness" directed no longer at the King and his

---

50. *See* J.H. Baker, *An Introduction to English Legal History* 601 (3d ed. 1990).

51. *See generally* Dubber, *The Police Power*, *supra* note 5, at 38–41.

52. *See generally* Thomas Vormbaum, *Einführung in die moderne Strafrechtsgeschichte* 95, 107 (2009) (citing Adolf Hertz, *Die Geschichte des Legalitätsprinzips* (Diss. Freiburg/Breisgau 1935)).

peace, but at the public (and its peace, or less archaically, its security, welfare, or "interests").[53]

The flexibility of *nullum crimen sine lege* in a police power model is matched by that of *actus non facit reum nisi mens sit rea*. Consider, for instance, the central role of possession offenses in American criminal law. The punishment of possession flies in the face of an *actus reus* principle (or "act requirement") since possession is not an act, but a status; to be in possession of an object is to stand in a certain relation to it, whether or not that relation is accompanied by an act of some kind or not. But nothing stands in the way of criminalizing possession under a police power model, which may regard possession of certain objects ("contraband") as an indicium of dangerousness, particularly when that possession is combined with some other status (felon, alien, prison inmate). The actus reus maxim then is addressed by definitional fiat, i.e., by simply *declaring* possession to be an act.[54] Possession offenses also illustrate the widespread flouting of the so-called mens rea requirement, both explicitly in the form of strict liability possession offenses[55] and implicitly through the common use of presumptions (running both ways, from some extraneous fact—proximity, say—to the fact of possession or from the fact of possession to some other fact—larceny, for instance).[56]

Keller *and the Legitimacy of Morals Offenses*

What is more, as *Keller* illustrates, the rootlessness of American criminal law extends beyond principles of the general part of criminal law, such as *nullum crimen sine lege* and *actus non facit reum nisi mens sit rea*, to its special part. The special part of American criminal law (or, rather, the special parts of the fifty-plus systems of American criminal law, including those of the states, the federal government, the District of

---

53. Under the Code, the judicial assessment of mens rea amounted to a rough preliminary diagnosis of dangerousness (under the Code's more differentiated, yet still coarse, taxonomy of purpose, knowledge, recklessness, and negligence), to be adjusted as necessary in light of an expert penological evaluation by the department of corrections. Model Penal and Correctional Code § 7.08 ("When a person has been sentenced to imprisonment upon conviction of a felony, whether for an ordinary or extended term, the sentence shall be deemed tentative . . . for the period of one year following the date when the offender is received in custody by the Department of Correction [or other state department or agency]."). *See generally* Markus D. Dubber, *Criminal Law: Model Penal Code* (2002).

54. Model Penal Code § 2.01(1), (4); N.Y. Penal Law §§ 15.00(2), 15.10.

55. These are possession offenses that require no mens rea whatsoever, or no mens rea with respect to some element of the offense—the "conduct" element or, more commonly, attendant circumstance elements such as the quality or quantity of the item possessed.

56. *See generally* Markus D. Dubber, *Policing Possession: The War on Crime and the End of Criminal Law*, 91 J. Crim. L. & Criminology 829 (2001).

Columbia, and the American military, not to mention the Model Penal
Code) likewise never underwent a fundamental critique and revision in
light of the basic principles of legitimacy underpinning the American
political project. American legislatures and courts simply continued to
criminalize the same conduct, or status, for the same reasons as their
English counterparts and predecessors. If anything, American state
officials displayed a particular zeal in performing their function as
custodians of *bonos mores et decorum*, i.e., as protectors of the public's
moral police, where police is used in the traditional sense of welfare,
well-being.[57]

Recall that *Keller* involved two so-called morals offenses, not only
the common law crime that gets all the attention, indecent disposition of
a dead body, but also a statutory one, adultery. *Keller* thus merely
illustrates the judiciary's long-standing contribution to the state's comprehensive moral police regime through criminal law. Turning, once
again, one's attention from the secondary issue of institutional competence (the who, or what) to the primary issue of state action (the why, or
whether) raises the question of the legitimacy of employing the state's
power to punish through criminal law, no matter who exercises it,
against behavior that threatens the public's moral "police" (or welfare).
John Stuart Mill's harm principle ("That the only purpose for which
power can be rightfully exercised over any member of a civilized community, against his will, is to prevent harm to others."), widely considered
the best candidate for a limiting principle of American criminal law, had
so little impact on American penal discourse that reports of its "collapse" may be less premature than misplaced,[58] not merely because Mill
did not formulate it until 1859, decades after the Founding Era, and
after the opportunity for fundamental critique it represented, had
passed.[59] That is not to say that the harm principle, even if it had exerted

---

57. The *Keller* judge's enthusiastic and even entrepreneurial protection of the community's moral police thus should not be discounted as an isolated deviation from a
universal norm of moral laissez-faire (judicial or legislative). *See generally* Dubber, *The
Police Power*, *supra* note 5, at 98–104, 127–28, 153, 197, 202, 205–06, 214. Judge Gates
showed a similar commitment to moral policing in other cases. *See, e.g., Lebanon County
Judge Condemns Pornography*, Reading Eagle (Lebanon, Pa.), Feb. 17, 1978, at 10 ("We
are fully aware that we are footprinting on new snow" by instituting obscenity proceedings
against an adult bookstore "a day or two after the state's new obscenity law became
effective."); *cf. supra* note 13 (case of Raul Valentin).

58. Bernard E. Harcourt, *The Collapse of the Harm Principle*, 90 J. Crim. L. &
Criminology 109 (1999).

59. Thomas Jefferson occasionally made remarks, in different contexts, notably his
insistence on the distinction between law and religion, that could be, but never were,
interpreted as precursors of Mill's principle. Jefferson also was the only member of the
Founding Generation to devote, however reluctantly, any significant time to the problem of
criminal law. His draft Virginia criminal law bill, however, notoriously failed to advance
beyond a promising general preamble; the bulk of the bill is an anachronistic gloss on Coke

greater influence, could have provided the special part of American criminal law—or any other criminal law system—with a principled foundation given its vagueness and unresolved relation to an account of law, as opposed to ethics.[60]

In this light, the question in *Keller* is not whether the trial court had the authority—or even the duty, as the Law Lords in *Shaw* would have it—to define new common law crimes in general, or offenses against *bonos mores et decorum*. Rather, the question is whether morals offenses in general could be legitimated. This question has remained remarkably unexplored in American legal and political discourse, undoubtedly because it had an answer as obviously affirmative as the question regarding the legitimacy of the state's power to punish as an instance of its power to police. The Supreme Court's opinion in *Lawrence v. Texas* is the exception to the otherwise universal rule, not only by striking down a specific morals offense, here homosexual sex, but also by drawing into question the legitimacy of morals offenses in general.[61] It is no surprise that the majority in *Lawrence* would have to invoke a principle that is as abstract and fundamental as it was previously unannounced, and all the more noteworthy for it:

> Freedom extends beyond spatial bounds. Liberty presumes an autonomy of self that includes freedom of thought, belief, expression, and certain intimate conduct.

The basic substantive question that underlies the institutional question explicitly addressed in *Keller*, and which is raised indirectly through *Keller's* invocation of Blackstone's classical definition of the English king-patriarch's power to police, cannot be resolved by restricting the power to punish through criminal law to the legislature. At bottom, the court-created morals offense of "indecent disposition of a dead body" in *Keller* faces the same legitimacy concerns as the legislature-created morals offense of adultery or, after the recodification of Pennsylvania criminal law in the wake of the Model Penal Code, the morals offense of "abuse of corpse."[62]

---

and Anglo–Saxon dooms. Markus D. Dubber, *"An Extraordinarily Beautiful Document": Jefferson's Bill for Proportioning Crimes and Punishments and the Challenge of Republican Punishment*, in *Modern Histories of Crime and Punishment* 115 (Markus D. Dubber & Lindsay Farmer eds., 2007).

60. For a critical discussion of the German concept of *Rechtsgut* (or law good), which is said to play this foundational role in German criminal law, see Markus D. Dubber, *Theories of Crime and Punishment in German Criminal Law*, 53 Am. J. Comp. L. 679 (2006).

61. 539 U.S. 558 (2003).

62. Pa. Crimes Code § 5510 ("Except as authorized by law, a person who treats a corpse in a way that he knows would outrage ordinary family sensibilities commits a misdemeanor of the second degree."); *compare* Model Penal Code § 250.10.

2

Erik Luna

The Story of *Robinson*: From Revolutionary Constitutional Doctrine to Modest Ban on Status Crimes

For much of American history, criminal law allowed punishment not only for conduct, such as theft or burglary or assault, but also for a person's status or condition or ascribed character, such as being a "common thief." Most obviously, punishing individuals for their reputation instead of their behavior, "not for doing, but for being,"[1] was the essence of vagrancy law. The crime of vagrancy had long been used against perceived threats to society, including people who were associated with specific offenses (e.g., gambling and prostitution) as well as those variously and colorfully described as rogues, vagabonds, tramps, and ne'er-do-wells. In one sense, these offenses were justified as super-inchoate preventive crimes: "A vagrant is a probable criminal," a federal court wrote in 1947, "and the purpose of the statute is to prevent crimes which may likely flow from his mode of life."[2] But often the socially disfavored state of being seemed sufficient for prosecution.

From the days of early English common law on, the list of status offenders included the "common drunkard" (or "habitual drunkard"). He was guilty of nuisance at common law and considered a vagrant under many statutory schemes in the United States. The offense of public intoxication was also old enough to be part of the common law received from England; Parliament explicitly criminalized this "Odious and Loathsome Sin" in 1606.[3] In the late nineteenth century, one American court categorized voluntary drunkenness as malum in se,

---

1. People v. Allington, 229 P.2d 495, 500 (Cal. Ct. App. 1951).

2. District of Columbia v. Hunt, 163 F.2d 833, 835 (D.C. Cir. 1947).

3. 4 James 1, c. 5 (1606); *see also* 4 William Blackstone, *Commentaries* *25–26.

"always wrong, morally and legally."[4] Although the crimes overlapped, public drunkenness was distinguishable from vagrancy through the persona of the common drunkard. The former offense involved an act, intoxication at a particular place and time, whereas the latter was a condition or what came to be fashionably called a "lifestyle," that is, the character of "a person whose general rule of life is that of drunkenness."[5]

The drug addict was a more recent addition to the litany of status offenders.[6] Public concern about narcotics is sometimes traced to the Civil War, when injured soldiers returned home with the so-called "army disease"—addiction to morphine. The problem was largely considered medical in nature, however, and the first national narcotics law still permitted a physician to prescribe drugs "in the course of his professional practice."[7] Even so, law enforcement and, eventually, the courts would interpret the federal regime as an outright ban, prohibiting a doctor from prescribing certain specified drugs to addicts and thereby foreclosing their only legal supply.[8] In time, all American jurisdictions would forbid the distribution, possession, and use of drugs such as heroin and cocaine, typically without exception or mitigation for the addict. By the early 1960s, a third of all states went even further by criminalizing addiction itself.[9] Some jurisdictions classified addicts as vagrants or disorderly persons, while others made it a distinct crime "to be or become addicted."[10] Either way, addicts were punished not for their actions but for their status or condition.

In the mid-twentieth century, jurists and legal commentators denounced status crimes as ineffective at preventing crime or solving profound social problems, and they balked at arrests based on mere suspicion of criminality rather than antisocial actions.[11] Despite historical pedigree, some scholars believed that the laws were unconstitutionally void for vagueness under the Due Process Clause, not unlike the crime

---

4. State v. Brown, 16 P. 259, 262 (Kan. 1888). For the distinctions among types of intoxication (e.g., voluntary vs. involuntary), see 2 Wayne R. LaFave, *Substantive Criminal Law* § 9.5 (2d ed. 2003).

5. Tatum v. State, 22 So. 2d 350, 351 (Ala. Ct. App. 1956).

6. As a pharmacological matter, alcohol is a "drug." For purposes of this chapter, however, the word "drug" will refer to illicit psychoactive substances such as cocaine, heroin, and marijuana. *Cf.* Margaret P. Battin et al., *Drugs and Justice* 14–20 (2008) (discussing definition of "drug").

7. Harrison Narcotics Act of 1914, Pub. L. No. 63–223, 38 Stat. 785, 786 (1914).

8. *See, e.g.*, United States v. Behrman, 258 U.S. 280 (1922).

9. *See* S. Doc. No. 84–120 (1956).

10. Mo. Ann. Stat. § 195.020 (1959).

11. *See, e.g.*, William O. Douglas, *Vagrancy and Arrest on Suspicion*, 70 Yale. L.J. 1 (1960).

of being a "gangster" that the Supreme Court had struck down years earlier.[12] A few status offenses were additionally objectionable on medical grounds. Researchers and health care professionals began to view alcoholism as a disease, making the age-old practice of punishing habitual drunkards more complicated and discomforting.[13] The same was true of the drug addict, with modern science recognizing addiction as a disorder that required treatment.[14]

Nonetheless, most penal codes retained status crimes, their violators filling jails and courthouses across the nation. As critics acerbically noted, vagrancy-type provisions served as street-sweeping devices, a means to banish the unwanted, tools to deal with suspicious characters, and a sort of "garbage pail of the criminal law."[15] Moreover, status offenders were social "diseases" in and of themselves. Addicts were "contagious," spreading drug addiction "with cancerous rapidity,"[16] and vagrancy was "a parasitic disease, which, if allowed to spread, will sap the life of that upon which it feeds."[17] For a while, the U.S. Supreme Court appeared unwilling to join the fray, dismissing a petition that challenged a California vagrancy statute.[18]

Against this background, Lawrence Robinson's arrest and conviction for his status as a drug addict was neither unprecedented nor inconsistent with prevailing drug laws and enforcement. In the early 1960s, however, the criminalization of addiction and the very idea of status offenses would be assailed on constitutional grounds, eventually landing in the Supreme Court. *Robinson v. California* would test whether government could continue to punish an individual for his status, his disease or condition, and his related conduct—and for a time, it would portend a revolution in criminal law doctrine.

Indeed, *Robinson* stands as a prime example of the Court's intermittent efforts to constitutionalize substantive criminal law. A few years earlier, the Court held in *Lambert v. California* that a felon must have

---

12. *See* Lanzetta v. New Jersey, 306 U.S. 451 (1939).

13. *See, e.g.*, E.M. Jellinek, *The Disease Concept of Alcoholism* (1960). For instance, the World Health Organization recognized alcoholism as a disease in 1951, and the American Medical Association did the same in 1956. *See* H.R. Rep. No. 91–1663, at 2 (1970).

14. *See, e.g.*, *Drug Addiction: Crime or Disease?* (Alfred R. Lindesmith ed., 1961); *Symposium on Narcotics*, 22 Law & Contemp. Probs. 1 et seq. (1957).

15. Caleb Foote, *Vagrancy–Type Law and Its Administration*, 104 U. Pa. L. Rev. 603, 631 (1956).

16. Rufus King, *Narcotic Drug Laws and Enforcement Policy*, 22 Law & Contemp. Probs. 113, 129 (1957) (quoting congressional report).

17. State v. Harlowe, 24 P.2d 601, 603 (Wash. 1933).

18. Edelman v. California, 344 U.S. 357 (1953).

actual notice of a statutory duty to register with law enforcement.[19] In turn, the landmark 1970 case of *In re Winship* required the prosecution to prove the defendant's guilt beyond a reasonable doubt,[20] a rule that was extended five years later in *Mullaney v. Wilbur* to preclude the state from shifting this burden to the defendant for any elements of the charged crime.[21] Although each decision raised expectations of a larger constitutional project, later judgments and the passage of time would recast the cases as outliers rather than outlines of a grand makeover. Two years after it was decided, *Mullaney* was effectively neutralized by *Patterson v. New York*, in which the Supreme Court concluded that a state may define facts or circumstances as "affirmative defenses" to be proven by the accused.[22] As dissenting Justice Felix Frankfurter predicted, *Lambert* would come to be viewed as "a derelict on the waters of the law,"[23] concerned solely about registration statutes and without any impact on criminal law doctrine more generally.

Maybe more than any other Supreme Court decision, *Robinson* had the potential to alter fundamentally the jurisprudence of crime and punishment in America, bringing the core of criminal law doctrine within the fold of constitutional law. But its promise would go unfulfilled, as the case was downscaled from a revolutionary spark to a modest principle. If at all, any constitutional reformation of criminal law would be decades away and would come through the oblique means of criminal procedure.

Robinson v. California

Since 1872, California's penal code covered the usual suspects of vagrancy, including the common drunkard.[24] For a decade, the addict was also explicitly listed as a vagrant, until the state's drug laws were moved to the Health and Safety Code in 1939. The new provisions prohibited the transportation, sale, and possession of certain "narcotics," including cocaine, opium, morphine, heroin, and marijuana.[25] There

---

19. 355 U.S. 225 (1957).

20. 397 U.S. 358 (1970).

21. 421 U.S. 684 (1975).

22. 432 U.S. 197 (1977). *But see infra* note 98 and accompanying text (referencing contemporary Sixth Amendment decisions).

23. *Lambert*, 355 U.S. at 232 (Frankfurter, J., dissenting).

24. Cal. Penal Code § 647 (provided in Arthur H. Sherry, *Vagrants, Rogues and Vagabonds—Old Concepts in Need of Revision*, 48 Cal. L. Rev. 557, 562 n.38 (1960)).

25. Cal. Health & Safety Code §§ 11001, 11712, 11713. By their medical definitions, cocaine and marijuana are not narcotics; they are, respectively, a stimulant and a hallucinogen. Moreover, the original statute only included *cannabis sativa L.*, a specific type of marijuana. Nonetheless, the California courts held that the state legislature had

was also a section criminalizing drug use or being under the influence of narcotics. Most importantly, this section made it a misdemeanor "to be addicted to the use of narcotics," punishable from ninety days to one year in the county jail.[26] The prosecution did not have to prove that an alleged addict had used drugs within the relevant jurisdiction, nor was it material that he was going through a state of withdrawal at the time of arrest.[27] "[A]ddiction is a chronic rather than an ordinary acute offense," a state court opined, "and one may be guilty of being a 'drug addict' at any time and place he is found so long as the character remains unchanged, although then and there innocent of any act demonstrating his character."[28] The addict remained a potential vagrant as well, only now as someone who could be regarded as a "dissolute person."[29]

During the 1950s, California officials were urged to adopt more humane and comprehensive approaches to the problems of drug addiction and chronic alcoholism. An initial bill to revamp the state's vagrancy law was vetoed by the governor, who believed the proposed legislation "removed from police control certain dangerous conduct, regulation of which is necessary in the public interest."[30] The drug addiction statute provided a powerful tool for law enforcement, permitting police searches and arrests without proof of drug possession, for instance, and allowing prosecutors to skirt venue requirements. Officials in the Los Angeles Police Department (LAPD) had stated that virtually all drug addicts were involved in other criminal activities.[31] As for increased arrests of drunkards, the police chief wryly responded that perhaps Los Angeles should adopt the system of other cities, "where drunks are left to die in the gutter."[32]

In early 1960, the California Supreme Court struck down the state's "common drunkard" provision as unconstitutionally vague,[33] providing more impetus for legislative reform. A new law would eliminate many of the state's status crimes, refocusing its penal code on behavior such as public intoxication.[34] In signing the law into effect, California's governor

---

intended to include all plants popularly known as "marijuana." *See* People v. Van Alstyne, 46 Cal. App. 3d 900 (1975).

26. Cal. Health & Safety Code § 11721.

27. *See, e.g.*, People v. Ackles, 304 P.2d 1032, 1032 (Cal. Dist. Ct. App. 1956).

28. People v. Jaurequi, 298 P.2d 896, 899–900 (Cal. Dist. Ct. App. 1956).

29. *Id.*

30. Sherry, *supra* note 24, at 569 n.67 (quoting letter from Gov. Edmund G. Brown).

31. *See, e.g.*, *The Narcotic Problem*, 1 UCLA L. Rev. 405, 510 (1954).

32. *Report on Mafia Stirs California*, N.Y. Times, May 3, 1959, at 46 (quoting LAPD Chief William H. Parker).

33. *See* In re Newbern, 350 P.2d 116 (Cal. 1960).

34. *See* Cal. Penal Code § 647(f).

declared "it is what a man does, not who or where he is, that defines the crime."[35] Still, the status offense of being a drug addict remained on the books as an instrument of law enforcement.

The Crime and the Trial Below

Lawrence Robinson was a twenty-five year old army veteran who lived in Los Angeles, purportedly spending the days with his mother and the nights with his grandmother.[36] On the chilly evening of February 4, 1960, Robinson picked up his "lady friend," Ruth Fairlur, in a car driven by Charles and Norma Banks. As the couples were looking for a place to cash Fairlur's paycheck, their car was pulled over by an unmarked police vehicle driven by Officers Lawrence Brown and S.T. Wapato of the LAPD's Wilshire Felony Unit. According to Officer Brown, the car had been stopped because its rear license plate was not illuminated as required by law. (In court, Brown would express additional concern about a recent spate of purse snatchings in the vicinity.) The driver, Charles Banks, got out of his green, four-door 1947 Nash and began talking with the police officers, who observed a fresh needle mark on the driver's left arm. When Banks admitted using narcotics, Officer Brown placed him under arrest. In the meantime, Officer Wapato approached the car, ordered the three passengers out, lined them up in front of an adjacent building, and told them not to talk. After searching the car and then the passengers themselves, the officers turned their attention to Lawrence Robinson.

They noticed that Robinson was perspiring heavily, had glassy eyes and pinpointed pupils, and generally appeared nervous. When asked by Officer Brown, Robinson supposedly said, "Yes, I use narcotics," although he claimed to be neither an addict nor a buyer. Instead, Robinson said he used drugs provided by his friends, initially stating that he last injected heroin two months earlier but then admitting that it had been only two weeks. Robinson was ordered to take off his coat and roll up his sleeves, revealing scabs, discoloration, and what appeared to be fresh needle marks on his arms. At that point, the officers placed Robinson under arrest, allowed the women passengers to go their way, and transported the two men to the police station for booking. The next day, Robinson was examined at the central jail by Officer Theodore Lundquist of the LAPD's Narcotics Division. In addition to observing Robinson's arms, Lundquist asked a series of questions about drug use, with Robinson disclosing that he injected heroin about three or four times a week and that his last fix had been at a gas station in Los Angeles a few days earlier.

---

35. *Police Here Drop Vagrancy Arrests*, S.F. Chron., June 2, 1961.

36. This account is based on testimony at Robinson's trial. *See* Record from Municipal Court of Los Angeles, Index, Robinson v. California, 370 U.S. 660 (1962) (No. 554) [hereinafter "Record"].

A misdemeanor complaint was filed against Robinson on February 5, charging him with using, being under the influence of, and being addicted to narcotics. The following day, he was represented by a deputy public defender for his arraignment. Robinson pleaded not guilty, demanded a jury trial, and was released after posting bail of $525. When his case was called for trial in March and again in April, Robinson appeared in court without an attorney—and both times the proceedings were continued. In May, he finally came to court with counsel: Samuel Carter McMorris, the attorney who had successfully argued *Lambert v. California* before the U.S. Supreme Court. With Robinson now represented by defense counsel, his trial was set for the following month.

On the afternoon of June 6, 1960, the case of *People of the State of California v. Lawrence Robinson* began before Municipal Court Judge Kenneth Holaday and a twelve-person jury composed of four men and eight women. Neither side made an opening statement, and Deputy City Attorney Sanford Gage simply called Officer Brown as the state's first witness. After Brown briefly described the events preceding Charles Banks's arrest, defense attorney McMorris objected to "the reasonableness and the legality of the arrest" and asked that the court hold a hearing on the matter. The motion was granted and the jury was excused from the courtroom, followed by a half-day or so of testimony and argument about whether the police had engaged in an unconstitutional search and seizure.

During the hearing, McMorris attempted to demonstrate that the car's unlit license plate and purported concerns about purse snatching were mere pretexts. He suggested that the real rationale of felony-unit agents, who "were not traffic officers and not in a traffic car and not dressed in uniform," was to rummage around for more serious crimes, presumably those involving drugs. Given the difficulties of drug enforcement, "officers tend to remember what they must remember and say what they must say, to gain a conviction," McMorris argued. "[T]his is a dirty business, and if they perjure themselves a little bit or forget or remember what they should, then it is justified by the fact that this is, in fact, a criminal."[37] In the distant future, the phenomenon of police perjury in suppression hearings would come to be known as "testilying,"[38] and the problem of pretextual stops would reach the Supreme Court in a remarkably similar fact-pattern.[39] As in modern court prac-

---

37. Record, *supra* note 36, at 45.

38. *See, e.g.,* Comm'n to Investigate Allegations of Police Corruption and the Anti-Corruption Procedures of the Police Dep't, City of N.Y., *Commission* Report 36 (1994).

39. *See* Whren v. United States, 517 U.S. 806 (1996) (reviewing constitutional challenge to a vehicle stop for minor traffic violations conducted by plainclothes drug agents in an unmarked car).

tice, Judge Holaday simply accepted Officer Brown's account and found
no constitutional violation in the traffic stop and subsequent investigation.

With this issue resolved, the jury was brought back into the courtroom and the trial resumed with Officer Brown on the stand, describing
the evidence of heroin injections on Robinson's arms, as well as the
defendant's admission to having used drugs in the past. Officer Lundquist was the next witness, recounting the physical examination of the
defendant's arms. Lundquist also testified that Robinson confessed to
injecting heroin on a regular basis and having used the drug a few days
before his arrest. Both officers identified pictures of Robinson's arms,
which were then admitted into evidence. Under cross-examination, Officer Lundquist conceded that the defendant had not appeared to be under
the influence of drugs or experiencing withdrawal symptoms. Moreover,
the officers had neither examined other parts of Robinson's body, nor
conducted a medical test for the presence of narcotics.

The prosecution rested at the close of the officers' testimony, triggering the nearly perfunctory defense motion for a directed verdict of
acquittal due to insufficient evidence, which the court summarily denied.
McMorris then called his client as the first defense witness. Robinson
denied using or being under the influence of narcotics on the night of his
arrest, or telling anyone that he had used narcotics. In fact, he denied
ever using drugs, period. The marks on his arms were not from injecting
heroin, the defendant claimed, but instead were the result of an allergic
reaction to "some overseas shots" he received while in the service. The
discolored spots would come and go, said Robinson, who then took off his
shirt before the jury to show various other marks on his body. As for
profuse sweating at the time of the arrest, "I am perspiring all of my
life," Robinson testified. "I automatically perspire."

The next witness, Ruth Fairlur, described the night of the arrest
and the less-than-courteous behavior of the officers. Fairlur also mentioned that she had known Robinson for three years, corroborating the
character of the spots on his body and how "he sweats just all over him."
On cross-examination, prosecutor Gage questioned Fairlur about what
the couples were doing in the car, whether she lived with the defendant,
and whether she had told the officers that her name was "Ruth Robinson," apparently to imply that they were not going to cash Fairlur's
paycheck and to cast doubt on "the type of person involved."

McMorris then called the defendant's mother, Ruby Robinson,
whose brief testimony confirmed the nature of the marks on her son's
body and his tendency to sweat. Finally, McMorris recalled the defendant to the stand, where he once again denied telling law enforcement
that he used drugs, but admitted on cross-examination that he might

have given the booking agent Fairlur's address as his own. With that, the defense rested.

Before closing argument, Judge Holaday had both counsel approach the bench and asked the prosecutor about his theory of the case. Gage responded that he did not think the state could establish Robinson was under the influence of narcotics at the time of arrest and he would therefore proceed only on the theory that the defendant was addicted to and used narcotics. At that instant, McMorris renewed his motion for a directed verdict of acquittal, claiming that the government had failed to prove either addiction or use, but the court denied the motion. The attorneys then gave their closing arguments, followed by the court reading the jury instructions.

Among other things, Judge Holaday informed the jury that although "it is a misdemeanor for a person either to use narcotics, or to be addicted to the use of narcotics," these two provisions "are not identical."

> That portion of the statute referring to the "use" of narcotics is based upon the "act" of using. That portion of the statute referring to "addicted to the use" of narcotics is based upon a condition or status.... A person may make use of narcotics once or for a short time without becoming or being addicted to the use of narcotics.

The judge then defined the concept of addiction:

> The word "addicted" means strongly disposed to some taste or practice or habituated, especially to drugs. In order to inquire as to whether a person is addicted to the use of narcotics is in effect an inquiry as to his habit in that regard. Does he use them habitually. To use them often or daily is, according to the ordinary acceptance of those words, to use them habitually. To be addicted to the use of narcotics is said to be a status or condition and not an act. It is a continuing offense and differs from most other offenses in the fact that [it] is chronic rather than acute; that it continues after it is complete and subjects the offender to arrest at any time before he reforms. The existence of such a chronic condition may be ascertained from a single examination, if the characteristic reactions of that condition be found present.[40]

The court also instructed the jury that once drug addiction is proven to exist prior to the date in question, "the presumption is that this status or condition continues until the contrary is shown," thus placing "upon the defendant the burden of showing his reformation" through actions that "display a real change of heart."

---

40.   Record, *supra* note 36, at 95.

On the morning of June 9, the jury retired to deliberate the case, and a little more than two hours later, it returned with a judgment: "We, the Jury in the above entitled cause, find the defendant guilty of the offense charged." This general verdict provided no clue as to whether the jurors believed that Robinson had used drugs, was addicted to the use of drugs, or both. Sentencing was held two weeks later. After denying the defense's obligatory motion for a new trial, Judge Holaday sentenced Lawrence Robinson to ninety days in county jail, followed by two years of probation. The defendant's notice of appeal was immediately filed, bail on appeal was set at $525, and he was released from custody that day after posting a surety bond.

The only direct review available to Robinson was in the Appellate Department of the Los Angeles County Superior Court. In a short opinion, the court rejected the defendant's arguments as foreclosed by its own recent decisions upholding the addiction provision. But it paused to note that the provision criminalizing the status of addiction might be unconstitutionally vague, akin to the crime of being a common drunkard that the California Supreme Court had struck down the year before. Although no further appeal was available, the court mentioned that habeas corpus review remained a possibility and made explicit that "[w]e would welcome such a test." Without issuing written opinions, the California Court of Appeal and the California Supreme Court rejected Robinson's habeas corpus petitions, thus leaving open only one avenue of relief: the U.S. Supreme Court.

In the U.S. Supreme Court

Samuel McMorris filed a notice of appeal with the Supreme Court, listing a variety of questions presented by his client's conviction. The case seemed to be headed for a pro forma denial. Chief Justice Earl Warren had placed it on a list of appeals warranting no review, and unless another member of the Court objected, the case would be turned down without any vote or discussion when the Justices met in conference. For some reason, however, Robinson's appeal was taken off the list, and Justice John Marshall Harlan eventually requested a delay in voting on the case in order to study it more thoroughly. After examining the trial record, Harlan concluded that the California statute was "capable of the most mischievous sort of abuse" and that the case "raise[d] serious constitutional questions," given that Robinson appeared to have been punished not for his conduct but only for his status as a drug addict.[41] With Harlan having convinced his colleagues to take the case, probable jurisdiction was noted on November 20, and *Robinson v.*

---

41. Tinsley E. Yarbrough, *John Marshall Harlan: Great Dissenter* 281–82 (1992).

California was transferred to the Supreme Court's docket for its 1961 Term.

Robinson's opening brief reiterated several pretrial and trial issues,[42] but the primary focus was the criminalization of addiction, offering a series of reasons why the state provision and thus Robinson's conviction were unconstitutional. The introduction to the argument section cited the recent change in California's vagrancy statute, suggesting that the only remaining vestige was the state's crime of addiction. The brief would later claim, among other things: critical phrases such as "be addicted to" were unconstitutionally vague; the ongoing nature of addiction placed defendants in a "double jeopardy trap"; the statute interfered with an addict's freedom of movement between jurisdictions; and it could impose ex post facto punishment, given that addiction might have developed before the law's passage.

These arguments were creative, if nothing else, but the eventual key to Robinson's case would be the brief's somewhat scattered discussion of foundational principles of criminal law doctrine. It assailed the criminalization of an individual's status as violating the traditional requirements of actus reus and mens rea, with a status crime lacking an external act by the defendant accompanied by a culpable mental state. "To punish a person for a condition or status is to incriminate him vaguely as 'bad,' 'immoral,' or 'lewd,'" the brief contended. Worse yet, the statute punished an involuntary status, drug addiction being a crime of compulsion rather than human volition.

The brief's crucial assertion was that the crime of addiction punished a defendant's physical and mental illness, suggesting that addiction was a disease as "a matter of universal definition." The defendant's brief compared drug addiction to insanity, and argued that to "penalize the condition of addiction as such is about as advanced as the burning at the stake of 'witches' (insane persons) during colonial days." It suggested that drug use by the addict might be the sole means to preclude "serious physical illness, collapse, and even death." Throughout, the brief railed about the irrationality of modern drugs laws and the need for treatment rather than punishment. "Counsel has made the most extensive research of this problem, and ventures to say that nowhere else in

---

42. *See* Appellant's Opening Brief, Robinson v. California, 370 U.S. 660 (1962) (No. 554), 1962 WL 115380. Among other things, the brief laid out the search and seizure argument presented at trial, prefaced by an allusion to the Cold War and an analogy to the Salem Witch trials, although culminating in a more orthodox attack on the vehicle stop as pretextual and the resulting search as tainted and overbroad. The brief also claimed there was insufficient evidence to support the defendant's conviction. Scar tissue and a few needle marks could not prove addiction, for instance, and there was no admissible evidence that Robinson had used drugs in Los Angeles in order to establish venue.

the world is addiction punished as such (except in a small minority of American states)."

To be sure, Robinson's opening brief at times reads more like a position paper or op-ed than a legal document, making all sorts of policy arguments and quoting extensively from articles, books, and reports. Its shotgun approach offered some rather dubious legal claims, and it cited more frequently to state cases and secondary authorities than to precedents of the U.S. Supreme Court. The eventual basis for the Court's decision, the Eighth Amendment ban on cruel and unusual punishment, was the very last argument made against the statute's constitutionality. It covered less than three pages, focusing primarily on the horrors of forced withdrawal and once again referring to the criminalization of addiction as "a modern example of the burning of witches at the stake."

At least some of this scattershot argument is understandable in context. In 1962, the U.S. Constitution placed relatively few constraints on criminal justice. The so-called "Warren Court revolution" was barely underway, with seminal cases such as *Gideon* and *Miranda* still to be decided—and, of course, these revolutionary decisions were about procedure, not substance. Until the Court decided Robinson's case, only the federal government was bound by the Eighth Amendment, its provisions having yet to be incorporated against the states. Moreover, the Cruel and Unusual Punishments Clause was understood as a ban on disproportionate sentences and certain methods of punishment (e.g., literal burning at the stake), not as a limitation on what could be a crime in the first place. It should come as little surprise, then, that defense counsel would throw out any number of legal arguments, ask for broad doctrinal extensions, and make a series of quasi-political statements, all to see what sticks. When it came to relevant Supreme Court precedents and historical support, there just was not much there. "Were we able to cite judicial authority," Robinson's reply brief quipped, "we would not have before us a case of first impression."[43]

As might be expected, the government's brief emphasized the absence of standard legal arguments for overturning Robinson's conviction.[44] The Supreme Court had upheld the validity of state drug regulations more than four decades earlier, and since then, the lower courts had "repeatedly noted the evils of illegal use of narcotics." The statutory terms were clear, using "simple words whose meanings should be known to all." In turn, there was no legal support for the notion that it violated the constitutional freedom of movement or the ban on ex post facto laws.

---

43. *See* Appellant's Reply Brief, Robinson v. California, 370 U.S. 660 (1962) (No. 554), 1962 WL 115382.

44. *See* Brief of Appellee, Robinson v. California, 370 U.S. 660 (1962) (No. 554), 1962 WL 115381.

Besides, Robinson "denies being an addict at all," the brief twice stressed. As for the double jeopardy and Eighth Amendment claims, the defendant had not been threatened by a subsequent prosecution, and ninety days in jail with two years of probation hardly amounted to cruel and unusual punishment. In any case, neither of these constitutional bans applied to the states.[45]

Most importantly, the government maintained that it was perfectly acceptable for California to punish drug addiction. There was "nothing novel" about status crimes, which had long been sustained in Anglo–American jurisprudence. Vagrancy laws had been upheld time and time again, the brief argued, and "in spite of the vigor" with which Robinson calls for their invalidation, "he has been unable to cite a single case in which a court has so held."[46] The crime of addiction was "the practical teeth" of the California statute, allowing law enforcement to deal with drug offenders when evidence of use or intoxication was wanting.

In addition, the government thought it was "preposterous" to claim that Robinson had been penalized for an involuntary status or that the statute was unconstitutional because it punishes some type of illness.[47] His first shooting of "that foreign poison was a voluntary act," as was every subsequent injection. There was nothing inappropriate about prosecuting Robinson for drug addiction, any more than prosecuting the pyromaniac who sets fires, for instance, or the kleptomaniac who steals another's property. "[T]hese crimes must subject their perpetrators to punishment in spite of the fact that they are associated with an illness." Nonetheless, the government's brief had made a critical concession: "a narcotic addict, particularly one addicted to the use of heroin, is in a state of mental and physical illness."

The stage was thus set for oral argument before the Supreme Court.[48] On April 17, 1962, Chief Justice Warren called the case, hearing first from Samuel McMorris. Although initially arguing procedural issues, McMorris expressed his willingness to "abandon or waive or withdraw from" these claims, because the "crux" of the case was the criminalization of addiction. Among other things, he emphasized that a status offense punishes a mere possibility or suspicion of misconduct without any act or omission by a defendant. Moreover, there was no "intent," presumably referring to the traditional mens rea requirement.

---

45. As will be seen below, *Robinson* would be the decision that incorporated the Eighth Amendment. The Double Jeopardy Clause would be applied against the states seven years later. *See* Benton v. Maryland, 395 U.S. 784 (1969).

46. Brief of Appellee, *supra* note 44.

47. *Id.*

48. An audio recording of oral argument in Robinson v. California is available at http://www.oyez.org/oyez/resource/case/332/audioresources.

McMorris suggested that a drug user no more intends to become an addict than a social drinker intends to become an alcoholic, or one engaging in sexual intercourse intends to catch a venereal disease. In fact, it was "uncontradicted" that drug addiction is a mental and physical illness, citing the government's admission on this point.

Although conceding the lack of legal precedent for his position, McMorris referred the Court to a couple of decisions invalidating status crimes on vagueness grounds, suggesting that key terms in the addiction provision might be equally problematic. He also discussed at some length the barbarity of the criminal justice system's "cold turkey" approach to addiction and the superiority of medical treatment, although only once referring to the former as cruel and unusual punishment. When asked by Justice Harlan whether there had been many prosecutions for addiction, McMorris replied, "Every day. It's a constant thing."

Deputy City Attorney William Doran argued the government's case. He went directly to the issue of addiction as a status offense, noting the history of the relevant statute and rejecting any analogy to vagrancy laws. This prosecution did not involve vagrancy concepts such as the "tramp," "ne'er-do-well," or "wanderer," Doran reminded, but instead "a man who was putting a foreign fire into his veins." Anyway, no case had invalidated the notion of punishing a status—courts had struck down a few vagrancy statutes, for sure, but the problem had been vagueness not status. When asked whether government could punish other addictions such as smoking cigarettes, Doran suggested that the question would be whether the law was a reasonable exercise of a state's police powers, and "there would appear to be a vast difference between heroin being injected into the veins and smoke being taken into the lungs."

As had occurred during McMorris's argument, the Justices voiced some concern over the distinction between drug use and addiction as well as the overlap between the two pertinent provisions. In response, Doran claimed that the addiction provision was crucial in "at least 85 or 90 percent" of the prosecutions under the California statute, given the practical difficulties of meeting the requisites of venue by proving an act of drug use in the relevant county. Although once again admitting that addiction was an illness, the Deputy City Attorney maintained that the status crime was indispensable "in the control of the use of narcotics."

The Supreme Court Decision

Notes of the Justices' private discussions and conference on the case offer some interesting insights.[49] Chief Justice Warren seemed concerned

---

49. *See* Bernard Schwartz, *Super Chief: Earl Warren and His Supreme Court* 439 (1983); Robinson v. California, *in The Supreme Court in Conference (1940–1985): The*

that the jury instructions did not distinguish between drug use and addiction, "and we don't know which ingredient the jury went on." Justice Hugo Black, on the other hand, had no problem with the instructions, did not think the statute was vague, and saw no other constitutional problem. Although Justice Harlan appeared unwilling to invalidate the statute merely because it criminalized a status—"[c]onventionally, it has been dealt with that way"—he might declare the law unconstitutional as applied in this case. Justice Potter Stewart thought the statute was "bad" on its face and would vote to strike it down in any application. Justice William Douglas agreed: "To the extent that one is a sick person, just being one can't be made a crime." In early April, Justice Frankfurter had been incapacitated by a stroke and did not participate in the case, leaving the possibility of an evenly divided Court: four votes for reversal and three for affirmance, with Justice Harlan leaning toward affirming the conviction as well.

In the end, positions would change and the vote would not be a close one, with the Supreme Court issuing a 6–2 decision on June 25, 1962, striking down California's crime of addiction.[50] Justice Stewart wrote the majority opinion, beginning with a summary of the case facts and the proceedings below. The opinion asserted that the "broad power of a State to regulate the narcotic drugs traffic within its borders is not here in issue," stressing that this question had been settled by the Court four decades earlier. Stewart then detailed the "variety of valid forms" that such regulation could take: criminalizing the manufacture, prescription, sale, purchase, or possession of narcotics; requiring compulsory treatment for drug addicts, including involuntary civil confinement backed by criminal sanctions; and establishing programs of public education on narcotics and socio-economic legislation to attack the precursors of drug crime. "In short, the range of valid choice which a State might make in this area is undoubtedly a wide one, and the wisdom of any particular choice within the allowable spectrum is not for us to decide," a caveat that would be repeated at the end of the opinion. Moreover, Justice Stewart noted that it would be a different case if the addiction provision had been construed to require proof of drug use, referring to the two separate crimes (use and addiction) charged in this case.

Here, however, the trial judge had instructed the jury that it could convict based on an individual's status as a drug addict, and the state court approval of this interpretation was binding on the Supreme Court. "California has said that a person can be continuously guilty of this offense, whether or not he has ever used or possessed any narcotics

---

Private Discussions Behind Nearly 300 Supreme Court Decisions 603–04 (Del Dickson ed., 2001).

50.   Robinson v. California, 370 U.S. 660 (1962).

within the State, and whether or not he has been guilty of any antisocial behavior there." As such, the apparently unavoidable question was whether government could make addiction itself a crime. In answering this query, Justice Stewart drew analogies from the briefs and oral argument:

> It is unlikely that any State at this moment in history would attempt to make it a criminal offense for a person to be mentally ill, or a leper, or to be afflicted with a venereal disease. . . . [I]n the light of contemporary human knowledge, a law which made a criminal offense of such a disease would doubtless be universally thought to be an infliction of cruel and unusual punishment in violation of the Eighth and Fourteenth Amendments.[51]

Drug addiction was in the same category, the opinion claimed, specifically mentioning the state's concession that addiction was a disease. "Indeed, it is apparently an illness which may be contracted innocently or involuntarily," as addiction could result from medical treatment and might even take hold from the moment of a person's birth. Ninety days incarceration was not cruel or unusual in the abstract, Stewart admitted, but "[e]ven one day in prison would be cruel and unusual punishment for the 'crime' of having a common cold." California's statute violated the Constitution by criminalizing the status of having an illness, drug addiction, with the Court explicitly applying the Eighth Amendment against the states for the first time.

Justice Douglas wrote a ten-page concurrence depicting the historic approach to mental illness and other diseases, now recognized as utterly inhumane. "If addicts can be punished for their addiction, then the insane can also be punished for their insanity. Each has a disease and each must be treated as a sick person." The concurrence also provided extended quotes and citations about innocently acquired addiction and the compulsions experienced by the drug addict. A particularly graphic quotation described the horrific symptoms of an addict, leading a life as "one of the walking dead." After mentioning that most states did not punish addiction, the concurrence noted that England had adopted a medical approach that decreased the number of addicts and concomitant crime. Appropriate medical treatment was subject to debate, of course, and Douglas conceded that punitive measures against an addict might be justified "when they relate to acts of transgression." Criminalizing addiction itself was a completely different matter. "This age of enlightenment cannot tolerate such barbarous action."

Justice Harlan penned a two-paragraph concurrence that joined the Court's judgment on narrow grounds. Given "the present state of medical knowledge," he was unprepared to deem it irrational for a state

---

51. *Id.* at 666.

to regard addiction as something besides an illness or to subject drug addicts to punishment. If addiction was necessarily associated with illegal drug possession or use, "it may surely be reached by the State's criminal law." However, the instructions in this case allowed the jury to convict Robinson for being an addict without proof of drug use, with addiction defined as a strong disposition or taste for a substance rather than actual consumption. "Since addiction alone cannot reasonably be thought to amount to more than a compelling propensity to use narcotics, the effect of this instruction was to authorize criminal punishment for a bare desire to commit a criminal act." For Harlan, such action was arbitrary and beyond the power of government.

Justice Tom Clark dissented, arguing that the California statute was part of a "comprehensive and enlightened program for the control of narcotism based on the overriding policy of prevention and cure." According to Clark, the state had adopted a graduated approach to the status of being a drug addict, beginning with the provision before the Court. It applied to those addicts who acted with volition and maintained the power of self-control, subjecting them to incarceration for no more than a year. If an addiction progresses beyond this "incipient, volitional stage," a different provision comes into play, allowing civil commitment of addicts for up to two years in a state hospital. "Each deals with a different type of addict but with a common purpose," namely, curing the addiction. But even if the law's purpose and effect were punishment rather than treatment, it would still be a constitutional response to the social harms of drug use and abuse, including the crimes associated with an addict feeding his habit. "Moreover, 'status' offenses have long been known and recognized in the criminal law," Clark concluded, citing to Blackstone's *Commentaries* and offering the crime of drunkenness as a "ready example."

Justice Byron White also dissented, emphasizing that Robinson was not being punished for "having an illness or for simply being in some status or condition." Instead, he was prosecuted for "the regular, repeated or habitual use of narcotics immediately prior to his arrest," with the crime of addiction allowing "convictions for use where there is no precise evidence of the county where the use took place." In White's view, there was no indication that the state would apply the statute to a "helpless addict," and there was no evidence that Robinson had lost his power of self-control. "The [majority] recognizes no degrees of addiction," however, and thereby bans "any prosecution for addiction regardless of the degree or frequency of use." White also protested that the Court's opinion "bristles with indications of further consequences," noting that if a state cannot punish an addict as such, it would seem equally unacceptable to punish him for drug use based on the same evidence proving his addiction. The decision thus left the states to wonder whether they may criminalize drug use at all, although "[t]hey will have to await a final answer in another case."

The Legacy of Robinson

The day after the decision was announced, a *New York Times* article described California's "unusual statute" and the equally unusual basis for its invalidation.[52] The Eighth Amendment's ban on cruel and unusual punishment "is seldom invoked in the courts, and observers had difficulty today remembering any case in which a criminal conviction had been reversed on that ground." After describing the underlying facts and majority opinion, the article mentioned that "Justice White's dissent drew particular attention" and quoted his arguments at length. In a short sidebar piece in the *Times*, Los Angeles City Attorney Roger Arnebergh said the decision would "greatly handicap our effort to curb the use of narcotics" and "would undoubtedly have an adverse effect on the state program for rehabilitation of narcotics addicts."[53]

At this point, an already extraordinary case took a bizarre turn. Immediately after the Court's opinion was issued, it was revealed that Lawrence Robinson had died of a drug overdose on August 5, 1961—many months before briefs were filed and oral argument was heard and nearly a year prior to the Supreme Court's decision.[54] The California Attorney General filed a petition arguing that all proceedings before the Justices had been moot in light of Robinson's death and asking the Court to vacate the decision consistent with its own precedent. Apparently, Samuel McMorris did not respond to the request for rehearing, which undoubtedly would have required some explaining on his part. Not only had he pressed the case before the Supreme Court after his client's demise, McMorris had also told the Justices at oral argument that Robinson was "still on probation at this time."[55] Nonetheless, the

---

52. *Drug Addiction Ruled No Crime: High Court Voids California Law Penalizing Use*, N.Y. Times, June 26, 1962, at 1.

53. *Action Seen as Handicap*, N.Y. Times, June 26, 1962, at 18.

54. *See* Amicus Curiae Brief of the Cal. Att'y Gen. in Support of Rehearing or Dismissal of Action at 2, Robinson v. California, 370 U.S. 660 (1962) (No. 554), 1962 WL 115379 (noting that, on the day *Robinson* was announced, the public press informed the California Attorney General's office of the defendant's death).

55. In a subsequent journal article, McMorris pooh-poohed the issue, arguing that "nothing could be gained by either side by dismissal or rehearing," given that "state and federal courts throughout the United States would have been immediately flooded with thousands of petitions" based on the Supreme Court's original decision. "[I]t is this very fact of [Robinson's] death which serves to make him a martyr to the cause of justice for the unhappy class of which he was a part." Samuel Carter McMorris, *The Decriminalization of Narcotics Addiction*, 3 Am. Crim. L. Q. 84, 87–88 (1964). In the coming years, however, McMorris would amass a record of legal misconduct and bar discipline, eventually leading to his disbarment. *See, e.g.*, McMorris v. State Bar of California, 672 P.2d 431 (Cal. 1983);

Court denied the petition without explanation. Justice Clark wrote a
short dissent joined by Justice Harlan and the author of the original
opinion, Justice Stewart, describing the Court's action as "but a mean-
ingless gesture utterly useless in the disposition of the case—the appellant being dead."[56]

This intrigue aside, the major issue was the decision's impact on
criminal justice throughout the nation. The Supreme Court had not
invalidated a sentence as too long or a mode of punishment as too crude,
but instead had held that something could not be a crime at all. In
Robinson, that something was being "addicted to the use of narcotics,"
but questions remained as to the scope of the Court's decision. Over the
next few years, a stream of legal commentary (including pieces by
Samuel McMorris!) would scrutinize every aspect of *Robinson* and offer
all sorts of interpretations. Part of the problem was the ambiguous
rationale for the Court's judgment, providing ideal material for scholarship. "As is evident from these writings," Professor Anthony Amsterdam
wrote in 1967, "*Robinson* can be read quite broadly, or quite narrowly,
or somewhere in between."[57]

A. *Potential Interpretations*

One interpretation focused on actus reus, the traditional act requirement of Anglo–American common law, which limits criminalization to
physical actions or, in some circumstances, omissions (a failure to act
when someone has a duty to do so). This understanding might then be
refined in a number of ways. *Robinson* might be a relatively simple
decision about jurisdiction or some sort of federalism concern, demanding proof that a defendant committed an affirmative act within the
prosecuting state. After all, the majority opinion had emphasized that
California's statute would imprison an addict "even though he has never
touched any narcotic drug within the State or been guilty of any
irregular behavior there."

More generally, the decision might stand for the proposition that
government cannot punish individuals for their status—who they are,
more or less—but only for what they do, that is, their conduct. The word
"status" appeared throughout the various opinions, suggesting that the
decision constitutionalized the status-conduct distinction. In so doing,
the Court may have implicitly adopted retribution as its favored moral

---

see also Edwin Chen, *Very Forgiving: State Bar's Discipline System Hit*, L.A. Times, Sept.
29, 1985 (discussing McMorris's disciplinary problems), *available at* http://articles.latimes.
com/1985–09–29/news/mn–19099_1_state-bar-act.

    56. Robinson v. California, 371 U.S. 905 (1962) (denial of petition for rehearing).

    57. Anthony L. Amsterdam, *Federal Constitutional Restrictions on the Punishment of
Crimes of Status, Crimes of General Obnoxiousness, Crimes of Displeasing Police Officers
and the Such as*, 3 Crim. L. Bull. 205, 236 (1967).

theory, allowing punishment only for an individual's past wrongdoing and not merely for a tendency to commit crimes in the future. This would comport with Justice Harlan's view that addiction was nothing more than "a compelling propensity to use narcotics," with the statute impermissibly punishing an addict for "a bare desire to commit a criminal act."

Another interpretation was premised on the idea of volition, susceptible to either a narrow tenet or instead a relatively broad principle. Under one conception, *Robinson* was about the ability to choose one's characteristics or condition: A state may only punish an individual's status if it is freely chosen and capable of being changed. Certainly, both Justice Stewart's majority opinion and Justice Douglas's concurrence noted that drug addiction could be acquired "innocently," with the latter also describing the difficulties of kicking the habit. Even the dissents had distinguished between "volitional" addicts and those who had lost their power of self-control.

A different conception of volition might lead to a much wider view of *Robinson*, one that prohibited punishment not only for a status but also types of behavior—specifically, conduct rendered involuntary by an individual's status or condition. To use Justice Stewart's memorable phrase, a ban on punishing "the 'crime' of having a common cold" presumably would cover the involuntary cough or sneeze as well. The same line of argument would apply to addiction, drawing upon language in *Robinson* describing it as a disease and analogizing it to a mental illness. If someone is a drug addict, his possession and use of an illicit substance and resulting intoxication are in some sense involuntary rather than the product of free choice, the unavoidable attributes of the addiction itself.

A final pair of interpretations would involve closer judicial oversight of the criminal justice system or carve out a new constitutional right for the courts to enforce. The former idea would require that the denomination and enforcement of crime be rationally related to some valid aim of punishment—deterrence, for instance—thereby applying a type of scrutiny analysis to criminal justice policies in the style of modern equal protection jurisprudence. At times, the Supreme Court briefs in *Robinson* employed the language of equal protection. More importantly, Justice Harlan had alluded to rationality review in his concurrence, concluding that the California statute was "an arbitrary imposition which exceeds the power that a State may exercise in enacting its criminal law."

A somewhat different but potentially more significant interpretation would recast the Court's decision as protecting a right of individual autonomy and privacy. As Professor Amsterdam suggested, "it probably matters little whether *Robinson* is conceived as the Eighth Amendment case it calls itself or the substantive due process case it appears to be."

> The Court's experience in the political-liberty field has given it both the theory and the precedents to support creation of new constitutional "rights" not tightly delimited by the constitutional text. . . . As the Court put it in announcing a "right to privacy" [in *Griswold v. Connecticut*], "specific guarantees in the Bill of Rights have penumbras, formed by emanations from those guarantees that help give them life and substance." . . . Assuming that the "emanations" of the concerns that gave birth to *Robinson* itself can be identified and tapped, there will be no lack of constitutional "penumbras" into which to tuck them.[58]

The right of privacy might implicate a wide-ranging freedom to control one's body, including consuming intoxicating substances, so long as no harm accrues to others. Ironically, speculation about such a right could draw upon Justice White's dissent in *Robinson*, where he pointed out that the majority had failed to mention the states' power to punish drug use, suggesting that this omission could not have been accidental.[59]

Myriad laws and practices were at stake, all depending on the interpretation of *Robinson*. Every statute that punished drug addiction would be unenforceable, unless one adopted the narrowest construction of the Supreme Court's decision and construed the relevant provision to require proof of drug possession or use. Various status offenses would also appear suspect, including vagrancy laws that punished "common drunkards," "rogues," "vagabonds," "idle and disorderly persons," and so on. If volition was the key to understanding *Robinson*, drug addicts could have a defense to possession and use—and it might limit public intoxication charges against alcoholics, for example, and prosecutions of the homeless for crimes such as loitering. A volition-based interpretation could even cover drug dealing or property crimes, with addicts claiming that they only sold drugs or stole from others in order to feed their habit.

In theory, a volition-based reading of *Robinson* could provide the basis for constitutionalizing the entire field of criminal responsibility. This might mean a national standard for insanity or a requirement that the states recognize any defense premised on involuntariness of action. To the extent that volition implicates an individual's intention or adver-

---

58. *Id.* at 234–35 (quoting Griswold v. Connecticut, 381 U.S. 479, 484 (1965)).

59. In a memorandum to Justice Douglas about *Griswold*—a case that struck down Connecticut's anti-birth control law—White would jest that *Robinson* might be relevant, "since there is an obvious addiction to sex involved and it is cruel and unusual punishment to deprive one of it or to permit only at the cost of having children. A grizzly [sic] choice." *Supreme Court in Conference, supra* note 49, at 802.

tence, a culpable mental state might be an obligatory ingredient of all crime. This understanding would make the common law mens rea requirement a constitutional rule, thereby calling into question the entire body of strict liability offenses. If instead the principle of *Robinson* were a penumbra (or an emanation?) of a right to autonomy and privacy, many so-called "victimless" offenses might well be unconstitutional, ending the criminalization of drugs, gambling, pornography, prostitution, and certain sexual relationships (e.g., adultery, fornication, and sodomy).

B. *Post*-Robinson *Case Law*

The broader predictions were, in Professor Amsterdam's words, "highly imaginative but probably extravagant." Many in the academy predicted that *Robinson* would shake American criminal justice to its core. For the most part, however, this forecast did not come to pass, with the lower judiciary taking a staid approach to interpreting and applying the Supreme Court's opinion. One could have anticipated that countless criminal defendants and inmates would share the scholarly exuberance by bringing *Robinson*-based constitutional challenges—and that most would fail. With the Eighth Amendment now applicable to the states, defendants and inmates raised federal claims against anti-recidivist statutes, long prison terms, indeterminate sentencing, prison discipline and transfers, parole procedures, and the death penalty. Almost all were rejected.

Challenges to particular crimes were only slightly more successful in light of narrow interpretations of *Robinson*. One decision upheld a gambling crime, rejecting defendant's argument that gambling was an addiction akin to drug addiction, by reading the Supreme Court's decision as merely banning punishment for diseases rather than invalidating status offenses in general.[60] Other decisions construed *Robinson* as simply constitutionalizing the status-conduct line, leaving untouched those statutes that criminalized behavior. For instance, sex offenders were convicted and punished for their misconduct, rather than their status or mental disorder.[61]

Attacks on vagrancy statutes did witness some victories, most of which relied upon the distinction between socio-economic status and affirmative conduct.[62] A few cases incorporated *Robinson* into a far broader constitutional argument: Vagrancy laws go beyond the state's police powers by punishing harmless conduct with a tenuous connection

---

60. Commonwealth v. Dyer, 32 Pa. D. & C.2d 194 (1963).

61. *See, e.g.*, People v. Schaletzke, 49 Cal.Rptr. 275 (Cal. Dist. Ct. App. 1966).

62. *See, e.g.*, Parker v. Municipal Judge of Las Vegas, 427 P.2d 642, 643 (Nev. 1967) (striking down a local vagrancy ordinance because "its effect is to make the status of poverty a crime").

to real crime and threats to public order.[63] In contrast, a decision out of
the District of Columbia upheld a vagrancy statute without any reference to *Robinson*, and the U.S. Supreme Court refused to hear the case
over a passionate but futile dissent by Justice Douglas.[64] "No overt act of
criminal dimensions is charged here," Douglas argued, and "I do not see
how economic or social status can be made a crime any more than being
a drug addict can be."

As might have been expected, the most prominent applications of
Robinson involved drugs. Several cases struck down state statutes punishing addiction, although sometimes struggling to discern the appropriate rationale. One decision pondered whether the Supreme Court's
language only required proof of the defendant's drug use within the
relevant jurisdiction, but it ultimately invalidated the state statute based
on the distinction between status and conduct.[65] Another court relied
upon both the jurisdictional language and a volition-based interpretation
of *Robinson*, striking down the state law because it would punish those
who acquired their addiction in another jurisdiction, or who had become
addicts by the innocent use of medically prescribed drugs.[66]

In general, though, courts across the nation would reject challenges
to crimes closely associated with addiction, such as drug use and possession. These cases tended to interpret *Robinson* as striking down punishment for the status of addiction or a crime without a voluntary act, but
the Supreme Court's decision would otherwise permit the criminalization of drug-related conduct. *Robinson* did not even seem to cover the
crime of drug intoxication. Although some might interpret the decision
as invalidating punishment without proof of harmful conduct, a court
could characterize being under the influence of drugs as itself antisocial
behavior, voluntarily induced, and posing a danger to society.[67] Decisions
also upheld convictions for conduct allegedly driven by addiction, such as
property crimes to finance a drug habit or congregating in public in
pursuit of drugs.[68]

Some of the most interesting and controversial decisions on addic-
tion-related behavior were issued by the U.S. Court of Appeals for the
District of Columbia. This was due in large part to the unique potential
for the D.C. Circuit to accept an expansive interpretation of *Robinson*. A
decade earlier, the court had adopted a novel insanity test in *Durham v.*

63. *See, e.g.*, Fenster v. Leary, 229 N.E.2d 426, 429–31 (N.Y. 1967).

64. Hicks v. District of Columbia, 197 A.2d 154 (D.C. 1964), *cert. dismissed as improvidently granted*, 383 U.S. 252 (1966).

65. *See* State v. Bridges, 360 S.W.2d 648 (Mo. 1962).

66. *See* People v. Davis, 188 N.E.2d 225 (Ill. 1963).

67. *See, e.g.*, State v. Margo, 191 A.2d 43 (N.J. 1963).

68. *See, e.g.*, People v. Borrero, 227 N.E.2d 18 (N.Y. 1967).

United States, holding that "an accused is not criminally responsible if his unlawful act was the product of mental disease or defect."[69] In conjunction with *Robinson*, this highly controversial insanity test might provide addicts a legal defense against drug crimes (e.g., possession) and related offenses (e.g., theft). Under the *Durham* standard, a defendant made out a viable insanity claim if his addiction was deemed a mental disease or defect—and *Robinson* indicated that it is (or at least could be) such an illness—and the unlawful act was a product of this addiction.

The D.C. Circuit's most significant post-*Robinson* decision involved alcohol rather than illegal drugs. In *Easter v. District of Columbia*, a homeless, chronic alcoholic had been convicted of public intoxication. Sitting en banc, the court unanimously agreed to reverse the conviction, though its members divided on the legal rationale.[70] Half of the judges were willing to apply *Robinson* as a constitutional ban on punishing an alcoholic for the crime of public drunkenness, with their opinion describing alcoholism as a disease that prevents its victims from controlling their drinking. But the concurring judges emphasized that the decision merely harmonized the public intoxication law with another statute, which declared "a chronic alcoholic is a sick person" and substituted treatment for criminal punishment. Moreover, one judge cautioned that the citizenry would not tolerate uninhibited public drunkenness and would demand police action as before.

Lacking sub-constitutional grounds for case resolution, some courts could not avoid *Robinson*-based Eighth Amendment challenges to public intoxication prosecutions. In *Driver v. Hinnant*, the U.S. Court of Appeals for the Fourth Circuit adopted a strong conception of volition in striking down the conviction of a chronic alcoholic for public drunkenness.[71] After recognizing alcoholism as a disease that compelled excessive drinking, the Fourth Circuit concluded that the defendant's presence in public was neither of his own will nor accompanied by a culpable mental state. Instead, it was likened to "the movements of an imbecile or a person in a delirium of a fever."[72] In contrast, several state court decisions upheld the prosecution of alcoholics for being drunk in public.[73] The statute did not punish the chronic alcoholic for his alcoholism, the Washington Supreme Court argued, but for being in public while drunk,

---

69. Durham v. United States, 214 F.2d 862, 874–75 (D.C. Cir. 1954); *see also* Janine Kim, *The Story of Clark v. Arizona: The Incredible Shrinking Insanity Defense*, in the present volume.

70. Easter v. District of Columbia, 361 F.2d 50 (D.C. Cir. 1966).

71. 356 F.2d 761 (4th Cir. 1966).

72. *Id.* at 764.

73. *See* Seattle v. Hill, 435 P.2d 692 (Wash. 1967); *see also* In re Spinks, 61 Cal.Rptr. 743 (Cal. Ct. App. 1967); People v. Hoy, 143 N.W.2d 577 (Mich. 1966).

which was consistent with *Robinson*'s "sharply delineated" distinction between status and conduct. The court was also unwilling to equate alcoholism with mental illness or physical ailments, balking at the idea that the offender's drinking and appearance in public were involuntary.[74]

C.   Powell v. Texas

In the years following *Robinson*, the Supreme Court seemed less than eager to confront the unanswered interpretive questions posed by its decision. As mentioned above, the Court refused to hear an Eighth Amendment attack on a District of Columbia vagrancy statute. A few months later, it rejected a similar challenge to California's public intoxication law, provoking Justice Abe Fortas to dissent from the denial of certiorari.[75] "It is time for this Court to decide whether persons suffering from the illness of alcoholism and exhibiting its symptoms or effects may be punished criminally therefore," Justice Fortas contended, later referring to *Easter* and *Driver* as support for declaring the practice unconstitutional. "The use of the crude and formidable weapon of criminal punishment of the alcoholic is neither seemly nor sensible, neither purposeful nor civilized," he argued, and "can be applauded only by the uninformed or the sadistic."

The time to examine this issue finally came during the 1967 Term, when the Court agreed to hear the case of *Powell v. Texas*.[76] On December 19, 1966, defendant Leroy Powell was arrested for public intoxication in Austin, Texas, and convicted the next day in city court.[77] In early April 1967, Powell received a de novo trial in county court, where he testified about his dismal four-decade history of alcohol use and abuse. Although he had a family and residence, Powell often slept on the sidewalk and in other public places. In fact, he had been arrested more than 100 times for public intoxication. The principal witness for the defense was David Wade, a psychiatrist with an expertise in alcoholism. He described the alcoholic as suffering from a disease that prevents him from resisting the consumption of alcohol, and whose appearance in public might be a symptom of the underlying illness. According to Dr. Wade, Powell was "a chronic alcoholic," who suffers from "an uncontrollable compulsion to drink" and "is not able to control his behavior," such as appearing in public.

The witness did acknowledge a debate within the medical profession as to whether alcoholism is an "addiction," or merely a strong habit

---

74. *Hill*, 435 P.2d at 698–701.

75. Budd v. California, 385 U.S. 909, 909–13 (1966), *cert. denied* (Fortas, J., dissenting from denial of certiorari). Fortas had replaced Justice Arthur Goldberg in 1965.

76. Powell v. Texas, 392 U.S. 514 (1968).

77. This interpretation of the facts can be found in the "Appendix" to Powell v. Texas, 392 U.S. 514 (1968), filed by appellant Powell in the U.S. Supreme Court.

predisposing one to drink. On cross-examination, Dr. Wade even conceded that Powell's first drink from a sober condition would be a voluntary exercise of will, with the defendant fully cognizant of the difference between right and wrong and the consequences of his drinking. Wade also admitted that the compulsion to drink, though "an exceedingly strong influence," is "not completely overpowering," and could not be distinguished from the pressures faced by a compulsive eater, for instance.

The trial judge ultimately found Powell guilty as charged, rejecting the Eighth Amendment claim that chronic alcoholism is an excuse to the crime of public intoxication. At the request of the defense, however, the judge entered findings of fact: "chronic alcoholism is a disease which destroys the afflicted person's will power to resist the constant, excessive consumption of alcohol"; "a chronic alcoholic does not appear in public by his own volition but under a compulsion symptomatic of the disease of chronic alcoholism"; and Powell "is a chronic alcoholic who is afflicted with the disease of chronic alcoholism."[78] Because he had no right to further review in state court, Powell appealed his case directly to the U.S. Supreme Court, which noted probable jurisdiction in early October 1967.

On June 17, 1968, the Supreme Court issued a decision affirming Powell's conviction, with Justice Thurgood Marshall announcing the judgment and delivering a plurality opinion joined by Chief Justice Warren and Justices Black and Harlan. After describing the case background, Marshall proceeded to reject the trial court's "findings of fact," which could not be sustained given, inter alia, the lack of agreement within the medical profession about what is meant by labeling alcoholism a disease.

> One of the principal works in this field states that the major difficulty in articulating a "disease concept of alcoholism" is that "alcoholism has too many definitions and disease has practically none." This same author concludes that "a disease is what the medical profession recognizes as such." In other words, there is widespread agreement today that "alcoholism" is a "disease," for the simple reason that the medical profession has concluded that it should attempt to treat those who have drinking problems. There the agreement stops.[79]

Alcoholics exhibited a broad, sometimes inconsistent range of symptoms, Marshall noted. Moreover, proponents of the disease conception relied

---

78. These findings roughly mirrored the syllogism adopted by the Fourth Circuit. *See* Driver v. Hinnant, 356 F.2d 761, 764 (4th Cir. 1966).

79. *Powell*, 392 U.S. at 522 (quoting E.M. Jellinek, *The Disease Concept of Alcoholism* (1960)).

upon empty phrases such as "compulsion" or "impulse" to describe the alcoholic's ultimate motivation to drink. Defendant Powell's situation was a case in point, where his first drink was a "voluntary exercise of will," yet undertaken by the "exceedingly strong influence" of a "compulsion" that was "not completely overpowering."

For Marshall, the juxtaposition of free will and compulsion had little meaning and instead represented the problematic interaction of distinct disciplines. "The definitional confusion reflects ... not merely the undeveloped state of the psychiatric art but also the conceptual difficulties inevitably attendant upon the importation of scientific and medical models into a legal system generally predicated upon a different set of assumptions." Besides, there was neither a consensus on treating alcoholism nor sufficient medical facilities to deal with indigent alcoholics. "Thus we run the grave risk that nothing will be accomplished beyond the hanging of a new sign—reading 'hospital'—over one wing of the jailhouse." A jail sentence is typically short, or at least limited in duration, thereby ensuring periodic release, whereas civil commitment may result in indefinite detention of an alcoholic until he is "cured." In this context, Justice Marshall concluded, the application of the criminal process was scarcely irrational or devoid of social value.

Finally, Marshall turned to the Eighth Amendment issue and the application of *Robinson*. The present case was entirely distinguishable from the Court's precedent, the opinion concluded, interpreting *Robinson* as a minimal prohibition on status crimes:

> [Appellant Powell] was convicted, not for being a chronic alcoholic, but for being in public while drunk on a particular occasion. The State of Texas thus has not sought to punish a mere status, as California did in *Robinson*; nor has it attempted to regulate appellant's behavior in the privacy of his own home. Rather, it has imposed upon appellant a criminal sanction for public behavior which may create substantial health and safety hazards, both for appellant and for members of the general public, and which offends the moral and esthetic sensibilities of a large segment of the community.... *Robinson* so viewed brings this Court but a very small way into the substantive criminal law. And unless *Robinson* is so viewed it is difficult to see any limiting principle that would serve to prevent this Court from becoming, under the aegis of the Cruel and Unusual Punishment Clause, the ultimate arbiter of the standards of criminal responsibility, in diverse areas of the criminal law, throughout the country

So interpreted, the "entire thrust" of *Robinson* was that punishment can only be imposed when an individual "has committed some act," "has engaged in some behavior," or, "in historical common law terms, has committed some actus reus." It did not constitutionalize a volition requirement or the doctrine of mens rea.

Nor was the plurality opinion willing to extend the Eighth Amendment to cover a status-related "condition"—in the present case, an alleged symptom (public intoxication) of a disease (alcoholism). After downplaying the reference in *Robinson* to innocently acquired addiction, Marshall averred that a reading of that decision as anything but a modest ban on status offenses could end up exculpating all forms of antisocial behavior. "If Leroy Powell cannot be convicted of public intoxication, it is difficult to see how a state can convict an individual for murder, if that individual, while exhibiting normal behavior in all other respects, suffers from a 'compulsion' to kill, which is an 'exceedingly strong influence,' but 'not completely overpowering.' " Even if such a principle were limited to alcoholism, it might bar government from punishing, for instance, a drunken assault by an alcoholic.

In Marshall's view, an extension of *Robinson* to the present case would "inexorably" impel the Court into creating a constitutional test for insanity. "If a person in the 'condition' of being a chronic alcoholic cannot be criminally punished as a constitutional matter for being drunk in public," then a person might be able to claim that "his unlawful act was the product of a mental disease or mental defect"—effectively substituting a constitutionalized *Durham*-type standard for a different insanity test under state law. Noting the difficulties the D.C. Circuit had experienced in applying *Durham*, the plurality refused to "freeze" the doctrine of mental illness through a national standard. Marshall concluded, "It is simply not yet the time to write the constitutional formulas cast in terms whose meaning, let alone relevance, is not yet clear either to doctors or to lawyers."

Justice Black, joined by Justice Harlan, penned a concurrence that criticized the claims for reversing Powell's conviction as sounding "more like a highly technical medical critique than an argument for deciding a question of constitutional law one way or another." An extension of *Robinson* to immunize conduct would be revolutionary and possibly devastating to the nation's criminal justice systems, but a limited ban on status offenses embodied the aversion of Anglo–American jurisprudence toward punishing mere desires or propensities. As such, Black argued, "our limitation of our *Robinson* holding to pure status crimes seems to me entirely proper."

In stark contrast was Justice Fortas's lengthy dissenting opinion, joined by Justices Douglas, Brennan, and Stewart. After a factual summary,[80] it described the "disease concept of alcoholism" and supporting

---

80. Justice Fortas's dissent bears some of the traits of the majority opinion it once was—before Justice White switched votes and penned a concurrence affirming the decision

medical knowledge. Along the way, Fortas was careful to delineate the limits of his position, noting that the case did not implicate police authority to stop and detain drunks found in public places, for instance, or the liability of alcoholics for crimes such as drunk driving, assault, theft, or robbery. Rather, it involved a person who suffered from a disease that compelled him to drink until the point of intoxication and led him to appear in public. For the dissenters, *Robinson* stood for the proposition that "[c]riminal penalties may not be inflicted upon a person for being in a condition he is powerless to change"—which was precisely what happened to defendant Powell.

Arguably, the most important opinion of all was that of Justice White. His concurrence in the result refused to adopt the rationale of either the plurality or dissent; instead, he would hold that *Robinson* could cover behavior but that the present case failed to meet the prerequisites for a valid Eighth Amendment claim. As for his interpretation of *Robinson*, White had the following to say:

> If it cannot be a crime to have an irresistible compulsion to use narcotics, I do not see how it can constitutionally be a crime to yield to such a compulsion. Punishing an addict for using drugs convicts for addiction under a different name. Distinguishing between the two crimes is like forbidding criminal conviction for being sick with flu or epilepsy but permitting punishment for running a fever or having a convulsion. Unless *Robinson* is to be abandoned, the use of narcotics by an addict must be beyond the reach of the criminal law. Similarly, the chronic alcoholic with an irresistible urge to consume alcohol should not be punishable for drinking or for being drunk.[81]

In the present case, however, defendant Powell was convicted not for drinking but for being drunk in public. Even assuming he was compelled to drink, there was insufficient evidence that the defendant was compelled to be in public while intoxicated. "On such facts," White argued, "the alcoholic is like a person with smallpox, who could be convicted for being on the street but not for being ill, or, like the epileptic, who would be punished for driving but not for his disease."

Particularly intriguing was White's recognition that *Robinson* might still prohibit punishment of the alcoholic for public intoxication. Homeless alcoholics may be both compelled to drink by their diseases and literally unable to avoid being in public places. "It is also possible that the chronic alcoholic who begins drinking in private at some point becomes so drunk that he loses the power to control his movements and for that reason appears in public." In either circumstance, and with an

---

below. *See, e.g.*, Mark Tushnet, *Thurgood Marshall and the Brethren*, 80 Geo. L.J. 2109, 2115–18 (1992).

81. *Powell*, 392 U.S. at 548–49 (White, J., concurring).

adequate evidentiary record, the Eighth Amendment might preclude
punishment for public intoxication. In a footnote, the concurrence also
suggested the potential implications for illegal drug use. "[S]uch a
construction of the Eighth Amendment would bar conviction only where
the drug is addictive and then only for acts which are a necessary part of
addiction, such as simple use," Justice White noted. "Beyond that it
would preclude punishment only when the addiction to or the use of
drugs caused sufficient loss of physical and mental faculties." None of
this applied to the present case, given that the defendant had "made no
showing that he was unable to stay off the streets on the night in
question." For these reasons, White joined the plurality in affirming
Powell's conviction.

D. *Post–*Powell *Case Law*

After the *Powell* decision was announced, the ACLU's Peter Hutt,
who had argued to overturn the conviction, said to Texas's lead counsel,
David Robinson: "You won on the facts of this case, but we won on the
law."[82] Presumably, Hutt was referring to the combination of Justice
White's concurrence and the four dissenting votes, which in appropriate
cases might lead the lower courts to find an Eighth Amendment violation in imposing punishment upon alcoholics and drug abusers for
conduct compelled by their respective addictions. Most legal commentators advocated this position in the wake of the Court's decision, arguing
for a post-*Powell* reading of *Robinson* that would go beyond a minimal
ban on status offenses.

Many, in fact, believed that such an extension would come in the
form of a third Supreme Court case that would tie up the loose ends left
by *Robinson* and *Powell*. After analyzing the earlier decisions in light of
punishment theory, Professor Kent Greenawalt suggested that "*Robinson* gives the Eighth Amendment a sufficiently wide reading to support
further excursions by the Court into questions of responsibility."[83] But
other scholars, such as Professor Herbert Fingarette, saw *Powell* as
constraining *Robinson* to a prohibition on pure status crimes only, with
any broader interpretation premised on slippery, unsound conceptions of
"disease" and "involuntariness."[84] In the coming years, the latter posi-

---

82. David Robinson, Jr., Powell v. Texas: *The Case of the Intoxicated Shoeshine
Man—Some Reflections a Generation Later by a Participant*, 26 Am. J. Crim. L. 401, 435
(1999).

83. Kent Greenawalt, *"Uncontrollable" Actions and the Eighth Amendment: Implications of* Powell v. Texas, 69 Colum. L. Rev. 927, 973 (1969). On the truly lighter side, one
scholar wrote a song for Leroy Powell, lyrically opining that the defendant's claim would
someday prevail before the Court. Gary V. Dubin, *The Ballad of Leroy Powell*, 16 UCLA L.
Rev. 139 (1968).

84. *See* Herbert Fingarette, *Addiction and Criminal Responsibility*, 84 Yale L.J. 413
(1975). Some media commentators saw *Powell* as part of a conservative trend on the

tion would prevail in the lower courts, with Justice Marshall's plurality opinion in *Powell* typically viewed as controlling and *Robinson* confined to a ban on status offenses.

As in the immediate aftermath of *Robinson*, a variety of post-*Powell* defendants would claim that their crimes fit within the now-narrower Eighth Amendment prohibition, including: compulsive gamblers indicted on tax violations, recidivists subject to enhanced punishment, juveniles declared delinquent for their youthful transgressions, previously deported aliens charged with illegal reentry into the United States, and all sorts of suspects accused of sex-related crimes. Almost all of these claims have been rejected by the courts, which typically find that the defendant was punished for his conduct rather than his status. A few decisions would acknowledge the possibility of a constitutional bar against punishing a status-related behavior, only to hold that a given defendant had not made a sufficient showing. Either way, the result was the same—the punishment did not violate the Eighth Amendment.

The rousting of homeless individuals is one area where *Robinson–Powell* claims have seen at least limited success. Federal courts in Los Angeles and Miami found it unconstitutional to punish homeless people for activities such as sleeping in public.[85] Both decisions relied upon *Robinson* and Justice White's concurrence in *Powell*, concluding that individuals could not be punished for acts or conditions that were unavoidable consequences of their status of homelessness. Other courts have rejected such interpretations in addressing claims of the homeless, concluding that the relevant laws and police enforcement were aimed at conduct rather than status, or that sufficient shelters existed for those living in public places, thereby rendering their behavior a matter of choice.[86]

Not surprisingly, alcohol and drugs have been frequent topics of *Robinson–Powell* litigation. One case held that a city ordinance making "drunkenness" a crime—regardless of whether it occurred in public or occasioned disorderly behavior—could not be applied to an alcoholic.[87] Another decision rejected *Powell*'s reasoning on state constitutional grounds, ruling that an alcoholic could not be prosecuted for being drunk

---

Supreme Court. *See, e.g.*, Fred B. Graham, *New Tide in High Court: A Trend to Conservativism is Discerned as Changing Issues Influence Pattern*, N.Y. Times, June 20, 1968, at A32.

85. *See* Jones v. City of Los Angeles, 444 F.3d 1118 (9th Cir. 2006); Pottinger v. City of Miami, 810 F. Supp. 1551 (S.D. Fla. 1992).

86. *See* Joel v. City of Orlando, 232 F.3d 1353 (11th Cir. 2000); Tobe v. City of Santa Ana, 892 P.2d 1145 (Cal. 1995); Joyce v. City & County of San Francisco, 846 F. Supp. 843 (N.D. Cal. 1994).

87. *See* State v. Fearon, 166 N.W.2d 720 (Minn. 1969).

in public.[88] Nonetheless, meritorious claims would prove to be the exception in public intoxication cases. Sometimes courts have found insufficient evidence that an alcoholic is compelled to drink or appear in public, for instance, although others simply concluded that the Eighth Amendment poses no bar to punishing an alcoholic who creates a safety hazard.[89]

Numerous court decisions have also rejected *Robinson*-based claims against drug-related crime. Some pointed out that a given defendant failed to prove he was an addict or was unable to control his actions, but others rejected the notion that the Eighth Amendment protects drug-related conduct at all. As was true after *Robinson*, the U.S. Court of Appeals for the District of Columbia issued the most noteworthy post-*Powell* decisions on drug crime and addiction. A few of its opinions expressed concern that the combination of drug addiction and the *Durham* insanity standard had fostered "trial-by-label" through the medium of expert testimony.[90] For several years, the court would struggle with the issue of whether an addict could be convicted of drug-related crimes such as illegal possession.

In 1972, the D.C. Circuit rejected the *Durham* rule in favor of one based on the insanity test promulgated by the American Law Institute's Model Penal Code.[91] The following year, the court en banc issued what might be described as the mother-of-all post-*Powell* decisions—covering 121 pages of the Federal Reporter, with six separate judicial statements varying in length from a three-sentence paragraph to a small monograph.[92] In that case, *United States v. Moore*, the court affirmed an addict's conviction for drug possession. The "plurality" opinion saw no limit to a constitutional principle exonerating the addict for his drug-related behavior. "The obvious danger is that this defense will be

---

88. *See* State ex rel. Harper v. Zegeer, 296 S.E.2d 873 (W. Va. 1982). Still another case invalidated a vagrancy statute that made it a crime to be a "habitual drunkard." *See* State v. Pugh, 369 So. 2d 1308 (La. 1979).

89. *See, e.g.,* People v. Kellogg, 14 Cal.Rptr.3d 507 (Cal. Ct. App. 2004); City of Portland v. Juntunen, 488 P.2d 806 (Or. 1971).

90. *See* Salzman v. United States, 405 F.2d 358 (D.C. Cir. 1968).

91. *See* United States v. Brawner, 471 F.2d 969 (D.C. Cir. 1972). In response to the successful insanity defense of John Hinckley, Jr. for shooting President Ronald Reagan in 1981, Congress eventually adopted a more stringent standard that abrogated the rule adopted by the D.C. Circuit in *Brawner*. *See* Insanity Defense Reform Act of 1984, 18 U.S.C. § 17. *See also* Kim, *supra* note 69.

92. United States v. Moore, 486 F.2d 1139 (D.C. Cir. 1973). As an aside, the defendant was originally represented by Peter Hutt, one of the ACLU-affiliated attorneys who had participated in *Easter, Driver,* and *Powell. See, e.g., supra* note 82 and accompanying text. When Hutt was named chief counsel to the Food and Drug Administration, the D.C. Circuit appointed Patricia Wald to argue defendant Moore's case. A few years later, Wald would be become a judge on the D.C. Circuit itself.

extended to all other crimes—bank robberies, street muggings, burglaries—which can be shown to be the product of the same drug-craving
compulsion."[93] Moreover, *Robinson* provided "no authority" for the
proposition that a defendant cannot be punished for his allegedly compelled acts, and the *Powell* plurality had interpreted the Supreme
Court's earlier decision in *Robinson* as banning status crimes only. With
addiction viewed as a mere craving or desire to use drugs, and the
addict's illegal possession deemed at least partially volitional, the Eighth
Amendment provided no defense to a drug prosecution.

Two concurring judges paused to consider Justice White's concurring opinion in *Powell* and his statement that drug possession or use by
an addict might be covered by *Robinson*. Taken as a whole, however,
White's reasoning and votes did not "undercut Justice Marshall's opinion on the constitutional permissibility of holding even narcotic addicts
for the intentional act of possession, without recognition of a new
defense of psychological dependence that poses difficult problems of
verifiability and widespread use."[94] Four dissenting members of the D.C.
Circuit saw *Robinson* and *Powell* as prohibiting punishment of an addict
for purchasing, possessing, and using drugs, while one judge would have
allowed a defendant to raise a defense to crimes indirectly related to
addiction, such as drug trafficking. These arguments were to no avail,
with courts across the nation essentially agreeing with the plurality
opinion in *Moore*: "Any widening of the Eighth Amendment rationale
should come from the Supreme Court."[95]

Concluding Thoughts

More than three decades later, the Justices have neither widened
the Eighth Amendment in this context nor provided the (initially) much
anticipated third decision to complete a *Robinson* trilogy. So is *Robinson*
just a ban on status crimes, with no other effect on American criminal
law? Is it like Samuel McMorris's other big case, *Lambert v. California*,
"a derelict on the waters of the law," standing as "an isolated deviation
from the strong current of precedents"?[96] Neither decision generated a
revolution in substantive criminal law. Since *Robinson*, the Eighth
Amendment has been a virtual dead letter outside of capital punishment,[97] and, in fact, Supreme Court decisions on constitutional criminal

---

93. *Moore*, 486 F.2d at 1147 (Wilkey, J., joined by MacKinnon & Robb, JJ.).

94. *Id.* at 1198 (Levanthal, J., joined by McGowan, J., concurring).

95. *Id.* at 1153 (Wilkey, J., joined by MacKinnon & Robb, JJ.).

96. Lambert v. California, 355 U.S. 225, 232 (1957) (Frankfurter, J., dissenting).

97. Only one modern Supreme Court decision has invalidated an adult defendant's
prison sentence as constituting cruel and unusual punishment. *See* Solem v. Helm, 463
U.S. 277 (1983) (striking down non-violent recidivist's sentence of life imprisonment

procedure have had a far greater influence on American criminal law doctrine.[98]

Although a claim to expand *Robinson* is unlikely to succeed today, the main obstacles do not rise from the terms of the Court's core opinions. After all, *Robinson* and *Powell* did not preclude an alcoholic or drug addict from raising a meritorious Eighth Amendment challenge against punishment for conduct proven to be an unavoidable consequence of an addiction.[99] In refusing to extend *Robinson*, the plurality opinion in *Powell* emphasized, inter alia, the lack of medical consensus as to what it means to say that alcoholism is a disease, the absence of agreement on the etiology and manifestations of the addiction, and the "definitional confusion" in trying to explain alcoholism in terms of compulsion.

Forty years later, however, medical professionals and scientific researchers have reached a consensus that addiction is a brain disease resulting from the interactions between the substance(s) ingested by the addict and key risk factors, including biochemistry and genetics, which produce long-term changes in the composition and function of the human brain.[100] They also agree that some behaviors are central components of the disease, especially compulsive use and related drug-seeking behavior.[101] In the words of one expert, "drugs change the brain and thereby produce uncontrollable, compulsive drug-seeking and use"[102]—a position consistent with modern science's recognition that physical disorders of the brain manifest themselves in conduct.

Despite the "logically appealing"[103] character of applying the Eighth

---

without the possibility of parole); *see also* Graham v. Florida, 130 S. Ct. 2011 (2010) (striking down juvenile offender's sentence of life imprisonment without the possibility of parole).

98. For instance, the Supreme Court's recent decisions on the Sixth Amendment jury trial right have limited judicial fact-finding for purposes of punishment and resulted in the invalidation of key aspects of sentencing guidelines in the federal and state systems. *See, e.g.,* United States v. Booker, 543 U.S. 220 (2005); Blakely v. Washington, 542 U.S. 296 (2004).

99. *See, e.g.,* People v. Kellogg, 14 Cal.Rptr.3d 507, 522–30 (Cal. Ct. App. 2004) (McDonald, J., dissenting); *see also supra* notes 85–86 and accompanying text (discussing homeless cases).

100. *See* Institute of Medicine, *Dispelling the Myths About Addiction: Strategies to Increase Understanding and Strengthen Research* 37 (1997).

101. *See, e.g.,* American Psychiatric Association, *The Diagnostic and Statistical Manual of Mental Disorders* 176 (4th ed. text rev. 2000); Robert C. Rinaldi et al., *Clarification and Standardization of Substance Abuse Terminology*, 259 J.A.M.A. 555 (1988).

102. Alan I. Leshner, *Understanding Drug Addiction: Insights from the Research, in Principles of Addiction Medicine* 47, 48 (2003).

103. *See* People v. Davis, 188 N.E.2d 225, 226 (Ill. 1963); *see also* United States v. Moore, 486 F.2d 1139, 1239 (D.C. Cir. 1973) (Wright, J., dissenting).

Amendment to immunize an addict's alcohol- or drug-related activities, there is no reason to believe that the contemporary definition of addiction in science and medicine would be welcome in the field of law. As noted in Justice Marshall's *Powell* opinion, the conflict stems from the disciplines' entirely different, largely incompatible worldviews. The medico-scientific perspective is deterministic, where events are the result of a complex set of antecedent factors, from biochemistry to genetics to human experience, making a given result almost inevitable. For the most part, concepts such as voluntariness are immaterial in medicine and science, which do not deal with the assignment of blame.

In contrast, criminal law and its principles of responsibility are built on a type of shallow philosophy and folk psychology. The much-contested concept of "free will"[104] assumes that individuals are acting of their own volition, making them fully responsible for their choices and ensuing conduct. Sometimes law is even prepared to open up the relevant time frame or hypothesize alternative courses of action in order to find a sufficiently voluntary decision—for example, the addict who freely chose to use heroin the first time he injected it into his veins or who continues to use the drug rather than enter a rehabilitation program.[105] Criminal law does all of this with the precise goal of ascribing blame and imposing punishment.

The tension between the disciplines continues in assessing culpability in criminal law, particularly with regard to mental illness.[106] But in the areas of alcohol, drugs, and addiction, the battle between legal and medical models has been over for decades, at least in the criminal justice system. Despite reasonable interpretations of Supreme Court precedent and the modern scientific understanding of addiction, *Robinson* and *Powell* are now understood as drawing a line between impermissible criminal sanctions for status and perfectly legitimate punishment for conduct. The sheer passage of time and the long line of lower court precedent to the contrary all but foreclose a different reading. In addition, subsequent Supreme Court opinions have not been particularly supportive of broader constitutional principles in the area of drugs,

---

104. *See, e.g.*, Stephen J. Morse, *The Non–Problem of Free Will in Forensic Psychiatry and Psychology*, 25 Behav. Sci. & L. 203 (2007).

105. *See, e.g.*, Richard C. Boldt, *The Construction of Responsibility in the Criminal Law*, 140 U. Pa. L. Rev. 2245, 2304–07 (1992); Mark Kelman, *Interpretive Construction in the Substantive Criminal Law*, 33 Stan. L. Rev. 591, 600–03 (1981).

106. *See, e.g.*, Clark v. Arizona, 548 U.S. 735, 774–75 (2006) (noting, inter alia, that a "diagnosis may mask vigorous debate within the profession about the very contours of the mental disease itself" and that "the consequence of this professional ferment is a general caution in treating psychological classifications as predicates for excusing otherwise criminal conduct"). *See also* Kim, *supra* note 69.

alcohol, and addiction.[107]

Although once seen as a radical constitutional doctrine with broad implications for criminal law, *Robinson* now stands as a modest ban on status crimes and not much more. A few years ago, Professor Sanford Kadish reflected on the "constitutional revolution that failed" in the Supreme Court:

> The *Robinson* decision could plausibly have been seen as a vital opening toward establishing lack of self-control as a constitutional bar to punishment. But not for long. Just a half dozen years later the Court closed the door [in *Powell*, limiting] *Robinson* to the kind of crime there in issue, namely one that made mere status—a propensity to abuse drugs—a crime. It rejected the broader reading of *Robinson* that one could not be punished for what is beyond one's power of control. *Powell* turned out to be the end of the Court's flirtation with the possibility of a constitutional criminal law doctrine.[108]

Other scholars agree. The doctrine in this area, "though of great theoretical interest, has no practical importance today," Professor Peter Low notes. "Nothing has come of it, and the Court has not gone on to find a 'voluntary act' principle in the Constitution."[109]

To be sure, *Robinson* did have some limited impact on political actors. For instance, Congress rejected criminalizing mere membership in the "Mafia" or "La Cosa Nostra" as part of its anti-organized crime statute (RICO) on the express ground that this would create a status offense in violation of the Court's ruling.[110] As for public policy, Professor Jesse Choper once suggested that *Robinson*, although "solv[ing] neither society's drug problems nor the plight of its victims," did spur some drug rehabilitation efforts by the states and the federal government.[111] Despite some positive developments, the quandary of how to deal with drug addicts and alcoholics, and their antisocial conduct, lingers to this day.

Nonetheless, history reminds us that a prohibition on punishing individuals for who they are (as compared to what they do) was not an altogether trivial development. As mentioned in the introduction, there

---

107. *See, e.g.*, Montana v. Egelhoff, 518 U.S. 37 (1996) (upholding ban on evidence of voluntary intoxication in criminal trials); Traynor v. Turnage, 485 U.S. 535 (1988) (finding that alcoholism can be "willful misconduct" for purposes of terminating government benefits).

108. Sanford H. Kadish, *Fifty Years of Criminal Law: An Opinionated Review*, 87 Cal. L. Rev. 943, 964–66 (1999).

109. Peter W. Low, *Criminal Law* 409 (2d ed. 2002).

110. *See* 116 Cong. Rec. 35,343–46 (1970).

111. Jesse H. Choper, *Consequences of Supreme Court Decisions Upholding Individual Constitutional Rights*, 83 Mich. L. Rev. 1, 42–44 (1984).

was a time when status offenses were standard fare for criminal prosecution—not just drunkards and drugs addicts, but also vagabonds, gamblers, prostitutes, beggars, and so on. *Robinson* could be seen as the first
step toward purging these crimes from American criminal codes, with
later decisions completing the process through other means, such as
striking down vagrancy laws as unconstitutionally vague.[112]

Robinson and *Powell* also stand as fascinating case studies in the
frailty of humankind. Of course, there are the stories of the defendants
themselves: Lawrence Robinson, who at trial denied ever using drugs
and then died of a heroin overdose before his case was heard by the
Supreme Court; and Leroy Powell, who was arrested more than 120
times for public intoxication over the course of two decades.[113] Then
there are the stories of those whose plight they represent—the countless
Americans who suffer from substance abuse and find themselves em-
broiled in the criminal justice system as a result. "While drunkenness
may be the occasion for the arrest," one judge wrote about the alcoholic's crime, "human inadequacy is the gravamen of the offense."[114]

This pre-*Powell* characterization still seems applicable today in
delineating the general dilemma posed by status crimes: punishing
individuals for their personal failings as measured by some societal
standard. It is one thing to rail against alcohol and drugs, to look down
upon those who use these substances and become addicted, to employ
the civil mechanisms of proactive anti-drug education and medical treatment, and even to invoke the unparalleled power of the criminal process
against the antisocial acts of an addict. But to punish someone for his
status alone—for being a drug addict or an alcoholic—is just not decent.[115] *Robinson* may not have revolutionized the criminal justice system
as a constitutional rule, but as a philosophical principle, it hardly seems
frivolous.

---

112. *See, e.g.*, Papachristou v. Jacksonville, 405 U.S. 156 (1972).

113. *See* C.L. Gaylord, *Whatever Happened to Leroy Powell?*, Case & Comment, Jan.–
Feb. 1981, at 28, 29 n.1 (mentioning that after being arrested approximately 100 times
between 1949 and 1966, Powell would be arrested twenty more times between 1967 and
1970).

114. John M. Murtagh, *Status Offenses and Due Process of Law*, 36 Fordham L. Rev.
51, 58 (1967).

115. *See, e.g.*, Joshua Dressler, *Understanding Criminal Law* 105 (4th ed. 2006)
("Essentially, the retributive message of *Robinson* seemed to be the following: Although
drug addicts constitute a danger to society and, therefore, it may be rational to incarcerate
some of them, it is indecent to punish them simply because they are sick.").

3

Joseph E. Kennedy

The Story of *Staples* and the Innocent Machine Gun Owner: The Good, the Bad and the Dangerous

Introduction

In the early evening of December 29, 1989, Harold Staples of Tulsa, Oklahoma, had just finished leading his local Cub Scout pack through their monthly meeting. Still wearing his pack leader uniform, he loaded his two sons and a couple of the remaining Cub Scouts into his car to go get some ice cream. As the garage door lifted he saw a phalanx of helmeted federal agents wearing flak jackets and carrying guns swarm into his garage. Locked in a gun safe in his basement downstairs was a rifle that the agents would use as a basis for charging Staples with illegally possessing a machine gun.

The raid on Harold Staples's home was the beginning of a case that would make its way to the Supreme Court and change how federal and state courts think about fundamental principles of mens rea. Staples claimed that he had not known his firearm was a machine gun, and the Supreme Court held that the government had to prove such knowledge in order to convict him under the National Firearms Act. Before the *Staples* case, public danger trumped traditional mens rea concerns in the interpretation of such federal criminal statutes. The *Staples* case changed that understanding. Staples's story of a potentially innocent defendant prosecuted for things he did not know transformed the way both federal and state courts interpreted criminal statutes with ambiguous mental state requirements. *Staples* established the proposition that courts should read knowledge requirements into statutes that criminalized conduct that would be otherwise innocent, particularly when serious punishment was at stake. To put it plainly although somewhat less precisely, if a defendant's conduct alone was not clearly criminal, the prosecutor had to prove that the defendant "knew what he was doing."

The Staples story contains within it many different stories. At the most abstract level, it is a story about how the law wrestles with visions of wrongfulness and dangerousness and how those two concerns compete with and shape one another. Doctrinally, it is a story about how the old legal concept of mens rea evolved in response to new social problems but then returned to the concerns that animated its original development. But it is also a series of more particular stories that do not neatly fit into grand narratives about cycles or inexorable historical trends. These ground level stories involve choices made by lawyers, law enforcement agencies, judges, and Staples himself. At the heart of the Staples case was a series of decisions that shaped the case in ways not evident from the four corners of the Supreme Court's opinions in the case: the government's decision to prosecute Staples based on a somewhat technical definition of machine gun; the defense's decision to mount an aggressive defense of moral as well as legal innocence and Staples's decision to turn down representation by the National Rifle Association before the Supreme Court and to keep the case away from the controversial gun politics of the time. Court documents, interviews with the people involved, and Justice Harold Blackmun's recently published papers on the case reveal the role that these choices played in the *Staples* decision.

But ultimately, the *Staples* decision was about character. Dangerous things are sometimes done by people who are otherwise good. Deciding what balance a legislature intended to strike between protecting the public and protecting the innocent requires a court to decide what sorts of people the legislature intended to imprison when it defined a crime. What moved the Court in *Staples* was a vision of good people going to prison for conduct that was poorly defined under a statute designed for dealing with the worst type of criminal.

Character is also the key to understanding the limits of *Staples*'s influence. Subsequent courts have resisted applying *Staples* to statutes that were not designed to deal with traditional criminal activity. For example, courts have divided over whether and to what extent to apply *Staples*'s presumption of a knowledge requirement to environmental criminal cases. The chord that *Staples* struck with judges seems to resonate most when people of good character are prosecuted under statutes designed for the very bad. These cases reveal something important about how notions of character relate to notions of danger. They also help explain the not-quite-constitutional status of mens rea principles.

Finally, a few strange developments took place after Staples won his case before the Supreme Court that deserve mention. After his Supreme

Court victory on the gun charges, Staples was indicted in federal court on fraud and theft charges that turned out to be baseless. Staples's AR–15 was also returned to him, even though the government had maintained to the Supreme Court that it was an illegally owned machine gun. These developments—which raise questions about why Staples was singled out for prosecution in the first place—do not fit neatly into orderly narratives about criminal justice. Rather they serve as subversive reminders that the competence and integrity of law enforcement cannot always be assumed.

The fuller story of the Cub Scout leader with the machine gun in his basement bears telling for all of these reasons.

Mens Rea and the Public Welfare Offense Doctrine before the Staples Case

Understanding the influence of the *Staples* decision requires understanding how mens rea changed in the years leading up to the decision. The general definition of the term had been in flux for some time. A series of Supreme Court decisions had also created a category of "public welfare offenses" to which the traditional mental state requirements of the criminal law did not apply. These decisions balanced traditional concerns about character and moral innocence against more instrumental concerns about the need to protect the public from the newly emerging dangers of a modern industrial economy. They left some basic questions unanswered, however, that the Court had to address in order to decide *Staples*.

Mens rea has too many meanings to succinctly define, but it emerged at common law with the idea of a guilty mind. Earlier conceptions of what was meant by a guilty mind differ from how most judges, legislators and lawyers think about it today, however. The common law descriptions were colorful but vague—vicious will, wickedness, malevolence. A guilty mind could simply be a "wrongful mind" in a general sense. For example, in *Regina v. Prince* the defendant was found guilty of eloping with an underage girl, his ignorance of her age notwithstanding. Under this early conception of guilty mind as wrongful mind it was enough that the defendant knew he was taking a daughter away without the consent of her father.[1] This earlier view of mens rea was rooted in judgments about character. Common law terms such as malice, wickedness and depraved heart alluded to moral judgments about character.

Over time, however, mens rea came to be understood more narrowly. In *Regina v. Faulkner*, for example, it was not enough for an arson conviction that the defendant was trying to steal rum when he knocked over the candle that started the fire that burned down the ship. The

---

1. R v. Prince, [1875] 2 L.R.C.C.R. 154.

guilty mind of the rum thief was too far removed from the guilty mind of the arsonist to justify the punishment for arson.[2] Mens rea came to be understood in terms of the relationship between a mental state and an element of an offense. Over time this more element-based approach to mens rea was reflected in the statutory definitions of crime. Yet the early concern with character never fully disappeared. As a result, mens rea took on a number of different meanings. Some of these reflected the earlier focus on character, such as a definition of general intent as a morally blameworthy state of mind. So, the narrower, element-based view of mens rea overshadowed but never completely eclipsed the earlier character-based view.

The fact that mens rea continues to be used in both ways reflects the tradeoffs involved between the two approaches. The element-based approach requires an assessment of the specific thoughts that accompany specific acts and offers a more precise and more objective basis for adjudication. In contrast, the character-based approach involves less structured and more subjective judgments. The character-based approach offers some advantages, however, if the definition of the crime resists reduction to specific psychological states about conduct, circumstances or consequences, and if it demands more contextual assessments of motive and morality. The continued appeal of both ways of thinking about mens rea complicates the judge's task of deciding what the legislature intended when it wrote a criminal statute.

An important example of the continued appeal of the character-based approach to mens rea is the criminal law's continued hostility to strict liability crimes. Strict liability crimes require little or no moral fault or mental awareness on the part of the defendant with respect to the facts that constituted the offense. While ignorance of the law was no excuse at common law, ignorance of the facts that made the offense wrongful usually was. Offenses that did not require this sort of "guilty knowledge" of the key facts were termed strict liability offenses. The common law abhorred such offenses, and judges interpreting modern statutes often presume that legislatures intended to require culpable mental states—even in the absence of explicit language to that effect. In practice, however, this presumption typically requires proof that the defendant knew *more* facts about the nature of his or her conduct. Indeed, the term "strict liability" rarely means in the criminal law what it means in tort. Strict liability in tort means that you are prima facie liable for any damage you cause. If your lion escapes his cage then you pay for the resulting damages even if you had every reason to believe that the lion was safely secured. True strict liability in criminal law would mean that you would be guilty of drug possession if someone

---

2. R v. Faulkner, (1877) 13 Cox Crim. Cases 550.

slipped an illegal drug into your pocket without your knowledge. Yet entirely unwitting conduct is almost never a crime. A "strict liability crime" typically means that you can be ignorant about some significant aspect of conduct, circumstances, or consequences of the crime but be guilty nonetheless. Statutory rape, for example, is often described as a strict liability offense because awareness that the boy or girl is under the age of consent is not an element of the crime the prosecution must prove. One must know that one is having intercourse, but one need not know that one is having intercourse with a minor in order to be guilty. The resulting criminal liability is described as strict because you are not required to "know what you are doing" in the ordinary sense of the words or even to "have reason to know."

The Public Welfare Offense Doctrine

The hostility to stricter forms of criminal liability began to weaken in the nineteenth century with the advent of so-called public welfare offenses suitable to an industrialized society. Statutes were passed and regulations promulgated that imposed criminal liability without fault, although the penalties were typically slight and often merely fines. Regulations about tenement conditions, food and drug safety, and traffic were paradigm examples of public welfare offenses. Since unsafe or unsanitary conditions could threaten the welfare of many people at once, the legislature was presumed to be deliberately omitting mental state requirements in order to ease the burden of proof of prosecutors, and to create the maximal incentive for those regulated to inform themselves about the nature of the activities in question. So crimes could be based on mere inattention—as opposed to conscious wrongdoing, recklessness or even negligence—in order to protect the public from the newly emerging and often poorly understood dangers of modern living.

Thus understood, the public welfare offense doctrine was an instrumental response to an instrumental problem. To deal with the dangerous conditions of industrial society where market pressures sometimes produced unsafe practices, legislatures adopted stricter forms of criminal liability to create stronger incentives for safe practices. The means of imposing criminal liability with little or no fault was justified by the ends of a safer society. Yet there was always more to the public welfare offense doctrine than simple instrumentalism. Richard Singer has pointed-ed out that many of the early public welfare offenses involved offenses with some moral component—such as laws dealing with minors.[3] Wayne LaFave has suggested that stricter criminal liability was in part simply an effort to make it easier for prosecutors to convict those who truly did act wrongfully. "Doubtless with many such crimes the legislature is

---

3. Richard G. Singer, *The Resurgence of Mens Rea: III—The Rise And Fall Of Strict Criminal Liability*, 30 B.C. L. Rev. 337, 363 (1989).

actually aiming at bad people and expects that the prosecuting officials, in the exercise of their broad discretion to prosecute or not to prosecute, will use the statute only against those persons of bad reputation who probably actually did have the hard-to-prove bad mind, letting others go who, from their generally good reputation, probably had no such bad mental state.''[4]

So, just as there are fundamentally two different ways of looking at mens rea—element-based and character-based—so, too, are there two different ways of looking at the public welfare offense doctrine. One can look at the doctrine as an instrumental response to especially dangerous activities. or as a moral response to especially bad people whose crimes are especially difficult to prosecute. To the degree that a judge assumes the legislature was concerned about especially dangerous conditions then the judge is apt to presume that the legislature intended stricter forms of criminal liability even if the risk of convicting a morally innocent actor is also great. To the degree that courts assume that the legislature was concerned with especially bad people, however, courts will only presume that the legislature intended stricter forms of criminal liability if they can readily imagine people of poor moral character being engaged in the proscribed conduct. Under such circumstances, courts will be less concerned about morally innocent offenders being convicted and more willing to trust the discretion of prosecutors and law enforcement, who they will presume are capable of identifying the truly bad.

The Supreme Court's decisions with respect to the mens rea requirements of federal regulatory statutes moved back and forth between these instrumental and moral visions of public welfare offenses in the years before the *Staples* decision. In a brief opinion in *United States v. Balint*, the Court interpreted a federal narcotics statute as not requiring proof of knowledge that that the drugs possessed were illegal even though the possible penalty was a five year term of imprisonment.[5] The Court instead found that Congress intended to "require every person dealing in drugs to ascertain at his peril whether that which he sells comes within the inhibition of the statute."[6] *Balint* framed the issue as a simple trade-off between public danger and potential innocence. "Congress weighed the possible injustice of subjecting an innocent seller to a penalty against the evil of exposing innocent purchasers to danger from the drug, and concluded that the latter was the result preferably to be avoided."[7] *Balint* made no mention of the history of strict criminal liability for offenses involving the sale of alcohol to minors, but it is hard not to

---

4. Wayne LaFave, *Criminal Law* 289 (5th ed. 2010).

5. 258 U.S. 250, 252 (1922).

6. *Id.* at 253–54.

7. *Id.*

wonder whether the *Balint* court saw those dealing in narcotics as morally suspect even if actually ignorant of the contents of any one shipment.

Twenty years later, in *United States v. Dotterweich,* the Court described the public welfare offense doctrine in almost purely instrumental terms.[8] The Court affirmed the misdemeanor conviction of a corporate officer whose company shipped adulterated and misbranded drugs in violation of the Food and Drug Act "though consciousness of wrongdoing be totally wanting."[9] The Court trusted prosecutors to make good decisions about when to hold corporate officers strictly liable and justified punishing someone who was not consciously doing wrong as necessary for the greater good. Thus, those who stood in "responsible relation to a public danger" were criminally responsible even if not aware of what they did wrong.

A decade later, in *Morissette v. United States,* the Court expressed much more concern with character and moral innocence.[10] Morissette, walking on a military firing range, collected empty artillery shell casings that he assumed were abandoned and later sold them. By law, the casings still belonged to the government, but the federal statute involved was ambiguous as to whether a defendant had to know that the property was still owned by another. The Court read into the theft law the traditional mens rea requirement for theft offenses and therefore reversed Morissette's conviction. In doing so, the Court articulated some boundaries for public welfare offenses. Criminal laws that dealt with the positive aggressions and invasions that were the original concern of the common law were not included and were subject to the presumption of traditional mens rea requirements. Second, the Court went on at some length to emphasize that public welfare offenses typically involved relatively small penalties and little stigma for those convicted.[11]

The *Morissette* Court also promoted the common law's traditional concern with wrongfulness to near constitutional status. In ringing phrases that have been cited by the Court as a bedrock principle in countless decisions, the Court described traditional mens rea requirements as almost akin to a principle of natural law.

> The contention that an injury can amount to a crime only when inflicted by intention is no provincial or transient notion. It is as universal and persistent in mature systems of law as belief in

---

8. 320 U.S. 277 (1943).

9. *Id.* at 280–81.

10. 342 U.S. 246 (1952).

11. *Id.* at 256.

freedom of the human will and a consequent ability and duty of the normal individual to choose between good and evil.[12]

Indeed, in subsequent decisions, different Justices would flirt with the idea that perhaps requiring a sufficiently culpable mental state was not just a statutory presumption grounded in common law tradition but a matter of due process grounded in the Constitution itself. These flirtations amounted to nothing, but the enduring appeal of *Morissette's* description of mens rea requirements as "no provincial or transient notion" speaks to the power of moral innocence as a continuing concern.[13]

Dotterweich and *Morissette* presented opposing visions of the public welfare doctrine. On one side was *Dotterweich,* with its responsible-relation-to-public-danger standard and its ends-justify-the-means logic. On the other side was *Morissette,* with its almost constitutional reverence for moral innocence and its plain hostility to stricter forms of criminal liability where prison was a possibility. An obvious question remained. What would the Court do when confronted with a public welfare offense involving both great danger to the public *and* a significant penalty?

In *United States v. Freed*, the Supreme Court answered that question. In that case, the Court found that the National Firearms Act, the very same statute under which Harold Staples would one day be charged, was a public welfare statute. The Court held that the government did not have to prove that defendant Freed knew that his hand grenade was unregistered in order to be convicted under the act, even though the offense carried a possible prison sentence of up to ten years.

Freed should have been a very perplexing case for the Court. The crimes covered under the National Firearms Act challenge the neat distinction that the *Morissette* Court tried to create between the "positive aggressions or invasions" that had been the traditional concern of the common law, and the newer regulatory offenses, which while dangerous in consequence, could be innocent in origin. What could be more positively aggressive than possession of a small bomb expressly designed for killing many people at once? By forbidding possession of machine guns, bombs, mortars, and bazookas, the National Firearms Act seemed to focus on the sort of evil character with whom the common law was originally concerned.

---

12. *Id.* at 250.

13. In this regard, *Morissette* resonates with the famous case of *Lambert v. California*, 355 U.S. 225 (1957). *Lambert* held that it violated due process to punish an ex-offender for failing to register as a felon upon entering Los Angeles, because the law and circumstances gave him no fair notice that he was obliged to do so.

Justice William Douglas's opinion for the majority in *Freed* dealt with this question of character in a somewhat oblique way. Douglas seemed to conflate the distinguishing criteria, describing Freed's possession as not innocent simply because it was so dangerous. "This is a regulatory measure in the interest of the public safety, which may well be premised on the theory that one would hardly be surprised to learn that possession of hand grenades is not an innocent act."[14] Here, Douglas seems to be saying that certain types of danger are less "innocent" than others. What is not spelled out is whether this is so because a single hand grenade is considered to be more dangerous than any single violation of a more mundane regulatory statute, or because a character judgment is being made about the sort of people who possess highly dangerous weapons without registering them. While the food executive in *Dotterweich* was assumed to be free of moral blameworthiness, *Freed* suggests—without spelling out why—that the moral innocence of a person who possesses a hand grenade should not be assumed.

Unlike food, drug and housing regulations, the National Firearms Act was in fact passed with highly dangerous criminals in mind. During the 1930s, "gangsters" carrying automatic weapons were literally termed "public enemies" who epitomized the most dangerous type of criminal. The National Firearms Act was passed to deal with such gangsters. Automatic weapons and explosive devices again became a great concern during the sixties and seventies, when various paramilitary groups bombed government buildings and used automatic weapons against police. Freed, in fact, was a member of a terrorist cell, although Douglas never mentioned this fact.[15] So *Freed* involved both a dangerous thing and a very bad man.

While Douglas thereby finessed the issue of character somewhat, Justice William Brennan, in his concurrence, dismissed it as irrelevant. Taking the narrower, element-based view, Brennan argued that mens rea did not require "knowledge that an act is illegal, wrong, or blameworthy." Rather, Brennan looked solely to the dangerousness of the items regulated in order to decide what Congress had intended.

> [T]he firearms covered by the Act are major weapons such as machine guns and sawed-off shotguns; deceptive weapons such as flashlight guns and fountain pen guns; and major destructive devices such as bombs, grenades, mines, rockets, and large caliber weapons including mortars, anti-tank guns and bazookas. Without exception, the likelihood of government regulation of the distribution of such

---

14. United States v. Freed, 401 U.S. 601, 609 (1971).

15. Richard Singer & Douglas Husak, *Of Innocence and Innocents: The Supreme Court and Mens Rea Since Herbert Packer*, 8 Buff. Crim. L.Rev. 861 (1999).

weapons is so great that anyone must be presumed to be aware of it.[16]

Here Brennan connects back to the sparer, instrumental logic of *Dotterweich*. Those standing in "responsible relation" to a public danger bear the burden of inquiry—of "knowing what they are doing" in the fuller sense of the words, not because they are of questionable character but because everyone is presumed to know that such activities are highly regulated.

Of course, it makes perfect sense that the dangerous items of the National Firearms Act would be closely regulated, but it also makes perfect sense that such dangerous offenses would carry severe penalties. Here the *Morissette* Court's assumption that public welfare offenses would carry slight penalties broke down. No one would imagine that possessing a bazooka would carry only a fine. Indeed, possession of a single unregistered hand grenade carried a possible sentence of up to ten years in prison. Entirely absent from either the majority or concurring opinions in *Freed* was any reference to the possible sentence under the Act. Punishing an oblivious hand grenade possessor too hard did not seem to concern anyone. The fact that neither Douglas nor Brennan even mentioned the fact that Freed was a would-be terrorist obscured whatever role character judgments may have played in their respective decisions.

The Court's next case clearly subordinated questions of character to concerns about public danger. In *International Minerals*, the defendant had been convicted of shipping sulfuric acid across state lines without the documents required by federal regulations. Even though the criminal statute stated that "whoever knowingly violates any such regulation" shall be fined or imprisoned, the Court held that knowledge of the regulations themselves need not be proved.[17] Writing again for the majority, Douglas defined public welfare offenses in terms of dangerousness.

> In *Balint* the Court was dealing with drugs, in *Freed* with hand grenades, in this case with sulfuric and other dangerous acids. Pencils, dental floss, paper clips may also be regulated. But they may be the type of products which might raise substantial due process questions if Congress did not require ... 'mens rea' as to each ingredient of the offense. But where, as here and as in *Balint* and *Freed*, dangerous or deleterious devices or products or obnoxious waste materials are involved, the probability of regulation is so

---

16. *Freed*, 401 U.S. at 616.

17. United States v. International Minerals & Chemical Corp. 402 U.S. 558, 559 (1971) (quoting 18 U.S.C. § 834(f)).

great that anyone who is aware that he is in possession of them or dealing with them must be presumed to be aware of the regulation.[18]

Aside from elevating the common law tradition of mens rea to a possible due-process issue, this paragraph is notable for the clarity with which it reduces the choice between traditional mens rea requirements and stricter forms of criminal liability to a simple question of dangerousness. If *Freed* hinted that the wrongfulness of possessing hand grenades played a part in lowering mens rea requirements, *International Minerals* suggested that innocents dealing with the dangerous, the deleterious, or the obnoxious had simply best be aware. In dissent, Justices Potter Stewart, John Harlan, and Brennan, however, deplored the possibility that a casual shipper ignorant of the regulations might be convicted as a "perversion of the purpose of the criminal law."[19]

Convicting morally innocent offenders had been an acknowledged cost of the public welfare offense doctrine since *Balint* and *Dotterweich*, but the casual shipper troubled Stewart and his fellow dissenters in a way that the ignorant hand grenade owner earlier that year had not, even though the casual shipper arguably presented the greater danger. A truckload of sulfuric acid could potentially be more dangerous to the public welfare than a single hand grenade, and the aggregate danger of all such shipments might well exceed the threat posed by all hand grenades illicitly possessed. Both the registration-requirement-ignorant hand grenade owner and the regulation-ignorant casual shipper would be equally morally innocent in an analytic sense, but the *International Minerals* dissent suggests that a more value-laden moral calculus may have been at work in *Freed*. Some types of innocence seemed more important than others to the Justices, perhaps because would be terrorists and casual shippers evoked very different visions of character.

Concerns about moral innocence once again became paramount in the Court's last two decisions in this area before *Staples*. *United States v. U.S. Gypsum Co. et al.* involved not grenades nor corrosive acids but illegally priced drywall. In that case, the Court decided that criminal antitrust violations of the Sherman Act did require proof of criminal intent.[20] Chief Justice Warren Burger's main point was that the inherent vagueness of the conduct element of the price-fixing prohibition made it particularly unsuitable for a lower mens rea requirement. "[T]he behavior proscribed by the Act is often difficult to distinguish from the gray zone of socially acceptable and economically justifiable business conduct."[21] A hand grenade is a hand grenade and sulfuric acid is sulfuric

---

18. *Id.* at 564–65.

19. *Id.* at 558.

20. United States v. U.S. Gypsum Co., 438 U.S. 422 (1978).

21. *Id.* at 441.

acid, but for the *Gypsum* majority, an illegally fixed price existed too much in the eye of the beholder to presume that no criminal intent was required. Moreover, illegal pricing involved conduct that was *neither* clearly morally wrong nor dangerous.

In *Liparota v. U.S.*, the Court refused to find a public welfare offense where the conduct was neither dangerous nor apparently "wrongful" in and of itself.[22] The Court reversed the conviction of a restaurant owner who had bought food stamps at a discount from an undercover federal agent in violation of federal regulations. A seven-Justice majority rejected the Government's position that no "evil-meaning mind" was required, holding that "to interpret the statute otherwise would be to criminalize a broad range of apparently innocent conduct."[23] The Court also emphasized that the activity involved had to be dangerous. "A food stamp can hardly be compared to a hand grenade, see *Freed*, nor can the unauthorized acquisition or possession of food stamps be compared to the selling of adulterated drugs, as in *Dotterweich*." *Liparota* emphasized that it was the dangerousness of the activity that justified the presumption that people would be aware that the activity was highly regulated. "In most previous instances, Congress has rendered criminal a type of conduct that a reasonable person should know is subject to a stringent public regulation and may seriously threaten the community's health or safety." Notably, the *Liparota* majority did not hold that the government had to prove that Liparota knew the specific regulations involved, only that he knew that what he was doing was "unauthorized *or* illegal" (emphasis added).[24]

Taken as a whole, in the years leading up to the *Staples* decision the Supreme Court's public welfare cases provided a reasonably clear framework for interpreting the mens rea requirements of federal regulatory crimes. The Court was willing to interpret federal regulatory statutes in a way that criminally punished innocent offenders when the danger was high (*Dotterweich*, *Freed*, and *International Minerals*), even when the penalty was potentially severe (*Freed*), but it was not willing to do so when there was no public danger (*Liparota*), and especially not when the conduct proscribed was vaguely defined (*Gypsum*). Absent public danger the Court might require a mental state that was merely wrongful, although not necessarily fully cognizant of the illegality involved (*Liparota*). These cases fleshed out a framework that struck a balance between the spare instrumentalism of *Dotterweich* and the near constitutional

---

22. Liparota v. United States, 471 U.S. 419 (1985).

23. The Court cited the example of someone who used food stamps to buy food from a store that "unknown to him, charged higher than normal prices to food stamp program participants." *Liparota*, 471 U.S. at 423–26.

24. *Id.* at 433–34.

reverence for traditional mens rea of *Morissette*. This delicate but reasonably clear balance between public danger and moral innocence would last until the *Staples* case reached the Court eight years later.

But fundamental questions about mens rea in federal regulatory statutes remained unanswered during the intervening years. Most of the recent cases involved questions of law or mixed questions of law and fact: knowledge of registration in *Freed* and knowledge of regulations in *Liparota* and *International Minerals*. The maxim that ignorance of the law did not excuse provided an easy basis for deciding cases when the issue could be framed as knowledge of the law. But what mental state would the Court require with respects to purely factual matters? Even the *dicta* in these opinions were maddeningly vague on this crucial point. Language in *International Minerals* stated that an offender who thought he was shipping distilled water and not sulfuric acid could not be convicted under the statute,[25] but what state of knowledge would be sufficient? That he was shipping sulfuric acid? A corrosive chemical? A regulated chemical? Language in *Freed* stated that an offender had to know that he possessed a hand grenade,[26] but a hand grenade is not easy to mistake for anything else other than a replica or a toy. To what degree did the government have to prove that the defendant knew what he was doing when a statute was silent or ambiguous with respect to mental state? To what degree could an otherwise "innocent" offender get punished for what he did not know about his conduct or circumstances? *Staples* would be the occasion for the Court to answer these questions.

The Lower Court Decision

Such was the state of Supreme Court jurisprudence on regulatory mens rea issues on the day that federal agents swarmed into Harold Staples's garage. The National Firearms Act included no mental state language. It simply stated that "[i]t shall be unlawful for any person . . . to receive or possess a firearm which is not registered to him in the National Firearms Registration and Transfer Record."[27] "Firearm" was a statutory term of art that included machine guns.[28] Whether Staples would be found guilty or innocent would ultimately turn on whether the Court read some sort of mental state requirement into the act, and whether the Court would require the government to prove that Staples knew some or all of the characteristics that brought his gun within the definition of a firearm that must be registered in order to be legal.

---

25. *International Minerals*, 402 U.S. at 563–64.

26. *Freed,* 401 U.S. at 614.

27. 26 U.S.C. § 586.

28. 26 U.S.C. § 5845(b).

Would the Court focus on the dangerousness of the items regulated, as the Court did with sulfuric acid in *International Minerals* and with hand grenades in *Freed*, and thereby find Staples to be in responsible relation to a public danger? Or would the Court see gun ownership as apparently innocent activity like the price-setting in *Gypsum* or the food stamps purchasing in *Liparota?*

How the Supreme Court decided that issue in turn would be influenced by how they viewed Harold Staples and his gun. Was Staples an innocent engaged in otherwise blameless conduct caught up in a hyper-technical regulatory scheme? Or was he the sort of dangerous person that the National Firearms Act had been passed to deal with? Was his firearm the sort of dangerous instrumentality whose possession—like the hand grenade in *Freed*—could hardly be considered innocent?

All cases get distilled and shaped through the trial and appellate processes. The facts discussed in the Supreme Court's decision in *Staples* were a subset of the larger mass of detail out of which the trial record was built. How facts are developed at trial can influence how a Supreme Court case gets decided in ways not always apparent from the resulting opinions of the Court. In the *Staples* trial facts were developed in two areas that shaped the Supreme Court's ultimate decision. The first was the set of particular difficulties involved in regulating the type of gun that Staples owned. The second was the character of Harold Staples.

The fact that the rifle for which Staples was prosecuted was an AR–15 was significant because the AR–15 was the sort of firearm that raised difficult interpretive issues under the National Firearms Act. The AR–15 was the civilian and semiautomatic version of the M–16, a military rifle that can fire either semiautomatically or automatically with the flip of a switch. But AR–15s could easily be converted into machine guns, and such converted machine guns presented a serious problem for law enforcement. Indeed, the National Firearms Act had been specifically amended in 1968 and 1986 to deal with the problem of such converted machine guns.

Distinguishing a semiautomatic AR–15 from an AR–15 converted to automatic on inspection can be surprisingly difficult. The AR–15 resembles the M–16 both externally and internally, and many parts are interchangeable between the two guns. M–16 parts are often used to build or repair AR–15s, because the civilian market is flooded with surplus M–16 parts which have been rejected by the military. Fitting an AR–15 with some M–16 parts would not necessarily make it a machine gun and would not be illegal: only certain combinations of parts would do the trick. The most crucial M–16 part in this respect is the autosear, a device whose only purpose in a gun is to make it fire automatically and which is essential for reliable automatic fire. For this reason, the autosear alone among all the parts of an automatic rifle must itself be registered under the National Firearms Act.

Even in the absence of an autosear, however, an AR–15 could still fire automatically under certain circumstances. Certain combinations of other M–16 parts could result in automatic fire depending on the age and condition of the parts involved and the type of ammunition used. Such automatic fire results when, after the first shot is fired, a part of the rifle slams back into place against the next bullet harder than it is supposed to. If the ammunition used has especially soft primers (a primer is a tube containing a small amount of starter explosive), the unusually great impact ignites the primer and results in a second shot. As long as the cycle repeats itself, the gun continues to fire even though the trigger is only pulled once. Such automatic fire was termed "slam fire" by ATF experts and as "hammer follow down malfunction" by defense experts in machine gun cases. The difference in terminology was not incidental. Describing the automatic fire as a malfunction allowed defense lawyers in this type of case to argue that the firearm was not a machine gun but a broken semiautomatic. Distinguishing a legal semiautomatic AR–15 from an autosear-less AR–15 machine gun simply by pulling the trigger was not an entirely reliable test either. Slam fire was not a reliable distinguishing criterion, because an AR–15 might or might not fire automatically with any single pull of the trigger, and it would not fire automatically at all unless soft primer ammunition was used.

Thus, while the issue that ultimately reached the Supreme Court was whether the government had to prove that Staples *knew* that his AR–15 was a machine gun, much of Staples's defense at trial was that his gun in fact *was not* a machine gun. The knowledge issue was logically a fallback defense that the jury would only reach if they concluded that Staples gun did, in fact, fire automatically.

Staples's AR–15 contained one M–16 part that was of particular importance, an M–16 selector switch. On M–16s, such selector switches allow the operator to select between automatic and semiautomatic fire. To thwart any effort to convert an AR–15 to an a machine gun, a metal stop had been put by the manufacturer onto the frame of Staples's AR–15, and this stop would have prevented an M–16 selector switch from moving all the way to the automatic setting. The stop on Staples's AR–15 had been filed down. While this modification alone—in the absence of an autosear—would not necessarily produce automatic fire, all experts agreed that it made it easier for the gun to slam-fire. What made the filed-down stop important was that it was the only modification to the AR–15 that might indicate to someone inspecting the outside surfaces of the gun that it was capable of automatic fire. It was also the clearest evidence that someone had modified the gun with an eye to converting it to a machine gun.

The *Staples* trial was not, however, merely a battle of the experts over technical distinctions between malfunctioning semiautomatics and converted machine guns. Staples's lawyer, Clark Brewster, made the case as much as he could about Harold Staples himself.

All good defense attorneys represent their clients zealously but not all believe in the legal or moral innocence of their clients (nor need they). But Brewster had personal reasons both for taking the case and for believing in Staples. In the late eighties, Brewster represented the wife of a local multimillionaire in a bitterly contested divorce case. One day a man came to see Brewster and told him that the husband was tapping Brewster's phone and was talking about having Brewster killed. The man further claimed that his business partner had tape recordings of the husband making statements to that effect. The man's business partner was none other than Harold Staples. Staples eventually came forward and testified in federal court against the husband, who was convicted of federal wiretapping and conspiracy charges.[29] Brewster believed that Staples may have saved his life by coming forward. And Brewster also suspected that the federal investigation of Staples may have been instigated in some fashion by former federal agents who had been employed by the husband during the divorce case. For this reason, Brewster—who enjoyed a successful civil practice—defended Staples all the way to the Supreme Court on a pro bono basis.

But there was a second reason why Brewster believed that Harold Staples might have been singled out for unfair treatment—a personal connection between Staples and a local ATF agent. The ATF agent who led the raid on Staples's house was Lewis Jobson. Jobson's son was Brian Jobson. The younger Jobson was a one time employee of Staples's carpet upholstery business and a close friend of Staples's nephew, who was the Jobson's next door neighbor. The nephew and the younger Jobson had fired hundreds of rounds through Staples's AR–15 and had both worked on the gun. Agent Jobson had his own AR–15, and some of the ammunition the younger Jobson had fired in the Staples's gun was taken from Agent Jobson's garage. At one point, his son even took the bolt from Agent Jobson's AR–15 and installed it in Staples's AR–15 in an effort to make it work better. Brewster suspected that Staples was being prosecuted as the result of some sort of bad blood between Agent Jobson and Staples, perhaps arising from the relationship between the two youths.

---

29. United States v. Grossich, No. 94–5167, 1995 WL 539439 (10th Cir. Aug. 31, 1995).

The assistant U.S. Attorney who prosecuted Staples, on the other hand, saw him differently. Neal Kirkpatrick, an experienced criminal prosecutor who had just joined the Tulsa office of the U.S. Attorney's office, remembered this as a straightforward case. "We really had no qualms about charging people possessing illegal weapons." Because of the filed-down stop on the selector switch, Kirkpatrick also believed that Staples knew that his AR–15 had been converted to automatic fire.

But there was more to the *Staples* prosecution than just the possession of an illegal weapon. When asked in an interview for this chapter whether there was a particular reason for federal law enforcement's interest in Staples, Kirkpatrick stated that there was but that he could not discuss the matter because it involved Grand Jury testimony that was still subject to secrecy rules. In fact, Staples was subsequently indicted in federal court in Tulsa on conspiracy charges relating to identity theft after his machine gun case was dismissed, although he was acquitted on all charges.

Clearly Harold Staples was anything but innocent in the eyes of the Tulsa U.S. Attorney's Office, and in this sense his prosecution fit naturally into both the instrumental and character-based vision of the public welfare offense doctrine. The case involved both a dangerous item—a machine gun—and a defendant thought to be a bad man whom prosecutors might otherwise have not been able to convict. For the defense, however, the *Staples* prosecution was a regulatory nightmare come true. An innocent man was being prosecuted on the basis of a hyper-technical distinction because vindictive law enforcement agents were abusing the discretion that low mens rea offenses permitted them.

Brewster's defense strategy was significantly shaped by his belief that Staples was not just legally innocent of the charges in a narrow, technical sense but innocent also of any wrongdoing and the likely victim of a vindictive prosecution. Defendants are often well advised not to testify in their own defense in criminal cases. In this case, Staples could not get on the stand to deny possession of the firearm, since it was found in his gun safe. And since the statute did not on its face require proof of knowledge of its automatic capability, there seemed little to be gained and everything to be lost from having Staples testify. Reasonable doubts about whether the gun was a machine gun could be raised through expert testimony and through the testimony of other people who had fired the gun. Even if Brewster was able to convince the judge to insert a mental state requirement into the jury instructions, the prosecution would bear the burden of proof on that issue and would not be able to argue any inference from Staples's decision not to testify.

Nevertheless, Harold Staples did testify at his own trial, and he denied that the AR–15 was even close to being a machine gun. From the very beginning of the case he maintained that the AR–15 was defective and would not even reliably fire semiautomatically. Government agents admitted during trial that when Staples was told during the raid that the AR–15 was being seized, he was incredulous. Staples told the agents that the gun was broken and did not work properly. He also asserted that the only reason they were taking the gun was that Agent Jobson did not want to leave the house empty handed.

Staples testified that he had bought the AR–15 legally at a Tulsa gun show six years earlier but immediately realized that it was defective.

> [I]t was the very first day that I purchased it.... I picked up some ammunition at the gun show. Being excited about buying it, I couldn't wait till I could get there and shoot it. I was very disappointed when I got to my father's farm. The gun wouldn't function. It would not function properly in the semiautomatic mode. The gun was defective in some way.

Staples said that the bolt would jam most times he fired a shot, requiring him to pull the bolt back before firing a subsequent shot. He tried without success to get the gun fixed, but he quickly lost interest in it when he could not get it working properly. He therefore gave it to his nephew, David Seebolt, to do with as he pleased. When Seebolt had to report for National Guard training, he gave the AR–15 back to Harold Staples to store in his gun safe.

Seebolt testified that he essentially took the gun over from his uncle with the understanding that he would try to get it to work. He described firing at least 1,000 rounds of ammunition through the gun and tinkering with it over the years in a fruitless effort to get the gun to fire properly.

Seebolt's frequent companion on these trips to the firing range was none other than Brian Jobson, the son of the Special Agent who led the raid on the Staples house. The two youths would often cut high school classes to fire the gun. Brian Jobson personally fired the gun three or four hundred times, frequently taking ammunition from his father's garage. At one point the younger Jobson even took his father's AR–15 down to the range in order to exchange parts between the guns in an effort to get the Staples gun working. Brian Jobson himself testified for the defense, as did another of Seebolt's school friends who had also fired the AR–15. All of the witnesses referred to the AR–15 as Seebolt's gun, and the testimony of all witnesses about the gun's capability was consistent: the AR–15 never fired automatically, rarely fired semiautomatically, and when it did fire semiautomatically it would inevitably jam after four or five shots.

The prosecution had no evidence to rebut any of this testimony. One issue in dispute, however, was the identity of the person who filed down the stop on the selector switch. A government agent testified that he noticed that the selector stop had been filed down at the time the gun was seized. Staples, along with all of the defense witnesses, testified that the stop had never been filed down while in their possession. An ATF photographer admitted that his photograph of the AR–15 showed what appeared to be tiny metal shavings around the stop. Brewster argued that the presence of these shavings suggested that the stop had been filed down by the federal agents shortly before the ATF photo was taken.

Ultimately the case came down to a battle over jury instructions. Questions of character and moral innocence were very much on the mind of Dale Cook, the trial judge, although he ultimately put aside his misgivings and refused the defense's requested instructions. The National Firearms Act defined as a machine gun "any weapon which shoots . . . automatically more than one shot, without manual reloading by a single function of the trigger."[30] The government's position was that any gun that fires more than one shot with a single pull of a trigger was a machine gun. Brewster argued that this would make the word "automatically" redundant in the statutory definition. In saying that a machine gun fires *automatically* more than one shot with a single pull of a trigger, Brewster argued that Congress meant to exclude from the definition of a machine gun firearms that fire more than one shot per trigger pull as the result of a malfunction. He illustrated his argument with the example of a hunter whose rabbit gun had "doubled"—fired twice with a single trigger pull. Brewster submitted proposed instructions from past patent law cases which defined "automatic" as a self-acting process that produced a certain and uniform or controlled result.

Judge Cook was taken with Brewster's hunting example, and agreed during a conference in chambers that the government's definition of automatic seemed unfairly broad.

> Your example of a person out there duck hunting, and the gun happens to fire twice when he pulls it once because it's an automatic loading gun as distinguished from an automatic firing gun. . . . What's the guy to do? Shoot at a duck, it shoots twice, and he suddenly has become a felon . . . [T]hat's disturbing, because our sense of fair play to people. [Sic] And it may be that the sense of fair play was such that the Congress just assumed that while it technically is a violation the ATF wouldn't prosecute them.

Implicit in Cook's response was an assumption about the type of person who could be prosecuted in such a case: an "innocent" and otherwise law-abiding hunter who would have no legal defense if the government decided to charge him. Nonetheless, Cook refused the de-

---

30. 26 U.S.C. § 5845(b).

fense's instruction and defined automatic fire as simply more than one shot resulting from a single trigger pull.

The use of this broad definition of automatic meant that the jurors would have to find Staples guilty if they concluded that the AR–15 was capable of slam fire during the time that it was in Staples's possession. Staples's only remaining chance of being acquitted was if the judge read a knowledge requirement into the statute. So Brewster asked for the following instruction: "An essential element of the offense of possessing a machine gun, is that the possessor knew that the gun would fire fully automatically and the burden is upon the Plaintiff to prove that specific knowledge." Judge Cook refused this instruction, too. His Circuit had resolved the knowledge issue in the National Firearms Act in *United States v. Mittleider*,[31] upholding an instruction that stated that "[i]t is not necessary for the government to prove that the defendant knew that the weapon in his possession was a machine gun within the meaning of the statute."[32] Judge Cook gave this instruction, but he also gave a further instruction that attempted to translate *Dotterweich's* responsible relation to a public danger standard into the context of federal firearm regulation.

> The Government need not prove that a defendant knows he is dealing with a weapon possessing every last characteristic which subjects it to regulation. It is enough to prove he knows that he is dealing with a dangerous device of such type as would alert one to the likelihood of regulation. If he has such knowledge, and if the particular item is in fact regulated, he acts at his peril.[33]

While simply following precedent in his circuit, Judge Cook was clearly troubled by the knowledge issue. During a chambers conference he told the attorneys that he had complained about this aspect of the law to one of Kirkpatrick's predecessors.

> It seems clear to me that what the Congress was doing is saying, look, this is what's unlawful, whether you know it or don't know it, and that's what's disturbing to me, and, of course, we take that into consideration in the sentencing phase.... [S]ome years ago, Ben Baker was the first assistant U.S. Attorney up here and I said, for goodness sakes, why don't you get some legislation that permits the Justice Department, the US. Attorney, an option whether to go a route that is a criminal violation or a pure civil violation that has a penalty where the person has no criminal background and has, you

---

31.   835 F.2d 769 (10th Cir. 1987).

32.   *Id.* at 774 (1987).

33.   Trial Transcript at 464 quoted in *Staples v. United States*, 511 U.S. 600, 604 (1994).

know, all of these things, but happens to be in the possession of this. It's kind of a victim of circumstance.[34]

In describing an unknowing defendant as a "victim of circumstance" more suitable for civil than criminal punishment, Cook was again envisioning certain types of defendants who were not otherwise criminals. Cook's recurring concern was that the wrong people could get convicted under the federal firearms scheme.

So in the end the jury was simply told to determine whether Staples possessed the gun and whether it was capable of firing more than one shot with a single pull of the trigger-all without regard to Staples's state of mind on the latter point. Given the jury instructions and the largely undisputed evidence that the gun could slam fire if fed the right ammunition, it was not surprising that Staples was convicted.

The jury verdict finding Staples guilty of unlawful possession of the AR–15 was returned a little less than a year after the post-Christmas raid on his house. Staples knew that he faced a possible prison term of up to ten years. Immediately after the verdict was read and court adjourned, Special Agent Jobson, who had not been called by either the prosecution or the defense, came by the defense table and said, "Merry Christmas."[35]

What happened at sentencing defies easy explanation. Under the federal sentencing guidelines in effect at the time, Harold Staples should have been sentenced to at least eighteen months in federal prison, even taking into account his lack of a prior criminal record. Instead, Cook sentenced Staples to a fine and probation. Court records indicated that Staples's offense level under the guidelines was reduced—and the permissible sentence thereby mitigated—because the judge found that the gun was only used for sporting purposes even though the relevant guideline provision clearly did not permit a "sporting purpose" downward departure for the possessor of a machine gun.[36] Neal Kirkpatrick believed that Cook was mindful that the knowledge issue might be successfully appealed and did not want to imprison someone whose sentence might be reversed. For their part, Brewster and Staples believed that Cook was genuinely troubled by the jury instructions he felt bound by law to give. Cook even went one step further and stayed the imposition of both the fine and the probation pending appeal.

The Tenth Circuit denied Staples's appeal. The mens rea issue that would eventually reach the Supreme Court was actually the easiest issue

---

34. Appellant's Principal Brief at 12.

35. Telephone Interview with Jennifer DeAngelis, Counsel for Harold Staples, October 7, 2009 (transcript on file with author).

36. U.S. Sentencing Guidelines Manual § 2K2.1 (2008).

for the Tenth Circuit panel to deal with, because the panel refused to reconsider the Circuit's prior decision in *Mittleider*.[37] The defense's arguments in favor of a knowledge requirement did draw a concurring opinion from one member of the panel who—like Judge Cook—seemed troubled by the idea that an otherwise blameless and law-abiding person could so easily be convicted. The concurring judge invited Staples to file for a rehearing en banc and concluded that "[p]rinciples of justice and fair play suggest that we ought to overturn *Mittleider* and let the jury decide whether the defendant knowingly possessed an *automatic* weapon."[38]

In this posture and on this record the case would go up for Supreme Court review. As a test case for the public welfare offense, the case seemed to involve neither great wrongfulness nor great danger. If Staples was involved in criminal activity aside from the firearm possession, nothing in the evidence produced at trial or sentencing suggested it. The evidence also did not suggest that he associated with criminal types—the two people who fired his gun the most were a National Guardsmen and the son of a federal agent—nor did the gun itself seem all that dangerous. It fired automatically only under ideal conditions and even then not all that reliably. In a very real sense, Staples's federal firearms conviction seemed hyper-technical. His gun was technically a machine gun because it could fire five shots in a row if kept very clean and given a very special type of ammunition, and he was technically guilty even if he had no idea that it had been converted. Even if his nephew and his friends had filed down the selector stop and converted the gun without Staples's knowledge, Staples would still be guilty under the jury instructions given because of his subsequent possession.[39] Two different federal judges had expressed misgivings about the sorts of people who could be convicted under the law as it was being interpreted. Those misgivings would prove to be prescient.

The Petition for Certiorari

In drafting their petition for certiorari, the defense logically focused on the only issue on which a circuit split existed—the mens rea issue. But in a sense mens rea was an odd basis for his claim, because the reason Harold Staples had no knowledge that his gun was automatic was

---

37. *Mittleider*, 835 F.2d at 608. The Court of Appeals took more time *rejecting an evidentiary* argument about the relevance of certain documents and another instructional argument about the meaning of "automatically."

38. *Id*. (Emphasis in the original.)

39. Clark Brewster considered this possibility at the time of the trial, and the jury may have as well. Without a knowledge instruction, however, it mattered not who converted the firearm as long as it was done before it came into Staples's possession. Interview with Clark Brewster, October 7, 2009 (transcript on file with author).

that the gun had not ever been automatic in the ordinary sense of the word and may never have been automatic in *any* sense of the word while in his possession. Indeed, the defense's certiorari petition snuck in suggestions that the gun was not clearly an automatic weapon in the first place.

> The split in the Circuit Courts of Appeals on the question of mens rea or *scienter* is not an academic problem, especially in cases where, as here, there is evidence that, though the accused knew he was in possession of a firearm in the lay sense of the word, he may not have known he possessed a firearm which, *as a result of physical modifications and special loading techniques, either was or had the potential to be a "firearm" within the meaning of the Act.*[40]

The reference to the "special loading techniques" and to the possibility that the gun may merely have "had the potential" to be a machine gun would be the first in a series of efforts to weave doubts about the conduct element of the offense into the defense's main argument that a higher mens rea requirement should be read into the statute.

A circuit split had indeed developed in the wake of *Freed* as to what level of knowledge the government had to prove in a machine gun prosecution. All parties agreed that the defendant had to at least know that he possessed a firearm of some sort, so a defendant who thought he had a toy gun could not be found guilty, but beyond this, a number of different approaches had developed. Some circuits had opted for a "strict liability" approach, holding that simply knowing you had a gun was enough. Others required that the defendant must specifically know that the gun was "a dangerous device of such type as would alert one to the likelihood of regulation," as did Judge Cook in the Staples case. Three circuits had taken a compromise approach, holding that knowledge had to be proved only if the weapon contained no "external indicia" that alerted the defendant to the likelihood of regulation under the Act. For converted machine guns this meant that knowledge had to be proved only if all the modifications rendering the gun automatic were internal and not visible to the eye. In effect, this hybrid approach took what would be an issue of fact that would bear on the knowledge issue—the absence or presence of external indicia of modification—and converted it into a threshold issue that determined whether knowledge need be proved at all. Only a single D.C. Circuit decision, *United States v. Harris*, required proof of knowledge in all cases that the firearm was in fact a machine gun.[41] Notably, two of the judges who signed the opinion—Ruth

---

40. Petition for a Writ of Certiorari at 26, Staples v. United States, 511 U.S. 600 (1994) (No. 92–1441) (emphasis added).

41. 959 F.2d 246 (D.C. Cir. 1992), *cert. denied* 506 U.S. 932 (1992).

Bader Ginsburg and Clarence Thomas—would be sitting on the Supreme
Court at the time that the Staples case was heard.

The defense asked the Court to adopt the D.C. Circuit's approach in
Harris and to require that knowledge of the firearm's relevant characteristics be proved in all cases. A more modest strategy would have asked
the Court to adopt the compromise approach which required that knowledge be proven only when no external indicia existed that a semiautomatic had been converted to a machine gun. But in this case the filing
down of the tiny stop on the AR–15's selector switch gave the defense
pause. If a court concluded that the filed down stop constituted an
external indicium of conversion, then Staples's conviction might still
stand because knowledge would not have to be proven. So this one piece
of evidence involving a tiny metal bump a few millimeters in size—the
authenticity of which the defense had bitterly contested from the beginning—led the defense to go for broke and to request that the Court go
with the one circuit that had imposed an across the board knowledge
requirement for all machine gun prosecutions.

The Solicitor General's Office also made an unusual and fateful
decision of its own: it joined Staples in requesting Supreme Court
review. The government's response to the defense's petition for certiorari emphasized that the majority of circuits did not require proof of
knowledge and that the compromise approach constituted a "narrow
exception" to this general rule. While not typical, acquiescing to Supreme Court review of a case that the government had won below was
not unprecedented. The government had opposed certiorari in similar
firearms cases and presumably acquiesced to certiorari in the Staples
case because it thought *Staples* a good vehicle for resolving the mens rea
issue in its favor. Seen in context, *Staples* allowed the government to
defend a relatively moderate position. In asking the Court to uphold the
Tenth Circuit's approach, the government was not seeking a strict
liability standard for anyone who knew that he had some sort of firearm
(as the defense had framed the issue in its petition) but was instead
asking that liability be imposed whenever a jury concluded that the
defendant possessed a weapon that should have alerted him to the
possibility of regulation.

The Supreme Court Decision

The stakes change when a case makes it to the Supreme Court. By
definition, a Supreme Court case is a matter of national importance, and
national players often get involved. The National Rifle Association
offered to take the case over from Brewster and represent Staples for
free. But even though he was still handling the case on a pro bono basis,
Brewster turned down the offer. Brewster was afraid that the NRA
would frame the case around gun rights and lose sight of the fundamen-

tal issues of wrongdoing and innocence that he thought were the key to winning. Brewster did not even want the NRA to file an amicus brief, although he did allow the association to put its offer of representation directly to his client. Staples remembers that the NRA promised to not only take over the case all expenses paid but to even fly him to D.C. for the argument. In the end, although generally pro-NRA himself, Staples refused to replace Brewster. Staples wanted to avoid a felony conviction at all costs, not take a stand for gun rights. He remembered trusting Brewster completely because Brewster had stood by him from the beginning. "If Clark Brewster had asked me to ride to hell with him, I would have jumped in the back seat."

The defense's merits brief focused heavily on the innocent nature of gun ownership. It argued that there was nothing suspect about owning an AR–15 that contained M–16 parts, and that owners of such guns were therefore not aware of the risks likelihood of regulation.[42]

> AR–15 semiautomatic sport rifles with M–16 selector switches are in the closets of thousands of citizens. These sport rifles are openly sold at gun shows across America to innocent purchasers who are unaware, as was the petitioner, that they are at risk of prosecution and substantial penalties that accompany felony crimes.

The brief went on to contrast the innocent nature of gun ownership generally and of owning AR–15s specifically with the Congressional purpose behind the National Firearms Act. "The intent of the National Firearms Act was to prevent violent crime and drug trafficking among the so-called 'criminal element' in American society." Since gun ownership in and of itself was an innocent activity, the best way to limit liability to this "criminal element" was to only prosecute those who knowingly possessed the firearms in question.

Along these lines, the defense argued that Staples was not the type of person that Congress had in mind when it passed the National Firearms Act. The brief distinguished Staples from the sorts of defendants in the circuit court cases where a knowledge requirement had been rejected: defendants who were involved in other criminal activity and who probably did know that they were dealing with a machine gun.

> [T]he petitioner before this Court does not deal in weapons, did not possess fifty guns, nor was his weapon seized in connection with illegal drug activity. The item seized was an AR–15 sport rifle, bought at the public gun show held annually in Tulsa, Oklahoma. The flaw in reasoning in the First, Fourth, Seventh, Eighth and Tenth Circuits is that they fail to differentiate between persons such

---

42. Brief of Petitioner, United States v. Staples, 511 U.S. 600 (1994) (No. 92–1441), 1993 WL 433033.

as the petitioner who have no felony convictions and who was totally unaware of the automatic capability of his 'firearm' as opposed to persons such as defendant Mittleider or Shilling who were dealing in weapons and/or narcotics and who clearly knew of the automatic capability of their weapons.

Whereas dicta in *Mittleider* and in some of the other circuit court decisions had, in fact, suggested that the defendants in these cases did know they had machine guns, here the defense's brief argued strenuously that Staples did not, even repeating arguments that Staples's AR–15 was not in fact a machine gun and implying that government agents may have filed down the stop on the selector switch.[43]

The defense's brief was clearly unconventional. It was all about innocence, a very risky move before the highest appellate court of the land whose paramount aim in granting review is not to right wrongs in individual cases but to shape the laws in ways that produce the greatest amount of justice in the aggregate of cases as a whole. During a moot court session organized by the NRA, the association's lawyers told the defense the Supreme Court would not care about the innocence of their client and that they needed to broaden the focus of their claim by making more rights-based arguments.

The NRA's reaction was understandable. The defense's brief did not contain even a single reference to the Second Amendment of the Constitution. The focus of the brief was not on rights but on character and innocence. For Staples and Brewster, the problem was not that the statute was being interpreted in a way that trampled on constitutionally protected rights; the problem was that the statute was being interpreted in a way that led to the wrong types of people being prosecuted.

The Government's brief took a more conventional approach: focus on the big picture, not the small details of the individual case before the Court, and especially focus on Congressional concern with machine guns in general. With respect to whether the AR–15 was truly a machine gun and to who filed down the stop on the selector switch, the Government noted that Staples had not challenged either the jury instruction defining machine gun or the sufficiency of the evidence in his petition for certiorari. Responses to the defense's claims of factual innocence and government misconduct were relegated to footnotes.[44]

The main theme of the Government's brief was that dangerous things justified stricter forms of criminal liability. Dangerousness was the key to reconciling the cases where the Court had and had not

---

43. "Photographs taken of the weapon months after seizure show metal filings evidencing a RECENT grinding of the switch." *Id.* at 17.

44. Brief for the United States at 8, Staples v. United States, 511 U.S. 600 (1994) (No, 92–1441), 1993 WL 433034.

interpreted federal statutes to dispense with traditional mens rea requirements in the past. "A defendant may be convicted of such offenses so long as the government proves that he knew the item at issue was highly dangerous and of a type likely to be subject to regulation."

The Government also argued that Congressional intent heavily favored its interpretation of the statute. Acknowledging that the National Firearms Act had been intended to deal with gangsters and other highly dangerous criminal types, the Government argued that keeping such weapons out of such hands had led Congress to impose stricter criminal liability for anyone possessing them. "Stringent regulation of machine guns, backed up by harsh penalties for failure to register, was thought to be the most effective means then available to the federal government to accomplish that end." With respect to Congressional intent, the government's brief cited convincing evidence that the National Firearms Act was explicitly pattered after the Harrison Anti–Narcotic Act—whose mens rea issues the Court had long ago settled in the government's favor in *Balint*—for the express purpose of making the statute easier to prosecute.

While largely instrumental in its logic, the Government's brief also took a more doctrinal approach; it justified stricter criminal liability on its own terms by characterizing the resulting form of liability as a de facto standard of negligence. "Congress enacted the NFA's provisions requiring registration and taxation of firearms to penalize 'neglect where the law requires care,' and thereby control the public danger posed by free circulation of hazardous weapons." Negligence converted the unknowing inheritor of a regulated firearm from an "innocent" to someone who is careless, a point the Government drove home with a lengthy quote from one of the circuit court decisions in its favor.

> [M]any persons must own old guns that may or may not be capable of automatic fire. Congress wants the automatic guns registered. That is going to happen only if the onus is on the owner. The approach [adopted by the courts below] requires the owner to investigate, and so leads to compliance with the law. The approach [proposed by petitioner in this case] converts ignorance into bliss. . . . Rational people would turn a blind eye, which would defeat the purpose of the statute.

Thus, the Government answered the defense's character argument with one of its own. Those who unknowingly possessed converted machine guns were not innocents, but careless people whose wrongful possession endangered the public.

Because Supreme Court Justices and their clerks rarely speak publicly about the inner workings of the Court, speculation about how the Court arrives at its decisions is based on the opinions written, the

Justices' comments in oral argument, and whatever publicly available papers from retired members of the Court exist. With respect to the *Staples* case, Justice Blackmun's papers contain much that is useful, including correspondence between the Justices and even Justice Blackmun's own notes from the Justices' conference on the case. The picture that emerges is of an early consensus for reversing Staples's conviction but one that required some negotiation to maintain.[45]

In a memo dated the day after the oral argument, Blackmun clerk Paul Oetken described the case as "a very close one." He observed that both parties had staked out relatively moderate positions, noting that the government was not seeking a "true strict liability standard." Despite describing the case as a close one, Oetken noted that "most of the law clerks and several of the Justices appear to be leaning in favor of reversal." Oetken also told Blackmun that he was troubled by the possibility of truly innocent possession. "Someone who has little or no knowledge of guns receives from a relative a gun with the capability of automatic fire and stores it in the attic. That person is subject to severe penalties (including ten years imprisonment) for merely having the gun, even if he does not know that it is a machine gun." Apparently Blackmun had confided that he thought Staples actually knew that the AR–15 was a converted machine gun, because Oetken suggested that Staples would probably be convicted on retrial even if the Court read in a knowledge requirement.

As Blackmun's notes from the conference reveal, Chief Justice William Rehnquist and Justice John Paul Stevens initially joined him in voting to affirm Staples's conviction, while the remaining six justices voted to reverse. At conference, Rehnquist commented that *Balint* supported the government's position. Stevens described the 1934 Firearms Act as a response to the gang situation in Chicago and agreed with Rehnquist that it was a strict liability measure in line with *Balint*. Justice Sandra Day O'Connor, who grew up around guns and hunting, disagreed, arguing that having semiautomatic weapons in the United States was not unlawful. Justice Antonin Scalia agreed with O'Connor and made a reference to the American tradition of gun ownership. Justice Anthony Kennedy thought Staples's conviction set a dangerous precedent. Justice David Souter said that *Balint* provided no support for the Solicitor General's position because it was not reasonable to expect the gun to be subject to regulation. Thomas agreed with this point. Ginsburg said that this was a difficult case but that she would vote to reverse. By the end of the conference, Rehnquist had switched his vote, thus creating the 7–2 majority reflected in the Court's eventual decision.

---

45. Box 637 of Justice Blackmun's papers at the Library of Congress. The author thanks Joseph Kennedy, his father, for locating and photographing Justice Blackmun's papers on the case.

Because he had now joined the majority, Rehnquist got to assign the writing of the opinion, and he assigned it to Thomas.

This 7–2 majority for the result held up, but the Justices' correspondence and the oral argument transcript suggest that the vote would have been closer and might conceivably have gone the other way if the case had been argued a little differently. Putting aside Rehnquist's unexplained ambivalence, Souter and Kennedy both raised substantive concerns with the opinion Thomas initially drafted, and Ginsburg and O'Connor signed only a concurrence

Ginsburg's decision to concur instead of joining in the majority is not fully explained in her correspondence or in concurrence, but she had said during the case conference that the decision was a difficult one for her. During oral argument, she had pushed the defense on the dangerousness of firearms: "[W]hy isn't this case more like the drug case, particularly the *Balint* case, than it is like the Food Stamps case? Because a gun is a dangerous instrument. Nothing dangerous about a Food Stamp." But she had also pointed out to the government that since guns generally had not historically been as closely regulated as drugs, "[y]ou don't have the same kind of congressional determination of dangerousness." After seeing the first draft of Thomas's opinion she wrote him that she would file a concurrence because she preferred "to say less rather than more in this case." Her short concurrence was narrowly drafted, focusing on the particulars of how the word "firearm" was used and defined in the statute and how the indictment in the case was worded.[46] What may have tipped the balance for Ginsburg were her concerns about the difficulty of determining whether a firearm was possibly a machine gun and thereby subject to government regulation, and here the defense's emphasis on the possibly defective nature of Staples's AR–15 seems to have made an impression. The one line she quoted in her concurrence from her previous circuit court decision in *Harris* noted that regulated weapons were often difficult to distinguish from unregulated ones.

The possibly defective nature of Staples's AR–15 also seemed to concern Justice Souter during the oral argument. When the government's lawyer suggested that the jury had rejected the theory, Souter pursued the point relentlessly until he established that the definition of machine gun that was given to the jury would not clearly have excluded a firearm that fired automatically as the result of a defect. Souter's point

---

46. Ginsburg argued that since "firearms" was a term of art in the statute that described highly dangerous weapons with special characteristics then the Government should have to prove knowing possession of such a weapon, not just of a firearm generally. *Staples*, 511 U.S. at 620–23.

was that strict liability should not apply to conduct that was vaguely
defined.

Justice Kennedy's correspondence with Thomas during the drafting
of the majority opinion made a different point and suggests that Brewster may have been right in steering clear of the Second Amendment
arguments. Kennedy asked Thomas to tone down language in Thomas's
original draft that seemed designed to set up future Second Amendment
cases. In his first draft Thomas wrote the following:

> [T]here is a long tradition of widespread lawful gun ownership by
> private individuals in this country, a tradition perhaps rooted in the
> unique experiences of a nation that was born from a colonial
> rebellion and that retained a frontier for the better part of its
> existence. [Citation omitted.]

The last clause of this sentence—the one describing the colonial
rebellion and prolonged existence of the frontier as unique national
experiences—was deleted from the final opinion at Kennedy's request.
Also deleted at Kennedy's request was a quote from one of the historical
sources in the footnote that read "In American history the gun has been
more than just present—it has been prominent." Finally, Kennedy asked
Thomas to change a phrase of the draft opinion from "owning a gun is
licit and blameless conduct" to "owning a gun can be licit and blameless
conduct." Kennedy explained these requests in what seems to be a
reference to the Second Amendment. "My reason for these suggested
changes is my concern that the opinion could be understood as some
indication of our position on other constitutional issues."[47]

Justice Souter also asked Thomas to qualify his language about the
innocence of firearms ownership somewhat. Souter asked Thomas to
include language emphasizing the dangerousness of the weapons that
Congress did deem to regulate. Thomas largely accommodated this
request, describing machine guns as "quasi-suspect" like the grenade in
Freed.

Perhaps Kennedy and Souter wanted to moderate Thomas's enthu-
siasm for guns in part because *Staples* was being decided at a time when
gun regulation in general and highly dangerous firearms in particular
were very much matters of public controversy. Earlier in 1993, in July—
after certiorari had been granted and only a few days before the defense
filed its brief—a deranged gunman killed eight people at a San Francisco
law firm using military-style, semiautomatic firearms with high-capacity
magazines. Calls for tighter regulation of firearms generally and assault

---

47. Justice Stevens pounced on the defense when it slipped in a reference to the
Second Amendment during oral argument. The defense abandoned the point, and no
further reference to the Second Amendment was made by anyone. Oral Argument at 5,
Staples v. United States, 511 U.S. 600 (1994) (No. 92–1441), 1993 WL 757643.

rifles in particular followed. In November, the same month that *Staples* was argued before the Court, two major pieces of gun legislation were passed in Congress. A ban on assault rifles passed the House and Senate two weeks before the *Staples* oral argument. The Brady Bill, which mandated background checks for the purchase of handguns, passed both houses of Congress the week before the oral argument and was signed by President Clinton the very day that *Staples* was argued. Taken together, these actions made November both the busiest month for government regulation of firearms in quite a while and a time when assault rifles in particular were very much on people's minds.

So there was an elephant in the chambers and the courtroom that no one was mentioning. Thomas's first draft referred to Staples's gun as an "assault rifle" even though both the Government and Staples's attorneys had scrupulously avoided use of that term. "Assault rifle" was changed to "rifle" in the subsequent drafts, even though the term was not mentioned in any of the Justices' correspondence. With the exception of a passing reference by Justice Souter in oral argument, none of the justices referred to either the Brady Bill or the Assault Weapons Ban in any way during oral argument, in correspondence, or—as far as we know from Justice Blackmun's notes—in conference.

Thomas's majority opinion drew a vigorous dissent from Stevens that was joined by Blackmun. Indeed, a few days after the case conference—and weeks before Thomas produced the first draft of his opinion—Stevens warned Thomas that he would need extra time to write a lengthy dissent because he considered the case "one of the most important—and most unfortunate—decisions of the Term." His letter also gave Thomas a short preview of his dissent and some further evidence of what had been said in conference. Stevens was troubled by the notion that "food stamps and machine guns are more analogous than hand grenades and machine guns." He also professed surprise about all of the concern that had apparently been expressed at the case conference about Staples's innocence and about the prospect of morally innocent offenders being incarcerated.

> I am also somewhat surprised that, after half a century of literal interpretation of this statute, clinching evidence of congressional intent is found in the possibility that a sentencing judge might abuse his or her discretion and send an unwitting owner of an inherited weapon to prison. Indeed, the judge in this case sentenced petitioner to probation and a fine despite that he appears hardly unwitting.

Clearly, Stevens expected morally innocent offenders to be sentenced leniently by trial judges, as he believed Staples had been. But Stevens also suspected that the "hardly unwitting" Staples had at least some idea that his AR–15 had been converted to a machine gun. Perhaps it was not a coincidence that the two dissenting judges in the case, Stevens and Blackmun, both believed that Staples was not, in fact, morally innocent.

Stevens's dissent made it clear that he saw *Staples* as a major case. Although he was writing for only two justices, Stevens's dissent ran sixteen pages in length, only four pages shorter than Thomas's majority opinion. Read in tandem, the two opinions map out both what was at stake in *Staples* and what seemed to get resolved.

Thomas's opinion gave the defense a sweeping win by affirming the D.C. Circuit's approach in *Harris*. No distinction was made between firearms with external indicia of special capabilities and those without. The opinion held that "the Government should have been required to prove beyond a reasonable doubt that he knew the weapon he possessed had the characteristics that brought it within the statutory definition of a machine gun."

Stevens's dissent emphasized dangerousness. He argued that the NFA "unquestionably is a public welfare statute," and that the dangerousness of the weapons regulated by the National Firearms Act justified presuming that Congress did not intend traditional mens rea requirements. Alluding to the Court's previous decisions in *Freed* and *Liparota*, Stevens questioned why the majority had reached "the rather surprising conclusion that guns are more analogous to food stamps than to hand grenades."

As if in dialog with Stevens, Thomas conceded from the outset that public welfare offense statutes typically "regulated potentially harmful or injurious items." But he interpreted the public welfare cases as requiring "at least that the defendant know that he is dealing with some dangerous or deleterious substance." In doing so he cited the *dicta* statement from *International Minerals* that a shipper who thought he was carrying distilled water instead of acid would not be liable and *Freed*'s *dicta* statement that a hand grenade possessor had to know that he possessed a hand grenade.

On this basis, Thomas denied that the National Firearms Act should be interpreted as creating public welfare offenses *in all cases*.

> [O]ur analysis in *Freed* likening the Act to the public welfare statute
> in *Balint* rested entirely on the assumption that the defendant *knew*
> he possessed a particularly dangerous type of weapon (one within
> the statutory definition of a 'firearm'), possession of which was not
> entirely 'innocent' in and of itself (citation omitted). The predicate
> for that analysis is eliminated when, as in this case, the very
> question to be decided is *whether* the defendant must know of the
> particular characteristics that make his weapon a statutory firearm.

In maintaining that whether a public welfare offense exists depends on whether or not a defendant knew what he was dealing with, Thomas finally answered the question that had been left vague in the Court's earlier cases about how much a defendant had to know about the facts of the offense. In Thomas's vision, the Court can only interpret something as a public welfare offense if it is are satisfied that the defendant's state of mind was not innocent to begin with.

Thomas then directly addressed the relationship between dangerousness and innocence that had been left ambiguous in *Freed*. He argued that dangerous things could also be innocent things and that guns were just such things.

> "That an item is 'dangerous' in some general sense, does not necessarily suggest . . . that it is not also entirely innocent. Even dangerous items can, in some cases, be so commonplace and generally available that we would not consider them to alert individuals to the likelihood of strict regulation. . . . Despite their potential for harm, guns generally can be owned in perfect innocence."

In a similar vein, Thomas rejected the notion that existing firearm regulation put defendants in such cases on notice. Noting that half of American homes had at least one gun, he questioned "whether regulations on guns are sufficiently intrusive that they impinge upon the common experience that owning a gun is usually licit and blameless conduct. . . ."

Stevens challenged the majority's preoccupation with moral innocence in the face of clear evidence of congressional intent for a stricter form of criminal liability for firearms. "To avoid a slight possibility of injustice to unsophisticated owners of machine guns and sawed-off shotguns, the Court has substituted its views of sound policy for the judgment Congress made when it enacted the National Firearms Act."[48] Such a preoccupation was, he argued, inconsistent with the basic idea of public welfare offenses. "The enforcement of public welfare offenses always entails some possibility of injustice."[49] Stevens also repeated the government's argument that ignorant offenders were not innocent because they were not completely without fault. "The dangerous character of the product is reasonably presumed to provide sufficient notice of the probability of regulation to justify strict enforcement against those who are merely guilty of negligent, rather than willful, misconduct."[50]

Stevens made a strong argument that Congress was not worried about morally innocent possessors of machine guns when it passed the

---

48. *Staples*, 511 U.S. at 624 (Stevens, J., dissenting).

49. *Id.* at 634.

50. *Id.*

National Firearms Act in 1934 Indeed, since hunting rifles of that era could not be readily converted to Tommy guns, Congress was not worried about an innocent hunter going to federal prison but was concerned that a gangster might escape prosecution by claiming innocent possession.

Ultimately, Stevens accused Thomas and Ginsburg of simply ignoring the intent of Congress in favor of the facts in the particular case before it. "[F]ollowing the approach of their decision in *United States v. Harris*, they have simply explained why, in their judgment, it would be unfair to punish the possessor of this machine gun."

Thomas, however, had a point that clearly extended beyond the somewhat compelling facts of the case before it—albeit one that did not directly address Congress's original intent. Speaking to the present, Thomas challenged Stevens's implicit distinction between "innocent" hunting firearms and would-be machine guns, noting that "[t]he Government does not dispute the contention that virtually any semiautomatic weapon may be converted, either by internal modification or, in some cases, simply by wear and tear, into a machine gun within the meaning of the Act."

The battle over the role that the principle of moral innocence should play in interpreting the National Firearms Act ultimately turned into a debate between Thomas and Stevens over what sort of guns were at issue. Thomas claimed that the government's position was that "guns in general are dangerous items" and that as long as a defendant knew that he possessed some sort of gun he could be prosecuted under the NFA under the public welfare doctrine. Stevens flatly accused both Thomas (and Ginsburg) of mischaracterizing the Government's position, citing passages from the Government's brief to the effect that only highly dangerous offensive weapons were at issue. Specifically, knowing possession of "a semiautomatic weapon that was readily convertible into a machine gun" was enough to place the possessor on notice of the possibility of regulation.

Limiting machine-gun prosecutions to those who knew they possessed a "readily convertible semiautomatic" would indeed have greatly reduced the chance that innocent hunters would be ensnared in federal prosecutions through no fault of their own. Thomas criticized this standard as an ad-hoc category of weapons with no foundation in either statutory text or in the Government's brief. He also considered this standard inherently vague, given that virtually all semiautomatics may be converted into automatic weapons. For Thomas, neither Congress by statute nor the ATF by regulation or ruling had ever made such a distinction between firearms, and this absence of regulation, combined with the statute's broad definition of machine gun, made the "doubling duck gun" that had worried the trial judge in the Staples case a legitimate concern. As long as the duck hunter knew that she had a gun and not a toy in her hands, she could be charged under the government's standard with possession of a machine gun if it fired two shots with a single pull of a trigger.

Stevens's best response to the innocent hunter hypothetical lay in the jury instructions that the government was defending in the Staples case. That instruction limited criminal liability to those who knowingly possessed "a dangerous device of a type as would alert one to the likelihood of regulation." The innocent duck hunter would only be convicted if the jury saw a duck gun as such "a dangerous device."[51]

Running through all of Thomas's arguments on these various points was a series of reminders that conviction under the National Firearms Act involved not simply a criminal conviction but a felony conviction that carried a possible prison sentence. Thomas finished his opinion with three pages arguing that the higher the penalty, the more reluctant courts should be to presume that legislatures intended low mens rea requirements. Stevens argued in reply that the statute in *Balint* carried a five year prison sentence and that sentencing discretion allowed judges to punish innocent offenders less severely. While acknowledging that such a rule was not consistent with *Balint*, Thomas nonetheless floated a trial balloon suggesting that the Court might in the future impose a clear statement rule on Congress in this area.

> In this view, absent a clear statement from Congress that mens rea is not required, we should not apply the public welfare offense rationale to interpret any statute defining a felony offense as dispensing with mens rea. We need not adopt such a definitive rule of construction to decide this case, however. Instead, we note only that where, as here, dispensing with mens rea would require the defendant to have knowledge only of traditionally lawful conduct, a severe penalty is merely a further factor tending to suggest that Congress did not intend to eliminate a mens rea requirement. In such a case, the usual presumption that a defendant must know the facts that make his conduct illegal should apply.

Interestingly, the language of this trial balloon would take on a life of its own over the years in lower court decisions holding that a severe penalty or felony conviction precluded strict liability.

---

51. Justice Thomas responded that such a question was a matter of law for judges and not fact for juries. Relying on juries to interpret such a general standard, he said, would result in open-ended regulatory liability. "[E]very regulatory statute potentially could be treated as a public welfare offense as long as the jury—not the court—ultimately determines that the specific items involved in a prosecution were sufficiently dangerous." *Staples*, 511 U.S. at 613, n.6. Justice Stevens replied that juries frequently applied just such general standards.

The Legacy of Staples

The *Staples* case has had an enormous impact. In federal courts, it has radically changed federal firearms prosecutions and raised persisting questions about the scope of the public welfare offense doctrine. *Staples* has also influenced how state courts interpret the mens rea requirements of their own criminal statutes.

The most immediate impact of the decision was, of course, on Harold Staples himself. The decision came down almost five years to the day after his sentencing, and Staples remembers thinking that had Judge Cook sent him to prison he would have already finished his sentence before the Supreme Court made its ruling. But Staples was not out of the woods yet. His case was remanded to the Tenth Circuit, where the same panel that affirmed his conviction had to decide whether to have Staples retried. Neal Kirkpatrick, the prosecutor at trial, remembers thinking that he could prove to a jury that Staples knew his AR–15 was a machine gun because of the filed down stop on the selector switch. Although Kirkpatrick did not know it, two members of the Supreme Court agreed with him on this point. Stevens had thought Staples "hardly unwitting," and Blackmun and his clerk both thought that Staples would be convicted under a knowledge standard. Yet the Tenth Circuit panel saw the trial evidence differently, ruling in the summer of 1994 that "no rational juror could find Mr. Staples guilty beyond a reasonable doubt of the offense charged" and ordering that Staples be acquitted of the machine gun charge.[52]

Staples fundamentally changed the prosecution and defense of cases under the National Firearms Act. Previously, only the D.C. circuit had required proof of knowledge of the characteristics that brought a weapon within the statute. *Staples* changed how the NFA was interpreted almost everywhere.[53] While most circuits subsequently held that the *Staples* knowledge requirement applied to all firearms, a few circuits initially tried to limit the knowledge requirement to cases where the illegal characteristics were not readily apparent, thus adopting the hybrid approach that neither party in the *Staples* litigation had sought.[54] By 1996, however, the Department of Justice instructed its prosecutors that in all NFA cases "the government should anticipate proving the defendant's knowledge of the NFA weapon's unlawful characteristics and request an appropriate instruction on knowledge."[55]

---

52. United States v. Staples, 30 F.3d 108 (10th Cir. 1994).

53. Stephen P. Halbrook, *Firearms Law Deskbook* (VOL. 1 2009), at 450.

54. *Id.* at 455.

55. *Id.*

Staples also influenced the way the Supreme Court looked at mens rea generally. The year after the *Staples* decision, the Court decided *United States v. X–Citement Video*. In that case the Court read a knowledge requirement into a federal child pornography statute, reversing the conviction of a video store operator who claimed that he did not know that an actress in one of his store's videos was underage. After concluding that the statute did not create a public welfare offense,[56] the Court cited *Staples* as reinforcing the conclusion in *Morissette* that "the presumption in favor of a *scienter* requirement should apply to each of the statutory elements that criminalize otherwise innocent conduct."[57] That presumption has been applied in numerous cases since then[58]

Staples's influence has also extended well beyond federal cases. As a case rooted not in constitutional but mens rea principles, *Staples* is only persuasive—not binding—authority in state court cases. But its widespread use by state courts suggest that *Staples* struck a chord that is deeply fundamental to our criminal jurisprudence, even if not constitutional. Numerous state courts have cited and quoted from *Staples* in reading additional mens rea requirements into state penal statutes. Most commonly, *Staples* is cited for the proposition that crimes that carry serious penalties or even any sort of felony conviction cannot be strict liability offenses.[59] The Supreme Court of Minnesota discussed *Staples* at length in holding that a statute prohibiting possession of a deadly weapon on school grounds required proof that the defendant knew he was on school property. "Applying this analysis to the facts here, we observe that knives as common household utensils are clearly not inherently dangerous, as they can be used for a myriad of completely benign purposes."[60]

Yet there are limits to how far the Supreme Court itself has been willing to extend *Staples*. Over time it has become clear that *Staples* only applies to those who would otherwise be innocent. Where the conduct at issue is itself wrongful and not innocent, then simply knowing you are engaging in that conduct is enough. Distinguishing *Staples* and *X–Citement Video* from a robbery case, Justice Thomas wrote that mens rea need only be read into a statute when "necessary to separate wrongful conduct from 'otherwise' innocent conduct."[61] The Court has also made

---

56. United States v. X–Citement Video, Inc., 513 U.S. 64, 71 (1994).

57. *Id.* at 72.

58. *See, e.g.,* United States v. Vilanueva–Sotelo, 515 F.3d 1234 (D.C. Cir. 2008); United States v. Cote, 504 F.3d 682 (7th Cir. 2007).

59. *See, e.g.,* Owens v. State, 352 Md. 663 (1999); State v. Bash, 925 P.2d 978 (Wash. 1996).

60. *In re* the Welfare of C.R.M., 611 N.W.2d 802, 810 (Minn. 2000).

61. Carter v. United States, 530 U.S. 255, 269 (2000).

clear that all that is required is *some* wrongful conduct. In *Dean v. U.S.*[62] , a bank robber who accidentally fired his gun during a robbery appealed a statutory sentence enhancement for discharge of a firearm on the grounds that under *Staples* the Court should read in a requirement that the discharge be intentional in order for the sentence to be enhanced. Writing for a 7–2 majority, Chief Justice John Roberts declined to give him the benefit of the *Staples* holding, because "the defendant is already guilty of unlawful conduct twice over: a violent . . . offense and the use . . . of a firearm in the course of that offense." In dissent, Justice Stevens objected to the imposition of additional criminal liability for accidental conduct, citing *Staples* for the proposition that "absent a clear statement by Congress that it intended to create a strict-liability offense," a mens rea requirement has generally been presumed in federal statutes.[63] The message from these cases is that *Staples* will be used to read in additional *mens rea* requirements only for those who are completely innocent, not simply partially innocent of some additional crime or enhancement.[64] In this sense, only those of manifestly good character need apply for relief under *Staples*.

Yet ironically, the impact of *Staples* on the public welfare offense doctrine itself is far from clear. Most notably, a battle has raged over whether and how far to apply *Staples* in environmental criminal prosecutions, resulting in a circuit split that the Supreme Court has thus far declined to resolve. In *United States v. Weitzenhoff*,[65] the Ninth Circuit had to decide whether a "knowing" violation of the Clean Water Act required proof of knowledge that the waste discharged was in excess of the amount authorized by permit. The Ninth Circuit read *Staples* as confirming the continued vitality of the public welfare doctrine for "obnoxious waste materials" and reasoned that "the dumping of sewage and other pollutants into our nation's waters is precisely the type of activity that puts the discharger on notice that his acts may pose a public danger."[66] While noting the *Staples* opinion's concern with harsh penalties, the Ninth Circuit noted also that it refrained from holding that public welfare offenses could not be felonies.[67]

---

62. 129 S.Ct. 1849 (2009).

63. *Id.* at 1858.

64. *See also* U.S. v. Wells, 519 U.S. 482, 498–99 (1997) (Declining to read a materiality requirement into a false statements statute, reasoning that one who knowingly makes a false statement to a bank with the intent to influence the bank is not engaging in trivial or innocent conduct even if that statement was not material to the bank's decision.)

65. 35 F.3d 1275 (9th Cir. 1993).

66. *Id.* at 1286.

67. *Id.* at 1286 n.7.

Yet a few years later the Fifth Circuit used *Staples* to read a knowledge requirement into an environmental case. In *United States v. Ahmad*,[68] the court reversed the conviction of a gas station owner who had unknowingly—albeit negligently—pumped gasoline into a sewer. The facts of the case literally reeked of public danger: the discharge resulted in the evacuation of a sewage treatment plant and two nearby schools out of fear of a "tremendous explosion" that might have resulted in "hundreds, if not thousands of deaths."[69] Ahmad claimed that he thought he was merely pumping out some water that had seeped into the bottom of his station's tank and that he did not know he was discharging gasoline at all. Reversing the conviction, the Fifth Circuit read *Staples* as holding that "the key to the public welfare offense analysis is whether 'dispensing with mens rea would require the defendant to have knowledge only of traditionally lawful conduct.'" Despite the enormous danger to the public evident from the facts, the Fifth Circuit concluded that no public welfare offense existed. "Following *Staples*, we hold that the offenses charged . . . are not public welfare offenses and that the usual presumption of a mens rea requirement applies."[70]

Whether and how a future Supreme Court might apply *Staples* to environmental statutes remains unclear. The Court declined review in an environmental criminal case where Justice Thomas made it clear that he thought *Staples* required reversing the conviction in an opinion dissenting from the denial of *certiorari*. The petition in *Hanousek v. United States*[71] challenged the conviction of a rock quarry supervisor whose backhoe operator accidentally struck a petroleum pipeline, resulting in the spillage of thousands of gallons of petroleum into the Skagway River. The Ninth Circuit affirmed his conviction on the grounds that the Clean Water Act was public welfare legislation. Noting the circuit split created by *Ahmad*, Thomas used *Staples* to argue that the public welfare doctrine did not apply to such environmental crimes arising out of ordinary industrial and commercial activities.

Responding to the Ninth Circuit's conclusion that a reasonable person would know that working around a pipeline would be highly regulated because of the threat to community health and safety, Thomas called into question the continued validity of the entire line of public welfare offense cases. "But we have never held that any statute can be described as creating a public welfare offense so long as the statute regulates conduct that is known to be subject to extensive regulation and

---

68.   101 F.3d 386 (5th Cir. 1996).

69.   *Id.* at 388.

70.   *Id.* at 391.

71.   528 U.S. 1102 (2000).

that may involve a risk to the community."[72] What Thomas says the Court has "never held" is almost exactly the definition of public welfare offense used by the Court during the thirty year span from *Dotterweich* to *Liparota*: highly regulated activities that involved public danger. Thomas concluded his dissent by calling for a reconsideration of any precedents that "contributed to the Court of Appeals' overly broad interpretation of this doctrine,"[73] a veiled concession, perhaps, that he was effectively asking the Court to overturn the public welfare offense doctrine. Yet Thomas raises a significant point that future decisions may have to resolve. As the extent of regulation in society expands, so too could the mens rea free zone created by the public welfare offense doctrine.

Conclusion

It is almost always easier to understand a story when you see how it ends. With respect to the public welfare offense doctrine, *Staples* and its progeny help us better understand the role that implicit judgments about character played in the earlier decisions. All of these earlier cases justified low mens rea requirements in terms of public danger. *Staples* and its progeny make clear, however, that danger is not a generic concept for the courts. Some types of danger, such as those at issue in food safety or environmental cases, involve widespread sickness, death or destruction emanating from a single act of carelessness. The instrumental logic for criminal punishment of the heedless is strongest in the face of this type of danger, and courts are more willing to presume that criminal liability is not limited to only those who knew what they were doing. Other types of danger involve bad people doing dangerous things under circumstances where their guilty minds may be difficult to prove. These people are perceived as dangerous because of their demonstrably bad character. Such was clearly the case with the National Firearms Act and may have been the case with the narcotics statute at issue in *Balint*. When courts interpret statutes designed to get at the dangers created by bad people, they are more likely to read in a mens rea requirement of wrongful knowledge if the conduct itself does not suggest the poor character of the people being prosecuted.

This concern with character also helps explain the "not-quite-constitutional" status of these mens rea concerns. Courts ultimately, and properly, are willing to defer to legislative judgment about whether the ends of avoiding environmental degradation or some other form of public danger justify the means of prosecuting potentially innocent offenders. For this reason, mens rea never achieved status as a due process concern

---

72. *Id.*

73. *Id.*

because the Supreme Court was loath to categorically rule that such ends could never justify the means. What the Court has created through the public welfare cases, and what it articulated most clearly in *Staples*, was a clear statement rule requiring Congress to state clearly its intent to impose a stricter form of criminal liability than was traditional. What *Staples* and subsequent cases make clear is that this desire for clear statement is at its strongest when statutes clearly designed for the very bad may end up being successfully used against the possibly good.

Epilogue

As for Staples himself, acquittal on the machine gun charges was not the end of his involvement with the criminal justice system. Two further developments took place: one raises questions about the system's integrity, and the other raises questions about its competence.

After his machine gun case was dismissed, Staples was indicted in federal court on conspiracy charges relating to an identity theft scheme. He claimed that he was being framed by law enforcement agents. Specifically, he claimed that he had been working as a confidential informant for the Tulsa Police Department in a criminal investigation of the very same men who were the primary witnesses against him in the federal case. Once again, Staples called Clark Brewster, and once again Brewster—who believed that this prosecution also was vindictive and baseless—represented him pro bono. At trial, Brewster subpoenaed the Tulsa detective with whom Staples claimed to have been working, but the detective denied all knowledge of Staples. Brewster then played for the jury a tape recording that Staples had made of some of his conversations with the detective confirming Staples's account. Staples was acquitted on all counts and has not been arrested since. He currently operates a bail bond agency in Tulsa.

Just as one should resist seeing court cases as the pre-ordained results of larger forces, so too, should one resist the tendency to see the universe in a grain of sand. Harold Staples may have been the victim of one or possibly two misguided or vindictive prosecutions. If so, his story might be representative of some larger trend or problem, or it might be simply an idiosyncrasy—a product of the mistakes or bad actions of a few government agents at a particular place and time. This also does not necessarily mean that the U.S. Supreme Court decision that bears his name was rightly decided. If Staples was wrongfully prosecuted, the most that can be said—but also the least that should be said—is that the case serves as a cautionary tale about what can happen when the law gives police and prosecutors great discretion about the type of people they prosecute by requiring little wrongfulness in the way of mental state on the part of the defendant. Whether at the end of the day that is a risk worth running to keep society safe in other regards is another matter altogether.

It is the nature of storytelling to try and make sense of the world in some way. Perhaps that is a tendency best resisted in telling fuller stories about Supreme Court adjudication in criminal cases, an enterprise that by its nature moves back and forth between the disordered world out of which criminal cases often emerge and the construction of doctrines that try to bring coherence to that world. One final incident illustrates this point. After his machine gun case was dismissed, Staples got a call from the U.S. Marshal's office asking him to come down to the federal courthouse and pick up his AR–15, even though the Government had maintained all the way to the Supreme Court that it was an illegal machine gun. Staples was so nervous about taking the gun out of the courthouse that he asked a Marshal to walk him to the parking lot and put the AR–15 in the trunk of Staples's car. When told for the first time in 2009 that the Government had returned the AR–15 to Staples, Clark Brewster laughed and aptly observed with respect to Staples's mens rea that "if he did not know before, he sure does now."

So this story ends with an image that exemplifies not the orderly or the morally instructive but the paradoxical and the ironic. The photograph that follows was taken in 2010 and shows Harold Staples holding the unregistered AR–15 "machine gun" whose seizure led him and the U.S. government to the Supreme Court and back twenty years earlier.

Photograph taken in 2010 of Harold Staples holding the unregistered AR–15 "machine gun" whose seizure led him and the U.S. government to the Supreme Court and back twenty years earlier.

4

Susan D. Rozelle

The Story of *Berry*: When Hot Blood Cools

It was 1974. Patty Hearst had been kidnapped by the Symbionese Liberation Army; Richard Nixon resigned in the wake of Watergate; people were reading *Zen and the Art of Motorcycle Maintenance* and a thriller by unknown author Stephen King called *Carrie. Blazing Saddles* was playing in the theatres, and "Killing Me Softly with His Song" won a Grammy for Song of the Year.

The feminist movement was gathering steam, and society was just beginning to reframe domestic violence as a crime justifying police intervention rather than as a private, family matter.[1]

In San Francisco, police officer Paul Higaki went to Kaiser Emergency Medical Hospital at 3 a.m. to talk with Rachel Pessah. Albert Berry had strangled her until she passed out, and then called her a cab to take her to the hospital. Officer Higaki felt really bad for Rachel, he said, because she was afraid of Albert, and there was nothing he could do about it. "I gave her information about battered women's shelters and therapists, and moved on to the next call." This kind of thing was routine. Nothing to lose sleep over, but depressing nevertheless: in the end Rachel became just another homicide statistic.[2]

The country felt the same way, it seems. There was no news coverage of Rachel's death to speak of, and Albert's trial, appeal, and the ultimate reversal of his murder conviction went more or less unnoticed at the time. But the story of *People v. Berry* reverberated through the voluntary manslaughter doctrine, challenging our view of what counts as

---

1. *See generally* Elizabeth M. Schneider, *Battered Women and Feminist Lawmaking* 3, 29 (2000) (identifying the beginnings of this change in the late 1960s, with much work taking place through the 1970s).

2. Telephone Interview by Ceara Riggs with Paul Higaki, Retired Law Enforcement Officer, S.F. Police Dep't (Sept. 27, 2010) [hereinafter Higaki Interview].

an adequate provocation to turn what would have been a cold-blooded murder into a lesser form of hot-blooded homicide.

The Courtship

Rachel Pessah was a slender, young widow working at Fantasia Bakery in San Francisco.[3] A Jewish Israeli girl, she was blonde and freckled and her customers asked for her. Married in Israel at the age of 17, she had come to the States with her new husband, Joe, settling easily into the rhythms of an active, California lifestyle. They went dancing, went camping, had picnics, and spent quality time with the family on both sides who lived nearby.

Only three years later, Joe died. He turned on the gas heater one night, and inexplicably it burst into flames. Horrified, Rachel tore Joe's jacket off of him, frantically beating the fires out, but he could not be saved. Losing her husband in such a traumatic way was understandably hard on Rachel. Nightmares about the fire haunted her. And she was only twenty years old. Three months passed by, and then Rachel met Albert Berry.

Albert was a cook at the Red Roof Inn across the street from the bakery. At forty-six, he was more than twice Rachel's age and a Christian to boot, but Albert was disarmingly handsome, even looked a little bit like her Joe. Thick, wavy hair tousled Albert's forehead, and wide eyes and sensuous lips belied his unsavory track record with life in general, and with women in particular.

Albert suspected his first wife—with whom he had two children—of cheating on him, though he never confronted her about it. She did leave him, but not necessarily for anyone else: she left in 1952, when Albert was convicted of possessing stolen goods. He served time until 1957 in Attica State Prison in New York (famous for its unusually dangerous criminal population and the deadly riot commemorated in the John Lennon song "Attica State"[4]).

Upon his release, Albert came back to San Francisco, where he met and within thirty days, married, his second wife, Carrol.[5] She bore him five children, but that relationship, too, was rocky. They were both

---

3. Unless otherwise indicated, the facts in this chapter have been drawn from the *Berry* record. For the presence of facts from additional sources, I am indebted to the diligent team of research assistants, Ceara Riggs and Christine Edwards, and to reference librarians Robert Brammer and Pamela Burdett. This chapter was supported by a grant from the Stetson University College of Law.

4. John Lennon, *Attica State, on* Some Time in New York City (Capitol Records 1972).

5. Although the trial transcript spells the name conventionally, "Carrol" is the spelling reflected in public records. *See, e.g.,* California Divorce Index, 1966–1984.

sleeping with someone else, engaged in a "mutual wife-swapping arrangement . . . that carried on for years," when she told him she was leaving him for the other man. She called Albert by the other man's name during sex one night—the implication from the way he told the story was that she had done it on purpose to taunt him—and he responded by going to the kitchen for a butcher knife. He returned to lie in bed with her "for quite a while, fighting what to do," before stabbing her in the stomach multiple times. She recovered, going on to marry that other man. He earned one—yes, *one*—more year behind bars. (Careful readers may have noticed: that was five years for possession of stolen goods, and one year for repeatedly stabbing his wife in the stomach.)

When Albert got out on probation in May of 1973, he lived with a woman named Jean Berk for a couple of months, and then with a woman named Justine Weldon for four or five more. His relationship with Justine ended when she locked him out, and he broke down her door. Albert's California Department of Corrections record shows a probation violation in mid-September that put him back in jail for almost two weeks; breaking down his girlfriend's door probably explains that entry. Albert's probation was restored in October of 1973, and Jean took him back in.

Toward the end of January 1974, Albert met Rachel. They married just four months later, on May 27 in Reno.

The Marriage

Albert testified that they made each other very happy, but from the outside, it certainly seemed to be an odd relationship. Three days after marrying, when most couples would be enjoying a romantic honeymoon getaway, Rachel took a six-week trip to Israel by herself. More oddly, Albert testified that on her way out, she asked him what he would do if she got pregnant there. He said she sent two letters while she was away: the first expressed how much she loved and missed him, and the second accused him of forcing her to marry him and demanded that he move out before she returned.

As Albert told the story on direct examination at trial, this turn of events was shocking, bewildering, and emotionally devastating. According to Rachel's brother, Jack Pessah, however, there was no mystery. Israeli citizens, men and women alike, all serve a few years in the military, and Albert had convinced Rachel that the only way she could go home to visit her family without being drafted was to marry a U.S. citizen. This explanation was never shared with the jury—Jack was a student at the time, classes had just started, and the prosecution decided it could win the case without calling him. As far as the jury was concerned, the marriage was followed by a trip and two letters, with no explanation at all for Rachel's apparent change of heart.

The Abuse

Rachel returned from Israel on Saturday, July 13. On the way back from the airport, she told Albert she had met someone else, a man named Yacob,[6] and she wanted a divorce. They fought, and as he explained, "She started getting on top of me, and she started scratching. . . . So to get her off me, I grabbed her by the throat and started choking her." In the aftermath, Albert said he would leave, "and she said, 'no, I don't want you to leave. . . . I need somebody. I don't want to be alone, [so] you can stay until [Yacob] is coming.'" Albert objected, "[a]nd she said, 'well you either can stay or I'm going to sign a report that you tried to kill me.'"

In the end, however, Rachel never did report this incident to the police. She went to the hospital, describing how she had tripped on her way off the plane and gotten tangled up in her purse strap. Albert, in contrast, seemed proud of his injuries and of how he had incurred them; at least, he was proud at the time. In Albert's retelling on direct, he portrayed himself as a reluctant combatant: he said he choked Rachel only after she attacked him first. One of Albert's co-workers, however, testified that Albert came to work that Sunday morning showing off his scratches and crowing that "he had tried to choke his wife and this is what she did to him to defend herself." And if she ever tried to leave him, the co-worker testified next, Albert said he was going to kill her.

An awful lot happened in the next week. Albert testified that he and Rachel went to Santa Rosa to check in with his probation officer, and spent the rest of the day at a fair before heading home. On the drive back, Albert said Rachel began caressing him, propositioning him, declaring that she could not wait until they found a motel but had to have him then and there. When Albert protested that there was nowhere to park, "[s]he got very mad and she said, 'Forget it.'" They rode in silence for a time, but "[e]ventually, we turned off and we had sexual intercourse. She insisted on it." Later that night Rachel informed Albert that she was in love with Yacob, and so she would not have sex with Albert again. "It was like she didn't know what she really wanted. . . . She wanted me and then she didn't."

The following day, they went to Lake Tahoe, and from Albert's perspective, Rachel's bizarre, provocatory behavior continued. She played blackjack while Albert hit the slots, and at some point, Albert offered Rachel a cigarette. She declined, only to turn to the man sitting

---

6. The trial transcript reads "Yako," an attempt to capture the Hebrew name more commonly transliterated as "Yacob."

next to her and pointedly ask for one of his. Red-faced, Albert yanked the obliging stranger's cigarette out of Rachel's mouth, broke it in half, and stalked off.

Despite the tiff, they left together. Albert did not like for Rachel to drive—he said she had a tendency to speed—but she refused to hand over the keys, threatening to report him to his probation officer for choking her if he did not let her do as she wished. Again, of course, this is Albert's story. As he told it, Rachel was the aggressor: taunting, provoking, holding his prior strangulation of her over his head as leverage to force him to do her will. A different picture of the balance of power in the relationship emerged on cross-examination, when the jury learned that Rachel had "begged and pleaded" with Albert's probation officer not to recommend his probation be revoked—and that Albert was standing right there with her when she had done so.

Regardless, both sides agreed that on that drive back from Tahoe, Rachel was the one behind the wheel when they hit a bicyclist. The rider smashed right through the windshield, coming to rest in the back seat, and they thought he was dead. Rachel was "completely out of her head . . . [and making] for the Yolo Causeway like she was going to jump off" before Albert pulled her back.

The cyclist lived, and Albert and Rachel spent the rest of the week in Sacramento, where they had followed him to the hospital at the University of California, Davis. Albert said he had Rachel seen there, as well, because her distress over the accident had her saying she wanted to kill herself. At the same time, she insisted that Albert tell people he had been the one behind the wheel, again, he said, threatening to report him to his probation officer if he refused.

On Sunday, July 21, Albert and Rachel returned to San Francisco. Albert testified that over the next two days, Rachel resumed the pattern. "One minute she wanted me to leave. One minute she wanted me to stay." And she needled him again in a number of ways: she wrote three or four letters to Yacob, and had Albert address the envelopes. On the twenty-second, they picked up the photographs Rachel had taken in Israel. First, she allowed him to look through them, then said, "This is one I better not let you see," before "she said, 'But oh, here.' And she made a point of showing" Albert the ones of her and Yacob. Despite the hurt this presumably would have engendered, Albert testified that the two of them then shopped together for a photo album to put the pictures in. Interestingly, Albert's description of the day's events in the taped statement he gave to police when he was arrested characterized the twenty-second as "a beautiful day," in which they had had "a beautiful time, no arguments, no problems. She was happy and I was happy."

In both his trial testimony and in that taped statement, Albert described another egregiously provoking event that evening, when they went out to dinner and saw a movie. They had "done some heavy petting" in the theater, and came home around midnight. In the early morning hours of Tuesday, July 23, Rachel said, "I was going to make love to you, but I'm saving myself for [Yacob]." "Besides, I think that I might be pregnant by him and if I have sexual intercourse with you, I don't know whether it will be your baby or his." Albert told her to "shut up" and got up to leave.

Albert told two different versions of what happened next. In his trial testimony, he said he "blanked out" before grabbing Rachel and choking her into unconsciousness. In both his taped statement to the police and in the testimony of the court-appointed psychiatrist, however, Albert included a bit more detail: Rachel threatened that if Albert were to leave her, " 'I'll go and sign that God damn report ... and have your probation officer put you in jail anyhow.' [A]nd I says, well, if ... you want to put me in jail for something, I might as well do something. So I grabbed her by the throat and she passed out and I quit."

Albert revived her with massage and by putting cold water on her face. They talked for about two hours, according to his testimony. Rachel's version differed slightly. She told Assistant District Attorney Paul Cummins that Albert "strangled her into unconsciousness ... at about 12:05 a.m. [and] when she came to her senses, the next thing that she remembers was at approximately 12:25 a.m. she looked at the clock, the Defendant choked her again." She said Albert had "kept her there for some time after." Both sides agreed that in the end, Albert called two cabs: Rachel went to the hospital, and he went to the Greyhound Bus station, moving his things out of the apartment and leaving them in a locker there.

It was while Rachel was at the hospital that she made her first police report against Albert. Officer Paul Higaki, who spoke with Rachel that night, was not sure what to make of her. He "didn't think she was making [the abuse] up," but suspected what had happened that night "might not have been as severe as she was claiming."[7]

Albert, meanwhile, had gone on to Jean Berk's place. He told her "he had tried to choke [his wife], ... and when he called Kaiser they wouldn't let him talk to her because she was talking to a police officer." In the morning, Jean "asked him why he had done it ... [and h]e said, 'Maybe I was trying to stop her mouth.' " She drove him downtown and went to work; he took a bus to Reno, taking $146 with him.

---

7. Higaki Interview, *supra* note 2.

The following day, Wednesday, July 24, Albert returned from Reno with forty-six cents. He called Rachel twice at home from the Red Roof Inn, both during the day and late into the evening turning into Thursday the twenty-fifth. He tried to talk her out of pressing charges, and she used her leverage, he testified, to bully him into making a tape recording stating that he "had forced her to marry" him, and that he "was driving the car at the time of the accident." She told him "that she never wanted to see [him] again, that [he couldn't] possibly love her, that [he] would kill her." "I told her she was crazy," Albert said.

July 25 was Rachel's birthday. She was twenty-one years old, and Albert or no Albert, she wanted a cake and some cookies. Still, she called her cousin, Fortunee Lichaa, who was working at the Fantasia Bakery that morning, to let her know she was on her way. When Rachel arrived safely, she asked Fortunee to please make sure, if she died, that she be buried in Israel, and she gave Fortunee her parents' phone number there.[8]

A little before 3 p.m., Albert went to the apartment because, he testified, "I wanted to talk to Rachel ... [to] see if I could get her to drop the charges." He was one block away when he saw Rachel emerge from a cab, go inside, and return having changed clothes. On cross-examination, he protested that he was not hiding from her, but was just too slow to catch up, and could not call out to her to wait for him because he was a block away. After she left, he entered the apartment. He took the pictures of Rachel and Yacob and hid them, together with some of Rachel's jewelry and the tape Rachel had forced him to make of the phone conversation from the night before. He ran out to buy some cigarettes, and then he settled down to wait. Morning came, but still no Rachel. Albert went out for more cigarettes, and returned to the apartment.

The Death

At 11 a.m. on Friday, July 26, Rachel came through the door. She had slept at a friend's house, but returned home as she had done the previous day to get more clothes.[9] Albert testified that she said, "Hello," and then "I suppose you have come here to kill me." He said, "Yes," and then "No," and then "Yes," and then "I really have come to talk to you." She screamed. He tried to stop her from screaming, but "she wouldn't stop.... We struggled and the next thing I knew I had a telephone cord around her neck." On cross, he admitted that he had used an electrical cord first, switching to the telephone cord in the midst

---

8. Telephone Interview by Christine Edwards with Fortunee Lichaa, Relative of Rachel Pessah Berry (Sept. 16, 2010) [hereinafter Lichaa Interview].

9. *Id.*

of strangling her. After it was over, he said, "I asked her why won't she get up and talk to me." He took her body into the bathroom, went into the kitchen, made a cup of tea, and sat down. "Rachel, come on," he said, "wake up. I want to talk to you." Then he locked the door behind himself, "put the key back up where we usually leave it," and left.

The prosecution's version was a little different. In Albert's taped confession to the police, he had said, "I deliberately waited to kill her. No pretense, no bullshit, no nothing." While he was waiting, he cut a black electrical cord into a convenient length to serve as a ligature. When she came through the door and screamed, he said on the tape, "I threw her down on the floor and I grabbed the cord. I said, 'now you'll shut the hell up, won't you.'" After she fell to the floor, still conscious but no longer struggling, he switched to the telephone cord. The interrogating officers asked him why he switched. The black cord, he explained, "kept slipping out of my hand."

The Discovery and Investigation

After Albert left the apartment, he went to Jean Berk's place, dropping off the key to that Greyhound Bus station locker and leaving a note. He spent several hours downtown and called Jean that night. The conversation was short. "I told her I had strangled Rachel," he testified, and she said, "Not again?" "Yes," he replied. "I think I've killed her." "How?" Jean asked him. "And he said, 'With a phone cord. . . . As of 11:30 this morning she's dead.'"

Jean did not call the police that evening: "There would have been no point," she testified at trial, lamely explaining that she did not know where Rachel would be. Instead, she called Bill Tuberville, Albert's former roommate, and Joe Grumich, her Buddhist spiritual leader. The next morning, when Rachel was not at the Fantasia Bakery, Jean, Bill, and Joe went to Rachel's apartment. They rang the bell, and when they got no answer, they went to the police.

Three officers came to investigate. Rachel's body was face down on the bathroom floor—Bill Tuberville caught a glimpse of her legs—and there was "a lot of blood around the body." Twin furrows traced the circumference of her neck. The only time Jean ever saw Rachel was as the officers carried her body out on the stretcher, covered by a sheet. Inspectors dusted for fingerprints and made note of the condition of the apartment. No signs of a struggle, really, not enough out of place to say whether that just might have been the way it was kept. There were dissolution of marriage papers and a police inspector's business card noting "warrant in process for Albert Berry" on the kitchen table, a key had been dropped on the floor, and there was a length of black cord tossed under the back stairs. There was a telephone on a front hall table;

its long extension cord boasted strands of hair stuck to it, and some "red brown spots which appeared to be blood." Unsurprisingly, both were consistent with Rachel's. The widths of the two furrows on her neck matched those of the electrical cord and of the telephone cord, respectively. With steady pressure, it would have taken between three and eight minutes for her to die. Since Albert had switched cords, it probably took Rachel longer.

The next morning, Sunday, July 28, Albert called Jean again, to say he had not seen anything in the paper about the killing. When she told him that police had found the body, he said he was "sorry that [Jean] was involved." His tone was "not flippant but kind of light" considering the gravity of the subject. Jean told the police about the phone call, and they were still at her place when the phone rang again. Again, it was Albert. Gently, Jean suggested turning himself in. He said "he didn't think he would," but then reconsidered. He would do that, he said, he just wanted to "take a couple of days to think" first. Jean handed the phone to the officer, and Albert told him the same. In the days that followed, Albert called Jean again, and wrote her two letters, too. That he "felt dead inside" was "an on-going theme."

Albert rattled around San Francisco for a few more days, staying in flophouses and visiting old haunts. There was a certain symmetry about his choice of locations: when Albert first came to San Francisco twenty years earlier, he had stayed at the National Motel, and the National Motel was the last place he stayed before being arrested.[10] He never did turn himself in, though; police caught up with him on Thursday, August 1, when he tried to pawn one of Rachel's gold bracelets.[11] Albert's confession was taped on that date. Understandably, the confession played a prominent role in the prosecution's case. Albert's last taped words were, "I knew damn well when I was waiting there for her, I'd probably kill her."

The confession, especially, made this an easy case for the prosecution. But something about the confession did not add up for public defender Geoffrey Brown. In fact, he thought, the confession made this case sound too easy. So much of the tape reflected depression, even suicidal tendencies. When Albert was first introduced to the inspector taking his statement, he announced he was going to make the inspector's job easy. He responded to the Miranda warnings and being asked if, "having these rights in mind, [he] want[ed] to talk," by saying, "[m]ight as well, what the hell." "What was in my mind at the time? I was going

10. Telephone Interview by Christine Edwards with Geoffrey Brown, Deputy Public Defender, City and County of San Francisco (Sept. 16, 2010) [hereinafter Brown Interview].

11. Lichaa Interview, *supra* note 8.

to kill her and go to the bridge.... I was tired of it all. Just tired of bullshit. Tired of trying. Tired of struggling." The officers never talked about what the charges might be, even protesting that making charging decisions was not their job. But Albert insisted. "You charge it murder in the first degree, premeditated, you got it, cause it doesn't matter, all right.... If that's what you want, you got it. It doesn't make any difference."

The Attempted Suicide

The talk of jumping off a bridge made perfect sense to Brown. When he met with Albert for the first time, Albert told him he "wanted the gas chamber."[12] As his trial date neared, jail staff gave Albert Valium on a regular basis to calm his nerves. Rather than taking it as prescribed, however, he hoarded the pills, and took them all at once on the eve of trial.[13] Around 1 a.m. on September 23, the deputy sheriff "noticed there was something wrong with him." Dr. Robert Cramer, the prison doctor, examined him, and told the court in chambers that morning that he had overdosed. Since Albert would not be able to assist with his own defense, trial was postponed until the next day. He was ordered back to the county jail, kept under observation for twenty-four hours—and not given any more Valium.

The Sham

On September 24, the day began with a hearing in chambers on Albert's competence to stand trial. Doctor Cramer examined Albert again, and declared him well. The drugs had worn off, and Albert knew where he was and why he was there. He appeared lethargic, however, and "[w]hen asked if he felt he could aid his attorney in choosing a jury, he stated that it didn't matter ... he had been convicted of felonies before." That lethargy, opined Dr. Cramer, was "highly motivated by secondary gains." In other words, Albert was pretending still to be affected by the Valium, hoping to buy himself more time. How could Dr. Cramer tell it was a sham? He is acting tired, explained the doctor, which is what most people think Valium does to you. Really, though, Valium is not a soporific; it does not make you fall asleep, as Albert seemed to be prone to doing that morning. Valium does, however, interfere with the ability to make fine motor movements: people lose the ability to tie their shoelaces, for example. Albert's fine motor skills were just fine. And although he looked pretty disheveled, that was ultimately his own doing: he had been the one to take the pills, and he was the one who was malingering now. The court decided not to grant another

---

12. Brown Interview, *supra* note 10.

13. *Id.*

continuance, reasoning that Albert would put on this same act whenever the trial went forward, and so today was as good a day as any.

Still, just to be on the safe side, Dr. Cramer stayed in chambers and watched as the lawyers debated the admissibility of Albert's prior conviction of assault with a deadly weapon for stabbing his second wife, Carrol. Albert was indignant during this discussion: "I paid that penalty. I pleaded guilty to it." How can it be the law, he demanded, "that you get punished twice for the same crime?" "I guess that is one way to put it," the judge admitted. The prior conviction came in.

"Having watched Mr. Berry participate in legal actions peripheral to the pending trial," Dr. Cramer dryly informed the court next, "It is my professional opinion that he is capable of aiding Counsel in his own defense and that there is no evidence of residual toxicity from his overdose of Valium."

The Judge

Trial Judge Claude D. Perasso got his juris doctorate from the University of San Francisco in 1953. He had originally been a civil trial lawyer, but then the Public Defender's Officer asked him to join, and he stayed for fifteen years. He was elevated to the bench in 1971. At the time of the *Berry* trial, he had almost twenty years of practice experience and three years of judging under his belt. For many years, his days took one of two forms: either he was handling between 50 and 100 cases on the criminal master calendar, or he was presiding over a criminal trial.[14]

The Prosecutor

Assistant District Attorney Gerhard Winkler was a graduate of the University of California at Berkeley. He had worked for the District Attorney for eight years, trying his first murder case in 1969.[15] Like Judge Perasso, Winkler had amassed significant experience by the time of the *Berry* trial, and opposing counsel respected him for his skills as a litigator. His cross-examination of defense expert Dr. Martin Blinder was "personal and poignant"; no doubt he had become emotionally invested in the case.[16] Winkler was also a creative thinker. It was his idea to count up the number of cigarette butts in the apartment, which the government established were likely to be Albert's with the rudimentary form of

---

14. Telephone Interview by Christine Edwards with the Honorable Claude Perasso, Retired Trial Judge, Superior Court of California (Sept. 15, 2010) [hereinafter Perasso Interview].

15. Telephone Interview by Christine Edwards with Gerhard Winkler, Assistant District Attorney, City and County of San Francisco (Sept. 16, 2010) [hereinafter Winkler Interview].

16. Brown Interview, *supra* note 10.

DNA testing that was available at the time. The government relied on that number to demonstrate for the jury how long Albert had been hunkered down in the apartment waiting for Rachel.[17]

Winkler said he has "two pet peeves: people who lie, and bullies. Albert Berry was both." Winkler never believed Albert's tales that Rachel taunted him with her feelings for Yacob, or came on to Albert sexually only to declare that she had changed her mind and was saving herself for Yacob. "According to everyone [he] interviewed, behavior like that would be completely out of character for Rachel."[18]

His coworkers in the homicide division of the District Attorney's office urged Winkler to offer Albert a plea deal for second degree murder, arguing that he would never get a conviction based on lying in wait.[19] Winkler insisted on the first degree charge, though, and eventually his passion for this theory of the case rubbed off on the whole team.[20]

The Defense Attorney

In his early 30s and recently married, Public Defender Geoffrey Brown would have taken that deal for second degree murder, if the DA's office had been able to convince Winkler to offer it. At the time, a second degree murder conviction carried a minimum penalty of five years, in contrast to today's fifteen. And while Brown shared Winkler's sympathy for the victim, his compassion extended to the defendant, too. Albert had genuinely suffered as a child,[21] and Brown was convinced that "much of what Al said about Rachel was true." Albert had committed a terrible crime, Brown would be the first to admit, but the whole story of what happened between Albert and Rachel was not as black-and-white as Winkler seemed to think it was.

More junior than Winkler, Brown earned his law degree from San Francisco Law School in 1970. Although he had "tried a few felony cases" before joining the Public Defender's office in October 1971, he had almost no experience with homicides when he was assigned to *Berry*. Especially in this case, with the kind of confusing, mutually destructive psychology that seemed to characterize the relationship between Albert and Rachel, the relatively green Brown could use a seasoned expert

---

    17. Winkler Interview, *supra* note 15.

    18. *Id.*

    19. "Lying in wait is defined as waiting and watching for an opportune time to act, together with a concealment by ambush or some other secret design, to take the other person by surprise." Trial Transcript at 387, California v. Berry, No. 88726 (Oct. 1, 1974) (quoting jury instructions).

    20. Winkler Interview, *supra* note 15.

    21. Brown Interview, *supra* note 10.

witness. He chose Dr. Martin Blinder, a man with an established reputation in the diminished capacity area.[22]

The Expert

Doctor Martin Blinder earned his medical degree at the University of Chicago in 1962. He interned at San Francisco General Hospital and completed his psychiatric training at the University of California Langley Porter, which included two international fellowships, one in London and one in Denmark. He had been in private practice since 1966, and held the title of Assistant Clinical Professor of Psychiatry at the University of California, among others. He also did "a fair amount of work for the Courts," offering opinions on people's mental health for prosecutors and criminal defense attorneys, as well as in civil suits involving issues like personal injury and child custody.

Blinder might be described as an arrogant witness,[23] though Brown today says Blinder does not deserve the negative attention he has been given. Brown remembers that Blinder gave him advice on jury selection, suggesting married jurors because they would be able to empathize with Albert.[24] "[V]ery short and very smart," Blinder was "a spellbinding storyteller."[25]

Winkler, on the other hand, thought Blinder was "disreputable." He was familiar with Blinder's testimony from other trials, and already did not like what he had heard. When Winkler learned Blinder's theory of the case in *Berry*, he thought it was crazy.[26]

The Trial Theories

Winkler's theory of the case, of course, was straightforward: Albert killed Rachel because she was going to leave him, just as he had told his co-worker he would. Winkler charged it as first degree murder based on premeditation and deliberation and lying in wait. After all, Albert had not seen Rachel even once in the three days before he killed her. He

---

22. *Id.* "Diminished capacity" has been used confusingly to mean different things. *See, e.g,* Joshua Dressler, *Understanding Criminal Law* § 26.01 (5th ed. 2009) (providing a concise overview of the term in its different guises). In *Berry*, the judge's instruction to the jury demonstrates that the phrase referred to psychiatric evidence showing the defendant did not form the required mens rea.

23. *Cf.* Michael Weiss, *Double Play: The San Francisco City Hall Killings* 346 (1984) (describing Blinder as "loung[ing] on the stand" in the context of a different, later case, in which "[i]t took nearly ten minutes for him merely to recite his degrees, his advanced training, his accomplishments and publications, the journals he edited, the medical schools and hospitals with which he was associated, and his expertise as a forensic psychiatrist").

24. Brown Interview, *supra* note 10.

25. Weiss, *supra* note 24, at 346–347.

26. Winkler Interview, *supra* note 15.

waited in the apartment for her for twenty hours. While he was waiting, he cut an electrical cord to strangle her with. He killed her as soon as she walked in the door. And he acknowledged in his taped confession that he had "deliberately waited to kill her." Case closed.

For the defense side, no effort was made to deny the strangling. Instead, Brown focused on Albert's mental state. The goal was simple: disprove premeditation and deliberation, and limit any conviction to some lesser homicide than first degree murder. Maybe evidence of provocation or diminished capacity would convince the jury to come back with second degree murder—maybe even with voluntary manslaughter.

Only two witnesses took the stand for the defense. First, Brown called Dr. Blinder. This story, Dr. Blinder explained, was a tale of mutual depression, mutual abuse, and mutually-assured destruction. Albert's relationships with women, beginning with his relationship with his mother, had consisted of "intense provocation of almost sadistic nature," and he was always "enormously dependent upon [these women] for all gratification." Dr. Blinder drew a connection between all the women with whom Albert had ever been involved, describing how one after the other, they each left him. "I think unconsciously he chooses certain kinds of women. I think he then imposes a certain kind of relationship upon them which leads them to do this.... [W]e have this pattern of enormous dependency on these woman and then rupture of the relationship with tremendous rage, almost uncontrollable."

Dr. Blinder testified that Rachel was suicidal after her first husband's death, and that "[s]he would deliberately tell [Albert] about other men in her life to make him jealous because his jealousy made her feel cared for and wanted or made her feel less depressed." Albert's feelings for Rachel were equally complicated. He described her as "a woman with a heart as good as gold," who "has no flaw ... but on the other hand she would taunt [him] with these other men." Dr. Blinder characterized this as a "sweet-sour kind of relationship," and yet another incarnation of the pattern of a woman telling Albert that she loved him before leaving him. The entirety of their courtship and married life consisted of "bitter fights ... coupled with active sexuality ... which is not unusual in these kinds of love-hate relationships." There was, as Dr. Blinder put it, "[a] sadomasochistic aspect to the relationship." She uses him to deal with her depression. He takes her abuse and abuses her back. She feels "this is her due ... as is often the case with people who are depressed and suicidal. And so they love and have sex with and punish each other. And this is characteristic of all of his relationships."

In the end, Albert's "passions, these rages, short circuited the rational, cognitive, reasonable part of him." "In other words," asked Brown on direct, "this was in some sense, in some odd sense, a victim-precipitated offense, is that correct?" "Yes," Dr. Blinder replied. Some-times, "people who are suicidal . . . in effect, invite someone to do them in."

Winkler had no patience for this. In a blistering cross-examination, he pointed out that Dr. Blinder had never met Rachel, that he had spent only two and a half hours with Albert, and that he had made no effort to verify anything Albert told him. Dr. Blinder took it in stride. "I don't by any means take what he says at face value. But when you get a total longitudinal history of this man, one can almost draw up the nature of his relationships with women without his telling you a great deal about them."

The only other defense witness was the star of the case, Albert Berry himself. It is always a tricky question, assessing whether a defendant should testify or not, but this time, Brown felt he did not have a choice. In his inexperience, Brown thought that the only way for Dr. Blinder to testify would be on the basis of evidence Albert provided, that if Albert did not take the stand, then Dr. Blinder would not have any foundation for his opinions. Many years later, Brown realized his mistake—Dr. Blinder could have testified without Albert. Even so, Brown says he would have made the same decision. The jurors should meet Albert, and Albert should tell them his story because, Brown said, "He was a screwball[, and] without him, there would be no human connection."[27]

Today, Brown says the climax of the trial was when Albert took the stand. In Brown's words, it was "not a particularly great performance. [Albert] just opened up and told everything, and the D.A. went after him."[28] Albert talked about his childhood: about being ignored by his mother; about his stay at a reform school where he was punished for talking at the dinner table by being "made to walk four or five hours with a fifty-pound sack of sand;" about being forced to commit "acts of homosexuality" by the other "inmates." He talked about his first two wives: how his mother rebuffed his attempts to introduce them to her; how he suspected his first wife of cheating on him; how she left him and he remarried; how his second wife said she was leaving him for another man; how she called him by the other man's name during sex one night; how he stabbed her. He talked about living with Justine next: how "[s]he locked [him] out one day[, and he] broke her door down." He talked about Rachel: how they met; how they married; how they fought; and how he killed her.

Albert concluded his direct by saying he was bent on "self destruction" when he made his confession to the police, testifying that after the

---

27. Brown Interview, *supra* note 10.

28. *Id.*

tape was turned off, he asked the investigating officers whether they had everything they needed for "the perfect premeditated murder case, murder one." On the stand, he said "a lot" of his taped confession was untrue. Like what?, asked Brown. "The fact that I laid in wait to kill Rachel was untrue because I did not. I had no intention of killing that woman."

Winkler opened cross-examination baldly: "How much money did you take from Rachel's purse after you murdered her?" Some back and forth later, the question was rephrased: "How much money did you take from Rachel's purse after you killed her?" "Thirty-three dollars," Albert said. Things went downhill for Albert from there. Whereas on direct, Albert said he had stabbed his second wife, Carrol, after she taunted him with her infidelity, Winkler got Albert to admit on cross that he had been similarly openly unfaithful to Carrol for many years, through that "mutual wife-swapping arrangement" that Albert had neglected to mention earlier. Winkler got Albert to admit that after stabbing Carrol that night, he told a psychiatrist he had thought to himself, "Die, you bitch." And although Albert testified on direct that Rachel repeatedly threatened to report him to his probation officer, Winkler got Albert to admit that when she actually spoke to his probation officer, she successfully "begged and pleaded" with the officer on Albert's behalf and that Albert watched her do it.

Perhaps most devastatingly, Winkler pointed out that on direct, Albert had failed to mention the black electrical cord he first used to strangle Rachel, and got Albert to admit having cut it while he waited for her. "And you cut it because that was what you were going to use to strangle Rachel, didn't you?" "Not necessarily," said Albert. Winkler changed the subject, and came back several pages later. "Why did you cut the black cord for (sic)?" "I had thought about it," Albert said.

Genuinely incensed that the defense would insinuate Rachel wanted to be killed, Winkler then called several rebuttal witnesses. First, Rachel's cousin, Mazel Pessah, testified that Rachel and her first husband, Joe, had a normal and happy marriage, with no bizarre sexual taunting. Of course she was affected by her husband's death, but Rachel had never given Mazel any reason to think she was suicidal; she was "very much" someone who "loved life." Next came cousin Fortunee Lichaa. She, too, testified that Rachel and Joe had a happy marriage and that Rachel absolutely was not suicidal. The day before Rachel's death, when she had gone to pick up her cake and cookies from the Fantastia Bakery, Fortunee wished her "many many happy" birthdays. And in response, Rachel indicated she was planning on at least fifty more: she said she would see Fortunee when she was seventy-one. Lastly, Winkler called Paul Cummins, the assistant district attorney who spoke with Rachel the day before she was killed about pressing charges against Albert for strangling her earlier. Rachel told him that she was afraid of Albert, that he "was a very violent man and she feared for her life." When asked about Rachel's demeanor, he said, "To me she appeared to be a normal person who was deathly afraid of the Defendant."

There is an old saw that advises lawyers never should ask a question to which they do not know the answer. On cross, Brown asked whether Rachel had told Cummins anything about her personal life, to which he responded that she had told him she was going to get a divorce. Brown asked if she said anything about wanting to marry someone else, presumably hoping for some mention of her infatuation with Yacob. "No, sir, she did not," Cummins said. "She just indicated she wanted to divorce the Defendant."

The Trial's End

Winkler's closing was both powerful and aggressive. He began traditionally, summarizing the definitions of premeditated murder and lying in wait, and reviewing the evidence to show how both had been fully satisfied. Having made his own case, he next turned to demolishing Albert's. Essentially, he said, Albert's defense was to blame the victim. In one of the more memorable lines from the trial, Winkler delivered his take on the defense argument: "poor Albert, look at the life he lived with such a bitch like Rachel for a wife. What else could the man do but kill her?"

Winkler accused Brown, too, of choosing male jurors, postulating that men might be more sympathetic to this strategy. "Maybe that is why we have nine men on the jury. Maybe that is why all the women kept getting excluded." He drew an objection for improper argument on that point; it would be two more decades before the U.S. Supreme Court would forbid using peremptory challenges[29] to exclude jurors because of their gender.[30] Even the State of California—reliably more protective of defendants' rights than the federal government—had not done so at the time of the *Berry* trial.[31]

---

29. Peremptory challenges allow lawyers to prevent prospective jurors from serving without any explanation at all, for any reason or no reason, so long as the challenge is not motivated by unconstitutional discrimination. *See, e.g.,* Batson v. Kentucky, 476 U.S. 79, 85–86 (1986).

30. J.E.B. v. Alabama, 511 U.S. 127 (1994) (reversing for constitutional violation where prosecutor used nine out of ten peremptory challenges to strike men from serving in paternity and child custody case).

31. California did come to this view much more quickly than the U.S. Supreme Court, ruling in 1978 that peremptory challenges could not be used to keep prospective jurors from hearing a case based on presumptions of "group bias." People v. Wheeler, 583 P.2d 748, 761–762 (Cal. 1978).

On the defense side, Brown asked the judge for a voluntary man-slaughter instruction, arguing that the evidence supported a claim that Albert had been provoked into killing Rachel. The judge disagreed, allowing talk of provocation only insofar as it might have defeated the premeditation and deliberation necessary for a first degree murder charge, establishing second degree murder instead.

The instruction to the jury read as follows:

When the evidence shows the existence of provocation that played a part in inducing the unlawful killing of a human being, you may consider the evidence of provocation for such bearing as it might have on the question of premeditation and deliberation and, there-fore, whether the murder was of the first or second degree.

Frankly, Brown was relieved. He had wanted a second degree murder charge all along, and would have had trouble structuring an argument for voluntary manslaughter. It was just as well that he did not have to.[32]

Brown's closing trod carefully, beginning with a nod to the horrific nature of the act committed, and a denial of any attempt to disparage Rachel. The goal, he said, had only been to show the jury "the strains and the tension and the frustrations that were on this sick man that brought his passions and ultimately dethroned all of his reason." In line with the judge's ruling, Brown emphasized that contrary to Winkler's characterization of premeditation or lying in wait, "this is a crime of passion." His argument was a simple plea for second degree over first degree murder. As he put it at the end of his closing, "rage and not forethought caused the death of Rachel Pessah Berry."

Winkler's rebuttal restated his essential points, and in his final remarks to the jury, he nicely summed up the case for first degree murder. Albert premeditated: "He said before he was going to kill her if she left him. She was going to leave him." And Albert had lain in wait: "He waited there twenty hours and he cut this weapon of destruction while he was there." He urged them to find Albert guilty of murder in the first degree.

It was lunchtime. The jurors ate, and returned to hear their instruc-tions. They deliberated for a little over two hours, and then asked to have two instructions re-read to them: the instruction on diminished capacity, and the one on lying in wait. The judge repeated those instructions.

As to lying in wait:

---

32. Brown Interview, *supra* note 10.

Murder which is immediately preceded by lying in wait is murder of the first degree. The term lying in wait is defined as a waiting and watching for an opportune time to act, together with a concealment by ambush or some other secret design to take the other person by surprise.

The lying in wait need not continue for any particular period of time provided that its duration is such as to show a state of mind equivalent to premeditation or deliberation.

To constitute murder by means of lying in wait, there must be, in addition to the aforesaid conduct by the Defendant, an intentional infliction upon the person killed of bodily harm involving a high degree of probability that it will result in death, and which shows a wanton disregard for human life.

As to diminished capacity:

If you find from the evidence that at the time the alleged crime was committed the Defendant had substantially reduced mental capacity, whether caused by mental illness, mental defect, intoxication, or any other cause, you must consider what effect, if any, this diminished capacity had on the Defendant's ability to form any of the specific mental states that are essential elements of murder in the first degree.

Thus, if you find that the Defendant's mental capacity was diminished to the extent that you have a reasonable doubt whether he did maturely and meaningfully premeditate, deliberate and reflect upon the gravity of his contemplated act or form an intent to kill, you cannot find him guilty of a willful, deliberate and premeditated murder of the first degree.

Sixteen minutes later, the jury came back with first degree murder.[33]

Albert was sentenced to life in prison.

The Appeal

Edward Suman represented Albert on appeal. He had been in the District Attorney's office for almost five years, and then left for a private practice doing criminal defense work.[34] He was appointed to represent Albert through the Private Defender Panel, California's system for providing indigents with representation.

Although Brown was skeptical about Albert's chances on appeal,[35] Suman believed he could get a reversal. He poured "infinite hours" into

---

33. They also found him guilty of the strangulation assault on July 23, 1974.

34. Telephone Interview by Christine Edwards with Edward Suman, Appellate Defense Counsel, Private Practice (Sept. 16, 2010) [hereinafter Suman Interview].

35. Brown Interview, *supra* note 10.

the effort, working at his office all day, and then heading to the San Francisco Law Library to do research at night. There was no electronic Shepardizing at the time, of course; verifying that a given opinion was still good law required painstaking cross-referencing by hand. Suman considered the *Berry* case worth the energy he put into it, though. He devoted months to the research, uncovering multiple mistakes he felt confident would earn Albert a second chance.[36] The result: a fifty-page brief filed with the intermediate appellate court asserting twelve independent errors, one of which was the failure to instruct the jury on voluntary manslaughter.

The Attorney General's office responded, and with respect to the voluntary manslaughter instruction, had this to say: "Since there was no evidence of provocation or heat of passion, the trial court correctly refused to instruct the jury on voluntary manslaughter." This portion of the government's brief began with a statement of the definition of a heat of passion killing:

> Voluntary manslaughter is the unlawful killing of a human being without malice upon a sudden quarrel or heat of passion. It is a willful act, characterized by sufficient provocation and by the absence of premeditation, deliberation and (by presumption of law) malice aforethought. To be sufficient to reduce a homicide to manslaughter, the heat of passion must be such as would naturally be aroused in the mind of an ordinary, reasonable person, under the given facts and circumstances, or in the mind of a person of ordinary self-control. . . . Furthermore, before a homicide may be classified as voluntary manslaughter, it must appear that there was no "cooling" period, that is, after the "heat of passion" was reasonably and justifiably engendered, "hot blood had not had time to cool" before the fatal act was committed, that is, the act that engendered the "hot blood" had occurred so shortly before the killing that reason had not had time "to resume its empire." (citations omitted)

"There is absolutely no evidence," the government's brief goes on to say, "which would have supported any instructions on this type of voluntary manslaughter. . . . If nothing else, the mere fact appellant waited in the apartment for more than 20 hours and had not seen his wife after he strangled her on July 23 until he killed her on July 26 is overwhelming proof there was a cooling period and that the killing could not possibly have occurred in a heat of passion."

The facts presented at trial certainly supported this conclusion. The last time Albert and Rachel had seen each other before he killed her was on their ill-fated movie night, which he reported began with her sexually taunting him and ended with his strangling her into unconsciousness.

---

36. Suman Interview, *supra* note 34.

Albert spent the next day gambling in Reno. The day after that, he called
Rachel twice to implore her not to press charges; he says she bullied him
over the phone. Twelve or fourteen hours passed before he went to the
apartment, ostensibly to plead his case in person, and just could not
catch up to her in time. He hid some of her possessions, and waited there
for her return for twenty more hours, making two cigarette runs and
cutting an electrical cord that he admitted on cross he "had thought
about" using to strangle her. In the end, three and a half days had
passed between the last time Albert had seen Rachel and the moment he
killed her; approximately thirty-four hours had passed between the last
contact of any sort and the killing. Albert waited by himself in the
apartment for the last twenty of those hours—ample time and circumstances to allow even the hottest blood to cool. This simply could not be
a heat of passion killing.

The Court of Appeal agreed, pointing out that Albert's own expert,
Dr. Blinder himself, testified on direct that he believed Albert formed the
intent to kill Rachel "hours" before he acted on that intent. Blinder
characterized Albert as suffering "a growing, malignant, persistent,
enduring kind of impulse. I don't see it as a sudden impulse." Although
California is careful to require that the words "premeditation and
deliberation" carry meaning, it is also frank in acknowledging that no
minimum amount of time must pass in order to satisfy those elements.
"There need be 'no appreciable space of time between the intention to
kill and the act of killing[;] they may be as instantaneous as successive
thoughts of the mind.' "[37] Together with the other facts outlined at trial,
the hours following Albert's formation of the intent to kill—during
which he thought about how he would strangle Rachel with the cord he
cut for that purpose—would be more than sufficient to establish the
premeditation and deliberation necessary for first degree murder, much
less to negate the heat of passion required for voluntary manslaughter.

This is why Brown accepted the trial court's initial denial of the
voluntary manslaughter instruction, and why he felt Suman's odds on
appeal were long. Even if Albert had been provoked by Rachel's taunting, the hours he spent alone in the apartment surely sufficed to support
a first-degree murder conviction based on lying in wait.[38] Still, Suman
petitioned for a hearing in the Supreme Court of California.

---

37. People v. Bender, 163 P.2d 8, 19 (Cal. 1945), *abrogated on other grounds by*
People v. Lasko, 999 P.2d 666, 672 (Cal. 2000). The *Bender* court takes some pains to
explain that while this is correct, it would be misleading—and indeed cause reversible
error—for this to be the only instruction a jury received on the meaning of the words
"premeditation and deliberation." *Id.* at 20–21.

38. Brown Interview, *supra* note 10.

The Reversal

To nearly everyone's surprise, the Supreme Court of California reversed and remanded for a new trial. Quoting established California law on voluntary manslaughter, the Court began by emphasizing that whether the defendant was acting under a heat of passion was a question for the jury. Even more pointedly, it laid out the case of *People v. Borchers*,[39] in which "evidence of admissions of infidelity by the defendant's paramour, taunts directed to him and other conduct, 'supports a finding that defendant killed in wild desperation induced by (the woman's) long continued provocatory conduct.'" Similar to Albert's story in *Berry*, the defendant in *Borchers* had been found to have been "aroused to a heat of 'passion' by a series of events over a considerable period of time." In light of this precedent, the Court readily characterized Albert's "testimony [as] chronicl[ing] a two-week period of provocatory conduct by his wife Rachel that could arouse a passion of jealousy, pain and sexual rage in an ordinary man of average dispositions such as to cause him to act rashly from this passion." [40]

As for the government's argument that the undisputed facts show a cooling period that would defeat a voluntary manslaughter claim, the Court replied only briefly: "The long course of provocatory conduct, which had resulted in intermittent outbreaks of rage under specific provocation in the past, reached its final culmination in the apartment when Rachel began screaming." Together with Albert's and Dr. Blinder's testimony that Albert "killed in a state of uncontrollable rage," the Court found "ample evidence in the record to support" a voluntary manslaughter instruction.[41]

Suman never met Albert in person, but recalls him as a good client. He was "cordial, with no hang-ups," even sending Suman a thank-you note to say how appreciative he was of the result.[42]

The Plea Bargain

By the time the California Supreme Court remanded for a new trial, it was December of 1976 and more than two years had passed. Brown began to gird himself for a second trial, reviewing what he had, and searching for new evidence to make their case. Winkler powerfully discredited the "victim-induced" argument the last time, so Brown concentrated on that angle.

---

39.   325 P.2d 97 (Cal. 1958).

40.   People v. Berry, 556 P.2d 777, 780–781 (Cal. 1976) (citation omitted).

41.   *Id.* at 781.

42.   Suman Interview, *supra* note 34.

Rachel had received psychiatric treatment at Kaiser Hospital, where she had gone when Albert strangled her the second time, and Brown subpoenaed those records. Sure enough, the psychiatric records revealed detailed accounts of her relationship with Yacob and of the depths of her depression.[43]

If they tried the case again, Albert would get a voluntary manslaughter instruction, and Brown now had additional evidence of Rachel's depressed mental state. But he could not change the fact that Albert had not seen Rachel for more than three days prior to the killing, had not talked to her for thirty-four hours prior, and had spent the last twenty hours prior waiting in the apartment for her with a cut electrical cord.

In the end, Winkler and Brown negotiated a deal for second degree murder—the very charge they might have agreed to at the outset if Winkler's office had managed to convince him to offer it. Again, the minimum sentence for a second degree murder conviction at the time was five years, and Albert had already served over two. It was an easy deal to make.[44]

The Immediate Impact

People v. Berry was a real "sleeper" of a case.[45] There was almost no press coverage of the crime at the time it happened—even Albert commented to Jean Berk on how there was nothing in the paper. He was not entirely right about that: the San Francisco Examiner and Chronicle ran a short blurb on page five of the local section two days after the killing naming Albert Berry (and his two aliases, Albert Perry and Alfred Johnson) as the suspect in the crime.[46] Still, that one blurb certainly would have been easy to miss.

"Not a single person" attended the trial as a supporter or interested party for either side, with scant attention paid even by the Israeli Consulate.[47] The only observers at all may have been a handful of high school students who stopped in briefly as part of a program to educate them about the court system. In fact, when Joe Grumich, the Buddhist spiritual leader whom Jean Berk called for moral support the day they discovered Rachel's body, was interviewed about the case for this book chapter, he said he was "shocked to hear [we were] interested."[48]

---

43. Brown Interview, *supra* note 10.

44. *Id.*

45. *Id.*

46. *Man Sought in Murder Questioning*, S.F. Examiner & Chron., July 28, 1974, at B5.

47. Brown Interview, *supra* note 10.

48. Telephone Interview by Christine Edwards with Joseph Grumich, Spiritual Advisor to Jean Berk (Sept. 15, 2010) [hereinafter Grumich Interview].

The newspapers at the time were filled with other stories. Inez Garcia was making headlines for tracking down and killing a man within an hour after he held her pinned while his friend raped her.[49] (She, too, incidentally, was convicted of second degree murder before winning a reversal on the basis of an erroneous jury instruction defining reasonable doubt.[50]) And the kidnapping of heiress Patricia Hearst by the Symbionese Liberation Army ate up a lot of column inches, as well. Primarily, though, *Berry* probably went unnoticed at the time because "San Francisco had a high homicide rate, and male chauvinism was prevalent."[51] When it came right down to it, it just was not all that unusual for a man to kill his wife.

The Long–Term Impact

Today, of course, *People v. Berry* is famous, at least among first-year Criminal Law students and others interested in the development of the provocation doctrine. Appearing in law school casebooks for its illustration of a "flexible" approach, both to the suddenness of the provoking event and to the "no cooling period" requirement, most students remember it as the case where the guy strangled his wife with a telephone cord.[52]

Interestingly, *Berry* itself did not mark a change in the law. Almost twenty years earlier, California had approved a voluntary manslaughter charge in the previously-mentioned case of *People v. Borchers*, where the "defendant was roused to a heat of 'passion' by a series of events over a considerable period of time." In *Borchers*, the "long continued provocatory conduct" justifying manslaughter rather than murder included the victim's "admitted infidelity, her statements that she wished she were dead, her attempt to jump from the car on the trip to San Diego, her repeated urging that defendant shoot her, [her foster son], and himself on the night of the homicide, and her taunt, 'are you chicken.' "[53] For this sort of thing—which boils down to "mere words," spoken over a

---

49. Much to the dismay of defense counsel, she shouted on cross-examination, "The only thing I'm sorry about is that I missed [the rapist]." *Changing Times, Changing Defenses*, Recorder (San Francisco), Dec. 1, 1997, at 10 [hereinafter *Changing Times*].

50. People v. Garcia, 126 Cal. Rptr. 275 (Cal. Dist. Ct. App. 1975). The retrial acquitted Garcia on the grounds of self-defense: the victim had threatened "to do worse to [her]" before she went in search of the men, and he was brandishing a knife when she shot him. *Changing Times, supra* note 49.

51. Winkler Interview, *supra* note 15.

52. A colleague joked that this is memorable today because students are unfamiliar with the idea of phones having cords. Conversation with Jamie Fox, Associate Dean of Faculty Development and Professor of Law, Stetson University College of Law (Fall Semester 2010).

53. People v. Borchers, 325 P.2d 97, 102 (Cal. 1958).

lengthy period of time, and during which time period the defendant had a significant chance to brood before he killed—to qualify for the mitigation from murder to manslaughter was a change from the traditional heat of passion doctrine indeed.

Until the late 1400s, the only homicide was murder, and its punishment was death. "Benefit of clergy" (originally exempting clergymen from jurisdiction of the secular court, later exempting anyone who could read) saved some from the gallows, but generally speaking, administering homicide law was very easy. Gradually, however, the unfairness of punishing all killers alike began to grate, and by the mid 1500s, the criminal law had developed a formal distinction between murder and manslaughter. Murder included all those killings accomplished with "malice aforethought," a legal term of art meaning intent to kill, intent to cause serious bodily injury, extreme recklessness manifesting depraved indifference to human life, and felony murder. Manslaughter, on the other hand, included those killings committed in the absence of malice aforethought: for example, killings committed in a heat of passion.[54]

The law of voluntary manslaughter, by which these heat of passion killings are measured, required three things: that the defendant commit the killing while feeling an actual heat of passion; that the passion the defendant was experiencing be a reaction to a sudden, provoking event; and that the provoking event be one a reasonable person would find provoking, as well. Succinctly put, "[v]oluntary manslaughter is a killing committed in an actual heat of passion, based on a sudden provocation, which was legally adequate to provoke a reasonable person."[55]

Originally, the list of legally adequate provocations was small: "mutual combat, violent assault, unlawful arrest, and witnessing one's wife in the act of [committing] adultery."[56] In fact, witnessing one's wife committing adultery was considered so appalling that a few states approved outright of killing the lover. In those places, such an act was considered "a justifiable homicide—not a crime at all."[57]

For the majority of jurisdictions that did condemn such killings, however, one thing by definition was not legally sufficient to mitigate murder to manslaughter: "words alone."[58] The idea had been that

---

54. Richard J. Bonnie et al., *Criminal Law* 856–857 (3d ed. 2010).

55. Susan D. Rozelle, *Controlling Passion: Adultery and the Provocation Defense*, 37 Rutgers L.J. 197, 198 (2005) (citing Richard J. Bonnie et al., *Criminal Law* 804 (2d ed. 2004)).

56. *Id.*

57. Cynthia Lee, *Murder and the Reasonable Man: Passion and Fear in the Criminal Courtroom* 20 (2003) (citing statutes in Georgia, Texas, Utah, and New Mexico).

58. Bonnie et al., *supra* note 54, at 887.

whatever was said, words alone could not even partially justify or excuse a homicidal response. More recently, the move has been to reject predetermined categories of what can and what cannot be adequate provocation. Instead, whether the event in question was adequately provoking to mitigate the crime from murder to manslaughter is left for the jury to decide[59]—even when the event in question consists of nothing more than someone talking: i.e., those "words alone."

This rejection of predetermined categories, including the possibility of provocation by mere words, was the state of the law in California at the time of *Berry*. As the California Supreme Court explained in the *Berry* decision, "there is no specific type of provocation required," and "verbal provocation may be sufficient."[60] But *Berry* is not in casebooks for allowing a provocation instruction based on words alone. The rejection of predetermined categories of what is and what is not adequate provocation had spread far and wide by then. The drafters of the Model Penal Code, who had begun their work in the 1950s and published the final product in 1962,[61] took this approach, and many jurisdictions, including of course California, had followed suit.[62]

Rather, the points for which *Berry* is famous flow from the two remaining, interrelated changes noted in *Borchers*: not only was the provocation there comprised of mere words, but (1) it took a long time for those words to be spoken, and (2) the defendant therefore had a considerable amount of time to think on those words before killing.

Traditionally, no amount of provocation would mitigate murder to manslaughter for a defendant who waited too long to kill. The concept is known as a "cooling period," and it loosely tracks the three-part requirement for provocation generally: the defendant's passion had not in fact cooled; the amount of time that passed between the provoking event and the killing was not so long as to consider the defendant's passion to have cooled as a matter of law; and if these first two are met, then it will be for the jury to decide "whether a reasonable person would have cooled off in the interval between the provocation and the act of killing."[63]

In contrast to the traditional formulation, *Berry*, like *Borchers* before it, involved not a "sudden" provocation, but a "long course of provocatory conduct." Albert killed, not in an immediate flush of emotion arising from Rachel's infidelity, sexual taunting, or threats to report him to his probation officer for strangling her before, but in the throes of

---

59. *Id.* at 889.

60. People v. Berry, 556 P.2d 777, 780 (Cal. 1976).

61. Bonnie et al., *supra* note 54, at A1.

62. *Id.* at 889.

63. *Id.* at 892.

that "growing, malignant, persistent, enduring kind of impulse" that Dr. Blinder described. Albert killed Rachel after not seeing her for three and a half days, spending the last twenty hours of those three and a half days alone, waiting for her. He killed her as soon as she came in the door, with nothing but her screams to serve as the final act of provocation.

By Albert's own account, Rachel began screaming that night after he acknowledged that he was indeed there to kill her—not an unreasonable thing to do for someone who has just been threatened, really. It is unclear whether "such predictable conduct by a resisting victim [c]ould constitute the kind of provocation sufficient to reduce a murder charge to voluntary manslaughter"[64] at the time *Berry* was decided. In 1980, the California Supreme Court declared unequivocally in *People v. Jackson* that "[n]o case has ever suggested" the victim's resistance to being killed could constitute the adequate provocation to mitigate murder to manslaughter.[65] Nevertheless, *Berry* certainly could be read that way; and a case in 1978 discussing *Berry* intimated the very same thing when it explained that Albert "killed his wife with the telephone cord in an attempt to keep her from screaming" without any comment on the supposed impropriety of the victim's screams being considered a provoking event.[66] Finally, the case *Jackson* cited in support of its declaration that a victim's resistance never could supply adequate provocation, *People v. Morse*, cannot be read to stand for that proposition at all. The defendant in *Morse* killed a fellow prisoner over a gambling debt. That victim owed a carton of cigarettes but could not pay, and so worked out an alternative payment plan in the form of desserts. He began refusing to pay these, as well, which naturally upset the defendant, but the event contended as the provocation for the killing occurred when the victim "had the temerity to [ask the defendant if he could] bum a cigarette."[67] Since asking for a cigarette is not analogous to screaming in protest at an attack, it is unclear exactly what the *Jackson* court had in mind when it cited *Morse*.

Donna Coker explains the apparent contradiction—*Berry*'s description of Rachel's screams as the final precipitating event that triggered a heat of passion killing, contrasted with the *Jackson* court's position that the victim's resistance cannot serve as a triggering provocation—as the result of *Berry*'s nature as a domestic violence case.[68] It simply never occurred to anyone that Rachel's screaming was the resistance of a

---

64. People v. Jackson, 618 P.2d 149, 169–170 (Cal. 1980).

65. *Id.*

66. People v. Johnson, 146 Cal. Rptr. 476, 478 (Cal. Ct. App. 1978).

67. People v. Morse, 452 P.2d 607, 620–21 n.15 (Cal. 1969).

68. Donna Coker, *Heat of Passion and Wife Killing: Men Who Batter/ Men Who Kill*, 2 S. Cal. Rev. L. & Women's Stud. 71, 126 (1992) [hereinafter Coker, *Heat of Passion*].

victim to being killed. In the context of domestic violence, Rachel's screaming sounded more like yet another piece of that long course of provocatory conduct by the shrewish wife against her husband that we had already heard so much about. Remember, Albert told Jean Berk that he had strangled Rachel before "to stop her mouth."

Leaving aside the question of whether the California Supreme Court simply failed to recognize Rachel's screams as the protests of a resisting victim, or whether the law on that point had in fact been established at all before *Berry* was decided, the primary question remains. Given that the move to allow a series of cumulative provocations with its concomitant time to think on them had happened at least two decades earlier in *Borchers*, why did *Berry* become the case famous for the proposition?

Cynthia Lee suggests that *Berry* is so widely taught because its facts are "so outrageous" that they "make[ ] us question the desirability of an open-ended reasonableness requirement."[69] The facts as described in the *Berry* opinion certainly are titillating. And in its focus on Rachel's behavior, rather than on the defendant's, we are invited to view the world through Albert's eyes. That the California justices' sympathies lay with Albert is abundantly clear.

Strangely, though, it is not the uniqueness of the facts in *Berry* that make it such a landmark case. It is their banality. The more one reads voluntary manslaughter cases, the more one reads about women who, it is claimed, taunted their killers with their infidelity, about women who were supposedly suicidal. Just like Albert, the typical domestic homicide offender has a prior record of violence, commonly involving prior acts of violence against his eventual homicide victim.[70] And just like Albert's,[71] the typical domestic homicide offender's true motivation seems to have less to do with his victim's infidelity than with her attempt to leave him.[72] In *Berry*, these banalities even repeated themselves. Albert had only just been released from custody for stabbing his second wife, Carrol, when he met and married Rachel. And what is his explanation for that prior conviction? Carrol had been unfaithful to him. More gallingly, she

---

69. Lee, *supra* note 57, at 45.

70. Coker, *Heat of Passion*, *supra* note 68, at 89.

71. Several commentators have made the point that *Berry* is not really about Rachel's infidelity at all, but instead about her efforts to leave the relationship. *See, e.g.*, Caroline Forell, *Homicide and the Unreasonable Man*, 72 Geo. Wash. L. Rev. 597, 605–606 (2004); Martha Mahoney, *Legal Images of Battered Women: Redefining the Issue of Separation*, 90 Mich. L. Rev. 1, 74 (1991).

72. *See, e.g.*, Victoria Nourse, *Passion's Progress: Modern Law Reform and the Provocation Defense*, 106 Yale L.J. 1331, 1343 n.80 (1997) (gathering data suggesting separation is better predictor of relationship violence than infidelity); Margi Laird McCue, *Domestic Violence: A Reference Handbook* 58–59 (2d ed. 2008) (finding battered spouse most in danger of being killed by abuser when leaving relationship).

had taunted him with that fact, calling him by her lover's name during sex.

If nothing else, it is a curious coincidence for Albert to have married two different women who would engage in such self-destructive behavior. As Cynthia Lee, in her signature understated fashion put it, "With this additional information [about Berry's past relationship violence], Berry's claim that he was reasonably provoked by Rachel's behavior is disingenuous."[73]

That Rachel's behavior, like Carrol's, can be viewed as "self"-destructive at all is the telling point. *Berry* is a morality play (a "passion" play?), in which the defendant and the California Supreme Court play the role of the traditional patriarchy, blaming the victim for her own demise, and considering the government's intrusion into the domestic sphere with great skepticism. Winkler carries water for the feminist movement, openly deriding these positions with his mocking, "Such a bitch for a wife. What could he do but kill her?" As shocking as this sounds—and as shocking as it was intended to sound, being the prosecutor's satirical representation of the defense position—"The Bitch Deserved It Defense" is frankly a common one in domestic violence cases.[74]

The Ironies

Two ironies have emerged in *Berry*'s legal wake. First, the *Berry* case today sometimes serves to protect women. Female defendants accused of killing their abusers under nonconfrontational circumstances that do not satisfy the traditional understanding of self-defense law's imminency requirement—when the abuser is sleeping, for example[75]—can point to *Berry* to support their claims of entitlement to a reduced charge of voluntary manslaughter rather than murder. The argument is that, like Albert, these women suffered a long course of provocatory conduct at the hands of their abusers, which culminated in the killing.[76]

---

73.   Lee, *supra* note 57, at 44.

74.   *See* Coker, *Heat of Passion*, *supra* note 68, at 104.

75.   For insightful elucidation of the position that self-defense law ought not be "expand[ed]" to accommodate non-confrontational killings by battered spouses, *see* Joshua Dressler, *Battered Women and Sleeping Abusers: Some Reflections*, 3 Ohio St. J. Crim. L. 457, 458 (2006). *But see* Joan Krause, *Distorted Reflections of Battered Women Who Kill: A Response to Professor Dressler*, 4 Ohio St. J. Crim. L. 555, 562 (2007) (suggesting battered spouse's belief of imminent threat from sleeping abuser could be reasonable).

76.   Suman Interview, *supra* note 34. *See also, e.g.,* Carolyn B. Ramsey, *Provoking Change: Comparative Insights on Feminist Homicide Law Reform*, 100 J. Crim. L. & Criminology 33, 34 (2010) (recognizing that "many battered women charged with murdering a violent spouse can successfully claim provocation under the excuse-based modern doctrine").

Indeed, some scholars have suggested limiting the voluntary manslaughter doctrine in ways that would deny the reduced charge to the Alberts of the world. If one of these suggestions were adopted, there could someday be a legal system under which battered women who kill their abusers would benefit from the mitigation to manslaughter, while batterers who kill their long-abused victims would not. One such proposal would limit provocation's mitigation to those defendants whose reason for killing "appeals to the very emotions to which the state appeals to rationalize its own use of violence,"[77] using the legality (or not) of the allegedly provoking act as a "strong measure" of the adequacy of the provocation.[78] The position is a nuanced one, but the general idea is that only illegal acts would be considered legally provoking. Another variant would limit provocation mitigation even further to situations in which the law itself permits the defendant to respond to the provoking event with some amount of force, following an imperfect self-defense paradigm.[79] Proposals such as these would nicely distinguish the woman who kills her abuser in order to escape the abuse from the man who kills his victim to prevent her from leaving. Coupled with *Berry*'s approach to allowing provocation to cumulate over time, future abusers would be denied a voluntary manslaughter instruction, while future abuse victims who kill their abusers to flee the relationship might qualify.

The second irony appears in *Berry*'s ultimate outcome, dramatically illustrating the value of plea-bargaining. Had there been a plea pre-trial, it would have been for the same second degree murder charge the parties settled on post-appeal. This next bit is heretical, but take note of the hypothetical premise with which the argument begins before judging: if one accepts Albert's version of events (understanding that for some readers to be a very big "if"), then second degree murder probably does most accurately capture the crime he committed. A bit more historical background may help to explain. In the late 1700s, Pennsylvania became the first state in the country to divide murder into degrees, carving out those murders committed "by means of poison, or by lying in wait, or by any other kind of willful, deliberate and premeditated killing," as among those kinds of murders that merit the death penalty.[80] This had the effect of narrowing the category of death-eligible homicides once again. First, all killings were capital crimes; then only murders (as opposed to manslaughters); now, only first degree (as opposed to second degree) murders.

---

77. Nourse, *supra* note 72, at 1338.

78. *Id.* at 1396.

79. Rozelle, *supra* note 55, at 227, 233.

80. Bonnie et al., *supra* note 54, at 868.

Whether one approves of the premeditation and deliberation distinction or not, that distinction marks the traditionally recognized difference between those killings considered to be the worst of the worst, and those considered to be only the second-worst. Those killings committed with premeditation and deliberation, by means of poison or by lying in wait, are akin to contract killings or murders for hire, where the killer is, for lack of a better word, dispassionate. According to Albert's trial testimony, and according to most jurisdictions' understanding of what constitutes adequate provocation, Albert did indeed commit murder rather than manslaughter—but it was second degree murder, not first.

Taking the facts as Albert presented them, he was not lying in wait to kill Rachel, but instead truly was ambivalent about what he was going to do. He "had thought about it," as he admitted, but killing her was not a deliberate and premeditated plan. In response to her supposition that he had come to kill her, he waffled: "Yes. . . . No. . . . Yes. . . . I really have come to talk to you." And then she screamed, and he could not stop her from screaming, and "the next thing [he] knew [he] had a telephone cord around her neck."

That Albert admittedly thought about killing Rachel while he waited in the apartment, and that he then struggled with his response when she accused him of coming to kill her, both fully support the jury's finding that he intended to kill. In other words, Albert possessed the mental state required for a murder conviction of some sort. But the "premeditation and deliberation" required for a first degree murder conviction means more than just intent.[81] And the ambivalence and waffling Albert testified he felt on the subject rank lower on that scale than the meticulous planning process and cool-headed rehearsings of a hired hitman.

To be clear, this interpretation accepts Albert's trial disclaimer of his taped statement to police. His additional commentary as reported in that taped statement—"now you'll shut the hell up, won't you?" and of course the directly contradictory, "I deliberately waited to kill her," both support the jury's finding of murder in the first degree. But if one thinks a reasonable jury could have believed Albert at trial—and credibility always is a matter for the jury[82]—then his trial testimony demonstrates a distinct lack of premeditation and deliberation.

---

81. People v. Bender, 163 P.2d 8, 18 (Cal. 1945), *abrogated on other grounds by* People v. Lasko, 999 P.2d 666 (Cal. 2000); Wayne R. LaFave, *Criminal Law* § 14.7(a) (5th ed. 2010).

82. Laura Hunter Dietz et al., *Credibility of witnesses; accuracy of testimony; weight and probative value of evidence*, 75A Am. Jur. 2d *Trial* § 624 (2010) ("The jury determines the credibility of witnesses.")

With an admission of guilt to the charge of second degree murder as the plea deal (almost) everyone wanted from the outset, and the plea that in the end everyone accepted, all the myriad judicial resources consumed by Albert's trial and appeals could have been conserved for other cases. If ever there were an argument for the value of plea bargaining, *Berry* epitomizes it.

The Social Context

Berry came at an eventful time in American social history. "Fifty years ago, domestic violence was not even recognized as a subject of study or as a legal problem—it was simply invisible. Marriage—the notion that husband and wife were one and that one was the husband—made domestic violence permissible and acceptable."[83] By 1920, early feminists had succeeded in abolishing laws expressly protecting a husband's "chastisement prerogative," but the societal sense of what was appropriate lagged half a century behind. It was not until the 1970s, about the time that *Berry* was decided, that consciousness truly began to be raised.[84]

It is hard for us today even to conceive of such a milieu: domestic violence awareness is taught in schools and advertised on subways; doctor's visits include routine questions about whether the patient feels safe at home, just as they include questions about drug use, exercise habits, and wearing seatbelts. But like the notion that the government has any business mandating seatbelt use, the idea that the government had any business interfering with a husband's discipline of his wife was a novel one until the disco era.[85]

As a result, through the 1970s and even into the 1980s, police officers actually ignored a lot of domestic violence calls, responding slowly when they did respond. In addition to being a private, family matter, domestic violence was considered to be one of the most dangerous kinds of call for police officers, presumably because of the inherent emotions involved in disputes among family members, together with the rightful objection of the parties to government intervention in their private affairs.[86] As Officer Higaki, who interviewed Rachel in the emergency room, tells it, "The officers' biggest concern [in responding to domestic calls] was injury to police officers."[87]

---

83. Elizabeth M. Schneider, *Domestic Violence Law Reform in the Twenty–First Century: Looking Back and Looking Forward*, 42 Fam. L.Q. 353, 353 (2008).

84. Jeannie Suk, *Criminal Law Comes Home*, 116 Yale L.J. 2, 11–12 (2006).

85. Schneider, *supra* note 83, at 354.

86. Joan Zorza, *The Criminal Law of Misdemeanor Domestic Violence, 1970–1990*, 83 J. Crim. L. & Criminology 46, 47, 51 (1992).

87. Higaki Interview, *supra* note 2.

Officer Higaki, too, was typical of the time period in thinking Rachel might have been exaggerating the danger she was in. Officers frequently responded less than whole-heartedly to abused women. In part, this followed from the general difficulty in understanding how it is that a battered wife could stay in an abusive relationship—Lenore Walker's groundbreaking work on the cycle of abuse and Battered Women's Syndrome not having been published until 1979[88]—together with a sense of futility born of seeing so many abuse victims over and over again, especially when those same victims so often refused to press charges.[89] Again, rather than on the perpetrator, the focus was on the victim; rather than ask why he hit, we asked why she stood in the path of his fist.

Police departments at the time explicitly discouraged arrests as a solution to the problem of domestic violence. The Oakland Police Department's *1975 Training Bulletin on Techniques of Dispute Intervention* is typical:

> The police role in a dispute situation is more often that of a mediator and peacemaker than enforcer of the law. In dispute situations, officers are often caught between an obligation to enforce the law on one hand, and on the other, the possibility that police action such as arrest will only aggravate the dispute or create a serious danger for the arresting officers due to possible efforts to resist arrest. Such a possibility is most likely when a husband or father is arrested in his home; he is upset in the first place, and if he is taken into custody in front of his family, desperate resistance can result to prevent loss of face. [Although t]here are some situations when there is no reasonable alternative but to arrest . . . [n]ormally, officers should adhere to the policy that arrests shall be avoided. . . . [If] one of the parties demands arrest, you should attempt to explain the ramifications of such action (e.g., loss of wages, bail procedures, court appearances) and encourage the parties to reason with each other.[90]

Momentum for reform was building, however. One of the very first domestic violence shelters in the country, Haven House, opened in California in 1964. The first book on domestic violence, *Scream Quietly or the Neighbors Will Hear*, was published in 1974. And the National Organization for Women formed a "National Task Force on Battered

---

88. Lenore E. Walker, *The Battered Woman* (1979).

89. Paul Friday et al., *Policing Domestic Violence: Perceptions, Experience and Reality,* 16 Crim. Just. Rev. 198, 199–200 (1991).

90. Del Martin, *Battered Wives* 93–94 (1981) (quoting Oakland Police Department's *1975 Training Bulletin*).

Women/Household Violence" in 1975,[91] the same year the Oakland Police Department's Training Bulletin was printed.

By 1976, the confluence of that prototypically old-school police attitude with a rising awareness of domestic violence inspired two class action lawsuits. Together, these suits hastened the swelling tide of a sea change for law enforcement. *Scott v. Hart*[92] in California and *Bruno v. Codd*[93] in New York each alleged that police officers systematically failed in their duty even to attempt to protect victims of domestic violence. In *Bruno*, the New York City Police Department's motion to dismiss drew a resounding denial:

> For too long, Anglo–American laws treated a man's physical abuse of his wife as different from any other assault and, indeed as an acceptable practice. If the allegations of the instant complaint— buttressed by hundreds of pages of affidavits—are true, only the written law has changed; in reality, wife beating is still condoned, if not approved, by some of those charged with protecting its victims.[94]

This ruling prompted a consent judgment in which the NYPD essentially agreed to enforce the law, promising "to respond swiftly to every request for protection and, as in an ordinary criminal case, to arrest the husband whenever there is reasonable cause to believe that a felony has been committed against the wife or that an order of protection or temporary order of protection has been violated." The NYPD agreed to additional measures, as well, including ensuring that officers would remain on the scene to prevent retaliation, providing social services, and disciplining any officers who refused to follow the new guidelines.[95] *Scott v. Hart*, the California case, settled in 1979 under similar terms.[96]

As word of these two agreements spread, policies in police departments across the country began to change. Joan Zorza, a staff attorney with the National Center on Women and Family Law, pointed to New Haven, Connecticut, Chicago, Illinois, and Atlanta, Georgia, as examples.[97] Mandatory arrest and no-drop prosecution policies, stipulating that officers must arrest and prosecutors must bring charges even over the victim's objections,[98] took root. Although Oregon enacted such a law

---

91. *Id.* at 7.

92. Scott v. Hart, No. C–76–2395 (N.D. Cal. filed Oct. 28, 1976).

93. Bruno v. Codd, 396 N.Y.S.2d 974 (N.Y. Sup. Ct. 1977).

94. *Id.* at 975–976 (citations omitted).

95. Bruno v. Codd, 393 N.E.2d 976, 980–82 (N.Y. 1979).

96. *Scott*, No. C–76–2395 (cited in Zorza, *supra* note 87, at 56 nn. 100–109).

97. Zorza, *supra* note 86, at 59 n.136.

98. Donna Coker, *Crime Control and Feminist Law Reform in Domestic Violence Law: A Critical Review*, 4 Buff. Crim. L. Rev. 801, 806 (2000).

in 1977—the first state in the nation to do so—it took several more years
and yet another lawsuit to convince actual police officers to comport with
its requirements.[99]

Hugely influential in prompting policy changes was the empirical
work of Larry Sherman and Richard Berk. Their research demonstrated
that arresting domestic violence offenders not only improved recidivism
rates for individual offenders, but also deterred others, lowering domestic violence rates across the board.[100] More states began enacting similar
laws, and by 1984, Congress got into the act with the Family Violence
Prevention and Services Act. Although the Act was defunded and reau-
thorization efforts have so far been unsuccessful,[101] its stated purposes
included increasing awareness of domestic violence; providing assistance
to victims; and training law enforcement agencies.[102] The Violence
Against Women Act followed in 1994, together with private efforts like
the Remember My Name project, sponsored by the national Coalition
Against Domestic Violence and *Ms. Magazine.*

The proliferation of these high-profile ventures demonstrated an
incredible amount of progress for domestic violence awareness in those
first two decades after *Berry*, but much remained to be done. Case in
point: in 1999, Texan Jimmy Watkins received only four months (albeit
with ten years of probation and a $10,000 fine) for killing his wife. She
had thrown Watkins out of the house for sexually assaulting a family
member, and her lover moved in the same day. Watkins called her
literally every few minutes from late that evening into the wee hours of
the next morning. His calls continued into the afternoon, culminating in
one in which he asked where in the house she was. When she obligingly
answered that she was in the kitchen, Watkins broke down the door,
shooting both her and her lover in front of their ten-year-old son.
Watkins fired repeatedly, stopping only when his gun jammed. He left
briefly, fixed the gun, and came back, shooting his wife five more times.
For this he got four months in jail, a fine, and probation. And that was
1999.[103] Writing in 2003, Cynthia Lee mused that "Watkins' probation-

---

99. Zorza, *supra* note 86, at 63–64.

100. Lawrence W. Sherman & Richard A. Berk, *The Special Deterrent Effect of Arrest for Domestic Assault*, 49 Am. Soc. Rev. 261, 270 (1984) (cited in Friday, *supra* note 79, at 199) (concluding that "arrest makes an independent contribution to the deterrence potential of the criminal justice system"). Later studies painted a more complicated picture. *See, e.g.*, Lawrence W. Sherman et al., *The Variable Effects of Arrest on Criminal Careers: The Milwaukee Domestic Violence Experiment*, 83 J. Crim. L. & Criminology 137, 139 (1992).

101. National Network to End Domestic Violence, http://www.nnedv.org/policy/issues/fvpsa.html (last visited Mar. 31, 2011).

102. 42 U.S.C. § 110, 10401 (2006).

103. Lee, *supra* note 57, at 42–43 (citing Texas newspaper reports). *See also* Ex parte Watkins, 73 S.W.3d 264, 266 (Tex. Crim. App. 2002). Elizabeth Rapaport convincingly

ary sentence ... is a reminder that even today, some people think a man's violent reaction to female partner infidelity is normal or reasonable."[104]

The Present Day

Have things improved in the last ten years? Would Jimmy Watkins receive more than four months and probation if he had killed his wife in 2010? Probably. A study by Laurie Ragatz and Brenda Russell surveyed over 400 people, providing participants with an abbreviated description of the facts in Watkins's case. The short version actually sounded much more favorable to Watkins than the fuller newspaper versions described above. Study participants were not told that Watkins had sexually assaulted a relative before being thrown out of the marital home. They were told instead only that the wife asked him to leave, then had sex with her lover that night. They were told that Watkins "learned of the affair through various phone calls," called his wife the next day to threaten her and her lover, and then walked into the home, fatally shooting his wife and wounding the lover.[105] The fact of the ten-year-old son's presence during the rampage also was omitted.

Ragatz and Russell's study was undertaken to investigate the influence of sex and sexual orientation on perceptions of heat of passion crimes, so the case scenario was varied to reflect a male defendant and a female victim, a female defendant and a male victim, two females, and two males, respectively.[106] In each variation, participants divided fairly evenly between convicting the defendant of second degree murder (46.3%) and convicting of voluntary manslaughter (48.8%).[107] Mean sentence lengths ranged from nine and a half to more than fifteen years.[108] In all instances, study participants in this far-more-sympathetic-to-the-defendant version of Watkins's killing meted out punishments far more severe than his real-life sentence of probation, with four months to serve.

It may be that society has finally caught up with Gerhard Winkler. He maintained all along that Blinder's theory that Rachel was "begging

---

documented this "domestic violence discount" in the death penalty context with her study of capital domestic violence homicides in *Capital Murder and the Domestic Discount: A Study of Capital Domestic Murder in the Post*-Furman *Era*, 49 SMU L. Rev. 1507 (1996).

104. Lee, *supra* note 57, at 43.

105. Laurie L. Ragatz & Brenda Russell, *Sex, Sexual Orientation, and Sexism: What Influence Do These Factors Have on Verdicts in a Crime-of-Passion Case?*, 150 J. Soc. Psychol. 341, 346 (2010).

106. *Id.* at 346.

107. *Id.* at 349.

108. *Id.* at 350.

to be killed [wa]s ridiculous."[109] Disheartening as it may seem to have to say so, one of the "most important insights" that has grown out of the increased attention given to domestic violence in the years following *Berry* is the revelation that "battered women are neither masochists nor provocateurs."[110]

Epilogue

Albert and Rachel's old address appears in an area called the Richmond. The locale is not noteworthy in itself, but just across the street lies Presidio Terrace, an "ultra-exclusive neighborhood" formerly inhabited by former Speaker of the House Nancy Pelosi and Senator Dianne Feinstein.[111]

The Fantasia Bakery went out of business, and is now a trendy café.[112]

Joe Grumich, the Buddhist spiritual leader Jean Berk called for support, still chants. He worked as a chef for over thirty years. Retired now, he volunteers at a thrift shop to stay active, sometimes performing with a group of "middle age men singing rock and roll and gospel" called the "Love Choir."[113]

Appellate attorney Edward Suman is still working. Married, he has a daughter, and he enjoys watching sports and traveling. He cautions that lawyering can be a bit of a thankless profession, pointing out that he never received any recognition for his work in *Berry*. He would advise "young lawyers out there to protect their reputation and work hard."[114]

Judge Perasso served on the California Superior Court for twenty years, retiring in 1991. As far as his experience in law school is concerned, he said only that he was "just happy to get through." His advice to the aspiring lawyer includes the following: "Study, do your own briefing, and be serious about whatever you do."[115]

Prosecutor Gerhard Winkler left the District Attorney's office to do civil litigation, then returned to the DA's office career criminals section for a short time. Next came a stint as counsel for Union Bank for five years, then more private practice, first as defense counsel for a large firm handling asbestos litigation, then on his own in San Jose doing medical

---

109. Winkler Interview, *supra* note 15.

110. Coker, *Heat of Passion*, *supra* note 68, at 74.

111. Email from Eileen Hirst, Chief of Staff, S.F. Sheriff's Dep't, to Ceara Riggs (Oct. 7, 2010) (on file with author).

112. Winkler Interview, *supra* note 15.

113. Grumich Interview, *supra* note 48.

114. Suman Interview, *supra* note 34.

115. Perasso Interview, *supra* note 14.

malpractice defense. Today, he is "ninety-nine percent retired," spending the other one percent of his time consulting on medical and legal
defense cases. He has taught trial advocacy at the University of California Hastings College of the Law. His advice to the aspiring lawyer is to
be creative. Married now, with three daughters, Winkler is a "family
man." Coincidentally, his middle daughter, 21, is reading the *Berry*
transcripts for fun, thinking she may want to be a lawyer. Even now,
Winkler "despises cowards who beat up on women." He tells his own
daughters "if a man abuses you, you leave immediately. You don't stick
around. They can never be trusted." Winkler is proud of his performance
in *Berry*. Despite being reversed, despite being criticized for his aggressive approach on cross with Blinder, he "wouldn't do it differently
today."[116]

Defense attorney Geoffrey Brown went on to become a "hot shot" at
the Public Defender's office. He was elected Public Defender six times,
running unopposed in all but one of those races. He served for over two
decades. Next, he was appointed Public Utility Commissioner, where he
served for six years. He enjoyed a period as the Dean of the John F.
Kennedy University College of Law (accredited in California, though not
nationally) from 2007–2009, but "the commute was too much." Now
retired, Brown still does some consulting work on utility law and
mediations. He is a widower, and his three daughters are all successful
professionals: one is a college professor teaching Chinese history, one is a
legal headhunter, and the other is in-house counsel at the Pacific Gas &
Electric Company.[117] Unquestionably, Brown has much to be proud of.
With respect to *Berry*, though, he is quick to acknowledge that he would
try the case differently today. He was young, he said, and inexperienced.
For his own part, he wishes he could go back and reconstruct the tape
Albert testified Rachel coerced him into making, stating that he forced
her to marry him and was the one driving the car when they hit the
cyclist. The tape had been described to the jury, but because it was
unplayable, jurors never had the benefit of hearing its contents for
themselves. Had Brown been able to reconstruct it,[118] he believes that
tape would have revealed Rachel ruthlessly browbeating Albert. That
tape would have made "a compelling case . . . for Al's assertion about
Rachel, debunked by Winkler."[119] More than anything, though, he wishes
Albert's probation officer had recommended Albert be sent back to

---

116. Winkler Interview, *supra* note 15.

117. Brown Interview, *supra* note 10.

118. Email from Geoffrey Brown, Deputy Public Defender, City and County of San
Francisco, to Christine Edwards (Oct. 31, 2010) (on file with author) ("My office in '74 was
not a model of forensic science").

119. Email from Geoffrey Brown, Deputy Public Defender, City and County of San
Francisco, to Christine Edwards (Oct. 23, 2010) (on file with author).

prison when he first violated his probation by strangling Rachel into unconsciousness. If only he had, Rachel might still be alive.[120]

Martin Blinder's career took off in a remarkable way. An expert witness in many high-profile cases, he is perhaps best known as the man behind the "Twinkie Defense." When Dan White killed San Francisco Mayor George Moscone and Supervisor Harvey Milk, Blinder testified for the defense. Arguing that the defendant's depression justified mitigation from murder to voluntary manslaughter on the grounds of diminished capacity, Blinder provided an explanation of depression that included, among other things, mention of the fact that White's formerly healthful diet had taken a precipitous turn for the worse. Taking this out of context, some misunderstood the testimony as a claim that junk food made White do it. The associated infamy still "bugs" him.[121] But it has not been all bad. Blinder's professional success is reflected in his popularity with talk show hosts Sally Jessy Raphael, Ted Koppel, Oprah Winfrey, and Larry King.[122] He authored the pre-eminent textbook in his field, *Psychiatry in the Everyday Practice of Law*, now in its fourth edition. In its very last section, in a chapter entitled, "Unorthodox Use of Psychiatric Testimony," Blinder briefly describes the *Berry* case, providing some excerpts of his own testimony under the heading "Mitigating psychiatric testimony in the criminal case where there is no formal mental illness."[123] He has authored other books, as well, in addition to being "a produced playwright … and a terrific jazz pianist."[124] Lasting interpersonal happiness has proven more elusive. Blinder's second wife committed suicide, and his first wife did, too—though she tried to kill him first. In 2001, he was engaged to a woman who showed great promise: she taught Bliss Flow Tantra.[125] But whether that promise was realized or not is something we may never know. After sharing the above details with a reporter whose published article highlights the compelling parallel between the violent romantic lives Blinder studies professionally and his own personal life,[126] Blinder seems to have had second thoughts about the way in which he interacts with the press. Called for this book chapter, he would say only, "I like to keep my

---

120. Brown Interview, *supra* note 10.

121. Mike Weiss, *Final Witness: Psychiatrist's Work Echoes in Personal Life; Doctor Known for Insanity Murder Defenses Was Almost Killed by Ex in Seemingly Insane Act*, S.F. Chron., May 20, 2001, *available at* http://articles.sfgate.com/2001–05–20/news/17600607_1_larry-king-eminent-mayor-george-moscone.

122. *Id.*

123. Martin Blinder, *Psychiatry in the Everyday Practice of Law* 1070–1072 (4th ed. rev. 2006).

124. Weiss, *supra* note 121.

125. *Id.*

126. *Id.*

professional and personal life separate, but thank you for extending me the courtesy of asking."[127]

Rachel's body was sent to Israel just as she had requested. Her cousin, Fortunee, said the family wanted her to get her wish.[128]

So what happened to Albert Berry? He began serving his sentence at the California Men's Colony in San Luis Obispo, "the happiest city in America,"[129] located about halfway between San Francisco and Los Angeles. In a few short months, his good behavior earned him a transfer to the minimum security unit. One more year in, and he began serving with the California Department of Forestry and Fire Protection, through which Department of Corrections inmate work crews contain forest fires, maintain conservation land, and perform other useful service out in the community. Paroled on October 30, 1980, he spent his last year under Corrections supervision on the streets of San Francisco, Modesto, and Stockton, California. Albert's final discharge came on October 30, 1981: six years behind bars plus one on parole.

Fifty-three years old and still a charmer, Albert lost no time in once again finding a mate. Immediately after his release from Attica State Prison back in 1957, he had met and within thirty days married his second wife, Carrol. After his release on probation for stabbing Carrol, it had taken Albert all of one year to meet and marry his third wife, Rachel. Less than nine months after his discharge for Rachel's murder, Albert met and married wife number four: Lorretta Joyce Estepp.[130]

Joyce, as she preferred to be called in her later years, was with Albert until the end.[131] There is no answer at the phone number listed for the last Mrs. Berry. One can only hope she fared better than the others. She certainly fared better than Rachel.

For fifteen years, Albert and Joyce made their home in Oakdale, California. Albert resumed his old occupation, working as a cook at Monty's Restaurant well past the usual retirement age. In December of 1997, though, he started to have trouble breathing. Diagnosed with congestive heart failure and its common companions, severe chronic obstructive pulmonary disease and pneumonia, Albert spent his last days in the hospital at Doctors Medical Center of Modesto.

---

127. Telephone Interview by Robert Brammer with Martin Blinder, M.D., Forensic Psychiatrist (June 1, 2011).

128. Lichaa Interview, *supra* note 8.

129. San Luis Obispo Chamber of Commerce, San Luis Obispo: Pure California, http://www.visitslo.com/ (last visited May 3, 2011).

130. Nevada Marriage Index, 1956–2005, *available at* Ancestry.com.

131. Albert's death certificate lists his spouse as "Joyce Berry," whose maiden name is shown as "Joyce L. Zumwalt." State of California, Certification of Vital Record, County of Stanislaus, Modesto, California, Certificate of Death for Albert Joseph Berry [hereinafter Death Certificate]. Loretta J. Zumwalt married and divorced Greg Estepp. Ancestry.com, California Marriage Index, 1960–1985 and California Divorce Index, 1966–1984. Interestingly, her divorce from Greg appears to have come one year after her marriage to Albert: the divorce is listed as July 13, 1983 and the marriage as July 25, 1982. Scrivener's error could account for the discrepancy: a divorce on July 13 followed by a Nevada marriage 12 days later seems more plausible than bigamy, though of course one never knows.

Rachel Pessah and her first husband, Joe Pessah, taken in Israel when Rachel was 17 years old. Reprinted by permission of Fortunee Lichaa, Rachel's cousin.

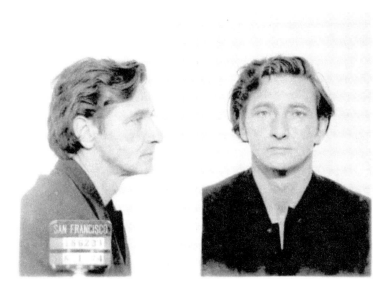

Albert Berry's mugshot taken in San Francisco, CA August 1, 1974.

Albert passed away on March 29, 1998, at the age of seventy,[132] his blood cooled for good.

---

132. Death Certificate, *supra* note 131.

5

Jeannie Suk

"The Look in His Eyes": The Story of *Rusk* and Rape Reform

The thing is, most of the time when you're coming pretty close to doing it with a girl ... she keeps telling you to stop. The trouble with me is, I stop. Most guys don't. I can't help it. You never know whether they really *want* you to stop, or whether they're just scared as hell, or whether they're just telling you to stop so that if you *do* go through with it, the blame'll be on *you*, not them. Anyway, I keep stopping. The trouble is, I get to feeling sorry for them. I mean most girls are so dumb and all. After you neck them for a while you can really *watch* them losing their brains. You take a girl when she really gets passionate, she just hasn't any brains. I don't know. They tell me to stop, so I stop.

—J.D. Salinger, *The Catcher in the Rye*

The thoughts of Holden Caulfield, the most popular adolescent character in American letters, have been read by virtually every young student coming of age in America. These words, published in 1951, capture something of the expectations about sex between men and women that prevailed into and beyond midcentury. Starting in the 1970s, under the influence of feminism, social attitudes changed significantly.

Like many guys of his time, Edward Salvatore Rusk of Baltimore, Maryland didn't take a girl's "no" to sex as necessarily meaning he had to stop, when he otherwise thought she was interested. He was convicted of rape at the cusp of legal transformation, when sexual behavior that had been commonplace and tolerated by the law was rapidly being recast as criminal. The story of *State v. Rusk* is the story of when and how a set of social norms of sex and dating became unacceptable. It is a story of the legal role and consequences of that social change.

September 21–22, 1977

The prosecuting witness was a twenty-one-year-old woman known as Pat. One Wednesday evening in the fall of 1977, she attended an alumnae meeting at the Catholic girls' high school from which she graduated. The Archbishop Keough School was on thirty acres of rolling land on the outer edge of Baltimore City. She worked as a secretary at an insurance company and had a two-year-old son. She was married but recently separated from her husband and living with her mother and child in the white middle-class suburb of Parkville, right outside the city. When the meeting wound down, it was still early and her classmate Terry Norman, whom she'd known since before high school, asked if she wanted to go down to Fell's Point with her.[1]

In downtown Baltimore, Fell's Point was a waterfront harbor district established in the colonial era. Cobblestone streets, quaint street lamps, and eighteenth- and nineteenth-century buildings provided the atmospheric backdrop for a busy commercial area teeming with shops, bars, and restaurants. On the National Register of Historic Districts, though not gentrified as it is today, Fell's Point by night was the place for young people to party. The noisy bars and clubs were frequented by students from Johns Hopkins, Goucher, and Loyola. Young professional, working-class, local, and suburban folks mixed there too. In the 1990s Fell's Point would become familiar to television audiences as the setting for the NBC series *Homicide: Life on the Street*.[2]

From a telephone booth, Pat called her mother, who was babysitting her son, to say she was going to Fell's Point with Terry but wouldn't be late. The two women drove in separate cars and arrived around 9:45 at a bar called Helen's, where Terry ordered Pat a screwdriver. After an hour of talking, the two friends decided to walk a few blocks to a different place, The Horse You Came In On, a two-hundred-year-old saloon where folk music was playing. After a half hour, they thought they would try another bar. At E.J. Bugs, they found a large crowd and a band playing.[3]

---

1. Unless otherwise indicated, the underlying story in this chapter is drawn from: State v. Rusk, 424 A.2d 720 (Md. 1981); Rusk v. State, 406 A.2d 624 (Md. Ct. Spec. App. 1979); Trial Transcript of Sept. 19–20, 1978, State v. Rusk (Baltimore City Crim. Ct. Part X) (No. 27732702/1977); Sentencing Transcript of Oct. 20, 1978, State v. Rusk (Baltimore City Crim. Ct. Part X) (No. 27732702/1977). When relying on sources other than these, I cite them at the end of a paragraph or several sentences containing the information used.

2. Telephone Interview with James Salkin, Attorney (Dec. 4, 2009) [hereinafter Salkin Interview I].

3. The trial transcript's misspelling of the establishment as "E.J. Buggs" was repeated in the judicial opinions.

Pat stood against a wall holding but not finishing her third screwdriver of the evening when she saw a man of medium height and build come over and say hi to Terry. Terry was talking to a guy she had met, but she glanced over to say "Hi Eddie" and resumed her conversation.

Eddie Rusk was a thirty-one-year-old veteran of the National Guard, which he had joined to avoid the Vietnam draft.[4] He had worked as a television repairman, and was trying to get his own shop. In the meantime, he was searching newspaper ads for used cars to buy, and fix up, to sell. The son of a wallpaper hanger, he was raised in an Irish–Italian family in a lower-middle-class East Baltimore neighborhood that became riddled with drugs over the years. Since separating from his wife, who had their child at seventeen and had drug abuse problems, he often stayed at his parents' house, where he had grown up. Eddie's parents had adopted his little daughter, who was a toddler.[5]

Eddie was out that night with his buddies Mike Trimp and Dave Carroll, friends since their teenage years when Eddie was the "Casanova of Woodlawn High" and the neighborhood boys had a club called "the Animals."[6] A mile away from his family home, Eddie rented a room with Mike for $80 a month in an apartment house they called their "pit stop." That night they were trying "to pick up some ladies." Eddie drank a couple of Millers. While his friends were getting something to eat, he stayed in the bar and saw a girl smiling at him. He walked over and struck up a conversation. They quickly discovered what they had in common: each was married and separated, and each had a two-year-old child.

According to Pat, after ten or fifteen minutes of talking to Eddie, she decided it was time for her to head home because she didn't want to stay out late. It was midnight, and she'd have to get up early with her toddler. As she was getting ready to leave, Eddie asked if she wouldn't mind dropping him off at home on her way. Thinking her friend Terry knew him, she agreed to give him a ride home. As they walked to her car, she told him, "I'm just giving a ride home, you know, as a friend, not anything to be, you know, thought of other than a ride."

Eddie, however, recalled that as Pat was getting ready to leave the bar, he asked her to go home with him. She said she couldn't because she had her car with her. He suggested they both take her car to his

---

4. *Deaths, Central Florida*, Orlando Sentinel, Nov. 10, 2006, at B6; Telephone Interview with Jo Ann Riccobono, Sister of Edward Rusk (Dec. 15, 2009) [hereinafter Riccobono Interview].

5. Riccobono Interview, *supra* note 4; Telephone Interview with Gina Sell, Daughter of Edward Rusk (Dec. 15, 2009) [hereinafter Sell Interview].

6. Riccobono Interview, *supra* note 4.

place and she agreed. Eddie's friends said they saw Pat walking down the street "snuggling up to him" and "hanging all over him."

During the twenty-minute drive, the two talked more about their children and separation from their respective spouses. According to Eddie, she suddenly asked, "You're not gonna rape me, are you?" Taken aback, he asked why she would say that, and she confessed she was raped once before. He sympathized, "It's a drag." She then asked, "You are not gonna beat me up, are you?" and explained that her husband used to beat her up. Again he said, "That's a drag."

Pat pulled up across the street from Eddie's apartment on the 3100 block of Guilford Avenue, a row of Romanesque turn-of-the-century stone houses, now divided into humble multiple dwellings. Charles Village, near Johns Hopkins University, was a residential area where students and young people lived, and it bordered an unsafe area.[7] Pat was unfamiliar with the neighborhood. Leaving the ignition on, she said "Well, here, you know, you are home." He invited her up to the apartment. She recalled the invitation being repeated and declined several times, and even explaining she couldn't even if she wanted to because she wasn't yet legally divorced and a private detective could be watching her movements. It was about 1:00 a.m.

Pat and Eddie each remembered what happened next differently. She recalled that he reached over, turned off the ignition, and took the keys. He got out, walked around to her side, opened her door, and said, "Now, will you come up?" She now felt she was in trouble and feared he was going to hurt her. She followed him upstairs to his room on the second floor of the apartment house. The building seemed dark, quiet, and empty, and she didn't see any lights on in the adjacent units.

Eddie, though, recalled that it was Pat herself who turned off the ignition, and he denied taking her keys. They sat in the car for a few minutes making out and then went upstairs to his room, she as willing to go up as he was to have her come up. He unlocked his door, offered her a seat, and left for a few minutes to use the bathroom, which was outside the apartment and down the hall. When he returned, she was still in the chair next to the bed. He switched off the light, because she said it was too bright. He sat on the bed across from her, and they started to kiss and caress, falling back on the bed together.

Pat recalled that when Eddie returned from the bathroom, she asked him, "Now, I came up. Can I go?" But he said he wanted her to stay. He still had her keys. He began to undress her and asked her to remove both their trousers, which she did. When they were both un-

    7. Telephone Interview with David Eaton, Retired Public Defender, Office of the Public Defender for Baltimore City (Dec. 3, 2009) [hereinafter Eaton Interview]; Salkin Interview I, *supra* note 2.

dressed on the bed, she begged him to let her leave: "you can get a lot of girls down there, for what you want." He kept saying no. She was scared, not because of what he said, but because of "the look in his eyes." She asked, "If I do what you want, will you let me go without killing me?" When she began to cry, he put his hands on her throat and started "lightly to choke" her. She asked, "If I do what you want, will you let me go?" and he said yes. She performed oral sex and had sexual intercourse.

According to Eddie, it was true that he suggested taking their clothes off, but she readily agreed. He denied putting his hands on her throat or choking her, lightly or otherwise. There seemed to be nothing wrong until after sex. It was only then that she "got uptight" and started to cry, saying, "You guys are all alike, just out for one thing." He tried to calm her down but she just wanted to leave. He walked her to her car and asked if she wanted to go out with him again. She said yes, having no intention to see him again, and when he asked for her telephone number, she said, "No, I'll just see you down Fell's Point sometime." She asked him for directions out of the neighborhood.

Pat stopped at a gas station to use the bathroom and then drove home. As she parked the car, she began to turn over in her mind what had happened, and what would have happened if she hadn't done what Eddie wanted. After sitting in the car thinking, she decided to go to the police. She drove to the nearby town of Hillendale, found a police car, and reported the incident. She went with an officer to Guilford Avenue where he spoke with Eddie's landlady and located his room.

Eddie had fallen asleep after Pat left. His friend Mike came in soon thereafter, around 2:00 or 2:30 a.m. Soon after that, Eddie was awakened by the police at his door. He was dumbfounded when he gathered the officer was there to arrest him for what had happened with Pat.[8] The next day, the landlady threw Eddie and his friend out of the apartment.

An examination at Baltimore City Hospital revealed semen on Pat's vagina but no unusual stretching or tearing. Her underpants and Eddie's bed sheets had semen but not blood.

Trial

James Salkin was a thirty-six-year-old prosecutor with the State's Attorney for Baltimore City. Born and raised in middle-class Jewish northwest Baltimore, he graduated from the University of Baltimore Law School after years of working in city government. His reputation as a prosecutor was intense and aggressive, but physically he was reed-thin, slight of stature, and asthmatic since childhood. In his Savile Row

---

8. Telephone Interview with Ira C. Cooke, Former Attorney (Dec. 7, 2009) [hereinafter Cooke Interview]; Eaton Interview, *supra* note 7; Riccobono Interview, *supra* note 4.

bespoke suits, custom-tailored shirts and bench-made shoes—acquired on trips to London with savings from his salary—he cut an unusual figure in the rough-and-tumble world of criminal court. He joked that Brooks Brothers was Mecca to him and he'd want to be buried there.[9]

In six years in the trial division, Salkin had prosecuted every imaginable kind of criminal case. He got Eddie Rusk's case on a routine assignment. He met the victim and heard her story. She seemed ordinary and unremarkable, if a bit foolish to go to a Fell's Point nightclub where guys were obviously looking to get laid. But she was sincere, even adamant about what happened. He thought that a jury would believe her. She wasn't weird or dislikable, as key trial witnesses sometimes were. Baltimore City was a tough place to win criminal trials because of the great distrust of law enforcement among the jury pool. Given his credible witness, the case was worth trying, but he told her the jury might well not convict. He charged Eddie with rape and with assault.

David Eaton was a seasoned public defender. Salkin thought of him as "a straight arrow, salt of the earth." Tall and preppy, he was an understated lawyer, even genteel in his manner. Hearing the story, Eaton did not think Eddie raped the woman. It was difficult to see what her intention was when she chose to give a ride to a man she'd just met at a Fell's Point bar, if not to go home with him. Perhaps she regretted having sex that night, and perhaps Eddie was not a gentleman, but without force, regrettable sex was not rape. Eaton thought the jury would see it this way.[10]

Salkin and Eaton were friendly in the small world of the Criminal Court of Baltimore, and they thought well of each other. Both saw the case as serious but routine, one of many they had together, and one of many in front of Judge Robert Karwacki, who knew them both by first name. Karwacki was a tough judge with a fine reputation. He moved dockets along and did not dawdle. You knew not to ask for postponements.[11]

Around the courthouse at this time there was a film shooting, *And Justice for All*, an Oscar-nominated courtroom drama starring Al Pacino as an attorney blackmailed into defending a corrupt judge accused of rape.[12] Salkin befriended the casting director and asked if he could be an extra. He was told to come the next morning to shoot a scene on the steps of the Baltimore War Memorial. But Salkin was supposed to start a felony arson trial that afternoon and the jury hadn't yet been selected.

---

9. Interview with James Salkin, Attorney, in Baltimore, Md. (Dec. 12, 2009) [hereinafter Salkin Interview II].

10. Eaton Interview, *supra* note 7.

11. *Id.*; Salkin Interview I, *supra* note 2.

12. *And Justice for All* (Columbia Pictures 1979).

In all likelihood the trial would continue the next morning. When he realized the trial was with Karwacki, though, he explained to the judge what he needed. Karwacki told him to start voir dire—he would make it happen. Three and a half hours later, the trial was completed and the jury's guilty verdict was in. Salkin was able to show up to shoot his part in the film's final scene, in which he walks by carrying a briefcase behind Pacino.[13]

At the start of Rusk's trial, both lawyers were called up to the bench and asked, "What's this case about?" Salkin recalls that after hearing a bit, Judge Karwacki said, "Jimmy, get rid of this piece of crap." When Salkin insisted it was a serious case and that he intended to try it, the judge simply said, "Fine, let's go." And so two days of trial began.

The jury had at least five women. Four jurors had police or corrections officers in their families. Two other jurors worked for the police. One of those was a police officer who worked in the same unit of the Baltimore City Police Department as the officer who had arrested Eddie. That juror was the only one Eaton challenged for cause, but Judge Karwacki denied the challenge based on the juror's statement that he'd be able to be fair and impartial.

Once the jury was seated, Salkin began his opening argument. "If this was a Perry Mason mystery, it would be the case of a foolish victim," he said. He focused on how Pat "volunteered to give [Eddie] a ride home," and he called her "a very, very foolish young lady" who was "stupid to get herself into this fix. But it's up to you to decide what happened after she was stupid and foolish," Salkin continued, "and whether it was rape, or not." The issue, he said, was whether "she volunteered to everything, or did she volunteer to things to a point, that is, to drive him to his place." Salkin argued that "she volunteered for nothing that took place thereafter." He asked the jurors to use common sense, and to ask themselves "what anyone has to gain, or lose, by testifying the way they do."

Eaton opened by stating, "Quite frankly, there is only one issue in this case: . . . was there a rape, or wasn't there?" Describing the events, Eaton told the jury that the room Eddie rented was "a place to socialize with members of the opposite sex if the occasion arose." Eaton said, "The evidence will be clear that there was an entirely voluntary situation on the part of these two adults; and there was no force, no violence, no threats, nothing involved. This was, to use a slang term, a pickup."

Pat was just as credible as Salkin expected her to be. In her testimony, she said she only agreed to give Eddie a ride home because she thought her friend knew him, and it was just a ride, nothing more.

---

13. Salkin Interview I, *supra* note 2.

She said he continued to insist she come up to the apartment even when she repeatedly declined. Finally he took her car keys from the ignition. When asked why she didn't try to run away instead of walking inside with him, she said, "I didn't know what to do. I was scared." She explained that once she was undressed, "I was really scared, because I can't describe, you know, what was said. It was more the look in his eyes."

Pat testified that she asked whether he would let her go without killing her if she did what he wanted. "Because I didn't know, at that point, what he was going to do; and I started to cry; and when I did, he put his hands on my throat, and started lightly to choke me." Several times during her testimony Salkin asked her to speak up because the jury could barely hear her. He asked, "As unpleasant as it may be, and I have discussed this, you have to tell the ladies and gentlemen exactly what took place. Tell us what he did. We're all adults." She said, "He made me perform oral sex, and then sexual intercourse."

Eaton's cross-examination began by questioning whether she had stayed out all night in the past. She said, "I stayed at a girlfriend's." He asked whether she had previously met people at Fell's Point. She said, "I've never met anybody I've gone out with. Met people in general, talking in conversation, most of the time people that Terry knew, not that I have gone down there, and met people as dates." He asked what her purpose was in going to Fell's Point that night. She said, "Just to have a few drinks with Terry. The reason we picked that, because she lived at the opposite end of town than I did, and it's midway between the two of us." Efforts to suggest she was a party girl didn't take.

She testified, "I even brought the subject up that even if I wanted to come up, which I didn't want to come up, I was separated. It would cause marital problems. I tried everything. I did not want to go up. I was very explicit in that." Asked if she feared her husband would find out she was with another man, she answered, "No, not as much as I was fearful that maybe I had someone following me that, you know, it can be an innocent thing. I'm driving someone home, and I told him, if I come up, you know, for a drink, I would be in trouble." She said it was a "likelihood" that she was being followed.

Eaton asked why she did then go up. She explained:

At that point, because I was scared, because he had my car keys. I didn't know what to do. I was someplace I didn't even know where I was. It was in the city. I didn't know whether to run. I really didn't think, at that point, what to do.

Now, I know that I should have blown the horn. I should have run. There were a million things I could have done. I was scared, at that point, and I didn't do any of them.

"What were you scared of?" She said, "Him."

"What were you scared that he was going to do?"

"Rape me, but I didn't say that. It was the way he looked at me, and said, 'Come on up, come on up'; and when he took the keys, I knew that was wrong. I just didn't say, are you going to rape me."

Asked why she removed her clothes, she said, "Because he told me to."

Finally, Eaton touched on divorce and custody. "Isn't it true that after you had sex with Mr. Rusk, you told him that you could lose your child, because of what you had just done; isn't that true?" She responded, "I said I could lose my child if that were taken—I don't remember what I said. I don't remember. I said something about losing my child. I don't remember what." That was Eaton's last question of Pat.

Pat's friend Terry Norman testified that she knew Eddie's face and name, "but I honestly couldn't tell you—apparently I ran into him sometime before. I couldn't tell you how I know him. I don't know him very well at all." It was rare for Pat to go out with her, she said. Pat's "mother didn't let her go out too often," and she "always had to leave around midnight." Terry also testified that Pat "doesn't usually drink. She usually just gets a drink, and plays with it. She rarely finishes it." Officer Hammett, the police officer who arrested Eddie, testified that Pat was sober at the time of the complaint.

At the end of the state's case, Eaton made a motion for judgment of acquittal, saying "there is no evidence of any weapon, any striking, any intimidation, from a physical standpoint. I think she said that she looked at him, and knew from looking at him, that she was going to be raped." Judge Karwacki denied the motion, citing evidence of "a taking of the car keys forcibly, a request that the witness accompany the Defendant to the upstairs apartment," and "a look in his eye which put her in fear." He also cited her "begging him to let her leave. She was scared. She started to cry. He started to strangle her softly she said. She asked the Defendant, that if she'd submit, would he not kill her, at which point he indicated that he would not."[14]

The next morning, the defense case began with Eddie's friend, Mike Trimp, who testified that at E.J. Bugs, "Eddie scored on a—you know, he picked up a chick." He explained that while Eddie "was rapping with a chick," he and Dave left Eddie at the bar. He later saw "Eddie walking down the street with a lady," and "she had both arms around him."

---

14. Pat's testimony, however, did not indicate that Eddie had actually answered her question whether he would let her go without killing her if she did what he wanted. She did testify, however, that Eddie responded "yes" to her question whether he would let her go if she did what he wanted her to do.

"She was all over him, man," Mike said. "I figured he scored," he explained, "You go out with three guys. Somebody scores, you know. That's the way it is." He testified that when he later returned to the apartment he shared with Eddie, "no questions were asked, you know. We just laughed, and cut up a little bit, and that was about it."

Eddie's other friend, Dave Carroll, also testified, "She had her arms around him, and he had his arms around her; and she was kind of like, you know, snuggling up to him like." He indicated that when Mike called him the next day to tell him that Eddie was arrested for rape, "I couldn't believe it, you know. I said, 'That's crazy.'"

Eaton thought Eddie's friends, who had motley criminal records for assault, drunk driving, alcohol possession, and marijuana smuggling, made a horrendous impression on the jury. Eaton had put on their testimony to establish that Pat was behaving amorously when she left the bar with Eddie, but Mike's testimony especially made Eddie look like a jerk.[15]

Eddie then chose to take the stand. According to his testimony, he asked Pat to go home with him, she agreed, and they walked out of the bar with their arms around each other. En route, in the midst of talking about their children, she asked if he was going to rape or beat her, confessing that she had been raped before and that her husband had beaten her. He testified that she had the car keys the entire time, readily came up to the apartment after making out in the car, and had sex; only afterward did she get upset and cry. He said that he never threatened or attempted to strangle her. He testified that in addition to her complaint about guys being "all alike" and "just out for ... one thing," she "said something about her child. We had a discussion earlier in the car on the way to my apartment about her kid; and she said that she was going through some kind of proceeding about getting her child, and then I think she said something about losing her child." He denied ever taking the car keys, giving threatening looks, or choking her.

Salkin asked Eddie about his criminal record, using the permissible formula for inquiring about criminal convictions to impeach a witness's credibility: "Since the age of 18 when you had a lawyer, or told the judge you didn't want a lawyer, have you ever been convicted of any crimes?" Eddie answered, "Possession of marijuana, and a battery, possession and transporting." Salkin did not elicit further details in front of the jury, such detailed questioning about priors was impermissible.[16] In fact, Eddie was referring to three previous crimes: In addition to a marijuana possession conviction, he had a federal jury conviction for smuggling and transporting marijuana from back when he had moved to California and

---

15. Eaton Interview, *supra* note 7.
16. Salkin Interview II, *supra* note 9.

recruited his neighborhood buddies to come out and bring drugs from Mexico to Baltimore, in his ambition to make money as a drug dealer.[17] On a separate occasion he was also convicted by a jury of battery, "for grabbing someone."[18] Salkin asked Eddie who a certain "young lady" who was present in the courtroom was, and Eddie answered that she was his girlfriend.

Salkin thought that when Pat agreed to give Eddie a ride, Eddie's mindset was that he was going to "get some action," and then he wouldn't take no for an answer. There could be a thin line between consent and non-consent, and Salkin believed Eddie crossed it that night. Eddie appeared to think he was God's gift, and he had an attitude that such a big deal was being made over a one-night stand. In contrast, Pat came across as guileless, demure, and unfamiliar with the ways of the city. Salkin thought it was believable that this girl was truly scared in the circumstance she described.[19]

Salkin's closing argument repeated his refrain that

> this was the case of a foolish victim ... She was dumb. She was stupid, and you may all say to yourselves, she asked for it. She got what she asked for. Any person who has a little common sense wouldn't get themselves in this predicament. It was almost foreseeable what Mr. Rusk was after, when he asked her to give him a ride home. It was predictable, what was going to happen. Nonetheless, it happened and what happened was a crime.

He also said, "It's easy to cry rape. It's hard to prove, and rape is an unprosecuted crime, because of what you have to go through to press charges against someone for rape, the humiliation of the whole thing, to go before your peers, and tell all of those gory details that took place." Salkin recited the many things Pat could have done to get away from Eddie that night. But he asked the jurors not to decide based on what they, "sitting here calmly and collectively" knew they "could have done." Instead he asked them to consider decisions in their own lives that they had regretted. "We can all reflect back and see the errors of what we did; but it's at the time what you are capable of doing to alleviate the situation. What's going through your mind."

---

17. *See* Rusk v. U.S., 425 F.2d 262, 263 (9th Cir. 1970) (per curiam) (indicating that Rusk was "convicted by a jury of conspiracy to smuggle and transport, and with smuggling of marihuana into the United States"); Telephone Interview with Rigg Kennedy, First Cousin of Edward Rusk (Dec. 17, 2009) [hereinafter Kennedy Interview]; Riccobono Interview, *supra* note 4.

18. This battery conviction apparently arose from a fight with a man in a bar, not a domestic incident or violence against a woman. Cooke Interview, *supra* note 8; Kennedy Interview, *supra* note 17; Riccobono Interview, *supra* note 4.

19. Salkin Interview I, *supra* note 2.

Eaton too attempted to conscript common sense. His closing argument asked,

> Now, basically, what is the testimony here to make any case at all? I have scratched my brain to figure it out; but the only thing I can think of in the testimony is that ... Mr. Rusk was lightly strangling her. Now, I ask you to use your common sense here. A person who is strangled lightly—I'm not sure what that means.... They were kissing, and hugging, and I think that's exactly what happened.

Eaton emphasized the absence of "force, or violence, or anything that would lead you to believe that this act was done against somebody's will or consent. So why are we here?" Eaton then explained that the "only thing that leads me to think that we are here for a purpose is that [Pat] was in a divorce situation of some sort." He explained,

> It was after the sexual act was finished, and completed, and she was leaving that she realized that she had done a foolish thing, that it may have cost her custody of her child or whatnot. That, ladies and gentlemen, is the only motive that I can think of for calling the police and telling that she had been raped.

When Salkin came back for rebuttal, he reemphasized, "It's so easy to second guess people sitting at home, sitting in a jury, calmly and deliberatively, with no pressure on you.... But every time a woman drives a man home, do you have to presume that sex is going to take place? Is that an absolute natural consequence of that?" Salkin argued that it didn't make sense that Pat would tell Eddie in the car that she had been raped and beaten before, and even ask him if he was going to rape her, but then still agree to have sex with him.

> Why did he take the keys out of the ignition? Why is one and one two? He wasn't about to take no for an answer, when he asked her to go up to the apartment.

> Macho, that's why he's here today. He's got macho with him. His manhood was insulted. That's what this case is all about. So he took the keys out of his ignition. I forgot to ask how tall he is, and how much he weighs; and you can guess yourselves. She's no equal to him. He's certainly going to dominate her physically.

He asked the jury not to condemn her simply because "she did not act the way that you would like her to act.... Sure you know what to do now. Sure she knows what to do now; but she didn't do it." Why in the world would she subject herself to this trial if she had not in fact been raped? Salkin dismissed the child custody motivation that Eaton had raised by pointing out that Pat had reported the incident that very night and had not waited to see if her husband found out about it. Finally,

Salkin said, "It's just as much a rape case as when you are dragging somebody off the street, or breaking into their home, and raping them."

Salkin knew that a trial was like playing cards—you got dealt a hand and you played it. A good trial lawyer won some cases he wasn't supposed to win based on the cards he was showing. In this case he felt he had no more than an even chance.[20]

Twelve Hungry Men[21]

In the jury instructions on the rape charge, Judge Karwacki explained:

> Submission to a compelling force or as a result of being put in fear is not consent. A woman is not expected to resist an attack at the expense of her life, or at the risk of serious bodily harm.... The kind of fear in the mind of the victim, which would reasonably render resistance unnecessary to support a conviction of rape, includes ... a fear so extreme as to preclude resistance, or a fear which well might render her incapable of continuing to resist, or a fear that so overpowers her that she does not dare resist.

After Judge Karwacki sent the jurors to deliberate, they sent him two questions. First, "Did the victim have to verbally let the Defendant know that the act was against her will in order for him to know it was a rape?" Judge Karwacki answered no. Second, "When the victim was testifying, and she said something about, if I do what you want me to do, will you give me my keys back. What did she say his reply was?" The clerk read aloud the relevant portion of Pat's testimony, which indicated that Eddie had answered yes to her question, "If I do what you want, will you let me go?"

After three and a half hours of deliberation, the jury returned guilty verdicts on both the rape and the assault charges. Eaton was surprised. Ninety percent of cases he tried could go either way, depending on the jury. Here the verdict was due to Salkin's skill, he thought. With another jury, the verdict could easily have gone the other way.

At the sentencing hearing a month later, Eaton moved for a new trial, because the case was "devoid of any real indicia of force or violence.... [F]rankly, I think it was Mr. Salkin's eloquence in closing arguments that swayed the jury." Eaton told the Court, "I frankly was quite surprised at the verdict. I know the Defendant was surprised; and frankly, I think that the jury had to really stretch awfully far to come back with a guilty verdict in this case." The only evidence of force was the light choking, but Eaton suggested that in an embrace, Eddie "may

---

20. Salkin Interview II, *supra* note 9.

21. With thanks to my colleague Mark Roe.

have in fact had his hands around her neck in a caress . . . and I would submit that this lady may have just considered this in her own mind to have been a threat." Judge Karwacki denied the motion.

In the sentencing hearing, it came out that Eddie had omitted to mention at trial two other prior convictions for possession of drug paraphernalia. Eaton admitted that Eddie had had drug problems which "emanated from his attempt to make some money." But Eddie was now attempting to establish himself in business with his own store. Eddie was "not in true fact a rapist," he said, as he had no "pattern" of "sexual deviation problems, or emotional problems which would lead to the acting out form of rape." Eaton said, "This man has learned what can happen when you pick up somebody in a bar in Fell's Point and take her home." Eddie then spoke: "I know I've been in a lot of trouble but I feel that . . . if you were to send me to do any time, it wouldn't help me at all; . . . I'm just starting to get myself together. I've got the shop, and things are starting to go good for me."

Salkin told the Court that Eddie had been "diagnosed as being of an anti-social personality." Assuming that the Court would not be inclined to give the maximum sentence of twenty years, Salkin recommended, considering Eddie's "very, very poor background, as a Defendant in criminal cases, and as a person, and as the individual he is," that he be sentenced to fifteen years in prison. Eaton, however, argued that "to put him in jail . . . would be a waste, because this man knows now that risks are attached to being alone with a young lady." He submitted that the Court should give Eddie a suspended sentence. Eaton argued, "If he goes to jail now, he loses his business. He loses his girlfriend, his personal life, it's gone; and I don't know what might happen to him. So I would ask the Court to make him the holder of his own jail cell key, and let him decide whether he can make it or not."

Judge Karwacki sentenced Eddie to ten years imprisonment for the rape, and five years for the assault, to be served concurrently. He said Eddie had "demonstrated a pattern of anti-social conduct, since he was in his late teens." The instant offense fit the pattern of "demanding constant gratification for each of his current whims." He said, "He wanted something, and he took it. What he took in this case was something that the lady involved did not want to give. It was her province to make that decision. It's a very serious thing." Judge Karwacki said Eddie would have to "resolve his behavior," and that "he's only going to be able to do that with some real development of insight into who he is, and who he wants to be. Because, if he's released on the streets at this time, in my judgment, he's a danger to the community."

Some members of the jury that convicted him were horrified. One juror, Sallie Boswell, eventually confessed to the *Sun* paper that there

was "no question in my mind that the man was innocent." She recounted that when jury deliberations started at 12:30 in the afternoon, the
first poll was 7–5 for conviction. It became a "knock-down, drag-out
fight" between this elderly female juror arguing for acquittal and a
young male juror arguing for conviction. This division, in which a
woman favored acquittal and a man favored conviction, was not anomalous. Indeed, the somewhat surprising conventional legal wisdom is that
female jurors tend to judge female rape complainants more harshly than
do male jurors.[22]

Eventually four jurors, and then finally Boswell, the last holdout for
acquittal, gave in.[23] According to this final juror, the jury would not have
convicted if only it had eaten lunch. As deliberations wore on for hours
with no lunch break offered, she was starving. In an uncanny echo of the
victim's testimony of submission to pressure, the juror told the *Sun*:

> By 4 o'clock, with nothing in my stomach since the night before, I
> finally caved in.... I know I shouldn't have given in. I know now
> that I should have spoken up in the courtroom. I should have
> insisted on getting lunch, but I didn't know what else to do, so I
> voted for conviction. I didn't think he'd get such a heavy sentence.

A court official the *Sun* questioned about the jurors' hunger claimed
that skipping lunch was "one of the tactics judges use to discourage
unnecessarily lengthy deliberations." Judge Karwacki denied this, however. He didn't give the *Rusk* jury a break before the start of deliberations because "not everybody has his lunch hour at 12:30." He would
have sent the jurors food had they requested it.

The hungry juror was pricked by conscience. She said, "I couldn't
sleep for months afterwards, I felt so bad. I've even had dreams about it.
I just can't get over it." She and another juror "felt so guilty about
sending him to jail when we knew he was innocent." She prayed Rusk
would win his appeal.

Intermediate Appeal

Bond pending appeal was set at $5,000. Tommy Braden was the
clerk in the courtroom throughout the trial. He was shocked when the
jury returned a guilty verdict. He thought Eddie got a raw deal and

---

22. *See, e.g.*, Sandra Benlevy, *Venus and Mars in the Jury Deliberation Room:
Exploring the Differences That Exist Among Male and Female Jurors During the Deliberation Process*, 9 S. Cal. Rev. L. & Women's Stud. 445, 449–50 (2000) (examining jurors' post-
verdict interviews and authored accounts, and finding that "female jurors were unsympathetic toward rape victims when the victim's character was at issue").

23. *See* Matt Seiden, *Juror Regrets Hunger Led to Rape Conviction*, The Sun
(Baltimore), Oct. 22, 1979, at C1 (quoting juror Sallie R. Boswell) (internal quotation
marks omitted).

wanted to help him. As Eddie was about to be taken to jail, Tommy got on the phone to Barry Udoff, a bail bondsman with an office nearby, and asked him to help. Udoff would come right away, even if the defendant couldn't pay him immediately. Clerks generally did not refer bonds—that was certainly frowned upon—so Udoff took the unusual phone call as an indication of how strongly the clerk felt that he'd seen an injustice. He bailed Eddie out and sent him home.[24]

Based on Tommy's perception that Eddie was railroaded, Udoff wanted Eddie to have a top-flight lawyer for his appeal. Udoff's friend was Ira Cooke, an ambitious new associate at the prominent Baltimore law firm, Melnicove, Kaufman & Weiner. Udoff and Cooke lived in the same apartment building, had kids of similar ages, and often socialized together. A Manhattan native, Cooke had settled in Baltimore as a high school English teacher and guidance counselor at the Park School, and then completed law school at the University of Baltimore. Just starting his legal career, he had already assisted in his firm's high-profile criminal defense of Democratic Governor Marvin Mandel—the first Jewish governor of Maryland—in a trial that ended with a mail fraud and racketeering conviction (he would be pardoned by President Reagan and eventually have his conviction reversed).[25] Cooke hadn't yet had a jury trial or appellate case of his own. He jumped at the chance to have his first appellate argument, and took Eddie's appeal without expecting payment.[26]

Eddie's story amazed him. Cooke believed rape was a crime of violence, not a sexual act. Yet there wasn't any violent behavior in this story. Why didn't Pat use the telephone in the room to call for help when Eddie left for several minutes to go to the bathroom? Why didn't she knock on adjacent neighbors' doors? At least four other people lived on the same floor and a dozen in the apartment house. He thought if these questions had been highlighted at trial, the jury would have acquitted.[27]

Worse, he believed Eddie really was innocent. Cooke viewed what happened in sociological terms, as a severe culture clash between a white-bread, middle-class suburban Catholic school girl and a rougher blue-collar wise guy. It also didn't help that the Guilford Avenue place had been depicted as a pad that Eddie rented just for luring and hooking up with girls, though in reality Eddie was living there much of the

---

24. Telephone Interview with Barry Udoff, President, Fred W. Frank Bail Bonds (Dec. 15, 2009).

25. *See* Robert Timberg, *Mandel Portrait Hung in State House*, The Sun (Baltimore), Oct. 14, 1993. http://www.baltimoresun.com/news/maryland/politics/bal-portrait101493,0,134817.story

26. Cooke Interview, *supra* note 8.

27. *Id.*

time.[28] But the charge was second degree rape, which was vaginal intercourse "by force or threat of force against the will and without the consent of the other person."[29] It simply could not be correct that Pat's completely subjective fear was enough to convict Eddie of the crime of rape.

Cooke's brief in the Court of Special Appeals of Maryland argued there was insufficient evidence to support a rape conviction. The encounter was "an attempted seduction," not rape. Despite "not a single threat nor a scintilla of force," the woman "did nothing but docilely and voluntarily accompany" Rusk to the apartment. Her fear was "simply an unreasonable subjective reaction by the prosecutrix to a situation in which *she placed herself.*" The brief focused on how Pat could have avoided the compromising situation, such as screaming, fleeing, or calling for help. Cooke wrote, "She elected to do nothing. She acquiesced. She agreed. . . . She offered no resistance despite the total, complete and abject absence of any force or threats of force." If she acted from fear, that fear was "unreasonably exaggerated," not reasonable.[30]

In November 1978, soon after Rusk's conviction, a dynamic new attorney general had won election in Maryland. Stephen Sachs was an unabashed liberal progressive who hired, promoted, and mentored record numbers of female attorneys during his tenure. Out of a dozen and a half criminal appellate lawyers in his office, Kathleen Sweeney, a young assistant attorney general only three years out of the University of Baltimore Law School, was assigned to argue the case on behalf of the state. A liberal feminist (though, as she explains, not the "bra-burning" kind), she was on the board of the Women's Law Center, a Maryland legal services organization devoted to advancing women's rights through litigation and community education.[31]

Rusk was a routine appeal in which a convicted defendant argued that the evidence was legally insufficient to support a conviction. Sweeney's argument in response was straightforward: It was the province of the jury as finder of fact to believe or disbelieve witnesses, observe their demeanor, and judge their credibility. The jury heard the evidence and believed the defendant forced the victim to have sex. Moreover, Cooke's brief all but ignored a crucial fact, namely the testimony that right

---

28. Cooke Interview, *supra* note 8; Riccobono Interview, *supra* note 4.

29. State v. Rusk, 424 A.2d 720, 720 (Md. 1981) (quoting Md. Code art. 27, § 463(a)(1)). First degree rape was the same, but with the presence of one or more aggravating factors including use of a weapon, infliction or threat of serious physical injury, and assistance by one or more other persons. Md. Code Ann. art. 27, § 462 (Supp. 1976).

30. Brief of Appellant at 9, 12, 21, Rusk v. State, 406 A.2d 624 (Md. Ct. Spec. App. 1979) (No. 1249).

31. Telephone Interview with Kathleen M. Sweeney, Associate Judge, District Court of Maryland, District I, Baltimore City (Dec. 2, 2009) [hereinafter Sweeney Interview].

before intercourse, Rusk lightly choked her—that was force. That the victim had opportunities to avoid her fate was not the point. He had taken her car keys; was she supposed to flee into the night in an unfamiliar neighborhood? Even short of screams or escape attempts, the evidence was sufficient for a rape conviction. It was also tellingly inconsistent that Rusk was appealing his rape conviction on the theory of insufficient evidence of force, but he wasn't appealing his assault conviction—an implicit admission that the encounter involved force. Sweeney didn't think the appellate court would have difficulty affirming the conviction.[32]

But after oral argument before a three-judge panel of the Court of Special Appeals came the surprising news that rather than issuing a panel decision, the Court would rehear the case en banc. The panel had voted 2–1 to affirm the conviction, and though most panel decisions went unreported, the judge who voted to reverse submitted the case for publication. The entire court then conferenced the case—a procedure designed to ensure that a case that would be binding precedent not be decided by only two judges—and determined that all thirteen judges should rehear the case.[33] Only a few times since the court's creation in 1966 had the entire court sat en banc. This unusual step meant *Rusk* was becoming a more significant case than the lawyers had realized.[34]

Sweeney's friend Deborah Chasanow (then Deborah Handel), a mere four years out of Stanford Law School, became chief of criminal appeals under Attorney General Sachs. The two women were aware that women were still somewhat of a novelty and unwelcome in some quarters of the legal profession. In Sachs's office, they were entrusted with a lot of responsibility, particularly in criminal cases. It was a heady place to be a young lawyer.[35]

Chasanow helped Sweeney prepare for oral argument. They wanted to keep the Court focused on the province of the jury.

At oral argument, in front of the thirteen judges, not one of them a woman, Cooke argued that the victim was unreasonable to feel so afraid that she had to submit to sex. He suggested that what the victim saw as light choking could have been a "heavy caress." He was trying to shift the issue from the *credibility* of what she said at trial to the *reasonableness* of how she perceived and reacted to the situation. This move had its

32. *Id.*; Brief of Appellee at 7, Rusk v. State, 406 A.2d 624 (Md. Ct. Spec. App. 1979) (No. 1249).

33. Telephone Interview with Alan M. Wilner, Retired Judge, Court of Appeals of Maryland (Dec. 3, 2009) [hereinafter Wilner Interview].

34. Cooke Interview, *supra* note 8; Sweeney Interview, *supra* note 31.

35. Telephone Interview with Deborah K. Chasanow, Judge, U.S. District Court for the District of Maryland (Dec. 3, 2009) [hereinafter Chasanow Interview].

lineage in the tradition of putting the rape victim on trial. It took enormous courage for a victim to report a rape because she was often scrutinized, blamed, and discredited in the legal process. Questioned by the judges whether the law of rape demanded that the victim's fear be reasonable, Sweeney criticized Maryland precedents that did so require and asked the Court to overrule them. The rapist took his victim as he found her.

Sweeney and Chasanow stood over the fax machine as it slowly pulsed out the decision of the en banc appellate court. As the two women read one page after another, they looked at each other in shock. They had lost. Not only had the Court reversed Rusk's conviction. The tone of the majority opinion was stunning.[36]

The Court's decision split 8–5. Writing for the majority was Judge Charles Awdry Thompson (he was nearly seventy years old and died three years later). Considering whether the light choking and being in a strange part of town late at night were "sufficient to overcome the will of a normal twenty-one year old married woman," Judge Thompson wrote, "We are not impressed with the argument." The "prosecutrix" said she was afraid and submitted because of "the look in his eyes." The Court supposed that the light choking could have been, as Cooke had suggested, a "heavy caress." All these facts and circumstances were insufficient "to cause a reasonable fear which overcame her ability to resist." Such lack of resistance meant there was insufficient evidence of the force necessary for a rape conviction.

Baltimore lawyers often associated judges' sensibilities with their geographical origins. Those from Maryland's urban areas tended to be more liberal and have less of the good-old-boy feel than those from rural areas. As if to reflect this basic social split of a small state, Judge Thompson hailed from the conservative Eastern Shore, and Judge Alan Wilner, who wrote for the five dissenters, came from a liberal Jewish neighborhood in northwest Baltimore City.[37]

The dissent began by stating "profound conviction" that the majority had "made a serious mistake."[38] The court's "baby" judge at forty two, Wilner was appointed to the bench from service as chief legislative aide to Democratic Governor Mandel.[39] When Maryland ratified the Equal Rights Amendment in 1972, the Governor had appointed Wilner

---

36. Sweeney Interview, *supra* note 31.

37. *Id.*; Cooke Interview, *supra* note 8; Wilner Interview, *supra* note 33.

38. *Id.*

39. *See* Lawrence F. Rodowsky, *Judge Alan M. Wilner, Public Servant: The Man Who Needs No Sleep*, 66 Md. L. Rev. 835, 838 (2007); David A. Maraniss, *Mandel Chief Aide Wilner Named to Appeals Court*, Wash. Post, June 23, 1977, at C2.

to a commission to implement it.[40] With that experience, he got a sense of the women's movement's goals, particularly the legal reform of sex offenses, one of the main projects of the commission.[41]

Judge Wilner, who had teenage daughters, had seen some rape cases before *Rusk* and was appalled at how judges often treated them, with little regard for what the victim was facing. The mindset of many older judges and lawyers was not much different from Sir Matthew Hale's seventeenth-century pronouncement that "rape is ... an accusation easily to be made and hard to be proved, and harder to be defended by the party accused, tho never so innocent."[42] When Judge Wilner read the circulated majority opinion, he thought enough was enough. The zeitgeist of the time was to reconsider many of the traditional views in the law. It was obvious the case would go up to the state's highest court, so it was important for him to lay out the other side.[43]

Judge Wilner's dissent focused on two points. The first was appellate restraint. In reversing the conviction, the majority substituted its own judgment of the evidence and invaded the province of the jury and trial judge. He wrote:

> We know nothing about Pat and appellant. We don't know how big they are, what they look like, what their life experiences have been. We don't know if appellant is larger or smaller than she, stronger or weaker. We don't know what the inflection was in his voice as he dangled her car keys in front of her. We can't tell whether this was in a jocular vein or a truly threatening one. We have no idea what his mannerisms were. The trial judge and the jury could discern some of these things, of course, because they could observe the two people in court and could listen to what they said and how they said it.

The second point was that the majority gave "new life to myths about the crime of rape that have no place in our law today." Wilner rebuked the majority for insinuating that Pat was "on the make," and that someone who had to wonder whether to report such an incident hadn't really been raped. Indeed Pat had explained that her hesitation was because she "didn't want to go through what I'm going through now." It was precisely the kind of callous attitude evinced in the majority opinion that made victims reluctant to report rape.

---

40. Rodowsky, *supra* note 39, at 838.

41. Wilner Interview, *supra* note 33. *See Legislation: Rape and Other Sexual Offense Law Reform in Maryland 1976–77*, 7 Balt. L. Rev. 151, 151 n.3 (1977).

42. 1 Matthew Hale, *The History of the Pleas of the Crown* *635 (1778).

43. Wilner Interview, *supra* note 33.

Judge Wilner held courts responsible for "ignorance and misunderstandings" about rape. He explained that while courts expected a rape victim to resist when attacked, studies showed that resistance was dangerous. Even government pamphlets advised that fighting back could provoke severe bodily harm. Thus Pat "offered the very type of verbal resistance that is prudent, common, and recommended by law enforcement agencies." Whether the fear that prevented her from resisting in other ways was reasonable was for the jury to determine, not the appellate court.

Finally, Judge Wilner said the majority "countermanded the judgment of the trial court and jury and declared Pat to have been, in effect, an adulteress." This criticism of the mention of her marital status brushed up against the story Eaton had told at trial about Pat's incentive to think of what happened as rape. This alleged motivation grew out of the mutually exclusive legal relation of rape and adultery—a byproduct of the traditional regulation of sex in which no legal sex could be had outside of marriage. If the sex was not rape, it would instead be consensual sex outside marriage, that is, adultery. Conversely, if it was rape, it would not be adultery.[44] As Eaton had explained, the trial testimony revealed that the distinction may have been important to Pat because she suspected her husband of trying to catch her in adultery, so as to win an advantage in a child custody fight.[45] Legally, the only way the events of that night would not be adultery for child custody purposes was if she was raped.

Though Rusk's trial had passed without notice outside the courthouse, the reversal of his conviction immediately drew public attention. For days the *Sun* paper ran articles reporting both criticism and praise of the decision.[46] Jurors who convicted Rusk, including the forewoman, came forward to say they were glad to see his conviction reversed.[47] Much press attention focused on the ambiguity of whether the facts of the case could be interpreted as seduction rather than rape. One reporter called Rusk's taking the keys out of the ignition "a little stunt I've seen a dozen times in the movies and since incorporated in the male hand-

---

44. *See* Anne M. Coughlin, *Sex and Guilt*, 84 Va. L. Rev. 1 (1998) (arguing that rape law's suspicion of rape complainants reflects the traditional legal regulation of sex, in which rape was a defense available to relieve women of criminal responsibility for consensual nonmarital sex—adultery and fornication).

45. *See, e.g.*, Davis v. Davis, 372 A.2d 231, 235 (Md. 1977) (holding that adultery is a relevant consideration in child custody awards but does not result in a presumption of parental unfitness).

46. *See, e.g.*, J.S. Bainbridge, Jr., *Rape Guilt Rules Set by High Court*, The Sun (Baltimore), Oct. 11, 1979, at D1.

47. *See* Seiden, *supra* note 23.

book of sexual etiquette."[48] Was he dangling them like "a suave Clark Gable," or more like a terrifying "Anthony Perkins"?[49]

The Court's decision was called "a major setback for the women's movement in its fight against the crime of rape."[50] Law enforcement and rape counseling organizations raised alarm that the decision would make rape convictions more difficult and deter women from reporting an already underreported crime.[51] Most rapes occurred in precisely this situation, between people who came into contact voluntarily. It was now the standard advice of rape prevention programs not to fight a rapist lest the victim be more seriously hurt or even killed.[52] The national trend was decidedly moving away from the traditional inquiry into whether the victim resisted.[53] But the Court was now saying women had to fight or else they wouldn't be considered rape victims, even if they did just what experts thought was appropriate.[54] Judge Wilner's dissent was immediately praised.[55] Women's groups even sent him letters of appreciation.[56]

Some time after Eddie won his appeal, he was walking down a Baltimore street. When he saw Pat, he traversed the street to face her. Angrily, he told her that his parents were forced to spend a fortune on his appeal because of her.[57] To the reporter who had written an article about his case in the *Sun* titled "Court Was Right to Throw out Rape Conviction,"[58] and also exposed the story of the hungry juror,[59] Eddie promptly wrote a letter:

---

48. Richard Cohen, *"Reasonable Fear" Ruling on Rape is Shocker*, Wash. Post, Oct. 16, 1979, at B1.

49. *See* Matt Seiden, *Court Was Right to Throw Out Rape Conviction*, The Sun (Baltimore), Oct. 22, 1979, at C1. One recalls Clark Gable's leading man in *Gone With the Wind* (Selznick Int'l Pictures 1939), and Anthony Perkins's title role in *Psycho* (Paramount Pictures 1960).

50. Seiden, *supra* note 49.

51. *See* Sandy Banisky, *Court's Rape Ruling Angers Counselors: "Reasonable Fear" Proviso Attacked*, The Sun (Baltimore), Oct. 12, 1979, at D1; Saundra Saperstein, *Md. Ruling Will Restrict Provable Rape Cases, Lawyers Say*, Wash. Post, Oct. 12, 1979, at C1.

52. *See* Banisky, *supra* note 51.

53. *See* Scott Flander, *Rape Ruling Condemned Locally*, Evening Capital, Oct. 13, 1979, at 1; Saperstein, *supra* note 51.

54. *See* Banisky, *supra* note 51.

55. *See, e.g.*, Leigh Bienen, *Rape III—National Developments in Rape Reform Legislation*, 6 Women's Rts. L. Rep. 170, 181 n. 66 (1980) (calling Wilner's dissent "knowledgeable").

56. Wilner Interview, *supra* note 33.

57. Kennedy Interview, *supra* note 17.

58. Seiden, *supra* note 49.

59. Seiden, *supra* note 23.

I'm glad that their [sic] was someone concerned enough to look past their nose at the circumstances of my case. What a nightmare. For the past two years you can't imagine what I've been through. My friends stuck behind me all the way. But it's funny how people who don't even know you personally, can make you feel like you have a contagious disease.[60]

He asked the reporter for help finding information about a fund that would help pay his legal bills in the event he'd have to defend against a further appeal:

It cost me a lot of money to get this far. Now their [sic] is talk by the Wemon's [sic] Movement to take my case to the Supreme Court. If this is true I have to pay my own way. "I don't think it's fair." A friend told me about the Playboy Foundation. It's suppose [sic] to be an organization set up by Playboy magazine to help people like myself.

The reporter answered his letter in two days, saying he would see what he could find out about the Playboy fund and promising, "If I've got any news for you, I'll give you a call."[61]

Highest Appeal

In the Attorney General's Office, Sweeney and Chasanow wrote a petition for certiorari to the state's highest court. The Court of Appeals's conference discussion on whether to grant cert in *Rusk* was very contentious. The custom was to reserve cert grants for cases of legal importance, but *Rusk* was a fact-bound appeal asking the Court to find there was insufficient evidence for a conviction. The case did not appear to present a significant broader issue of law. But the case was garnering a lot of press coverage, indicating important public interest. Three out of seven judges voted to grant cert, which was all it took.[62]

The two women assistant attorneys general proposed that Sachs argue the case in the Court of Appeals himself. Having the Attorney General personally argue a seemingly run-of-the-mill appeal arising from a two-day criminal jury trial would send a strong message that much was at stake. There were some old men on that court and they needed to be educated. *Rusk* was one of only a handful of cases Sachs chose to argue personally in the Court of Appeals during his tenure as attorney general.

---

60.   Letter from Edward S. Rusk to Matt Seiden (Oct. 22, 1979) (on file with author).

61.   Letter from Matt Seiden to Edward S. Rusk (Oct. 24, 1979) (on file with author).

62.   Telephone Interview with John C. Eldridge, Retired Judge, Maryland Court of Appeals (Dec. 29, 2009) [hereinafter Eldridge Interview]; *see also* Md. Code Ann., Cts. & Jud. Proc. § 12–203 (West 2009) (providing that the Court of Appeals shall grant certiorari if it finds review "desirable and in the public interest," and that the number of judges required to grant "may not exceed three").

which otherwise consisted of arguments in federal court, including three successful ones in the U.S. Supreme Court.[63]

The position of attorney general in Maryland was traditionally filled by someone who essentially ran as a running mate to the candidate for governor. Sachs however had won election on his own, without being the "French Fries to a Big Mac." The former U.S. Attorney for Maryland, he ran for attorney general with the campaign slogan, "I'm *your* lawyer." He promised a new, proactive kind of attorney generalship representing the people.

Sachs thought the *Rusk* jury reached the right result, but he recognized it was a close case under current law. It was a case with which to confront the mistreatment of victims that haunted the administration of rape law. The strength of his case lay in the invocation of traditional judicial principles of appellate restraint and respect for the institutional role of jury. But Sachs's principal interest was not in these procedural points. Rather it was in the substantive law and policy at issue: women were entitled to be respected and believed, as victims of rape no less than any other crime. As an elected official who would soon run for governor, he knew the case was politically good for him to take on. The women's movement was in flower, and women's groups were an important constituency. Though ten years earlier he might have thought the movement was a fad, he was now an unapologetic feminist. He was married to a feminist lawyer and he had a daughter. He was proud that three generations of his family's women—wife, daughter, and mother-in-law—marched together for abortion rights.

When the opposing sides set out to write an agreed statement of facts for briefing in the Court of Appeals, they disagreed about how the statement should refer to Pat. Cooke called her the "prosecutrix." But Sweeney thought she should be called the "victim"—to Sweeney's ears, "prosecutrix" was derogatory. Courts had the habit of using the term for rape complainants but almost never for other kinds of crime victims. It perversely sounded like a prosecutorial version of a dominatrix, yet it referred to a woman who was far from that, a victim of sexual domination. The term proved to be more of a sticking point than the facts. The two sides eventually compromised on something more neutral: they would call Pat the "prosecuting witness."[64]

The Attorney General's brief strongly emphasized Pat's alarm, terror, intimidation, paralysis, and helplessness. It played up Eddie's commandeering of her car keys, and repeatedly mentioned the strange,

63. Telephone Interview with Stephen H. Sachs, Retired Partner, WilmerHale (Dec. 4, 2009).

64. *See* Brief of Appellant at 3, State v. Rusk, 424 A.2d 720 (Md. 1981) (No. 142); Sweeney Interview, *supra* note 31.

threatening, menacing "look in his eyes." The brief acknowledged the existence of several plausible interpretations of events. But "[i]t was the jury ... which was best able to weigh the impact of 'the look in his eyes' because it was the jury which saw those eyes. It was only the jury which could evaluate the meaning of 'light choking.' " The reasonableness of her fear could not be gauged from a cold transcript; the jury had effectively found her fear reasonable. The brief attacked the intermediate appellate court for belittling the light choking, for mocking her hesitation to report the crime, and for "skepticism drawn from its own experience, imagination and preconceptions in order to supplant the jury's judgment with its own." This was judicial activism.[65]

Cooke began to receive invitations to speak publicly about *Rusk* and was often greeted by highly critical audiences. Egocentric by his own account with a sense of invincibility, he began to realize this was becoming a significant case of social policy, rising well beyond his client's conviction—but Eddie himself hadn't had a clue in the world that he was committing rape. Cooke had not seen a judicial opinion making as much use of non-legal sources as Judge Wilner's dissent. Cooke perceived the Attorney General as a cutting-edge liberal activist, and this case was for the left wing of his constituency. Eddie was getting caught in a perfect storm of a social movement.[66]

Cooke took a close look at the seven judges on the Court of Appeals and set out to tailor his argument to the ones he could win. Rita Charmatz Davidson was the first and only woman on the Court—a dyed-in-the-wool feminist out of liberal Montgomery County. Harry Cole was the first and only African American judge on the Court, and very liberal. Lawrence Rodowsky was known to be close with Rusk's trial judge, Karwacki, a fellow Pole. Cooke expected to lose these three judges' votes. But he expected to pick up the remaining four judges, who he thought were good-old-boy types.

With women's groups and rape-counseling organizations in attendance at oral argument, he stood and said, "May it please the Court, my name is Ira C. Cooke." Judge Rita Davidson cut him off, he recalls. "I know who you are, Mr. Cooke, and I've been waiting for a year to have this conversation with you." He saw that the judges expected the lone woman on the Court to take the active lead in questioning. She chastised him for suggesting that "light choking" or even a "heavy caress" in a moment of passion was not force. Cooke got softballs from the rest.

Attorney General Sachs knew all the judges personally, some very well. He'd been friends with Rita Davidson for over a decade, from before her judicial appointment. Both were left-wing Jews in Maryland

---

65. *See* Brief of Appellant at 12–17, State v. Rusk, 424 A.2d 720 (Md. 1981) (No. 142).

66. Cooke Interview, *supra* note 8.

Democratic politics who attended Yale Law School, she in the 1940s and he in the 1950s. There was no question how she would vote here.[67]

At oral argument, Sachs was particularly sensitive to the presence of Judge Rodowsky, his former law partner from private practice, and Chief Judge Robert Murphy, whom he knew well from public service. He thought those two were the "real lawyers" on the Court and would be receptive to his institutional argument about the roles of juries and appellate courts.[68]

He was right. The Court of Appeals' decision was 4–3 to reinstate the conviction. The majority opinion by Chief Judge Murphy explicitly embraced Judge Wilner's dissent in the intermediate court. While it was correct to require that a victim's fear be reasonable, the Court held, the question of reasonableness was for the jury, and a jury could rationally find the elements of rape established here, "with particular focus on the actual force applied by Rusk to Pat's neck." A victim's resistance was unnecessary where she was restrained by fear of violence. "Just where persuasion ends and force begins in cases like the present is essentially a factual issue."

Judge Cole's impassioned dissent is now infamous:

While courts no longer require a female to resist to the utmost or to resist where resistance would be foolhardy, they do require her acquiescence in the act of intercourse to stem from fear generated by something of substance. She may not simply say, "I was really scared," and thereby transform consent or mere unwillingness into submission by force. These words do not transform a seducer into a rapist. She must follow the natural instinct of every proud female to resist, by more than mere words, the violation of her person by a stranger or an unwelcomed friend. She must make it plain that she regards such sexual acts as abhorrent and repugnant to her natural sense of pride.

Judge Cole thought there was no evidence here inconsistent with "ordinary seduction of a female acquaintance who at first suggests her disinclination." He belittled her testimony that Rusk " 'started lightly to choke' her, whatever that means." Judge Cole didn't see evidence that the fear that constrained her from resisting was created by anything the defendant did. He said, "[T]his was not a child. This was a married woman with children, a woman familiar with the social setting in which these two met." Getting out of her car and walking up to his room,

67. Telephone Interview with Stephen H. Sachs, Retired Partner, WilmerHale (Jan. 8, 2010) (hereinafter Sachs Interview).

68. *Id.*

"[s]he certainly had to realize that they were not going upstairs to play Scrabble."

Despite the vocal mobilization of women's groups around the case after his victory below, Cooke had thought the Court of Appeals would decide in his favor. As expected, Cooke lost Davidson and Rodowsky, but he couldn't understand how he lost good-old-boys Murphy and Eldridge. He thought Davidson, the Court's first woman, must have lobbied them to make up the majority.[69] Unbeknownst to Cooke, however, Eldridge was one of the judges who had voted to grant certiorari in *Rusk*, and was no stranger to the women's movement. As Governor Mandel's chief counsel in the early 1970s, Eldridge had taken a leading role in making Maryland one of the first states to ratify the federal Equal Rights Amendment and to pass its own, which he drafted.[70]

The unexpected dissent by Judge Cole, the first African American on the Court, was also intriguing. Cole was generally protective of the rights of criminal defendants, but it was a surprise to Cooke that that tendency would predominate here.[71] Cooke thought the Court was engaged in a most dangerous sort of judicial activism. It seemed that rape had in effect become a strict liability offense. A woman's subjective fear was now enough to convict a man of rape—even a guy who had no idea he was doing anything wrong. By recasting regular dating behavior as the crime of rape, the forces of the women's movement, in concert with legal elites, were flipping the rules of engagement. They flipped them on Eddie Rusk.

After the Case

Women's groups prominently celebrated the Court of Appeals decision in the press. It was called a "vote in favor of women being believed."[72] The president of the Women's Law Center called the decision "terrific," because it "recognizes the current-day realities of life."[73] Cooke told the *Sun* that Rusk was "a victim of changing social times and changing social attitudes about relationships between men and women. . . . Rusk is a guy caught in the middle of a changing time. That's his only crime."[74]

---

69. Cooke Interview, *supra* note 8.

70. Eldridge Interview, *supra* note 62.

71. Cooke Interview, *supra* note 8.

72. Scott Flander, *High Court Reversal in Rape Case Hailed*, Evening Capital (Annapolis), Jan. 14, 1981, at 33 (quoting Karen Goldman Lyon, head of the Sexual Offense Crisis Center) (internal quotation marks omitted).

73. *Women's Groups Praise Court's Ruling on Rape*, The Post (Frederick), Jan. 15, 1981, at D–8 (quoting Sally Gold) (internal quotation marks omitted).

74. Michael Olesker, *Edward Rusk: Rapist or Victim?*, The Sun (Baltimore), Mar. 1, 1981, at B1 (internal quotation marks omitted).

Eddie's cousin, a struggling actor in Hollywood, attempted to pitch a biopic about him to some screenwriters he knew.[75] Popular liberal *Sun* columnist Michael Olesker got a pitch from an "agent" who told him:

> This guy is hot. He's a character. He's crazy. You gotta meet him, you'll love him. You gotta write about him. What we're gonna do, we're gonna make a commodity out of him. We're gonna market him. We're gonna do a book, right? And then we're gonna do a movie. We figured it out already. For the movie, we want Cindy Williams as the girl, and Donald Sutherland to play Rusk.... Rusk's the victim, man.[76]

Cooke was about to take Eddie to surrender himself for his prison sentence but still had not relinquished the thought that he could get him a new trial. Olesker's *Sun* column gave him an idea.[77] The column included an interview with the victim. Pat was quoted saying she was "easily frightened" and that she left her husband "because he kept beating me up." She said that night with Rusk she couldn't scream because he choked her to keep her quiet; the only reason she testified in court that the choking was "light" was that the prosecutor told her not to bring up the choking because she didn't have any marks on her neck.[78] In her first public mention of the marks, she now claimed the police didn't note the marks because "they were getting ready to get off duty. They were changing shifts. They were in a rush to get off, and they really didn't care."[79] Prosecutor James Salkin, however, told the *Sun* that the victim said even that night there were no marks, and that he instructed her not to embellish the story in court.[80]

The column quoted Rusk as well: "Look, she didn't give in a hundred percent. I mean, what girl does? I mean, she didn't just lay down and say, take me. It was like, you know, you've been to bed with women, and they have second thoughts." Asked about the choking, he said "I might have had my hands anywhere . . . I was just getting down with her.... But I didn't rape her. I don't do that. I could bring in a thousand girls I've known and didn't rape."[81]

---

75. Kennedy Interview, *supra* note 17.

76. Michael Olesker, *Convicted Rapist Gets Agent—Watch For Movie at Your Local Theater*, The Sun (Baltimore), Feb. 8, 1981, at B1 (quoting Rusk's agent) (internal quotation marks omitted).

77. Cooke Interview, *supra* note 8.

78. Olesker, *supra* note 76 (internal quotation marks omitted); Olesker, *supra* note 74.

79. Olesker, *supra* note 76 (internal quotation marks omitted).

80. Olesker, *supra* note 74.

81. Olesker, *supra* note 76. (internal quotation marks omitted).

With little popular sympathy for his client, and outflanked by the power of both the state and the press, Cooke seized on deviations of Pat's printed interview from her trial testimony. He filed a motion for a new trial claiming she had recanted her testimony, and he sought access to Olesker's notes of the interview. Cooke felt overwhelmed when the *Sun*'s top First Amendment lawyers came to court to oppose his request for the notes. The judge came up with a Solomonic ruling: Olesker had to answer questions on the stand and read aloud from his notes, but Cooke was not allowed to examine the notes himself.[82]

Olesker thought this litigation was a desperate publicity stunt.[83] But Cooke believed (and still believes) that had the *Sun* produced those notes, he could have gotten Eddie a new trial.[84] After three decades as a respected and provocative columnist, Olesker resigned from the *Sun* in 2006 when it came to light that some of his columns used language from other journalists' work without attribution.[85] Cooke now suspects that the column about *Rusk* embellished the victim's words to make the incident seem more violent.

Some time after *Rusk*, Maryland's appellate judges—the thirteen on the Court of Special Appeals, and the seven on the Court of Appeals— were all invited to a party at the Governor's house. Judge Wilner, author of the dissent in the intermediate court, recalls that Judge Cole, the dissenter in the highest court, approached and started "giving him the business" about his opinion in *Rusk*. That is, until Mrs. Cole overheard and started giving her husband the business about *his* opinion in the case.[86]

One morning as Eddie was preparing to begin his prison sentence, his aunt called and told him to turn on the television. Pat was on a talk show talking about *his* case.[87]

A Crime of Violence

State v. Rusk came at the turning point of a massive legal revolution in relations between American men and women.[88] In the period between

---

82. Cooke Interview, *supra* note 8; Telephone Interview with Michael Olesker, Writer (Dec. 17, 2009) [hereinafter Olesker Interview].

83. Olesker Interview, *supra* note 82.

84. Cooke Interview, *supra* note 8.

85. Howard Kurtz, *Sun Columnist Dismissed; Attribution Issues Cited*, Wash. Post, Jan. 5, 2006, at C4.

86. Wilner Interview, *supra* note 33.

87. Riccobono Interview, *supra* note 4; Email from Ira C. Cooke, Former Attorney, to Jeannie Suk, Assistant Professor of Law, Harvard Law School (Dec. 20, 2009) (on file with author).

88. Cassia Spohn & Julie Horney, *Rape Law Reform: A Grassroots Revolution and Its Impact* 17 (1992) ("In the past twenty years, we have witnessed a virtual revolution in rape

the 1977 incident in the Guilford Avenue apartment and the 1981 decision of the Maryland Court of Appeals, the women's movement was making major progress nationally in the reform of rape law.[89] Feminist critique of the 1970s had brought attention to rape and the myriad problems of traditional sexism that beset its adjudication.[90] By the time *Rusk* was decided in 1981, every state had considered and most states had passed some rape reform laws.[91] Among the basic reforms debated was the substantive definition of the crime and how the crime was proven. These reforms implicated fundamental questions of what sexual relations between men and women should be.

Rape at common law was "carnal knowledge of a female forcibly and against her will."[92] Proof of the required elements of force and nonconsent inevitably focused factual inquiry on whether the woman physically resisted the man's advances. Without evidence of her "utmost resistance," "earnest resistance," or at least "reasonable resistance," the prosecution would fail to establish either or both of the required elements, making it difficult to almost impossible to get a rape conviction.[93] Though eventually most states eliminated the *requirement* that a rape victim resist her attacker, her resistance or lack thereof was still relevant in the proof of force or nonconsent.

Abolition of the resistance inquiry was one of the rape reform movement's most important goals.[94] Advocates were increasingly convincing legislatures, courts, and law enforcement officials that the victim's resistance should be not only unnecessary to prove rape, but also discouraged because it increased her risk of bodily harm or death.[95] Many legal actors, institutions, and scholars were adopting the view that resistance was dangerous.[96] This became the position of many police

---

law in the United States."); *cf.* Jeannie Suk, *At Home in the Law: How the Domestic Violence Revolution is Transforming Privacy* (2009).

89. Spohn & Horney, *supra* note 88, at 20 (calling rape reform "a key item on the feminist agenda").

90. *See, e.g.,* Susan Brownmiller, *Against Our Will: Men, Women, and Rape* (1975). Major targets of feminist critique of rape law included the requirement that a rape victim resist her attacker; the requirement that a rape victim's testimony be corroborated by another witness; the refusal to punish rape by a husband; the impeaching of victims' testimony with evidence of prior sexual conduct; and the definition of rape to require physical force. For a review of rape reform goals, see Spohn & Horney, *supra* note 88.

91. *See* Bienen, *supra* note 55, at 171.

92. 4 William Blackstone, *Commentaries* *210.

93. *See* Michelle J. Anderson, *Reviving Resistance in Rape Law*, 1998 U. Ill. L. Rev. 953, 962–65.

94. *Id.* at 974.

95. *See id.* at 968–69.

96. *See id.* at 968–80.

departments, the U.S. Department of Justice, and the American Law Institute.[97]

Judge Wilner's dissent in the Court of Special Appeals reflected this tide against a proof-of-resistance requirement in rape law. But today Judge Wilner believes his opinion's reliance on then existing studies purporting to show that resistance was inadvisable has turned out to be incorrect; later studies have purported to show that fighting back rather than remaining passive increased chances of avoiding rape, and that victims of completed rape were more seriously injured than victims of attempted rape.[98] Studies have also claimed that victims' resistance, compared to passivity, is correlated with decreased psychological injury.[99] It is, however, open to serious question whether empirical studies (particularly those purporting to use quantitative data), given their inherent limitations, could provide sound support for a resistance doctrine or for instructions on whether to resist a would-be rapist.[100]

Shifting empirical claims notwithstanding, reformers' initial beliefs about the dangers of resistance served a more general rape reform agenda, which was to move the focus of inquiry away from what the victim did or did not do, and toward the conduct of the defendant. The systematic mistreatment of rape complainants, in the tradition of putting the victim on trial and suggesting her dubious sexual virtue, provoked the reform movement for passage of rape shield laws that now limit the extent to which victims can be cross-examined about their sexual history.[101]

---

97. *See* Nat'l Inst. of Law Enforcement and Criminal Justice, *Forcible Rape: A National Survey of the Response by Police* 22 (1977) (reporting results of a study indicating that "[r]ape victims who resisted were more likely to be injured than ones who did not"); Rusk v. State, 406 A.2d 624, 635 n.15 (Md. Ct. Spec. App. 1979) (citing a police pamphlet advising that "attempts at self-defense, such as screaming, kicking, scratching . . . usually have provoked the rapist into inflicting severe bodily harm on the victim"); Model Penal Code § 213.1 (1980) ("[R]esistance may prove an invitation to danger of death or serious bodily harm.").

98. Wilner Interview, *supra* note 33. *See also* Anderson, *supra* note 93, at 981–82 (citing Pauline B. Bart & Patricia H. O'Brien, *Stopping Rape: Successful Survival Strategies* 33, 35, 42–43 (1985); M. Joan McDermott, U.S. Dep't of Justice, *Rape Victimization in 26 American Cities* 38, 40, 43 (1979); Gary Kleck & Susan Sayles, *Rape and Resistance*, 37 Soc. Probs. 149, 160 (1990)).

99. *See* Anderson, *supra* note 93, at 987–91 (citing studies).

100. Studies comparing injuries suffered by victims of completed rape to those suffered by victims of attempted rape may provide little information about whether encouraging potential victims to resist reduces injury. The links from such encouragement to physical resistance to a reduced chance of a completed rape are difficult to study. For example, it is hard to see how statistical techniques could adequately account for the possibility that women who would be inclined to resist may be inherently less likely to suffer physical or psychological injury than those who would be inclined to be passive.

101. *See, e.g.*, Michelle J. Anderson, *From Chastity Requirement to Sexuality License: Sexual Consent and a New Rape Shield Law*, 70 Geo. Wash. L. Rev. 51 (2002); Vivian D.

The lingering attitude that such reforms meant to address was on display in Judge Cole's dissent, which found Pat's behavior to fall short of that of a genuine rape victim. His litany of what a woman "must" do if she was legally to "transform a seducer into a rapist" demanded that she "follow the natural instinct of every proud female to resist, by more than mere words, the violation of her person," and "make it plain that she regards such sexual acts as abhorrent and repugnant to her natural sense of pride." Twenty or perhaps even ten years earlier, these sentiments might have been in the judicial mainstream. By 1981, they were becoming antiquated and time has not been kind to them since. Indeed a common reaction of today's readers to Judge Cole's recounting of the victim's testimony that Rusk " 'started lightly to choke' her, whatever that means," and his remark that she "certainly had to realize that they were not going upstairs to play Scrabble," is revulsion at how recently and openly judges evinced such dismissive and disrespectful attitudes.

Still, the ideas embedded in these sarcastic formulations implicate the problems with which rape reformers have grappled. Reformers noticed that the law did not prohibit much intercourse that many women experienced as nonconsensual where the intercourse did not involve what the law deemed to be force or threat of force. There was too often a discrepancy between female experience and the law's definition of rape—especially among acquaintances. If the traditional rapist was an armed stranger in a dark alley, rape reform raised the salience of the unwelcome sexual advance by a date or a friend. Moreover, a range of socially acceptable, even expected, male dating behavior—nonviolent intimidation, aggressive pressure to have sex, sex with an intoxicated woman, sex with an unequal in power—might be criminally regulated, as rape or a lesser sex crime, to change these sexual mores.

Rusk exemplifies its era's project to redefine and expand the range of conduct that falls under the criminal rubric. The Maryland Court of Appeals' view that there was sufficient evidence of "force" on facts that would not satisfy traditional rape law concepts of force was a victory for the feminist reform agenda then gaining momentum. Consistent with expansion of the meaning of "force" to enable more conduct to be criminally punished, some reformers advocated that the force requirement in criminal rape or sexual assault statutes be eliminated. Some state legislatures have done so, while most states have seen courts broaden what is considered forcible.[102] The anxiety of judicial activism

Berger, *Man's Trial, Woman's Tribulations: Rape Cases in the Courtroom*, 77 Colum. L. Rev. 1 (1977).

102. *See, e.g.*, Fla. Stat. § 794.011(5) (providing that a person commits a felony of the second degree if he commits "sexual battery" without consent and "does not use physical force and violence"); N.Y. Penal Law § 130.25(3) (defining rape as sexual intercourse without consent); Wis. Stat. § 940.225(3) (making sexual intercourse without consent a

visible in *Rusk* reflected a general post-Warren Court era anxiety about judges, as opposed to legislatures, making major social changes. This unease led feminist reformers to focus more on legislative reform.

A cultural shift in emphasis that emerged was from physical violence, to forms of not-necessarily-violent power that might nonetheless be conceivable as "force."[103] But this development has also produced some tension with the well-known 1970s feminist idea that rape is "a crime of violence," not sex.[104] For some who have taken seriously (or literally) the notion that rape is a crime of violence, it seems odd that sex without at least the threat of physical violence might be punished as rape. But what we have seen is the socio-legal transformation of the notion of violence itself, so that forms of power in sexual relationships— physical, emotional, psychological, intellectual, or economic—can be thought of as violence by other means.[105] Relatedly, some feminists have critiqued the idea of rape as a crime of violence, not sex, instead emphasizing precisely the sexual subordination entailed in the injury and thus the importance of nonconsent to sex, with or without physical

---

felony); *See also* Michelle J. Anderson, *All–American Rape*, 79 St. John's L. Rev. 625, 629–33 (2005) (finding that nonconsensual sex without force is a felony in fourteen states and a misdemeanor in eight states). In New Jersey, the statutory requirement of "force" is satisfied by the force inherent to sexual penetration. In the Interest of M.T.S., 609 A.2d 1266, 1277 (N.J. 1992).

103. *See* State v. Rusk, 424 A.2d 720, 726 (Md. 1981) ("[F]orce may exist without violence." (quoting Hazel v. State, 157 A.2d 922, 925 (1960))). *Compare, e.g.*, Commonwealth v. Mlinarich, 498 A.2d 395, 400 (Pa. Super. 1985) ("The term 'force' . . . when used to define the crime of rape, [has] historically been understood by the courts and legal scholars to mean physical force or violence."), *with id.* at 413 (Spaeth, J., dissenting) ("[T]he legislature did not mean force in the limited sense of 'to do violence to,' and *did* mean force in the more general sense of 'to constrain or compel by physical, moral, or intellectual means or by the exigencies of the circumstances.' "). Self help books encouraged women to see non-violent coercion as force. *See The Boston Women's Health Book Collective, The New Our Bodies, Ourselves: A Book By and For Women* 103 (1984) ("Men use different kinds of force against women, from pressuring us for a 'good night kiss,' to withdrawal of economic support from wives, to using weapons.").

104. *Compare, e.g.*, Brownmiller, *supra* note 90, at 376 (arguing that women experience rape as an "act of violence"); Cassandra Wilson, *Interview with a Feminist Lawyer, in* Rape: The First Sourcebook for Women 137, 140 (Noreen Connell & Cassandra Wilson eds, 1974) (explaining that reframing rape as a crime of physical assault would help eliminate obstacles to prosecuting rape), *with* Catharine A. MacKinnon, *Feminism Unmodified* 86 (1987) ("So long as we say that [normal forms of sexuality] are abuses of violence, not sex, we fail to criticize what has been made of sex, what has been done to us *through* sex, because we leave the line between rape and intercourse . . . right where it is."); Stephen J. Schulhofer, *Unwanted Sex* 114 (1998) (criticizing rape law's "narrow focus on violence rather than on sexual autonomy").

105. Pennsylvania, for example, has legislatively defined the "forcible compulsion" required for rape explicitly to encompass "physical, intellectual, moral, emotional or psychological force, either express or implied." 18 Pa. C.S.A. § 3101.

violence.[106]

Several decades after *Rusk*, the idea that a woman's acquiescence to not-quite-violent pressure may make a man a rapist is still difficult for many to stomach. Perhaps that explains the Maryland Court of Appeals' "particular focus on the actual force applied by Rusk to Pat's neck"—the only explicit suggestion of physical violence.[107] The state's decision to prosecute Rusk, though, likely did not hinge on that detail, given the other facts such as the taking of the keys, the intimidating look, and the affirmative answer to Pat's question whether he would let her go if she did what he wanted.[108] The light choking was a remnant of the kind of physical force that rape law traditionally demanded, in a case that became important for the suggestion that physical force or threat there-of, light or otherwise, might be unnecessary to establish "force" in rape. *Rusk*'s double-speak, suggesting rape could be nonviolent ("the look in his eyes") but also emphasizing the one existing violent detail (light choking), implicitly recognizes that when law shifts basic social concepts—here, the notion of violence entailed in the term "force"—and thereby resists people's ordinary intuitions, they may not buy it.[109]

In that vein, the ambivalence of *Rusk*'s signals bears note. First, *Rusk* ultimately affirmed the rape conviction, but a majority of the twenty-one judges at the three different levels of adjudication did *not* think there was legally sufficient evidence of rape.[110] Second, the story of the hungry jurors makes it at least ironic that *Rusk* featured such emphasis on appellate deference to the jury. Third, Rusk's appeal based on insufficiency of the evidence seemed to the lawyers and judges to be highly fact-bound, and centered on factual details like the taking of the car keys, the light choking, and the "look in his eyes"; but *Rusk* nevertheless became a case of legal importance involving the changing understanding of concepts like force and reasonableness in rape law.

---

106. *See* MacKinnon, *supra* note 104, at 86; Schulhofer, *supra* note 104, at 280.

107. *Cf.* Susan Estrich, *Rape*, 95 Yale L.J. 1087, 1113 (1986); Stephen J. Schulhofer, *Taking Sexual Autonomy Seriously*, 11 L. & Phil 35, 47 (1992) (wondering what "would have been the result if this one factual detail had been missing").

108. *See* Email from Stephen H. Sachs, Retired Partner, WilmerHale, to Jeannie Suk, Assistant Professor of Law, Harvard Law School (Dec. 29, 2009) (on file with author) ("[E]ven absent 'lightly choking' I believe there was a rape, although it was a much closer case. Yes, I would have argued this hypothetical case in the COA."); Email from James Salkin, Attorney, to Jeannie Suk, Assistant Professor of Law, Harvard Law School (Dec. 30, 2009) (on file with author) (indicating that "light choking" might have come up "pre trial or for the first time while [the victim] was on the witness stand").

109. *Cf., e.g.*, Jeanne C. Marsh, Alison Geist & Nathan Caplan, *Rape and the Limits of Law Reform* (1982) (finding Michigan's 1975 rape reform statute relatively unsuccessful in its goal of extending criminal prohibition to behavior that was previously permissible).

110. Estrich, *supra* note 107, at 1113.

Fourth, even if *Rusk* vindicated the rape reform position by affirming the rape conviction, the Court of Appeals remained fixated on force as physical force, and did not eschew the requirement that the victim's fear have been reasonable. That is why the decision somewhat disappoints the reformist challenge to traditional rape law. Perhaps this is why *Rusk*'s most quoted opinion is not the majority, but rather Judge Cole's dissent, which seemingly embodied the traditional sexism of rape law. For many, the dissent's dismissal of the victim's fear is the most salient aspect of the case, drawing repeated comment—so much that it is often treated as if it, rather than the vindication of rape reform, were *Rusk*'s legacy.[111]

Finally, though, even the meaning of this dissent was complicated, coming as it did from the first African American judge to serve on Maryland's highest court. "Traditional sexism" does not suffice to provide its context. Having grown up in segregation-era Baltimore and become a veritable pioneer as a state senator and judge, Judge Cole was attuned to the serious bias against African American defendants in criminal courts, and the notorious racial politics of prosecutions against African American defendants falsely accused of raping white women.[112] Coming of age in the South, he no doubt knew the ease with which African American men could be falsely convicted. This is not to say that Judge Cole's race can, by itself, explain his views here, but his experience alters somewhat the meaning of his insistence that the accuser should have manifested robust resistance. From this perspective, the concern might be that making it easier to prove rape by eroding the resistance requirement could aggravate intransigent and troubling race bias in rape law. Even deeper, though, this perspective might lend itself to greater sensitivity to the interests and rights of those accused of rape. It also highlights a split in the Left that feminist law reform revealed, between feminists and champions of criminal defendants' rights. The interaction of race and rape was not on the surface of *Rusk* because both the defendant and the victim were white, but nevertheless it is an unseen dimension of Judge Cole's dissent that was instantly understood, even if inchoately, by judicial colleagues and lawyers in the case.[113]

---

111. *See, e.g.*, Coughlin, *supra* note 44, at 40 (discussing *Rusk* as an "infamous example" of a rape victim being judged for putting herself in a situation where she was likely to be pressured to have sex); Estrich, *supra* note 107, at 1113–14 (criticizing the dissenters' view of the reasonable woman as demanding that she not be "a woman at all" but a "real man").

112. Telephone Interview with Alan M. Wilner, Retired Judge, Court of Appeals of Maryland (Dec. 29, 2009). Judge Cole died in 1999.

113. *E.g., id.*; Sweeney Interview, *supra* note 31; Cooke Interview, *supra* note 8; Sachs Interview, *supra* note 67.

Epilogue

State v. Rusk was a routine trial that evolved into an important test of the bounds of social and legal change. At trial, prosecutor and public defender alike had no inkling of implications beyond the jury's verdict, let alone the cause of feminism and the rape reform movement.[114] The trial judge says he does not remember the case at all.[115] But what began as an ordinary criminal-court jury trial came through the appellate process to herald legal transformation in relations between the sexes.

The trajectories of the judges and lawyers involved seem eerily to reflect the morality tale of shifting power in an epochal struggle. Judge Robert Karwacki moved on from the trial court to serve on the state's intermediate appellate court and eventually its highest court. Judge Alan Wilner became chief judge of the intermediate appellate court, and then was elevated to the highest court of Maryland. His *Rusk* dissent has been one of his most noted opinions.[116] Today the author of the Court of Appeals majority opinion, the late Chief Judge Robert Murphy, has his name on the courthouse, and *Rusk* is considered part of his contribution to defining and clarifying Maryland's substantive criminal law.[117] Judge Lawrence Rodowsky served as chair of the Maryland Select Committee on Gender Equality. His efforts to eliminate gender bias in the judicial system, especially in the education of judges and attorneys about domestic violence, family law, and sexual harassment, have been celebrated by bench and bar as highlights of his career.[118] Judge Rita Davidson, Maryland's first female appellate judge, was lionized as a judicial pioneer after her untimely death from cancer.[119] Four women judges have followed her on the Court of Appeals.

Attorney General Stephen Sachs was reelected to office the year after his success in *Rusk*. He later ran for governor of Maryland, in a Democratic primary in which both he and the winning candidate sought the support of women's groups. He is now a retired litigation partner at WilmerHale where he had a criminal, tax, and securities practice.[120] The

---

114. Eaton Interview, *supra* note 7; Salkin Interview I, *supra* note 2.

115. Telephone Interview with Robert Karwacki, Retired Judge, Maryland Court of Appeals (Dec. 2, 2009).

116. *See, e.g.*, Kim Lane Sheppele, *Legal Storytelling*, 87 Mich. L. Rev. 2073, 2095 (1989).

117. Lawrence F. Rodowsky, *The Opinions of Chief Judge Robert C. Murphy*, 56 Md. L. Rev. 626, 628 (1997).

118. Peter F. Axelrad et al., *Tributes to Judge Lawrence F. Rodowsky*, 60 Md. L. Rev. 785, 790–97 (2001); *Judge Rodowsky Awarded for Exemplary Efforts to Achieve Gender Equality*, 2.4 Justice Matters: A Publication of the Maryland Judiciary 4 (1999).

119. *A Tribute to Judge Rita C. Davidson*, 19.5 Md. Bar J. 13 (1986).

120. Sachs Interview, *supra* note 67; http://www.elections.state.md.us/elections/1986/candidates_1986/primary_gov.html; http://www.wilmerhale.com/steve_sachs/.

two women Assistant Attorneys General who worked with him on *Rusk* are both judges. Within a decade of the case, Kathleen Sweeney became a Maryland district court judge in Baltimore,[121] and Deborah Chasanow a federal magistrate judge. President Clinton then appointed Chasanow to the Federal District Court for the District of Maryland, of which she is now chief judge.[122] In 2004, she received the highest honor of the Women's Bar Association of Maryland, an award named for Judge Rita Davidson.[123] Before leaving the State's Attorney's Office for private practice in Baltimore, Rusk's prosecutor Jimmy Salkin was promoted to the Violent Crimes Unit. There he worked dozens of homicide cases with Ed Burns, the homicide detective who would later co-produce *The Wire*, an HBO television series about the Baltimore worlds of drug rings, police, politics, public schools, and the media.[124]

Eddie Rusk's lawyers have not fared as well. Both have been disbarred. After retiring from a long career as a respected public defender, David Eaton shocked the Baltimore legal community when he was accused of stealing funds from a mentally retarded friend for whom he was a longtime financial guardian. Eaton pleaded guilty to perjury and theft in 2002, and received a three-year suspended sentence.[125]

Ira Cooke kept in touch with Eddie, visited him in prison, and even invited him to his home after he got out. In addition to his career as a litigator, Cooke's prominent portfolio came to include lucrative lobbying for unpopular interests such as bail bondsmen, mortgage lenders, landlords, and the gaming industry. A powerful but controversial figure in Maryland, he was troubled over the years with substance abuse, bankruptcy, accusations of forgery and fraud, and a contempt ruling for misreporting finances in one of his divorces. In 2004, he was convicted by a California jury of conspiracy, grand theft, and commercial bribery for allegedly participating in a kickback scheme that defrauded a mental health clinic for which he was consulting.[126] His conviction was reversed on appeal due to multiple trial errors including prosecutorial misconduct.[127] At the time of this writing, he was doing volunteer work at a

---

121.　See http://www.msa.md.gov/msa/mdmanual/32dc/html/msa11860.html.

122.　*See* http://www.mdd.uscourts.gov/publications/JudgesBio/chasanow.htm.

123.　*See* http://www.wba-md.org/RCDaward.aspx.

124.　Salkin Interview I, *supra* note 2.

125.　Laurie Willis, *Disbarred Lawyer is Sentenced in Theft: He Controlled Funds of Learning–Disabled Man*, The Sun (Baltimore), Feb. 8, 2002, at 3B.

126.　Jeffrey Anderson, *California Scheming: Maryland Lobbyist Ira Cooke Indicted in California on Charges of Conspiracy, Theft, and Bribery*, Balt. City Paper, Oct. 29, 2003, http://www2.citypaper.com/eat/story.asp?id=4652; Van Smith, *Un–Cooke-d*, Balt. City Paper, Feb. 2, 2005, http://www2.citypaper.com/printStory.asp?id=13069.

127.　People v. Cumberworth, No.F047243, 2006 WL 3549939 (Cal. App. 5 Dist. 2006).

men's halfway house and awaiting the decision of the Court of Appeals (the same court in which he lost *Rusk*) on his reinstatement to the Maryland bar so he could practice law again.[128] His daughter is a Baltimore Legal Aid lawyer who represents battered women.[129]

Until they were contacted for this story, none of the lawyers and judges involved in *Rusk* realized they had played a role in such a long-lasting legacy—a case studied closely by students and teachers of criminal law and feminist legal theory. So how did it become a canonical case?

At the time of *Rusk*, the crime of rape was barely taught in law schools, despite being one of the most controversial social issues of the day.[130] Stephen Schulhofer, then a recently tenured University of Pennsylvania professor, was joining a new edition of Sanford Kadish's dominant Criminal Law casebook as coauthor.[131] As part of the law-and-society movement, Schulhofer strongly believed that the teaching of law should be connected to real social problems, not abstracted from realities of social life. When he came across *Rusk* in the advance sheets of the Criminal Law Reporter, he realized it was "the perfect vehicle" for bringing a discussion of modern date rape into the curriculum, and getting beyond the traditional teaching of rape just as an instance of the mistake of fact doctrine.[132]

His senior coauthor, who had co-written the first edition of the casebook in 1962,[133] initially resisted his proposal to create a whole chapter devoted to the crime of rape. No other casebook had such a chapter; criminal law pedagogy at the time had moved away from treating specific substantive crimes and toward general principles of just punishment. Also, the topic of rape was broadly considered too explosive for the dispassionate pedagogy of the law school classroom. But Kadish was soon persuaded and the 1983 edition made *Rusk* the centerpiece of its new chapter. Schulhofer recalls that "the decision to include rape was very controversial at the time and triggered much protest from the then-

---

128. Van Smith, *Lobbyist Ira Cooke Wants His Law License Back*, Balt. City Paper, Oct. 3, 2008, http://www2.citypaper.com/news/story.asp?id=16805; Telephone Interview with M. Albert Figinski, Attorney, Law Offices of Peter G. Angelos (Dec. 4, 2009); Email from Ira C. Cooke, Former Attorney, to Jeannie Suk, Assistant Professor of Law, Harvard Law School (Dec. 25, 2009) (on file with author).

129. Cooke Interview, *supra* note 8.

130. *See* Susan Estrich, *Teaching Rape Law*, 102 Yale L.J. 509, 509–10 (1992).

131. Sanford H. Kadish, Stephen J. Schulhofer & Monrad G. Paulsen, *Criminal Law and Its Processes: Cases and Materials* (4th ed. 1983).

132. Email from Stephen J. Schulhofer, Robert B. McKay Professor of Law, New York University School of Law, to Jeannie Suk, Assistant Professor of Law, Harvard Law School (Jan. 12, 2010) (on file with author).

133. Sanford H. Kadish & Monrad G. Paulsen, *Criminal Law and its Processes* (1962).

older generation of criminal law teachers."[134] One longtime user of the casebook even took Schulhofer aside at a conference to explain that he had stopped teaching from it because the chapter caused trouble: if he skipped rape, students objected, and if he taught rape, it went badly.[135] But soon other casebooks and teachers followed in using *Rusk* to open up serious consideration of rape as a substantive crime.[136]

Susan Estrich was a young Harvard professor who had been the first female president of the Harvard Law Review—and before that, a victim of rape. She made her first major scholarly contribution in 1986 with a *Yale Law Journal* article, "A Study of Rape Law as an Illustration of Sexism in the Criminal law."[137] She used the story of Pat and Eddie to criticize the law's demand that the rape victim be "reasonable"—in effect, "one who does not scare easily, one who does not feel vulnerability, one who is not passive, one who fights back, not cries." In short, "not a woman at all," but "a real man."[138] The *Rusk* dissent, she said, showcased this male perspective on how women should react when faced with unwanted sex. She also criticized the typical judicial inability to "understand force as the power one need not use," and hence the majority's need to emphasize the "light choking" to see the encounter as a rape.[139] Since then, *Rusk* has been a flashpoint for criminal and feminist legal scholars.

Pat's own later story is not known. Perhaps it is to be expected, even by design, that a rape complainant, whose surname was not in the judicial opinions, and whose identity was obscured in her contemporaneous press interviews, would remain inaccessible. We are left to surmise how her life went after the media flurry when she dropped out of public view. As far as we know, she and Eddie never encountered each other after he got out of prison, and she would be fifty-two years old at the time of this writing. Perhaps she went on to have a relatively normal life, and did not lose custody of her son in her divorce as she had feared. If we were to project on her some common tropes associated with rape victims, we might imagine years of rape counseling, relationship problems, and bouts of fear and anxiety. Whether or not the experience affected her inner life, because of our developed social norms of shielding

---

134. Email from Professor Schulhofer, *supra* note 132.

135. Telephone Interview with Stephen J. Schulhofer (Jan. 15, 2009).

136. *See, e.g.,* John M. Brumbaugh, *Criminal Law and Approaches to the Study of Law* (1986); John Kaplan & Robert Weisberg, *Criminal Law: Cases and Materials* (1986); Lloyd L. Weinreb, *Criminal Law: Cases, Comment, Questions* (4th ed. 1986).

137. Estrich, *supra* note 107, at 1090.

138. *Id.* at 1114. *See also* Susan Estrich, *Real Rape* 63 (1987) (calling *Rusk* "one of the most vigorously debated rape cases in recent volumes of the case reporters").

139. Estrich, *supra* note 107, at 1115.

rape victims from exposure, the case in which she played a pivotal role as a young woman need not have been salient to her social persona afterwards, or even known to friends. Those expectations of privacy (or shame), particular to the social construction of *rape* victimhood, also prevent this story from providing a richer picture of her life.

In letters from prison, Eddie maintained he was innocent of rape. To his cousin, Eddie wrote of his daughter, who was six when he began his prison sentence. "She's really growing up fast! I haven't seen her for 4½ years—I only get to see her in photos. It's a real drag watching her grow up in pictures. I don't want her to know I'm in prison, especially for a charge like this." About his conviction, he said in the same letter: "I'm hopeful of clearing myself of these charges. An old girlfriend of mine just hired an attorney for me. He's an investigative lawyer. He's looking into this girl's background. He says he believes he can get a new trial for me. He's already talked with the girl's ex-husband who says the girl's a total bitch and says he'll testify for me in court if I get a hearing."[140]

Back when his appeal was pending, Eddie's parents had moved away with his daughter from their Baltimore home to Florida, in part to get away from the embarrassment of their son's rape conviction. He was able to get a transfer to serve the last part of his sentence in a Florida prison near his family. His daughter remembers visiting him there as a young child and being told that her dad couldn't be home with her because he was in the army.[141] He served a total of six and a half years and was released in 1987, just as his encounter with Pat was beginning to shape the teaching of rape law in classrooms all over the country.

When Eddie got out of prison, he resumed buying and selling cars for a living in Baltimore. His daughter, who was twelve, continued to grow up with his parents in Florida, though he sometimes sent money for her support and she occasionally visited him. In prison he had become unhealthily overweight. In 2000 when he became so sick with diabetes and dystonia (a neurological movement disorder) that he could no longer work, he moved to Florida to live with his parents, sister, and daughter. He was now on disability and abusing narcotics and prescription drugs. He badgered family members for money. His daughter, a dental assistant who had a young son, felt her father "brought a lot of stress" when he moved in. People close to him thought he had a kind and generous heart, but he was often angry. He was occasionally violent when he'd been drinking. Both his sister and his daughter reported domestic violence incidents to the police. His daughter eventually got a trespass warrant barring him from the home.[142]

---

140. Letter from Edward Rusk to Rigg Kennedy (Jun. 7, 1985) (on file with author).

141. Sell Interview, *supra* note 5.

142. Kennedy Interview, *supra* note 17; Riccobono Interview, *supra* note 4; Sell Interview, *supra* note 5.

After serving time for rape, Eddie had a number of additional convictions, for battery, petty theft, reckless driving, and cocaine possession, but he did not go to prison again. Just three months before his death, he was arrested for domestic assault. To the end, he remained bitter about doing the years in prison for a crime he didn't think he committed. He believed the rape conviction ruined his life. Eddie died at age fifty-nine, alone in a rented trailer in Port Orange, Florida. A week later, neighbors smelled his corpse and called the police. His little grandson, who loved and looked up to him, was told that grandpa died and went to heaven.[143]

---

143. Sell Interview, *supra* note 5.

6

Donna Coker & Lindsay C. Harrison

The Story of *Wanrow*: The Reasonable Woman and the Law of Self–Defense

Introduction

On February 23, 1976, Yvonne Wanrow, a Native American woman and single mother, sat in the Olympia courtroom of the Washington Supreme Court, awaiting the argument of her case. She had been convicted of first-degree assault and second-degree murder, and after her conviction was reversed by the Court of Appeals, the prosecution had appealed to the state's highest court.

Wanrow's supporters packed the courthouse for her hearing. Hundreds of Native Americans sat on the floor and crowded around the back of the courtroom to watch the arguments and demonstrate their support.[1] Many of the supporters had come by caravan to Olympia. On the

---

1. Interview with Yvonne Swan, in Inchelium, Wash. (Sept. 2002) (hereafter "Swan Interview"). Yvonne is now known by her maiden name Swan, rather than her married name Wanrow. Our research relies on the complete appellate record; interviews with Yvonne (Wanrow) Swan, her sister Alice Stewart, feminist activists Marge Nelson and Polly Taylor who worked on Yvonne's national defense organizing effort, Yvonne's trial attorney Eugene Annis, her appellate attorneys Elizabeth Schneider and Nancy Stearns, Beth Benora with the National Jury Project, and former Chief Justice of the State Supreme Court of Washington Robert Utter; archival documents and pictures from the Free Yvonne Wanrow campaign from Marge Nelson and Polly Taylor's collections and from the Center for Constitutional Rights (on file with author). Donald Brockett, then Spokane County Prosecuting Attorney and Fred Caruso, then deputy prosecutor, represented the state throughout the entire legal proceedings against Yvonne. Both are now retired. Caruso spoke with us briefly, but declined to be interviewed at length about the case. We were unable to reach Brockett. Comments from interviewees were made in the interviews noted here unless otherwise indicated. We are extremely grateful for the generosity of each of these individuals and for University of Miami law librarian Robin Schard's invaluable archival research assistance. We are also grateful for the helpful comments given us by

eve of the appeal, they had shared a meal of cooked salmon baked over
an alder-wood fire prepared by the Puyallup Tribe. Wanrow's two young
lawyers, Elizabeth Schneider and Nancy Stearns, were there. Native
American folksinger Floyd Westerman serenaded the group. The following day, the supporters so flooded the courtroom that many spilled into
the aisles, and many others were forced to wait outside the courthouse.
As Schneider and Stearns sat at the counsel's table waiting to argue
Wanrow's case, the sound of traditional Native American drumming
could be heard throughout the hushed courtroom.[2]

The fundamental question before the court was whether Wanrow
had received a fair trial when the judge restricted her ability to make out
a self-defense claim. Wanrow, who stood five feet four inches tall,
weighed 120 pounds, and at the time of the incident was wearing a cast
on her foot, shot and killed William Wesler, an intoxicated[3] sixty year old
white man and accused child molester who towered more than six feet
tall. Wanrow argued that she killed Wesler in self-defense when he
entered her friend's home intoxicated and uninvited, ignored loud demands to "get out," and after approaching the bedside of her young
nephew, moved toward her.

Wanrow's now-famous case enters law school textbooks on the issue
of what constitutes a fair trial for *women*. The jury instruction at her
trial encouraged jurors to determine the reasonableness of Wanrow's
fear from the standpoint of a man facing an unarmed attacker, rather
than a small female, untrained in the use of her fists to defend herself.
But race and racism were as important to the fair trial question in
Wanrow as were gender and sexism. In Spokane, Washington, where
Wanrow's trial took place, much of the white population harbored racist
attitudes regarding Native Americans.[4] Furthermore, anti-Indian senti-

---

Elizabeth Schneider, Martha Mahoney, and Zacchary Coker–Dukowitz, and the tireless
efforts of Sonia Ramos, Felicia Martin, Tara Lora, Cossette Charles and Linda Kirk.

   2. Tim L. Hanson, The Falls, Feb. 27, 1976; Swan Interview, *supra* note 1.

   3. The coroner testified at trial that Wesler's blood alcohol level was .27 and that a
level of .3 or .35 would result in convulsions.

   4. Swan Interview, *supra* note 1 (recounting her own experiences and that of other
Native Americans in Spokane). In preparation for a potential retrial in 1977, Wanrow's
lawyers secured the assistance of the National Jury Project to conduct a survey of a sample
of registered voters to determine likely bias in the jury pool. When asked to identify the
primary cause of poverty among American Indians, nearly half chose answers that
exhibited racist stereotypes: lack of ambition (32%) and lack of ability (14%). In addition,
41% agreed with the statement, "An Indian who carries a handgun is probably looking for
trouble"; 43% agreed with the statement, "The reason most Indians get into trouble is that
they drink too much"; however, 68% agreed that "Indian people have as much respect for

ment was at a fever pitch at the time of Wanrow's trial because of the widespread negative publicity accompanying the concurrent American Indian Movement (AIM) occupation of Wounded Knee. There, in a seventy-one day standoff beginning on February 27, 1973, AIM protested government mistreatment of Native Americans by taking over the site of an infamous 1890 massacre of Lakota Indians by federal troops.

Wanrow's case raised fundamental questions about the significance of race and gender in understanding the "reasonable man" standard that governed the law of self-defense. She and her lawyers would come to challenge the meaning of "reasonableness" in the jury instruction and the gendered language in which it was phrased, both of which suggested that a struggle between two men exemplified the legal definition of reasonableness. The shift in law that resulted from Wanrow's appeal recognized in the clearest terms possible that the circumstances and experiences of *women* must be accounted for if a jury is to determine the "degree of force which . . . a reasonable person in the same situation . . . would believe is necessary."[5]

For her lawyers, the case would represent more than a standard challenge to a criminal conviction. *Wanrow* became a powerful means of putting feminist theory into action to fight gender bias in the criminal justice system, and marked the beginning of what came to be called "women's self-defense work."[6] Many of the attorneys and law students who worked on Wanrow's case became leaders in the legal community and the legal academy.[7] They would expand the women's rights movement from the struggle against overt discrimination against women to the recognition that gender bias poses more subtle hurdles for female defendants in criminal cases.

For members of feminist organizations and AIM, the case represented a compelling example of racial and gender injustice in the criminal justice system. Her cause was first taken up by AIM members who spread the word through Native American newspapers and gatherings, participated in events to raise funds for her defense, and provided her with social support. It was soon promoted by feminists across the country, several of whom drove to Washington to organize popular support for her defense among non-Indians and who supported the work

---

the law as white people." *See* Aff. of Beth M. Bonora, founding member and president of the National Jury Project, State v. Wanrow, No. 20876 (Wash. Super. Ct. 1973).

5. State v. Wanrow, 559 P.2d 548, 557 (Wash. 1977).

6. Elizabeth M. Schneider, *Battered Women and Feminist Lawmaking* 33 (2000). Schneider defines "women's self-defense work" as "legal reform and legal advocacy on the hurdles that women defendants face concerning choice of defense." *Id.*

7. *See infra* p. 221 (describing the work of CCR attorneys including Wanrow's co-counsel, Stearns and Schneider); *infra* p. 243 and note 84 (describing the work of Susan Jordan, Cris Arguedas, and Mary Alice Theiler).

of the Defense Committee for Yvonne Wanrow, created by Wanrow and her sisters. These activists were able to raise funds for her defense and to draw national attention to her case, and that of other women who claimed they acted in self-defense in killing a male attacker. Wanrow became the subject of national attention, including being the focus of a public television documentary.[8]

AIM organizing was at its peak the year that Wanrow's case went to trial, and much of that organizing focused on problems of anti-Indian racism in the criminal justice system. In the years between Wanrow's trial and the resolution of her appeal, the women's movement brought unprecedented national attention to the failure of the state to respond to high levels of male violence against women. The analysis of race and sex oppression offered by these movements mirrored Wanrow's own experiences. She came to understand her personal struggle as a part of a larger struggle for racial and gender equality. She credits this understanding and her activism with preventing her from being "swallowed up" by the pain of her own circumstances.

Yvonne's Story

Yvonne Wanrow was born in 1943 on the Colville Reservation, approximately 113 miles northwest of Spokane, Washington. The U.S. government called the reservation "Colville," although the residents were actually descendants of twelve different Native nations: Colville, Nespelem, San Poil, the Lake, the Palus, the Wenatchi, the Chelan, the Entiat, the Methow, the southern Okanogan, the Moses Columbia and the Nez Perce of Chief Joseph's Bands.[9] Tribal enrollment in the Confederated Tribes of Colville stands today at about 9,065, with over 5,000 persons living on the Reservation.

Wanrow was the seventh of eight children. Her father farmed, hunted for wild game, and found paid work when he was able. Her mother frequently acted as an interpreter for elderly Native Americans. Through this work, Wanrow's mother became an activist against U.S. "termination" policy. The long-term goal of this policy was to "terminate" any special status for Native Americans, but it was functionally a program of forced assimilation in which tribal governments were sometimes disbanded, federal health care and education services were discontinued, and many residents of reservations were encouraged or coerced to relocate to urban centers.[10] Young people were given a stipend and

---

8. *See, e.g.*, Christine La Beau, *When A Woman Fights Back* (KCPQ television broadcast 1980).

9. Confederated Tribes of the Colville Reservation Home Page, http://www.colville tribes.com/facts.php (last visited Sept. 30, 2012). All facts regarding Colville are drawn from this official website.

10. *See* Felix S. Cohen, *The Erosion of Indian Rights, 1950–1953: A Case Study in Bureaucracy*, 62 Yale L.J. 348, 383–84 (1953).

one-way bus tickets to urban destinations, where they were enrolled in vocational schooling.

In 1966, Wanrow, newly divorced with two young children, became a part of the government's termination policy. The Bureau of Indian Affairs (BIA) gave Wanrow a ticket to San Francisco and paid for schooling in fashion design, the closest thing she could find to her real passion—art. Wanrow wanted to bring her two children with her, but BIA officials told her it would be better if she left them at home with her parents; she could send for her children once she was settled. While Wanrow was in San Francisco, state child protection authorities took her children from her parents and placed them in foster care.[11] Wanrow sought to have her children join her. The authorities told her that she would first have to obtain an apartment, a job, and a babysitter. By 1967, she had accomplished all three, and Darren, who was four, and Julie, who was three, began living with Wanrow in San Francisco.

With the added responsibility of child care, Wanrow began attending school part-time and working part-time as an assistant designer. Three weeks after her children arrived, however, her daughter Julie died suddenly of encephalitis. This lesson in tragic uncertainty was one that was to stay with Wanrow. Years later, she reflected on the impact of Julie's death:

> [Julie's death] was so devastating that I spent a lot of time worrying about my son. And then when I had another daughter Yvette, whenever one of them got sick, I would quit my job right away, and then I'd go on welfare so that I could stay home with my children. And then when they'd get well, and everything seemed to be going well, then I'd go out and get a job.

After Julie died, Wanrow quit school, left San Francisco, and reconciled with her ex-husband. She gave birth to her third child, Yvette, during this period. The reconciliation with her ex-husband did not last, though, and Wanrow was once again on her own with two young children. She returned briefly to her home town of Inchelium, and then, in the summer of 1971, she moved to Spokane to finish her art degree.

When Wanrow moved to Spokane, the area had a relatively large Native American population because of its proximity to a number of

---

11. It was not unusual during this period for Native American children to be removed from their homes by child protection authorities and placed in foster care or adoptive homes. In some states, between 25–35% of Native American children were removed sometime during their lifetime. See H.R. Rep. No. 95–1386, at 9 (1978), *reprinted in* U.S.C.C.A.N. 7530, 7531. As a result of these widespread removals of Indian children, in 1978 Congress passed the Indian Child Welfare Act, which mandates a preference for the placement of Native American children in Native American homes and confers exclusive jurisdiction to the tribe in child custody proceedings involving an Indian child residing or domiciled on the reservation. *The Indian Child Welfare Act,* 25 U.S.C. §§ 1901–63 (2000).

reservations, including the Colville Reservation. Wanrow remembers the anti-Indian racism in Spokane, particularly evident in the relationship between the local Native American population and the Spokane police. She recounted years later:

> There was a lot of anti-Indian sentiment. . . . I was always bailing people out of jail, and I was always helping people out of predicaments and sheltering people. . . . Indian people were not popular [with the police in Spokane.] It seems like they were the ones that always got arrested and got put in jail. My brother was maced. . . . [From] family members and friends, I would hear where [the police] would just beat them up whenever they could. I'm not saying all of the police, but [even] a little is too much racism.

By the time Wanrow arrived in Spokane, her daughter Yvette was nearly two and her son Darren was eight. The only housing Wanrow could afford was in a neighborhood that was known for its high crime rate. Wanrow felt vulnerable and afraid and, thinking she could not count on the police to protect her, she purchased a gun in the hope that it would provide some safety.

The Story of Native American Activism in the 1970s

Wanrow's case occurred at a time of extreme inequalities for Native Americans and at a time of unprecedented Native American activism. According to a U.S. government study published in 1976, 50% of Native Americans living on reservations were living in poverty as were one-third of *all* Native Americans—both on and off reservations. This was a much higher poverty rate than for any other group in the United States.[12] The rates of victimization of violent crime were higher as well.[13] Conditions on many reservations were bleak, but conditions for Native Americans in urban centers were also difficult.[14] In the communities that bordered Native American nations, anti-Indian racism was particularly

---

12. U.S. Department of Health, Education, and Welfare, *A Statistical Portrait of the American Indian: A Report for the Intra–Departmental Council on Indian Affairs, DHEW, Concerning Current Directions in Employment, Income, Education, and Health Care for the One Million American Indians in the United States* (1976).

13. *Id.* These disparities continue to exist. According to a Department of Justice report, the rate of crime victimization for American Indians is more than twice the rate for the U.S. as a whole. *See* Lawrence A. Greenfeld and Steven K. Smith, Bureau of Justice Statistics, *American Indians and Crime* (1999), *available at* http://bjs.ojp.usdoj.gov/content/pub/pdf/aic.pdf (last visited Sept. 30, 2012). American Indian women in particular are more likely to be the targets of violence than the average American. *See* Pamela J. Kingfisher, *The Health Status of Indigenous Women of the U.S.: American Indian, Alaska Native, and Native Hawaiians*, Ctr. for Research on Women and Gender, Univ. of Illinois at Chicago (1996).

14. *See* James S. Olson and Raymond Wilson, *Native Americans in the Twentieth Century* 140–45 (1986).

virulent.[15] As the movements against the Vietnam War and for racial justice emerged in the 1960s, young, predominantly urban Native Americans were inspired to organize for Native American rights.

AIM was hardly the largest or most well established Indian civil rights organization, but its confrontational style of politics made it the most visible to many Americans.[16] AIM members first focused their efforts on the harmful effects of termination policies, including the loss of Native American identity, the diminution of tribal governments, and the loss of federal assistance for education and health care. They also actively fought police harassment.[17]

In 1972, AIM activists organized a national caravan to Washington, D.C., called the "Trail of Broken Treaties." The caravan, which eventually included over 1,000 persons,[18] was intended to raise national awareness of the harms of federal policies concerning Native Americans. The participants presented the federal government with a twenty-point program calling for "renewal of treaty rights and treaty making power, reconstruction of Indian communities, and a complete revival of tribal sovereignty." AIM members occupied the Bureau of Indian Affairs building from November 1 until November 5, when the protestors and the federal government negotiated an agreement providing them with amnesty and financial assistance. National coverage of the takeover was intense and, while AIM had many non-Indian supporters, it also gained many detractors. Sentiment among Native Americans was also mixed, with many local tribal government officials denouncing AIM's militant tactics.

Four months later, when highly regarded Sioux elder Ben Black Elk died, hundreds of Native Americans including several AIM members attended his funeral on the Pine Ridge reservation in South Dakota,

---

15. For example, AIM organizers responded to a homicide that occurred in 1972 in Gordon, Nebraska, near the Pine Ridge reservation. An Oglala Sioux man named Raymond Yellow Thunder was dragged into an American Legion hall, stripped of his clothing from the waist down, and forced to dance at gunpoint for the amusement of the crowd. He was then stuffed into the trunk of a car in February freezing temperatures, where he died of exposure. His assailants were charged with only second-degree manslaughter and released without bail. Leonard Crow Dog and Richard Erdoes, *Crow Dog: Four Generations of Sioux Medicine Men* 165 (1995).

16. *See* Paul Chaat Smith and Robert Allen Warrior, *Like a Hurricane: The Indian Movement from Alcatraz to Wounded Knee* 114–15 (1996).

17. AIM members noted, for example, that Native Americans comprised 70% of the inmate population in the Minneapolis city jail, but only 10% of the population of the city. John William Sayer, *Ghost Dancing the Law: The Wounded Knee Trials* 28 (1997).

18. Unless otherwise noted, the description of the events involved in the "Trail of Broken Treaties," the occupation at Wounded Knee, and all related quotes are taken from Smith and Warrior, *supra* note 16.

near the site of the 1890 Indian massacre at Wounded Knee.[19] By this
point "the Pine Ridge Reservation was ripe for a major confrontation."[20]
Tribal Chairman, Richard Wilson, was widely accused of corruption and
AIM leader, Russell Means, had called for Wilson's impeachment. In
response, Wilson banned AIM leaders from the reservation and hired a
group of local men—called the "goon squad" by AIM activists—who
harassed local AIM supporters. Tribal members, particularly older "tra-
ditionalists," had previously joined younger AIM activists in an unsuccessful attempt to gain assistance from the federal Bureau of Indian
Affairs (BIA) to end what they believed to be the cronyism and corruption of Wilson's tenure. This unlikely coalition met again after Black
Elk's funeral. The decision was made to drive to the nearby site of
Wounded Knee, where they gathered at the mass grave site for the 200
Lakota who were killed in 1890 by U.S. troops. Meanwhile, sixty-three
U.S. marshals and many FBI agents were dispatched to the Pine Ridge
reservation because of fears of a violent clash between supporters of AIM
and those of Wilson.[21] Over 100 AIM members and supporters took over
the town, consisting primarily of a store and museum, with some
members looting the store. A priest and the store owners were held
hostage. Within a short period of time, FBI agents and U.S. marshals
had sealed off the site. AIM issued a statement to the federal government demanding hearings on the U.S. government's unilateral revoca-
tion of the 1868 Treaty with the Lakota and Cheyenne. They also
demanded an investigation of corruption in the BIA. A seventy-one day
standoff followed which ultimately resulted in 562 arrests and 185
federal indictments. The occupation of Wounded Knee was front page
news all over the country and "received more attention during its first
week than the entire previous decade of American Indian activism
combined."[22]

AIM efforts would intersect with Wanrow's trial in several ways.
During the period leading up to her trial, front page headlines decried
AIM conduct at Wounded Knee. Indeed, the occupation ended on the
second day of her trial. Wanrow's attorneys would later argue that the
negative publicity about AIM's Wounded Knee occupation undermined
Wanrow's ability to get a fair trial. On the other hand, AIM ultimately
took up Wanrow's cause, helping to raise funds for her defense and

---

19. In 1890, fearful of the growing popularity of the Ghost Dance Movement, a
religious movement premised on the belief that dead loved ones would rejoin living
relatives and bring back Native American dominance, U.S. soldiers killed over 300
Minneconjou Sioux, including women and children, at Wounded Knee, a small town in the
Pine Ridge Indian Reservation. Smith and Warrior, *supra* note 16, at 97.

20. Sayer, *supra* note 17, at 29.

21. *Id.* at 31.

22. Smith and Warrior, *supra* note 16, at 207.

create awareness of the inequalities she and her lawyers sought to rectify. Through her association with AIM, Wanrow too would eventually become an activist for Native American issues.

The Story of the Lawyers

While organizations like AIM were fighting to secure rights through social protest, civil rights attorneys were organizing to support those movements through litigation. In November 1966, civil rights lawyers William Kunstler, Arthur Kinoy, Morton Stavis, and Ben Smith founded the Center for Constitutional Rights (CCR).[23] CCR was founded to provide "a privately funded legal center [to] . . . undertake innovative, impact litigation on behalf of popular movements for social justice." As former CCR attorney and Wanrow's co-counsel Professor Elizabeth Schneider explained, "[W]e asserted rights not simply to advance legal argument or to win a case but to express the politics, vision, and demands of a social movement. . . ."[24]

By the early seventies, CCR had added a contingent of women lawyers that expanded the focus of the Center's work to embrace civil rights work on behalf of women.[25] Nancy Stearns, hired in 1969, was soon joined by Rhonda Copelon and Janice Goodman. Elizabeth Schneider would begin work as a summer intern in 1971, and would join CCR full time after graduation in 1973. The Center's commitment to working for women's rights was groundbreaking. CCR was among the first, if not *the* first, of legal organizations to make women's rights a major focus of work.[26] But the Center's commitment to hiring women lawyers to carry out that work was equally pioneering. Women, at the time, were only 3% of U.S. lawyers admitted to practice.[27] Those women who were fortunate enough to be admitted to law school soon discovered that there were few

---

23. The background information regarding the Center for Constitutional Rights is taken from CCR's website. *See* http://ccrjustice.org/about-ccr (last visited Sept. 30, 2012).

24. Schneider, *supra* note 6, at 30.

25. These were not the first women attorneys to join CCR. Harriett Rabb worked with CCR from its founding in 1966 until 1969. She would later head up the Employment Rights Project at Columbia Law School, bringing one of the first round of employment sex discrimination cases against major New York law firms. Cynthia G. Bowman, *The Entry of Women into Wall Street Law Firms: The Story of Blank v. Sullivan & Cromwell, in* Women and the Law Stories (Elizabeth M. Schneider & Stephanie M. Wildman, eds., 2011) 415, 428.

26. *See* CCR Fortieth Anniversary video interview with Stearns and Copelon, *available at* http://www.law.cuny.edu/faculty-staff/RCopelon.html. Two more projects soon followed: the ACLU Women's Rights Project, headed by Ruth Bader Ginsberg, was established in 1971; Equal Rights Advocates was established in 1974. Cynthia Fuchs Epstein, *Women in Law* (2d edition 1993) at 137–38.

27. *See* Barbara A. Curran, *Women in the Law: A Look at the Numbers* 8 (1995).

firms that would hire them.[28] As late as 1968, prestigious Wall Street firms were hiring only a handful of female summer clerks—and then putting them to work *in the typing pool*.[29] Even the civil rights bar was practically an all-male club, and local Legal Services jobs were often the only attorney positions available to women who wanted to do public interest work.[30]

Stearns, Goodman and Schneider were graduates of New York University Law School,[31] which by the late 1960s had emerged as a leader in educating women lawyers.[32] In 1967, the year Nancy Stearns graduated, women made up 12% of NYU's entering class.[33] That number will sound low to law students today, but it was nearly three times more women than the average female enrollment in law schools nationally. By 1968, the year Goodman started law school, the number of women at NYU had jumped to 16%, and it jumped again in 1970, the year Schneider enrolled.[34]

The four women who created CCR's women's rights practice were an extraordinary group. All were civil rights activists before they entered law school[35] and it was this commitment that inspired them to enroll. Just a few years out of school, these women were critical players in a feminist vanguard that revolutionized law as well as legal education. Janice Goodman helped to change legal education while in her first year

28. *See* Bowman, *supra* note 25, at 419. In 1964, 90% of the law firms in contact with NYU regarding hiring interviews refused to even interview women. *Id.* (citing Erwin O. Smigel, *The Wall Street Lawyer: Professional Organization Man?* (1964)).

29. *Id.* at 422. A 1969 survey of NYU Law women alumni documented the following remarks made by hiring attorneys to women applicants: "We hire some women, but not many"; "Women do not become partners here"; "Are you planning to have children?" Women were also told that women's salaries would be less than men's. *Id.* at 423.

30. Interview with Schneider and Stearns, *supra* note 1.

31. Copelon was a Yale Law School graduate.

32. Only Howard University had a higher percentage of women law students in 1967 than did NYU. Epstein, *supra* note 26, at 54.

33. Fred Strebeigh, *EQUAL: Women Reshape American Law* 16 (2009).

34. *Id.* The first increase was the result of changes in military draft laws which no longer allowed deferment for men enrolled in graduate school. The second increase occurred after the federal government delayed federal monies to Universities who discriminated against women in violation of federal rules governing government contracts. *Id.* at 17.

35. Goodman and Stearns had been organizers for the Student Non–Violent Coordinating Committee (SNCC), founded by African American civil rights activists in 1960. In 1964, SNCC organized the Freedom Summer action in which large numbers of mostly white students assisted with registering African American voters in Mississippi. Susan Brownmiller, *In Our Time: Memoir of a Revolution* 12 (1999); Interview with Schneider and Stearns, *supra* note 1. Schneider had been a member of the Students for a Democratic Society (SDS) while in college. Interview with Schneider and Stearns, *supra* note 1.

of law school when, in 1968, she and classmate Susan Deller Ross founded the Women's Rights Committee (WRC). The original goal of WRC was to challenge the male-only rules for NYU's most prestigious and valuable scholarship, the Root–Tilden.[36] Some of the scholarship holders as well as a professor and former dean opposed opening the scholarship to women because they could not share in the male camaraderie formed by activities such as "throwing water balloons at each other while running nude through the all-male Root–Tilden residence."[37] In a presentation to the faculty, Goodman and Ross warned that they would file suit against the school if the scholarship was not opened to women. Within days, NYU invited women to apply for Root–Tilden scholarships. As Professor Cynthia Bowman describes:

> [W]ith a heady sense of possibility and power from this quick victory, the WRC went on to attack one problem after another over the next couple of years—exclusion of women from the steam room in a residence hall, sexist remarks by faculty in class, recruitment and admission of more women students, recruitment of women faculty (there were none), and the addition of a course in women and the law to the curriculum in 1970, the first in the nation.[38]

Copelon became a leading litigator and activist in the field of women's international human rights. She was instrumental in changing the human rights framework to recognize crimes against women including rape and domestic violence as violations of human rights. Her victory in *Filártiga v. Peña–Irala*[39] established the right of victims of gross human rights abuses committed abroad to bring suit against abusers in U.S. courts based on customary international law. In *Harris v. McRae*,[40] Copelon challenged the constitutionality of the federal prohibition on using government funds for abortions; although the initial challenge succeeded, the U.S. Supreme Court ultimately reversed the victory. She

---

36. Strebeigh, *supra* note 33, at 18–19.

37. *Id.* at 17.

38. Bowman, *supra* note 25, at 421–22. In April 1970, WRC organized a meeting of women law students from seventeen schools, resulting in the formation of the National Conference of Law Women (NCLW). In the next year's hiring season, NCLW gathered data on sex discriminatory hiring practices of major Wall Street firms. This data formed the basis for the first gender discrimination law suit to be brought against a major law firm. (Harriet Rabb, formerly with CCR and then a clinical teacher at Columbia, represented the plaintiffs.) *See generally id.* Goodman would later co-found one of the first feminist law firms in the U.S. *Id.* at 442.

39. Filártiga v. Peña–Irala, 630 F.2d 876 (2d Cir. 1980).

40. The case is described in wonderful detail in Rhonda Copelon and Sylvia A. Law, *'Nearly Allied to Her Right to Be'—Medicaid Funding for Abortion: The Story of Harris v. McRae, in* Women and the Law Stories 207 (Elizabeth M. Schneider & Stephanie M. Wildman eds., 2011). For more information about Copelon, *see* http://www.youtube.com/watch?v=5izkuWAk3DY&feature=related.

was a member of the founding faculty of CUNY Law School, the co-founder of the school's International Women's Human Rights Clinic, and the founder of the Women's Caucus for Gender Justice—an international organization that successfully advocated for the inclusion of gender crimes in the International Criminal Court.[41]

Beginning in 1970, Stearns, who would be Wanrow's co-counsel with Elizabeth Schneider, led a groundbreaking and successful state-by-state litigation strategy challenging anti-abortion laws.[42] A brilliant litigator, Stearns was among the first to bring multi-plaintiff suits to challenge abortion as sex discrimination,[43] suits that included "an especially sophisticated rendering of the equality claim under the Nineteenth Amendment."[44] She would reprise her arguments in an amicus brief filed in *Roe v. Wade*.[45]

---

41. Kate Gallagher, *On the Cutting Edge: CUNY Law's International Women's Human Rights Clinic* (2000), *available at* www.law.cuny.edu/faculty-staff/RCopelon/cutting-edge.pdf.

42. *See, e.g.*, Abramowicz v. Lefkowitz, No. 69 Civ. 4469 (S.D.N.Y. 1970) (dismissed as moot when the state legislature eliminated the challenged abortion statute); Plaintiffs' Brief, *Abramowicz v. Lefkowitz* (March 9, 1970), *reprinted in* Before *Roe v. Wade*: Voices that Shaped the Abortion Debate Before the Supreme Court's Ruling 140 (Linda Greenhouse & Reva B. Siegel eds., 2010).

43. Greenhouse and Siegel write:

Whereas previous equal protection arguments had focused on the disparity in access to abortion between wealthy and poor women, the *Abramowicz* brief represents one of the first attempts to argue that the abortion right is essential to ensure equality between men and women. At the time the brief was written, the Supreme Court had yet to strike down any law on equal protection/sex discrimination grounds.

Greenhouse and Siegel, *supra* note 42, at 140. The strategy that Stearns and her colleagues adopted in these cases, and the one she would apply again in an amici brief in *Roe*, was revolutionary. They argued that anti-abortion laws violated Fifth- and Fourteenth–Amendment Equal Protection, the Eighth Amendment prohibition against cruel and unusual punishment, the Thirteenth Amendment prohibiting involuntary servitude, and the Nineteenth Amendment's guarantees of women's political rights. Rather than represent physicians—as had been the practice in earlier suits seeking to liberalize abortion restrictions, Stearns and co-counsel brought the suit on behalf of women as a class. Rather than argue to loosen abortion restrictions to *protect* women, they argued that women had a *right* to control their own reproduction.

44. Robert C. Post & Reva B. Siegel, *Legislative Constitutionalism and Section Five Power: Policentric Interpretation of the Family and Medical Leave Act*, 112 Yale L. J. 1943, 1991 n. 145 (2003). Post and Siegel quote the following from Stearns' complaint filed in Rhode Island v. Israel, No. 4605 (D.R.I. June 22, 1971):

The Nineteenth Amendment recognized that women are legally free to take part in activity outside the home. But the abortion laws imprison women in the home without free individual choice. The abortion laws, in their real practical effects, deny the liberty and equality of women to participate in the wider world, an equality which is demanded by the Nineteenth Amendment.

45. Brief Amicus Curiae of New Women Lawyers, et al. at 1, Roe v. Wade, 410 U.S. 113 (1973) (No. 70–18), 1971 WL 134283.

Schneider began law school in 1970. Though only three years separated Stearns's last year of law school from Schneider's first, their experiences were worlds apart. Women now represented a significant voice in law school politics at NYU and the focus of that voice was increasingly to challenge sex discrimination. Like Goodman, many of the activists who entered law school in those intervening years were deeply influenced by a revolution that began in civil rights work for racial justice and in the New Left anti-war movements. Frustrated with the ways in which women were disregarded and relegated to supporting roles in these organizations,[46] women began to organize for women's rights and to articulate a demand for "women's liberation."

Schneider was involved in civil rights and anti-war activism while in college, but it was not until the year after she graduated with a master's in political sociology from the London School of Economics that she became deeply involved in the women's movement. When Schneider returned to the U.S., she went to work for the Vera Institute for Justice, a criminal justice reform think tank. Soon, she was meeting with feminist lawyers like Jan Goodman, who urged her to attend law school. Persuaded that "there was a need for women to go into law," Schneider chose NYU "because there was this group of [activist] women who were already there." Schneider clerked at CCR both summers while in law school, working with Goodman, Stearns, and Copelon—her "heroines." "[The] critical mass of Nancy, Jan, and Rhonda ... really created a women's presence [at CCR]."[47] When she graduated, Schneider joined CCR fulltime, and she would work there for nine years. During those years at CCR, and the years that followed when she taught in the Constitutional Law Clinic at Rutgers School of Law–Newark, Schneider would be involved in numerous cases—either representing a party or, as often was the case, representing amici curiae. The cases included work with Stearns and Copelon on groundbreaking civil rights claims of race and sex discrimination, as well as challenges to government misconduct, labor union representation, and criminal representation.[48] But it was her

---

46. SNCC history provides an example. When Goodman volunteered for Mississippi Freedom Summer in 1964, she was the director of inner-city programs for Girl Scouts and had years of organizing experience. Volunteering was a brave move; three organizers had just been killed when the call came out for more volunteers. Despite Goodman's experience, her arrival (and that of her colleague, Susan Brownmiller) was met with derision by SNCC's field secretary: "Shit! I asked for volunteers and they sent me white women." Brownmiller, *supra* note 35, at 14–15. The same year, Mary King and Casey Hayden, SNCC volunteers, anonymously wrote a paper entitled "The Position of Women in SNCC," in which they criticized the "assumptions of male superiority" true of the general society and mirrored in the leadership of SNCC. The paper was ridiculed. It resurfaced the next year in an expanded version and this time the authors dared to sign their name. In 1966 it became the subject of intense conversation at a national SDS conference. *Id.*

47. Interview with Elizabeth Schneider and Nancy Stearns, *supra* note 1.

48. *See, e.g.,* Drew Municipal School District v. Andrews, 507 F.2d 611 (5th Cir. 1975), *cert. granted*, 423 U.S. 820 (1975), *cert. dismissed*, 425 U.S. 559 (1976) (CCR

work for the civil rights of women—in criminal as well as civil court-rooms—for which she is best known. She would become an internation-ally recognized expert on women's rights generally, and an expert on legal responses to domestic violence, in particular. She would author the prizewinning book *Battered Women and Feminist Lawmaking*, co-author a law school casebook on domestic violence, and consult for the U.N. Secretary General's *In–Depth Study of All Forms of Violence Against Women*.[49] This work began with *Wanrow*.

The Stories Converge:
The Story of State v. Wanrow

Though the facts surrounding the killing of William Wesler were sharply contested at trial, there was no real disagreement about what occurred the evening before his death.[50] On August 11, 1972, Yvonne Wanrow left her two children at the home of her friend Shirley Hooper so that she could go to a doctor's appointment. She had a broken foot and was wearing a cast. This was the first day that she was allowed to put weight on her foot. Wanrow's car broke down after her doctor's appointment, so she caught a ride to her home and called Hooper to say that she would be late to pick up her children. Hooper told her that they could spend the night, and Wanrow agreed to pick them up the next day.

Shirley Hooper lived in a small house in a mostly industrial area of town.[51] Because there were only a few residences, the area was lonely and grew very dark at night. But Hooper's reasons to be afraid went beyond her unfriendly environs. Only months earlier, her seven year old daughter had been sexually molested. Her daughter refused to identify the attacker, but the physical evidence was clear: the young child had contracted a venereal disease. Then, just a few nights before the day of the killing, Hooper saw a man crouching near the front of her house.

---

attorneys Copelon, Schneider, Morton Stavis, and Stearns, along with Legal Services lawyers, brought a successful challenge on behalf of African American women who were fired or not hired due to a school policy of not employing unwed mothers); Delfin Ramos Colon v. U.S. Attorney for the District of Puerto Rico, 576 F.2d 1 (1st Cir. 1978) (Schneider and co-counsel filed a motion for the appointment of a special prosecutor and investigation of proceedings against the U.S. Attorney's Office for the District of Puerto Rico on the basis that the government acted in bad faith in prosecuting petitioner for his political beliefs, knowing that it had insufficient evidence for the charge); *see also* Schneider, *supra* note 6, at 29 (describing CCR women's rights cases).

   49. See Schneider, *supra* note 6; Elizabeth M. Schneider, Cheryl Hanna, Judith G. Greenberg & Clare Dalton, *Domestic Violence and the Law: Theory and Practice* (2d ed. 2008); Women's Rights Section, United Nations Division for the Advancement of Women, *The Secretary–General's In–Depth Study on All Forms of Violence Against Women* (2006).

   50. The facts and witness statements described in this section are from the *Wanrow* Trial Transcript, unless otherwise noted.

   51. Swan Interview, *supra* note 1.

And only the night before, her bedroom window screen had been slashed for the second night in a row. It was a hot August night, and it seemed clear to Hooper that the person who slashed her screen was trying—or planning—to break into her house. Hooper told Wanrow about the prowler incident that morning when Wanrow dropped off her children, but she kept the information about her daughter's abuse to herself.

At some time after 6 p.m., Hooper called Wanrow in a panic. Hooper needed Wanrow to come over right away, and she wanted Wanrow to bring her gun.[52] William Wesler, her neighbor next door, had tried to grab Wanrow's son, Darren. Darren had broken free of Wesler's grasp and run to Hooper's house, leaving his bicycle behind. Just as Darren appeared breathless at Hooper's door, Wesler arrived claiming "I didn't touch the boy." Hooper recognized Wesler; he was the man she had seen hiding near the front of her house a few nights earlier. But the most terrifying revelation was yet to come. While Wesler stood on Hooper's front porch, Hooper's seven year old daughter told her that Wesler was the man who had molested her.

Hooper's landlords Mr. and Mrs. Joseph Fah[53] were at her house when Wesler appeared at Hooper's door. They were there to replace her slashed bedroom window screen. Hooper also had Joseph Fah look at her front porch light which had stopped working. Fah found that the bulb was fine; the problem was that someone had unscrewed it from the socket.

Joseph Fah recognized Wesler. He told Hooper that Wesler had attempted to molest the child of a prior tenant of the same house and that he had heard that Wesler had been committed to Medical Lakes, the state hospital for the mentally ill.

Hooper called the police and officers came to the house and took her statement. Despite Hooper's insistence that Wesler posed a threat to her safety and that of her children, the officers refused to arrest him. They told her that she would have to go to the District Attorney's office on Monday to file a complaint. Fah suggested that if Wesler returned, Hooper should "conk him on the head" with a baseball bat to which the police responded, "Yes, but wait until he gets in the house." The police also suggested that Hooper sprinkle flour by her bedroom window so that if someone tried to break in, his footprints would be captured in the flour.

Wanrow tried to convince Hooper that it would be safer if she and the children all came to Wanrow's house, but Hooper insisted that she

---

52. Hooper testified that it was Wanrow's idea to bring the gun, while Wanrow testified that it was Hooper's idea.

53. The woman is referred to only as "Mrs. Joe Fah" in the trial transcript. Trial Transcript at 268, State v. Wanrow, No. 20876 (Wash. Super. Ct. 1973).

wanted to stay in her own home. When Wanrow got off the phone with Hooper, she grabbed her crutches, milk and clothes for her children, a six-pack of beer, and, with some reluctance, her gun, and she took a cab to Hooper's house. On the way, she left a note at a friend's house, asking her to come to Hooper's house to help them. Wanrow arrived at Hooper's house at about 9 p.m. Darren rushed to hug her. He showed her the bruise on his arm from where Wesler had grabbed him. He said that he had entered Wesler's house because Wesler promised to show him how his dog ate cat food. Unbeknownst to Wanrow at the time, Darren's story matched the facts of complaints reported to the police as early as 1969. In three separate incidents, children and their parents reported to the police that Wesler had lured children into his house with promises of candy, cigarettes, or other treats and that once inside, Wesler had sexually assaulted them.[54]

The police were no longer at Hooper's house when Wanrow arrived, but the Fahs were still there making home repairs. Soon the Fahs left, and Wanrow and Hooper faced the night alone, sleeping next door to an identified child molester who Hooper believed had tried to break into her house. After putting the five children to bed, Wanrow and Hooper continued to rehearse the events of the day, becoming more and more frightened at the prospect of spending the night without a car and without more adults. They thought of several people they might call and finally settled on calling Wanrow's sister Angie Michel and Angie's husband Chuck. The Michels and their three young children arrived at Hooper's house at about eleven at night. There were now eight children in the house ranging in age from a few months old to eight years old.

The adults were jumpy and nervous. They stayed awake, drinking beer and talking, going over and over the events of the day. They could see Wesler's house from Hooper's back porch, and they spent considerable time watching his house for signs that he was coming over. Wanrow carried her gun in the waistband of her pants. When day began to break, Wanrow and Hooper noticed that Chuck Michel, who had been sitting on the back porch alone for some time, was no longer in the house.

---

54. The *Wanrow* case record reveals that in 1969 there were two prior reports of Wesler perpetrating child sex abuse and a third report alleging that he gave children beer and cigarettes. Ironically, only the last (and less serious) allegation resulted in criminal charges. He was found guilty of vagrancy, ordered to serve ninety days in jail with eighty-eight days suspended on good behavior, and was additionally ordered not to have any children in his house. The police officer's notes state that it was impossible to bring charges for the two alleged incidents of sexual abuse, because the children were unable to remember the dates on which the alleged acts of molestation occurred. Report No.421154 filed on May 31, 1969; Report No. 438565 filed on Dec. 15, 1969; Report No. 4213684 filed on May 29, 1969, in *State v. Wanrow* case file.

According to Wanrow, about thirty minutes after noticing Michel's absence, she saw him in the front yard with two men she did not recognize.[55] When one of the men, later identified as Wesler, appeared at the front door, Hooper began screaming, "I don't want that man in here!" Wesler, who was a large man and who was visibly intoxicated at the time, ignored Hooper, walked into the house, and moved towards the couch where Angie Michel's son was sleeping. Awakened by Hooper's screaming, the boy began crying. Wesler continued to approach him and, according to Hooper's testimony, said, "My, what a cute little boy."

Wanrow testified that she rushed to the front porch to call for Chuck Michel's assistance, but he did not respond. She turned to reenter the house. She testified at trial as to what happened next:

A: I had the gun in [the waistband of] my pants.... I was walking on this cast. And I turned around, and all of a sudden he was there.

Q: About how close to you was he when you saw him?

A: Close. Just—I could have touched him.

Q: And did he continue to make any movement ... toward you ...?

A: ... To me it seemed like he was coming right at me. He was just there, you know.

Q: Then what did you do?

A: I pulled the trigger of the gun.

Q: Do you remember grabbing hold of it?

A: No, I don't remember (crying).[56]

Wanrow also fired three shots at Wesler's friend, David Kelly, hitting him once in the right arm. She testified at trial that she didn't remember firing at Kelly. The only memory she had of him was seeing a man running down the street and thinking that the man was hurt.

After Wesler was shot, Hooper called the police and both Hooper and Wanrow spoke with the police dispatcher. During the conversation, Hooper stated: "Please come to 2903 E. Gordon, there is a guy broke in and my girlfriend shot him." Wanrow then took the telephone and told the police operator that she had shot two people. She repeatedly urged the police to "hurry up" because she was afraid that they were in danger: "I'm the only one that has a weapon and the guy might come

---

55. Chuck Michel testified that he went to Wesler's house and accused him of molesting children and that Wesler suggested that they go together to Hooper's home to "get the whole thing straightened out." Wesler's companion, David Kelly, testified that it was *Michel's* idea to go to Hooper's house. Wanrow testified that she did not know that Michel went to Wesler's house.

56. *Wanrow*, Trial Transcript at 300.

back with another gun."[57] The dispatcher told her that they had received
a call from an injured man who was presently at a nearby service
station. Wanrow responded, "We warned you—we told you guys." Neither Hooper nor Wanrow realized that the 911 call was being recorded.
When the police arrived shortly thereafter, Wanrow was arrested and
charged with second-degree murder in the death of Wesler and first-
degree assault for the shooting of Kelly. She spent three nights in jail
before she was released on bond and her case was assigned to a public
defender. Years later, Wanrow vividly recalled her first meeting with her
defense attorney:

> I didn't get a good feeling about him because he didn't seem willing
> to defend me. . . . He painted a gloomy picture. . . . I was sitting in
> his office, and my leg was still in a cast, and I must have looked
> really . . . pitiful. I felt small, anyway, because he was such a big
> man. . . . I tried to encourage him to go to trial for me. He said,
> "Yvonne you know you're guilty." I couldn't believe it, this was my
> lawyer! I just looked at him. I said, "But I don't *feel* guilty."

Nevertheless, in October 1972, Wanrow took her lawyer's advice and
entered a guilty plea. She recalled feeling that she "was up against the
whole system, and it was all non-Indian to me, so I just thought the
worst." About two months after entering her guilty plea, while awaiting
her sentencing hearing, Wanrow talked by phone with her nephew,
Jimmy Swan, who offered to send her money for an attorney. He told
her "Don't let them railroad you, get an attorney with the money I'm
sending you, fight it like an Indian." Wanrow, who was raised Catholic
and attended Catholic schools, turned to her childhood priest Father
Doyle for advice. Doyle recommended she contact local attorney Eugene
Annis. Father Doyle had watched Annis in court and thought he was
smart and tough. Annis was a young lawyer with a diversified litigation
practice. Annis agreed to take the case, in part because he thought there
were unique circumstances in the case that did not warrant a second-
degree murder conviction.[58] He had handled a number of criminal cases
before, but this was to be his first murder trial.[59] Wanrow retracted her
guilty plea in December 1972,[60] and entered a plea of not guilty, which
was later amended to include a plea of not guilty by reason of insanity.[61]
Wanrow's trial began on May 7, 1973.

---

57.   *Wanrow*, Trial Transcript at 13 (transcribing from the 911 tape).

58.   Annis Interview, *supra* note 1.

59.   Annis Interview, *supra* note 1.

60.   On Feb. 2, 1973, the Court granted defendant's motion and allowed her to
withdraw the plea. Washington allowed a defendant to substitute a plea as a matter of
right if the substitution motion was filed prior to judgment (RCW 10.40.175) or if the
defendant showed a prima facie defense on the merits.

61.   Annis recalls that initially Brockett contemplated charging Wanrow with first-
degree premeditated murder, but Annis was able to persuade him to pursue the lesser
second-degree murder charge. Annis Interview, *supra* note 1.

The morning that Wanrow's trial was to begin, Annis was horrified to read the following in the local Spokane newspaper:

> Yvonne Wanrow . . . is being charged in the death Aug.12 of William E. Wesler. . . . Mrs. Wanrow had pleaded guilty to the charge last year but changed the plea to innocent.[62]

The jury had been allowed to return home the prior evening. Annis moved for a mistrial, arguing that the potential prejudice to Wanrow was significant. The trial court denied the motion. The court then questioned jurors about the newspaper article, but the questions were not transcribed. The transcript includes only this summary statement:

> Following the recess the jury was returned to the courtroom and asked [as a group] . . . whether they had read or learned anything about the case from [local newspapers] and the response was negative.[63]

The Spokane County Prosecutor Donald Brockett and deputy prosecutor Fred Caruso represented the state. The prosecution's theory of the case was that Wanrow had lured Wesler to Hooper's house with the intent of killing him in revenge for his abuse of Hooper's child and his attempt to molest Darren. The state's case relied heavily on the testimony of Hooper and Kelly. Hooper's statement to the police immediately following the shooting largely corroborated Wanrow's description of events: Wesler entered her home uninvited; Hooper screamed for him to leave. To this, she added that she saw Wanrow "kinda reach" for Wesler, after which she (Hooper) went to the kitchen and did not see Wanrow shoot Wesler.[64] Her only comment regarding Wanrow's behavior earlier in the evening was that Wanrow and Chuck Michel "were arguing and making things worse than what it really should have came out to be." But at trial, Hooper's testimony changed. She said that earlier in the evening, Wanrow had said she was going to "fix" Wesler and at a different time had insisted, "We are going to get it over with." In addition, Wanrow had said that she knew how to handle the police because they were just like California police, adding, "I have done it before; I have pleaded insanity." Hooper added that just before the killing, she saw Wanrow grab Wesler's arm and lead him to the front door. Hooper turned her back and returned to the kitchen. Then she heard the gun go off. She ran to the living room and saw Wanrow

---

62. Appellant's Brief at 53, State v. Wanrow, No. 20876 (Wash. Super. Ct. 1973); *see also* State v. Wanrow, Trial Transcript at 31 (motion for mistrial).

63. *Wanrow* Trial Transcript at 31–32.

64. Statement of Shirley Kay Hooper taken by Detective Al Hales, Aug. 12, 1972, Misc. 72–54656 (in court file for State v. Wanrow).

leaning over Wesler and heard Wanrow say, "You will never molest another son—another child, you son-of-a-bitch."

Kelly testified that when he and Wesler arrived at Hooper's house, two women—one of whom was Wanrow—invited them inside to have a drink. They declined, and Kelly went to the side of the house with Chuck Michel to see the flour Hooper had placed under her bedroom window, per police instructions. Wesler told Kelly that he was going to knock on the door and clear things up with Hooper whom neither Kelly nor Wesler had yet seen. Kelly returned to the front of the house just a few minutes later and entered the house with Chuck Michel. Wesler was already inside. As testified to by all the other witnesses, Kelly testified that Hooper was screaming for Wesler to leave. According to Kelly, Wanrow then told Hooper to "shut up, he ain't bothering anybody." Contradicting his prior statement to the police that Wanrow was carrying her gun in the waistband of her pants, Kelly testified that Wanrow left the room, returned with a gun in her hand, went to the front door to shut the door—not to call for Michel, as Wanrow testified—and then turned and fired on Wesler. After shooting Wesler, she turned the gun on Kelly. Kelly said that he then ran out the front door and as he was running, he heard Wanrow say, "Come back here, I have another one for you."

The prosecutors contended in closing arguments that Wanrow's calm demeanor immediately after the killing, as captured in her 911 call to the police, suggested that she planned the killing. Didn't she seem calm on the 911 call tape? Didn't she say, "We warned you guys"? Doesn't that sound like a planned killing?

The defense attacked Hooper's credibility by presenting evidence that Hooper had become hostile to Wanrow some time after the homicide as the likely result of her boyfriend's hostility towards Wanrow's family. Hooper's boyfriend, Melvin Talou, was the ex-husband of Wanrow's sister Angie Michel. Wanrow had no prior criminal record, so it made no sense that she would say that she had pled insanity before. It was Talou who had a criminal record. And it was Talou who forbade Hooper from talking with Wanrow's defense counsel, telling counsel that Hooper wasn't going to talk to him, adding for good measure, that he hoped Wanrow "gets it" (i.e., is convicted). As to Kelly's testimony, the defense pointed out that no other witnesses recalled Kelly being inside the room at the time Wanrow shot Wesler, though all recalled seeing Kelly running across the front yard after the shooting. No other witnesses testified to hearing Wanrow tell Hooper to "shut up" or to her saying to Kelly, "come back here, I have another one for you." In fact, the other witnesses testified that the front door was propped open by a box of old records and that closing the door would have required Wanrow to move the box—an improbable scenario, given that Wanrow was hobbling on a cast and, according to Kelly, holding a gun in her hand. Further, it strained belief that Kelly and Wesler would have just stood there while Wanrow, moving slowly on her cast, walked through the room and directly past them holding a gun, or that Kelly could have run from inside the living room through the front door where Wanrow was standing, without knocking Wanrow down on his way out the door.

After each side had presented its case, the court delivered jury instructions setting forth the law of self-defense. Wanrow was charged with first-degree assault for the shooting of Kelly and felony murder for Wesler's death, with assault (on Wesler) serving as the predicate felony. Washington law was unusual in allowing assault to serve as a predicate felony for felony murder.[65] As a result, the prosecutor did not have to prove that Wanrow intended to kill Wesler. He only needed to prove that she intentionally used force against or intentionally inflicted bodily injury on Wesler and that she used a weapon likely to produce bodily harm.

If Washington's felony murder law was unusual, the self-defense law was not. Washington law provided that a person is justified in the use of deadly force against another person if he honestly and reasonably believed that he was in imminent danger of serious bodily injury or death and that the use of such force was necessary to avoid the danger. But in applying this fairly standard American legal doctrine requiring that the response to a perceived threat be proportional to the threat, the trial judge in Wanrow's case construed it in a way arguably narrower than standard doctrine—and certainly narrower than what American law would become in the years after this case. In Instruction 10, the *Wanrow* court directed the jury to consider only those acts and circumstances occurring "at or immediately before the killing."

The court's proportionality instruction read as follows:

> When there is no reasonable ground for the person attacked to believe that his person is in imminent danger of death or great bodily harm, and it appears to him that only an ordinary battery is all that is intended, and all that he has reasonable grounds to fear from his assailant, he has a right to stand his ground and repel such threatened assault, yet he has no right to repel a threatened assault with naked hands, by the use of a deadly weapon in a deadly manner, unless he believes, and has reasonable grounds to believe, that he is in imminent danger of death or great bodily harm.[66]

---

65. State v. Harris, 421 P.2d 662 (Wash. 1996). The law in most jurisdictions was that assault "merged" with the murder charge and therefore could not serve as a predicate felony for felony murder.

66. State v. Wanrow, 559 P.2d 548, 558 (Wash. 1977) (italics in original) (quoting Jury Instruction 10).

The jury, composed of five women and seven men—all of them white—deliberated for twenty-three hours. The trial court had ruled that the 911 tape was not to enter the jury deliberation room. The jury twice requested to hear the tape again, and twice the court denied the request. But when the jury asked a third time, the court relented. A mere forty-five minutes after receiving the tape, the jury returned a verdict of guilty.[67] The verdict was delivered on Mother's Day, May 13, 1973. Nearly forty years later, Annis remembers vividly that several women on the jury were in tears as the verdict was read.

Wanrow appealed her conviction to the Intermediate Court of Appeal. On appeal, Annis argued that the trial courts' decision to admit the 911 tape was error under a new Washington State law that made it unlawful for a municipality to record private communications between individuals without the consent of all participants to the conversation.[68] Annis also argued that the trial court erred in denying his motion to call an expert witness on Native American culture, in refusing to grant a mistrial on the basis of prejudicial pretrial publicity, and in its jury instructions on self-defense. The court allowed Wanrow to be free on bail pending her appeal.

Two years after the trial verdict was reached, the Court of Appeals issued its opinion.[69] Its holding would hardly have foretold the ultimate legacy of the case. The Court reversed Wanrow's conviction, finding that Washington's privacy statute prevented the introduction of the 911 tape made without Wanrow's awareness. The Court rejected Wanrow's arguments that the trial court erred when it failed to admit expert testimony regarding Native American culture, and said not a word about whether the self-defense instruction was faulty.

With her initial appeal won, Wanrow waited to see if the prosecution would appeal the appellate court decision to the Washington Supreme Court, bring charges again, or (the least likely outcome of all) drop the case. While awaiting the government's decision, Wanrow attended the Wounded Knee-related trial of AIM member Russell Means in 1975. She was impressed with what she saw in Means's lawyer, CCR attorney Bill Kunstler. After watching Kunstler in action, Wanrow thought, "I wish I had *that* lawyer.... [I wanted] to see if I could get him to take my case."

---

67. Eugene Annis believes that the tape was particularly "damning evidence." He remembers that as a witness Wanrow seemed too "intellectual" and less warm than she was in other settings. Thus, the prosecutor's argument that she sounded "cool" and calculated on the phone was consistent with her demeanor on the stand. Annis Interview, *supra* note 1.

68. State v. Wanrow, 538 P.2d 849, 851 (Wash. Ct. App. 1975) (discussing RCW 9.73.030).

69. *See Id.* at 852–53.

Wanrow sought the help of Floyd Westerman, a well-known Native American country folksinger and AIM activist with whom she was romantically involved. Westerman had rallied many Native American people to attend Wanrow's hearing at the Court of Appeals, and she thought he would be able to help arrange a meeting for her with Kunstler. Westerman was traveling to New York, and though she had only enough money for a one-way ticket, Wanrow arranged to go with him.

Once in New York, Wanrow met with Kunstler, who told her, "I read the papers that you gave me and I see some . . . women's issues in there." Kunstler told Wanrow that he thought that the women attorneys at CCR would be interested in taking her case, but if they declined, he would agree to represent her.

Wanrow then met with Schneider and Stearns. Nearly thirty years later, she still remembers how impressed she was with their sensitivity to the gender politics of her case, but also to its inevitable racial politics. Stearns and Schneider decided to take the case in part because the accused was a Native American woman and they were familiar with the issues of anti-Indian racism likely to be present in a criminal trial in Spokane. Their choice was solidified by the fact that Wanrow was an incredibly motivated client who had already organized a significant defense committee in support of her case.

Already overjoyed at her meetings with the CCR attorneys, Wanrow found further good fortune in New York when Westerman introduced her to the actor and singer Harry Belafonte, who bought her a ticket home.

The Appeal

The state filed an appeal with the Washington Supreme Court on September 25, 1975. Annis, who was still Wanrow's attorney of record, filed a brief arguing that the trial court's self-defense instruction was in error because it "fail[ed] to clearly indicate that the jury must judge the appellant's actions from the circumstances as they reasonably appear to the appellant at the time of the alleged illegal act."[70] Annis's brief also stated that "[the instruction] fails to unambiguously require the jury to consider the circumstances as they would have confronted a reasonable man in the appellant's position."[71] Annis further argued that, although the instruction may have included the key elements of self-defense, "the proper parts are so submerged in prejudicial language as to render the instruction as given ineffective."

---

70. Brief of Respondent at 45, State v. Wanrow, 559 P.2d 548 (Wash. 1977) (No. 43949).

71. *Id.* (emphasis in original.)

On February 11, 1976, having substituted as Wanrow's counsel, Schneider and Stearns filed a supplemental brief with the Washington Supreme Court.[72] As Schneider later noted, it was only after reading the trial transcript, that she and Stearns realized that

> [t]he judge's instructions [on self-defense] had prevented the jury from considering Yvonne Wanrow's state of mind, as shaped by her experiences and perspective as a Native American woman, when she confronted Wesler. The jury had not been presented with evidence concerning the general lack of police protection in such situations, the pervasiveness of violence against women and children, the effect on Wanrow of her belief that Wesler was a child molester, Wanrow's lack of trust in the police, and her belief that she could successfully defend herself only with a weapon. Moreover, the judge's instruction directed the jury to apply the equal-force standard and prevented them from considering Wanrow's perspective when it evaluated her claim of self-defense.[73]

The brief "grew out of a political analysis of gender discrimination." The theory that emerged "brought together diverse strands of feminist analysis and theory concerning gender bias in the criminal justice system."[74]

In their brief, Schneider and Stearns argued that "Instruction [number 10] not only fails to inform the jury that the standard to be applied is that of Yvonne Wanrow's own perspective . . ., but, in effect, it established an erroneous, sex-stereotyped and inflexible standard which directed the jury to exclude Respondent' [sic] own perspective."[75] This resulted from a set of erroneous statements included in Instruction 10. Each misstatement, they argued, was likely reversible error in its own right, but *combined*, these statements did further egregious harm to Wanrow's right to a fair trial.

First, the court's instruction that the jury consider only those acts or circumstances occurring "at or immediately before the killing" contradicted Washington law requiring the jury to consider *all* the circumstances surrounding the incident in determining whether the defendant had reasonable grounds to believe grievous bodily harm was about to be

---

72. Annis filed the response brief before Schneider and Stearns were substituted as counsel. The court granted them permission to file a supplemental brief. The state filed a motion to strike the supplemental brief on the grounds that, in contravention of the court's order, the brief went beyond the issues presented in Annis's initial brief. The court denied the motion.

73. Schneider, *supra* note 6, at 30.

74. *Id.* at 3–4.

75. Supplemental Brief of Respondent at 1–2, State v. Wanrow, 559 P.2d 548 (Wash. 1977) (No. 43949).

inflicted. Requiring the jury to focus exclusively on acts that occurred "at or immediately before the killing" prevented jurors from considering the very evidence necessary to judge the reasonableness of Wanrow's belief that she needed to defend herself or another. This language would prevent jurors from considering most of the events that occurred within twenty-four hours of the homicide: Wesler had grabbed her son; Hooper's daughter had identified Wesler as the man who had sexually assaulted her; Hooper's landlord had stated that Wesler had molested a prior tenant's young son; Hooper had told Wanrow about seeing someone she thought was Wesler crouching in the bushes outside her home the week before; someone had twice attempted to break into Hooper's home in the previous four days and had cut the screen on her bedroom window; someone had unscrewed her front porch light; and the police had refused to arrest Wesler on charges of child sexual assault or attempted kidnapping. By contrast, within the limits of Instruction 10, what events and circumstances might the jury consider? Wesler, a large sixty-year-old man standing six feet ten inches, had entered Hooper's residence despite her screaming for him to leave; Wesler had been intoxicated when he entered the house; he approached Wanrow's young nephew on the couch; he remarked that the boy was cute; Wanrow was five feet four inches, a small woman, had a leg in a cast and had been using a crutch; Wanrow had gone to the door to call for Chuck Michel's assistance and received no reply; when she turned around, Wesler was right in front of her and seemed to be coming towards her.

More boldly, Schneider and Stearns argued that the second error in Instruction 10 was the court's failure to instruct the jury to determine the defendant's reasonableness from the perspective of a reasonable person in the defendant's situation, as the defendant understood the situation. Gender, they argued, was a critical part of Wanrow's situation. They explained that gender roles have

> relegated women to a position of second-class citizenship with respect to their abilities to defend themselves. Women have been denied equal opportunity to education, access to physical training, and athletics.... Women have been discouraged from learning how to physically defend themselves ... and are socialized to be less active physically, to display physical aggression less overtly, and to be more sensitive to physical pain than boys.

As a result of this socialization, women "experience great anxiety when confronted with a situation where they must display aggression." The attorneys referred to research on rape supporting the view that women experienced a complete loss of confidence in their ability to protect themselves from a physical attack. They cited research showing the grossly inadequate criminal justice response to child abuse and rape of women.[76] They explained that society's failure to protect women from male violence should play an important role in defining women's reasonable assessment of danger. And they argued that the effects of gender socialization and experiences of inadequate police protection were evident in Wanrow's case: she was a small woman, facing a child molester, and facing him without state assistance because the police had refused to intervene.

Third, defense counsel argued that the proportionality component of Instruction 10—including the language "he [the defendant] has no right to repel a threatened assault with naked hands, by the use of a deadly weapon in a deadly manner . . ."—was erroneous because it created a standard "more appropriate to a fist fight between two men, than a physical confrontation between a large drunk man and a small woman on crutches." The distinction between an "ordinary assault" and a "deadly assault" might be a "meaningful distinction when the victim and assailant are both men, accustomed to the notion of physical assault. . . . [B]ut women do not have the same history or experience." Furthermore, "[t]he very notion of a 5'4" woman standing her ground and repelling the threatened assault of a 6'2" man without reliance on a weapon is absurd." They also noted that the instruction's persistent use of the male pronoun to refer to the defendant further encouraged the jury to think of reasonableness in terms of what a male defendant would do and believe.

The CCR lawyers thus challenged the homicide law applied in Wanrow's trial as de facto gender biased. Implicit in the CCR brief was the notion that gender bias exists not only when facial distinctions are made between men and women, but also when the paradigm examples that inform legal categories are experiences that are mostly those of men and not women.[77] As Schneider later explained, she and her fellow CCR

---

76. *See* Supplemental Brief, *supra* note 75. Schneider and Stearns cited research finding that only 29% of rapes that were reported in 1975 in Spokane resulted in an arrest and only 35% in 1976; in April, 1977, only 35 arrests (5%) were made as a result of 590 calls to police by women complaining of domestic violence. Police enforcement of child molestation laws, according to the defense brief, was "apparently characterized by a similar unwillingness to intervene and prosecute." *Id.* at 15–16 (citing De Francis, *Protecting the Child Victim of Sex Crimes Committed by Adults*, 35 Federal Probation 15 (1971)).

77. Similar arguments regarding the ways in which criminal law reflects a "male" point of view would be made by later feminist scholars. *See, e.g.,* Donna Coker, *Heat of Passion and Wife Killing: Men Who Batter/Men Who Kill*, 2 S. Cal. Rev. L. & Women's Stud. 71 (1992) (arguing that the paradigm examples and emotions embodied in voluntary manslaughter's heat of passion enshrine male concepts and male experience of reasonableness, rather than women's); *see generally* Susan D. Rozelle, *The Story of* Berry: *When Hot Blood Cools*, this volume; Cynthia Lee, *Murder and the Reasonable Man: Passion and Fear in the Criminal Courtroom* 277 (2003) (urging mechanisms such as "switching" to overcome the fact that "certain defendants, namely, majority culture defendants, are able

attorneys developed a "legal argument for women's 'equal right to trial,' which maintained that the law of self-defense was biased against women." She wrote:

> The argument was based on our knowledge of the particular problems that women who killed men faced in the criminal justice system: the prevalence of homicides committed by women in circumstances of male physical abuse or sexual assault; the different circumstances in which men and women kill; stereotypes and other misconceptions in the criminal justice system that brand women who kill as 'crazy'; the deeply ingrained problems of domestic violence, physical abuse, and sexual abuse of women and children; the physical and psychological barriers that prevent women from feeling capable of defending themselves; and stereotypes of women as unreasonable.[78]

Meanwhile, as Schneider and Stearns were hard at work on their brief, Wanrow was gathering additional support for her cause. She and her sisters, all talented artists and craftswomen, organized the Defense Committee for Yvonne Wanrow. The sisters used their fashion design know-how to create fashion shows in order to raise money and publicize Wanrow's plight. The shows were successful. During one show, Wanrow met the famed singer Buffy Sainte–Marie, herself of native ancestry. Saint–Marie gave Wanrow a check and told her to work with her publicist to get the word out about her case. The result was a five-page press release that Wanrow and her team began feeding to the feminist and the Native American press.

While publicists and feminist activists helped Wanrow connect with alternative newspapers, community organizers, and women's movement activists, Wanrow continued to work with Native American activists, most importantly AIM members and members of the Native American Church. As a result, Wanrow's message began to spread through a diverse, national network.

Throughout the process, Wanrow worked collaboratively with her attorneys, Schneider and Stearns. Years later, Wanrow recalled:

> I liked the team of women lawyers because they educated me on every step of the way; they'd explain it and they'd look at me and say, 'do you understand Yvonne?' ... But yet ultimately it was my choice. As the defendant, I had the choice as to which direction the case should go.... [With] any of the male attorneys, I felt like a dummy sitting there.... I grew up with four sisters.... There was

---

to rely on dominant social norms of masculinity, race, and sexual orientation to bolster their claims of reasonableness while others cannot").

78. Schneider, supra note 6, at 31.

a natural built-in sisterhood, so I never had to explain myself to women or sisters ... And so it made sense that I had a team of women lawyers.

The Washington Supreme Court Decision

The Supreme Court of Washington issued its decision in *State v. Wanrow* on January 7, 1977. The decision was a 5–3 victory for Wanrow and her attorneys. A majority of the court, composed of five justices, affirmed the appellate court's ruling that the recorded 911 call was inadmissible.[79] A plurality, consisting of four justices, held that the trial court committed reversible error in the jury instruction on self-defense.[80] One of the five who found error in admitting the tape filed a concurrence that said nothing about the self-defense instruction. Three justices dissented, arguing both that the tape was admissible and that the self-defense instruction was proper.

Though only a plurality found fault with the self-defense instruction, their opinion came to have a dramatic effect on American law. The plurality's opinion first stated that the trial court erred in directing the jury to consider only those acts and circumstances occurring "at or immediately before the killing," stating in clear terms that "[t]his is not now, and never has been, the law of self-defense in Washington. On the contrary, the justification of self-defense is to be evaluated in light of *all* the facts and circumstances known to the defendant, including those known substantially before the killing."[81]

The opinion next explained that Instruction 10 contained "an equally erroneous and prejudicial statement of the law" insofar as it directed the jury to evaluate the reasonableness of Wanrow's fear without considering how her gender might have colored her perspective.

> In our society women suffer from a conspicuous lack of access to training in and the means of developing those skills necessary to effectively repel a male assailant without resorting to the use of deadly weapons. [The jury instructions do] not make clear that the defendant's actions are to be judged against her own subjective impressions and not those which a detached jury might determine to be objectively reasonable.

The plurality further explained that the error in Instruction 10 was not only in its establishment of an objective standard for judging reasonable-

---

79. *Wanrow*, 559 P.2d 548, 555 (Wash. 1977).

80. Justice Robert C. Finley died unexpectedly a month after oral argument in the case, so only eight justices participated in the decision. *See* http://templeofjustice.org/justices/past/james-m-dolliver.

81. *Wanrow*, 559 P.2d at 555. Subsequent quotes in this section are from the published opinion unless otherwise indicated.

ness, but also in its "persistent use of the masculine gender," accepting the argument of Schneider and Stearns that such gendered language "leaves the jury with the impression the objective standard to be applied is that applicable to an altercation between two men."

Ultimately, said the plurality, the trial court's use of an entirely "objective" self-defense standard violated Wanrow's right to equal protection of the law.

> The impression created—that a 5 4 woman with a cast on her leg and using a crutch must, under the law, somehow repel an assault by a 6 2 intoxicated man without employing weapons in her defense, unless the jury finds her determination of the degree of danger to be objectively reasonable—constitutes a separate and distinct misstatement of the law and, in the context of this case, violates the respondent's right to equal protection of the law. The respondent was entitled to have the jury consider her actions in the light of her own perceptions of the situation, including those perceptions which were the product of our nation's 'long and unfortunate history of sex discrimination.'

Since Wanrow's perception of the situation on the morning of the murder was colored by her own experiences with societal sex discrimination,

> until such time as the effects of [discrimination] are eradicated, care must be taken to assure that our self-defense instructions afford women the right to have their conduct judged in light of the individual physical handicaps which are the product of sex discrimination. To fail to do so is to deny the right of the individual woman involved to trial by the same rules which are applicable to male defendants.

Perhaps an even greater significance of the decision for American criminal law lies in a crucial nuance about the standard for self-defense—the principle that the opposite of the erroneous "reasonable man standard" is *not* what people think of as a "subjective" standard. Although the *Wanrow* court seemed to have announced that it was error for the trial court to apply an "objective" standard of reasonableness, the Court did not mean that Washington law embraced a completely subjective test that would simply ask whether the defendant actually and honestly believed deadly force to be necessary. Rather, the opinion in *Wanrow* expressly stated that the jury was to determine the " 'degree of force which ... *a reasonable person* in the same situation ... seeing what (s)he sees and knowing what (s)he knows, ... would believe is necessary.' " What the *Wanrow* court recognized was that an instruction that encouraged jurors to judge a female defendant's reasonableness vis-à-vis a male standard of conduct and belief was not an "objective" standard, but a particularized male standard. The misnamed "objective" standard was therefore not supplanted by a subjective standard, but rather by a more accurate objective standard that takes into account the context of the defendant's background and situation. In other words, the Court replaced a standard that appeared to be objective but was in fact quite biased with a standard that might be mistaken for subjective but was in fact far less biased than its predecessor.

Despite the desired result, the victory for Wanrow was partial. The Washington Supreme Court affirmed the ruling of the Court of Appeals that the trial court did not abuse its discretion in declining to allow expert testimony on the relevance of Wanrow's Native American culture to her self-defense claim. In addition, the Court declined to rule on the argument that Wanrow suffered prejudice because of pretrial publicity and racial bias generated by publicity critical of AIM and other Native American activist efforts. Nevertheless, Schneider, Stearns, and Wanrow were satisfied with the win.

The prosecutors, on the other hand, were furious with the Court's recitation of the facts from the defense perspective without acknowledging that these facts had been controverted by the prosecution. In a strongly worded pleading, Brockett and Caruso filed a petition for rehearing, arguing that there were serious misstatements of fact in the majority opinion which

> [a]lthough ... not ... crucial to a determination of the legal issues involved, ... [are] of great importance in light of the national attention this case has received, with the facts often being exaggerated, misreported, and portrayed in a one-sided manner more favorable to the defendant than she is truly entitled to. The effect of such inaccurate reporting is to challenge the very integrity of our judicial system."[82]

On April 5, 1977, the Washington Supreme Court denied the State's petition for rehearing.

The Immediate Aftermath

Nancy Stearns later recalled, "The truth is we were stunned when we got the opinion.... We thought we were right, [but] in a million years I don't [think] we thought we'd get that opinion." The criminal defense bar and feminist activists were stunned as well. Soon, Schneider and Stearns were fielding calls from criminal defense attorneys, feminist

---

82. Petition for Rehearing at 1–2, State v. Wanrow, 559 P.2d 548 (Wash. 1977) (No. 43949). Years later, former Deputy Prosecutor Fred Caruso, in response to questions about the *Wanrow* case, would note that "as a matter of courtesy," when a court cites to facts that are in dispute, the court should acknowledge the fact of doing so. Interview with Caruso, *supra* note 1.

and civil rights activists, and defendants from around the country, seeking their assistance with women's self-defense cases. Most of the calls regarded women charged with killing abusive current or former boyfriends or husbands—the legal context which was not present in *Wanrow* and yet with which *Wanrow* is now strongly associated.

While Schneider and Stearns were dealing with the national attention being paid to the case, Prosecuting Attorney Donald Brockett filed new charges against Wanrow for second-degree murder in the death of Wesler and first-degree assault for the shooting of Kelly.[83]

With a potential new trial on the horizon, Wanrow's attorneys needed additional expertise on their team. A National Lawyers Guild member and Washington state criminal defense attorney, Mary Alice Theiler, joined the defense team, along with leading San Francisco civil rights and criminal defense lawyer, Susan Jordan.[84] Stearns moved on to other CCR cases, but Schneider, now four years out of law school, stayed with the *Wanrow* case.

Wanrow's attorneys filed a motion to dismiss the charges on the basis of police misconduct. They argued that it was not in the interest of justice to charge Wanrow since, had the police responded appropriately to Hooper's call for assistance, Wanrow would never have needed to defend herself. No court in Washington had ruled that police policy—in this case, a policy of failing to aggressively pursue the alleged perpetrators of child sexual abuse—could constitute police misconduct. The court denied the motion to dismiss. As the new trial neared, members of the Defense Committee for Yvonne Wanrow, spearheaded mostly by Native American women, re-doubled their efforts at organizing and fund-rais-

---

83. The charge was again felony murder. Wanrow's attorneys challenge to the constitutionality of Washington's felony murder statute was rejected by the Washington State Supreme Court. State v. Wanrow, 588 P.2d 1320 (1978).

84. Jordan was well known for her defense of Inez Garcia, charged with killing a man who was an accomplice to her rape. *See infra* note 91. She and Schneider, with the assistance of Cris Arguedas, would write the first law review article to describe the biases that affected cases involving women's claims of self-defense against a male attacker. See *infra* note 87 and accompanying text. Jordan died in a plane crash in 2009. Her remarkable accomplishments as a trial lawyer and activists are described at http://ukiahcommunity blog.wordpress.com/2009/05/30/remembering-susan-jordan-hal-bennett/

Cris Arguedas, then a law student at Rutgers and intern for CCR, would become one of the leading criminal defense attorneys in the country. *See* Peter Lattman, *Cris Arguedas in the Spotlight*, The Wall St. J. L. Blog (Oct. 6, 2006, 10:59 AM), http://blogs.wsj.com/law/2006/10/06/h-p-ii-cris-arguedas-in-the-spotlight/. Theiler, founding partner of the Seattle law firm, Theiler, Douglas, Drachler & McKee, practiced labor law and other civil litigation before becoming a federal magistrate for the U.S. District Court in the Western District of Washington. *See* http://www.wawd.uscourts.gov/courthouseinformation/MagistrateJudges.htm.

ing. Activists from around the country came to Spokane to support Wanrow.[85] They met with local church groups and women's organizations, sponsored fund-raising events, held press conferences, collected signature petitions, wrote letters to the Governor on Wanrow's behalf, and coordinated communication with members of the national Wanrow Defense Committee.

Native American rights organizations continued to be an important part of the movement on Wanrow's behalf. These activists collaborated with other civil rights activists to organize events such as a Native Women's Benefit "to honor Yvonne Wanrow and the struggles of native women."[86] The movement even reached an international audience, with organizations in Peru, Ethiopia, Iran, Grenada, and South Africa sending statements of support. The attorneys expanded their efforts to assist other similarly charged women, speaking at conferences and other fora. Schneider teamed with co-counsel Susan Jordan and law student Cristina Arguedas to write the first law review article explaining the feminist critique of the self-defense doctrine and the strategy used in the *Wanrow* case.[87] By 1978, CCR attorneys had joined with the National Jury Project[88] to create the Women's Self–Defense Project. Project members consulted on more than 100 cases, most of them involving women charged in the deaths of an abusive intimate partner or ex-partner.[89] A book grew from the Project's work, offering a practical guide for lawyers representing women charged with homicide who had killed male abusers in self-defense.[90] Entitled *Women's Self–Defense Cases: Theory and Practice,* the book focused on what became the overwhelming majority of

---

85. Interview with Marge Nelson and Polly Taylor, *supra* note 1. Nelson and Taylor traveled from their home in Minneapolis to Spokane, joining many other activists from all across the country. Their notes from the time state: "When we arrived, there seemed to be a lot of suspicion and hostility toward Yvonne from local feminists.... We set out to remedy these feelings and have." *See Major Foci of Our Work,* archives of Marge Nelson and Polly Taylor, *supra* note 1.

86. Sherrie Cohen, *Native Women's Benefit to Free Yvonne Wanrow, in* Off Our Backs: A Women's Newsjournal, April 30, 1979, at 6. The event was organized in D.C. and featured Floyd Westerman, civil rights activist Bernice Reagon, speakers from the Women of All Red Nations (WARN), the Native American Women's Association, AIM singers and drummers, and leading AIM activist Russell Means.

87. *See* Elizabeth M. Schneider and Susan B. Jordan, with the assistance of Cristina C. Arguedas, *Representation of Women Who Defend Themselves in Response to Physical or Sexual Assault,* 4 Women's Rts. L. Rep. 149 (1978).

88. The National Jury Project, founded in 1975, engaged in research and education regarding the jury system and "assisted lawyers and defendants in all phases of the trial process." *Women's Self–Defense Cases: Theory and Practice* xv fn ** (Elizabeth Bochnak ed. 1981).

89. *Id.* at xvi.

90. *Id.* Similar work is currently undertaken by the National Clearinghouse for the Defense of Battered Women. *See* http://www.ncdbw.org/.

women's self-defense cases—cases involving battered women. Schneider and Jordan co-authored a chapter.

The Social Significance of the **Wanrow** *Decision*

Although Wanrow did not defend herself against an intimate abuser,[91] the plurality opinion would ultimately provide a crucial tool for victims of domestic violence who acted to defend themselves against their abusers. At the time of Wanrow's trial in May 1973, victims of domestic violence were virtually invisible. The first newspaper accounts of battered women did not occur until the following year, 1974.[92] But by the time the Washington Supreme Court decided her case in 1977, violence against women, and rape and wife abuse in particular, had become the focus of intense public attention, feminist activism, and some legislative action. Erin Pizzey's 1974 book, *Scream Quietly or the Neighbors Will Hear*, chronicled the experiences of battered wives in England and received significant attention in the United States. Susan Brownmiller's famous book on society's response to rape, *Against Our Will*, one of the books cited in the Washington Supreme Court opinion, was published in 1975. In 1976, U.S. activist Del Martin published *Battered Wives*, describing the plight of thousands of U.S. women. That same year, the first set of state laws concerning wife abuse were enacted, the federal government allocated $700,000 for domestic violence intervention, and the results of the first national survey on spousal violence were announced.

A "media flurry" about wife-beating hit the national press in the late seventies. As historian Elizabeth Pleck describes: "Magazine and newspaper articles were emblazoned with close-up photographs of women's bruised faces and blackened eyes.... Television soap operas and police dramas featured sympathetic portrayals of abused women that diminished public apathy." In 1976, lawyers brought class action suits in Oakland, California, and New York City, claiming that police refusal to

---

91. Two other contemporaneous cases involving women who claimed self-defense in response to male attackers received widespread publicity as a result of the efforts of feminist activists and attorneys. Joan Little, an African American woman in North Carolina, killed a white jailer whom she testified was attempting to rape her at the time of the killing. *See* State v. Little, No. 75–CRS–32405 (N.C. Super. Ct. Aug. 15, 1975). Inez Garcia killed an accomplice to the man who raped her. Garcia's conviction for murder was overturned on appeal and Susan Jordan, the attorney who would join Wanrow's defense team, represented her in the second trial. Jordan successfully argued that Garcia killed in self-defense. People v. Garcia, No. CR–4259 (Super. Ct. Cal. 1977).

92. Elizabeth Pleck, *Domestic Tyranny: The Making of Social Policy Against Family Violence from Colonial Times to the Present* 182 (1987). Unless otherwise noted, Pleck is the source for the information in this section regarding the modern U.S. response to domestic violence.

respond to domestic violence calls was sex discrimination.[93] In 1977, the year of the *Wanrow* opinion, "the New York Times carried forty-four articles on wife beating, ranging from stories about hotlines and shelters to the trials of women who had murdered their assaultive husbands."[94]

This attention to violence against women grew directly from the activism and methods of the women's movement. Indeed, as Pleck writes, "[t]he rebirth of feminism was necessary for the rediscovery of wife beating." Consciousness-raising meetings and "speak-outs" encouraging women to tell personal stories revealed the ubiquity of violence against women—in homes, offices, and on the street. These stories prompted activists to investigate the causes of violence more broadly and to challenge the failure of the state to respond adequately.

The years that immediately followed the *Wanrow* decision brought even more national attention to the prevalence of violence against women. The House, the Senate, and the U.S. Civil Rights Commission held hearings on domestic violence.[95] President Jimmy Carter opened the Office of Domestic Violence,[96] and leading radical feminist author and activist Andrea Dworkin published her now-famous essay on her own experiences of battering entitled *The Bruise That Doesn't Heal*.[97] Newsweek magazine and other national newspapers ran stories on battered women who killed abusers in self-defense.[98]

The Legal Significance of the Wanrow *Decision*

The central importance of the *Wanrow* decision for the development of legal doctrine is the fair trial issue raised by Jury Instruction 10. The Washington court recognized that experiences related to a woman's gender are a part of the "context" in which a female defendant kills and that failure to so instruct the jury will result in the application of an implicit male definition of reasonableness.

---

93. *See* Susan Schechter, *Women and Male Violence: The Visions and Struggles of the Battered Women's Movement* 159–61, 337 n.10 (1982).

94. Pleck *supra* note 92, at 189.

95. *Domestic Violence: Prevention and Services*, Hearing on H.R. 2977 Before the Subcomm. on Select Education of the H. Comm. on Education and Labor, 96th Cong. (1979); *Domestic Violence 1978* Before the Subcomm. on Child and Human Development of the S. Comm. on Human Resources, 95th Cong. (1978); Carol A. Bonosaro, et. al., *Battered Women: Issues of Public Policy, A Consultation Sponsored by the United States Commission on Civil Rights* (Jan. 30–31, 1978), *available at* http://www.eric.ed.gov/ERICWebPortal/contentdelivery/servlet/ERICServlet?accno=ED177450.

96. Pleck *supra* note 92, at 196.

97. Andrea Dworkin, *The Bruise That Doesn't Heal*, Mother Jones, July 1978, at 31.

98. *See, e.g.*, *Wives Accused in Slayings Turning to Self–Defense Pleas*, Wash. PostJerrold K. Footlick, *Wives Who Batter Back*, Newsweek, Jan. 30, 1978, at 54.

However, the *Wanrow* case and the activism that surrounded it had an impact that went far beyond the change in doctrine. Not only did the case open up a new line of argument, but perhaps more importantly, defense attorneys began to understand female homicide defendants differently. Before *Wanrow*, self-defense was not seen as a viable defense strategy for battered women who killed their abusers. The contexts in which women were likely to kill in self-defense were not the paradigmatic stories that informed either cultural or legal narratives of self-defense. As Schneider later wrote, because gender was not seen as relevant to the reasonableness of a woman's defense against a male attacker, "both women defendants and the lawyers representing them were likely to perceive these cases as appropriate for (and thus claim) insanity or impaired-mental-state defenses rather than self-defense.... Both women defendants and their lawyers were not likely to argue self-defense because they could not perceive the women's actions as reasonable."[99]

In recognizing a woman's right to have the jury view the facts from a more realistic perspective, the *Wanrow* decision

> moved the political work to a different level; it posed the political questions of what a woman's perspective might be, whether there was a distinct women's perspective, and what equal treatment might look like. It focused further legal work on the disparate hurdles that limited women defendants' choice of defense—particularly the various ways women's experiences were excluded from the courtroom—and laid the foundation for remedial political and legal strategies.[100]

Subsequent Washington Supreme Court decisions underscored the necessity of making "the subjective self-defense standard '*manifestly* apparent to the average juror.' "[101] Recognizing that a male paradigm could infect juror decision making in a number of ways—in a proportionality instruction or in the persistent use the male pronoun—Washington courts required that instructions *specifically* call attention to the requirement that jurors place themselves in the circumstances of the defendant including the gender of the female defendant.[102]

---

99. Schneider, *supra* note 6, at 32. Recall that Wanrow's trial lawyer argued that she was not guilty by reason of insanity as an alternative to her self-defense claim.

100. *Id.* at 33.

101. State v. Allery, 682 P.2d 312, 314 (Wash. 1984) (quoting fromState v. Painter, *infra* note 103).

102. *See, e.g.*, State v. Crigler, 598 P.2d 741 (Wash. Ct. App. 1979) (reversing conviction of domestic violence victim who killed her abuser on the basis that jury instructions requiring that an "overt act" occur "at or immediately before the killing" that justified the use of deadly force contradicted the *Wanrow* requirement that the jury look to *all* the circumstances); State v. Bailey, 591 P.2d 1215 (Wash. Ct. App. 1979) (reversing conviction of domestic violence victim who killed her abusive husband, because the court failed to instruct the jury to determine reasonableness "in light of all the facts and

In one such case, Janice Painter received a new trial after claiming self-defense in the killing of her stepson, Ted.[103] Painter, who was forty-six years old, physically frail due to a back injury, and sometimes used a crutch, alleged that her stepson had several times threatened to rape and murder her and her children. Ted, a Vietnam veteran, was 145 pounds, 30 years old, and "strong and wiry." According to Painter, on the fatal day, Ted became abusive to her, then prevented her from calling the police for assistance by punching her and knocking her crutch out from under her, thereby causing her to fall and strike her back on the furniture. After she fell, she was unable to stand up. Ted continued to advance towards her telling her to "Go ahead and shoot," even after she warned him, "Stay back or I'll shoot." The Court of Appeals, citing *Wanrow*, reversed her first degree murder conviction. The appellate court noted that the trial court *properly* instructed the jury to determine the reasonableness of Painter's fear of imminent death or great bodily injury from the standpoint of "a reasonably and ordinarily cautious and prudent woman ... seeing what she sees and knowing what she knows."[104] But the effects of this instruction were "completely undermined" by the trial court's proportionality instruction defining "great bodily harm" as "an injury of a more serious nature than an ordinary striking with the hands or fists."[105] This instruction "injected an impermissible objective standard." Although the proportionality instruction had been approved in a series of prior cases, the Court noted that those cases "were decided before *State v. Wanrow*."[106]

Not every Washington trial court embraced the reasoning of the *Wanrow* plurality. When Sherry Lynn Allery was tried in the shooting death of her husband, the trial court was unsympathetic to defense counsel's reliance on *Wanrow*, noting that the opinion did not express the views of a majority of the justices and asserting that it did not correctly state the law.[107] The trial court concluded: "If my brothers upstairs [members of the Washington Supreme Court] ... are going to

---

circumstances known to the defendant" and to "view the circumstances as they reasonably might have appeared to the defendant at the time"). The *Bailey* court further noted "a woman defendant should be entitled to have jury instructions framed in the feminine gender in order to convey to the jury that they consider her actions in the light of her own perceptions and experience." *Bailey*, 591 P.2d at 1214.

103. State v. Painter, 620 P.2d 1001, 1004 (Wash. Ct. App. 1980). The Washington State Supreme Court declined to review the appellate court decision. 1981 WL 190850 (Wash.)

104. *Painter*, 620 P.2d at 1003.

105. *Id.* at 1004.

106. *Id.*

107. Ellen Yaroshefsky, *State of Washington v. Sherrie Lynn Allery: Victory Despite Conviction, in* Trial Stories at 14 (Michael E. Tiger & Angela J. Davis eds., 2008). Yaroshefky, now a law professor at Cardozo School of Law, represented Allery at trial.

write some law on the subject, they ought to write clearly and ought to remember not only what they write but read what other people write."[108] The Washington State Supreme Court answered the challenge. Quoting the appeals court decision in *Painter*, the court held that the trial court erred when it gave a self-defense instruction that failed to make "the subjective self-defense standard 'manifestly apparent to the average juror.' "[109] A self-defense instruction must order the jury "to consider the conditions as they appeared to the slayer, taking into consideration all the facts and circumstances known to the slayer at the time and prior to the incident."[110] Unlike the split opinion in *Wanrow*, this time the court was unanimous in firmly establishing the *Wanrow* plurality decision into Washington law.[111]

The emphasis in *Wanrow* on the importance of gender in the law of self-defense has since appeared in decisions by many other state courts. For example, the New Jersey Supreme Court reversed the manslaughter conviction of Ellen Gartland. Citing *Wanrow* as persuasive authority, the Court held that the trial court erred when it failed to instruct the jury to consider how "a reasonable woman who had been the victim of years of domestic violence would have reasonably perceived on this occasion that the use of deadly force was necessary to protect herself from serious bodily injury."[112] Courts have also cited *Wanrow* in underscoring the relevance of the decedent's history of violence against the defendant to a determination of the reasonableness of a defendant's perception of the need to use deadly force to defend herself.[113] Still other courts have cited *Wanrow* for the proposition that jury instructions on self-defense should not use the male pronouns "he" and "him" to refer to a female defendant.[114]

---

108. *Id.* at 21 and 44.

109. *Allery* 682 P.2d 312, 314, 314 (Wash. 1984) (quoting State v. Fischer, 598 P.2d 742 (1979)).

110. *Id.* As in many cases, the *Allery* court risked blurring this point with the unfortunate use of the word "subjective," but the full wording of the decision clarifies the key implication of *Wanrow*.

111. Two of the justices who dissented in *Wanrow* joined the unanimous decision in *Allery*. Nearly 30 years later, former Chief Justice Utter explained their switch as the result of "changes in society's attitudes" regarding domestic violence. He noted that at the time of *Wanrow*, not much was known about violence against women, but by the time *Allery* was decided, there was a great deal more public awareness. Interview with Utter, *supra* note 1.

112. State v. Gartland, 694 A.2d 564, 575 (N.J. 1997).

113. *See, e.g.*, State v. Dokken, 385 N.W.2d 493 (N.D. 1986) (reversed conviction because trial court erred in excluding evidence of prior abuse of the defendant by the victim.)

114. *See, e.g.*, State v. Hennum, 428 N.W.2d 859, 867 (Minn. Ct. App. 1988) (stating that a self-defense instruction should be gender-neutral, but declining to reverse on this basis).

Despite these important changes in the standard for self-defense, sex stereotypes, and stereotypes of battered women in particular, continue to influence judicial interpretations of legal standards. A study conducted fourteen years after the *Wanrow* decision underscored this point. In 1991, Professor Holly Maguigan reviewed all appellate homicide cases involving a convicted female defendant for whom evidence of domestic battering was proffered and who claimed self-defense at trial.[115] Maguigan's focus was not on judging the fairness of trial outcomes, but rather on judging the fairness of the trial process: Were these defendants allowed to present to the jury the evidence and the social context of their actions and were they granted legal instructions on the relevance of that context to their claims of self-defense?[116]

Maguigan discovered that these cases were reversed on appeal nearly five times more often than was generally true for homicide convictions: 40% compared to 8.5%. What accounted for this dramatic difference in reversal rates? In case after case, appellate courts reversed because trial courts were simply unable or unwilling to fairly apply standard self-defense law to battered women defendants.[117] Trial courts were inclined to see these defendants as vigilantes, even though the overwhelming majority of them faced a direct confrontation—that is, the classic self-defense scenario.[118] Maguigan concluded that contrary to popular notions that self-defense doctrine failed to adequately address the circumstances under which women kill abusers, it was the unfair *application* of standard self-defense doctrine that prevented these defendants from receiving a fair trial. This was the case despite the fact that most jurisdictions require the jury to view reasonableness from the circumstances of the defendant (as *Wanrow* would require), most of the cases studied were straightforward confrontation cases and thus should

---

115. Holly Maguigan, *Battered Women and Self Defense: Myths and Misconceptions in Current Reform Proposals*, 140 U. Pa. L. Rev. 379, 394 (1991). The search of appellate cases was limited to those where "(1) the defendant was a woman, (2) the defendant was accused of killing her spouse or lover, (3) there was evidence of a history of abuse of the woman by the man, (4) the defendant claimed to have acted in self-defense, (5) the defendant was convicted." Two hundred and twenty-three cases were identified. *Id.* at 393–94.

116. *Id.* at 383.

117. Maguigan concludes that "in most jurisdictions, to the extent that [battered women making self-defense claims] ... are precluded from getting a self-defense instruction, from presenting evidence of a history of abuse or expert testimony, and from having the jury instructed on the relevance of that evidence, the preclusion is the result of unfair application of existing law and not [due to the law's] ... structure or content." *Id.* at 458.

118. *Id.* at 394. Cases were identified as "confrontation" cases if there was evidence for all of the following criteria: "(1) the man (decedent) was awake [at the time of the homicide]; (2) he behaved in a way that the woman interpreted as posing an imminent or immediate threat of death or serious injury to her; and (3) there was evidence that she did not provoke his behavior by unlawful conduct and was not the initial aggressor." *Id.* at 4.

not have presented an imminence problem, and most jurisdictions "reject the notion that the proportional force rule operates to forbid use of a weapon against an unarmed attacker."[119]

Frequently, the problem in these cases was that courts were focused on the legally irrelevant question of why a battered woman "stayed" in an abusive relationship.[120] Take, for example, the rule on "imminence." In order to successfully assert a claim of self-defense, a defendant must reasonably believe that she is in *imminent* danger of losing her life or suffering great bodily harm. But as Professor Victoria Nourse's empirical study of cases found, rather than a narrow focus on the imminence of the risk of death or serious bodily injury, as the doctrine required, courts used the "imminence" requirement as a proxy for a number of other concerns—concerns that were often illegitimate under the state's legal doctrine.[121] In cases involving battered women, Nourse discovered that courts confused the *proper* question of the imminence of the threat with the *improper* question of why the defendant had remained in an abusive relationship.[122] This kind of "pre-confrontation retreat" rule, as Nourse pointed out, is contrary to the law and disadvantaged battered women as compared to other homicide defendants. As Nourse described, "We do not ask of the man in the barroom brawl that he leave the bar before the occurrence of an anticipated fight, but we do ask the battered woman threatened with a gun why she did not leave the relationship."[123]

Race: The Limits of Wanrow

Though a stunning success, the *Wanrow* decision also demonstrates the limits to which courts were willing to go to ensure a defendant's right to a fair trial. Washington Supreme Court Justice Robert Utter authored the gender-focused plurality decision in *Wanrow*, but when

---

119. *Id.* at 417. Maguigan notes that some jurisdictions rejected this notion "decades before Wanrow was decided," but whatever the history, it is clear that the current majority rule is that "the reasonableness of a defendant's degree of force is decided on a case-by-case basis and that use of a weapon against an unarmed attacker is not *per se* disproportionate." *Id.*

120. *See* Martha R. Mahoney, *Legal Images of Battered Women: Redefining the Issue of Separation*, 90 Mich. L. Rev. 1 (1991) (describing the ways in which law and culture create a false dichotomy between "staying" and "leaving" and thus fail to recognize women's acts of agency—even acts of separation, unless their actions are successful in stopping the violence).

121. Victoria F. Nourse, *Self-Defense and Subjectivity*, 68 U. Chi. L. Rev. 1235, 1236 (2001).

122. *Id.*

123. *Id.* at 1238. Nourse provides the following example: Barbara Watson was on the ground with her husband's hands around her neck when she killed him, yet the trial court determined that the threat against her was not "imminent" because of the long course of physical abuse that characterized the marriage. *Id.* at 1247.

Justice Utter was asked about the case more than thirty years later, it was the anti-Indian racism of Spokane County that was uppermost in his mind.

> Those were the times of *strong* anti-American–Indian sentiment in Spokane County. The prosecutor prosecuted [Wanrow] under the murder statute. The judge instructed the jury and the jury found her guilty.[124]

Further evidence of anti-Indian sentiment is found in Utter's description of the process he used to persuade his colleagues to uphold the appellate court's reversal of Wanrow's conviction.

> [T]he other justices wanted to affirm the conviction. It started out 8–1. I was the lone dissenter. But one by one I was able to get one more vote, and one more vote. Finally, Bob Hunter from Ephrata was the last vote I needed for a 5–4 majority. Bob was a wonderful guy, heart as big as the whole outdoors. . . . And he said, "You know, sometimes you've got to pull up your socks and be a judge." So he voted [with] . . . me, *although that was his constituency over there on the east side.*[125]

In an interview conducted for this chapter, Justice Utter explained that his remarks regarding "the east side" referred to the strong anti-American Indian sentiment present in the east side of the state, the part of the state that had supported Justice Hunter's election to the bench.

Consistent with Justice Utter's recollection, Wanrow's lawyers also believed that anti-Native American prejudice was central to the fair trial concerns at issue in Wanrow's case, but there were limited ways in which to make those concerns cognizable on appeal.[126] They were left

---

124. John Hughes, *Robert F. Utter: Justice's Sailor*, An Oral History (2009), Washington State Legacy Project, at http://www.sos.wa.gov/legacyproject/oralhistories/Robert Utter/pdf/complete.pdf (emphasis in original).

125. *Id.* (emphasis added). It is not surprising that more than thirty years after the fact, Justice Utter would fail to remember that the decision was 5–3, rather than 8–1, and only 4 justices joined the plurality decision finding error with the self-defense instruction.

126. It is not clear that Annis would have been successful had he challenged the racial makeup of the jury. At the time of trial (1973), explicit exclusion of African Americans from jury service would have been unconstitutional, *see, e.g.,* Strauder v. West Virginia, 100 U.S. 303 (1879); Glasser v. United States, 315 U.S. 60 (1942); Carter v. Jury Comm'n, 396 U.S. 320 (1970). Further, the Court had stated in cases such as *Smith v. Texas,* that the jury pool must be "representative of the community." *Smith,* 311 U.S. 128 (1940). But it was not until 1975 that the Court ruled that the Constitution required that the pool from which a jury is chosen be a "cross-section" of the community. Taylor v. Louisiana, 419 U.S. 522 (1975) (finding the exclusion of women from jury service to be unconstitutional). And it was not until the 1979 case of *Duren v. Missouri* that the Court fleshed out the defendant's burden to establish a prima facie violation of the fair-cross-section requirement. *Duren,* 439 U.S. 357 (1979). Even under current law, the racial composition in Wanrow's case would not have been a constitutional violation unless she

with two legal arguments. First, they argued that the trial court erred when it rejected Annis's motion for a mistrial on the basis of the prejudice occasioned by newspaper reports of Wanrow's withdrawn guilty plea published on the eve of trial. Washington law required a court to examine the "entire context" to determine the impact of prejudicial publicity. In their supplemental brief, Stearns and Schneider expanded the frame of Annis's argument for error by arguing that "[t]o get a true sense of the probable impact of the newspaper account" the court had to take into consideration the "context" which included "the constant [negative] press coverage of the occupation of Wounded Knee."[127] The attorneys argued that the possibility of prejudice was particularly strong in Wanrow's case because "although Indians represent the largest minority in the Spokane area, the white majority has no real understanding of Indian history or culture." The case presented an "inflammatory context" because it involved "an Indian woman charged with killing one white man and injuring another," yet the court did not even voir dire the all-white jury properly to determine the likely impact of the newspaper article.

The second defense argument that was related to Wanrow's American Indian identity was that the trial court erred when it disallowed expert testimony regarding Native American culture.[128] Annis's proffer at trial explained that the expert would testify that within Indian culture there is a "strong feeling of respect for elders," and if "an older person, who should be respected and revered, ... would take advantage of a younger [child] ... or try to perform an unnatural sex act on that younger child, ... that would strike at the very core of the Indian and his culture, ... and [you would expect] a more severe reaction to such conduct ... than there might be in the Anglo–Saxon culture." Further, "there is an especially close relationship between the Indian female and

---

could demonstrate that Native Americans were systematically excluded from the jury pool from which the ultimate petit jury was drawn or that in the selection of the ultimate trial jurors from that pool the prosecutor used peremptory challenges in a racially discriminatory fashion that violated equal protection. *See, e.g.,* Batson v. Kentucky, 476 U.S. 79 (1986); Powers v. Ohio, 499 U.S. 400 (1991). Several features of jury pool selection make it likely that Native Americans are underrepresented. *See,* Kevin K. Washburn, *American Indians, Crime and the Law,* 104 Mich. L. Rev. 709 (2006) 748–49 (Native Americans are underrepresented in federal jury pools because jurors are chosen from voting rolls, poverty among Native Americans is significant, and poor individuals are less likely to register to vote.)

127. Supplemental Brief of Respondent, *supra* note 75. Schneider and Stearns cited as examples of negative publicity a local newspaper article published a month before her trial that quoted a Congressman referring to AIM members as "goons or gutter rats" and "hoodlums."

128. The trial judge concluded, "I just feel to bring in the standards of another culture, when we are here under the same standards in relationship to this individual, would be insufficient relevance to allow it." *Wanrow* Trial Transcript at 452.

her children," Native American mothers are often "over protective [of their children]" and "more protective" than are Anglo–Saxon mothers.[129] Annis argued that this evidence was relevant both to Wanrow's self-defense claims and her insanity claim: "[T]hese factors would very much bear on the claim that she was fearful, reacting in this manner in self-defense, and that she may have reached an hysterical point and was unable to control her conduct or know the consequences of her act." It was important for the all-white jury to hear the evidence because "no one on the jury is Indian, and [they] may not understand the Indian culture, and may not appreciate the additional stress and strain that would have been placed on this woman...."

Admittedly, Annis's proffer was not a model of clarity, mixing arguments for the relevance of the testimony to the sincerity of Wanrow's fear for the purposes of a self-defense claim, her mental state for the purposes of an insanity claim, while also suggesting—rather obliquely—that the testimony was relevant to the reasonableness component of self-defense. A somewhat rehabilitated argument for the testimony's relevance to self-defense might go something like this: the very idea that an elder—Wesler was in his sixties when he was killed[130]—would engage in sexual conduct with a child would be extremely disturbing and frightening. This response would then accentuate the fear that Wanrow felt when she waited all night to see what Wesler would do, when Wesler ignored Hooper's demand that he "get out of the house," when Wesler appeared to be approaching a sleeping boy, and when Wesler appeared to be coming towards her. As was true with the gender argument, the claim was that without an understanding of this context, the jury would be unable to weigh the sincerity of Wanrow's fear as well as its reasonableness.

On appeal, Annis summarized the argument:

In offering such expert opinion, the defendant asks no special consideration. Rather, she asks only to be allowed to present to the jury the fundamental facts about herself—facts the jury would be expected to know and reasonably assume to understand about any white culture defendant—but which the jury could not know about an Indian culture defendant. The claim of error in excluding expert testimony is based on the right of the appellant to have her defense considered on an equal basis with defendants who have been raised in a dominant American culture group.[131]

---

129. *Id.* at 451. The remaining quotes are also from the trial transcript.

130. Arraignment and Plea from Oct. 18, 1972, State v. Wanrow, No. 20876 (Wash. Super. Ct. 1973)

131. Brief of Respondent, *supra* note 70.

The Washington State Supreme Court found no error in the trial court's decisions on these defense motions. For the court, Wanrow's experiences as a woman were critical to the jury's ability to understand her perceptions of the circumstances surrounding the homicide, but her experiences as a *Native American* woman were not. In contrast, Wanrow, her lawyers, and her supporters believed that her Native American identity was central to understanding the facts of the homicide—central to understanding why she was in reasonable fear for the safety of her children and herself when Wesler moved towards her and central to understanding the biases of the criminal justice system.[132] The courts who heard Wanrow's case failed to understand that gender and culture are not separate experiences, but rather "intersecting" experiences, as Professor Kimberle Crenshaw would later write.[133] The courts presumed that the jury could meaningfully understand Wanrow's experience "as a woman" apart from her experience as a *Native American* woman, "as if the perspective of the defendant's gender could be isolated from the perspective of her culture[,]"[134] when, in fact, it could not.

Conclusion

On April 26, 1979, just days before Wanrow's new trial was to begin, Wanrow reached an agreement with the State in which she pled guilty to manslaughter and second degree assault. She received a suspended sentence of five years probation, and one year of community service. In the end, Wanrow served only three days in jail—the three days that immediately followed her arrest.

For Yvonne Wanrow, the seven years in the criminal justice system were transformative. In that time, she became romantically involved with the actor, singer/songwriter, and AIM activist, Floyd Westerman. She and Westerman became parents to a daughter, born in May 1974,

---

132. One startling example of that bias is found in the sentencing hearing that followed Wanrow's conviction. At sentencing, the court allowed the expert testimony regarding Native American experience that it ruled inadmissible at trial. The expert witness testified that Indians are instilled with the belief that as one grows older, one becomes wiser, and therefore a mother's reaction when an older person sexually abuses a child "can be drastic." On cross-examination, Brockett asked if she meant that an Indian mother in such a situation "behaves basically like an animal?" The expert witness replied, "I did not say this. We are homo sapiens." Sentencing Hearing, State v. Wanrow, No. 20876 (Wash. Super. Ct. 1973)

133. *See* Kimberle Crenshaw, *Mapping the Margins: Intersectionality, Identity Politics, and Violence Against Women of Color*, 43 Stan. L. Rev. 1241, 1243 (1991) ("the experiences of women of color are frequently the product of intersecting patterns of racism and sexism"); *see also*, Angela P. Harris, *Race and Essentialism in Feminist Legal Theory*, 42 Stan. L. Rev. 581 (1990).

134. Holly Maguigan, *Cultural Evidence and Male Violence: Are Feminist and Multiculturalist Reformers on a Collision Course in Criminal Courts?*, 70 N.Y.U.L. Rev. 36, 81–82 (1995).

whom they named Chante. Her defense had been the subject of benefit concerts by such well-known performers as Buffy Sainte–Marie and Rita Coolidge. She and her sister Alice had developed clothing lines and organized fashion shows to raise money for her defense fund and to raise awareness about her case.

Wanrow had become an activist for Native American rights and for other women who claimed self-defense in the killing of a male aggressor.[135] She joined AIM leaders as a speaker at conferences, rallies, and "Indian Awareness Week" activities on college campuses.[136] She presented at an International Tribunal on Crimes Against Women in Brussels, and she traveled to Germany at the invitation of the International Indian Treaty Council and other European organizations. When she returned from Germany, she traveled to Cleveland to offer support in the defense of Kathy Thomas, an African American woman on trial for killing her abusive husband.[137] At the time of this writing, more than thirty-five years after her case was concluded, she continues to be a leading activist on Native issues ranging from protection of Colville lands from strip mining to support for the Native American Church and for AIM.[138]

Wanrow recounted the importance of her own consciousness-raising and involvement in the larger Native American struggle:

> If you don't create this exterior awareness for yourself, you're going to get bogged down in your own little struggle, swallowed up by it, eventually you'll probably give up. That was what saved me, to focus on something else; minimize my personal struggles. It put me in solidarity with other Indian people. Instantly, I was sympathetic to AIM, I understood it as being a spiritual movement. American Indian movement, that doesn't sound like any military force to me. It sounds like the wind. It sounds like a spirit, a spirit of defense. We are in defense of our land, our life, our human rights. There's nothing wrong with self-defense and self-defense is not a crime.... When I got up to speak eventually on my own behalf, that was the main thrust of my talk. That Indian people are defending their rights and their land. As a person, I'm defending my rights as a

---

135. A. Debeste, *Fighter for Women's Rights Tells her Story of Self–Defense*, Seattle Post Intelligencer, April 8, 1983, at B11.

136. Swan Interview, *supra* note 1.

137. *Letter from Yvonne Wanrow*, Akwesasne Notes (September 1977), from Nelson and Taylor archives, *supra* note 1. Wanrow was brought to Cleveland by the Gold Flower Defense Committee, a coalition of organizations supporting the right of women to act in self-defense. *See Self–Defense Rights to Be Focus of Talks*, The Plain Dealer, May 19, 1978, at 5A., from the Nelson and Taylor archives, *supra* note 1.

138. *See* a recording of Swan's talk at an AIM conference at http://www.youtube.com/watch?v=aLqpQsbRf2I.

mother. A mother that's defending her children and other people in that home.

As Wanrow became a public person, she engaged in soul-searching. "[I] just examined my life ... because I knew if I decided to become a public figure I would be representing my people whether or not they delegated me to do that." She explains:

> I grew. I got a new Spirit. I got a strong Spirit.... [My] case forced me to change, and how I changed. I broadened my thinking. I felt less sorry for myself. I found ways to positively find help, and help myself, plus help others at the same time.... [W]hen I was introduced to different people that were active in bringing about social justice in Indian Country, I felt aligned with them, with their struggle, ... and I felt good and I felt optimistic. I felt strong. I didn't feel alone.

Yvonne's children, her sisters, and her nieces wished her well as she departed Spokane for her hearing before the Washington State Supreme Court in Olympia, Washington (2/22/76). Front row, left to right: Yvette Swan, Viola Michel, Jamie Michel, Marcella Michel, Ana Tomeo, Aurora Michel, Chante Westerman, Lisa Swan. Back row, left to right: Bethley Jo Walters, Pamela Ludwig, Yvonne Swan Wanrow, Darren Swan (in tree), Alice Stewart.

Nancy Stearns, Elizabeth Schneider, and Yvonne Wanrow hope for victory on the eve of oral arguments before the Washington State Supreme Court (2/22/76).

Yvonne Wanrow and Floyd Red Crow Westerman, taken in Inchelium, Washington (1977).

Yvonne drew the picture which appeared on the cover of letters sent by
Yvonne Wanrow's Defense Committee (3/76) (from the personal archives
of Polly Taylor and Marge Nelson.)

Crowds gather outside the Washington Supreme Court building while
the court conducts hearings on matters following the court's reversal of
Yvonne's conviction (2/11/78) (from the personal archives of Polly Taylor
and Marge Nelson.)

A drumming circle was formed by supporters gathered outside the Washington Supreme Court hearing on motions following the court's reversal of Yvonne's conviction (3/13/78). The circle includes Native American civil rights activists Steve Robideau (kneeling to the right), Harold Belmont (sitting), and Roque Duenas (facing the camera looking down) (from the personal archives of Polly Taylor and Marge Nelson.)

Elizabeth Schneider, Susan Jordan, and Cris Arguedas meet with Yvonne to prepare for a second trial (1979).

7

Janine Young Kim

The Story of *Clark*: The Incredible Shrinking Insanity Defense

In the early morning hours of June 21, 2000, in Flagstaff, Arizona, seventeen year-old Eric Michael Clark shot and killed police officer Jeffrey Moritz, possibly under the delusion that the officer was a space alien out to capture and kill him. Three years later, Clark would be convicted of first-degree murder, and three years after that, the Supreme Court of the United States would affirm his life sentence. But the story of *Clark v. Arizona* properly begins in 1981, when John Hinckley attempted to kill President Ronald Reagan in order to impress actress Jodie Foster. Hinckley's acquittal by reason of insanity began the aggressive process of shrinking the insanity defense across the United States, eventually prompting the Justices of the U.S. Supreme Court in the *Clark* case to wonder: Is it wrong to kill a Martian? The oddness of this inquiry, taking place in the dignified chamber of the highest court in the land, rather colorfully illustrates the highs and lows of the endless American quandary over insanity and crime, and the role that psychiatry may play in making the distinction. Despite the fantastical quality of some of the facts and questions raised in *Clark*, the case offered some measure of clarity on the status of the insanity defense since John Hinckley's controversial trial. Moreover, it implicated just about all of the various doctrines that address criminal responsibility, including mens rea, diminished capacity, and the guilty-but-mentally-ill verdict.

The Criminally Capable Mind

The current state of the insanity defense in the United States traces back to the 1981 presidential assassination attempt by a mentally disturbed man named John W. Hinckley, Jr. After watching the film *Taxi Driver* repeatedly, Hinckley became obsessed with Jodie Foster, the actress who played a child prostitute in the film.[1] Hinckley stalked Foster, phoning her and leaving her letters and poems in failed attempts to gain her attention. Hinckley then decided that a presidential assassination would finally move her to take notice of him. (In *Taxi Driver*, the protagonist attempts an assassination on a presidential candidate after being rejected by a woman.) Hinckley first targeted President Jimmy Carter in 1979 during Carter's reelection campaign, but he was arrested for gun possession at the Nashville airport in 1980 (he paid a fine and was released) and temporarily gave up his plan.[2] Then on March 30, 1981, Hinckley fired at President Ronald Reagan outside a Hilton in Washington, D.C., wounding him and several others.

Hinckley's trial lasted six weeks and involved teams of expert witnesses who evaluated his mental state. All of the experts agreed that Hinckley was mentally disturbed, but they differed as to the severity of his condition.[3] The defense argued that Hinckley's mental illness left him totally incapable of intellectually or emotionally appreciating the wrongfulness of his conduct or of conforming his conduct to the requirements of law.[4] The government countered that Hinckley's act was premeditated ("Hinckley had bought a gun; followed President Carter; traveled to Washington; left a note stating his intentions; selected Devastator bullets from among the ammunition he had on hand; waited for President Reagan to leave the hotel; and fired six shots at the President."[5]), suggesting a man functional enough to make a plan and follow through.

There was, indeed, no doubt that Hinckley intended to kill a human being, the mental state (or "mens rea") required for the crime of attempted murder. Hinckley himself never claimed otherwise. Rather, his defense was that although he intended to kill, he should be acquitted because he possessed an *additional* mental state or condition that qualified him for an affirmative defense: legal insanity. The defense of insanity, like other affirmative defenses, exonerates a defendant even if the prosecution proves all of the elements of the offense beyond a reasonable doubt. Evidence of premeditation helped to establish Hinckley's intent to kill, which was not in dispute, and his clear-headedness,

---

1. *Taxi Driver* (Columbia Pictures 1976).

2. During this period, Hinckley went to New York to grieve for John Lennon, who had been shot and killed by a mentally disturbed fan who identified with the protagonist of J.D. Salinger's *A Catcher in the Rye. See* Peter W. Low et al., *The Trial of John W. Hinckley, Jr.* 26 (1986).

3. *See id.* at 27.

4. *See* Vincent J. Fuller, United States v. John W. Hinckley, Jr., 33 Loyola L.A. L. Rev. 699, 701 (2000). Vincent Fuller was lead counsel for Hinckley's defense.

5. Jonathan B. Sallet, *After* Hinckley: *The Insanity Defense Reexamined*, 94 Yale L. J. 1545, 1548 (1985).

which was. Both of these states of mind were relevant to determine the ultimate issue: Hinckley's culpability for his acts. The defendant acquitted on the basis of his affirmative defense of legal insanity is civilly committed to a mental health institution until he no longer poses a danger to society. The defendant who negates the mens rea element of a crime is acquitted without condition.

In June 1982, after deliberating from Friday afternoon to Monday evening, the jury returned a "not guilty by reason of insanity" (NGRI) verdict. The verdict surprised even Hinckley, who was then committed to St. Elizabeth's Hospital.[6] Hinckley's acquittal provoked widespread outrage, including from President Reagan, who later went before the Senate Judiciary Committee to propose restricting the insanity defense.[7] Even more anomalously, some of the Hinckley jurors themselves also appeared before the Senate Subcommittee on Criminal Law to explain the verdict.[8] After numerous hearings on the issue, Congress passed the Insanity Defense Reform Act of 1984, which states that a person is legally insane if "at the time of the commission of the acts constituting the offense, the defendant, as a result of a severe mental disease or defect, was unable to appreciate the nature and quality or the wrongfulness of his acts."[9] This was, in essence, a return to the *M'Naghten* rule, which had been the prevailing standard for insanity in American jurisdictions until the 1960s, but which, as discussed below, then temporarily receded from American law.

A.   *The History of* M'Naghten

The *M'Naghten* rule itself originates from a botched 1843 assassination attempt on the Prime Minister of England by Daniel M'Naghten, a Scottish woodcutter, who mistakenly killed the Prime Minister's secretary instead. M'Naghten was allegedly suffering from paranoid delusions and believed that he was being stalked and persecuted by the Tory government.[10] He pleaded not guilty. M'Naghten called several witnesses

---

6.   According to Lincoln Caplan, Hinckley expected to be convicted and had written a statement to be read at his sentencing. *See* Lincoln Caplan, *The Insanity Defense and the Trial of John W. Hinckley, Jr.* 101 (1984). The verdict also developed an unexpected racial dimension. The *Hinckley* jury happened to be all black, except for one member who was white. When public furor erupted after the verdict, one juror responded "that she and the others had understood their job, and had done it with particular fairness, as only a black jury . . . could." *See id.* at 102.

7.   Norman J. Finkel, *Insanity on Trial* (1988).

8.   *See* Caplan, *supra* note 6, at 102.

9.   18 U.S.C.A. § 17(a) (2009).

10.   There is some evidence to believe that M'Naghten may not have been delusional in his fear of Tory spies. *See* Finkel, *supra* note 7, at 17–18 (describing Richard Moran's research revealing that Prime Minister Robert Peel did in fact send a number of agents to

to describe his state of mind around the time of the murder. Nine medical experts also testified on behalf of M'Naghten, two pronouncing their conclusions without prior examination, relying solely on evidence they heard over the course of the trial.[11] The prosecution offered no counter medical evidence and eventually withdrew the case. The jury returned a not guilty verdict, and M'Naghten was committed to an insane asylum, where he died twenty-two years later.

In a parallel to the Hinckley case, an outraged House of Lords summoned the Justices of the Court of Common Pleas to answer questions on the law of insanity and excuse. Chief Justice Tindal (who had presided over M'Naghten's trial) spoke for all but one of the judges when he answered as follows:

> [T]he jurors ought to be told ... that to establish a defence on the ground of insanity, it must be clearly proved that, at the time of the committing of the act, the party accused was labouring under such a defect of reason, from disease of the mind, as not to know the nature and quality of the act he was doing; or, if he did know it, that he did not know he was doing what was wrong.

Chief Justice Tindal went on to clarify that the knowledge of right and wrong must not be merely abstract but in reference to "the very act with which he is charged."[12]

Unlike Congress in the aftermath of *Hinckley*, the House of Lords did not take it upon itself to revise the law of insanity in England. But the *M'Naghten* case signified the "formalization of the insanity plea."[13] And whereas before *M'Naghten*, judges gave varied instructions and constructions on what constitutes legal insanity (e.g., describing the insane accused as a "wild beast" or a "mere instrument in the hands of Providence," or one who does not know "what he is about" or the difference between right and wrong), the judges before the House of Lords in Daniel M'Naghten's case spoke with one voice to define the applicable law.[14]

This did not mean, however, that the law of insanity had suddenly become settled and clear. Even in 1843, there were concerns that the *M'Naghten* rule might lead to too many acquittals, that doctors would

---

Glasgow to undermine the growing Chartist movement and that these agents engaged in bribery, assault, harassment, and kidnapping).

11. *Id.* at 18–19. Finkel also describes how the experts were allowed to make legal conclusions about M'Naghten's culpability. *Id.* at 18.

12. R v. M'Naghten (*Daniel M'Naghten's Case*), (1843) 8 Eng. Rep. 718 (H.L.).

13. Joel Peter Eigen, *Witnessing Insanity: Madness and Mad–Doctors in the English Court* 3 (1995).

14. *See id.* at 40–46.

supplant the jury, and that the definition of legal insanity was too narrow to account for the varied manifestations of mental illness that were being studied by the "medical men" of the day. These basic disagreements continue to dog the defense to the present time.

The *M'Naghten* rule was also criticized for failing to clarify what it means to be legally insane and therefore not responsible for one's actions. The meaning of the words "know" and "wrong," in particular, have been subject to great debate. From the announcement of the rule onward, commentators have also disagreed on its basic composition. Some describe it as excusing those afflicted with at least one of two different types of incapacity: cognitive ("as not to know the nature and quality of the act") and moral ("did not know he was doing what was wrong"). Under this view, the two prongs of the rule work independently; a person who does not understand the nature and quality of his act will be deemed insane even if he knew that his act was wrong. Others, however, have suggested that the question of insanity as a practical matter turns on the moral prong of the rule, either because the cognitively incapacitated will (almost) always be morally incapacitated also (if a person does not even realize that striking a person can cause pain or injury, how can he know that doing so is wrong?), or because the moral issue is what really lies at the heart of the defense. Indeed, courts and commentators have long followed a custom of referring to the *M'Naghten* rule as the "right-wrong test."

In the United States, the *M'Naghten* rule was the predominant test of legal insanity but it was not the only one. As early as 1869, New Hampshire articulated the broadly-worded product test, which required only that the criminal act was "the offspring or product of mental disease in the defendant."[15] From 1954 to 1972, the District of Columbia also used the product test to determine the insanity of defendants.[16] Other jurisdictions began supplementing the *M'Naghten* rule with the control test, deeming a defendant insane if he does not *know* right from wrong or if he cannot *choose* right from wrong. To those who would use still another test, excusing defendants unable to control so-called "irresistible impulses," the *M'Naghten* rule was overly strict, expressing an already outdated understanding about madness and its effect on human behavior.

In 1955, the American Law Institute (ALI) offered its own formulation of the insanity test, one that combined and rephrased both the *M'Naghten* rule and the control test. The ALI test described the insane defendant as one who lacks "substantial capacity either to appreciate the

---

15. State v. Pike, 49 N.H. 399 (N.H. 1870).

16. Durham v. United States, 214 F.2d 862 (1954) (adopting the product test); United States v. Brawner, 471 F.2d 969 (1972) (overruling *Durham*).

criminality [wrongfulness] of his conduct or to conform his conduct to the requirements of law."[17] This was clearly a more lenient standard than the *M'Naghten* rule, not only because of the addition of a control component ("capacity ... to conform his conduct to the requirements of law") but also because it (1) required appreciation rather than mere knowledge of criminal wrongdoing, and (2) accepted substantial incapacity in place of total incapacity. In proposing this new standard, the ALI rejected the product test that had been favored by the D.C. Circuit a year earlier. The ALI definition of legal insanity was soon adopted by a majority of the states and the federal circuit courts. It was also the test that acquitted Hinckley.

The liberalization of the insanity defense that occurred during the 1950s–'70s reflected a shift in the public's perception of the mentally ill. The early 1950s saw "an abrupt upsurge of interest and faith in psychiatry and related fields."[18] This was in part due to large numbers of World War II veterans returning home with psychological damage, and also to pharmacological innovation that promised new avenues of treatment and even cure.[19] Within the criminal law, this cultural shift led to policies that assimilated the latest in social science and psychology, emphasizing treatment and rehabilitation rather than crude punishment of the criminal. The ALI's Model Penal Code, published in 1962 and containing the insanity test described above, exemplified the jurisprudence of its time. Its adoption in so many American jurisdictions was testament to the then-current belief that science could provide a neutral, universally-applicable test that could bring order to the legal chaos that had developed around mental illness and crime.

While the 1950s may have marked the beginning of this progressive movement, it also foreshadowed its end. It was a time when juvenile delinquency became a source of growing public concern and even fear.[20] (The two competing cultural strains are depicted in the popular 1961 musical, *West Side Story*, which tells the story of rival gangs in New York City and features a comical song called "Gee, Officer Krupke" sung by gang members blaming poor upbringing for their criminal ways— "Our mothers all are junkies/Our fathers all are drunks"; "Golly Moses, natcherly we're punks!" The "judge" in the number declares, "This boy don't need a judge, he needs an analyst's care!"[21]) By the late 1960s, rising crime rates and urban riots placed crime control at the top of the

---

17. Model Penal Code § 4.01 (1962). The bracketed term "wrongfulness" could substitute for "criminality" to designate more clearly appreciation of moral, as opposed to legal, wrong.

18. Thomas Maeder, *Crime and Madness* 73 (1985).

19. *See id.* at 73–74.

20. *See* Lawrence Friedman, *Crime and Punishment in American History* 449 (1993).

21. *West Side Story* (United Artists 1961).

political agenda,[22] as public sentiment shifted again. Some states had already changed, or were in the process of changing, their insanity defense laws by the time John Hinckley was facing trial, but it was his 1982 acquittal that served as the catalyst for broad and immediate reform.

Like the federal government, the states responded to the public outrage by tightening their insanity laws. Many jurisdictions followed the federal example and reverted back to the traditional *M'Naghten* rule. Some also shifted to the defendant the burden to prove insanity, in contrast to the Hinckley trial, where the burden lay on the government to prove beyond a reasonable doubt that the defendant was not legally insane. Others modified their commitment procedures in an effort to make the defense a less attractive option for the accused, reversing reforms that took place during the mental health advocacy movement of the 1960s and '70s.[23]

Perhaps most controversially, a significant number of states adopted a "guilty but mentally ill" (GBMI) verdict, supplementing the NGRI verdict which is the traditional means for the jury to recognize the impact of severe mental illness on criminal responsibility. The GBMI verdict was designed to reduce the number of insanity acquittals by offering the jury an alternative verdict that promises longer confinement of the offender while still offering treatment for his mental disease.[24] A person found GBMI is likely to receive some degree of psychiatric care in prison (although resources for this treatment vary greatly) but must complete serving the full sentence even after he is cured of the illness. This outcome contrasts with a person found NGRI, who is committed to a mental facility only until he is deemed no longer a danger to himself or society.

All of these measures to limit the insanity defense existed before 1982, but the *Hinckley* case brought them into focus as viable methods to curb the "abuses" that were occurring in insanity trials. It did not matter to this very public and emotional debate that insanity defenses were rare, and successes rarer still.

Four states—Idaho, Kansas, Montana, and Utah—abolished the insanity defense entirely as an excuse from responsibility for crime. Instead, they allowed defendants to offer mental illness evidence only to disprove the existence of the requisite mens rea element in the offense

---

22. *See* Friedman, *supra* note 20, at 450–51.

23. *See* Henry J. Steadman et al., *Before and After* Hinckley 33 (1993) (describing the rejection of automatic and indefinite commitment of insanity acquittees during the 1960s and '70s).

24. *See* Christopher Slobogin, *The Guilty But Mentally Ill Verdict: An Idea Whose Time Should Not Have Come*, 53 Geo. Wash. L. Rev. 494, 495 (1985).

charged. These states thereby laid out an alternative use of mental illness evidence that will be crucial to the discussion of the *Clark* case below—namely, its use to cast reasonable doubt on whether the crime, as defined by the statutory elements, had occurred in the first place. The Nevada legislature similarly attempted to abolish the defense in 1995, but its highest court struck down the law and declared the insanity defense to be "a well-established and fundamental principle of the law of the United States."[25] Relying on both the federal and state constitutions, the Nevada Supreme Court found that the insanity defense is necessary to give defendants due process of law, and it reinstated the law that had been in place before 1995—the *M'Naghten* rule.

B. *Diminished Capacity*

The insanity defense is not the only means by which a defendant can raise the issue of his mental capacity to commit crime. Several jurisdictions have also recognized the diminished capacity defense, although there is some confusion about how the defense operates. This is because there are in fact two different doctrines that fall under the single term "diminished capacity"; the first is an affirmative defense and the second a failure-of-proof defense. The affirmative defense variant of diminished capacity treats the defendant's claim of mental illness as a lesser form of the insanity excuse and is often limited to homicide cases where a defendant may be found only partially responsible for the crime. It is most closely associated with the California Supreme Court's 1966 decision in *People v. Conley*, a doctrine-muddying decision holding that evidence of mental disorder is admissible to disprove the often ill-defined notion of "malice" built into the traditional definition of murder.[26] Despite the language of "malice" addressed in *Conley*, Professor Joshua Dressler has characterized this case as adopting an affirmative defense of diminished capacity because the court there reversed a premeditated murder conviction by a jury that had already heard psychiatric evidence and found that the required mens rea existed.[27]

Although some criticized *Conley* as establishing an illegitimate, judicially-crafted excuse, it was not until 1978 that the diminished capacity defense became most controversial with the infamous murder

25. Finger v. State, 27 P.3d 66, 84 (Nev. 2001).

26. 411 P.2d 911 (Cal. 1966). In *Conley*, the state Supreme Court held that even if a person ostensibly kills with premeditation, he is entitled to an instruction saying that he might not be guilty of any kind of murder if because of intoxication and a "dissociated" mental state caused by emotional turmoil, he so lacks an awareness of his obligation to obey the law that he does not exhibit the requisite "malice aforethought."

27. According to Dressler, the court did this by adopting an unusually robust interpretation of the "malice aforethought" required for murder. Joshua Dressler, *Understanding Criminal Law* 399–400 (4th ed. 2006).

trial of Dan White.[28] Accused of killing San Francisco Mayor George Moscone and Supervisor Harvey Milk, White asserted the successful, but largely mythic, "Twinkie defense." White's position has been mischaracterized and trivialized as a claim that eating Twinkies drove him to kill. In fact, he argued that he shot Moscone and Milk in the heat of passion and that he suffered from clinical depression over the loss of his job. He also claimed that his depression had led to his consumption of large amounts of junk food, which caused a chemical imbalance that mitigated the "malice" required even for second-degree murder. White was convicted of voluntary manslaughter, the verdict provoking widespread public outrage.[29] In response, the state legislature effectively overruled *Conley* by abolishing the diminished capacity affirmative defense.[30]

While California's legislative action after the Dan White case seems to suggest that diminished capacity is easy enough to repudiate, the situation is more complicated. There is a second variant of diminished capacity that has proven to be more stubborn because of its relationship to the criminal law concept of mens rea and the constitutional law concept of due process. Under diminished capacity as a failure-of-proof defense, evidence of mental incapacity is used to rebut the prosecution's case on the defendant's mental state. In other words, a defendant may argue that his mental illness prevents him from forming the requisite mens rea to commit the crime. Unlike the affirmative defense of diminished capacity, where the defendant argues for partial responsibility for the crime, this second version is a claim of total innocence.

Abolition of diminished capacity in this second sense thus raises significant concerns. Excluding mental illness evidence (short of legal insanity, that is), which is what abolition of diminished capacity would entail, could lead to the conviction of a defendant who did not actually possess the mens rea required for the crime because his mental condition rendered him fundamentally incapable of possessing it. This result would violate certain basic tenets of criminal law—in particular, our common understanding that a person cannot be found guilty of a crime unless all of the elements of the offense are satisfied. In this way, a legislature wishing to limit mental illness evidence to insanity cases must confront

---

28. *See* Miguel A. Mendez, *Diminished Capacity in California: Premature Reports of Its Demise*, 3 Stan. L. & Pol'y Rev. 216, 218–19 (1991).

29. *See* Suzanne Mounts, *Malice Aforethought in California: A History of Legislative Abdication and Judicial Vacillation*, 33 U.S.F. L. Rev. 313, 354 (1999).

30. *See* Mendez, *supra* note 28, at 219. The legislature amended Cal. Penal Code section 189 to say that in establishing premeditation, it "shall not be necessary to prove the defendant maturely and meaningfully reflected upon the gravity of his or her act," and also amended section 187 to say, "Neither an awareness of the obligation to act within the general body of laws regulating society nor acting despite such awareness is included within the definition of malice."

the discomforting possibility that at least some defendants will be punished on the basis of a legal fiction about their states of mind.

Perhaps more importantly, abolition creates a potential due process problem. Restricting the defendant's use of mental illness evidence to challenge the existence of mens rea makes it harder for the defendant to mount a defense and makes it correspondingly easier for the prosecution to convict. It would therefore seem to violate the principles enunciated in *Chambers v. Mississippi*,[31] which held that the exclusion of exculpatory evidence may violate due process, and *In re Winship*,[32] which imposed the beyond-a-reasonable-doubt burden of proof on the state. Of course, allowing mental illness evidence to negate mens rea makes it easier for defendants to avoid punishment even if they are not so incapable as to be deemed insane, and a state legislature could well decide that this result is undesirable. After all, a person acquitted through diminished capacity is free to rejoin society, whereas a person acquitted by reason of insanity is almost always committed to a mental institution. But while easing the defendant's burden is largely a choice based on policy, easing the prosecution's burden is a decision that triggers constitutional scrutiny. As we shall see below, the U.S. Supreme Court has had to strike a delicate balance between the interests protected by *Chambers* and *Winship* and the political prerogative of the states in defining substantive criminal law.

C.   *Arizona Law*

After the Hinckley decision, Arizona, the home venue of the *Clark* case, was out in front of most other states in seeking to both curtail the insanity defense and abolish diminished capacity. Unlike the majority of states, Arizona had never expanded its insanity law beyond the basic *M'Naghten* rule, so it was already considered to be one of the most restrictive jurisdictions on the issue. Nonetheless, the public uproar over *Hinckley*, as well as two other notorious local cases involving the insanity defense, led the state to amend its law in 1983 to shift the burden of proof to the defendant to prove insanity by clear and convincing evidence.[33]

A decade later, another unpopular insanity verdict prompted Arizona to change its law once again. A Tucson man by the name of Mark Austin was tried and acquitted for the 1989 stabbing death of his

---

31.   410 U.S. 284 (1973).

32.   397 U.S. 348 (1970).

33.   Before the 1983 amendment, Arizona imposed the burden of proof on the prosecution to prove sanity beyond a reasonable doubt. *See* State v. McLoughlin, 652 P.2d 531, 537 (Ariz. 1982). The U.S. Supreme Court had previously decided that a state may require the defendant to carry the burden of proof on an affirmative defense. *See* Leland v. Oregon, 343 U.S. 790, 797–99 (1952).

estranged wife, Laura Griffin–Austin. Even though evidence suggested that he bought materials for the murder, watched her from outside her home, and then surprised her at the door, Austin argued that he did not possess the requisite cognitive capacity under the *M'Naghten* rule to be found legally sane and responsible for the crime. The jury acquitted him, and Austin spent six months in a psychiatric hospital before being conditionally released.[34]

Shortly thereafter, the legislature passed "Laura's Law," named after Mark Austin's victim and championed by her grieving parents. Laura's Law made two noteworthy changes in Arizona's insanity law. First, it narrowed the definition of legal insanity by eliminating the cognitive prong of the *M'Naghten* rule. Thus, Arizona recognized a defendant as insane only "if at the time of the commission of the criminal act the person was afflicted with a mental disease or defect of such severity that the person did not know the criminal act was wrong."[35]

Second, Laura's Law replaced the NGRI verdict with a "guilty except insane" (GEI) verdict. Although Arizona's GEI verdict may sound similar to the GBMI verdict other states adopted post-*Hinckley*, Arizona's law differs because GEI *replaced*, rather than supplemented, the NGRI verdict. Recall that in jurisdictions with the GBMI verdict, the jury typically has the option to find a mentally ill defendant *guilty* but mentally ill or *not guilty* by reason of insanity. In Arizona, however, a mentally ill defendant could not be acquitted of the crime because the law no longer recognized an NGRI verdict. Instead, a defendant who managed to prove himself insane under the narrowed redefinition of Laura's Law nonetheless would be found guilty of the crime. Put another way, while GBMI reduced insanity acquittals, Arizona's GEI law effectively eliminated them.

The passage of Laura's Law suggests that Arizona may have one of the toughest laws in the nation when it comes to the criminally insane. Whether there is any substance behind this suggestion is debatable, however. The shift from NGRI to GEI is largely symbolic, a means to label an insane defendant "guilty" but preserving essentially the same outcome: commitment for mental health treatment until such time as the defendant is no longer dangerous.[36]

---

34. *See* Kim Smith, *Mental Health Will Be a Tough Issue in Cop–Killing Case*, Ariz. Daily Star, June 15, 2008, at B1.

35. Arizona Rev. Stat. § 13–502(A). This section of the statute also excludes a number of mental disorders—for example, psychosexual disorders and impulse control disorders—from satisfying the requirements for legal insanity.

36. *See* Renée Melançon, *Arizona's Insane Response to Insanity*, 40 Ariz. L. Rev. 298, 314–15 (1998).There is at least one important difference between a GMBI conviction and

Regarding Arizona's redefinition of legal insanity, whether it works a substantive change depends on one's view of how the full *M'Naghten* rule separates the sane from the insane. As described above, many believe that the moral prong forms the "heart" of *M'Naghten* while the cognitive prong is merely redundant or superfluous. Under this view, Laura's Law did nothing more than eliminate verbiage in the traditional formulation of the rule. On the other hand, to those who argue that the two prongs of the *M'Naghten* rule are independent, Arizona's redefinition effects a significant change to the detriment of mentally ill defendants. These conflicting interpretations would be a key issue in Eric Clark's case.

If its revised insanity law fails to distinguish Arizona as especially harsh toward mentally ill defendants, the state's abolition of diminished capacity helps to push it over the top. In *State v. Mott*, the Arizona Supreme Court affirmed a trial court's decision to exclude expert testimony on battered woman's syndrome in the case of a woman accused of child abuse and first-degree felony murder.[37] In that case, Shelly Mott claimed that the reason she failed to take her dying daughter to the hospital was that her condition of battered woman's syndrome prevented her from forming the intent (i.e., purpose or knowledge) required for child abuse, which served as the predicate offense for her first-degree felony murder conviction.[38] Although Mott's defense depended on her mental illness, she was not asserting the insanity defense. Instead, Mott was arguing that she was not guilty of the crime in the first place—and therefore would not need any affirmative defense such as insanity—because she lacked the mens rea required for guilt.

The Arizona Supreme Court rejected Mott's claim as being rooted in diminished capacity. It noted that though Arizona homicide law was modeled on the Model Penal Code, the state legislature had declined to adopt the Code's provision specifically allowing a defendant to offer evidence of "mental disease or defect . . . to prove that the defendant did not have a state of mind that is an element of the offense."[39] Observing that the state legislature had "declined to adopt the defense of diminish-

---

Arizona's GEI statute: unlike a GMBI sentence, a defendant convicted of GEI may be released once he is found no longer dangerous, though he will continue to be monitored until the end of his sentence term by a psychiatric security review board who may return him to custody if his condition deteriorates. A GEI defendant who remains insane and dangerous beyond the term of his sentence may be re-committed under the state's civil commitment statute. *See* Ariz. Rev. Stat. Ann., § 13–3994(J) (2011).

37.   931 P.2d 1046 (Ariz. 1997).

38.   At trial, Dr. Cheryl Karp offered to testify that "[Mott's] history of being abused, in conjunction with her limited intelligence, prohibited her from being able to decide to take [her daughter] to the hospital." *Id.* at 1050 (footnote omitted).

39.   *Id.* (citing Model Penal Code § 4.02(1) (1962)).

ed capacity when presented with the opportunity to do so,"[40] the court went on to declare that "Arizona does not allow evidence of a defendant's mental disorder short of insanity either as an affirmative defense or to negate the mens rea element of a crime."[41]

The combination of Arizona's insanity redefinition and the *Mott* rule has potentially harsh consequences for a mentally ill defendant. The truncated GEI definition may mean that fewer defendants can meet their burden to prove insanity and the *Mott* decision forecloses the only other avenue available to demonstrate the accused's lack of culpability. The result is to leave mentally ill defendants in the worst possible condition: convicted of the most serious charge without the promise of psychiatric care during incarceration. Such was the legal landscape when Eric Clark, a teenager suffering from paranoid schizophrenia and a belief in alien invasion, faced first-degree murder charges in the courts of Arizona.

Eric Michael Clark

Eric Michael Clark appeared to be an ordinary middle-class teenager with a promising future. He had good grades, played running back for the varsity football team at Flagstaff High School, and was popular enough to be voted to the homecoming court in his freshman and sophomore years. He was easy-going, a good sport on and off the field. He dreamed of becoming a professional athlete, but believed that a college education was more important for his long-term goals. He had a loving family and many friends.[42]

But in late 1998, when he was sixteen years old, Clark began to show signs of mental disturbance. After a house fire that temporarily displaced the family to an apartment building, he refused to drink tap water for fear of lead poisoning and drank only from bottles that he bought and opened himself. He became moody, angry one minute and sobbing the next. He began expressing suicidal thoughts and stated that he would not live past the age of twenty. Alarmed by Clark's increasingly

---

40. *Id.* at 540.

41. *Id.* at 1051. Mott's conviction was overturned by a federal district court judge on the grounds that the exclusion of the battered woman's syndrome evidence was a denial of due process. *See* Mott v. Stewart, No. 98–CV–239, 2002 WL 31017646 (D. Ariz. Aug. 30, 2002) (unpublished decision). Arizona declined to retry her on the murder charge and accepted a guilty plea on child abuse. *See* John Gibeaut, *A Matter Over Mind*, 92 A.B.A. J. 33 (Apr. 2006).

42. Much of the factual information contained in this chapter is based on a facsimile of Terry Clark's log of Eric Clark's incarceration history and observed behavior, a telephone interview conducted by the author with Terry Clark and several of Eric Clark's attorneys, and emails sent by Terry Clark to the author (documentation on file with author). *See also* Pauline Arrillaga, *Arizona Justice and Mental Illness; High Court to Hear Insanity Case Debate*, Ft. Wayne J. Gazette, Apr. 16, 2006, at A7; Gibeaut, *supra* note 41.

erratic behavior, his parents admitted him to a mental health center for three days in June of 1999 and arranged for counseling thereafter. Although doctors at the center suggested that Eric might be displaying symptoms of schizophrenia, David and Terry Clark were not prepared to accept the possibility that their son was experiencing anything more serious or permanent than teenage angst and drug abuse. (Clark tested positive for marijuana at the center). By fall 1999, the once popular athlete no longer received calls from friends and sat alone at lunchtime. Even his brother and sister avoided him. Clark quit football, stopped going to school, and took correspondence courses from home. He also obsessed about Y2K and even purchased $1700 worth of survival gear with his father's debit card.

When New Year's Day passed without incident, Clark seemed to return to his old self and went back to school. But soon, he began to express other, stranger fears—this time, about aliens taking over his town of Flagstaff. He told his surprised parents that he believed they were aliens, too, and he could prove it if they brought him "some tools". He thought that his food, water, and clothes were poisoned, so he refused to eat or wash at home, and he would wear multiple layers of protective clothing without changing them. His appearance and hygiene suffered. Clark also believed that his air was poisoned, and he eventually kept a bird in his car as a warning system. He would later say that the bird became useless because the aliens had replaced its lungs with robotic ones. He hung beads and chimes attached to fishing line around his room to alert him of intruders. He also became increasingly child-like, clinging to his mother in public and decorating his room with Disney posters. He was once found sleeping with a machete under his pillow and, later, with a gun.

In April 2000, Clark was arrested on drunk-driving and drug charges when he was found with forty-two tabs of LSD. The county deferred the prosecution, however, to later that year when Clark would turn 18 and be eligible for a harsher sentence.[43] Then several weeks after this incident, he approached some people at a local park and boasted how he would lure the police by firing off his pistol and "start picking them off like a sniper" with rifles.[44] He had become so odd by this point that hardly anyone believed what he said.

---

43. Jeffrey Moritz's widow later unsuccessfully sued the county, claiming that it was "grossly negligent" for forgoing immediate prosecution. *Widow of Slain Officer Suing Coconino County*, The Ariz. Republic, Jan. 9, 2001, at B2. Because of the potential conflict of interest between the civil suit and Clark's prosecution, Clark was prosecuted by the Arizona Attorney General's office. *Id.*

44. Respondent's Brief at 3, Clark v. Arizona, 548 U.S. 735 (2006) (No. 05–5966), 2006 WL 565617.

Although his parents tried to get him into treatment centers and counseling, Clark insisted there was nothing wrong with him. Terry Clark even consulted her lawyer to have her son immediately prosecuted for the April 2000 incident so that he would be forced to obtain help, and she also called numerous treatment facilities during this period of time. On the day before the shooting, Terry Clark again talked to her lawyer, this time about having Clark involuntarily committed. That night, Clark and his parents went to dinner at a Sizzler restaurant—one of the few places where he would eat—and saw the movie *Shaft*. He seemed to be doing well, and Clark's parents allowed him to stay for a second film while they returned home. At some point later that night, Clark went home, got the keys to his brother's truck, and left again.

At about 4:30 a.m. on June 21, 2000, Jeffrey Moritz, a thirty-year-old officer for the Flagstaff Police Department, was called to the University Heights area of southwest Flagstaff after residents called to complain about a pickup truck playing loud music. One resident recalled that Clark circled the block over twenty times. As the prosecution would point out during the trial, Clark's music of choice that morning was Dr. Dre's *2001*—"a rap CD ... contain[ing] many antisocial attitudes as part of the lyrics."[45] Officer Moritz pulled Clark over and told the dispatcher that he was approaching the driver. Less than a minute later, Clark fired several shots from his .22–caliber revolver, hitting Officer Moritz through the armhole of his bulletproof vest and severing his aorta. Officer Moritz managed to return fire as Clark fled on foot, but the officer died at the scene. He was the first police officer in the city of Flagstaff to be killed in the line of duty. He had a two-year-old son, and shortly after his death, his wife learned that she was pregnant with their second child.[46]

By 5:00 a.m., the police traced Clark's abandoned vehicle to his residence and discovered that he was missing. An intensive sixteen-hour manhunt ended the next evening when Clark was found close to his home. He attempted to run, but he surrendered when he saw the laser sight of an officer's gun aimed at his chest. Clark's gun was discovered in a nearby yard, hidden inside a knit cap. After his arrest and while alone in an interview room, Clark sang to himself and mumbled incoherently, repeating phrases like "take me to heaven" and "end this torment" and saying that he did not want to be poisoned anymore.[47] While in the

---

45. 2 Joint Appendix at 115–16, 548 U.S. 735 (2006) (No. 05–5966), 2006 WL 282161. The movie *Shaft* was also portrayed during trial as a movie about violence and corrupt police.

46. According to newspaper accounts at the time, thousands of people attended Moritz's funeral and lined the streets during the motorcade. *Slain Officer Honored*, The Ariz. Republic, June 27, 2000, at B1.

47. 1 Joint Appendix at 27, 42, 43, 548 U.S. 735 (2006) (No. 05–5966), 2006 WL 282160.

Flagstaff jail, Clark also bit his jailer and "just started flailing like he was out of it."[48] Although Clark generally refused to talk about the events of June 21 and about the aliens he thought were trying to poison him, he did tell his parents two months after the shooting that Flagstaff was a "platinum city" inhabited by over 50,000 aliens and only bullets could stop them.[49]

Unsurprisingly, in light of his April arrest, the police and media initially portrayed Clark as a drug-addled delinquent.[50] But it quickly became clear that Clark was suffering from serious mental illness. Indeed, soon after his arrest, Clark was committed to the Arizona State Hospital because he was deemed to be "gravely disabled and a danger to himself and others."[51] In a separate hearing, Judge H. Jeffrey Coker determined that Clark was incompetent to stand trial.[52] He was hospitalized for almost three years before Judge Coker found him fit to stand trial—with the help of antipsychotic drugs—in 2003. Over time, Clark became less fearful of aliens and, in one interview, explained that they came to Earth for the benign purpose of interplanetary trade in broccoli and sugar.

The Trial

Clark's eleven-day bench trial for first-degree murder finally began on August 5, 2003, before Judge Coker. Bryon Middlebrook, one of Clark's trial attorneys, publicly explained that a bench trial was favored because of the "complexity of the evidence."[53] The notion that expert testimony can confuse the jury is hardly new, and courts have by turns both doubted and vouched for the jury's ability to sort through complex and conflicting evidence. Perhaps more important from a trial lawyer's perspective, however, is the statistic that the vast majority of insanity acquittals occur through prosecutor stipulations and bench trials.[54] Ju-

---

48. *Slaying Suspect Won't Provide Needed Samples*, The Ariz. Republic, Dec. 8, 2000, at B1 (quoting the county sheriff).

49. According to Flagstaff's official website, the city had a population of 52,894 in 2000. *See* City of Flagstaff (government website), *Census Facts, available at* http://www.flag staff.az.gov/index.aspx?NID=1095. It would appear, then, that Clark believed the overwhelming majority of the people in Flagstaff were actually aliens.

50. Clark, in fact, did have a juvenile record dating back to 1995 for selling marijuana. *Teen Still Uncharged in Killing*, The Ariz. Republic, June 23, 2000, at B1.

51. Petitioner's Opening Brief at 7 n.17, 548 U.S. 735 (2006) (No. 05–5966), 2006 WL 282168.

52. A person is incompetent to stand trial if "as a result of a mental illness, defect, or disability, the person is unable to understand the proceedings against him or her or to assist in his or her own defense." Ariz. R. Crim. Pro. 11.1.

53. *Bench Trial Set in Officer's Slaying*, The Ariz. Republic, Jul. 9, 2003, at B9.

54. *See* Ann C. Gresham, *The Insanity Plea: A Futile Defense for Serial Killers*, 17 Law & Psychol. Rev. 193, 198 (1993).

ries are the most skeptical adjudicators of insanity claims, and there would have been additional concerns about going to the jury in a highly publicized and emotionally charged case like Eric Clark's.

At trial, the prosecutor, David A. Powell, painted a picture of a mentally ill and drug-addicted teenager who boasted to his friends that he would lure and shoot a police officer, and then carried out his plan two weeks later by creating a noise disturbance that called Officer Moritz to the scene. Powell demonstrated that at the time of the shooting, Officer Moritz was in uniform, drove a marked patrol car, and turned on his lights and siren to pull Clark over to the side of the road. He also called witnesses who testified that on the night before the shooting at dinner and at the movie theater, Clark looked lucid— relatively speaking. A crucial element of the case was that the prosecution agreed from the start that Clark suffered from paranoid schizophrenia and was psychotic before, during, and after the shooting. But the state nevertheless argued that his illness did not stop him from orchestrating a deadly ambush on a police officer.[55] The state's expert testified that Clark "knew that he was committing a criminal act" and was probably intoxicated when he shot Officer Moritz.[56] Indeed, during his closing argument, Powell urged the judge to picture Clark "with a joint in [his] mouth, . . . a bottle of something in [his] hand, and . . . a gun in the other hand."[57]

The defense strategy, on the other hand, was almost entirely based on Clark's history of mental illness, which was presented through lay and expert witnesses who had observed the defendant at various times during the preceding five years.[58] Clark sought to use evidence of his

---

55. Powell did not seek the death penalty in light of Clark's age and acknowledged mental illness. After Clark's trial, the Supreme Court held in *Roper v. Simmons*, 543 U.S. 551 (2005), that capital punishment may not be applied to murderers who killed when they were under 18 years of age.

56. 2 Joint Appendix, *supra* note 45, at 159, 163.

57. *Id.* at 304. The defense expert attempted to explain Clark's drug abuse by testifying that schizophrenics often use drugs as a way to quell their symptoms. 1 Joint Appendix, *supra* note 47, at 25. The prosecutor, on the other hand, suggested that Clark's substance abuse may have caused his mental illness. 2 Joint Appendix, *supra* note 45, at 306.

58. Accordingly, the defense never argued that Clark did not commit the shooting, although he had told one of his doctors that he was at Lake Powell (located about 140 miles north of Flagstaff) with a girl he met at the movies when the shooting occurred. 1 Joint Appendix, *supra* note 47, at 55. The defense did explore, however, the theory that the shooting was the accidental result of a struggle over Clark's weapon. Memorandum Decision (unpublished), State of Arizona v. Eric Michael Clark, No. 2000-0538, at 5–6 n.4 (Ariz. Ct. App. Jan. 5, 2005). No factual support for this theory is apparent from the record. On the contrary, evidence indicated that Officer Moritz was shot from a distance of at least two feet and may have been taking evasive action at the rear of his vehicle when he was struck. *Id.*

mental illness both to negate the mens rea required for first-degree murder and to prove by clear and convincing evidence that he was "guilty except insane." Arizona's first-degree murder statute required proof that Clark intentionally or knowingly killed a law enforcement officer who was acting in the line of duty. Clark contended that at the time of the shooting, his paranoid schizophrenia led him to believe that he was killing an alien and not a police officer. Clark's GEI defense required that he prove that he suffered from a "mental disease ... of such severity that [he] did not know the criminal act was wrong."[59] Clark attempted to show that his paranoid delusions about aliens undermined his judgment to such a degree that he did not know right from wrong when he killed Officer Moritz. It should be noted that Clark's objective was never acquittal. Instead, he conceded from the first that the facts of his case demonstrated he was guilty, except insane, of a lesser form of homicide.[60]

As the prosecution pointed out at trial, Clark's attempt to negate mens rea using mental illness evidence clearly ran up against the *Mott* rule of exclusion. Clark's defense attorney responded by arguing that the *Mott* rule unconstitutionally prevented Clark from presenting a complete defense. Judge Coker ultimately allowed the defense to present mental illness evidence related to Clark's capacity to form intent because, he explained, there was no jury to confuse and such evidence "goes to the insanity issue" for which it was admissible.[61] He stressed, however, that he was bound by the law of *Mott* to restrict its consideration to the insanity determination.[62] The defense expert testified that Clark genuinely believed that aliens were in Flagstaff impersonating humans and that he was incapable of planning an ambush; indeed, the psychiatrist did not believe Clark was capable of planning much of anything at that period of his life.

On September 3, 2003, Clark was found guilty of first-degree murder. Judge Coker did not revisit the *Mott* issue, simply concluding that although Clark suffered from a mental disease, "it did not ... distort his perception of reality so severely that he did not know his actions were

---

59. Ariz. Rev. Stat. Ann. § 13–502(A) (2011).

60. Clark's attorney argued before the U.S. Supreme Court that Clark should have been found guilty of second-degree murder or manslaughter because he believed he was killing a space alien, not a police officer. This position confused the Justices since Clark's belief, if true, would also clearly negate the mens rea required for second-degree murder: the intent to kill a human being. Oral Arg. at 20–23, 548 U.S. 735 (2006) (No. 05–5966), 2006 WL 1085873.

61. Had there been a jury hearing the case, the judge would presumably issue an instruction charging the jury to limit its consideration of mental illness evidence to the question of insanity.

62. 1 Joint Appendix, *supra* note 47, at 9.

wrong.'"[63] The judge also explained that his decision to convict rested on a number of facts presented at trial, including the statements Clark had made about shooting police officers at the park, his act of driving around with music blaring to draw the victim to the scene of the crime, the fact that he avoided capture for sixteen hours despite an intense manhunt, and his ability to comply with instructions after his arrest. A month later, Clark was sentenced to life imprisonment with no possibility of release for twenty-five years, the minimum sentence for the offense. During much of his trial and sentencing, Eric Clark slept, possibly because of his medications.[64]

On state appeal, Clark argued, among other things, that Arizona's insanity statute violated due process by omitting the cognitive prong of the *M'Naghten* rule.[65] In an unpublished opinion authored by Judge G. Murray Snow, the Arizona Court of Appeals rejected this argument, stating that there is no constitutional requirement to recognize the insanity defense and that, in any case, the states are free to define the defense in any way they choose.[66] Judge Snow went on to observe that the cognitive prong adds little to the *M'Naghten* rule, since anyone who is cognitively impaired under the traditional test would suffer the requisite moral impairment as a matter of course. Judge Snow also ruled that the trial court was bound by *Mott* to reject mental illness evidence as it relates to mens rea and that he lacked the authority to overturn the decision of the Arizona Supreme Court.

The Arizona Supreme Court denied discretionary review without comment. The stage was set for an appeal to the Supreme Court of the United States. Clark's petition for certiorari raised two questions about the relationship between criminal guilt and mental illness. The first asked whether the U.S. Constitution requires Arizona to recognize, at a minimum, the two-pronged *M'Naghten* rule of insanity in its GEI statute. The second asked whether Arizona may exclude mental health evidence in determining a defendant's mens rea and still comply with the demands of due process.

---

63. 2 Joint Appendix, *supra* note 45, at 334.

64. One of Clark's trial attorneys later testified that his client was on Haldol, describing him as "sleep[y]" and "not there" during the trial. First Amended Petition for Writ of Habeas Corpus, No. CV–09–8006–PHX–JAT (JRI), at 61. *Clark v. Ryan* (submitted 6/8/09) (on file with author.)

65. Clark also argued that (1) there was insufficient evidence to support his conviction; (2) the trial court abused its discretion in finding that he did not meet his burden of proving legal insanity; and (3) his sentence of life imprisonment constitutes cruel and unusual punishment under the Eighth Amendment. All of these arguments were rejected. Memorandum Decision (unpublished) at 1, 2, No. 2000–0538 (Ariz. Ct. App. 2005).

66. *Id.*

The Supreme Court Decision

Certiorari was granted in the case of *Clark v. Arizona* on December 5, 2005, and it created a media stir. One could say that murder and insanity were in the air but not because of Eric Clark's wild beliefs about aliens in Flagstaff. By bizarre coincidence, at that very time, media outlets were commemorating the 25th anniversary of John Lennon's murder at the hands of Mark Chapman, a deranged fan who believed the novel *A Catcher in the Rye* held the answers to his actions.[67] In addition, some commentators anticipated that a Supreme Court decision on the insanity defense might affect the retrial of Andrea Yates, the notorious Texas woman who—exactly a year and a day after Clark shot Moritz—drowned her five children in the bathtub of their home and claimed she suffered from schizophrenia and postpartum psychosis.[68]

But the *Clark* case was notable on its own. After all, Clark was asking the Supreme Court to constitutionalize the much-maligned insanity defense, and a decision in his favor would, in the view of many, have a significant effect on the criminal laws of the states. The *Clark* case presented the type of substantive criminal law question that the Court had studiously avoided for decades under the leadership of the late Chief Justice William Rehnquist, who championed federalism principles and states' rights. There was no reason to think that much would change under new Chief Justice John Roberts, who seemed to be cut from the same conservative cloth. On the other hand, the two justices who were most openly skeptical about the constitutional status of the insanity defense—Justices Rehnquist and Sandra Day O'Connor—were no longer on the bench.[69]

Clark argued that the Arizona law violated his due process rights in three ways. First, the rewrite of the *M'Naghten* rule to exclude the cognitive prong violated due process because the rule in its entirety had

---

67. Although Chapman's lawyers believed that he would be acquitted of the murder by reason of insanity and initially asserted the defense, Chapman later changed his mind and pleaded guilty to second-degree murder. *See* Sally Frank, *Eve Was Right to Eat the "Apple": The Importance of Narrative in the Art of Lawyering*, 8 Yale J. L. & Feminism 79, 99–100 (1996).

68. Yates was convicted in 2002 and sentenced to life imprisonment, but in December 2005, she was waiting to be retried because of false testimony given by Dr. Park Dietz, an expert witness who had also testified for the prosecution in the *Hinckley* case. *See* Caplan, *supra* note 6, at 75. At the retrial, she was found not guilty by reason of insanity. *See* Peggy O'Hare & Mary Flood, *Decade Brought Infamous Cases We Can't Forget*, Houston Chron., Jan. 1, 2010.

69. *See* Ake v. Oklahoma, 470 U.S. 68, 91 (1985) (Rehnquist, J., dissenting) (observing that "[i]t is highly doubtful that due process requires a State to make available an insanity defense to a criminal defendant"); Foucha v. Louisiana, 504 U.S. 71, 88 (1992) (O'Connor, concurring) (suggesting that states are free "to determine whether, and to what extent, mental illness should excuse criminal behavior").

achieved the "fundamental" status that merits extraordinary respect in constitutional law.[70] Second, the *Mott* rule, which prevented him from offering mental illness evidence to negate the specific intent mens rea "knowingly or purposely killing a police officer," violated his due process rights. Third, even if the rewrite of the insanity defense standard and the *Mott* rule were separately constitutionally permissible, in combination they were not.

With respect to the substance of the insanity rule Clark was urging on the Supreme Court, his position could be described as decidedly modest. Ironically, Clark was actually fighting to preserve the *M'Naghten* rule, which had historically been the go-to standard whenever the insanity defense seemed to stray too far in protecting the criminally insane. Accordingly, Clark was hardly trying to break new ground; he was arguing instead for what had been widely viewed as the stingiest definition of legal insanity available at common law. The fact that the *M'Naghten* rule was both narrow and enduring helped Clark's case, since it was his contention that the test had acquired "fundamental" status and thus formed part of the Constitution's due process guarantee. Clark also was not challenging Arizona's decision to hold insane defendants guilty. Thus, a victory before the Supreme Court would only mean that Clark would be afforded a chance to be found guilty except insane and committed to a mental facility under the full *M'Naghten* rule.

In his certiorari petition to the Supreme Court, Clark put his insanity defense claim first in order, but the order of argument changed by the time he submitted his opening brief. Perhaps because his lawyer realized that the Supreme Court was unlikely to declare any minimal constitutionally required definition of insanity (no matter how narrow the definition) for the states,[71] Clark led his opening brief with the claim that the exclusion of mental illness evidence relevant to his state of mind at the time of the shooting prevented him from presenting a complete defense, the effect of which was to impermissibly lift the state's burden to prove the mens rea required for first-degree murder. As described above, the *Mott* rule's effect on the doctrine of diminished capacity may violate well-established principles articulated in *Chambers* and *Winship*.

---

70. A doctrine or principle becomes part of the due process guarantee under the U.S. Constitution when it is "so rooted in the traditions and conscience of our people as to be ranked as fundamental." Patterson v. New York, 432 U.S. 197, 201–02 (1977). To determine whether fundamental status has been acquired, courts primarily look to historical practice. *See* Montana v. Egelhoff, 518 U.S. 37, 43 (1996).

71. Clark conceded in his opening brief that "[t]he Court *justifiably* gives great deference to state legislative judgment in defining crimes and their elements when challenged as violations of substantive Due Process." Petitioner's Opening Brief, *supra* note 51, at 26 (emphasis added).

Clark noted that at trial, Arizona used both the ambush theory—that Clark played loud music in order to lure a police officer for the purpose of killing him—and Officer Moritz's displays of authority (uniform, patrol car, sirens, and lights) to prove that Clark intentionally or knowingly killed a law enforcement officer in the line of duty. Clark now claimed that he was prevented from providing an alternative version of the facts—that he had the music blaring to drown out the voices in his head, that he was not functional enough to plan an ambush, that he believed aliens sometimes disguised themselves as the police—because this alternative version was rooted in his mental illness. Without considering mental illness, therefore, the trier of fact was left with only one explanation of the events: that of the prosecution.

Clark's brief ended with a third due process claim. He argued that even if Arizona could constitutionally truncate the *M'Naghten* rule or exclude mental illness evidence that goes to mens rea, it could not do both at the same time because the two restrictions in combination unconstitutionally constrain the defense. Noting that even those states that have completely abolished the insanity defense allow mental illness evidence to rebut the prosecution's case on criminal intent (thereby subjecting the prosecution's case to full adversarial testing), Clark suggested that Arizona was a constitutional outlier in its treatment of mentally ill defendants.

Multiple amicus briefs were filed in support of Clark, including by the American Psychiatric Association, American Psychological Association, and the American Academy of Psychiatry and the Law, which filed a joint brief (APA joint brief) addressing both the procedural and substantive due process issues. The APA joint brief expressed serious concerns about the application of the *Mott* rule arguing that the rule precludes consideration of evidence that is perhaps more reliable than most given that it is the result of "expert study and experience."[72] Interestingly, the APA joint brief did not aggressively pursue the revival of *M'Naghten*'s cognitive prong; instead, it broadly referred to the common law's tradition of excusing a mentally ill defendant who "lacks rational appreciation of the wrongfulness of his conduct." Distinguishing the law's "formulation" from its "core," the APA joint brief urged the Court to recognize a "natural interdependence of the 'wrong' and 'nature and quality' components" of the *M'Naghten* rule.

Arizona's position, which had the support of the United States and several other States as amici curiae, could be summed up in one sentence: the insanity statute and the *Mott* rule both reflect policy decisions within the discretion of the state. In response to Clark's attack

---

72. Amicus Brief for the APA et al. at 17, Clark v. Arizona, 548 U.S. 735 (2006) (No. 05–5966), 2006 WL 247277.

on its insanity statute, Arizona argued that not only does a state have the discretion to define insanity as it sees fit, it also has the discretion not to recognize an insanity defense at all. In addition, Arizona pressed the state appellate court's reasoning that the moral prong constitutes the "heart" of the *M'Naghten* rule, rendering the cognitive prong superfluous to the inquiry and confusing to the jury.

Arizona's position was that its decision to restrict the use of mental illness evidence, was also a policy decision within the province of the states. This argument rested on *Montana v. Egelhoff*,[73] in which the Court upheld the murder conviction of a defendant who was not permitted to introduce evidence that his voluntary intoxication rendered him unable to form the mens rea required for a murder conviction. In the concurring opinion by Justice Ruth Bader Ginsburg that decided the case, Montana's exclusionary statute was viewed as a constitutionally permissible decision by the state legislature to redefine the mens rea element of the state's criminal offenses "to eliminate the exculpatory value of voluntary intoxication."[74] Exclusion was therefore valid because the evidence was no longer relevant to disproving the crime. According to Arizona, the *Mott* rule did no more than what the Montana statute accomplished in *Egelhoff*.

As critics of *Egelhoff* have noted, however, redefining the offense of murder to exclude consideration of facts such as intoxication that negate mens rea essentially transforms murder into a strict liability offense for defendants affected by the relevant condition. Justice Ginsburg said as much in *Egelhoff* when she wrote that Montana's statute allows conviction for murder if the prosecution can prove "that the defendant killed 'under circumstances that would otherwise establish knowledge or purpose "but for" [the defendant's] voluntary intoxication.' "[75] Under *Egelhoff*, the prosecution's burden to prove every element beyond a reasonable doubt remains untouched in only a technical sense—that is, only because the statute purports to reduce the burden of proof on the mens rea element to zero by eliminating the element altogether.[76] This move may superficially avoid the *Winship* problem since Montana's redefinition "extract[s] the entire subject of voluntary intoxication from the mens rea inquiry," rendering the disputed evidence logically irrelevant.[77]

---

73.   518 U.S. 37 (1996).

74.   *Id.* at 58–59. *Egelhoff* is a recent example of the Court's effort to define the contours of the constitutional requirement announced in *In re Winship* that the state bears the burden of proof *on each material element of a criminal charge.*

75.   518 U.S. at 58.

76.   *See* Ronald J. Allen, *Foreward:* Montana v. Egelhoff—*Reflections on the Limits of Legislative Imagination and Judicial Authority*, 87 J. Crim. L. & Criminology 633, 640 (1997).

77.   518 U.S. at 58; *Id.*

But it raises a host of other concerns, especially since the decision plunges into doubt the well-established assumption that a serious crime carrying a significant penalty, such as murder, requires a guilty mind.[78]

Egelhoff underscored the great power that, under our constitutional and federal system, legislatures have to define the elements of crimes and to thereby determine what evidence is relevant to proof of those elements. Therefore, it was hardly a surprise when the Supreme Court ruled against Eric Clark. Justice David Souter wrote the majority opinion, joined by Chief Justice Roberts and Justices Antonin Scalia, Clarence Thomas, and Samuel Alito. It was joined in part by Justice Stephen Breyer, who wrote a separate concurring opinion recommending remand.[79] First, the majority concluded that Clark failed to establish that the *M'Naghten* rule represents a fundamental principle of justice under the due process clause. In doing so, the opinion referred to the diversity of definitions found in American jurisdictions and held that "no particular formulation has evolved into a baseline for due process."[80] It then went on to affirm Judge Snow's ruling that Arizona's insanity statute did not differ materially from the *M'Naghten* rule since "a defendant can . . . make out moral incapacity by demonstrating cognitive incapacity."[81] Accordingly, Clark was not legally "shortchanged," as evidenced by the fact that the trial court admitted all of his mental illness evidence— including testimony bearing on his cognitive incapacity.[82]

The equivalency asserted by the majority between a one-pronged and a two-pronged rule depended on a broad reading of Arizona's insanity statute: one that required the defendant to "have understood that he was committing the act charged and that it was wrongful."[83] Thus, under Arizona law, a man squeezing his sister's neck would be found legally insane if he believed he was squeezing a lemon, for his cognitive incapacity rendered him unable to recognize his action as morally wrong. In addition, according to the majority's reading, a man who shot his sister believing he was shooting a dog would also have an insanity defense even though he might have known shooting a dog was wrong. This is because although he knew that he was doing something wrong, he did not also "[understand] that he was committing the act

---

78. *See* Morrisette v. United States, 342 U.S. 246 (1952).

79. Although the decision did not elicit surprise, some found it remarkable that the majority opinion was penned by Justice Souter, who was known to be especially protective of criminal defendants' rights. *See* Scott P. Johnson, *The Judicial Behavior of Justice Souter in Criminal Cases and the Denial of a Conservative Counterrevolution*, 7 Pierce L. Rev. 1, 3 (2008).

80. Clark v. Arizona, 548 U.S. 735, 752 (2006).

81. *Id.* at 753.

82. *Id.* at 753–757.

83. *Id.* at 754 n.23.

charged"—here, the murder of his sister. The moral prong completely subsumes the cognitive prong only because the Court recognized that a precondition to the knowledge of right and wrong is knowledge of what one is actually doing.[84] Thus, neither abstract knowledge that killing a human being is wrong, nor more specific knowledge that what one irrationally thinks one is doing is wrong, suffices to defeat an insanity claim. Whatever the Arizona legislature may have intended with its revisions to the state insanity law, the Supreme Court's integrated interpretation brought it in line with the *M'Naghten* rule as Chief Justice Tindal explained it in 1843.

The Court also rejected Clark's second due process claim on the mens rea issue. The majority offered its own reading of Arizona law here as well, construing the *Mott* decision as restricting only expert psychiatric evidence as opposed to all evidence of mental illness. Moreover, the majority read *Mott* to limit only expert *opinion* evidence about mental illness (e.g., diagnosis) and its effect on the defendant's capacity to form the requisite mens rea, leaving experts free to offer so-called "observation" evidence—that is, testimony about what the defendant did or said, his behavior and tendencies, etc.[85]

These distinctions may have come as a surprise to the parties. Although some mention of expert versus lay testimony, as well as fact versus opinion testimony, came up during oral arguments, the mention was in passing and no distinction among observation, mental-illness, and capacity evidence was ever argued by the parties or the many amici. The Court's evidentiary restriction also raised questions about the role of the psychiatrist at trial, since the majority seemed to exclude precisely that which makes the psychiatrist's testimony unique and important: her expertise in diagnosis and the effects of mental illness. After all, lay witnesses arguably could offer observation evidence just as effectively and thereby render the expert, in this context, superfluous.

The majority's novel evidentiary classification proved significant in two ways. The trial court appeared to believe that *Mott* disallowed the use of any mental health evidence to negate mens rea, making no distinction between observation evidence and expert opinion evidence. Thus, it was error for the trial court "to have applied *the Mott* restriction to *all* evidence offered by Clark for the purpose of showing what he

---

84. This may be a broader interpretation of the statute than Arizona urged at oral arguments. There, Arizona conceded that there may be a tiny number of cases affected by the absence of the cognitive prong, but argued that the legislature is entitled to disregard such anomalies in drafting the law. *See* Oral Arg. at. 29, 30.

85. This appears to be contrary to Arizona's position during oral arguments that *Mott* restricts all mental illness evidence, whether from expert or lay witnesses. Oral Arg., *supra* note 60, at 34–35.

called his inability to form the required mens rea."[86] However, the majority concluded that Clark failed to make his objection to the exclusion of observation evidence clear in the state courts because his arguments were generally worded to encompass expert opinion and capacity evidence as well as observation evidence. Relying on this finding, the majority decided that the question was not properly before the Court.[87]

Second, the Court reframed the issue as one of restricting (rather than wholly excluding) expert opinion evidence to the insanity inquiry. In other words, the fact finder could use expert opinion evidence to determine whether the defendant met his burden to prove GEI, but could not use the same evidence to determine whether the state carried its burden to prove the mens rea for first degree murder. Accordingly, *Mott*'s effect, if not intent, was to ensure that a criminal defendant is held to the statutory requirements of Arizona's insanity law, which places on the defendant the burden of proving, by clear and convincing evidence, that he lacked the capacity to distinguish right from wrong. If Arizona were to be forced to allow broad expert opinion evidence, observed the majority, the defendant would be able to avoid shouldering this heavy statutory burden by using the same evidence simply to cast reasonable doubt on the prosecution's case on mens rea. The majority held that Arizona may prevent this outcome by rejecting expert opinion evidence relevant to the issue of mens rea, especially because such evidence is more a matter of debate and judgment than fact. Its potential to mislead and confuse the jury therefore justified Arizona's decision to limit its admissibility to a context in which the defendant carried the burden of persuasion. In a footnote, the majority emphasized further the pragmatic nature of the insanity defense by observing that a state may justifiably be concerned that mentally ill criminals will avoid treatment and incapacitation by disproving mens rea in the manner Clark proposed to secure an outright acquittal.[88]

The majority never addressed Clark's final argument that the two rules combined violated due process.

Justice Anthony Kennedy, joined by Justices John Paul Stevens and Ruth Bader Ginsburg, wrote a spirited dissent over the *Mott* issue. The dissent began by attacking the evidentiary categories established by the majority as "the Court's own invention," stating that it was "unrealistic, and most unfair, to hold that Clark's counsel erred in failing to antici-

---

86. 548 U.S. at 760 (emphasis added).

87. Justice Breyer dissented in part, preferring to remand the case to determine whether the majority's reading of *Mott* accords with Arizona's understanding of that decision and whether the trial court properly applied it.

88. 548 U.S. at 778 n.45.

pate so novel an approach."[89] The new categories, moreover, were both artificial and unsustainable since observation evidence about what a mentally ill defendant did or said often becomes explicable and relevant through expert opinion testimony.

Justice Kennedy's dissent also pointed out that expert testimony relevant to the mens rea determination goes to a factual matter—that is, whether Clark knew he was killing a police officer—rather than to a judgment about criminal responsibility which lies at the heart of the insanity defense.[90] Thus, according to the dissent, the fact/judgment distinction drawn by the majority operates with less force in this context. In addition, the dissent agreed with Clark that Arizona's exclusionary rule impermissibly lifted the prosecution's burden of proving mens rea, since "the right [to have evidence considered on an element of the offense] is not respected by allowing the evidence to come in only on an issue for which the defendant bears the burden of proof."[91]

The dissenting opinion did not discuss the constitutionality of Arizona's insanity statute since the dissenters would have reversed on the *Mott* issue. It was clear during oral arguments, however, that Justice Kennedy agreed with Arizona's position on its insanity law. While questioning the state attorney general, Justice Kennedy indicated that he was struggling to imagine a scenario where the omission of the cognitive prong would make a difference in the outcome of an insanity case, and observed that all of the evidence Clark wanted to introduce had come in under the moral prong of the *M'Naghten* rule.

Reactions and Analyses

The *Clark* decision was not well-received by commentators. The majority opinion has been called "inexplicable,"[92] "tortured,"[93] and "gummy."[94] The justices of the majority have been accused of, at best,

---

89. 548 U.S. at 782.

90. In the *M'Naghten* case, where the role of the psychiatrist was also questioned, Chief Justice Tindal assured the House of Lords that "the medical man...cannot in strictness be asked his opinion [as to the defendant's state of mind at the time of the commission of the crime] because [the question] involves the determination of the truth of the facts deposed to, which is for the jury to decide, and the [question is] not merely [a question] upon a matter of science, in which case such evidence is admissible."

91. *Id.* at 797.

92. Susan D. Rozelle, *Fear and Loathing in Insanity Law: Explaining the Otherwise Inexplicable* Clark v. Arizona, 58 Case W. Res. L. Rev. 19, 20 (2007).

93. Ronald J. Allen, Clark v. Arizona: *Much (Confused) Ado About Nothing*, 4 Ohio St. J. Crim. L. 135, 135 (2006).

94. James J. Kilpatrick, *Who is Looney Now? Who Knows?*, Tulsa World, Aug. 6, 2006, at G4.

insensitivity and, at worst, animus, toward the mentally ill.[95] Although some, like Arizona's attorney general, celebrated the outcome as "a victory for states' rights and for the victim's family,"[96] critics have been decidedly more numerous and vocal. Two professional groups—mental health experts and lawyers—were particularly interested, and ultimately disappointed, in the case.

Given the Supreme Court's characterization of mental health testimony as misleading and unreliable, it is no wonder that the *Clark* ruling dismayed members of the mental health professions. Indeed, one commentator described Justice Souter's opinion as a "kick in the stomach" to the writers of the APA joint brief.[97] Others have suggested that the decision is infected with bias against psychiatry, criminal defendants, or both.[98] The idea that a young man could be locked up for first-degree murder when everyone agreed he was a schizophrenic who was actively psychotic at the time of the killing surely struck many in the profession as, at the very least, odd.[99]

The legal profession was no less critical of both the outcome and the reasoning behind the Court's ruling. Some saw the decision as condoning unequal treatment of mentally ill defendants. As Professor Susan Rozelle put it, "defendants who did not know that their victims were police officers will be acquitted—unless the reason they did not know was a mental illness."[100] Chief Justice Roberts inadvertently illustrated this point during oral arguments when he suggested that Clark could have explained the loud music "by showing that . . . he was in a rock band, and wanted to play the music . . . to advertise the concert, not to lure the police."[101] Of course, Clark could *not* have defended his case that way because those were not the facts; he did not have an explanation for his

---

95. *See* Kim Smith, *Justices Uphold Ariz.'s Limits on Insanity Defense*, Ariz. Daily Star, June 30, 2006, at A1; Rozelle, *supra* note 91, at 29.

96. Smith, supra note 94 (quoting Arizona's Attorney General Terry Goddard).

97. Alan A. Stone, *Psychiatric Testimony and the Insanity Defense*, 25 Psychiatric Times 4 (Apr. 1, 2008).

98. *See, e.g.*, Paul S. Applebaum, *Law & Psychiatry: Insanity, Guilty Minds, and Psychiatric Testimony*, 57 Psychiatric Serv. 1370–1372 (Oct. 2006). Critics were quick to cite to *Barefoot v. Estelle,* 463 U.S. 880 (1983), in which the Supreme Court held that expert testimony about future dangerousness at capital sentencing was admissible even if likely to be inaccurate because it will undergo adversarial testing.

99. The only person who seemed to express doubts about Eric Clark's mental illness was Dan Moritz, the victim's father and a psychologist. *See* Pauline Arrillaga, *Arizona Justice and Mental Illness*, Ft. Wayne J. Gazette, Apr. 16, 2006, at A7.

100. Rozelle, *supra* note 91, at 51–52; *see* Sherry F. Colb, *At the End of its Term, the Supreme Court Denies Mentally Ill Defendants' Right to a Fair Trial*, FindLaw (July 12, 2006), http://writ.news.findlaw.com/colb/20060712.html (observing that *Clark* "singles out the mentally ill for treatment that is worse").

101. Oral Arg., *supra* note 60, at 19.

behavior other than mental illness and therefore he was effectively forbidden from offering any (truthful) explanation.

Legal commentators also anticipated that Justice Souter's categories of mental illness evidence would sow confusion and eventually break down. The line between observation and opinion can be vanishingly thin, especially when the observation is made by an expert.[102] And as Professor Peter Westen pointed out, the attempt to restrict observation and opinion testimony is likely to lead to complications in jury instructions.[103] Moreover, the *Clark* case may encourage more misleading and unreliable testimony from behavioral experts because it forces them to give evidence that is divorced from their expertise, which lies in diagnosis and explanation of aberrant behavior.[104] If indeed Arizona and the Supreme Court aimed to exclude opinion evidence because of the purportedly speculative nature of that evidence, *Clark* may well exacerbate the problem.

But the fiercest criticism was saved for the majority's reasoning on the *Mott* rule's effect on the relative burdens of proof at trial. Commentators have almost been universal in condemning Justice Souter's justification of *Mott*'s exclusionary rule as a permissible way of effectuating the state's decision to place on the defendant the burden to prove insanity. Justice Souter was not wrong when he explained that allowing mental illness evidence to negate the requisite mens rea would lighten the mentally ill defendant's statutory burden to exculpate himself only by proving insanity by clear and convincing evidence. (Indeed, if the defendant were successful on the mens rea element, he would not need to prove insanity at all since there would be no crime for the insanity defense to excuse.) But Justice Souter seemed rather indifferent to the fact that *disallowing* mental illness evidence to negate the requisite mens rea would lighten the *prosecution's* burden to prove every element of the charged offense beyond a reasonable doubt, contrary to *Winship* and its progeny.[105]

---

102. *See* Rozelle, *supra* note 91, at 45–46; Christopher Slobogin, *The Supreme Court's Recent Criminal Mental Health Cases: Rulings of Questionable Competence*, 22 Crim. Just. 8, 13 (2007); Stephen J. Morse & Morris B. Hoffman, *The Uneasy Entente between Legal Insanity and Mens Rea: Beyond* Clark v. Arizona, 97 J. Crim. L. & Criminology 1071, 1104 (2007).

103. *See* Peter Westen, *The Supreme Court's Bout with Insanity:* Clark v. Arizona, 4 Ohio St. J. Crim. L. 143, 162 n.59 (2006).

104. *See* Steven K. Erickson, *Mind Over Morality*, 54 Buff. L. Rev. 1555, 1581–82 (2007). Of course, it is debatable whether exclusion of unreliable or misleading evidence is indeed Arizona's primary aim. There is no question that the post-*Hinckley* period of legal development in insanity law has been more focused on securing convictions than on improving the integrity of the trial process.

105. *See* Westen, *supra* note 102, at 143 (articulating the issue in *Clark* this way).

The Court not only declined to meaningfully address the due process demands of *Winship*, it also declined to use the *Egelhoff* rationale. Recall that in *Egelhoff*, the Court sidestepped a due process claim by ruling that the state of Montana's homicide law disallowing the use of evidence of involuntary intoxication to negate a purpose or knowledge mens rea was an acceptable means of defining the crime of murder, rather than an evidentiary rule impermissibly lightening the prosecution's burden to prove every element of the crime.[106] Why didn't the Court take the same route here, holding that Arizona had simply defined murder to require knowledge or purpose to kill a police officer except when the defendant lacked purpose or knowledge due to a condition of mental illness?

The answer is likely rooted in the differences between the historical treatment of mental illness and voluntary intoxication. Voluntary intoxication has long been thought irrelevant to finding a "guilty mind" in the common law, while mental illness has long been considered significant and may have achieved fundamental status. It is one thing to eliminate the subjective mens rea inquiry where the defense is based upon the voluntarily induced condition of intoxication. It is quite another to apply this kind of reasoning to a mental illness that is involuntarily suffered. Thus a *Clark* decision that followed the *Egelhoff* reasoning would have been radical indeed.

Although at least one scholar has criticized the Court for forgoing *Egelhoff*'s reasoning,[107] following *Egelhoff* probably would have had broader implications for the mens rea inquiry in cases like Eric Clark's. Rather than excluding all diminished capacity evidence by redefining the offense of murder, the *Clark* majority approached *Mott*'s restriction as an evidentiary rule and thereby preserved the admission of "observation" evidence, specifically described as:

> testimony from those who observed what Clark did and heard what he said; ... testimony that an expert witness might give about Clark's tendency to think in a certain way and his behavioral characteristics. This evidence may support a professional diagnosis of mental disease and in any event is the kind of evidence that can be relevant to show what in fact was on Clark's mind when he fired the gun.[108]

By reading *Mott* narrowly and treating the issue as an evidentiary question, Justice Souter retained the possibility for mentally ill defen-

---

106. As Justice Ginsburg stated in *Egelhoff*, such a decision "does not lighte[n] the prosecution's burden to prove [the] mental-state element beyond a reasonable doubt ... for [t]he applicability of the reasonable-doubt standard ... has always been dependent on how a State defines the offense that is charged." 518 U.S. 58 (internal quotations omitted).

107. *See* Slobogin, *supra* note 102, at 12.

108. *Clark*, 548 U.S. at 757.

dants in future cases to present evidence that goes directly to what was or was not actually on their minds when they acted—which is, in the end, all that is meant by proof and negation of mens rea. To be sure, the absence of expert opinion evidence will make it harder for the jury to understand and contextualize the state of mind of a mentally ill defendant. But Justice Souter appears to have assumed (or allowed that it is reasonable to assume) that evidence limited to what Clark did and said, and to Clark's own tendencies and characteristics, is more closely linked to his actual state of mind than expert opinion evidence, which at best speculates on what Clark may have been thinking based on the common traits and experiences of schizophrenics. Thus, Justice Souter justified the exclusion of opinion evidence, not because it cannot negate mens rea (since a person who is not capable of intending x could not have actually intended x) but because a state is permitted to reasonably conclude that such evidence is suspect.

The Court was also wary of Clark's *Mott* claim as an attempt to create a diminished capacity defense, contrary to Arizona's legislative intent. In the oral argument, both Justice Souter and Chief Justice Roberts suggested that by relying on "diminished-capacity evidence," Clark attempted to do "by the front door"—rebutting mens rea—what he was not allowed to do "by the back door"—forcing Arizona to recognize a diminished capacity defense.[109] Indeed, at one point, Justice Souter asked Clark's attorney whether it would be permissible for a state to conclude that mental illness evidence short of insanity is not relevant to criminal responsibility because otherwise, "everybody's going to have an excuse, and there isn't going to be any criminal law."[110] This exchange seemed to suggest that Justice Souter was skeptical not only of Clark's attempt to constrain Arizona's power to define its criminal laws, but also of the diminished capacity doctrine itself. Perhaps, then, by rejecting Clark's *Mott* claim Justice Souter was simply creating room for the states to finally be rid of this relatively new, confusing, and unpopular defense (and along the way, chastening the profession of forensic psychiatry for its role in promoting it[111]), and this singular policy focus

---

109. Oral Arg., *supra* note 60, at 17, 19

110. Oral Arg., *supra* note 60, at 17–18. Justice Souter's question is reminiscent of Mark Twain's comment that "[i]nsanity certainly is on the increase in the world, and crime is dying out." *See* Mark Twain, *A New Crime, in* Sketches, New and Old (1875), *available at* http://www.gutenberg.org/files/3189/3189–h/p4.htm#newcrime.

111. The *Clark* case probably did have some effect on professional discussions of ethical standards in forensic psychiatry. *See, e.g.,* Stephen J. Morse, *The Ethics of Forensic Practice: Reclaiming the Wasteland*, 36 J. Am. Acad. Psychiatry & L. 206 (2008) (discussing the limits of psychiatric contribution to legal questions on mental states). In this article, Professor Morse recommends that forensic psychiatrists refrain from giving diagnoses because it is "potentially misleading and confusing [to] the jury." *See id.* at 215.

overrode the practical conflict that arose between the Court's rulings in *Clark* and *Winship*.

One could say that with so much attention being paid to the evidentiary issue, Clark's substantive due process claim attacking Arizona's single-pronged insanity test has been overlooked by legal commentators. With respect to this issue, the *Clark* court held that "no particular formulation has evolved into a baseline for due process, and . . . the insanity rule, like the conceptualization of criminal offenses, is substantially open to state choice."[112] This ruling apparently struck observers as not only unsurprising, but unremarkable. The proposition that states have broad powers to define the criminal law is, indeed, so familiar to lawyers that it has become banal. The mental health profession also seemed mostly unconcerned; for example, the American Psychiatric Association declared in its most recent position statement on the insanity defense that it does not favor any particular formulation "so long as the standard is broad enough to allow meaningful consideration of the impact of serious mental disorders on individual culpability."[113]

The few, and sometimes only passing, commentaries on this issue reflect varied perspectives on the Court's ruling. Indeed, it is unclear whether the Court focused on the wording or the substance of the *M'Naghten* rule when it decided that it had not achieved fundamental status.[114] It seems implausible, however, to conclude that Clark was urging the Supreme Court to bind the states and the federal government to the exact wording of *M'Naghten*.[115] But if his claim goes to substance—namely, that due process requires consideration of *at least* cognitive and moral incapacity when a defendant's sanity is in question—then the Court's description of the "significant differences" among U.S. jurisdictions is simply wrong. By the majority's count, as of 2006, seventeen states and the federal government employed a "recognizable version" of *M'Naghten*, seventeen followed the ALI version (which explicitly accounts for "lack of awareness of what [the defendant] is doing" via explanatory notes), and three combined *M'Naghten* with the control test. That means that thirty-four states plus the federal govern-

---

112. 548 U.S. at 752.

113. American Psychiatric Association, *Insanity Defense Position Statements*, available at http://www.psych.org/Departments/EDU/Library/APAOfficialDocumentsandRelated/PositionStatements/200703.aspx.

114. *See* Westen, *supra* note 102, at 147–48 (noting the difference between form and substance in the Court's *M'Naghten* analysis).

115. Nonetheless, the amicus brief of the States of Massachusetts, Alabama, Arkansas, Colorado, Delaware, Hawaii, Indiana, Michigan, Montana, Ohio, Oklahoma, Oregon, Pennsylvania, South Carolina, South Dakota, and Texas, in support of Arizona, frame Clark's argument in just this way. *See* Amicus Brief of the States at 7–8, Clark v. Arizona, 548 U.S. 735 (2006) (No. 05–5966), 2006 WL 575249.

ment considered both cognitive and moral incapacity to determine legal insanity. If the Court's secondary argument that cognitive incapacity is subsumed by moral incapacity is accepted, then the number swells to forty-four. Moreover, one can easily argue that cognitive and moral incapacity is subsumed by New Hampshire's broad product test. That leaves only Alaska, which adopted only *M'Naghten*'s cognitive prong, and the four states that abolished the defense altogether.[116] To be sure, adherence to the *M'Naghten* rule is not universal, but this tally hardly describes significant variety in criminal insanity laws away from *M'Naghten*. By setting up a straw claim that places form over substance, the Supreme Court avoided having to decide whether due process requires both prongs of the *M'Naghten* rule.

The Court's assertion that the moral capacity prong "in practical terms" excuses the cognitively incapacitated is also vulnerable to challenge, depending as it does on a disputed reading of the Arizona statute.[117] Some commentators have argued that the "plain language" of the statute belies the Supreme Court's interpretation and suggest that the statute's reference to moral incapacity requires only abstract knowledge of right and wrong.[118] This was Clark's interpretation of the statute as well. Of course, the Supreme Court's integrated reading may in fact be correct, but there is some reason to question it. Arizona truncated the *M'Naghten* rule in response to Mark Austin's acquittal, which was believed to have been grounded on the rule's cognitive prong.[119] This, together with the general trend toward restricting the insanity defense to favor the prosecution, suggests that the Arizona legislature may have been doing more than merely "streamlining" the law to ease jury deliberation.[120]

Even if the Court has the correct reading, juries may nevertheless fail to apply the law as the Court read it in the *Clark* case. Some of Arizona's recent insanity cases reveal that the jury hears only the wording of the statute with no supplementary explanation about how a defendant's moral capacity to judge right from wrong necessarily depends on his cognitive capacity to understand his actions. Meanwhile, at least one post-*Clark* conviction seems to have been based on testimony regarding the defendant's abstract knowledge of right and wrong. Practically speaking, then, these cases suggest that the jury may be more

---

116. 548 U.S. at 749–52.

117. 548 U.S. at 753–54.

118. *See* Rozelle, *supra* note 91, at 39–40 & n. 120; Melançon, *supra* note 36, at 304–05.

119. *See* Melançon, *supra* note 36, at 304.

120. 548 U.S. at 755 n.24 (citing Ariz. H.R., Jud. Comm. Notes 3 (Mar. 18, 1993)).

confused than ever about the law they must apply.[121] Notwithstanding the Court's assertion that Arizona's statute does not materially differ from the *M'Naghten* rule, the state's one-pronged formulation creates greater risk that cognitive incapacity will be disregarded.

Conclusion

Much like *The Incredible Shrinking Man*[122] who, though becoming ever-smaller, remains an intact and whole human being, so does, apparently, the shrunken insanity rule of Daniel M'Naghten's case. Despite the Supreme Court's pronouncements, the *Clark* decision demonstrates how central that rule is to our understanding of responsibility and sanity, regardless of how "fundamental" it is in the technical constitutional sense. After all, the whole survived even when halved. Still, it is hard not to feel that the rule has been diminished, or at least changed, in some meaningful way.

The Supreme Court's interpretation reduces Arizona's amendment to a symbolic gesture, but symbols matter greatly in an area of law as expressive as the criminal law. The abandonment of *M'Naghten*'s cognitive prong, together with the rejection of "opinion" evidence in determining mens rea, signals the law's turn toward the moral and away from the scientific in answering one of its most basic questions: identifying responsible agents who may be subject to condemnation and punishment. This may be as it should be; Professor Stephen Morse has argued that criminal responsibility is based upon "folk psychology," which is unscientific but no less legitimate for its critical role in our understanding of ourselves as persons that act according to reason and, thus, according to law.[123] Even if Morse is right, so long as our definition of

---

121. *See, e.g.*, State v. McGee, No. 1 CA–CR 07–0681, 2009 WL 223117 (Ariz. Ct. App. Jan. 29, 2009) (unpublished decision); State v. Roque, 141 P.3d 368 (Ariz. 2006). The *McGee* case, especially, reveals continued confusion about what it is the defendant needs to know as wrongful under the test. The court, affirming the defendant's conviction, found noteworthy the following exchange between the prosecutor and an expert witness for the defense:

Q. But Jack McGee did know that killing a person or a human being was wrong.

A. Maybe—In an intellectual sense, I'd say he probably did; but in this case—And again, we may be dealing with—with a mental illness where the logic is being distorted—he did not believe this action was wrong.

Q. But he knew that killing a person would be wrong.

A. Yes, I would say so.

McGee, 2009 WL 223117. In *Roque*, one of defendant's arguments was that the jury should have been instructed that Arizona's insanity statute includes the first prong of the *M'Naghten* rule. In rejecting that claim, the Arizona Supreme Court held that "Arizona's definition encompasses only the second prong" and cited *Clark*. 213 Ariz. at 214.

122. *The Incredible Shrinking Man* (Universal Int'l Pictures 1957).

123. *See* Morse, *supra* note 110, at 209.

legal insanity encompasses mental illness, as it must, the law will have to create space for science to inform even this most normative of judgments. *Clark v. Arizona* represents one effort to map this fraught terrain.

It is worth noting that the Supreme Court's reticence to define a constitutional minimum definition of insanity does not necessarily extend to other areas of criminal law. One year after the *Clark* case, the Supreme Court confronted the issue of legal insanity again in *Panetti v. Quarterman*.[124] *Panetti* involved a Texas death row inmate who claimed that he was insane and therefore ineligible for execution according to the Eighth Amendment's prohibition against cruel and unusual punishment. Expert testimony indicated that Panetti, a schizophrenic, understood that the state was about to execute him for the murders he committed but he also "believe[d] in earnest that the stated reason is a 'sham' and the State in truth wants to execute him 'to stop him from preaching.' "[125] Panetti's claim relied on *Ford v. Wainwright*, which set forth a substantive standard of insanity for purposes of carrying out the death penalty as lack of comprehension, because of mental illness, of "the reasons for the penalty or its implications."[126] In *Panetti*, the Court held that comprehension embraces more than mere knowledge of the fact of execution and its causal relation to the underlying conviction; it requires a level of understanding that allows "the offender [to] recognize at last the gravity of his crime" by dint of the severest punishment.[127] *Panetti* demonstrates that in the capital punishment context, at least, the Court is willing to acknowledge that an appreciation of the nature and quality of one's actions and circumstances is indeed crucial to the condition of sanity.

As for Eric Clark, he did not give up. After the Supreme Court's decision against him, he filed for post-conviction relief. One of his claims was that he had ineffective assistance of counsel because his defense attorney failed to object to the trial court's exclusion of "observation" evidence.[128] Ironically, it was the dissenting opinion in Clark's case that would come back to thwart him again. The Superior Court of Arizona

---

124. 551 U.S. 930 (2007).

125. *Id..* at 954–55.

126. 477 U.S. 399, 417 (1986).

127. 551 U.S. at 958.

128. *Petition for New Trial Denied in Flagstaff Murder Case,* U.S. State News, Mar. 15, 2007, *available at* 2007 WLNR 5070321. Clark also claimed that counsel was ineffective for failing to raise the issue of Clark's competency once counsel realized that Clark was sleeping during the trial. Clark's trial attorney testified that his performance was indeed deficient in this regard, but the judge attributed the admission to the bond that counsel had formed with his client. Order at 8, Arizona v. Clark, No. CR 2000–0538, (Ariz. Super. Ct. Mar. 15, 2007).

denied his petition because an attorney cannot be faulted for failing to "predict the [Supreme] Court's own invention." The judge was quoting Justice Kennedy.

Clark remains incarcerated in state prison in Arizona. Although he was briefly placed in the mental health unit for treatment, he has recently been moved back to the maximum-security unit where he has spent most of the last seven years.[129] He has trouble handling interactions with other inmates—he has a number of minor and major infractions of prison regulations on his record[130]—and has often been placed in isolation. Even though Clark continues to exhibit odd behaviors and bizarre beliefs (e.g., he sometimes hallucinates and an adverse reaction to one of his medications has caused him to believe that he is turning into a woman), prison officials have determined that he is malingering. Clark is classified as posing the highest possible risk to the public and the institution under the prison's risk assessment system, and is ineligible for mental health services.[131]

---

129. Email from Terry Clark to author on April 8, 2010.

130. *See* Ariz. Dep't of Corrections, E. Clark Inmate Data, *http://www.azcorrections. gov/inmate_datasearch/results_Minh.aspx?InmateNumber=180165 & LastName=CLARK & FNMI=E & SearchType=SearchInet* (last visited Nov. 20, 2011).

131. *Id.*

8

Gabriel J. Chin

The Story of *Jacobson*: Catching Criminals or Creating Crime?

In *Jacobson v. United States*,[1] the Supreme Court narrowly but resoundingly reaffirmed the entrapment defense, exonerating the defendant because the crime had been induced by government action. The five justices in the majority applied the defense as a matter of law, even though a jury had considered and rejected it. They applied it to one of the most unsavory and unsympathetic crimes in the U.S. Code, receipt of child pornography. The Court accepted the argument even though a successful entrapment defense results in complete dismissal of criminal charges; thus, they allowed the defendant to go free. But the crime occurred only after the defendant, whose sole record was a decades-old DUI, had been repeatedly solicited by the government over a period of twenty-six months. The Court believed that had he been left alone, this crime likely would never have happened. Under the circumstances, the Court concluded, the defendant was entitled to be discharged.

Entrapment is a fairly recent addition to criminal law. The reason for its late development is simple. Until the process of expanding criminal liability reached a certain stage of development, government instigation of ordinary crime arose infrequently.[2] On the one hand, even members of the underworld could not easily be enticed into an impromptu rape, robbery, murder, arson, or other common-law felony, so such instigation on the part of law enforcement would rarely be rewarding. On the other hand, a successful proposal would be intrinsically dangerous if the crime reached the stage of a prosecutable attempt, which

---

1. 503 U.S. 540 (1992).

2. Some of this history is recounted in Rebecca Roiphe, *The Serpent Beguiled Me: A History of the Entrapment Defense*, 33 Seton Hall L. Rev. 257 (2003).

generally required something more than mere preparation.[3] For an innocent person to be raped, robbed or killed would be tragic, and embarrassingly so because it would have happened at government request.

Over time, however, legislatures created new crimes as new areas of economic and personal life were subjected to government regulation. For example, certain forms of drugs and alcohol were regulated or prohibited. After African American boxer Jack Johnson's triumph over "Great White Hope" Jim Jeffries was captured on film, Congress banned the interstate transportation of boxing films.[4] Federal authorities prohibited the mailing of obscenity and contraceptives. In the last quarter of the nineteenth century, the federal government began to regulate immigration for the first time. In short, as the modern regulatory and administrative state developed, criminal laws were enacted as adjuncts to civil regulation of social and economic behavior, and activities that one day were perfectly legal, the next day were deemed serious crimes. This was especially true under federal law, as the scope of federal legislation and regulation grew exponentially from the late Nineteenth Century through the New Deal.

Many of these new crimes took place behind closed doors or without the participation of a direct victim who might make a report to the authorities, or both. Accordingly, affirmative government investigation would be necessary to ferret them out. However, some of these new crimes were not subject to the same general moral condemnation as were traditional offenses—they were malum prohibitum rather than malum in se. Accordingly, a wider group of people were potentially subject to criminal liability. Therefore, entrepreneurial law enforcement techniques became more necessary and effective, but also more likely to capture persons not otherwise criminally inclined. A person who would never help a neighbor, say, carry a kidnap victim into the basement, might well help lug a case of bootleg gin. Indeed, a person who might never possess alcohol at all when left to her own devices might do so at the instigation of a "friend."

Another factor that led to the entrapment defense was the emergence during this era of modern police forces. At the federal level, such agencies as the Treasury Department were given special police forces (the Secret Service began with a goal of protecting the integrity of federal currency) that ultimately got involved in "morals" legislation such as drug and alcohol law. At the same time, municipal police forces grew into modern law-enforcement agencies. But just as these forces

---

3. Edwin Keedy, *Criminal Attempts at Common Law*, 102 U. Pa. L. Rev. 464 (1954).

4. Barak Y. Orbach, *The Johnson–Jeffries Fight 100 Years Thence: The Johnson–Jeffries Fight and Censorship of Black Supremacy*, 5 N.Y.U. J. L. & Liberty 270 (2010).

became more powerful and professionalized, they also became more subject to corruption as they enforced "morals" crimes, and as police agents began to infiltrate criminal enterprises, temptation and opportunity for both corruption and crime-inducing artifices grew.[5]

This new legal context raised the question: Should government have unrestricted power to make a criminal out of almost anyone? Of course, the question could be reversed: When should a person who voluntarily committed a crime get off the hook merely because the government had some involvement?

Several doctrines are potentially applicable to deal with the same basic problem of criminal conduct induced by a third party. The widely-accepted defense of duress is an important one; the Model Penal Code version grants a defense "if the actor engaged in the conduct charged to constitute an offense because he was coerced to do so by the use of, or a threat to use, unlawful force against his person or the person of another, that a person of reasonable firmness in his situation would have been unable to resist."[6]

Another defense, though one that is not widely applicable, is entrapment by estoppel. A person cannot be convicted if she reasonably relied on advice from a government official that particular conduct is legal. A contrary rule "would be to sanction the most indefensible sort of entrapment by the State—convicting a citizen for exercising a privilege which the State clearly had told him was available to him."[7]

Some courts also recognize a due process-based defense of "outrageous government conduct." The very few cases successfully advancing this theory suggest only genuinely extreme conduct gives rise to the defense. Merely providing contraband, say, drugs or drug precursors, is insufficient.[8] A Ninth Circuit decision held the defense was sufficiently pleaded when the defendant claimed the police jailed him on false charges, arranged for high bail, and, through government informants, gave him the opportunity to earn bail money by selling cocaine. The defendant was then charged with conspiracy to deal drugs.[9] Some judges and commentators have proposed that undercover investigations targeting individuals should be impermissible unless based on reasonable suspicion, but this restriction has been largely rejected.

---

5.   Roiphe, *supra* note 2, at 260–70.

6.   Model Penal Code § 2.09(1).

7.   Raley v. Ohio, 360 U.S. 423, 438 (1959). See also Model Penal Code § 2.04(3)(b) ("A belief that conduct does not legally constituted a defense is a defense to prosecution for that offense based on such conduct when [a defendant] acts in reasonable reliance on an official statement of the law, afterward determined to be invalid or erroneous").

8.   United States v. Russell, 411 U.S. 423 (1973).

9.   United States v. Bogart, 783 F.2d 1428 (9th Cir. 1986).

All of these defenses are like entrapment in that they are legal manifestations of the idea that the government should not too readily be able to make criminals out of persons who otherwise would have obeyed the law. But as entrapment law has evolved, it has applied in situations of government inducement not readily captured by these alternatives.

The earliest federal case recognizing the defense of entrapment is *Woo Wai v. United States*,[10] decided by the Ninth Circuit in 1915. Woo Wai was charged with helping bring in Chinese immigrants from Mexico. *Woo Wai* represented a new kind of law enforcement. The offense differed from traditional crimes in that entry of Chinese had been legal until the fairly recently enacted Chinese Exclusion Act and the other anti-Asian immigrant measures that followed. Because immigrant smuggling was "victimless," it might have generated less moral condemnation from the judiciary than robbery or arson.

The underlying facts were that a federal immigration agent hired a detective to entice Woo Wai, who was suspected of involvement in illegal importation of immigrants, to join a money-making scheme. Ironically, the agent's real goal was to place Woo Wai in a situation where he would disclose information about certain other federal agents who were suspected of corruption. The detective staged a meeting between Woo Wai and some local inspectors in which he proposed that Woo Wai smuggle immigrants across the Mexican–U.S. border and pay the inspectors a bribe. Woo Wai protested the illegality of this action and, for over a year, resisted several importuning pleas, and the inspectors' proposal of various specific plans for the smuggling. But, finally, he assented.

The court reversed on two separate grounds. The first was that because the government officials had never intended that the proposed importation occur, there was never any prospect of a crime to which Woo Wai would be a party. This ground reflected a common law concept that preceded modern entrapment law but often reached similar results, a notion of "consent." This was really a private law doctrine whereby the purported victim of the crime vitiated any criminal liability by staging the supposedly criminal event. Victim consent of this type operated as a defense, whether the staging party was a private entity (like an employer catching a filching employee) or a government agent.[11] This consent doctrine did not survive the expansion of inchoate criminal liability under modern law, where a person can still be guilty of attempting or

---

10.   223 F. 412 (9th Cir. 1915).

11.   The seminal case for this doctrine is an English decision, *Egginton's Case*, (1801) 168 Eng. Rep. 555 (P.C.), which was then widely followed in the United States. *E.g.,* People v. Collins, 53 Cal. 185 (1878) (where police decoy participates in burglary, there is in legal effect no burglary at all).

conspiring to commit a crime even if his supposed confederates have already begun cooperating with the police.[12]

But the more innovative ground, reflecting a modern public law version of entrapment, was that the government's action here violated "sound public policy" and that it "is not within the spirit of the Criminal Code" for an officer to be the originator of the proposed criminal plan.[13] The court held that because Woo Wai agreed to participate in the crime only as a result of the government's persistent efforts to persuade him, he was not guilty.

The predicate for the officials' efforts in *Woo Wai* was the Supreme Court's declarations, starting in the 1890s, that authorities were not bound by any provision of the Constitution or other law to limit their activities to investigation of past crimes. The Supreme Court held that U.S. Postal Inspection Service—a law enforcement agency frequently involved in litigation of claims of entrapment—could mail envelopes containing money to see if they would be purloined by letter carriers.[14] The Court also held that postal inspectors could submit mail orders to companies thought to be selling illegal products, and any contraband obtained could be used in a prosecution.[15] So some governmental participation in criminal activity was legal, and *Woo Wai* was simply the first federal case to consider where to draw the line. Before long, it was Prohibition, the major context in which entrapment doctrine developed, that led the Supreme Court itself to face the line-drawing problem.

The Supreme Court first recognized the defense of entrapment in *Sorrells v. United States*,[16] a liquor case decided during Prohibition. C.V. Sorrells, a factory worker in Canton, North Carolina, had served in the Thirtieth Division of the U.S. Army in France during World War I. He was suspected of running rum, although he was well-known in his town for never drinking himself. A prohibition agent posing as a tourist visited Sorrells at his home, truthfully claimed to be a veteran of the same unit, and, over an hour or more, repeatedly asked Sorrells to get him some liquor. Finally, Sorrells acquiesced, leaving his home and returning a few minutes later with a $5 jug, when he learned that this "old war buddy" was no friend.

The Court held that the trial court had erred in refusing to charge the jury on the defense of entrapment. It based its decision not on any

---

12. *See* United States v. Jimenez–Recio, 537 U.S. 270 (2003).

13. *Id.* at 274–75.

14. Montgomery v. United States, 162 U.S. 410 (1896); Goode v. United States, 159 U.S. 663 (1895).

15. Price v. United States, 165 U.S. 311 (1897); Rosen v. United States, 161 U.S. 29 (1896); Grimm v. United States, 156 U.S. 604 (1895).

16. 287 U.S. 435 (1932).

provision of the Constitution but on statutory construction: "We are unable to conclude that it was the intention of the Congress in enacting this statute that its processes of detection and enforcement should be abused by the instigation of government officials of an act on the part of persons otherwise innocent in order to lure them to its commission and to punish them."[17] The Court implied that the entrapment defense was not its own creation, but rather an actual, if implicit, decision of Congress. The elements of the defense, the Court explained, were "that the particular act was committed at the instance of government officials" and not the "predisposition and criminal design of the defendant," which may involve "an appropriate and searching inquiry" into the defendant's conduct.[18] Whether entrapment was established was to be submitted to the jury for its determination. The court identified the "controlling question" as "whether the defendant is a person otherwise innocent whom the government is seeking to punish for an alleged offense which is the product of the creative activity of its own officials."[19]

Although entrapment is conceptually related to other defenses, cases like *Sorrells* highlight the distinctions. Entrapment, unlike duress, requires no force or threat. It differs from entrapment by estoppel, because no known government agent need assure the defendant of the legality of the conduct. Entrapment requires nothing so egregious as "outrageous government conduct"; wheedling and social pressure may be sufficient.

Sherman v. United States,[20] decided in 1958, also involved deployment of federal law to suppress a substance, in this case, drugs. Defendant Joseph Sherman had been approached in a clinic by a fellow addict where both were being treated for addiction. Sherman's acquaintance, Kalchinian, turned out to be working with agents of the Bureau of Narcotics. Kalchinian repeatedly asked Sherman, over a period of time, for help obtaining heroin. Kalchinian claimed that treatment was not working and that he was suffering symptoms of withdrawal. Finally, Sherman agreed, and purchased heroin that he and Kalchinian shared on several occasions. Sherman was arrested.

The Court held that Sherman had been entrapped as a matter of law, discharging him in spite of the jury's consideration and rejection of the entrapment defense.

> The function of law enforcement is the prevention of crime and the apprehension of criminals. Manifestly, that function does not include the manufacturing of crime. Criminal activity is such that stealth

---

17. *Id.* at 448.

18. *Id.* at 451.

19. *Id.* at 451.

20. 356 U.S. 369 (1958).

and strategy are necessary weapons in the arsenal of the police officer. However, "A different question is presented when the criminal design originates with the officials of the government, and they implant in the mind of an innocent person the disposition to commit the alleged offense and induce its commission in order that they may prosecute."[21]

"[T]o determine whether entrapment has been established," said the Court, "a line must be drawn between the trap for the unwary innocent and the trap for the unwary criminal."

In *Sherman*, there was no question of government inducement; Kalchinian came up with the idea of purchasing drugs and persuaded Sherman to carry it out. Rather, the issue was Sherman's *predisposition*. The Court noted that Sherman made no profit on the sales, and that no narcotics were found in his apartment when it was searched. More problematic were Sherman's two drug convictions, one nine years old, the other five, but, said the Court, these were "insufficient to prove that [Sherman] had a readiness to sell narcotics at the time Kalchinian approached him."[22]

Sorrells and *Sherman* applied what has come to be known as the "subjective" test for entrapment, requiring inducement of the transaction by the government and the lack of "predisposition" by the defendant. Two powerful concurrences, by Justice Owen Roberts in *Sorrells* (joined by Justices Louis Brandeis and Harlan Stone) and Justice Felix Frankfurter in *Sherman* (joined by Justices William Brennan, William Douglas, and John Harlan), urged the Court to focus instead on "the conduct of the police and the likelihood, objectively considered, that it would entrap only those ready and willing to commit crime."[23]

Advocates of the "objective" approach viewed the idea that the defense was premised on an unexpressed legislative intent to be "sheer fiction"; it was better grounded on the court's supervisory authority over federal law enforcement.[24] Accordingly, many advocates of the objective test would give enforcement, as with the exclusionary rule, to judges rather than juries.[25] Although the Supreme Court has definitively adhered to the subjective test, legislatures and courts in the states are divided, most following the Court's subjective approach, some the objective test, and some a hybrid where both the court and the jury consider

---

21. *Id.* at 372 (quoting *Sorrells*, 287 U.S. at 442).

22. *Id.* at 375.

23. *Id.* at 384 (Frankfurter, J., concurring).

24. *Id.* at 379–80.

25. *Sorrells*, 287 U.S. at 457 (Roberts, J., concurring).

the defense in turn.[26] But whether the Court in *Sorrells* invented the defense or not, it is clear that the Justices identified an idea that American jurisprudence was eager to embrace; some form of the entrapment defense is now recognized by statute or court decision in virtually every jurisdiction in the United States.

The difference in focus between the subjective and objective approach has led to a scholarly debate about whether entrapment is analytically part of criminal law or criminal procedure. Under the objective test, where the critical issue is the conduct of the police, entrapment could be understood as a member of the family of procedural regulations of law enforcement behavior, like, say, the Fourth Amendment. On this view, entrapment prevents conviction for reasons other than the defendant's lack of culpability.

By contrast, the subjective approach, with its focus on predisposition, examines the defendant's mental state. Therefore, the focus is on culpability. Mens rea and culpability are questions of substantive criminal law. Under this approach, a conclusion that entrapment has been made out is a conclusion that the defendant does not deserve to be punished. The majority approach, and the approach in the Supreme Court, is subjective. Therefore, at least doctrinally, entrapment is properly understood as a matter of substantive criminal law in most jurisdictions.

The great mystery of entrapment law is the meaning of the key concept of predisposition.[27] Because the defense was created as a matter of statutory interpretation, Congress is free to clarify it, and the states are free to shape it as they wish, but Congress has not acted, and the states, for the most part, have adopted some variant of the ideas contained in the early Supreme Court decisions. Accordingly, courts and lawyers still struggle with the meaning of a term of art created in 1932 that turns out to be difficult to construe.

Predisposition cannot mean "disposition" in the sense that an individual's character makes them capable of committing a particular crime. Because entrapment is an affirmative defense, by definition, it is irrelevant except in cases where the fact finder concludes that the defendant voluntarily engaged in the prescribed conduct with the necessary mens rea. Thus, at least by the time of the crime the defendant was willing to engage in the illegal conduct. Presumably many people would not sell illegal substances regardless of any persuasion, enticement or encouragement short of physical compulsion. Sherman and Sorrells, by

---

26. *See* Paul Marcus, *The Entrapment Defense* § 1.05 (4th ed. 2009).

27. *See* Louis Michael Seidman, *The Supreme Court, Entrapment, and our Criminal Justice Dilemma*, 1981 Sup. Ct. Rev. 111.

contrast, were at some level ready to commit the crime, yet the defense was available to them.[28]

Predisposition also cannot exist simply because a defendant has actually engaged in the conduct in the past. Sherman was "predisposed" to drug use; he'd been convicted of it before and was in treatment because he was a recent user and therefore offender. If he had lost interest in taking drugs, there would have been no reason for him to be in treatment. Yet, Sherman was not "predisposed" as the Supreme Court used the term. Sorrells, too, had a remarkable knowledge of the illicit market in moonshine even if he was in fact a teetotaler. These defendants were clearly not "innocent" in any absolute sense, yet the Court referred to both as innocent for purposes of applying the entrapment defense.[29]

The Investigation of Keith Jacobson

The facts of *United States v. Jacobson* are like a drawing that dramatically changes form depending on how you look at it. On the one hand, the record suggests that Keith Jacobson was a law abiding person who, had the government simply left him alone, would likely have lived his entire life without ever committing a crime. On the other hand, with no direct physical coercion, Jacobson purchased child pornography, something that most people would not have done no matter how many solicitations and entreaties they received. It is little wonder that this case split a panel of the U.S. Court of Appeals for the Eighth Circuit, the Circuit sitting *en banc*, and then the Supreme Court itself. A total of thirteen judges rejected the defense, and seven accepted it, including five on the Supreme Court.

The underlying events are fairly clear, if complex.[30] In 1984, lifelong bachelor Keith Jacobson lived in Newman Grove, Nebraska, a town of

---

28. In addition, "if the entrapment defense were truly concerned with the culpability of the individual defendant and protecting those who were not predisposed to commit the crime, then the defense should be available to those who were lured into committing crime by private parties, and not just by government agents." Michael L. Piccarreta & Jefferson Keenan, *The Entrapment Defense*, 8 Crim. Just. 13, 58 (Summer 1993).

29. *Sherman*, 356 U.S. at 376; *Sorrells*, 287 U.S. at 448 ("otherwise innocent").

30. These facts are drawn from the parties' briefs, from newspaper accounts, from a September 21, 2004 interview with George Moyer, a June 14, 2010 interview with Paul Larkin, and a May 21, 2010 interview with Keith M. Jacobson. *See* Dirk Johnson, *Farmer Caught in a Pornography Trap Feels Vindicated, but at a Cruel Cost*, N.Y. Times, Apr. 19, 1992; David Thompson, *Nebraska Man is "Overjoyed" With Decision*, Omaha World Herald, Apr. 6, 1991 at 1; Paul Tash, *Entrapment, or Service to the Public?*, St. Petersburg Times, Dec. 2, 1991, at 1A; David Thompson, *Madison Attorney Back to Earth*, Omaha World Herald, Nov. 18, 1991, at 9; Paul Goodsell, *Porn Sting of Nebraskan is Defended*, Omaha World Herald, Nov. 7, 1991, at 1; Ruth Marcus, *Fair Sting or Foul Trap?*, Wash. Post Nov. 6, 1991, at A1.

about 800 where he was born in 1930. Jacobson was retired from a career in the U.S. Army which included service in Vietnam and Korea. His duties in the service included working for the newspaper *Stars and Stripes*; during a stint in Italy, he appeared as an extra in the 1968 film *The Devil's Brigade*, starring William Holden. He held a B.A. in Public Administration from Upper Iowa University. In Newman Grove, Jacobson worked for a local shopping newspaper for a while, then drove a school bus, grew soybeans and corn on his eighty-acre family farm, and served as the treasurer of the Zion Lutheran Church.

Also in 1984, Jacobson ordered the magazines *Bare Boys I* and *Bare Boys II* and a list of adult book stores by mail order from a San Diego business called Electric Moon. At the time, purchase and possession of these magazines violated no federal law even though they featured naked photographs of boys; they did not depict sexual conduct of any kind. Accordingly, they were not legally obscene.[31]

It was legally significant that Jacobson ordered the magazines in February, because the law in this area changed in the middle of 1984. In 1982, *New York v. Ferber*[32] held that the First Amendment did not prohibit criminalizing possession of non-obscene but sexually oriented materials involving minors. Although Congress had regulated transportation of some child pornography before *Ferber*,[33] Congress prohibited receiving non-obscene sexually explicit materials involving minors only in May 1984, the effective date of the Child Protection Act of 1984.[34] Thus, what Jacobson did perfectly legally in the winter, was a crime by spring. Later in 1984, California police found Jacobson's name and address when searching Electric Moon. This information brought Jacobson to the attention of the federal authorities.

Jacobson described himself as bisexual, but said he never had a gay relationship. In January 1985, Jacobson received a letter purportedly from the "American Hedonist Society," along with a membership application containing a survey of sexual attitudes. The documents proposed that Americans had the "right to read what we desire, the right to discuss similar interests with those who share our philosophy, and finally that we have the right to seek pleasure without restrictions being placed on us by outdated puritan morality." Jacobson responded, noting

---

31. *See* United States v. X–Citement Video, 513 U.S. 64, 74 n.4 (1994) ("The *Miller* test for obscenity asks whether the work, taken as a whole, 'appeals to the prurient interest,' 'depicts or describes [sexual conduct] in a patently offensive way,' and 'lacks serious literary, artistic, political or scientific value.' ") (quoting Miller v. California, 413 U.S. 15, 24 (1973)).

32. 458 U.S. 747 (1982).

33. Protection of Children Against Sexual Exploitation Act of 1977, Pub. L. No. 95–225, 92 Stat. 7 (1978).

34. Pub. L. No. 98–292, 98 Stat. 204 (1984).

that he was interested in pre-teen sex, but that he was opposed to pedophilia. The "American Hedonist Society" was in actuality a U.S. postal inspector trolling for persons interested in child pornography.

In May 1986, over a year later, Jacobson received a sexually oriented solicitation from "Midlands Data Research," and he replied that he was "interested in teenage sexuality." A couple of months later, Jacobson got a letter and survey from "Jean Daniels," director of the "Heartland Institute for a New Tomorrow" (HINT), a purported lobbying organization "founded to protect sexual freedom and freedom of choice. We believe that arbitrarily imposed legislative sanctions restricting your sexual freedom should be rescinded through the legislative process." The Heartland Institute was another front organization. Jacobson completed and returned the survey, again expressing interest in "pre-teen sex-homosexual." He also stated, "Not only sexual expression but freedom of the press is under attack. We must be ever vigilant to counter attack right wing fundamentalists who are determined to curtail our freedoms."

Jacobson received a thank-you note from Jean Daniels of HINT, along with a list of names and addresses of persons with similar interests, but Jacobson did not initiate correspondence with any of them. Using the pseudonym "Carl Long" (one of the names listed in the Jean Daniels' letter), a postal inspector wrote to Jacobson. Jacobson replied twice, in letters that did not discuss child pornography, and then stopped replying to Long's letters.

In March 1987, the Customs Service mailed Jacobson a brochure for child pornography materials. He placed an order which was never filled. Also in March 1987, a postal inspector sent a brochure from the "Far Eastern Trading Company" offering to send a catalog. Jacobson requested one, and he received it in May 1987. From that catalog, Jacobson ordered *Boys Who Love Boys*, which, according to the catalog, involved "11 and 14 year old boys" who "get it on in every way imaginable. Oral, anal sex and heavy masturbation. If you love boys you will be delighted with this."

On June 16, 1987, Jacobson found a notice in his post office box, and exchanged it for an envelope containing *Boys Who Love Boys*. Postal inspector Calvin Comfort, who had conducted most of the investigation, observed Jacobson pick up the magazine and obtained a warrant to search Jacobson's home. Comfort, accompanied by customs agents and the local sheriff, confronted Jacobson at his home, and searched the residence. In addition to *Boys Who Love Boys*, Comfort found the *Bare Boys* magazines, and the fabricated correspondence from the government, but no other child pornography related materials.

Jacobson was indicted in September 1987, and in April 1988, was tried by jury before Chief Judge Lyle E. Strom of the U.S. District Court for the District of Nebraska. He was charged with violation of 18 U.S.C. § 2252(a)(2), that is, with knowingly receiving through the mails sexually explicit material depicting a minor.

Jacobson retained attorney George H. Moyer, Jr., a graduate of the University of Nebraska law school, whose general practice included matters ranging from agricultural law to workers compensation. Moyer got the case when Jacobson walked into his office, and he represented Jacobson throughout the case. Moyer, the third of four generations of Moyers who practiced in the same firm, called himself "a little old county seat lawyer," but was described by a fellow attorney as "probably one of the shrewdest trial lawyers in the state." At trial, Moyer raised the defense of entrapment, but the jury rejected it.

Jacobson was sentenced to three years' imprisonment, suspended in favor of two years' probation and 250 hours of community service.[35] Jacobson discharged his community service by painting a church garage and working at the town library. He was fired from his school bus driving job, although there was no evidence that he engaged in misconduct with children; "I'm not the kind of person who wanted to get involved with kids that way. I never have and I never would," he said. He was forced to sell his share of the family farm to his sister to pay his $25,000 in legal fees.

Jacobson explained his purchase of child pornography by saying, "They kind of worked on me.... I bought it. It's something I regret doing, [but] I just figure I was kind of gullible at the time." The case "just destroyed my life. It destroyed the way I viewed myself."

In spite of Jacobson's conviction, the Newman Grove community stood by him. The local newspaper wrote that "[m]ost any of us could be set up for such a sting;" his pastor stated that "he's always been an honorable person and we supported him."

The Lower Court Decisions

Jacobson appealed the conviction to the U.S. Court of Appeals for the Eighth Circuit. A panel of the Eighth Circuit decided the appeal on January 12, 1990. Senior Judge Gerald W. Heaney wrote an opinion that was joined by Chief Judge Donald P. Lay. They began with facts that must have made the defendant and his counsel optimistic, noting that he is "currently living on a family farm and supporting his parents. Jacobson served in the Korean and Vietnam Wars, for which he received the Bronze Star and Army Commendation Medal. He has no criminal

---

35.   United States v. Jacobson, 893 F.2d 999, 1000 (8th Cir. 1990).

history, with the exception of a conviction for driving while intoxicated in 1958."[36] They ordered the conviction reversed.

At this stage, *Jacobson* was not decided as an entrapment case; the gist of the opinion was that the government should not have initiated the investigation of Keith Jacobson because they "had no evidence giving rise to a reasonable suspicion that Jacobson had committed a similar crime in the past or was likely to commit such a crime in the future."[37] The majority reasoned first that the legal 1984 purchase of nudist magazines "(1) . . . was not evidence of predisposition and did not give rise to a reasonable suspicion based on articulable facts that Jacobson had committed a crime in the past or was likely to commit a crime in the future; (2) the government must have reasonable suspicion based on articulable facts before initiating an undercover operation directed at a person; and (3) since the undercover operation was improper, Jacobson's conviction must be set aside."[38]

The purchase of the *Bare Boys* magazines, said the Circuit Court, did not establish reasonable suspicion. Its probative value was diminished because the purchase was entirely legal: "[w]hen an individual engages in legal conduct and no additional or extrinsic evidence exists to give rise to a reasonable suspicion of predisposition, the government may not target that individual, no matter how distasteful the lawful conduct may be."[39]

The court recognized that "the use of undercover operations is indispensable to the achievement of effective law enforcement," but, it said, "the potential harms of undercover operations call for the recognition that there must be some limitation on the indiscriminate use of such government targeting."[40]

Judge George G. Fagg dissented, asserting that the majority "has declared war on the government's power to initiate undercover investigations." He answered in the majority's terms, rejecting the idea that reasonable suspicion was an indispensable prerequisite for initiating an undercover investigation, instead arguing that an investigation was valid unless the defendant could show that it violated due process. "In my opinion, the panel has borrowed from the rule of probable cause to arrest, and from the rule of particularized suspicion that governs brief investigatory detentions, for the singular purpose of narrowing the government's power to initiate undercover investigations. Needless to

---

36. *Id.* at 999–1000.

37. *Id.* at 999.

38. *Id.* at 1000.

39. *Id.* at 1000.

40. *Id.* at 1002.

say, law enforcement decisions to conduct undercover investigations are not controlled by fourth amendment doctrine." Application of the proper due process standard, said Judge Fagg, would lead to affirmance, because "[the] government possessed well-grounded reasons to believe that an investigation aimed at Jacobson would uncover criminal behavior."[41]

Disappointed with the result, the Department of Justice successfully sought rehearing en banc. En banc, Judge Fagg reversed roles, authoring the decision for an eight-judge majority which addressed three issues precisely and succinctly.[42] First, the court said that no reasonable suspicion was necessary before the government could undertake an undercover investigation against an individual; the only general limitation was due process. And due process would invalidate an investigation, or a decision to investigate, "only when the [g]overnment activity in question violates some protected right of the defendant."[43] Since Jacobson made no such claim, the presence or absence of a factual basis for investigation was irrelevant.

Second, the court rejected Jacobson's claim that the government's conduct during the investigation was sufficiently outrageous that it violated his due process rights. The court recognized that in earlier decisions, a majority of the justices stated that outrageous governmental conduct could invalidate a conviction.[44] However, "because the government may go a long way in concert with the investigated person without violating due process, the level of outrageousness needed to prove a due process violation 'is quite high.' "[45] The court noted that the "postal inspectors did not apply extraordinary pressure on Jacobson. The inspectors merely invited Jacobson to purchase pornographic material through the mail.... Unlike face-to-face contacts, Jacobson easily could have ignored the contents of the mailings if he was not interested in them."[46]

Finally, the court dismissed Jacobson's claim that he had been entrapped as a matter of law. The jury necessarily rejected the entrapment claim by convicting Jacobson, and the court said it was entitled to do so. "The government presented ample evidence that the postal inspectors only provided Jacobson with opportunities to purchase child

---

41. *Id.* at 1003.

42. United States v. Jacobson, 916 F.2d 467 (8th Cir. 1990) (en banc).

43. *Id.* at 469 (quoting Hampton v. United States, 425 U.S. 484, 490 (1976)).

44. *Id.* at 469 (citing *Hampton*, 425 U.S. at 492–95 and United States v. Russell, 411 U.S. 423, 431–32 (1973)).

45. *Id.* at 469 (quoting Gunderson v. Schlueter, 904 F.2d 407, 410 (8th Cir. 1990) and citing United States v. Musslyn, 865 F.2d 945, 947 (8th Cir. 1989) (per curiam)).

46. *Id.* at 470.

pornography and renewed their efforts from time to time as Jacobson responded to their solicitations."[47]

Judges Lay and Heaney, the panel majority, could get none of their colleagues to join them en banc. Indeed, at this point, they did not even fully agree with each other, dissenting in separate opinions on separate grounds.

Chief Judge Lay's dissent argued that Jacobson had established entrapment as a matter of law, because he was not predisposed. "From the uncontroverted facts in this case, it is readily apparent that Jacobson was not predisposed to commit the crime of receiving through the mails sexually explicit materials depicting a minor." Although in response to the inquires arranged by the government Jacobson expressed an interest in pre-teen sex magazines,

> [b]ased on Jacobson's prior history, it is not clear that he would knowingly and voluntarily violate the law by purchasing obscene materials.... The government invested considerable time and money to prosecute a man who would never have committed a crime but for the government's encouragement. The government should not concentrate its efforts on incriminating innocent individuals; rather it should strive to suppress criminal behavior."[48]

Judge Heaney agreed that "[h]ad the Postal Service left Jacobson alone, he would have, on the basis of his past life, continued to be a law-abiding man, caring for his parents, farming his land, and minding his own business."[49] He adhered to the view that the legal doctrine that gave rise to a defense was that "the government must have ... a reasonable suspicion before instituting an undercover sting directed at an individual." However, the only case he cited was a Ninth Circuit decision which was then being reheard en banc. The en banc Ninth Circuit ultimately vacated the relevant portion of the decision, leaving that legal argument without supporting precedent.[50]

Judge Heaney also elaborated on the argument that the government conduct was outrageous. The prosecution "was the culmination of the Postal Service's two and one-half year campaign to induce this heretofore law-abiding farmer to violate the obscenity laws."[51] "In my view," concluded Judge Heaney, "the government's investigation and prosecution of Jacobson amount to the deliberate manufacture of a crime that

---

47. *Id.* at 470.

48. *Id.* at 471 (Lay, J., dissenting).

49. *Id.* at 471 (Heaney, J., dissenting).

50. *Id.* at 472 (citing United States v. Luttrell, 889 F.2d 806, 813 (9th Cir. 1989), *vacated in relevant part en banc*, 923 F.2d 764 (9th Cir. 1991)).

51. *Id.* at 474.

would never have occurred but for the Postal Service's overzealous efforts to create it."[52]

The Supreme Court Decision

Although George Moyer, Jacobson's attorney, had never appeared before the Supreme Court, and was not even admitted to the high court when the Eighth Circuit affirmed the conviction, he had participated in dozens of appeals to the Nebraska Supreme Court and in other cases in the Eighth Circuit. Moyer sought certiorari in a petition containing seven grounds, advancing various forms of the outrageous government conduct defense, the absence of reasonable suspicion, and entrapment. Justice John Paul Stevens picked the case out of the pile of thousands of mostly hopeless certiorari petitions. Jacobson initially did not receive the necessary four votes, but Justice Byron White asked for a re-vote, and Stevens and Justices Thurgood Marshall and Harry Blackmun agreed that the case should be reviewed.[53] According to his biographer, Justice White was "[t]roubled by the government's behavior ... ; his preliminary view of the record was that Jacobson had been harassed by government agents run amok."[54]

The grant of certiorari was limited to the question of whether Jacobson had established entrapment as a matter of law.[55] The parties' briefs focused the issues. Moyer insisted that the predisposition required by *Sorrells* and *Sherman* was not a "sexual, pharmaceutical or political" interest, but rather "intent to commit the crime."[56] In addition, "predisposition 'must appear before anything at all occurs respecting the alleged offense.' "[57]

The brief also attempted to distinguish the government's efforts in this case from other types of stings on the ground that these crimes might never have occurred but for government facilitation. Jacobson was caught in a "national program in which the postal authorities would actually solicit, advertise, sell, manufacture and deliver child pornography."[58] "The Government has become the number one commercial

52. *Id.* at 476.

53. Joyce Murdoch & Deb Price, *Courting Justice: Gay Men and Lesbians v. the Supreme Court* 410 (2001).

54. Dennis J. Hutchinson, *The Man Who Once Was Whizzer White: A Portrait of Justice Byron R. White* 420 (1998).

55. Jacobson v. United States, 499 U.S. 974 (1991).

56. Petitioner's Brief at 16, Jacobson v. United States, 503 U.S. 540 (1992) (No. 90–1124) 1991 WL 535304.

57. *Id.* at 16–17 (quoting United States v. Williams, 705 F.2d 603, 618 n.9 (2d Cir. 1983)).

58. *Id.* at 28.

purveyor of child pornography in the United States. Government created publications are the only publications in the United States today which advertise, sell, offer to purchase or exchange child pornograph[y]."[59] "Lonely old men who may harbor 'private fantasies' are not within the statute's ambit. Although the government has a duty to protect children by suppressing the market for child pornography, the Government cannot first create the market by tempting the innocent, but vulnerable and then justify prosecution by claiming it is merely suppressing the market."[60]

Solicitor General Kenneth W. Starr's brief (signed by, among others, Paul A. Larkin, Jr., who would argue the case for the United States) responded that evidence of predisposition need not involve criminal offenses. Although Jacobson's receipt of the *Bare Boys* magazines "did not violate federal law . . . that fact does not deprive his mail order purchase of those magazines of evidentiary significance on the issue of his predisposition to receive *Boys Who Love Boys*."[61]

One part of the Solicitor General's brief and subsequent oral argument defended the conviction on grounds that sound more in duress than entrapment. The Solicitor General addressed the argument that the government induced the crime, noting that postal inspectors did not apply extraordinary pressure or coercion,[62] and arguing that entrapment was made out only if "the government's behavior was such that a law-abiding citizen's will to obey the law could have been overcome,"[63] or an "average person could not resist."[64] Such behavior would include grave threats, fraud, or extraordinary promises.[65] "Petitioner concedes that he was neither 'coerced' nor 'force[d]' into committing the crime."[66]

---

59. Petitioner's Reply Brief at 11 n.5, Jacobson v. United States, 503 U.S. 540 (1992) (No. 90–1124) 1991 WL 535306. Here, Moyer cited Lawrence Stanley, *The Child Pornography Myth*, 7 Cardozo Arts & Ent. L.J. 295, 324 (1989). The Stanley article is a well-researched and scholarly argument for the idea that the problem of child pornography had been greatly exaggerated, and that the commercial market had long since dried up. Unfortunately, the credibility of that article has been profoundly impeached by an undisclosed conflict of interest: Mr. Stanley was himself reportedly deeply involved with sexual images of children, and actual children, giving rise to numerous scrapes with the law, including, reportedly, some convictions. *See* Stanley v. United States, 932 F. Supp. 418 (E.D.N.Y. 1996); Robert Stacy McCain, *Porn Lawyer Charged in Brazil Girls Case*, Wash. Times, July 24, 2002, at A09.

60. Petitioner's Reply Brief, *supra* note 59, at 20.

61. Brief for the United States at 29, Jacobson v. United States, 503 U.S. 540 (1992) (No. 90–1124) 1991 WL 535305.

62. *Id.* at 12, 15.

63. *Id.* at 18 (quoting United States v. Kelley, 748 F.2d 691, 698 (D.C. Cir. 1984)).

64. *Id.* at 17.

65. *Id.* at 20 (citing United States v. Evans, 924 F.2d 714, 717 (7th Cir. 1991)).

66. *Id.* at 25.

Several prominent groups filed amicus briefs. Newt Gingrich, Henry Hyde, Richard Armey, Rick Santorum and other members of Congress filed a brief emphasizing the importance of undercover investigations in catching pedophiles, as did the National Center for Missing and Exploited Children. Legendary Northwestern Law Professor Fred Inbau, inventor of a widely used police interrogation technique, was one of the signers of the brief of Americans for Effective Law Enforcement, which argued that there had been no entrapment and that reasonable suspicion was not required before initiating an undercover investigation.

The ACLU, Nebraska Civil Liberties Union, and the National Association of Criminal Defense Lawyers filed a brief supporting Jacobson; three out of four authors would become law professors by 2011. Pace Law Professor Bennett L. Gershman was counsel of record; with him on the brief were ACLU lawyers john a. powell who became a professor of law at Ohio State, and William B. Rubenstein, who joined the faculty at UCLA (and is now at Harvard).

Moyer prepared for the argument by returning to law school. University of Nebraska College of Law Professor Richard Harnsberger, who had taught Moyer when Moyer was a student, invited him to appear before a moot court of fellow Nebraska professors, including Josephine Potuto and William Lyons along with Professor Harnsberger. Moyer also spent several hours being questioned by a student seminar at Washington and Lee School of Law.

As befits a case attracting such distinguished amici, the case received significant media attention. It was the subject of a February 16, 1992 *60 Minutes* segment, narrated by Mike Wallace and featuring George Moyer, entrapment expert and William and Mary law professor Paul Marcus, and a supervisor from the Postal Inspection Service. The latter acknowledged to Wallace that "the dealers of child pornography have virtually been eliminated in this country," which made authorities choose to target consumers to dry up the demand side of the market.

The case was argued before the actual Supreme Court on November 6, 1991,[67] with Keith Jacobson in the audience, as he had been at the Eighth Circuit. George Moyer appeared for Jacobson and Paul A. Larkin Jr. argued for the United States.

One issue for the Justices was the evidentiary import on the issue of predisposition of legal purchase of disreputable items. When Moyer proposed that "you cannot assume that somebody is going to engage in criminal activity, knowing that it's criminal, just because he has engaged in that activity when it was legal," Justice Scalia responded, "It depends

---

67. See Transcript, Jacobson v. United States, 503 U.S. 540 (1992) (No. 90–1124) 1991 WL 636288, available on line at http://www.oyez.org/cases/1990–1999/1991/1991_90_ 1124/argument.

on what that activity is. If it's that kind of an activity, just as if it would have been cocaine, I think one may, one may suspect that this is a person who does not care that much about societal norms."[68] But Larkin admitted that "if what you're asking is do I have any change in the law cases where on day—on a certain day something that was not previously illegal became illegal, I don't have any case dealing with that problem."

The Justices also alluded to the defense of entrapment by estoppel, when the government gives an individual the idea that conduct is legal, then prosecutes them for it.[69] Larkin stated that an undercover officer could say "to somebody this is, you know, a new designer drug and it's not yet been listed on the Attorney General's . . . prohibited list, in that context the defendant I don't think is able to say that the Government misled him." Justice Scalia replied, "You just lost me, Mr. Larkin. I think you've gone too far now." This conduct would not quite constitute entrapment by estoppel, which requires reassurance of legality by the police or another government actor known to the defendant as a public official. However, Justice Scalia was right, in that courts treat assurances of legality, even by an informer, as at least relevant to evaluation of entrapment.[70]

The Justices were also interested in how a decision for Jacobson would affect other common investigative techniques. Moyer suggested that a government pawn shop seeking to purchase stolen goods would be perfectly permissible even though there was no particular evidence about anyone who might come in, because the predisposition would be evident; indeed, by hypothesis, the person would have actually committed the theft, burglary, or robbery, or would have knowingly received stolen goods, before any contact with the government. Moyer also said that placing an ad for child pornography in a magazine would be entirely an acceptable investigative method, because the only people who would respond would be those who already had an interest in such material.

After the argument, Jacobson stated to reporters that Americans had a right to be "let alone unless you're involved in a type of criminal activity. I was not running any kind of pornographic enterprise. I just figure that if I had been left alone I wouldn't have bought it." Jacobson added; "I'm not saying I did the right thing here. I did make a mistake."

On April 6, 1992, the Court reversed Jacobson's conviction in a 5–4 decision written by Justice White for himself and Justices Blackmun, Stevens, David Souter and Clarence Thomas. The description of the

---

68. Is it possible that Justice Scalia did not know that cocaine was once sold over the counter and included in widely used patent medicines, such as Coca Cola? *See* David Musto, *The American Disease: Origins of Narcotic Control* 3, 7 (3d ed. 1999).

69. *See* United States v. Batterjee, 361 F.3d 1210 (9th Cir. 2004) (applying doctrine).

70. People v. Juillet, 475 N.W.2d 786, 794 (Mich. 1991).

Court's consideration of the case in the book *Courting Justice* shows that many minds were changed after argument. Justice Sandra Day O'Connor was assigned to write a 7–2 affirmance; only White and Stevens supported reversal. *Courting Justice* suggests that "White's very human argument swiftly swept Blackmun and Thomas to Jacobson's side."[71] Justice Souter supplied the controlling fifth vote. Justice O'Connor's majority opinion became a dissent, and Justice White's dissent a majority opinion announcing reversal.

The central legal ruling in *Jacobson* was the particular moment that the government was required to prove that predisposition existed: "Where the Government has induced an individual to break the law and the defense of entrapment is at issue, as it was in this case, the prosecution must prove beyond reasonable doubt that the defendant was disposed to commit the criminal act prior to first being approached by Government agents."[72] The dissenters claimed this was a novel holding; the majority claimed that it was existing law. Neither was able to cite to a specific clear holding from a Supreme Court case, although in *Sherman*, the Court held that the question was the defendant's disposition "at the time [the agent] approached him."[73] In any event Paul Larkin conceded the point for the United States at oral argument.[74] This holding is important because it limits the ability of law enforcement to engage in long periods of grooming and luring potential targets.

An equally important development was the rigor with which the Court enforced the principle. The Court recognized that even someone who was ultimately persuaded to do something quite wrong could nevertheless be the beneficiary of the defense.

Ordering and receipt of *Bare Boys*, it declared, was not enough to prove predisposition: "It may indicate a predisposition to view sexually oriented photographs that are responsive to his sexual tastes; but evidence that merely indicates a generic inclination to act within a broad range, not all of which is criminal, is of little probative value in establishing predisposition."[75] It was also significant that what Jacobson did was lawful. "Evidence of predisposition to do what was once lawful is

---

71. Murdoch & Price, *supra* note 53, at 412 (citing Hutchinson, *supra* note 54, at 421). A book about Justice Clarence Thomas's contentious confirmation hearings suggests that his experience made him more sympathetic to Jacobson: "A former clerk explained that after all Thomas has gone through, the justice was especially sensitive to the overreaching powers of prosecutors." Jane Mayer & Jill Abramson, *Strange Justice: The Selling of Clarence Thomas* 358 (1994).

72. Jacobson v. United States, 503 U.S. 540, 549 (1992).

73. 356 U.S. 369, 375 (1958).

74. 503 U.S. at 549 n.2.

75. *Id.* at 550.

not, by itself, sufficient to show predisposition to do what is now illegal, for there is a common understanding that most people obey the law even when they disapprove of it. This obedience may reflect a generalized respect for legality or the fear of prosecution, but for whatever reason, the law's prohibitions are matters of consequence."[76] This conclusion is eminently consistent with the finding of entrapment in *Sherman*, where the defendant had previously been convicted of using drugs, precisely the same conduct at issue in the prosecution, but was nevertheless not predisposed as a matter of law.

The Court also emphasized the political nature of the inducement. "[T]he strong arguable inference is that, by waving the banner of individual rights and disparaging the legitimacy and constitutionality of efforts to restrict the availability of sexually explicit materials, the Government not only excited petitioner's interest in sexually explicit materials banned by law but also exerted substantial pressure on petitioner to obtain and read such material as part of a fight against censorship and the infringement of individual rights."[77] "[T]he two solicitations in the spring of 1987 raised the spectre of censorship while suggesting that petitioner ought to be allowed to do what he had been solicited to do."[78] Given Jacobson's experience working on newspapers, the Court's conclusion that a First Amendment argument could have been influential was quite reasonable. In 2010, Jacobson referred to a portion of the solicitation that indirectly suggested legality; "their lawyer said this was not illegal."

Thus, Jacobson's compliance at the end of the process did not suggest predisposition at the beginning. "The evidence that [Jacobson] was ready and willing to commit the offense came only after the Government had devoted 2 ½ years to convincing him that he had or should have the right to engage in the very behavior proscribed by law."[79] The Court concluded: "In their zeal to enforce the law ... Government agents may not originate a criminal design, implant in an innocent person's mind the disposition to commit a criminal act, and then induce the commission of the crime so that the Government may prosecute."[80]

The Court made clear that its holding was based largely on the long period of persuasion. Other investigative techniques, where a mere opportunity is presented, would not constitute entrapment. Accordingly, an agent "may offer the opportunity to buy or sell drugs," and if the

---

76. *Id.* at 551.

77. *Id.* at 552.

78. *Id.* at 552.

79. *Id.* at 553.

80. *Id.* at 548.

government "simply offered petitioner the opportunity to order child pornography through the mails, and petitioner—who must be presumed to know the law—had promptly availed himself of this criminal opportunity, it is unlikely that his entrapment defense would have warranted a jury instruction."[81]

Justice O'Connor dissented in an opinion joined by Chief Justice Rehnquist and Justice Kennedy, and joined in part by Justice Scalia. The dissent understood the facts quite differently. "Keith Jacobson was offered only two opportunities to buy child pornography through the mail. Both times, he ordered. Both times, he asked for opportunities to buy more."[82] Unlike *Sherman* and *Sorrells*, there was no face-to-face contact; merely mailings which could have been discarded. The questionnaires and solicitations were not sinister efforts to create a kiddie-porn aficionado where none existed before, but were instead designed to screen out innocent recipients; they were legitimate efforts "to make sure he was generally interested in the subject matter."

The dissent objected to the idea that predisposition had to exist before the operation started; instead "the inquiry is whether a suspect is predisposed before the Government induces commission of the crime, not before the Government makes initial contact with him."[83] One problem with the majority's rule might be that it would be "misread by lower courts as well as criminal investigators as requiring that the Government must have sufficient evidence of a defendant's predisposition *before it ever seeks to contact him*." This would amount to a requirement that "the Government must have a reasonable suspicion of criminal activity before it begins an investigation, a condition that we have never before imposed." But the dissent's warning dispelled any danger of misreading the majority opinion, and no circuit now requires reasonable suspicion before beginning an investigation.

The dissent also feared that the case would give rise to a proliferation of entrapment defenses:

> a bribetaker will claim that the description of the amount of money available was so enticing that it implanted a disposition to accept the bribe later offered. A drug buyer will claim that the description of the drug's purity and effects was so tempting that it created the urge to try it for the first time. In short, the Court's opinion could be read to prohibit the Government from advertising the seductions of criminal activity as part of its sting operation, for fear of creating a predisposition in its suspects.[84]

---

81. *Id.* at 549–50.
82. *Id.* at 554.
83. *Id.* at 556–57.
84. *Id.* at 557.

GABRIEL J. CHIN

GABRIEL J. CHIN

321

Of course, the twenty-six-month cultivation process Jacobson experienced is easily distinguishable from these scenarios. But apart from that, the principle of the majority's decision might justify a response that the government should not systematically "advertise the seductions of criminal activity" to persons who are presently unseduced. If the enticements would fail, then prohibiting them is no loss. If they work, then more business is generated for the criminal justice system, but only among people who evidently would not otherwise have committed crimes.

The government had sent out child pornography advertisements to many people, including many who were not prosecuted because they never ordered from the front organizations. If the postal inspector who appeared on *60 Minutes* was right, there was little danger that any of the targets would have ordered child pornography from anywhere; it was commercially unavailable. (Remember, *Jacobson* was litigated before the rise of the Internet, which became a new distribution channel for this material.) Yet, it is conceivable that some of the targets were encouraged by the arguments and suggestions, but found an outlet for their newly enhanced prurient interests elsewhere.[85] To create actual pedophiles in order to prosecute non-pedophiles is a poor trade.

The dissent also challenged the majority's conclusion that purchase of *Bare Boys* was insufficient to prove predisposition; instead, "this should have settled the matter." Because of the majority's emphasis on the legal nature of the purchase, the dissent suggested that perhaps the majority was adding a new element: "Not only must the Government show that a defendant was predisposed to engage in the illegal conduct, here receiving photographs of minors engaged in sex, but also that the defendant was predisposed to break the law knowingly in order to do so."[86] But this objection was a misunderstanding of what the majority did; the majority explicitly upheld the idea that ignorance of the law is no excuse.[87] Justice Scalia did not join this part of the dissent.

The relevant question is not whether the government has knowledge of prior criminal conduct or other evidence of predisposition before beginning the investigation, but whether the predisposition in fact existed at the time of the initial government contact. Thus, in an

---

85. Amy Adler, *The Perverse Law of Child Pornography*, 101 Colum. L. Rev. 209, 212 (2001) ("I suggest that child pornography law and the eroticization of children exist in a dialectic of transgression and taboo: The dramatic expansion of child pornography law may have unwittingly heightened pedophilic desire.")

86. 503 U.S. at 559–60.

87. *Id.* at 550 (noting that defendants "must be presumed to know the law"); *Id.* at 551 n.3 ("We do not hold, as the dissent suggests . . . that the Government was required to prove that petitioner knowingly violated the law. We simply conclude that proof that petitioner engaged in legal conduct and possessed certain generalized personal inclinations" is insufficient to prove predisposition beyond a reasonable doubt).

undercover drug purchase or sale, the government may not even know the names of potential targets, but if individuals propose or agree to criminal transactions when first meeting the (undercover) police, predisposition is clear.

The majority also had a compelling argument that the lawful nature of Jacobson's prior conduct was relevant. Of course, prior conduct of the same or similar nature is often probative, unless there is some reason that deprives it of evidentiary value about the defendant's state of mind at the relevant time. It is relevant to predisposition that a person charged with unlawful possession of an automatic weapon often eagerly possessed automatic weapons in the past, but much less so if the possession was lawful, say, incident to service in the Marine Corps or with a proper license. It is relevant to predisposition that a person charged with a drug offense is a prior drug user, less so if they, like Sherman, are in treatment to kick the habit. That a person had sexual contact with a fourteen year old when they themselves were fourteen says little about whether they would do so as an adult. And it is suggestive of predisposition that an individual is interested in certain kinds of sexual materials or has purchased them in the past, but less so if they did so legally.

All past acts diminish in probative value with the passage of time, because if they are not repeated, they show that any predisposition no longer exists or has been, until the governmental involvement, successfully resisted. Obedience to the law in spite of a contrary impulse is certainly conduct that the government should respect and encourage,[88] and it is probably true as an empirical matter that the overwhelming majority of criminal impulses are resisted.

In this case, there is a basis for speculating about what would have happened without governmental involvement. Keith Jacobson had a contact for this material, Electric Moon, and a list of adult bookstores. If he had not merely an abstract interest in this material but also an inclination to purchase it illegally, he could easily have attempted to do so without the government's help. The fact that legal materials and correspondence were found in the search of his house, but no other child pornography, goes a long way to showing that any curiosity Jacobson had had been sated, until the government came on the scene.

The Immediate Impact of Jacobson

Many newspaper editorials praised the Court's decision. No mainstream outlet had any sympathy for child pornography of course, but

---

88. Renunciation or abandonment is a defense in some jurisdictions to criminal attempt or conspiracy. *See* Model Penal Code § 5.01(4) ("It is an affirmative defense [to the crime of criminal attempt] that [the defendant] abandoned his effort to commit the crime or otherwise prevented its commission, under circumstances representing a complete and voluntary renunciation of his criminal purpose").

editors did support the idea that people were entitled to be left alone unless they committed a crime. The *Washington Post* called the government's conduct "entrapment, plain and simple."[89] The *Denver Post* editorial was entitled "Postal Snoops Went Too Far," and described "federal law enforcement gone berserk."[90] The *Chicago Tribune* decried "Fighting Crime by Inducing It."[91] Columnist Clarence Page wrote that "[t]he cleverness of the mailed bait would astonish Wile E. Coyote."[92] *The New York Times* proposed that federal agents be required "to obtain court warrants, similar to search and wiretap orders, before setting up traps and stings."[93] Locally, the *Omaha World–Herald* editorialized that Jacobson "never should have been arrested or charged."[94]

The U.S. Attorney for the District of Nebraska claimed that *Jacobson* "will not change anything with regard to traditional law enforcement sting operations," but this view was optimistic. The 1980 Attorney General's Guidelines on FBI Undercover Operations[95] differed from those in effect by 2002.[96] The revisions reveal some minor changes in phraseology—entrapment "must" be scrupulously avoided instead of "should"; the "illegal" nature of the activity should be apparent to potential participants instead of "corrupt." But there is also a change in the definition of entrapment, which now tracks the language of *Jacobson*: "Entrapment occurs when the Government implants in the mind of a person who is not otherwise disposed to commit the offense the disposition to commit the offense and then induces the commission of that offense in order to prosecute." Law enforcement agencies across the country had no choice but to confront the implications of *Jacobson*, and ensure that their investigative techniques were within the law or bear the consequences.

The Continuing Importance of Jacobson *Today*

Jacobson may also be important simply because the defendant's sexual orientation did not destroy his chances before the Court. According to authors Joyce Murdoch and Deb Price, "[b]efore 1992, a Supreme

---

89. Editorial, *Entrapment, Plain and Simple*, Wash. Post, Apr. 10, 1992, at A26.

90. Editorial, *Postal Snoops Went too Far*, Denver Post, Apr. 15, 1992, at 6B.

91. Editorial, *Fighting Crime by Inducing It*, Chi. Trib., Apr. 7, 1992, at 16.

92. Clarence Page, *Government Went to Obscene Lengths*, St. Louis Post Dispatch, Apr. 9, 1992, at 3C.

93. Editorial, *Entrapment Out of Control*, N.Y. Times, Apr. 8, 1992, at A24.

94. Editorial, *Justice For Nebraskan*, Omaha World–Herald, Apr. 7, 1992, at 16.

95. *Attorney General's Guidelines on FBI Undercover Operations* (Dec. 31, 1980), reprinted in Select Committee to Study Undercover Activities of the Department of Justice, S. Rep. 97–682, at 551 (1982).

96. *The Attorney General's Guidelines on Federal Bureau of Investigation Undercover Operations* (May 30, 2002).

Court majority opinion never expressed the slightest empathy for any homosexual."[97]

The case was also important for criminal law. In the words of Judge Richard Posner, *Jacobson* "changed the landscape" and "breathed new life into the entrapment defense."[98] Before *Jacobson*, "the courts of appeals had been drifting toward the view ... that the defense of entrapment must fail in any case in which the defendant is 'willing' in the sense of being psychologically prepared to commit the crime for which he is being prosecuted, even if it is plain that he would not have engaged in criminal activity unless inveigled or assisted by the government."[99] This approach, said Judge Posner, "cannot in our view be squared with *Jacobson.*"

Professor Paul Marcus opined that *Jacobson* brought entrapment "back from the [almost] dead."[100] In the wake of *Jacobson*, Professor Marcus explains, "many courts have exhibited a willingness, rarely seen before, to find entrapment as a matter of law where government involvement is extensive."[101] Predictably, many of these cases involve drug stings.[102] *Sorrells* and *Sherman* both involved entrapment with respect to substances; among the most famous modern cases of entrapment were the acquittal of automobile executive John DeLorean on cocaine charges, and of Washington, D.C. mayor Marion Barry for using crack. Juries and courts, it seems, can be sympathetic to claims of entrapment in drug cases, perhaps because they imagine that many people could be similarly targeted. Also appearing in drug cases with some regularity is the doctrine of sentencing entrapment. In such cases, the crime itself is not the product of entrapment, but police induce the target of the sting to traffic larger amounts than they normally would, in order to generate a higher sentence. In such cases, some courts have disregarded the amounts induced by police efforts.[103]

---

97. Murdoch & Price, *supra* note 53, at 406.

98. United States v. Hollingsworth, 27 F.3d 1196, 1198 (7th Cir. 1994) (en banc).

99. *Id.* at 1198.

100. Paul Marcus, *Presenting, Back from the [Almost] Dead, the Entrapment Defense*, 47 Fla. L. Rev. 205 (1995).

101. *Id.* at 225.

102. *See, e.g.*, United States v. Brooks, 215 F.3d 842 (8th Cir. 2000) (Heaney, J.); United States v. Martinez, 122 F.3d 1161 (9th Cir. 1997); United States v. Skarie, 971 F.2d 317 (9th Cir. 1992); United States v. Groll, 992 F.2d 755 (7th Cir. 1993) (vacating guilty plea to allow assertion of entrapment defense to drug and firearm charge); United States v. Beal, 961 F.2d 1512 (10th Cir. 1992); Madera v. State, 943 So. 2d 960 (Fla. Dist. Ct. App. 2006); Curry v. State, 876 So. 2d 29 (Fla. Dist. Ct. App. 2004); Dial v. State, 799 So. 2d 407 (Fla. Dist. Ct. App. 2001); People v. Kulwin, 593 N.E.2d 717 (Ill. App. Ct. 1992); State v. Johnson, 511 N.W.2d 753 (Minn. Ct. App. 1994).

103. *See, e.g.*, United States v. Vierra, 426 F. Appx. 484 (9th Cir. 2011); U.S. Sentencing Guidelines § 2D1.1, note 14 ("If, in a reverse sting (an operation in which a

Other cases follow *Jacobson* in child pornography cases involving elaborate stings,[104] and even in the more serious circumstance of attempted sex crimes against children. Citing *Jacobson*, Judge Alex Kozinski wrote for a panel of the Ninth Circuit finding entrapment as a matter of law where the defendant had been convicted of crossing state lines for the purpose of engaging in sex acts with a minor.[105] The sting was similar to the one used against Jacobson, but taken to a higher level of intensity. The defendant answered an online ad for an adult sex partner. He initially responded with confusion to his email correspondent's insinuations about his role as the "special man teacher" for the teen and pre-teen children of his pen pal, but, after much prodding, ultimately agreed to have sexual contact with them. He was sentenced to 121 months after he traveled from Florida to California to carry out this plan, but the Ninth Circuit reversed. In the words of *Jacobson*, the defendant was an "otherwise law-abiding citizen who, if left to his own devices, likely would never have run afoul of the law." "There is surely enough real crime in our society that it is unnecessary for our law enforcement officials to spend months luring an obviously lonely and confused individual to cross the line between fantasy and criminality."[106] The Nebraska Supreme Court reached the same result on similarly disturbing facts.[107]

Courts have found entrapment as a matter of law for other offenses. The Florida Supreme Court found entrapment in a case where adult videos were rented to a minor;[108] the Indiana Court of Appeals found entrapment as a matter of law when a driver responded to a street solicitation from an undercover vice officer.[109] The Florida District Court of Appeals[110] and the Fifth Circuit[111] have found entrapment as a matter of law in financial cases.[112]

---

government agent sells or negotiates to sell a controlled substance to a defendant), the court finds that the government agent set a price for the controlled substance that was substantially below the market value ..., thereby leading to the defendant's purchase of a significantly greater quantity ... than his available resources would have allowed him to purchase ..., a downward departure may be warranted."); Derrick Agustus Carter, *To Catch the Lion, Tether the Goat: Entrapment, Conspiracy and Sentencing Manipulation*, 42 Akron L. Rev. 135 (2009).

104. Farley v. State, 848 So. 2d 393 (Fla. Dist. Ct. App 2003).

105. Poehlman v. United States, 217 F.3d 692 (9th Cir. 2000).

106. *Id.* at 705.

107. State v. Canaday, 641 N.W.2d 13 (Neb. 2002).

108. Munoz v. State, 629 So, 2d 90 (Fla. 1993).

109. Ferge v. State, 764 N.E.2d 268 (Ind. Ct. App. 2002).

110. State v. Finno, 643 So. 2d 1166 (Fla. Dist. Ct. App. 1994).

111. United States v. Sandoval, 20 F.3d 134 (5th Cir. 1994).

112. *See also* People v. Karraker, 633 N.E.2d 1250 (Ill. App. Ct. 1994) (weapons charge; entrapment as a matter of law).

Jacobson has not proved to be prominent in the Supreme Court itself. The Court has decided no entrapment cases since 1992.[113] Indeed, the decision has been cited only twice, both times for peripheral points, and both times by Justice Stephen Breyer, who wrote a major entrapment decision citing *Jacobson* while on the First Circuit.[114]

With the 2010 retirement of Justice John Paul Stevens, of the *Jacobson* majority, only Justice Thomas remains on the Court. Of the dissenters, Justices Scalia and Kennedy still serve. Six members of the Court then have never had a chance to address the doctrine, at least as justices. Accordingly, the future of the defense in the Supreme Court is not clear.

The Court's impassioned decision in *Jacobson* gives rise to an interesting question that the Court may never answer. Doctrinally, *Jacobson* rested on the reasoning of *Sorrells*, namely that the entrapment defense was available as a matter of statutory construction.[115] The Court could apply it because Congress has never purported to eliminate the defense. But what if it did? If Congress explicitly authorized the government to "originate a criminal design, implant in an innocent person's mind the disposition to commit a criminal act, and then induce commission of the crime to that the Government may prosecute,"[116] something the Court has clearly considered quite unjust, the Court would be forced to explain whether government creation of crime in this manner was consistent with the due process clause and other constitutional limitations.

A narrower but important question is presented by prosecutions arising from the "War on Terror." Many terrorism prosecutions are based on affirmative undercover investigations,[117] sometimes involving inducement and government-supplied weapons or materials. Entrapment is often raised in these cases, and courts generally hold that entrapment

---

113. However, in 1994, the Court decided another case involving the mental state required for violation of 18 U.S.C. 2252, the statute Jacobson was charged with violating. In *United States v. X–Citement Video*, 513 US 64 (1994), the Court held as a matter of statutory interpretation that conviction required proof that the defendant knew that the sexually oriented material dealt with children rather than adult performers.

114. *See* Dixon v. United States, 548 U.S. 1, 25 (2006) (Breyer. J., dissenting) (citing *Jacobson* in dissent about burden of proof for duress defense); United States v. Jimenez Recio, 537 U.S. 270, 276 (2003) (Breyer, J.) (citing *Jacobson* in decision interpreting scope of conspiracy statute); United States v. Gendron, 18 F.3d 955 (1st Cir. 1994) (Breyer, C.J.) (discussing *Jacobson* extensively in entrapment case). The Supreme Court cited *X-Citement Video* eighteen times by June 2010.

115. Jacobson v. United States, 503 U.S. 540, 553 (1992).

116. *Id.* at 548.

117. Jon Sherman, *"A Person Otherwise Innocent": Policing Entrapment In Preventative, Undercover Counterterrorism Investigations*, 11 U. Pa. J. Const. L. 1475 (2009).

is available.[118] Yet, in *Sorrells* itself, the Court intimated that in extreme cases entrapment would be unavailable: "We have no occasion to consider hypothetical cases of crimes so heinous or revolting that the applicable law would admit of no exceptions."[119] Thus, the Model Penal Code makes the defense "unavailable when causing or threatening bodily injury is an element of the offense charged"[120] when the target of the violence is the person other than the one perpetrating the entrapment. It may be that the Court will have to consider entrapment in the terrorism context, where the penalty is extreme because of the nature of the crime, but the crime occurred solely because of the inducement and encouragement of government agents.

After the Decision

The surveys, letters, and advertisements Jacobson received had been part of a national postal investigation called "Project Looking Glass." In 1991, the Postal Service claimed that 147 convictions resulted from the investigation, including thirty-five cases where there was evidence that the defendants were molesters or producers of child pornography. Four targets committed suicide.[121] Tragically, the lead investigator, postal inspector Calvin Comfort, himself committed suicide in 1999, leaving a note suggesting that he was despondent over stress from his job.[122]

Keith Jacobson, not surprisingly, was relieved by the reversal of his conviction. "I felt like a big weight had been lifted from my shoulders," he said in 1992. "Now, I want to get on with my life, live a normal life. I plan on staying around here. I plan not to get involved in that kind of thing. I will watch my mail more closely."

As of 2010, Keith Jacobson is seventy-nine and healthy. After the decision, as he had hoped, he largely returned to his normal life. He resides in the same Newman Grove home, inherited from his parents, that he lived in when arrested in 1987. He maintains his military ties as a member of the local American Legion color guard. A University of Nebraska football season ticket holder, he enjoys watching his grand-nieces and nephews play high school sports. He remained a private person after the Supreme Court decided his case. In 1994, he joined a busload of Nebraskans for a trip to New York City to march in a parade celebrating the twenty-fifth anniversary of the Stonewall Riots, which

---

118. United States v. Al–Moayad, 545 F.3d 139, 153–54 (2d Cir. 2008).

119. Sorrells v. United States, 287 U.S. 435, 451 (1932).

120. Model Penal Code § 2.13(3).

121. For a critical discussion of Project Looking Glass, see Douglas O. Linder, *Journeying Through the Valley of Evil*, 71 N.C. L. Rev. 1111 (1993).

122. *Milwaukee Postal Inspector Found Dead In His Parked Van*, Wis. St. J., Apr. 2 1999, at 3C.

marked the beginning of the gay rights movement in the United States. He says he has not been arrested for anything since 1987.

George Moyer practices law with his son, Michael, a 2000 graduate of Creighton Law, as Moyers have been doing in Madison County, Nebraska since 1886.

Paul Larkin became a federal law enforcement officer after leaving the Solicitor General's office, and is now in private practice.

Further Reading:

Ronald J. Allen, Melissa Luttrell & Anne Kreeger, *Clarifying Entrapment*, 89 J. Crim. L. & Criminology 407 (1999).

Fred Warren Bennett, *From* Sorrells *to* Jacobson: *Reflections on Six Decades of Entrapment Law, and Related Defenses, in Federal Court*, 27 Wake Forest L. Rev. 829 (1992).

Anthony Dillof, *Unraveling Unlawful Entrapment*, 94 J. Crim. L. & Criminology 827 (2004).

Paul Marcus, *The Entrapment Defense* (4th ed. 2009).

Richard H. McAdams, *The Political Economy of Entrapment*, 96 J. Crim. L. & Criminology 107 (2005).

9

Robert Weisberg

The Story of *Rizzo*: The Shifting Landscape of Attempt

Introduction

The iconic opinion is so brief that it is best to review the whole thing before turning to the back story. The opinion opens with the greatest inter-branch-damn-with-faint-praise in American legal history. In the tart, terse words of the New York Court of Appeals:

> The police of the city of New York did excellent work in this case by preventing the commission of a serious crime. It is a great satisfaction to realize that we have such wide-awake guardians of our peace. Whether or not the steps which the defendant had taken up to the time of his arrest amounted to the commission of a crime, as defined by our law, is, however, another matter.[1]

What did the police do wrong? Here were the brief facts summarized by the Court:

> Charles Rizzo, the defendant, appellant, with three others, Anthony J. Dorio, Thomas Milo and John Thomasello, on January 14th planned to rob one Charles Rao of a payroll valued at about $1,200 which he was to carry for the United Lathing Company. These defendants, two of whom had firearms, started out in an automobile, looking for Rao or the man who had the payroll on that day. Rizzo claimed to be able to identify the man and was to point him out to the others who were to do the actual holding up. The four rode about in their car looking for Rao. They went to the bank from which he was supposed to get the money and to various buildings

---

1. People v. Rizzo, 158 N.E. 888, 888 (N.Y. 1927). I am indebted to Stanford Law Librarians Erika Wayne and Rachael Samberg for their extraordinary help with archival research.

being constructed by the United Lathing Company. At last they came to One Hundred and Eightieth Street and Morris Park Avenue. By this time they were watched and followed by two police officers. As Rizzo jumped out of the car and ran into the building all four were arrested. The defendant was taken out from the building in which he was hiding. Neither Rao nor a man named Previti, who was also supposed to carry a payroll, were at the place at the time of the arrest. The defendants had not found or seen the man they intended to rob; no person with a payroll was at any of the places where they had stopped and no one had been pointed out or identified by Rizzo. The four men intended to rob the payroll man, whoever he was; they were looking for him, but they had not seen or discovered him up to the time they were arrested.[2]

The defendants were charged with and convicted of attempted first-degree robbery. Rizzo appealed to the Appellate Division, where he lost by a 2–1 vote, and then won a successful hearing before the Court of Appeals, where, notably, Judge Benjamin Cardozo joined a unanimous opinion by Judge Frederick Crane.

The holding was straightforward—though perhaps deceptively so. As the Court of Appeals explained, state law defined attempt as any action "done with intent to commit a crime, and tending but failing to effect its commission." The court added that "the word *'tending'* is very indefinite." Moreover:

> It is perfectly evident that there will arise differences of opinion as to whether an act in a given case is one *tending* to commit a crime. "Tending" means to exert activity in a particular direction. Any act in preparation to commit a crime may be said to have a tendency towards its accomplishment. The procuring of the automobile, searching the streets looking for the desired victim, were in reality acts tending toward the commission of the proposed crime. The law, however, has recognized that many acts in the way of preparation are too remote to constitute the crime of attempt. The line has been drawn between those acts which are remote and those which are proximate and near to the consummation. The law must be practical, and, therefore, considers those acts only as tending to the commission of the crime which are so near to its accomplishment that in all reasonable probability the crime itself would have been committed but for timely interference.[3]

Drawing the line between what we call "preparation" and attempt is a highly contestable enterprise, in part because it elides related but somewhat different concerns: (a) How much sheer temporal or physical

---

2. *Id.* at 888–89.

3. *Id.* at 889 (emphasis in original).

proximity to the final act is a public threat?; (b) At what point of
interruption of the ultimate crime can we say there was a high enough
probability that the crime would have occurred absent the interruption?;
and (c) How much action do we need to corroborate independent
evidence we have of the defendant's intent to do the crime? Throughout
the twentieth century courts proffered a wide variety of doctrines to help
resolve these questions, doctrines under such evocative names as the
"physical proximity doctrine," the "dangerous proximity doctrine," the
"indispensable element test," the "probable desistance test," the "abnormal step approach," and the "unequivocality test," all culminating in
the Model Penal Code's "substantial step test."[4] The *Rizzo* court's
formulation, full of vague (or flexible) words, is more of a standard than
a rule. On its face, it might permit a finding of attempt well before the
so-called "last act," but as applied on the *Rizzo* facts, it makes it difficult
to prove attempt liability much before that point. On the whole, the
movement of recent decades has been to move the line somewhat earlier
in time to make conviction easier, and, as discussed below, the Model
Penal Code (MPC) formulation exemplifies that trend.[5]

Rizzo appears in many casebooks because it so piquantly illustrates
the significance of the choice among these tests. But *Rizzo* offers further
refinements for our understanding of attempt law, as well. It underscores how the substantive criminal law of attempt necessarily relies on
various rules of criminal procedure—laws governing when and how the
police intervene before the final act, or how the police elicit mental state
evidence from the suspect or his or her accomplices. So changes in
attempt law partly reflect changes in the other realms of legal doctrine,

---

4. United States v. Mandujano, 499 F.2d 370, 373 n.5 (5th Cir. 1974).

5. Two other major principles of attempt law have remained relatively constant over
time. First is the degree of punishment for attempt. How much we punish attempt may
depend on the rationale for punishment. As Professor Joshua Dressler explains, a "culpa-
bilty-retributivist" would punish a failed attempter just as severely as a successful one,
because he has exhibited the same culpability. A "harm-retributivist" would grade punishment only according to the actual harmful effect of the failed attempt—perhaps in terms of
threat to public order and repose. A utilitarian focused on deterrence might punish the
attempter just as much as the successful criminal because ex ante criminals expect to
succeed; but some utilitarians might suggest a lesser punishment for attempt so as to give
a failed attempter an incentive to desist from a second effort. *See, e.g.* Joshua Dressler,
Understanding Criminal Law 381–84 (6th ed. 2012). As if "averaging out" these ratio-
nales, American jurisdictions generally punish attempts less severely than successful
crimes, often setting the sentence at roughly half that for the completed crime, or, if the
penal code grades felonies by degree of punishment, one degree lower than the completed
crime. *Id.* at 381. Second, a virtually universal rule is that the attempter must exhibit
purpose with respect to the completion of the crime. Thus, for example, where grossly
reckless conduct that results in death can constitute murder, a person who undertakes a
grossly reckless act that that by chance does not kill the potential victim is not guilty of
"reckless attempted murder" (though there might be liability for some form of reckless
endangerment). *Id.* at 492–93.

including rules of search and seizure and interrogations, and various in-trial rules of evidence. *Rizzo* also illuminates the venerable issue of "impossible attempts," illustrating how impossibility, often seen as an exotic side issue to the more conventional forms of attempt law, may actually be an inseparable part of the general law of attempt, distinguishable only by rhetorical artifice. Finally, *Rizzo* helps set the stage for the now-dominant MPC rule and particularly the MPC's procedural innovation. Given the unavoidable vagueness of any definitional distinction between preparation and attempt, one way to induce greater rigor and uniformity is through rules governing the trial judge's preliminary decision whether sufficient evidence of attempt exists to even get the question to the jury. The MPC's mechanism for guiding this preliminary decision points a procedural way out of the substantive morass of attempt law that the *Rizzo* court found itself in.

To understand how this eccentric case illuminates the historical evolution of attempt law, a fair amount of reconstruction of the contested facts and issues, as well as the bizarre events at trial, is necessary.

The Story

The setting is mid-winter in the dense urban ethnic world of the Bronx, a maze of streets that play a role in the klutzy meanderings of a gang that could never seem to find a victim. As *The New York Times* for January 15, 1927, reported, the police deserved credit for having "frustrated a payroll holdup . . . [by four men] well supplied with pistols and ammunition."[6] The ring leader was a "boy," Charles Rizzo, whose father Anthony was a partner in the very business whose payroll he allegedly sought to steal. The *Times* reported that the elder Rizzo refused to believe that his son would do such a thing, but, said the *Times*, the younger Rizzo had confessed to the police at the stationhouse, admitting that his $14 per day salary had not satisfied him. And in a virtually literary coincidence, this was not the only successful robbery thwarted by the local police that week. Apparently there had been a string of payroll robbery holdups, and just two days earlier five men were arrested for a failed robbery of the Bronx National Bank. Nor were the Rizzo gang the only extremely feckless criminals: The same day a youthful would-be robber brandished a pistol at the owner of a used-clothing dealer in the Bronx, using a gun that turned out to be unloaded and dysfunctional, and the victim put up his hands so quickly that he hit the bandit's nose, causing him to drop the gun and flee.[7]

The *Rizzo* trial includes some conflicting narratives that depict the charmingly bumbling incompetence of the parties but also a fair amount

---

6. *Another Robbery Is Foiled In Bronx*, N.Y. Times, Jan. 15, 1927, at 17.

7. *Id.*

of bumbling and cheap drama in the trial itself. Along the way, the trial narrative underscores how now-anachronistic investigative and trial procedures made the conviction possible.

The characters: Charles Rizzo was 23, single and living with his parents, and had no priors. He had occasionally worked as a lather and had been a union member since his teens. John Thomasello, 22, was a baker and was married and had some petty larceny priors.[8] Thomas Milo, 23, did some kind of driving for a living, and had, ominously for him as it later turned out, a prior burglary conviction. Anthony Dorio, 20, was a chauffeur with no priors. Rizzo had known the others for varying times, though in all cases fairly casually. Charles Rao was a boss lather in charge of several jobs that day, and he moved from site to bank and back, transporting money for payroll at each site. Frank Previti was a shareholder in the business and occasionally carried payroll himself. Charles Rizzo's father was a shareholder in United Lathing, and Charles Rizzo's brother Joe Rizzo worked for the business as a payroll agent.

On January 18, 1927, the defendants were indicted by a Bronx Grand Jury.[9] At arraignment on January 20, they pleaded not guilty. The indictment contained a count of attempted grand larceny[10] as well as attempted first-degree robbery.[11] The case was then tried in Bronx County Court before Judge Albert Cohn. The trial ran from February 7 through the verdict on February 16 and sentencing the next day.

Although, as discussed below, many of its procedural events now seem anachronistic in light of Warren Court constitutional rulings, one aspect of the case consistent with modern procedural law is that each defendant had separate counsel.[12] Rizzo actually had two key lawyers,

---

8. The *Times* reported that Thomasello had also been implicated in some hold-ups as part of the "Sheik Gang," although he was not prosecuted for those.

9. Throughout this chapter, record citations are to the record of Case on Appeal, *People v. Rizzo*, 158 N.E. 888 (N.Y. 1927) [hereinafter, COA], which includes the trial transcript, Appellant's Brief [hereinafter AB], and Respondent's Brief [hereinafter RB].

10. The judge ultimately granted a defense motion to dismiss this count. COA, *supra* note 9, at 342–43. Although no explanation was given, the judge might have viewed this as duplicative with the robbery, or possibly even thought that the dollar amount of intended theft was uncertain under the facts.

11. Under the New York statute, the possible robbery was first-degree both because weapons were used and because each defendant had accomplices. The indictment uses the colorful language of the time, saying that the attempt included weapons "loaded with gunpowder and leaden bullet." COA, *supra* note 9, at 4–5. Confusingly, the indictment also contains language that seems to allege an actual assault on Rao, alleging that he "feloniously did make an assault...," *id.* at 4, although that count was later dismissed. Notably, the defendants were never charged with conspiracy, *see infra* text accompanying note 28.

12. A couple of times the judge requested or allowed one counsel to cover briefly for an absent counsel for another client, at the time of initial appearances of counsel, COA,

John Zoetzl and John DePasquale (the latter argued the appeal). The trial testimony mostly consisted of predictable direct and cross-examination of the officers, and reports of the defendants' statements. The exchanges among the judge, District Attorney Israel Adlerman, and the various defense lawyers were robust and often sarcastic.[13] The trial was a highly spirited affair, hardly lacking in adversarialness, with fascinatingly sarcastic exchanges between the District Attorney and Zoetzl, lawyer for Rizzo, and Dorio's lawyer, O'Brien, including barbed expressions of mutual disbelief and brute insult.[14]

Though the key police witness, Officer Walter Sullivan, testified with benefit of hindsight of the supposed confessions, his description of the observable facts was mostly uncontested.[15] He and fellow officer Cronin happened to observe a Paige automobile with four men in it traveling in the opposite direction. Aside from a vague reference to the Paige going slightly fast—though perhaps barely twenty miles per hour—nothing in the record explains the reason for their suspicion. The

---

supra note 9, at 17–18, but even for purposes of closing argument, *Id.* at 344, although one defense lawyer did express concern about a possible conflict. *Id.* at 20–21. Of course in cases like this, rife with the possibility (and actuality) of antagonistic defenses and cross-accusations, conflicts can create problems that the Supreme Court would later view as Sixth Amendment violations. Cuyler v. Sullivan, 446 U.S. 335 (1980). As will be evident below, even with separate counsel those problems can affect the case when the defendants are joined in a single trial.

13.   Things quickly became more heated, as in this exchange between defense lawyer O'Brien and the District Attorney:

O'BRIEN: "I have been waiting patiently to hear some evidence."

DA: "Well, you will hear a lot before you get through."

O'BRIEN: "Not up to the present time."

DA: "Be patient. The worst is yet to come."

O'BRIEN: "Go Ahead."

DA: "Every cloud has a silver lining." COA, *supra* note 9, at 24–25.

Later, Adlerman rephrased a question apologetically, and O'Brien replied, "I object to the apology."

DA:"To the what?"

O'BRIEN: "To the apology."

DA: "I am not apologizing to anyone." *Id.* at 46.

At another point, Zoetzl said to the defendant Rizzo about his injury,:

"They did not take you to the Morgue after you had been hit." "No sir."

Adlerman interrupted: "He is not dead yet, Mr. Zoetzl." *Id.* at 335.

14.   In his closing argument, Adlerman said of O'Brien that "he represents people when he knows they are a guilty as a dog." When O'Brien understandably objected, the trial judge observed that the comment was "a little outside of the record" but within the "latitude" of acceptable argument. *Id.* at 348–49.

15.   *Id.* at 27–76.

facts were that the police made a U-turn and followed the Paige for a couple of miles on Southern Boulevard, then Boston Road, then East Tremont Avenue. Along the way, they picked up another officer, Gush, who was on foot patrol, and with Officer Gush in the car, they pulled up next to the Paige when the Paige stopped at the a construction site on 180th Street. Amid some conflicts even among state witnesses, we can discern their story to be: Rizzo jumped out of the Paige and entered the building, possibly through a window. Officer Sullivan followed Rizzo into the building, while Officers Cronin and Gush ordered the others out of the car. Sullivan, unable to locate Rizzo, returned outside. As the three officers grabbed and handcuffed Dorio, Thomasello, and Milo, they extracted loaded revolvers from the latter two. Officer Sullivan struck Thomasello in the head with Milo's gun because Thomasello had dropped his hands and turned threateningly toward Officer Cronin. Officer Sullivan then reentered the building, this time with Officer Cronin, and there they confronted Rizzo, apparently crouching on a pile of debris. When Rizzo failed to keep his hands up as the police demanded, Officer Cronin struck him hard with a blackjack, causing bleeding. Meanwhile Gush managed to maintain control of the others with handcuffs. The arrests were completed by about 2 p.m. Then the unknowing Rao—the intended robbery victim—showed up, presumably wondering what in the world was going on.[16] The suspects were then driven to the Westchester Avenue station house. For the next three hours, the suspects were detained there and questioned by Police Inspector Duane and District Attorney Adlerman, who would ultimately try the case.

Perhaps the gist of the prosecution case, beyond these facts, came from the statements Dorio, Thomasello, and Milo gave at the station house.[17] The four arrestees had initially met the night before at a cafeteria. Ultimately they all went to Thomasello's nearby apartment, where they played cards. In the course of their conversations, Rizzo told them he had a plan to rob a payroll agent the next day, Rao—or possibly Frank Previti, who also carried payroll. They all agreed to the plan, letting Rizzo take the lead and deciding to split the proceeds evenly, which Rizzo guessed at a figure of several thousand dollars in cash. They would use a Paige automobile that Dorio happened to have stolen a few days earlier and kept available for such opportunities. After Dorio switched plates on the Paige, the four set out in the morning. Alas, Rizzo had miscalculated both time and place. The foursome zig-zagged around the Bronx like a Frogger video game,[18] but whatever jobsite they went to, they found no one carrying any payroll. Perplexed, Rizzo and the other

---

16.   The record does not tell us what Rao said on arrival.

17.   *Id.* at 150–57, 165, 175–79.

18.   They traveled to worksites ranging at least from 140th Street in the South Bronx to 204th in the North Bronx, with at least one stop in between. *Id.* at 22.

three drove to the bank. Rizzo alone went inside and asked a bank clerk, Palmer, whether the payroll had been picked up by Rao—and was told it had not. The team ultimately went to the jobsite at 180th Street and Morris Park Avenue, where the above events occurred.

Rizzo himself gave a statement at the police station, but later disavowed memory of the statement,[19] claiming that he was dizzy from the earlier blackjacking and from a second blow administered at the station house, this time with sticks. The record confirms that Rizzo was bleeding at the police station and that later that evening he was given medical attention after an ambulance was summoned. As recorded by a stenographer, McMahon, Rizzo's station house confession gave a somewhat different version of the preceding events.[20] He said that in the course of the conversation the evening of January 13, the others became aware that he had connections to and knowledge of the United Lathing Company and its payroll agents and that they implored him to accompany them the next day and to point out the likely robbery victim—Rao. But, said Rizzo, his only self-interest in the event was to meet with some agent who would pay him the $77 he was owed for work past due, or, conversely and at worst, he was a vaguely interested participant in the plan hatched by the others, but had no expectation of any particular payout. The next day, Dorio did the driving; Thomasello and Milo had their own guns. Rizzo denied that he had observed that Dorio had switched plates from another car. Rizzo said that he was indifferent as to the split of any anticipated proceeds: "If I didn't get anything I would not have given a damn either."[21] If that were true, he still might be liable as an accomplice, depending on what version of complicity mens rea rules applied.[22] But Rizzo added that "these guys are supposed to be tough guys and I didn't want anything to do to do with them."[23] By that reckoning, he might have clearly the mens rea for robbery or possibly proffered a duress defense. As a counter-explanation, Rizzo said that when he went to the bank it was solely to inquire about his brother, Joe Rizzo, who was a paymaster for the firm.[24]

---

19. *See infra* text accompanying note 52.

20. COA, *supra* note 9, at 183–88.

21. *Id.* at 187.

22. In the famous case of *United States v. Peoni*, 100 F.2d 401 (2d. Cir. 1938), Judge Learned Hand said the accomplice is only liable where he participates in the crime with the desire that it succeed, most obviously where he has a material stake in the venture. In a famous opposing case, Judge John Parker held that so long as the defendant knows that his participation will enhance the possibility of success, he is guilty even if he has no personal stake in success. Backun v. United States, 112 F.2d 635 (4th Cir. 1940).

23. COA, *supra* note 9, at 187. According to Cronin, Rizzo also said that he "thought" the others were going to do a hold up and that "he was kind of suspicious, but that they did not say anything to him about what they were going to do." *Id.* at 83.

24. This is what Joseph Rizzo said in his own testimony. *Id.* at 246–47.

Then there was Rizzo's actual trial testimony,[25] which amended the story slightly—adding the possible motive that he needed money to pay Thomasello for gambling losses incurred the night before. But in that testimony Rizzo also disavowed—or disavowed any memory of—the station house confession, stressing that at the time he was dazed from the beating (with a blackjack) he received at 180th Street and then the beating (allegedly with sticks) at the station house.[26]

Attempt Law: Procedure And Substance

In cross-examining the key police witness, one of the defense lawyers initiated the following colloquy, which was important both substantively and rhetorically:

Q: Do you think that is a very peculiar way of attempting to hold up somebody, by going into a cashier or paying teller, into a bank, and saying, "Is John Jones' payroll ready yet?" . . .

A: I do not.

Q: In the course of your experience as a police officer, that is very common?

A: No sir.

Q: You know that in this case in order to get a conviction they must perform some overt act; you know that, don't you? In other words, you cannot be arrested for thinking, can you? . . .

Q: Until you placed Rizzo under arrest, or placed any of these defendants under arrest on January 14, 1927, did they do anything as far as an attempted hold-up was concerned, outside of riding in a car and one defendant going into an unfinished building . . . ?

A: No, sir.[27]

Obviously, the prosecution's narrative is that this arguably innocent-looking conduct is explained by—and, in turn, corroborates—a nefarious plan to pull off a violent crime. Some attempt cases involve observable conduct more inherently suspicious-looking than this. But *Rizzo* illustrates that in attempt cases the prosecution often must find and rely on more direct evidence of the defendant's thinking and technical mental state. And to do that police and prosecutors may have to rely more heavily on investigative tools than would be the case for

---

25. *Id.* at 273–90.

26. *Id.* at 287. In addition, the defense put on friendly testimony contradicting evidence that he had ever asked about the whereabouts of any payroll and instead averring that he was simply seeking back pay and asking where he might find his brother, Joe Rizzo, who might have been able to pay him. *Id.* at 225, 230, 386.

27. *Id.* at 61–62.

proving a completed crime. So examining just how the police got the "intent" evidence in *Rizzo* is important to understanding attempt law.

The only reason the prosecutor was able to convince the New York jury in this case was that the police made an initial temporary seizure, not a true arrest, of the defendants without any need for probable cause. The police were then able to exact confessions from the suspects without the obstacle of the then-inconceivable Fifth Amendment rules we associate with *Miranda*. The prosecutor also did so in a joint trial where the rules of hearsay were applied so loosely that cross-imputation of statements against the four defendants occurred throughout the trial, barely constrained by feckless jury instructions that would become constitutionally insufficient some years later. The case thereby illustrates an unstated and perhaps overlooked reason for the then-very strict level of proof to which the prosecutor was put under the law of attempt: that in the absence of conduct very close to the completion of the crime to corroborate bad intent, the police might resort to legal, but morally questionable, procedures to establish that intent. Conversely, on the very facts of *Rizzo*, a modern prosecutor might have been able to prove attempt under any of the modern definitions of attempt that allow strong proof of intent to make up for any shortage of conduct evidence, and at least would have had a legally sound basis for thwarting a crime for which they had very weak predictive evidence. This is because a key doctrine of Fourth Amendment law, one that had not been articulated in 1927, might have permitted the stop of the car anyway, and, if physical brutality were avoided, might have resulted in evidence sufficient to prove attempt under the more liberal MPC formulation.

Obviously one thing that made it easier for Rizzo's prosecutor was that there were multiple defendants, each providing the best possible source of evidence against the others. I will note below how the prosecution worked this opportunity to its advantage. But one corollary to the multi-actor attempt case is the possibility that the prosecution can seek a conspiracy charge instead of or in addition to attempt. That way, the reports of actions or communications that establish intent toward the ultimate crime might suffice for conviction even if the defendants have stayed well on the safe side of the preparation/attempt boundary. In *Rizzo,* the evidence that supported the conviction would have established the criteria for conspiracy, and that charge was available under New York Law. But it apparently was never contemplated by the prosecutor,[28] presumably because the penalty in New York was relatively trivial[29] and

---

28. The jury instructions in the case at one point use the term "conspire," but only as a descriptive term in explaining attempt doctrine. *Id.* at 375.

29. State conspiracy laws are often much more limited than federal conspiracy law, and often, as in New York, may take the form of a unitary crime, the sentence fixed without regard to the possible sentence for the completed crime. So New York Penal Law,

possibly because it might have been deemed mutually exclusive with attempt.[30]

Search and Seizure

Consider the sequence of events that made it at least plausible to try the defendants for attempt. We have, roughly speaking, three categories of evidence: (1) All the conduct observable by the police, which chiefly includes (a) the driving activity, (b) the group's presence at the location where the intended victim would eventually arrive, and (c) Rizzo's entrance into the building, which appears to be flight from officers; (2) the guns found on two of the suspects; and (3) the confessions. So how did the police legally (if so) develop this chain of evidence?

As for the purely observable conduct, here the police means of investigation is obviously the most innocuous. Modern students of criminal procedure can readily parse what the police did. Whatever caused Officers Sullivan and Cronin to be suspicious of the defendants and to turn their car around and follow the Paige, even under modern Fourth Amendment law the police would not have needed to shoulder any burden to justify what they did. Following a car is not a "search" or "seizure" requiring any Fourth Amendment criteria to be proved. But when the police arguably stopped the car by pulling up next to it,[31] and possibly when they entered the building after Rizzo, they may have been undertaking a seizure. Did they have legal grounds for a seizure at that point, based on inferences they drew when they were merely following the car? The defense questioned Sullivan as to just how fast the Paige was going, and the answer that it received, a "great rate of speed," was left fairly unchallenged.[32] Sullivan testified that the driver looked "suspi-

Art. 54, Sec. 580 stated: "If two or more persons conspire (1) to commit a crime ... each of them is guilty of a misdemeanor." Notably, the "crime" of conspiracy is in a unitary section with other traditional forms of conspiracy, such as "maliciously to indict another for a crime ... to cheat or defraud," or to interfere with trade. N.Y. Penal Law of 1909, ch. 88, § 580 (codified at N.Y. Penal Code § 580) (repealed 1965). Only in the case of treason would conspiracy become a felony. N.Y. Penal Law of 1909, ch. 88, § 581 (codified at N.Y. Penal Code § 581) (repealed 1965).

30. Double jeopardy doctrine does not bar multiple punishment for conspiracy and attempt because while both are inchoate crimes, neither is a lesser-included offense of the other, *e.g.,* State v. Verive, 627 P.2d 721 (Ariz. 1981), but New York law may nevertheless have viewed the two crimes as merging.

31. The facts are somewhat ambiguous as to whether the police car cut the Paige off and forced it to stop, or merely pulled up next to the Paige after the suspects stopped on their own. COA, *supra* note 9, at 93.

32. *See Id.* at 27–28. Defense counsel did push the point at least rhetorically, asking the police witness, "Is that what you saw these defendants do on Jan. 14, 1927, speed for a distance of two miles—the car and then one of the defendants goes into an unoccupied building or an incomplete or unfinished building; that is the extent of this evidence, is that right?" *Id.* at 62.

cious," but he said this in a desultory fashion, acknowledging that he drew no inference about what the driver was thinking.[33] Perhaps the rather trivial suspicion they had at that point justified entry into an arguably non-public building, but the key issue is of course the next phase: the physical constraint on Rizzo, the order to put his hands up, the attack on him when he allegedly did not comply, the constraint on the others, the extraction of their weapons, and the striking of Thomasello. These actions were crucial steps in the ultimate case because they led to the discovery of the weapons, and, more importantly, to the later confessions.

These questions hardly troubled the police or ultimately the court, nor were they ever raised by the defense as matters of procedural rights. If anything, there was merely some questioning of police witnesses as to what made them suspect the men were up to no good. Significantly, those questions were viewed as solely relevant to the substantive question of whether the acts and implicit mental state supported the attempt charge. But reflecting on the possible procedural grounds for establishing the substantive elements of the attempt charge is crucial to understanding attempt law in its wider legal context.

Under modern law, the police would have had two legal ways of legitimating these arguable seizures and searches. If we characterize this set of police actions as full arrests and searches, they would be legal— even without a warrant—so long as the police had probable cause to believe a crime had occurred. (That was also the law of New York at the time, under rules that are thoroughly consistent with contemporary constitutional doctrine.[34]) But the question of probable cause at that point is entangled with the *substantive* question of when preparation morphs into attempt, because even though probable cause is a lesser standard than trial proof beyond a reasonable doubt, the police would have had to have grounds for interpreting the suspects' actions as having already crossed the preparation/attempt divide.

---

33. *Id.* at 50–51. In opening argument the District Attorney began to say that as the police followed the car, they "suspected this automobile ...," but O'Brien interrupted this sentence and said, "You cannot prove suspicion or suspect." The trial judge then observed, "I do not know whether he can or not. It may be that he may be able to prove that some of these defendants were suspected of something." *Id. at* 24.

34. Under the New York Code of Criminal Procedure, a peace offer could make an arrest without a warrant if a felony has been committed or was happening in his presence, and if he gave notice of intent to arrest and the suspect resisted or tried to flee, the officer could use all reasonable means to complete the arrest. N.Y. Crim. Proc. Law of 1881, ch.3–4, §§ 168–77 (codified at N.Y. Code Crim. Proc. §§ 168–77) (current version at N.Y. Crim. Proc. Law 140.10). Although the arrest law does not explicitly address searching the arrestee, the traditional search-incident to arrest doctrine would surely have permitted a fully body and clothing search for evidence or weapons so long as the there was probable cause for the arrest itself.

Our modern student of criminal procedure would rightly note that under current law the police had an alternative way of characterizing and thereby justifying their actions under the Fourth Amendment. Since the famous 1968 case of *Terry v. Ohio*[35] we have known that if the police can meet a lesser burden of showing "reasonable cause" to suspect that individuals have committed, are in the process of committing, or even are about to start committing a crime, the police can temporarily detain them and, if they reasonably fear the individuals are armed (a test easily met), they can frisk them for evidence of weapons. And, ironically, the roots of the *Terry* decision significantly lie in the law and practice of New York as they existed at the time of *Rizzo*.[36] Under then-New York law, the prosecutor, if asked, could probably have justified these constraints and the grabbing of weapons as "stops" or "detentions" without any need to establish probable cause for arrest.[37]

Scant 1920s era case law forthrightly addresses in any detail the standards governing stops or frisks. But there was a fairly clear doctrine approving police conduct where the officer "merely detained the person temporarily for the purpose of searching him, presumably to ascertain whether he had a weapon upon his person."[38] The most useful case is *People v. Rivera*.[39] This case was handed down well after the 1920s and just after a new 1964 law, section 180–a,[40] legislatively ratified the New York stop-and-frisk practice. But *Rivera* was expressly decided under pre-section 180 law because it dealt with events that happened before the statute's enactment, and the court there observed a long tradition of permitting detentions under common law doctrine and statutes of other states.[41] As for the "frisk" part of the equation, *Rivera* clarified that an officer may pat down the suspect (to insure the officer's own safety), and if he/she feels a weapon, then can proceed with a search for it.[42] As one

---

35. Terry v. Ohio, 392 U.S. 1 (1968).

36. *See id.* at 10–11, nn. 3–5 (discussing New York case law as a source of the holding).

37. Another way of parsing this under modem law was that if the police were otherwise justified in seizing or searching Rizzo in the building, they were allowed to at least temporarily detain the others in to have them available for arrest if the acts against Rizzo ended up implicating all of them. *See* Michigan v. Summers, 452 U.S. 692 (1981).

38. People v. Marendi, 107 N.E. 1058, 1060 (N.Y. 1915). *Marendi* relied upon Crim. Proc. Code, Section 167 defining "arrest." The 1928 edition of the annotated code for Section 167 itself cites *Marendi* for the proposition that "merely detaining a person and searching him for concealed weapons does not constitute an arrest." N.Y. Code Crim. Proc. 48 (1928).

39. 201 N.E.2d 32 (N.Y. 1964).

40. Act of Mar. 2, 1964, ch. 86, sec. 2, § 180–a, 1964 N.Y. Laws 111 (codified at N.Y. Code Crim. Proc. § 180–a) (current version at N.Y. Crim. Proc. Law § 140.50).

41. 201 N.E.2d 32 at 34–36.

42. *Id.* at 35.

expert commentator later observed, "The police also have the right to take investigatory action and frisk a person as an incident to lawful inquiry where the conduct of the person in question is suspicious and the policeman suspects he is exposing himself to danger when he stops to question him."[43] Notably, neither this nor any other authority lends any meaning to the term "suspicious."

So assuming the stop-and-frisk doctrine was settled in New York in 1927,[44] the police may have acted legally—so long as the requisite reasonable suspicion was established. The observable conduct up to the point of the car stop seems unlikely to meet the "reasonable suspicion" standard, and if we add the police claims about Rizzo's own allegedly furtive conduct in the building, not much more gets added.[45] So perhaps

---

43. Hon. Eugene R. Canudo, Criminal Law of New York 32 (1967). Another commentator observed:

> The court, recognizing that New York's recent stop-and-frisk laws was not in effect at the time of the particular events, stated that the validity of the frisk rested on the initial right to make the summary street inquiry. The authority of the police to stop and question in the circumstances of the case was perfectly clear, since the "business of the police is to prevent crime if they can"; prompt inquiry into suspicious or unusual street action is an "indispensable police power in the orderly government of large urban communities." Comment, Police Power to Stop, Frisk, and Question Suspicious Persons, 65 Colum. L. Rev. 848, 848–49 (1965) (quoting *Rivera*, 201 N.E.2d at 34).

44. After the new statute was enacted, there was some dispute as to whether the common law stop-and-frisk doctrine of *Marendi*, as described in *Rivera*, was indeed settled law or whether the new statute was really creating the doctrine. Indeed, the new statute was controversial enough that some suggested it violated Article 1, Section 12 of the New York Constitution, the state equivalent of the Fourth Amendment. *See* Note, The "No–Knock" and "Stop and Frisk" Provisions of the New York Code of Criminal Procedure, 38 St. John's L. Rev. 392, 398 (1964).

45. As reflected in the defense cross-examination of Sullivan, the dispute over this point in the narrative achieved an Abbott and Costello quality:

DEFENSE: "Did you see Rizzo in the building?"

SULLIVAN: "At that time?"

DEFENSE: "At any time you were in the building did you see Rizzo in the building?"

SULLIVAN: "I did."

DEFENSE: "Where did you see him?"

SULLIVAN: "Standing in on a pile of debris, a pile of wood and dirt."

DEFENSE: "Did you talk to him?"

SULLIVAN: "Cronin spoke to him?

DEFENSE: "I thought you left Cronin and this other officer in the car which was parked on the opposite side of the street where this building was."

SULLIVAN: "I did."

DEFENSE: "You ran into the building?"

SULLIVAN: "I ran into the areaway of the building."

only the most generous reading of police power made this attempt prosecution possible at all. Worse yet, as noted earlier, if the seizures of the men were deemed to be arrests—and they surely were arrests once the suspects were transported to the station house—then the case would only be salvageable for trial if *probable* cause were evident at that time. Further, as noted above, that probable cause requirement would put even more pressure on the evidentiary value of the men's suspicious actions to show that they were already well along the way towards completion of a robbery—of a nonpresent victim.

But its odd and questionable facts aside, *Rizzo* illustrates how procedural law informs attempt law. Ultimately, stop and frisk doctrine became embedded in American constitutional law, not just in *Terry* but also (to reinforce the irony) the companion pair of cases called *Sibron v. New York* and *Peters v. New York*.[46] In those cases, the Supreme Court declined to address the facial validity of the New York statute, section 180–a, but, as did *Terry*, cited *Rivera* in declaring the virtues of a flexible, nontechnical standard for situational judgments that police could legitimately make.[47] So for decades now American police have had broad power to undertake invasive investigation even when they merely suspect some crime may be afoot or imminent. And that power has important implications for attempt law. Under a regime of stop-and-frisk, police who encounter what they believe is a crime-in-progress have two ways of helping the prosecution win a conviction for attempt. First, if the observable action appears to cross the preparation/attempt line, they may have probable cause to arrest for the "completed" crime of attempt. But in addition, even if the observable action has not progressed that far, a stop-and-frisk might enable the police to elicit admissions from the suspects, and those admissions might then add to the observa-

---

DEFENSE: "Did you finally get to the building?"

SULLIVAN: "I did."

DEFENSE: "When you got into the building you saw Rizzo?"

SULLIVAN: "Not at that time."

DEFENSE: "Well, at some point you saw Rizzo on a pile of debris?"

SULLIVAN: "That is right."

DEFENSE: "In the corner?"

SULLIVAN: "That is right."

DEFENSE: "At the time when you saw Rizzo on this pile of debris, was Cronin there?"

SULLIVAN: "He was."

COA, *supra* note 9, at 52.

46. 392 U.S. 40 (1968).

47. *Id.* at 64.

ble action to establish probable cause for attempt and thus permit arrest at that second point.

The more general point is that the police officers' success getting admissible evidence may depend on where on the continuum the substantive law draws the preparation/attempt distinction. A more liberal attempt actus reus will likely mean that police have a lighter burden in finding probable cause for arrest, while a stricter rule will have the converse result. Of course even if they intervene too early they might still be using their stop-and-frisk power legally and not fret over a foregone lost prosecution, because they will at least be preventing a crime. On the other hand, if, as in the *Rizzo* case, the court draws the preparation/attempt boundary fairly late along the continuum, might the police be tempted to delay intervention to ensure a conviction, thereby taking a risk that they intervene too late to save a victim from harm? In any event, the interaction of attempt doctrine with procedure in these situations surely influences the temptations, incentives, and strategies of law enforcement.

The Confessions

The most obvious procedural anachronism in the case involves the confessions themselves. We can focus on Rizzo's, although similar issues arise with the other defendants'. In 1927, of course, the privilege against self-incrimination was decades away from even being held applicable in state prosecutions,[48] much less construed to require the rules of the *Miranda* decision.[49] In theory, Rizzo might have raised one version of a constitutional attack on the interrogation—under the Due Process Clause. As of 1927, some law indicated that the admission of a truly coerced, involuntary confession would violate defendant's constitutional due process rights.[50] It would seem that if Rizzo had been struck by the police, his confession would have failed the due process standard, certainly if the beating was done immediately before or with the intent to extract the confession. Even absent facts sufficient to make out a constitutional claim, Rizzo could argue, and did argue, that the effect of the beating rendered his thinking insufficiently clear-headed to make the confession reliable. The police fairly readily admitted to the beatings they administered,[51] while purporting to minimize the effect of the

---

48. The privilege was not deemed applicable to the States through the Fourteenth Amendment until Malloy v. Hogan, 378 U.S. 1 (1964), and *Miranda* was decided in 1966.

49. Miranda v. Arizona, 384 U.S. 436 (1966).

50. Bram v. United States, 168 U.S. 532 (1897). The major due process case in this vein came a few years after *Rizzo*: Brown v. Mississippi, 297 U.S. 278 (1936).

51. Officer Cronin admitted he struck Rizzo with a blackjack when the suspect allegedly violated an order to keep his hand up, even after Rizzo announced that he had no gun. COA, *supra* note 9, at 106–07. There was no serious denial that Rizzo visibly bled

beatings on the suspects' free will.[52] Officer Sullivan found no trouble
conceding the beating while insisting that the confessions were voluntary.[53] The prosecution put on the police stenographer, McMahon, who
was allowed to read the whole of all the defendants' confessions to the
jury. In fact, the only serious objections involved concerns about the
accuracy of the stenography, with a vague implication by one of the
defense lawyers that the transcript had been cooked.[54] The trial transcript has some indecisive colloquy about just how severe the beatings
were,[55] or whether the circumstances of the confession, at least at the
station house, were suspicious.[56] Later, after Rizzo took the stand in his

---

from the beating. Later, the stenographer who recorded Rizzo's confession at the station
house testified that at that point Rizzo did not mention the beating but nevertheless
conceded that he saw cuts on Rizzo at that time and that an ambulance was eventually
called for him. *Id.* at 192–93.

52. Defense lawyer O'Brien had the following colloquy with Officer Sullivan:

DEFENSE: "When you got to the Westchester station house you asked them certain
questions?"

SULLIVAN: "I did."

DEFENSE: "They responded voluntarily?"

SULLIVAN: "They did."

DEFENSE: "Told you the truth?"

SULLIVAN: "Yes."

DEFENSE: "Anybody touch them?

SULLIVAN: "Yes, I hit the defendant Thomasello . . . I hit the defendants Thomasello
with the butt of a gun that I had taken from Milo, on top of the head." . . .

DEFENSE: "There was no resistance as far as any of the defendants was concerned in
giving up these guns, was there?

SULLIVAN: "Only that while I was taking the gun from the defendant Milo, the
defendants Thomasello dropped his hand and turned toward them." *Id.* at 58–59.

Later, cross-examining Rizzo, Adlerman challenged Rizzo on whether there had been a
second beating, at the station house, saying: "Why, don't you know the only time you were
hit was on the sidewalk at 180th Street and Morris Park Avenue?" *Id.* at 326.

53. An exchange on cross-examination:

DA: "Every question propounded to these defendants, whether it was in the station
house or on the way to the station, was answered freely."

SULLIVAN: "It was." *Id.* at 60.

54. *Id.* at 181–82. One phrasing imputed to Rizzo might have caused a jury to doubt
the authenticity of the reported confession. Asked by the interrogator how Thomasello and
Milo might have known about the payroll, "They surmised about it. . . ." *Id.* at 311–12.
Historical analysis of linguistic patterns would be necessary to determine whether Rizzo,
who had no high school education, would have used the word "surmise."

55. Officer Sullivan said he was unsure on what part of the body Officer Cronin
struck Rizzo. *Id.* at 69.

56. One of the defense tacks in challenging Rizzo's station house confession was to
suggest that the prosecutor may have manipulated the defendant or contrived it, because

own defense, he was cross-examined in a bizarre way, Adlerman essentially reading the confession back to him, asking him whether each statement was true.[57] Rizzo's response was that he had no recollection of the contents of his alleged statement because of the beatings he suffered at the crime scene and at the station house.[58] It takes little understanding of Fifth Amendment law to recognize that on the facts alleged about the beatings—indeed on the facts fully admitted by the police—Rizzo's and the others' statements would have violated any reading of *Miranda*. Even if they had been given *Miranda* warnings (an inconceivable requirement at the time),[59] a voluntary waiver of rights after the beating would have been impossible for the State to prove. That does not mean that the defendants had no way to fight the confessions. They had a way, and they tried it. But under the law at the time, except in the rarest instances where the coercion was so brutal as to violate due process, judges tended to allow the confession to be reported to the jury and then give the *jury* a chance the decide whether the defendant's statements were involuntary. Thus, the jurors had several options, at least in theory. They could have chosen to disregard any confession they deemed involuntary—assuming this is psychologically possible for jurors. They could have deemed the confession to be factually false, precisely because it was beaten out of a terrified suspect. Or, even if they had thought the police tactics brutal and unfair, they still could have viewed the confession as factually reliable.

After the jury had in effect twice heard Rizzo's confession, in his summation one of the defense lawyers argued that the "so called

---

the key questioning was done by District Attorney Adlerman himself, who had been called to the station. In fact, the defense tried to establish that the police absented themselves from the interrogation room while Adlerman questioned Rizzo. *Id.* at 65, 67–68, 160. The police, argued the defense, played no role on the interrogation and the word "holdup" was never uttered in their presence. *Id.* at 68, 174. In fact, Officer Cronin admitted that the police had never taken steps to book all the arrestees for attempted robbery, but that Adlerman had decided to do so. *Id.* at 99. The defense also sought to establish that Rizzo was never made aware of the identity of the questioner, *Id.* at 162, and that Adlerman had "terrorized" the stenographer into testifying in full favor of the prosecution. AB, *supra* note 9, at 67. As a corollary, the defense averred that Adlerman should have taken the stand to rebut the contentions of the bearings at the station house but regrettably could not because of the principle that lawyers should not be themselves be witnesses in cases where they serve as counsel. *Id.* at 65.

57. COA, *supra* note 9, at 306–27.

58. Rizzo testified that when he got to the station house he was beaten with sticks and punched in the jaw. *Id.* at 281.

59. When defense counsel asked the stenographer whether there was "anything said about any admissions being made by him that night that might be used against him," Adlerman interrupted to say that "There is no law that requires it." *Id.* at 170. Later he added that there was no requirement that after Rizzo confessed he be given a transcript to read and sign. *Id.* at 191.

admissions were obtained by force or fear."[60] But Adlerman took his turn arguing:

> I trust and hope, gentlemen, that you are not going to be misled in the case because of the attack that has been made upon these police officers in hitting Thomasello and Rizzo. You have heard no complaints from [sic] Thomasello's beating. Counselor O'Brien did not say that Thomasello was so badly hurt. Did Thomasello know what he was talking about when he answered his questions and then stated that Rizzo was the man that planned this whole thing?[61]

And then came the judge's charge to the jury, following the judge's own summary of the contents of the confessions:

> Under our law the confession of a defendant ... can be given in evidence against him unless made under the influence of fear produced by threats ... but it is not sufficient to warrant his conviction without additional proof that the crime charged has been committed. It is claimed ... that any statements obtained from the defendants ... were taken under the influence of fear produced by threats and preceded by blows struck on two of the defendants. It is for you to say, gentlemen, whether or not these statements or confessions made by each of these defendants were voluntary statements not given under the influence of fear or produced by threats. If the statements were voluntary statements made freely and without any influence of fear produced by threats or bodily harm, then, gentlemen, they are competent evidence in the case.... If ... you are satisfied from the evidence that these statements were obtained or these confession were obtained by under the influence of fear produced by threats, whether express or implied, then, gentlemen, you must under the law disregard those confessions.[62]

Moreover, the judge went on to remind the jurors that the force used by the police was a lawful use of their force if necessary to quell resistance to a lawful arrest.[63] It was left to one of the defense lawyers to make a somewhat obligatory, hopeless pitch before the jury that "these so-called admissions were obtained through force or fear," but that was

---

60. *Id.* at 347.

61. *Id.* at 366.

62. *Id.* at 379–80.

63. *Id.* at 380–81. If anything, the most litigated issue about the confession involved the venerable corroboration requirement, whereby a conviction cannot rest upon a confession that has not been substantially corroborated by other evidence. The judge's explanation of that rule and the proof of the prosecution's corroborative evidence essentially removed that issue from the case. *Id.* at 379–81.

simply a way of urging the jury to find the confessions unreliable, rather than any kind of suppression motion.[64]

On appeal, Rizzo's attack on the confession shows up in rather desultory fashion under a generic final claim that "[f]or other reasons the defendants did not have a fair trial."[65] But this claim was always really about factual arguments made before the jury; the appeal does not cite any clear rule of law barring admission of the confessions. In its own brief the State re-narrated the facts of the arrests and interrogation of Rizzo himself and proclaimed that the evidence "shows conclusively that the confession taken by the District Attorney was voluntarily made by the defendant[66] and that when the defendant made his confession he was still in full possession of all his faculties."[67]

And so the confession question stood, or, in effect, would have stood. When the Court of Appeals reversed the conviction solely on the ground that the police had interrupted the scheme before Rizzo had crossed the line into attempt, it mooted any possible procedural claim about the confession. But left intact was the power of the State at the time to engage in what now seems like unconscionable tactics to elicit a confession to help boost a "mere preparation" case into an attempt case. Moreover, even the modern *Miranda* restraints on interrogations, the considerable power of police to extract confessions plays a key role in establishing attempt, especially where, as discussed below, the preparation/attempt line has been moved up somewhat earlier along the continuum.

Complicity and its Effects

Winning admission of individual confessions was clearly the key to the prosecution's case against Rizzo and his alleged confederates. But equally useful was finding ways that the facts averred in the defendants' individual statements could be summed up into an overall picture and could be used against all the defendants. The interaction of attempt law, accomplice liability, and rules of procedure is thus another important dimension of the case. Of course many cases of attempt involve a single suspect, but the relationship of attempt law and complicity doctrine is mutually revealing. For one thing, at a fairly abstract level, both involve difficult issues of causation. In attempt cases the question is whether the individual is to be punished even where by definition, she never causes the ultimate harm. In complicity cases, the contributory role of any one accomplice may be uncertain as a matter of necessary or sufficient cause

64. *Id.* at 347.
65. AB, *supra* note 9, at 64–69.
66. RB, *supra* note 9, at 72–78.
67. *Id.* at 75.

of the ultimate harm; hence some of the classic complicity cases turn on drastically easing the causation requirement so as to (arguably) elevate an attempt to aid into full causal responsibility.[68]

But the most practical link between attempt and complicity is simply that accomplices are often the best sources of information about the mental state of each other, and so the cross-admissibility of evidence, especially of confessions, can be crucial in multiple-attempter cases, and the admissibility issue then turns, yet again, on rules of procedure as much as substantive doctrine. *Rizzo*, again, is illustrative.

The first procedural matter is the one of joint trial. Separate trials for the defendants in *Rizzo* might well have accomplished the same result but would have been costly in terms of prosecution resources and the risk that witness testimony would not maintain consistency. The rules of joinder permit a joint trial of alleged accomplices to the same crime.[69] Moreover, under both traditional and current rules, where defendants' cases are initially joined by the prosecutor it would take a heroic argument to persuade a judge to nevertheless grant a motion to sever the cases to avoid undue prejudice resulting from the possibility of mutually inconsistent defenses.[70]

In any event, no such request was ever made in *Rizzo*. Prosecutors have ways of playing off defendants against each other so as to maximize the number or severity of the convictions in the case, and Adlerman was hardly subtle about his goals here. Judges have considerable power, in theory at least, to alert the jury to the dangers of unfair cross-imputation of evidence, but such jury admonitions are of questionable value— and the legal regime of 1927 exhibited much more confidence in the efficacy of these admonitions than would be the case now. The *Rizzo* case was rife with such moments of possible prejudice, and the prosecution certainly took every opportunity to impute any inculpatory facts against all, especially Rizzo. Moreover, the judge may have been unusually disingenuous in assuming the jury instructions would work in this particular case. Some of those moments involved evidence other than confessions or admissions. Thus, when Officer Sullivan described taking a gun from Milo's pocket and produced the gun for the jury, Zoetzl objected to this "as not binding on the defendant Rizzo, there being no evidence that Rizzo was there at the time that this occurrence took

---

68. *See* State v. Tally, 15 So. 722 (Ala. 1894) (whether defendant as accomplice to murder for blocking warning message to victim turns on whether "the aid in homicide can be shown to have put the deceased at a disadvantage, to have deprived him of a single chance of life which but for it he would have had . . .").

69. *See* Fed. R. Crim. P. 8.

70. *See* Fed. R. Crim. P. 14; Zafiro v. United States, 506 U.S. 534 (1993) (severance only warranted where joinder endangers specific trial-type right of defendant; prospect of antagonistic defenses insufficient).

place." The trial judge replied that "it is taken subject to connection. I do not know whether the testimony will be adduced to connect it."[71] Later, when Adlerman introduced evidence that Dorio had stolen the Paige car some days before his involvement with Rizzo, the judge temporarily allowed this evidence in as part of the "res gestae" of the attempted robbery,[72] but later made clear that the jury deciding the attempted robbery charge should only consider the change of plates (that occurred after Dario's meeting with Rizzo) and disregard the car theft.[73]

But of course the most damning evidence was in the form of out-of-court statements. Even under the law at that time, the hearsay rules provided some limitation against the prejudicial effect of introducing such statements. In that light, it is interesting that while the trial court's rulings, as noted below, seem anachronistic with regard to confessions, the trial judge was extremely punctilious about the risk of hearsay, frequently admonishing witnesses to restate their answers to avoid hearsay problems, even without a lawyer's request.[74] By contrast, when it came to the defendants' admissions to the police (and to Adlerman at the station house), the court relied on limiting instructions rather than ruling those inadmissible. Indeed, the court was forced to give such limiting instructions numerous times because Alderman inserted statements allegedly made by co-defendants as frequently as he could.

Thus, when Adlerman asked Officer Sullivan, "Will you tell this jury what the defendant Dorio said to you before you got into the station house and after you got into the station house?," Zoetzl objected that the testimony would be "incompetent, irrelevant, and immaterial" as against Rizzo. The trial judge then said: "The jury is now instructed that the statements made by Dorio after his arrest are only admissible against Dorio...."[75] When Sullivan testified that Dorio said, " 'I am come into this innocently. I have been gorialled [sic] by these other three men,' " defense counsel again objected, and the trial judge replied, "The same ruling that the Court made before applies with respect to all of this witness' testimony relative to the statement made by Dorio to him."[76]

---

71. COA, *supra* note 9, at 30–31. The same thing happened when Officer Gush presented one of the guns on the stand. Id. at 124.

72. *Id.* at 36–37. The term "res gestae" ("things done") refers to the events at issue, or all the steps contemporaneous with part of the conduct constituting the crime, thus marking the scope of potentially relevant evidence. Black's Law Dictionary 1335 (8th ed. 2004).

73. *Id.* at 355.

74. When Sullivan began to say, "I told Detective Cronin ...," O'Brien objected and the judge immediately admonished the witness, "Do not say what you told him. What did you do ...?" *Id.* at 28.

75. *Id.* at 35.

76. *Id.* at 36.

Later still, Officer Cronin testified to statements by Dorio whereby Dorio said he was suspicious about things that Rizzo and the others said to him. Now ritually, Zoetzl objected and the court replied, "Yes, it must be only as against Dorio."[77] More dramatically, when Officer Cronin was reporting on what Dorio said to the police at the station house, O'Brien's objection was met yet again by the court's desultory limiting instruction ("Yes, it is immaterial as to Rizzo, but competent as to Dorio"). But when Cronin then said, "Dorio told me about the job that Milo and Thomasello has done in New Rochelle," O'Brien even asked for a mistrial. The judge then simply repeated the standard limiting instruction.[78]

The history of legal doctrine in regard to this issue of cross-imputation is very simple. In 1927, if the defense had pushed harder on the unfairness of allowing the jury to hear one defendant's out-of-court statements as implicating others, the reply would have been that the limiting instructions given by the judge were quite sufficient. As late as three decades later, in *Delli Paoli v. United States*,[79] the Supreme Court held that there was no constitutional problem with this practice, at least as long as the standard jury admonition was given. The defendant in *Delli Paoli* claimed that an out-of-court admission by a co-defendant was not only hearsay against him, but also a violation of the Sixth Amendment's Confrontation Clause. And where such an out of court statement is in effect a confession to a crime, it is devastatingly influential on a jury and therefore hugely prejudicial to the defendant raising the claim. But the Court expressed confidence that a limiting instruction would obviate any Confrontation Clause problem. Then just a decade later, the Supreme Court changed its mind in *Bruton v. United States*.[80] Weaving its way through a variety of cases involving confessions and the efficacy of limiting instructions, the Court declared unconstitutional the practice that was used in *Rizzo*:

> In joint trials, . . . when the admissible confession of one defendant inculpates another defendant, the confession is never deleted from the case and the jury is expected to perform the overwhelming task of considering it in determining the guilt or innocence of the declarant and then of ignoring it in determining the guilt or inno-

---

77. *Id.* at 83. Other examples appear throughout the trial transcript. When the stenographer read a statement by Dorio that he recalled Rizzo inquiring about the payroll, Zoetzl objected that it "is not a statement of Rizzo." The court admonished the jury to disregard any possible relevance to Rizzo. *Id.* at 153–54. See also *id.* at 164 (same in regard to Milo statement); *Id.* at 175 (same in regard to Thomasello statement).

78. *Id.* at 117–18. Somewhat improbably, Adlerman suggested that the defense had "opened to door" to this testimony, and O'Brien replied, "It must be a swinging door."

79. 352 U.S, 232 (1957).

80. 391 U.S. 123 (1968).

cence of any co-defendants of the declarant. A jury cannot "segregate evidence into separate intellectual boxes." . . . It cannot determine that a confession is true insofar as it admits that A has committed criminal acts with B and at the same time effectively ignore the inevitable conclusion that B has committed those same criminal acts with A.[81]

As for limiting instructions:

> The fact of the matter is that, too often, such admonition against misuse is intrinsically ineffective, in that the effect of such a nonadmissible declaration cannot be wiped from the brains of the jurors. The admonition therefore becomes a futile collocation of words, and fails of its purpose as a legal protection to defendants against whom such a declaration should not tell. . . . The government should not have the windfall of having the jury be influenced by evidence against a defendant which, as a matter of law, they should not consider, but which they cannot put out of their minds.[82]

The Court also addressed the common argument in favor of joint trials that "the benefits of joint proceedings should not have to be sacrificed by requiring separate trials in order to use the confession against the declarant. Joint trials do conserve state funds, diminish inconvenience to witnesses and public authorities, and avoid delays in bringing those accused of crime to trial."[83] But the Court rejected that argument:

> We still adhere to the rule that an accused is entitled to confrontation of the witnesses against him and the right to cross-examine them. . . . We destroy the age-old rule which in the past has been regarded as a fundamental principle of our jurisprudence by a legalistic formula, required of the judge, that the jury may not consider any admissions against any party who did not join in them. We secure greater speed, economy and convenience in the administration of the law at the price of fundamental principles of constitutional liberty. That price is too high.[84]

In any event, in *Rizzo*, the defendants had to rely on faith in the judge's admonitions. And that faith, especially Rizzo's own, may have been undermined by Adlerman's closing flourish. The District Attorney appears to have been fairly confident of convictions against Thomasello,

---

81. *Id.* at 130–31 (quoting *People v. Arand,* 407 P.2d 265, 271–72 (Cal. 1965)).

82. 391 U.S. at 129 (quoting *Delli Paoli v. United States,* 352 U.S. 232, 247–48 (1957)) (Frankfurter, J. dissenting).

83. 391 U.S. at 134.

84. *Id.* at 134–35 (quoting *People v. Fisher,* 164 N.E. 336, 341 (N.Y. 1928)) (Lehman, J., dissenting).

Milo, and Dorio, so his aim was at Rizzo, especially Rizzo's claim of having been witless or duped or manipulated by the others. Adlerman's acerbic, vitriolic closing argument tried to depict Rizzo as the mastermind who avoided any risk of being seen holding a gun, but whose information about the payroll route was the absolutely necessary key to success.[85] And at the heart of Adlerman's argument was his unapologetic exploitation of cross-imputation:

> What is the evidence? You cannot separate these statements that have been taken in the Twenty–Third Precinct. You have got to read them together. Who was the directing influence that ordered Dorio to go to these different jobs under consideration? Was it Dorio? No, Dorio did not know where those jobs were being constructed. Was it Thomasello? Thomasello did not know where these jobs were being constructed. The one man that knew it is the man that had the information because of the intimate connection with the United Lathing Company. . . . You have in evidence here a statement made by the defendant Thomasello, the statement made by the defendant Dorio and the statement made by the defendant Milo, and their statements jibe in every particular with the statements made by Rizzo. Their statements stand uncontradicted, undeniable and unquestioned.[86]

Decades after *Rizzo*, a multiple-defendant attempt case might have put the prosecution to a hard choice. It could avoid all these *Bruton* problems at the huge cost of holding separate trials for each defendant. Conversely, It could enjoy the economies of a single trial—and still exploit possible indirect or implicit opportunities of cross-imputation that are outside the scope of *Bruton*—by sacrificing a co-defendant's out-of-court statements that implicate other defendants.[87] Yet another possibility of course, which appeared not to interest Adlerman, would be to cut cooperation deals with the minor players in the scheme in exchange for live testimony against the key villain.[88] But beyond all these particu-

---

85. COA, *supra* note 9, at 354–56.

86. *Id.* at 357, 361.

87. A possible compromise under modern law is to bring in the out-of-court statement against the party who made it, but to redact that part of the statement that implicates others. Gray v. Maryland, 523 U.S. 185 (1998). But that solution requires semantic maneuvers that might not pass court muster.

88. In *United States v. Jackson*, 560 U.S. 112 (2d Cir. 1977), one of the accomplices in a planned bank robbery turned informer when she was arrested on a separate charge. She began cooperating by faking participation in the bank robbery; she was thereby able to help the police thwart the crime before it was completed and then could offer live testimony. By contrast, in *United States v. Buffington*, 815 F.2d 1202 (8th Cir. 1987), the informant was not allowed to testify because the prosecution violated a court order to give timely notice of the witness's appearance. The jury convicted anyway, but the Court of Appeals reversed

lar speculations, the general point is that in cases of equivocal observable action, once again the state of procedural law helps determine whether the attempt conviction can be won.

The Meaning of Attempt

The Trial Ruling

Once all the confession evidence came in, the pivotal moment in the trial became the judge's instructions on the definition of attempt. Those instructions merit careful reading:

> To think ... of a crime, does not constitute an attempt; to prepare for the commission of a crime does not constitute an attempt to commit a crime. If three or four men congregate together in a given place and agree among themselves that they will commit, let us say, the crime of robbery, and if, after having that conference, they stopped, the law says that is not enough to establish the crime of robbery in the first degree, nor does that arise even to the dignity of an attempt to commit the crime of robbery in the first degree.
>
> .... The law requires that there be some overt act, some open act committed in pursuance of their prior agreement to carry out the intention which existed in their minds. Whenever the intention exists, followed by acts apparently affording prospect of success and tending to render the commission of the crime effectual, the accused brings himself within the letter and the intent of the statute.... In such cases the accused has done his utmost to effectuate the commission of a crime, but fails to accomplish it for some cause not previously apparent to him.
>
> The question whether an attempt to commit a crime has been made is determinable solely by the condition of the actor's mind and his conduct in the consummation of his design. So far as the culprit is concerned the felonious design and action are then just as complete as though the crime could have been or in fact had been committed.[89]

An alternative wording was offered as well:

> Whenever the acts of a person have gone to the extent of placing it in his power to commit the offense unless interrupted in them, but such interruption prevents his present commission of the offense, at least then he is guilty of an attempt to commit the offense, whatever may be the rule as to his conduct before it reached that stage.[90]

---

because the residual physical evidence on which the prosecution had to rely was insufficient to support conviction.

    89. COA, *supra* note 9, at 374–75.

    90. *Id.* at 376.

If we stop reading at this point, the instructions might seem so vague as to be unhelpful. If we try to align the judge's doctrinal definition with the taxonomy of common law tests noted above, it may appear in the middle along a continuum. The variations among those standards is hard to discern. "Physical proximity" and "dangerous proximity" put more emphasis on how close the acts are toward completion, whereas the "unequivocality test" puts more explicit emphasis on the defendant's mental state.

The New York instruction seems to put some emphasis on intent but treats it as a fact independently established, a necessary but not sufficient condition. If this is the case, then the key issue became the degree of movement toward the crime. In effect, the question calls for a thought experiment. Imagine that we are watching the defendant on a videotape, and the tape stops at the instant just before he was interrupted. Would the viewer of the tape at that moment predict a fair likelihood of success for the defendant? In hazarding that prediction, the viewer would have to take into account the range of possible things that could happen between this last observed act and the ultimate goal that might in the ordinary course of events thwart success—including both exogenous events and the possible change-of-mind by the defendant. Thus, the defendant need not have engaged in the *last* act needed to succeed, but he must have crossed what we might consider a point of no return toward completion.

The New York instruction used in *Rizzo* was probably a fair averaging out of all the common law formulas. In that sense, it may seem too vague to give the jury the help it might want. But the substance of the instruction has procedural significance. Imagine that the defense had made more than a superficial effort to dismiss the attempt charge, at the start, middle, or end of the evidence, rather than take its chance on persuading the jury to acquit. It takes a fairly precise set of crime elements for a judge to readily conclude that no reasonable jury could find the elements proved beyond a reasonable doubt. If the standard is as vague as this one is, and if there are facts on both sides of the case—as the admission of the confessions ensured was true here—then the judge has little basis for keeping the issue from the jury.

On the other hand, the judge went on to reframe the instruction in light of the facts of the case. The judge said that if the jurors found that the defendants

> conspired to commit the robbery, . . . to hold up a man who had a payroll in his possession, and that they had secured weapons for the purpose of carrying out that intent which existed in their minds; that the next morning after that conspiracy had been already formed they left 142d street and entered an automobile; that they

effected the change of license plates on that automobile; that thereafter they went to several places to seek for an intended victim, the
man who carried the payroll, and that if they had not been inter-
cepted by police officers they would have completed the crime of
robbery in the first degree but for the interception and interruption
by police officers . . . you should find them guilty.[91]

Here the judge might seem to be giving the jury *too much* help,
suggesting that the key prosecution facts, if true, necessarily supported
the attempt charge. As a result, once the jury heard and believed the
confessions, a verdict of guilty may have been unavoidable.

The Appeal

Rizzo's Argument

Was the jury verdict right? Given the instruction, it seems implausible to deny that there was sufficient evidence to find the defendants
guilty beyond a reasonable doubt. The "insufficiency of evidence" test is
traditionally so deferential to the trier of fact that Rizzo's best hope
would have been to find some way to identify an error of law and not
erroneous findings of fact. So how did the defense attack the verdict?
Rizzo's appellate arguments did not explicitly attack the jury instruction
as having stated the wrong legal standard. Rather, the appeal framed the
issue as what might best be called a mixed question of law and fact, by
which the evidence failed to establish the crime. But to make this claim,
defense had to reframe the facts in such a way as to identify a distinct
legal boundary around the facts. At the very least he had to classify
precedent into affirmed and reversed attempt cases and show that the
fact pattern in his case resembled the facts patterns in the reversed
group. Better yet, in doing so he had to argue that this classification
could generate at least a discernible legal boundary, even if not a
crystalline doctrinal difference.

In effect, Rizzo had three possible strategies. First, he could insist
that his testimony at trial and the benign version of the evidence argued
by his lawyers cast reasonable doubt on whether he, at least, had ever
formed the intent to rob anyone. Even if the others had hoped to deploy
him as their guide towards finding a vulnerable payroll victim at a
conducive time and place, he himself was only dimly aware of being so
used and was motivated by the desire to collect his back pay for his own
use or at worst to pay off a small gambling debt.

Second, and more fruitfully for the appeal, he could concede the
malign version of the facts testified to by the others and not entirely
rebutted by his own alleged confession, but then try to interpret the

---

91. *Id.* at 376.

relevant doctrinal precedents as implicitly establishing something close to a last act test. From Rizzo's perspective, the available precedential material was at best equivocal for this purpose. In his way were various cases from New York and elsewhere that endorsed attempt convictions for conduct short of the last or penultimate act. Conversely, even some cases reversing attempt convictions could be read as still not requiring a very late act but just finding a lack of great resolution in the defendant's mind, at a point where a fair amount of action was still needed to go from the final observed act to the necessary ultimate one.[92] The fact-specificity of most of these holdings did not offer Rizzo much help. To draw the doctrinal line that would enhance his cause, the brief focuses on the fact that Rizzo was interrupted before he ever encountered Rao, so that there were still several steps yet to be taken before completion. Thus it avers: "[T]here was much to be done when the defendant was apprehended . . .";[93] It adds: "In the case at bar there were many things that might have happened between the last act of the defendant and the crime intended which would have prevented the crime."[94] Rizzo then cited the famous *Commonwealth v. Peaslee* opinion by Justice Oliver Wendell Holmes as at least implying the requirement of something close to the last act test.[95] By that reckoning, the case might flunk any of the standard phrasings of the preparation/attempt line, at least if those lines were pushed by this interpretation pretty close to the last act test. Even if at the moment of interruption the intent to help rob was in Rizzo's mind, what Holmes in *Peaslee* called a *"locus penitentioe,"* an "opportunity for repentance," had not yet been passed.[96] The appellate brief certainly tries this reading of the cases, but this effort requires an artificial enumeration of steps yet to be taken. After all, had Rao shown up just a moment earlier or the police been just a bit slower, the confederates might have needed just the single step of pulling out their guns to rob him.

Hence, Rizzo had to revert to a third strategy—to draw a qualitative or categorical line through the cases, arguing that no attempt conviction could stand where the circumstances made it literally impossible for the

---

92. AB, *supra* note 9, at 34–36.

93. *Id.* at 36.

94. *Id.* at 40. The appeal noted that Rizzo might have given up and gone home if Rao had not soon shown up at the 18th Street site. COA, *supra* note 9, at 186–87.

95. AB, *supra* note 9, at 35, quoting *Commonwealth v. Peaslee*, 59 N.E. 55, 56 (Mass. 1901): "Obviously new considerations come in when further acts on the part of the person who has taken in the first steps are necessary before the substantive crime can come to pass. In this class of cases there is still a chance that the would-be criminal may change his mind."

96. *Id.*

next steps to succeed. Thus, we see in the appellate brief some of the following language:

> But the question here presented, that of the possibility ever committing the crime of attempt to rob where the intended victim is not shown to have been within sight or hearing or range or anywhere near or in proximity to defendant, seems never to have been passed upon in the state.[97]

> How can it possibly be said that there can be an attempt to commit a crime, the essential ingredient or foundation of which is accomplishing the purpose by force or fear, when there is no one present to put in fear or to exercise force against?[98]

> [H]ere defendant is found guilty of doing something which he never intended and which it was wholly impossible for him to do....[99]

This was a crucial maneuver by the appellant. The jury instruction did not require that the defendant have committed the last or penultimate possible acts, so that proximity to the final crime could have been a matter of degree. Worse yet, if the confessions about intent were to be believed, a reasonable jury could surely have found that whatever steps were yet to be taken, would have been taken absent interruption by police. So the appellate maneuver was to turn a matter of degree into a categorical distinction: If the crime alleged was supposedly the robbery of Rao at 180th Street, and if Rao was not there, then no matter how many further steps were taken, the crime could not have been succeeded.

To render this impossibility defense less abstract, Rizzo tried to thread his way through key background cases to argue they support this defense. His position was that the physical presence of the victim is the key variable in the cases.[100] This is the meaning of the term "present commission" as derived by the trial judge in this case and inserted into the jury instruction.[101] Thus, in *People v. Sullivan*, Judge Edgar Cullen opined:

> If one with intent to shoot another should procure a pistol for that purpose, that alone might not amount to an attempt to shoot him. It may be that if after procuring the pistol he took a conveyance to the residence of his intended victim, still that would not constitute an attempt. But if after this with his design unchanged he approaches the person he intends to shoot but is seized before he can draw the

---

97.   AB, *supra* note 9, at 23.

98.   *Id.* at 23.

99.   *Id.* at 22.

100.   *Id.* at 34–35.

101.   COA, *supra* note 9, at 376.

pistol, I think he is properly punished as having attempted to commit the crime.[102]

Rizzo, of course, wanted to read *Sullivan* as declaring "impossibility" cases as a wholly separate category, and as making physical proximity the criterion of "possibility." But there is a contrary way of reading *Sullivan* that renders the notion of "impossibility" a misleading distraction, a reading by which finding a sufficient sum of act and intent evidence is a matter of degree, and by which proximity becomes at most a relevant factor, and by no means a decisive one. By that reckoning, factual differences between Rizzo's case and Sullivan's could make affirmance of the former's conviction perfectly consistent with reversal of the latter's.

But then another New York case presented a much greater challenge to Rizzo's lawyers. In *People v. Du Veau*, (the only cited New York case where the charge was attempted first-degree robbery), a defendant was arrested when he and a supposed accomplice (who had turned police informer) arrived at the victim's place of business, where the robbery was to occur.[103] The court upheld Du Veau's conviction, straightforwardly holding that the defendant's solicitation of the accomplice was an act clearly tending, however futilely, toward commission of the crime. A court inclined to be generous to accused attempters could certainly have framed *Du Veau* as an instance of impossibility even more plausibly than Rizzo's, since the sting operation terminated any conceivable chance of success for the crime. Therefore, in upholding the conviction, the *Du Veau* court was rendering the impossibility issue irrelevant and providing strong support to the State. *Du Veau* thus effectively equated sting cases with the more numerous empty pocket cases, where accused pickpockets generally failed to persuade the courts that their cases were really examples of nonpunishable "impossible" attempts.[104]

Thus, Rizzo's problem here was twofold: First, he had little precedent available to support his reading of impossibility doctrine. Second, as a conceptual matter "impossibility" is a very unstable line to draw. On

---

102. 65 N.E. 989.993 (N.Y. 1903). In his effort to seal up the category of spatial place, Rizzo cited *Peebles v. State*, 28 S.E. 920 (Ga. 1897), where the defendant poisoned a well to kill the victim, but the poison was discovered before the victim showed up. As described by Rizzo, the key relevant fact was that "the intended victim was not in insufficient proximity to the danger." AB, *supra* note 9, at 32.

103. 94 N.Y.S. 225 (N.Y. App. Div. 1905).

104. AB, *supra* note 9, at 34. Rizzo tried to use physical proximity to distinguish the pickpocket cases as well: "These cases are all distinguishable from the instant one in that in each the proper object or subject of the crime was present and available and close enough to the defendant and in sufficient proximity for him to work his designs upon." *Id.* But phrases like "close enough" seem to concede that these are indeed just matters of degree, and while Rizzo succeeded in 1927, this rationalization, as discussed below, now seems artificial and anachronistic. *See infra* text accompanying notes 128–29.

that second score, in trying to reframe his case as one of impossibility, Rizzo was reflecting an approach common in attempt cases throughout the twentieth century, and to some extent one continuing today. This approach views conventional attempt cases as ones where the State must establish clear intent to do the crime and sufficient action to meet whatever version of the preparation/attempt doctrine applies, but treats "impossibility" cases as a separate species altogether. Often using such classic examples as the pickpocket with his hand in an empty pocket, or the shooter who aims at a pillow thinking it is his enemy's head, many casebooks insert so-called impossibility cases as a supplementary unit in their attempt chapters[105] or describe it as a formal defense to an attempt charge.[106] But almost all efforts to make sense of this supposedly separate category come to failure. In the end, the *Rizzo* case thereby at least indirectly helps illustrate the better approach to this issue—to recognize that under a proper understanding of attempt law, impossibility may not be a separate category at all.

The Impossibility Question

Notably, New York actually did have important precedent on the impossibility issue, although it was never cited in the *Rizzo* pleadings or opinion. In the oft-excerpted case of *People v. Jaffe*,[107] after the police learned of a theft that was to end with selling the stolen goods, a sting was arranged and the putative buyer was caught. The court overturned a conviction for attempted receipt of stolen property because the goods "lost their character as stolen."[108] *Jaffe* was reviewed in the extremely useful case of *Booth v. State*.[109] There on similar facts, another state court ruled that there could be no punishable attempt to receive a stolen coat when the police were already informed of and in control of the situation because the coat had lost its character as stolen. The great value of *Booth* is that it articulates the difficulty that was raised less systematically by the State in *Rizzo*: The impossibility doctrine does not have a coherent definition or boundary.

Booth notes that the impossibility concept goes back at least as far as early Victorian England, where the courts at first rejected liability in the generic pickpocket/empty pocket cases,[110] but later started changing

---

105. *See e.g.,* Sanford Kadish, Stephen Schulhofer & Carol Steiker, *Criminal Law and Its Processes: Cases and Materials* 575–88 (8th ed. 2007).

106. *See, e.g.,* Joshua Dressler, *Cases and Materials on Criminal Law* 770–89 (5th ed. 2009) (calling impossibility a "special defense").

107. 78 N.E. 169 (N.Y. App. Div. 1906).

108. *Id.* at 169.

109. 398 P.2d 863 (Okla. 1964).

110. *See e.g.,* Regina v. McPherson (1857) 169 Eng. Rep. 975; 1 D. & B. C. C. 197. In the words of Baron Bramwell: "The argument that a man putting his hand into an empty

their view in favor of liability.[111] Once imported into American law, impossibility doctrine led to a very questionable sorting of generic situations into supposedly distinct categories called "factual impossibility," where attempt was chargeable and "legal impossibility," where it was not. As the *Booth* court lamented:

> What is a "legal impossibility" as distinguished from a "physical or factual impossibility" has over a long period of time perplexed our courts and has resulted in many irreconcilable decisions and much philosophical discussion by legal scholars.

> The reason for the "impossibility" of completing the substantive crime ordinarily falls into one of two categories: (1) Where the act if completed would not be criminal, a situation which is usually described as a "legal impossibility," and (2) where the basic or substantive crime is impossible of completion, simply because of some physical or factual condition unknown to the defendant, a situation which is usually described as a "factual impossibility."

> The authorities in the various states and the text-writers are in general agreement that where there is a "legal impossibility" of completing the substantive crime, the accused cannot be successfully charged with an attempt, whereas in those cases in which the "factual impossibility" situation is involved, the accused may be convicted of an attempt. Detailed discussion of the subject is unnecessary to make it clear that it is frequently most difficult to compartmentalize a particular set of facts as coming within one of the categories rather than the other.[112]

---

pocket might be convicted of an attempt to steal appeared to me at first plausible; but suppose a man, believing a block of wood to be a man who was his deadly enemy, struck it a blow intending to murder, could he be convicted of attempting to murder the man he took it to be?"

111. R. v. Ring [1892] 17 Cox C. C. 491; 66 L. T. N. S. 300.

112. *Booth*, 398 P.2d at 870. *Booth* offered these admittedly unhelpful case summaries: Examples of the so-called "legal impossibility" situations [citations omitted] are:

(a) A person accepting goods which he believes to have been stolen, but which were not in fact stolen goods, is not guilty of an attempt to receive stolen goods.

(b) It is not an attempt to commit subornation of perjury where the false testimony solicited, if given, would have been immaterial to the case at hand and hence not perjurious.

(c) An accused who offers a bribe to a person believed to be a juror, but who is not a juror, is not guilty of an attempt to bribe a juror.

(d) An official who contracts a debt which is unauthorized and a nullity, but which he believes to be valid, is not guilty of an attempt to illegally contract a valid debt.

(e) A hunter who shoots a stuffed deer believing it to be alive is not guilty of an attempt to shoot a deer out of season.

Examples of cases in which attempt convictions have been sustained on the theory that all that prevented the consummation of the completed crime was a "factual impossibility" are:

The *Booth* court concluded that, given this traditional taxonomy, it had to overturn the conviction, but it did so reluctantly: "The defendant in the instant case leaves little doubt as to his moral guilt. The evidence, as related by the self-admitted and perpetual law violator, indicates defendant fully intended to do the act with which he was charged."[113]

The Court therefore quoted with admiration, and urged legislatures to adopt, the then-new Model Penal Code provision on the issue:

(1) Definition of Attempt. A person is guilty of an attempt to commit a crime if, acting with the kind of culpability otherwise required for commission of the crime, he:

(a) purposely engages in conduct which would constitute the crime if the attendant circumstances were as he believes them to be; or,

(b) when causing a particular result in an element of the crime, does or omits to do anything with the purpose of causing or with the belief that it will cause such result, without further conduct on his part; or,

(c) purposely does or omits to do anything which, under the circumstances as he believes them to be, is a substantial step in a course of conduct planned to culminate in his commission of the crime.[114]

Note that this statutory language renders moot irrelevant any distinct concept of impossibility. So long as the act conceived by the malefactor is one which is condemned by a criminal statute, he can be guilty of attempt if the intent and sufficient act are proved.

The State's Response

In the Respondent's Brief in *Rizzo*, the State lawyers sounded quite confident that an affirmance was on the way. Reviewing all the cases cited by the appellant, the State read them all as straightforward applications of the conventional standards for attempt law reflected in the various verbal formulations of the preparation/attempt distinction, and as perfectly well summarized by the trial judge's "tending to render

---

(a) The picking of an empty pocket.

(b) An attempt to steal from an empty receptacle.

(c) Where defendant shoots into the intended victim's bed, believing he is there, when in fact he is elsewhere.

(d) Where the defendant erroneously believing that the gun is loaded points it at his wife's head and pulls the trigger.

(e) Where the woman upon whom the abortion operation is performed is not in fact pregnant. *Id.* at 870–71.

113. *Id.* at 872.

114. Model Penal Code § 5.01(1) (1985).

the commission of the crime effectual" instruction in the case. The State lawyers were happy to recite various versions of the preparation/attempt distinction and then view the various outcomes as case-specific. From that perspective, affirmance of the conviction in this case was close to a simple matter of deference to jury fact-finding under the highly deferential insufficiency-of-evidence standard. The State stressed that various "proximity" tests were all matters of degree, and in particular re-read the *Peaslee* opinion as supporting the view that the act before interruption need not be the last or even penultimate act contemplated:

> But some preparations may amount to an attempt. It is a question of degree. If the preparation comes very near to the accomplishment of the act, the intent to complete it renders the crimes so probable that the act will be a misdemeanor, although there is still a locus penitentioe, in the need of a further exertion of the will to complete the crime.[115]

The State then confidently tackled the impossibility issue head on by essentially deconstructing it. Its key point was that it was all a matter of categorization. There was the possibility of "present commission" if we imagine that absent interruption the defendants would have stayed there until Charles Rao arrived or have pursued a payroll elsewhere. The State thereby offers the key logical argument against any impossibility doctrine: Anything incomplete action can be called "impossible" to complete if we frame the situation narrowly enough. The State's argument thus anticipates the demise of "impossibility" as a distinct legal category or the blending of a broad category of factual impossibility into conventional MPC-type attempt law. "In all probability, under the circumstances, defendant Rizzo and his confederates would have waited for Rao's appearance, had they not been interrupted by the police."[116] As for the pickpocket and other attempted theft cases discussed—and supposedly finessed—by the appellant, the State happily cited the affirmance of convictions in those cases as proof that there is no "impossibility defense" at all.[117]

---

115. Commonwealth v. Peaslee, 59 N.E. 55, 56 (Mass. 1901).

116. RB, *supra* 9, at 40.

117. *Id.* at 40–41. The cases range from empty pocket attempted theft cases, *e.g.*, People v. Moran, 25 N.E. 412 (N.Y. 1890) to attempted abortion where the woman turned out not to be pregnant, *Commonwealth v. Taylor*, 132 Mass. 261 (1882). As the brief quoted from *Moran*, 25 N.E. at 412–13:

> Whenever the animo furandi exists, followed by acts apparently affording a prospect of success and tending to render the commission of the crime ineffectual, the accused brings himself within the letter and intent of the statute. To constitute the crime charged there must be a person from whom the property may be taken; an intent to take it against the will of the owner; and some act performed tending to accomplish it,

In this regard, the Respondent's brief relies heavily on *Stokes v. State*,[118] a very articulate opinion that underscores the view that attempt doctrine cannot avoid reliance on fairly general, case-sensitive standards:

> It is useless to undertake to reconcile the authorities on the subject of what constitutes an attempt, or what is an overt act, within the meaning of the section in question. It is equally impossible for us to undertake to lay down any rule on this subject which would serve as a guide in all future cases. To a very great extent each and every case must stand on its own facts. The text-books and decisions are noted for their lack of harmony. It is impossible to decide any case on this subject without doing violence to some author or some adjudicated case. Therefore all we can hope to do is to follow the best authorities and to clear up the subject as best we can, so far as the laws of this state are concerned.[119]

The *Stokes* court also stressed that drawing too sharp—and late—a line between preparation and attempt might cause police to risk public safety in order to ensure a righteous arrest:

> Must the citizen be required to imperil his existence up to the time of the actual menace before he can claim the protection of the law and procure the punishment of the offender? The mere buying of the gun would be preparation, and not attempt. The mere buying of a gun and loading it might not constitute an attempt. But when the facts show, in furtherance of the design, that a gun has been procured and loaded, and the party so procuring and loading the gun has armed himself and started out on his mission to kill, but is prevented from carrying out his design by such extraneous circumstances as that the party he intends to kill does not come to the point where he expected to carry out his design, or if the party designing to kill is arrested and prevented from carrying out the design, he is clearly guilty of the attempt. The public welfare and peace are better subserved, and the lives of citizens better protected, by the holding that these acts constitute criminal attempt, as in fact they do, than would any attempted refinement of the law which would result in a contrary view. . . .

> But, whenever the design of a person to commit crime is clearly shown, slight acts done in furtherance of this design will constitute an attempt, and this court will not destroy the practical and common-sense administration of the law with subtleties as to what constitutes preparation and what an act [must be] done toward the

---

and when these things occur, the crime has, we think, been committed whether property could, in fact, have been stolen or not. . . .

118. 46 So. 627 (Miss. 1908).

119. *Id.* at 628.

commission of a crime. Too many subtle distinctions have been drawn along these lines for practical purposes. Too many loopholes have been made whereby parties are enabled to escape punishment for that which is known to be criminal in its worse sense.[120]

And then the *Stokes* court dismissed the issue of impossibility as a phantom:

> In McClain on Criminal Law, § 226, it is held: Where there is the intent to commit, and an act is done tending to effect the commission thereof, the attempt is punishable, although by reason of extraneous circumstances the actual commission of the crime is impossible....
>
> ... All the authorities hold, that, in order to constitute an attempt, the act attempted must be a possibility; and counsel for appellant argue from this that the appellant could not have committed this crime at the time he was arrested, because Lane [the intended victim] was not even there, and therefore, they say, no conviction could be had. It was no fault of Stokes that the crime was not committed. He had the gun, and the testimony warrants the conclusion that it had been taken for the purpose of killing Lane. It only became impossible by reason of the extraneous circumstance that Lane did not go that way, and, further, that defendant was arrested and prevented from committing the murder. This rule of the law has application only to a case where it is inherently impossible to commit the crime. It has no application to a case where it becomes impossible for the crime to be committed, either by outside interference or because of miscalculation as to a supposed opportunity to commit the crime which fails to materialize; in short, it has no application to the case when the impossibility grows out of extraneous facts not within the control of the party.[121]

The rhetoric here is elegant, as the court demonstrates that any case of failed criminal effort can be viewed in retrospect as having been impossible to achieve if we take the extraneous interrupting circumstances as fixities in the universe. On the other hand, it tempts us with its throwaway point about some acts being "inherently impossible" to achieve, never telling us what might fall into that category. Traditional law school pedagogy often posits such cases. What if Jane, who is eighteen years old, wrongly thinks she is still seventeen and votes in an election? Has she attempted illegal underage voting? Or is this attempted crime truly impossible because Jane will absolutely never be able to violate this law? Or should we fear that her demonstrable willingness to flout the law might find another feasible criminal goal? As for a law

---

120. *Id.* at 628–29.

121. *Id.* at 629.

school classic, what if Bill, who believes in voodoo, uses voodoo technique to harm his enemy? If we assume voodoo cannot work, has Bill nevertheless attempted an assault? Might we fear that he will someday realize he needs a more efficacious weapon?[122] What if Zeke misunderstands the First Amendment and believes it is a crime to insult the Mayor. If he publicly shouts that the Mayor is a fool, has he attempted a crime? What crime? These amusing hypotheticals of course make heroic assumptions about the willingness of bad people to announce their intentions or about our ability or desire to explore their mental interiors. But they do put some intellectual pressure on us to decide what the real goal of attempt law is. Is it to punish the morally culpable who take serious steps toward carrying out their illicit desires? Or is it to deploy the tools of law enforcement and prosecution to thwart dangerous people before they commit some irredeemable harm? Or some combination?

But setting aside these intellectual temptations to explore the meaning of the "inherently impossible," the *Stokes* opinion sums up the common sense of the State's position in *Rizzo*. Unfortunately for the State, however, the Court of Appeals in the *Rizzo* case was not persuaded.

Conclusion: The Rizzo Opinion and After

In 1927, courts were very divided on how to analyze, much less resolve, the varieties of attempt cases. New York's highest court in *Rizzo* took a distinctly narrow, and pro-defendant, view of attempt law. The opinion recites some of the old chestnut formulations of the preparation/attempt boundary:

> Felonious intent alone is not enough, but there must be an overt act shown in order to establish even an attempt. An overt act is one done to carry out the intention, and it must be such as would naturally effect that result, unless prevented by some extraneous cause."[123]

> There must be dangerous proximity to success.[124]

> An act, in order to be a criminal attempt, must be immediately, and not remotely, connected with and directly tending to the commission

---

122. The voodoo hypothetical is not entirely hypothetical. *See* John Kaplan, Robert Weisberg & Guyora Binder, Criminal Law Cases and Materials 712 (7th ed. 2012) (citing case from Mississippi where arrest was made in such a case; but cf. Model Penal Code § 5.05(2) providing for mitigation of sentencing in attempt cases where conduct "is so inherently unlikely to result or culminate in commission of a crime that neither such conduct nor the actor presents a public danger").

123. People v. Rizzo, 158 N.E. 888, 889 (N.Y. 1927) (quoting *People* v. *Mills,* 70 N.E. 786, 789–90 (N.Y. 1904)).

124. *Id.* (quoting *Hyde v. United States* 225 U.S. 347, 388 (1912)).

of an offence.[125]

The acts constituting an attempt as coming *"very near* to the accomplishment of the [crime]."[126]

And as those precedents applied to the facts before it, the Court concluded:

> To constitute the crime of robbery, the money must have been taken from Rao by means of force or violence, or through fear, The crime of attempt to commit robbery was committed if these defendants did an act tending to the commission of this robbery. Did the acts above describe come dangerously near to the taking of Rao's property? Did the acts come so near the commission of robbery that there was reasonable likelihood of its accomplishment but for the interference? Men would not be guilty of an attempt at burglary if they had planned to break into a building and were arrested while they were hunting about the streets for the building not knowing where it was. Neither would a man be guilty of an attempt to commit murder if he armed himself and started out to find the person whom he had planned to kill but could not find him. So here these defendants were not guilty of an attempt to commit robbery in the first degree when they had not found or reached the presence of the person they intended to rob.[127]

There is a kind of doctrinal "takeaway" in the opinion. The Court first acknowledges the case-specificity of attempt law: "The method of committing or attempting crime varies in each case so that the difficulty, if any, is not with this rule of law regarding an attempt, which is well understood, but with its application to the facts."[128] But then, following the case-parsing of the Appellant's Brief, the Court speaks in spatial images of "remoteness" and "proximity" and infers from the pattern of cases under this loose doctrine what it calls the "immediate nearness" rule.[129] Without quite committing to a last act or penultimate act test, the Court straightforwardly announces that "nearness" is the key criterion. Of course "nearness" is not only vague, it is ambiguous in that it can be viewed spatially and temporally at the same time. Moreover, the Court never makes any effort to explain *why* this is or should be the rule.

---

125. *Id.* (quoting Halsbury, 9 Laws of England 259).

126. *Id.* (paraphrasing and quoting *Commonwealth v. Peaslee*, 59 N.E. 55, 56 (Mass. 1901)).

127. People v. Rizzo, 158 N.E. 888, 889 (N.Y. 1927).

128. *Id.*

129. *Id.*

The Court is clearly loath to punish attempt when, despite the evidence of intent, the perpetrators had not advanced very far along the preparation/attempt continuum. But its abruptly conclusory holding leaves it open to multiple and partly conflicting readings. Did the Court accept that Rizzo and his accomplices were morally repugnant but too incompetent to warrant state intervention? Had the police intervened before the point at which we could be confident that the men had truly resolved to commit the crime? Did it allow the men a margin of error to exhibit Hamlet-like indecision? Less plausibly, was this a civil liberties-focused decision in which, while never condemning the police actions here, the Court wanted to dissuade the police from violating the liberty and autonomy of citizens who had not yet caused any demonstrable harm? Or did the Court, while never using the word "impossibility," accept the idea that this case fell into a distinct category whereby, as framed and frozen at the moment of interruption, this was an instance of "legal impossibility." Finally, since the Court nowhere says that the trial judge had misinstructed the jury on the formal elements of the crime, it implicitly holds that a finding of attempt, whether one calls it a question of fact or a mixed question of fact and law, is one on which a jury may merit little deference. Was the Court rejecting the usually deferential insufficiency standard, ruling, in effect, that the trial judge should have yanked the case from the jury? Did these facts so fail the "nearness" test that no reasonable jury could find attempt proved beyond a reasonable doubt?

Whatever the explanation, *People v. Rizzo* stands as a key moment in the history of attempt law—but it ultimately was on the wrong side of history. A generation later, the Model Penal Code formulation was enacted and became fairly dominant across the nation.[130] As noted above, the articulation of the basic elements of attempt under the MPC renders the impossibility doctrine mostly irrelevant. Most cases that could be framed as arguably "impossible attempts" can now be prosecuted as attempts so long as intent and sufficient action are established. Furthermore, the MPC makes it plausible to identify punishable attempt at a relatively early stage on the preparation/attempt line. But the MPC accomplishes those goals with some very sophisticated legal innovations.

For those criminal efforts that fail or are interrupted before the last necessary act occurs, the key question under the MPC is whether the person "purposely does or omits to do anything that, under the circumstances as he believes them to be, is an act or omission constituting a substantial step in a course of conduct planned to culminate in his commission of the crime."[131] Here the key term is "substantial step." It

---

130. Dressler, *Understanding Criminal Law, supra* note 5, at 413.

131. Model Penal Code § 5.01(1).

replaces the old term "overt act," and serves as the MPC's basic definition of the actus reus of attempt. The main role of a "substantial step" is to corroborate intent, and so the focus of MPC attempt law would seem to be on the defendant's mens rea.[132] In that sense, the MPC navigates its way between the moral concern with discerning a culpable state of mind and the instrumental concern with thwarting danger. The drafters thought no greater precision was desirable or even possible, and they make no reference to the last or penultimate act. But the drafters still recognized the need to give further guidance to prosecutors, courts, and juries, and they did so with an unusual combination of substance and procedure. The key innovation in the MPC is that it draws from many of the classic attempt fact patterns a taxonomy of types of conduct that could be fairly viewed as substantial steps, and it enumerates them in some detail, and at the same it declares how application of the substantial step doctrine should be allocated between judge and jury:

> (2) ... Conduct shall not be held to constitute a substantial step ... unless it is strongly corroborative of the actor's criminal purpose. Without negativing the sufficiency of other conduct, the following, if strongly corroborative of the actor's criminal purpose, shall not be held insufficient as a matter of law:
>
> (a) lying in wait, searching for or following the contemplated victim of the crime;
>
> (b) enticing or seeking to entice the contemplated victim of the crime to go to the place contemplated for its commission;
>
> (c) reconnoitering the place contemplated for the commission of the crime;
>
> (d) unlawful entry of a structure, vehicle or enclosure in which it is contemplated that the crime will be committed;
>
> (e) possession of materials to be employed in the commission of the crime, that are specially designed for such unlawful use or which can serve no lawful purpose of the actor under the circumstances;
>
> (f) possession, collection or fabrication of materials to be employed in the commission of the crime, at or near the place contemplated for its commission, where such possession, collection or fabrication serves no lawful purpose of the actor under the circumstances;

---

132. In this regard, the drafters of the MPC viewed the proper focus of attempt law as the subjective culpability of the attemper, not on the dangerousness of his actual conduct: "The proper focus of attention is the actor's disposition." American Law Institute, Model Penal Code, Comment to § 5.01, at 298 (1985).

(g) soliciting an innocent agent to engage in conduct constituting an element of the crime.[133]

This rule gives judges three key chief mandates. First, if the prosecutor can make a reasonable preliminary case that one of the classic
forms of pre-completion conduct has occurred, the judge must send the
case to the jury. Second, the rule *allows* the judge to dismiss the case if
none of the forms of conduct can be proved, though it might allow the
judge to let the case go forward if some unlisted form of conduct seems
"substantial" enough. Third, once the case does go to a properly instructed jury, the trial judge and any appellate court presumably should
let a conviction of attempt stand so long as it meets the traditional
sufficiency of evidence test.

And how would Charles Rizzo et al. have fared under the MPC test?
We can safely say they would not have fared well. Ironically, the comic
narrative of their automobile travels around the Bronx might establish
the searching or following or reconnoitering—or even the lying in wait—
under (a), (b), or (c), although if their guns were *legally* possessed
perhaps (e) and (f) would not apply. And if those actions were enough to
get the case to the jury, and if all the confession evidence were still to
come in, then a jury verdict of guilty would be (1) likely and (2) almost
surely unassailable on appeal under the usual sufficiency of the evidence
standard. On the other hand, changes in procedural rules, most notably
the advent of *Miranda*, and, as a fallback, the *Bruton* rules, might have
rendered inadmissible any evidence of the nature of, or the possible
intent behind, preliminary but arguably substantial steps. Of course,
were modern police to encounter the very same circumstances that
Sullivan and Cronin saw on the Bronx streets in 1927, they might still
choose to exert their *Terry* power to detain the suspects and take steps
that might thwart the crime, even if they are unable to develop evidence
that could justify arrest or conviction.

A Coda

In 1927, New York's sentencing rules for attempted first-degree
robbery were very flexible and severe, and highly contingent on the
background, especially the criminal records, of defendants. By virtue of
these rules, after a brief hearing on aggravation and mitigation, the trial
judge gave Thomasello a sentence of 10 to 20 years, Milo 25 years, and
Rizzo and Dorio each 7½ to 15 years. One would think that all of them
would have appealed, given the extremely severe sentences, yet history
records only the appeal of Rizzo. Perhaps, as the scion of the lathing
firm, Rizzo alone had access to funding for the appeal. But when the
Court of Appeals reversed Rizzo's conviction, obviously recognizing no

---

133.   Model Penal Code § 5.01(2).

retrial was possible because the state had already taken its best shot at proving attempt, the Court took the unusual step of acknowledging a moral dilemma it had no legal power to solve on its own.

> A very strange situation has arisen in this case. I called attention to the four defendants who were convicted of this crime of an attempt to commit robbery in the first degree. They were all tried together upon the same evidence, and jointly convicted, and all sentenced to State's prison for varying terms. Rizzo was the only one of the four to appeal to the Appellate Division and to this court. His conviction was affirmed by the Appellate Division by a divided court, two of the justices dissenting, and we have now held that he was not guilty of the crime charged. If he were not guilty, neither were the other three. As the others, however, did not appeal, there is no remedy for them through the court; their judgments stand, and they must serve their sentences. This of course is a situation which must in all fairness be met in some way. Two of these men were guilty of the crime of carrying weapons, pistols, contrary to law, for which they could be convicted. Two of them, John Thomasello and Thomas Milo, had also been previously convicted, which may have had something to do with their neglect to appeal. However, the law would fail in its function and its purpose if it permitted these three men whoever or whatever they are to serve a sentence for a crime which the courts subsequently found and declared had not been committed. We, therefore, suggest to the district attorney of Bronx county that he bring the cases of these three men to the attention of the Governor to be dealt with as to him seems proper in the light of this opinion.[134]

The Court of Appeals was not alone in viewing this as a dilemma to be passed on to another branch. According to a dramatically headlined newspaper story (*3 Youths Innocent, But Can't Be Freed*), the head Bronx District Attorney, Mr. McGeehan, admitted that he was "puzzled as to the action he should take.... I do not feel that it would be fair to embarrass the Governor with a request for a pardon for these men.... I have decided to ask the court in Bronx County to act next week when I will have the men brought down on a writ of habeas corpus."[135]

The equity issue seems to be a kind of accidental aspect of the case, but it indentifies an important point of jurisprudence. Attempt law shares with accomplice law questions of how to impute liability when the harm against which the substantive law is aimed never occurs. Because

---

134. *Rizzo*, 158 N.E. at 890. Ironically, Adlerman himself prefigured this quandary when he attacked Rizzo as the ringleader-mastermind and said to the jury that "if Rizzo is going to be acquitted here, acquit the other three." COA, *supra* note 9, at 357.

135. *3 Youths Innocent, But Can't Be Freed*, N.Y. Times, Dec. 11, 1927, at N1.

attempt law then becomes so heavily dependent on mens rea and on preliminary acts that may confirm mens rea, it raises the possibility of differential liability among accomplices to an attempt.

In any event, while we do not know the fate of the District Attorney's habeas corpus maneuver,[136] the moral dilemma was resolved when the fear of embarrassing the State's chief executive proved unfounded. On January 30, 1928, shortly before he became the Democratic Presidential nominee against Herbert Hoover, New York Governor Al Smith announced the pardoning of Thomasello, Milo, and Dorio.[137]

This picture of a 1927 Paige sedan is likely similar to the one that Rizzo and his accomplices drove. The picture is part of the Richard Paige collection and is available at the *<http://www.wcroberts.org/Paige_History/1927_Paige.html>*, last visited Oct. 15, 2012).

---

136. Thanks to the colorfully named website politicalgraveyard.com, we do know something of the fate of the District Attorney himself. Adlerman, like many prosecutors, next became a judge (of the City Court in the Bronx), and he died in 1941 at age 62.

137. Pardon certificates signed by Governor Smith (on file with author).

10

Leo Katz

The Story of *Tally*: Judge Tally and the Problem of the Superfluous Accomplice

Scottsboro, Ala., Feb. 19–(Special)– This afternoon at 5:20 the argument closed in the sensational, most tragic, and most interesting preliminary trial that was ever before a Jackson county court. The argument was begun at 8 a.m. by Judge Richard Walker for the State, then followed in succession Capt. Shelby, Virgil Boudin, Geo. Hunt and Judge Richardson for the defense and then closed in a two hour speech by Col. Clift for the State. Such an array of legal talent was never before equaled in this county. Solicitor Hunt did not speak. The case was tried before Probate Judge Bridges. A few minutes after the argument closed the court decided to give the defendants bail and fixed the bond of each of $7000 $28,000 for the four. Public sentiment and opinion is very much divided. Business here for the past two weeks has been almost on a stand still. Little is being said by the natives, but a good deal of thinking is being done. *—The Daily Advertiser, Montgomery, Alabama February 19, 1894*

What Happened

The killing. There lived in the Alabama town of Scottsboro, circa 1893, a married man named Robert C. Ross, who entered into an affair with an unmarried young woman named Ann Skelton This Ann Skelton had four intemperate brothers, who blamed Ross for seducing their sister and resolved to kill him. For a while, Ross went into hiding outside of Scottsboro, but then he felt compelled to return because his wife had fallen ill. He stayed for just a few days, secluded in his house, evidently hoping no one would learn of his return, and then sought to leave again.

Accompanied by some family friends, everyone armed to the hilt, he drove his horse-drawn coach to the nearby town of Stevenson, there expecting to catch the train to Chattanooga. He never made it onto the train: The Skelton brothers had learned of his whereabouts, managed to catch up with him in front of the train depot, and finished him off in a hail of bullets.

The telegram. The killing became a *cause célèbre* in Alabama. Not because of any of the facts I have described so far, very little about which sets this killing apart from many other un-celebrated ones. Nor even because the Skelton name enjoyed some prominence in these parts. The reason rather was a somewhat tangential aspect of the case, which gave it both its tabloid and its legal interest. The Skelton brothers had a second sister, who happened to be married to a prominent Alabama judge, one John B. Tally. Tally had learned about the Ross affair and apparently approved of the way the Skeltons were about to deal with it. Although he did not actually participate in the killing, he did get involved in it in a more marginal way, and thereby gave rise to the thorny legal issue for which this case entered the casebooks.

While Ross was traveling to Stevenson and the Skelton brothers were chasing him there, one of Ross's cousins found out what was going on and decided to send a warning telegram to Stevenson telling Ross "Four men on horseback with guns following. Look out." Judge Tally happened to see this cousin of Ross just as he was leaving the telegraph office and easily guessed what he must have been doing there. Tally thereupon decided he would try to prevent the warning telegram from reaching Ross. He did so by mailing a telegram of his own to the telegraph operator of Stevenson, whom he knew. Tally's telegram read: "Don't let the party warned get away. Say nothing. Signed John B. Tally." Both telegrams arrived in Stevenson, and Ross never got his warning. Whether that was on account of Tally's request, or because there simply wasn't time enough to get it to him, was unclear—and became the subject of much debate and litigation.

What the Authorities Did About It

First, "William L. Martin, the Attorney General of the State of Alabama, in his own proper person, and for the said State, filed [an] information in writing against the said John B. Tally, as Judge of the Ninth Judicial Circuit of the State of Alabama, setting forth and charging that the said defendant has been guilty of willful neglect of duty and of an offense involving moral turpitude while in said office of Judge of the Ninth Judicial Circuit."[1] The information was presented to a grand jury, not, it seems, for the immediate purpose of trying Tally for murder—although that of course was supposed to happen as well—but

---

1. Information filed by Alabama Attorney General, William L. Martin (on file with author).

for the purpose of laying the foundation for an impeachment proceeding against him to get him removed from his judicial office. The indictment began with a more detailed recounting of the above-summarized facts, to-wit:

> That on Sunday the 4th day of February, 1894, in the county of Jackson, State of Alabama, John Skelton, Robert S. Skelton, Walter A. Skelton and James Skelton unlawfully and with malice aforethought killed Robert C. Ross, at Stevenson in said county of Jackson, by shooting him with a gun, that said Tally is and was at the time of said homicide the brother-in-law of the three last named Skeltons; that on said day and about the hour of six o'clock in the morning the said Robert C. Ross left the town of Scottsboro in said county traveling a distance of about eighteen miles to the town of Stevenson in said county at which point he intended to board a railroad train for some point beyond; that within one hour after the departure of said Ross from said town of Scottsboro on said Sunday morning as aforesaid, the said John Skelton, Robert S. Skelton, Walter A. Skelton and James Skelton armed themselves with guns, mounted horses and set out from said town of Scottsboro in pursuit of the said Ross and for the purpose of overtaking him and taking his life, and in pursuance of such purpose the said Skeltons did overtake the said Ross and did take his life, at said town of Stevenson, at or about the hour of eleven o'clock on said Sunday morning.[2]

The indictment charged Tally, first, with failing to restrain the Skeltons from their endeavor when it was his duty and within his power to do so. More concretely, it alleged

> that at and prior to the time when the said Skeltons left said town of Scottsboro in pursuit of said Ross as aforesaid, said Tally, who was there and present, knew of the intention and purpose of the said Skeltons to take the life of the said Ross and said Tally then and there had the capacity and power to exercise a restraining and controlling influence over the said Skeltons in the matter aforesaid and to prevent the commission by them of the said homicide; but said Tally then and there willfully failed to take any step to compel the said Skeltons to desist from their unlawful purpose to take the life of said Ross.[3]

The indictment's second complaint against Tally was that he had actively encouraged the Skelton's in their plan.

The third complaint, finally, related to the telegram, namely:

---

2. *Id.*

3. *Id.*

that after the said Skeltons had set out in pursuit of the said Ross
... and before the result of their ... pursuit was known to him, ...
Tally went to the telegraph office in the town of Scottsboro for the
purpose of their guarding against the transmission of any telegraphic message which would cause interference with the Skeltons in the
execution of their purpose ..., and while ... Tally was at [the]
telegraph office, one E. H. Ross, after being informed that the ...
Skeltons were in pursuit of ... Robert C. Ross, handed to the
telegraph operator at that office a message to be transmitted to ...
Robert C. Ross, at Stevenson, warning him that the ... Skeltons
were in pursuit ..., and to be on the lookout for them [;] Tally ...
read or learned the contents of said message of warning whereupon
[he] invited and handed to the operator to be transmitted to William
Huddleston at Stevenson, a message in words and figures substantially as follows: "Don't let the party warned get away. Say nothing.
Signed John B. Tally." which said message was then ... transmitted
to the said Huddleston at Stevenson, immediately after the transmission of the ... message of warning from ... E.H. Ross to Robert
C. Ross, and said two messages were at once viewed by the telegraph
operator at Stevenson who was none other than the said Wm.
Huddleston[;] ... Tally intended, by means of his ... message to
... Huddleston, to hinder the delivery to by him of said message of
warning ... and to aid and abet the ... Skelton[s] in their purpose.[4]

How the Trial Went

The indictment was followed by a trial of a highly unusual sort.
Since it was not a murder trial but an impeachment proceeding, it was to
take place before the Alabama Supreme Court, the Justices sitting as
both the finders of fact and of law. To compound the unusual nature of
the proceedings, the court, "to facilitate the hearing of the case, and to
subserve convenience and necessity of the witnesses, ... consented to
take the evidence and hear the arguments ... at Huntsville, near the
scene" of the crime, *but not to do so while sitting as a court.* As the court
explained it, "we were careful, while sitting at Huntsville as individual
members of the court, and not as the court itself, to avoid the attempted
exercise of all judicial power. Hence it is that we made no rulings as to
the admissibility of testimony except of a tentative and advisory nature,
and hence it is also that much incompetent testimony was received,
subject to objections noted at the time and ... now to be stricken out
and excluded." It insisted that "[t]his course, under the circumstances,
the triers of the facts and the judges of the competency of proposed
testimony being the same, and under a necessity, for the most part, to
know what the offered testimony is before passing upon its admissibility,

---

4. *Id.*

whether the ruling is to be presently or subsequently made, involved no prejudice, to either party and we believe, facilitated the hearing in this instance."[5]

The resulting fairly informal proceeding is described in three "Specials" to Montgomery's *Daily Advertiser*, the paper of record—three articles, which despite their grammatical deficiencies, incomplete sentences, missing quotation marks, and general air of unkemptness (or perhaps because of these), I could do no better than to quote in full:

> **HUNTSVILLE, JULY 3—(SPECIAL)**—Interest increases in Judge Tally's impeachment trial as the evidence begins to be more germane to the issue. Thirteen witnesses were examined today, all of Scottsboro.
>
> John Calloway, colored, was in the employ of Ross as a family servant, and went in a hack with the Ross party to Stevenson to take charge of valises. Calloway did not know anything of any contemplated trouble when they left Scottsboro, and Ross gave him no intimation of it, or where they were going. Supposed Ross was going away south by way of Sand Mountain, like he did when he left about the 7th of January.
>
> The remainder of the evidence of the witnesses, except the last three, was confined to the movements of the Skelton boys in Scottsboro on the morning of February 4th, about the streets getting guns, horses and who was seen with them and when leaving.
>
> C.W. Hunt testified to seeing Judge Tally and Bob Skelton together at the latter's office Saturday evening, February 3rd, but thought nothing unusual of it.
>
> Several of the other witnesses saw Judge Tally on the streets of Scottsboro Sunday morning talking to Bob for a few minutes.
>
> Gregory was coming from Chattanooga on a train with Judge Tally Friday night before the killing. Judge Tally had been off holding court and was telling witness about the number of murder trials he had before him. Witness remarked that they would likely have some killing in Scottsboro, and Judge Tally asked:
>
> "Why do you think so?"
>
> Witness replied:
>
> "Well, Ross has come back home and the Skelton boys are on the war-path."

---

5. State v. Tally 15 So. 722, 724 (Ala. 1894).

This latter was from mere street talk and rumor. Judge Tally said to witness that he did not think Ross would remain in Scottsboro or leave, or something like that.

Matt Snodgrass was at gold's livery stable early Sunday morning, February 4th. Judge Tally's son came and got one horse, a boy named John, and Jim Skelton got three. John's horse was ridden by one of the Skelton boys, as stated by one of the witnesses and Gold stated that Judge Tally paid for this horse, together with other items in account, and it was a frequent thing for Mrs. Tally to order horses from the stable.

No part of the foregoing evidence showed that Judge Tally knew what the Skelton boys was up to or had any knowledge of his son getting the horse, or anything about it.

Whitner, telegraph operator, stated that after the passenger train going west passed Sunday morning the 4th of February, Ed Ross asked him to go down to the office which was in the freight depot about one hundred or so yards below the passenger depot, that he wanted to send a message. They went down together and he sent this telegram for him to R.C. Ross, Stevenson, about 10:25.

"Four men on horseback in pursuit, armed, lookout."

Ed Ross said to me:

"I don't want any one to know anything about this," and went out.

Judge Tally came in before Ross finished writing the message and handed it to him (Whitner). Judge Tally wrote a message and called in Judge Bridges, who was passing. They talked privately a few minutes when Judge Tally came back and handed me his message which read (witness quoting from memory as to both the messages) William Huddleston Stevenson, "Don't let party warned get away. Say nothing."

The original telegram sent by Judge Tally is lost and cannot be found. Witness missed it when he checked up the files on February 6th. When Judge Tally handed his telegram to witness he said it had connection with the one you have in your hand, meaning the Ross telegram.

Judge Bridges testified that in the conversation before alluded to when Judge Tally wrote the message, Judge Tally said to him in substance:

"What do you reckon that young man, or fellow, the operator would think if I should tell him that I would put him out of this room before he should send that telegram" to which witness protested when he said:

"I do not want that telegram sent and I am going to send this one." showing witness the one he had written to Huddleston. Witness' recollection is that it was given to Whitner.[6]

HUNTSVILLE, JULY 5—(SPECIAL)—Upon the convening of court this morning the defendant, Judge Tally, was placed on the stand and his examination consumed most of the day. He made a manly, straightforward statement, acquitted himself most creditably and an able, adroit cross-examination failed to weaken it in any material point.

His statement went into details of where he was during January and up of February 4th, where he had held court, when he came home and why. There never was any understanding between he and Skeltons, that he was to be telegraphed to while away from home. He never knew or heard that Skeltons intended any violence to Ross until after they had left Scottsboro on the 4th of February.

The first intimation he ever had of Ross's relations with Annie Skelton was the 4th of January. On the 6th he asked Bob about it and read the letters he had from Ross to Annie. They agreed that the plan to be pursued was to get Annie home, let Ross go away, and save the publicity of the scandal and the life of her old mother. In this conversation, Dave Skelton was present and he spoke of killing Ross but witness never saw Dave again till after the killing and this was the only time violence to Ross was ever mentioned by Skelton to his knowledge.

On the 3rd of February he again saw Bob and discussed the way to find where Annie was and agreed to get Brown, Ross's attorney, or Dr. Rorex, his family physician, to see Ross and find out. Saw Bob Sunday morning about 8 o'clock on horse-back, asked him twice where he was going and he would only say "Up the road."

After he had gone some time, his wife told him what was up and that was the first he knew of it. His wife sent their son to the stable for the horse, John, without his knowledge or intimation whatever.

Judge Tally then told all about going to the depot telegraph office and then running into Judge Bridges, and while he did not recollect what passed exactly, as they detailed they might remember better, owing to his trouble and great mental strain

---

6.   The Daily Advertiser (Montgomery, Ala.), on dates indicated.

at that time. Remember only saying to Rorex: "I am so broke up I don't know what to do." Was alarmed for his brother-in-law and sent a telegram to Huddleston, knowing he was Mayor, to have Ross arrested, believing if Ross was advised of Skelton's coming, his party, if they got to Stevenson first, would place themselves in position to kill the Skeltons as they came up. Can't tell why I used the language I did; I saw afterwards it was not such as I thought to have used and went back to change it, but the operator was gone. Used words, 'say nothing,' to prevent publicity of scandal and to avoid to trouble with the Skelton boys by my interference.

Went to the telegraph office after the killing to get the address of Sinclair Randall of the Conservatory of Music at Cincinnati who had previously telegraphed him that Annie was there. Never had telegram file any time alone. Gooch Dieus, brother Odd Fellow of Ross went to his house Friday afternoon before the killing at Ross's request. Through Jim Kyle. Ross wanted me to get this withdrawal card which I was to do next Monday night and see him Tuesday. He asked me what people said as to where Annie Skelton was and I told him some said she was in Scottsboro with the Skeltons and some said he, Ross, had her somewhere. Ross replied that the Skeltons did not, but he knew where she was and would see her again. I advised to stop that or the Skelton boys would kill him and he replied "It was worth the risk."

Jim Skelton seeing me at Ross's asked me Saturday night if Ross told me where Annie was and I said no, but that he said he knew and would see her again. He then asked me to see Ross and find out where she was which I was to do the next Saturday. Am a friend of both Ross and the Skeltons.[7]

HUNTSVILLE, JULY 6—(SPECIAL)—The evidence in the Tally impeachment trial was concluded this afternoon at 4:30 o'clock and the argument will be made tomorrow, but the opinion of the court will be announced later at Montgomery. Attorney General Martin and Judge R W Walker will present the argument for the prosecution and Hons. John A Turk of Gunersville and David D. Shelby of this city, for the defense.

W J Tally, brother of Judge Tally, was in Stevenson the 4th of February and saw the shooting. Did not know where the Judge was and had no agreement to be there that day. Had not seen or heard from him since the 17th of January, when they

7. *Id.*

buried their mother. Had just left Ross when the firing began, and thought he was shooting at him, turned and asked him

"What are you shooting at me for?"

James, Robert and Walter A "Tot" Skelton where introduced and all consistently corroborated Judge Tally as to when they first heard of the relations between Ross and heir sister Annie; the plan to get her home, to keep the matter hushed and let Ross leave the country without violence. This agreement and plan was adhered to up to Sunday morning, the 4th of February. Neither of them ever at any time spoke to Judge Tally about any other feature of the matter. There was no agreement or understanding whatever with Judge Talley to send a telegram to Stevenson nor one to be sent him, Judge Tally did not know from them where they were going that morning, nor their purpose, for they did not know when they left where they would go.

They first thought Ross would cross the river and go south as formerly, until they saw back tracks leading to Stevenson, when they then thought he was to meet their sister Annie there and followed him to prevent it.

Walter stayed Saturday night at Bob's; got up very early and met the train east-bound. It is his habit to rise early and like others in town, to meet trains. He saw the Ross party between 5 and 6 o clock at his stable with guns, arranging to leave, and watched their track to see their direction. Went to Bob and tried to get a horse to pursue them, but he refused one, saying that was no use; too far ahead; can't overtake them. Then went to see Mrs. Tally, and she sent her son to get me a horse from the stable and brought to me half mile from town. Did not see Judge Tally.

All three gave details of getting horses and guns and leaving to pursue Ross only to prevent his going to meet their sister Annie. Agreed in that before leaving.

Bob corroborated Judge Tally as to the letter, his asking him (witness) where he was going and not telling him. Bob, Jim and John overtook Walter about a mile and a half out of town. Bob's relations with Ross were of the friendliest character, and he thought Ross the best friend he had on earth. Jim slept at Judge Tally's Saturday night, where he lived. He eat no breakfast. He was corroborated by John Proctor, a young lawyer who lived at Judge Tally's and who roomed and slept with Jim.

Proctor went to bed at his usual time, 10 or 11, and Jim had already gone to bed. Proctor saw none of the Skeltons Sunday morning except Jim. Eat breakfast and dinner about the time stated by Judge Tally who was there.

The Skelton boys stated they first saw the Ross party back when crossing the creek about one mile west of Stevenson. Bob and Jim got down, hitched their horses and walked up on the opposite side of the railroad from the road the hack went, walked fast and ran part of the way.

When Bob got to the depot platform he saw Ross get out and shake hands with Will Tally. When I saw Bloodworth's gun leveled on me I dodged down, raised up and fired at him. Then saw Ross trying to shoot me across his horses and I fired at him. Next saw Ross at the coal house with gun in his hand, when John fired and killed him. Under the excitement I went up and about him again when down, for which I am sorry. At that time, I did not know whether my brothers had been hurt or killed in the fight. Bloodworth was the first one who made any demonstration to shoot.

Jim was fifty feet behind Bob. Saw him dodging and then shoot.

The first Walter saw was Bloodworth's gun up and then heard gun fire. Bloodworth ran and I then fired at Ross. I then stepped back behind a telegraph pole to fixe cartridge, which got hitched. I then saw John shoot Ross.

In rebuttal, State proved by J P Harris of Scottsboro that he learned from Jesse E Brown first where Annie Skelton was and the on February 2nd Ross told him where he was and that Ross said he was done with the Annie Skelton affair and was going to move to Harnsville, Ga. to live, that he had trouble enough.

Jesse E Brown proved that Ross told him about the 12th of January that Annie Skelton was at the Conservatory of Music in Cincinnati and he (Brown) told this to a number of people in Scottsboro. About that time, Mrs. Tally was at his house to see him, to learn where she was but he was away from home. Wrote her a note he would give her any information he could.

The letters were introduced subject to exceptions, and will be argued.[8]

What the Court Concluded

The court's opinion is a long one, as homicide cases go. But of course this was no mere homicide case: It involved a judicial impeachment, and

---

8. *Id.*

it required lengthy fact-findings of the sort not usually recorded in judicial opinions, because they are typically matters for a jury. The fact-finding process turned up some amusing-to-intriguing tidbits. We learn for instance that the first lawyer Tally consulted had also served as Ross's lawyer—a quaint reminder of the small town interconnectedness of all actors in this drama. We learn of this tidbit because the question arises whether communications between Tally and the lawyer are covered by the attorney-client privilege. (The court says yes.) In the same vein, we learn another amusing small town fact: the telegraph operator in Stevenson, one Huddleston, the fellow who received Tally's instruction not to deliver the warning telegraph, was not merely the town's telegraph operator but also its mayor.

We also learn some intriguing facts about the trial itself, which the newspaper—in its open sympathy for the defendants—failed to mention: how, in the course of his testimony, Tally was caught in a barefaced lie concerning the contents of his telegram:

> The original of [Tally's telegram] was placed on a file in the office at Scottsboro. Two days after, a search was made for it, and it could not be found, and has never been found. The one man in the world most interested in its destruction, the respondent in this case, in the meantime had had an opportunity to abstract it, he having had access to this file, and gone through the messages on it, for the purpose, he said then, and says now, of finding the address of a person to whom he had sent a message some days before. And on the preliminary examination of the Skeltons before the probate judge of Jackson county, of the murder of Ross, Judge Tally was called and examined as a witness for them, and before a copy of this message was produced by the operator, and hence at a time when Judge Tally was not aware that a copy was in existence, this question was put to him: "You didn't send any dispatch that morning to Stevenson?" And his answer was: "Yes, Sir, I sent one, but not about this matter. It was to a friend about another matter, nothing concerning this case."[9]

A final curious tidbit is the tortured interpretation by which Tally attempts to put an innocent face on that seemingly irrebuttably incriminating telegram. He argues, for instance, that when he wrote "Do not let the party referred to get away" he only meant that Ross was to be given the warning telegram but then immediately arrested—by Huddleston, who was of course not only the telegraph operator, but also the sheriff. Ridiculous, said the court:

> The word "arrest" is a most common one, and in almost universal use. We cannot conceive of any man, and especially not of a lawyer

---

9. State v. Tally 15 So. 722, 728 (Ala. 1894).

and a judge, employing any other word and especially when a resort is had to telegraphic communication express the idea which this suggestion imputes to Tally, a lawyer and a judge. Then, too ... there was no ground for Ross's arrest.[10]

Nor is the court much moved by Tally's claim that his use of the phrase "Say nothing" was merely meant to keep Huddleston from disclosing "his [Tally's] connection with the message."

Before getting to the heart of the matter, the court then makes a number of somewhat puzzling legal points. It explains at some length why neither Tally nor the Skeltons are entitled to the partial defense of provocation, which would have reduced their guilt from murder to manslaughter. Too much time had passed, the court says, between the time they learned of Ross's affair with Annie and the time at which they chose to act. What is strange about the court's discussion of provocation is why they think it is necessary. Since they are merely investigating whether Judge Tally deserves to be removed from office, it seems relatively insignificant whether he was involved in a murder or a "mere" manslaughter. Surely committing manslaughter is sufficient for removing him.

Another oddity is the court's handling of the charge that Tally was willfully derelict in his judicial duties when he participated in this killing. Since he was not acting in his capacity as a judge, it seems very peculiar to describe what he did as a dereliction of his judicial duties. To be sure, his misconduct disqualifies him from continuing as a judge, but not because he was thereby derelict in his judicial duties. Now, as it turns out, the court ultimately dismisses this charge, but on some other ground, namely that Tally did not actually know about the Skeltons' endeavor as they left town, and thus was in no position to try to restrain them. (But what about trying to restrain them by sending *them* a warning telegraph via the Stevenson office?)

A final oddity has to do with the court's disposition of Tally's testimony about his true, and as he insisted, benign intentions in sending the telegram; They rejected the testimony under a bizarre rule of evidence that disallows a person from testifying as to his own past thoughts.

The heart of the case is of course the issue of complicity. The court concludes that Judge Tally did not become an accomplice by virtue of any encouragement he gave the Skeltons:

There is ... no affirmative evidence that Judge Tally knew, until after the Skeltons had gone, that they intended to take the life of Ross. There were circumstances proved which, unexplained might

---

10. *Id.* at 734

have justified, indeed, would have justified, the inference that he did. But explanations have been made which are either affirmatively satisfactory or cast such reasonable doubt on the conclusions to which without the explanation the circumstances would have led us, that we do not feel justified in adopting the conclusion. For instance, the hiring of the horse which Walter rode. As presented by the state, in all its boldness, that fact was most incriminating. But when taken in connection with the fact [that it was really ordered by his wife, while he was still asleep]; that it was charged to him because ordered by his wife, and paid for by him, after the circumstances of the hiring and use of the animal had been used in the public mind to connect him with the tragedy, because by the course of previous dealing between him and the liveryman, in respect of orders by his wife, he was under both a moral and a legal obligation to pay, its probative force against him is utterly destroyed. The presence that morning of Walter Skelton is a circumstance of suspicion, and would be of incrimination, but for the fact which is shown by other evidence than Tally's and against which nothing has been offered affording a contrary inference even, that Walter had come and gone before Tally got out of bed, in an upstairs room. Again, the naked fact that John came there after Tally had arisen, armed and mounted, has of course a natural tendency to show that Tally knew the purpose of such unwonted and warlike preparation on that day, when to ride about the country with guns is such an unusual thing. But according to the testimony, not only of Tally and Robert Skelton, but also of Mr. Shelley, a witness for the defense, and of Mr. Snodgrass, a witness for the state, the respondent [i.e. Tally] was at that time in his barn lot, or next it, in the side street, from which point he could see neither James Skelton in the house nor his gun standing against the front gate, nor his horse hitched in the street in front of the house and gate. . . .

We conclude this part of the case by saying that we do not find that Judge Tally had any knowledge of the intention of the Skeltons to kill Ross before or at the time of their departure or pursuit of him.[11]

Whether Tally was an accomplice thus comes down to answering two questions about what he did *after* the Skeltons had left town in pursuit of Ross. One is legal; the other factual. The legal question was simply: "[I]s it essential to Tally's guilt [that his actions] contributed to the effectuation of the [Skeltons'] design to the death of Ross?"[12] (And if not essential, what sort of contribution is required for Tally to be

---

11. *Id.* at 731.
12. *Id.* at 735.

guilty?) The factual question then simply is whether by sending his
telegram he acted in the requisite way.

It is the answer to the first question that made this case important.
The court concludes that Tally's contribution to Ross's death

> need not contribute to the criminal result in the sense that but for it
> the result would not have ensued. It is quite sufficient if it facilitat-
> ed a result that would have transpired without it. It is quite enough
> if the aid merely rendered it easier for the principal actor to
> accomplish the end intended by him and the aider and abettor,
> though in all human probability the end would have been attained
> without it. If the aid in homicide can be shown to have put the
> deceased at a disadvantage, to have deprived him a single chance of
> life, which but for it he would have had, he who furnishes such aid is
> guilty, though it cannot be known or shown that the dead man, in
> the absence thereof would have availed himself of that chance, as
> where one counsels murder, he is guilty as an accessory before the
> fact, though it appears to be probable that murder would have been
> done without his counsel; and as, where one being present by
> concert to aid if necessary is guilty as a principal in the second
> degree, though, had he been absent murder would have been com-
> mitted, so where he who facilitates murder even by so much as
> destroying a single chance of life the assailed might otherwise have
> had, he thereby supplements the efforts of the perpetrators and he is
> guilty as principal in the second degree at common law, and is
> principal in the first degree under our statute, notwithstanding it
> may be found that in all human probability the chance would not
> have been availed of, and death would have resulted anyway.[13]

As to whether Tally did in fact "put the deceased at a disadvantage,
[and] deprived him [of] a single chance of life, which but for it he would
have had," the court says yes. Huddleston, the court concludes, might
well have delivered the warning telegram, if not dissuaded in doing so by
Tally's countermand:

> [Ed Ross's warning of his kinsman] reached Huddleston ..., we
> suppose, about five minutes—certainly not more than ten minutes—
> before Ross arrived at Stevenson. Immediately upon the heels of it,
> substantially at the same time, Tally's message to Huddleston was
> received by the latter. Ed Ross's message imported extreme urgency
> in its delivery and Tally's to Huddleston though by no means so
> intended, emphasized the necessity and importance from the stand-
> point of duty, for the earliest possible delivery of Ed Ross's message
> to Robert C. Ross; and it was the manifest duty of Huddleston to
> deliver it at the earliest practicable moment of time. Huddleston

---

13. *Id.* at 736.

appears to have appreciated the urgency of the case, and at first to have intended doing his duty. Upon receiving the two messages, he went at once without waiting, to copy them, to the Stevenson Hotel, which is located very near the telegraph office in question, on the assumption that [Ross] might already have arrived. We are to presume a purpose to do what duty enjoins until the contrary appears; and we therefore shall assume that Huddleston intended to deliver the message to Ross, or to inform him of its contents, had he been in the hotel. Not finding him there (for he had not yet reached Stevenson).

Huddleston returned to the door of the depot, upstairs, in which was the telegraph office. By this time the command which Judge Tally had laid upon him had overmastered his sense of duty, and diverted him from his purpose to deliver Ed Ross's message to Robert. . . .[14]

And if Ross had gotten the warning, would that have saved his life? Quite possibly, the court concludes. To be sure, the court acknowledges, "being [forewarned], and not knowing of the immediate proximity of the Skeltons, it may be that Ross would have alighted as he did, exposed himself to the Skeltons' fire as he did, and been killed as he was." On the other hand, "he might then and there have put himself under the protection of Huddleston, as an officer of the law, and had the bystanders, those in the immediate neighborhood, of whom there were several, summoned to help protect him. This might have saved his life; it was a chance that he had." And even if he had not done that, "yet, when the first shot was fired, Ross would have known that the man who fired it was one of the Skeltons, and that three others of them were present in ambush, armed with guns to take his life." Had the warning been so delivered, the court surmises, it would probably have led Ross to make a dash for the nearby Union hotel, rather than remaining out in the open, as he did. "[I]n making that effort he would have gone away from the lurking places of his enemies, and he would not, as he did in his ignorance of the true situation, have placed himself where John Skelton, at close quarter, could and did shoot him to death from behind his back."[15] But whether things would or would not have played out exactly in this way, the court says is not really important:

> [W]hether he would or would not have reached a place of refuge we need not inquire or find. The knowledge that he would have had if the telegram of Ed Ross had been delivered to him, when it could and should have been delivered, of the pursuit of the Skeltons, together with the knowledge which would have been imparted to him by the report of the first shot in connection with the contents of

---

14. *Id.* at 739.

15. *Id.*

the message would instantly have advised him of the extent of his danger, a danger which he could not combat, which was deadly in character, and from which he would naturally have been at once impressed the only hope of escape lay in immediate flight. That was a chance for his life that this knowledge would have given him. That was a chance of which the withholding of this knowledge deprived him. [In other words,] Ross's predicament was rendered infinitely more desperate, his escape more difficult, and his death of much more easy and certain accomplishment by the withholding from him of the message of Ed Ross. This withholding was the work of Judge Tally. An intent to aid the Skeltons to take the life of Ross actuated him to it. The intent was effectuated. They thereby were enabled to take him unawares, and to send him to his death without, we doubt not, his ever actually knowing who sought his life, or being able to raise a hand in defense, or to take an advised step in retreat.[16]

Why the Case Became Important

Ordinarily, one is liable for a crime if one caused some harm—at least where the crime in question is a "result crime," like homicide or the infliction of some other kind of loss. (Not all crimes are "result crimes": some simply require the doing of something—like gambling, or the sale of illegal drugs.) That means that the defendant's actions must be such that "but for" these actions the harm would not have occurred, and the harm must not be "too remote or accidental to have just bearing" on his culpability. In other words, the harm must be "proximate." Put differently yet, he must have made a contribution to the eventual outcome that was both crucial and direct.

This at least is how we deal with things when assessing the guilt of a solitary actor committing a crime. Matters grow more complicated where several people collaborate in the commission of a crime. At first glance, it is not easy to say why anything really has changed. It would seem natural to still insist that for the participant in a jointly committed crime to be liable for that crime he must have made a crucial and direct contribution to the harmful outcome. What that would mean in the context of the *Tally* case is that Judge Tally could not be liable for the death of Ross unless (a) "but for" his intervention Ross would not have died, and (b) his intervention fairly directly led to that death. Neither (a) nor (b), it seems, are met. (a) is not met because we cannot be sure beyond a reasonable doubt that if the warning telegram whose delivery he tried to block had in fact reached Ross, he would have managed to escape the Skeltons. It is possible that he would have, according to the various scenarios laid out by the court. But those are just possibilities.

---

16. *Id.*

We simply cannot be as sure as we usually insist on being before finding someone guilty. Even if we could be sure that the warning telegram made a crucial difference to the outcome, we still would have reason to doubt whether Tally's intervention *directly* caused Ross's death. The problem is that between Tally's intervention and Ross's death a further set of actions intervened, those of the Skeltons. Ordinarily, the intentional actions of human beings are held to break the chain of proximate causation between the defendant's actions and the ultimate outcome.

The doctrine so clearly announced in *Tally* dispenses with this usual approach when it comes to complicity. It is not the first case to so hold. But it is particularly explicit, and it does so in the context of a case in which the difference that principle makes is particularly obvious. This caused the Model Penal Code drafters to cite the case in their commentary to the newly proposed complicity section,[17] whence it made its way into the leading casebooks as the staple case on actus reus of complicity, that is, on the question of what contribution a crime participant must have made before he can be reckoned an accomplice. American casebooks typically present the *Tally* holding as an unequivocal statement of the black-letter law on the subject, although in fact the principle of the case is far from universally accepted.

But let us begin with exploring why it is accepted at all. (Thereafter I will turn to the reasons why some jurisdictions reject the principle.) Why should we not generally insist that the participant in a crime not be held liable for its commission unless he made a causal contribution to its commission? Why are we willing to hold Tally liable even though we are not sure that his actions made a difference? And even if we could establish that his actions made a difference, is it not clear that he still would not have proximately caused Ross's death, since the Skelton's actions so clearly were an intervening cause?

Brief reflection should make it clear that we could not possibly require that in order for someone to qualify as an accomplice he must have a proximate connection to the criminal harm. Just think of someone who hires another person to commit a murder. It seems clear that the person hiring the killer should be as liable as the killer himself. If we insisted on a proximate connection between the accomplice and the ultimate harm, we would not be able to convict him: The killer's actions would be an intervening cause. Indeed this is surely the key reason the complicity doctrine was invented, to make it possible to impose liability

---

17. Model Penal Code § 2.04 fn. 29 (Tentative Draft No. 1 1953). The footnote, combined with pertinent introductory clause from text, reads: "[The inclusion of attempts to aid may go in part beyond the present law,] In cases where preconcert is lacking and liability at common law would have been based upon 'constructive presence' signalized by actual aid, though even here the aid need not have been essential to success. See e.g., State v. Tally."

in such cases despite the presence of an intervening cause. Now one might wonder why the law has not simply eliminated the intervening act doctrine which makes it impossible to impose liability in such cases. Why does the law take the roundabout path of creating the complicity doctrine merely for the purpose of suspending the intervening act doctrine? The answer is that the complicity doctrine does not merely dispense with proximate causation. It imposes various alternative requirements, most importantly, that the defendant be an *intentional*, as opposed to a reckless or knowing participant in the crime, but others as well.

But although brief reflection might convince one that complicity must dispense with the intervening act doctrine, it is by no means clear why it must also dispense with the "but for" requirement, as the *Tally* court so clearly and emphatically does. To dispense with the "but for" requirement is to say that the defendant can be held liable even though he did not really make a difference to the outcome. That is a rather drastic widening of the scope of liability. Why do that? Why not insist that one cannot be an accomplice unless one made a difference? Why not insist that the prosecution prove that those various scenarios envisioned by the court in which Tally's warning telegram would have made a difference really would have happened beyond a reasonable doubt? And if that cannot be proven, why treat the case any differently from any other case in which causation cannot be proved beyond a reasonable doubt?

Sometimes it is suggested that the reason for the loose actus reus requirement is that complicity has a very strict mens rea requirement. In other words, because we do not allow someone to count as an accomplice unless he acted intentionally (as opposed to merely knowingly or recklessly which is sufficient for other crimes), we compensate for that, as it were, by requiring less in the way of a causal contribution. Of course that really is not much of an argument: What makes such a compensatory step necessary at all?

Another equally makeshift argument is sometimes invoked: At common law, an accomplice could only be held liable for the crime of the principal. In other words, someone assisting in a manslaughter could only be held liable for manslaughter, even though he might himself have the mens rea of murder. His liability is said to be entirely derivative.[18] If we imposed liability on someone simply because he made a difference to the outcome of a crime, it is not clear why we do not simply hold him liable for causing a harm, regardless of the actions of the intermediary. This argument too is not particularly convincing: We don't *have* to make

---

18. Contemporary law is different. *See, e.g.,* Pendry v. State, 367 A.2d 627 (Del. 1976).

complicity liability derivative. Why do we choose to, in addition to dispensing with the usual requirement of factual causation?

Yet another makeshift argument focuses on the difficulty of figuring out whether someone made a difference when we are considering group action. Defendant continues his affair with a woman knowing, or perhaps even hoping, this might strengthen her resolve to kill her husband. Answering the but-for question here will be excruciatingly difficult. And it seems strange that all that much should turn on it. Luck matters elsewhere in the law, but here it would seem to start to matter excessively. Jurisdictions that do impose a causal requirement end up having to draw hair's breadth distinctions between a case in which the defendant hands a bank robber a drink which serves to refresh him, and a case in which the defendant by doing so inadvertently distracts the robber from his task—finding complicity in the former case and no complicity in the latter. Here is a further argument sometimes made against relying on causation as a criterion for complicity: Common law tended to distinguish between different levels of participation, between, that is, accessories, principals in the first degree and principals in the second degree, instigators, etc. If we think that complicity is simply a matter of causation, those distinctions cease to make sense: Everyone has caused the outcome, everyone has done so with an intent to bring about the outcome, how can some forms of causation count for more than other forms? On the other hand, Anglo–American law has largely abandoned the distinction between these different forms of complicity, perhaps in recognition of the difficulty of distinguishing between these different forms of causation.

A more convincing reason for dispensing with "but for" causation in the complicity setting is, I think, the following: Actions by collectivities have an obvious yet easily overlooked property: each participant tends to be relatively superfluous. When several people rob a bank, assault someone, or produce a fraudulent document, then subtracting any one of them from the enterprise would not change the outcome much. It might slightly diminish the harm done, if that. In economic parlance, the "marginal product" of each participant is quite low. And if we add up the marginal contributions of each participant they will not, as the economists say, "exhaust the total output." To make this more concrete: Suppose four people collaborate in the drafting of a fraudulent prospectus for the sale of securities. Each of them inserts a separate lie into the document. Each, in other words, is the cause of a particular misrepresentation. The harm wrought by the document is, let us say, $1,111. Without any one lie, the harm would only be a dollar less. Without two of the lies it would be $11 less; without three of the lies, $111 less. In other words, the first lie in the document does the bulk of the damage. (Which lie is that? It could be any one of them. As long as there is one lie, $1,000 worth of damage will result.) The second adds another $100 dollars worth in damages, and so on down the line. If we simply held every participant liable for the harm that would not have resulted but for his participation, each would only be liable for $1. The total liability would be $4. Yet their collaboration in fact resulted in $1,111 worth of damages. If we dispense with causation, we will be able to say about each that he is responsible for the entirety, and that seems to come much closer to the level of blameworthiness each has exhibited.

This is the unarticulated argument for the Tally court's view of the actus reus of complicity. But is it compelling? It is formidable, to be sure, but there are some significant reasons to be wary of it as well. Here are a few of the principal ones:

1. Ordinarily criminal law treats a criminal who tries but fails to bring about a criminal result more leniently than it treats someone who brings the result about. In other words, attempts are judged to be less blameworthy than completed crimes. The essence of an attempt would seem to be that the defendant tried to cause a certain outcome but failed. Ordinarily this involves cases in which the outcome the defendant desired does not come about because something went awry. But in unusual cases, the attempt may go awry because the desired event happens on its own. If the defendant takes aim at his target, the bullet misses, but the victim minutes later has a heart attack (not of fright but quite unrelated to the shooting), the defendant will only be liable for the attempt. Or, as happened in an actual case, the defendant took aim at an enemy lying on the ground, whom he took to be alive, but who in fact was already dead (having been shot by someone else). Here too the defendant is merely held liable for an attempt, since he did not succeed in bringing about the desired result, that result already having arrived on its own. It would seem that complicity cases like *Tally* are like that. If the defendant tries to make a contribution to the crimes planned by some others, but his contribution is basically irrelevant, because the outcome would have happened in pretty much the same way even if he had not intervened, he would really just seem to be like one of those attempters who try but fail because success comes to them independently.

2. Suppose that the threat facing Ross were of a somewhat different nature than the one he actually faced. Suppose he faced a natural disaster. In other words, picture someone like Ross in a mountain cabin, about to be overtaken by a tornado. Another person, knowing what is afoot, tries to send him a warning. Tally steps in and takes steps to prevent the warning from reaching Ross. Ross then falls victim to the tornado. When all is said and done, let us suppose we do not know whether the warning telegram would

have reached Ross, absent Tally's intervention, whether the warning would have led Ross to take any action in response, and whether it would have allowed him to escape the tornado in time. Under these circumstances, could Tally be convicted of having caused Ross's death? No, of course not. In this scenario, Tally would be charged as a principal for the murder of Ross, and that charge requires proof beyond a reasonable doubt that he actually caused Ross's death. Now what is the difference between this case and the real *Tally* case? Only the fact that in this case Tally was "assisting nature," rather than assisting human actors. Why should that make such a difference?

3. Consider a case in which the defendant is forced at gunpoint to assist in someone else's crime. In other words, he is turned into an accomplice by virtue of a deadly threat. To make this more concrete, suppose someone had forced Tally at gunpoint to send the telegram by which he sought to prevent Huddleston from delivering the warning telegram. Do we think Tally should go along with the demand? I should think so; Since it is not so likely that his telegram will make a difference to Ross's life, but he himself is certain to be killed for sure unless he accedes to the demand, it seems perfectly reasonable for him to proceed. But that suggests that we do not really believe that assisting in a wrong is on a par with actually causing that wrong. After all, we would not allow Tally to take actions that are certain to result in Ross's death just to save his own life.

4. Finally, there is this difficulty: If we decide that causation is not required to make someone an accomplice, then what exactly *is* required? The *Tally* court suggests that what is required is action that *might* under the right circumstances have made a difference, even if in actual fact it did not. There may, in a given situation, be a lot of people whose actions might have made an adverse difference to the victim, but under the circumstances did not. Many of those people might even have a desire for the victim's death. But it would be strange if all of them were to count as accomplices. To make this more concrete, picture the following: A group of assassins is simultaneously firing at the victim. Watching them from nearby is an uninvolved bystander who thoroughly approves. Is that person an accomplice? He has the requisite mens rea, i.e., an approving attitude toward what the principals are doing. What about his actus reus? Is he doing something which under the right circumstances might have made an adverse difference to the victim, though not in the actual circumstances? Well, suppose he happens to have in his possession—unbeknownst to the assassins—some extra ammunition which he intends to make available to them in case they run out.

Then under the right circumstances he could have made a difference. But should that really be enough to transform the bystander in to an accomplice? Surely not.

One could try to refine the *Tally* court's test so as to escape such difficulties. One might for instance say: The real reason for dispensing with causation when it comes to complicity is the "overdetermination" problem discussed above, the fact that we do not want a series of wrongdoers off the hook just because any one of them would have been superfluous to the outcome (lest we need to let off each of the Skeltons because each and everyone of them by himself was dispensable to the outcome.) Perhaps then we should distinguish cases in which an approving bystander makes no difference because of overdetermination and cases in which he makes no difference because he is totally irrelevant to the outcome, the way that bullet-playing bystander is. That seems like a reasonable test, but it is going to require us to draw some mighty fine lines. What are we to do for instance in the proverbial case where someone shouts encouragement at a deaf would-be assassin. Is this a case of "overdetermination" or of "ineffectuality"? It might seem at first glance like the latter. But then consider the case of someone shouting as part of a large group, all of whom are encouraging the hearing perpetrator, and but for whose encouragement he would not be acting as he is. Here too the actor's shouts cannot be heard, not because the perpetrator is deaf, but because his encouragement is drowned out by the shouts of the others. This now seems like a case of overdetermination, rather than ineffectuality. It is one of overdetermination because if we subtracted away some of the other shouters, we would eventually arrive at a point where the defendant's encouragements could be heard and would make a difference to the outcome. So the test for distinguishing overdetermination from ineffectuality might be put this way: we ask whether by subtracting other participants' actions from the setting, the defendant would eventually become a but-for cause of the adverse outcome. But is it not true that if we withdraw the principal's deafness from the setting, we would arrive at a point where the encourager's shouts would make a difference? That inference seems to suggest that he really stands in an overdetermination relationship to the outcome, rather than one of ineffectuality. And what of the defendant who shouts into the din, full well knowing that he cannot be heard? For that matter, what if Tally understood that what he was doing was really pointless but would serve to put him in good standing with his in-laws?

These are not unanswerable arguments. Or rather, these arguments don't clearly carry the day, and rejoinders can be made. And rejoinders to those rejoinders, and so on. My point here is simply to make it clear that the issue is a thorny one, and that whichever side one takes, one is going to be stuck with some counterintuitive implications. The side the

Tally court took avoids one kind of counterintuitive result, perhaps the most important kind, namely that of letting all participants in a collaborative criminal enterprise off the hook simply because they "overdetermined" the outcome, so that every participant considered individually was superfluous and therefore cannot be said to be the "but for" cause of the eventual harm. Alas, this particular counterintuitive result is avoided only at the price of accepting other ones, like those I delineated.

What Happened Thereafter

Was Judge Tally ultimately tried and convicted of murder? Were the Skeltons? One would think the answers to these questions would not be hard to come by. Alas, they are. No further recorded opinions in the matter shed light on it. And the Montgomery *Daily Advertiser*, which so faithfully reported the impeachment proceedings, makes no further mention of it. A family newsletter circulated among present-day descendants of the Skeltons states that no one was ever convicted, that one of the brothers fled, and that the others were acquitted; but it is hard to be sure. If indeed Alabama juries refused to convict Tally or the Skeltons in the teeth of overwhelming evidence of their guilt, that makes what happened next all the more ironic.

What happened next was that Ross's widow brought a wrongful death suit against Western Union, charging that the company's negligence (or rather, its agent Huddleston's negligent failure to deliver the warning telegram) had caused her husband's death. This time the Alabama juries were willing to find against the defendant. The first time a jury found against Western Union, the trial court set the verdict aside and ordered a new trial, presumably because it found the verdict to be against the weight of the evidence. The second time, the court gave the jury peremptory instructions to find for the defendant. Ross's widow appealed and lost.

The appellate court did not think that Western Union had been negligent or that it had in any way caused Ross's death. On the issue of negligence, the court said this:

> [Considering] the message from Judge Tally to Huddleston in connection with the Ross message, we think that Huddleston was justified in assuming that the men following Ross were pursuing him for the purpose of arrest, and that he (Huddleston) was expected to aid in holding him (Ross) in Stevenson until the arresting party should overtake him. He was the mayor of Stevenson, and Tally was a judge at Scottsboro—both peace officers. Therefore a slight delay on the part of Huddleston would seem to be justified as a reasonable precaution under all the circumstances ...

[Moreover] [t]here was only the briefest time between the very earliest moment at which the Ross telegram could have been delivered to Ross, and the shooting. There is evidence to show that the telegrams were being placed in the envelopes and directed at the time the firing commenced. . . .

[In addition,] Robert C. Ross, the person to whom the message was addressed, was not a resident of the town of Stevenson, nor was he in fact the in the town of Stevenson at the time the message was received at the Stevenson office. As the message was directed to no particular street, or locality within the delivery limits of the town, it was the duty of the telegraph company to deliver a written copy to Ross promptly on his calling at the telegraph office, and, failing Ross's early call at the office, to deliver such written copy to him by messenger within a reasonable time after the agents of the company should be informed that Ross was be found at some locality in the town of Stevenson. Ross arrived in the town of Stevenson soon after the message reached the Stevenson office, and was evidently proceeding directly to that office when he was waylaid, shot, and killed without there intervening sufficient time in which the telegraph company could have delivered a copy of the message to him, even if the company was charged with notice of his arrival in town as soon as he came in sight of the telegraph office. Conceding that the message sufficiently notified the company of the importance of speedy delivery, still the company was not charged with the duty of sending out messengers with copies of the message to watch for the arrival of Ross; and, unless charged with such duty, it is clear it was guilty of no negligence.[19]

The court's finding is of course completely at variance with that of the Alabama Supreme Court, which had concluded that Huddleston was obliged to do his utmost to get the warning telegram to Ross the moment he entered town, and had only failed to do so because he decided to do Judge Tally's bidding. This court, by contrast, concludes that Huddleston was obliged to do no such thing—because he could assume that the men pursuing Ross simply wanted to arrest him, and because he was acting with perfectly appropriate celerity in placing the telegram in an envelope for later delivery and in waiting for Ross to pick it up or to send it to him once informed of his whereabouts.

The court also argued that there really was no proven causal link between Huddleston's failure to deliver the telegram and Ross's death. First, it said, there was no proven "but for" connection:

If Ross had received the telegram, would it have prevented his death? It appears from all the facts in the case that the Skelton

---

19. Ross v. Western Union, 81 F.676, 678 (5th Cir. 1897).

brothers were close on his track, and, even if Huddleston had exercised the most extraordinary diligence, and had gone to meet him with the telegram, it is barely possible, but hardly probable that Ross would have escaped his pursuers.[20]

Second, the court said, there was no "proximate" connection, because of the Skeltons' intervening actions:

If another and independent force intervened to bring about the death of Ross, it will be the responsible cause, even conceding the failure of the telegraph company to deliver him the message from E H Ross in time for it to serve as a warning. The new and independent force would be, in law, the proximate cause, and, if the company's neglect could be said to be a cause at all, it would be remote and ineffective.... The company did not start the Skeltons in pursuit of Ross. The Skeltons, for reasons of their own, were acting on entirely independent lines, without any kind of connection with the telegraph company. Much authority might be cited in this line, but so unusual are the facts of this case that it must be controlled by recognized principles, rather than by any direct authority on anything like similar facts.[21]

One might well wonder why the court makes so much of the lack of a causal connection. Why could it not proceed in the same way as the Alabama Supreme Court with regard to Judge Tally and dispense with a causal nexus on the ground that this was a case of complicity? Why not say, in other words, that Huddleston was an accomplice of Tally and the Skeltons and therefore did not need to make a causal contribution to the death to be held liable? To be sure, this was not a criminal case, but the concept of complicity exists in tort law just as much as in criminal law, and is dealt with in largely parallel fashion. The likely reason the judges did not take this course is that they had not found the defendant, Huddleston, to have intentionally aided the Skeltons or Judge Tally. After all, they did not even find him to have engaged in a negligent wrong—a fortiori they could not find him to have engaged in an intentional one. Absent an intention, he could not be thought of as an accomplice, and the causal requirement could not be finessed the way it is in cases of complicity.

Whether or not one is persuaded by the appellate court's analysis, one can well understand the court's eagerness of overturn the jury verdict. Alabama juries had apparently exonerated all direct participants in the murder, the Skeltons and Judge Tally. The only party an Alabama jury seemed willing to hold liable was Western Union. The comparative injustice of letting this outcome stand would seem to give entirely new meaning to the old adage about blaming the messenger.

---

20. *Id.*

21. *Id.*

11

Mario L. Barnes

The Story of *Rahman*: Religious Advocacy at the Intersection of Crime and Free Speech

'This case is not about religion or about great social issues of the day ... It's a simple case of men who planned a war of urban terrorism. They planned to slaughter people as they traveled between New York and New Jersey or sat in office buildings while there were ticking time bombs underground.'

Robert Khuzami, Former Federal Prosecutor[1]

'Dr. Abdel–Rahman is not being charged because of anything he did ... he is charged with conspiracy only because of his words—words uttered as religious teachings, words protected by the Constitution.'

Lynne Stewart, Sheik Omar Abdel–Rahman's Defense Counsel[2]

Introduction

The above quotes offer competing descriptions of how the words of an Islamic religious leader were or were not responsible for encouraging the actions of a domestic terrorist cell, whose activities included an attempt in 1993 to destroy New York City's World Trade Center. Today, this is not the attack on that famous structure that is most indelibly engrained upon American citizens' collective consciousness. Several years before the massively destructive terrorist acts of September 11,

---

1. Statement from the opening remarks of prosecutor in *U.S. v. Rahman*. *See* Robert L. Jackson, *Terror Plot Trial Opens for Sheik, 11 Followers*, Los Angeles Times, Jan. 31, 1995, at 20. Khuzami is currently the director of the Division of Enforcement of the U.S. Securities and Exchange Commission.

2. Statement from the opening remarks of the defense in *U.S. v. Rahman*. *See id.*

2001, leveled the World Trade Center and left the Pentagon smoldering, defendants in another case—*U.S. v. Rahman*—foreshadowed the domestic devastation that could result from violence ostensibly waged in the name of religion.[3]

When tried in a federal court in the Southern District of New York, the *Rahman* case was the largest terrorism trial in U.S. history.[4] The acts of the co-defendants were not ultimately as destructive as the April 1995 Oklahoma City bombing of the Alfred P. Murrah Federal Building in downtown Oklahoma City, which took place during the course of the *Rahman* trial. Still, as a case of domestic terrorism, and one tied to a bombing that killed seven and injured over 1000 people at an iconic New York structure, the *Rahman* case was closely monitored by the media and government officials. The trial lasted from January to October of 1995, and was presided over by Judge Michael Mukasey. At the conclusion of the trial, Sheik Omar Ahmad Ali Abdel–Rahman, a blind Islamic scholar and cleric who was the leader of the Jersey City Al–Salam Mosque, and nine other co-defendants were convicted of multiple terrorism-related offenses.

Of particular interest, all ten defendants were convicted of a number of inchoate crimes, including a rarely charged and somewhat controversial Civil War-era offense—seditious conspiracy—which criminalizes the use of force or waging of war against the United States.[5] Defendant Abdel–Rahman was additionally convicted of soliciting and conspiring to commit the murder of then Egyptian President Hosni Mubarak, soliciting an attack on U.S. military installations, and conspiracy to bomb various other sites in New York City.[6] While the 1993 bombing of the World Trade Center was considered an "extension of his conspiracy,"[7]

---

3. This chapter is substantially based on the record from the appeal of the trial court judgment. *See* U.S. v. Rahman, 189 F.3d 88 (2d Cir. 1999). When relevant, the district court case from the Southern District of New York is also referenced. *See* 861 F.Supp. 247 (S.D.N.Y. 1994).

4. *See* Richard Bernstein, *Biggest U.S. Terrorist Trial Begins As Arguments Clash*, New York Times, Jan. 31, 1995, at A1.

5. The Civil War era statute made it punishable for two or more persons to conspire to overthrow the government of the United States, or to levy war against or impede the execution of the laws of the United States. Conspiracy Act of 1861, ch. 33, § 12, Stat. 284 (1861). For an analysis of the offense, see Catherine Tarrant, *To "Insure Domestic Tranquility": Congress and the Law of Seditious Conspiracy, 1859–1861*, 15 American Journal of Legal History 107–23 (1971).

6. 189 F.3d at 103.

7. Lisa Anderson, *Sheik, Nine Others Found Guilty in N.Y. Bomb Plot, U.S. Hails Verdict*, Chicago Tribune, Oct. 2, 1995, at 1; Laurie Mylroie, *Study of Revenge: The First World Trade Center Attack and Saddam Hussein's War Against America* 187 (2001) ("Although the Trade Center bombing was among the counts in the seditious conspiracy charge against Shaykh Omar et al., none of those convicted of the second bombing

other of Abdel–Rahman's followers were charged and convicted of offenses directly related to that bombing, in separate federal trials.[8]

Although seditious conspiracy may seem an exotic crime involving unusual political circumstances, understanding its operation is highly salient in the study of criminal law. Not only does seditious conspiracy have a long and fascinating legacy in American history, it also illustrates, in a dramatic context, the fundamental principles and complexities of general conspiracy law. As discussed below, they include a number of key features that offer significant prosecutorial advantage: the ability to link far-flung individuals into mutual, escalating, and vicarious liability; special procedural advantages (such as joint trials and a relaxed hearsay rule); and the possibility of separate punishment for a preparatory crime even when the object crime is ultimately committed. Further, although jurisdictions vary in the scope of their conspiracy laws, federal prosecutors enjoy the broadest possible reach of conspiracy doctrine. Moreover, because conspiracy is an inchoate crime often dependent on communications designed to motivate others towards a common object, conspiracy necessarily raises questions about the border of free speech protection, and no specific version of conspiracy does this so sharply as the seditious kind.

During the trial, Abdel–Rahman was identified as the leader of conspiratorial activities designed to effect a war of urban terrorism, the purpose of which was *"jihad"* against Egypt and the United States.[9] Abdel–Rahman actually began to organize the *jihad* in 1989, prior to his arriving in the United States. In Egypt, his Islamic fundamentalist followers were in a violent conflict with the Egyptian government;[10]

conspiracy was charged with actually having participated in the Trade Center bombing.") (emphasis in the original).

8. Prior to the trial in *U.S. v. Rahman*, four other co-conspirators—three of whom were Abdel–Rahman's followers—were convicted of the World Trade Center bombing in a separate trial in 1994. *See* U.S. v. Salameh, 152 F.3d 88 (2d Cir. 1998) (Mohammad A. Salameh, Nidal Ayyad, Ahmad Mohammad Ajaj, and Mahmoud Abouhalima were convicted and sentenced to 240 years in prison for their part(s) in the World Trade Center Bombing). Another co-conspirator, Abdul Rahman Yasin, who allegedly helped to make the bombs used in the attack on the World Trade Center, was indicted but fled to Jordan and was not tried. *Id.* at 108. Two other co-conspirators, who were instrumental in planning the attack and driving the van containing the explosives to the World Trade Center garage, were tried and convicted in a trial in 1997. *See infra* note 46.

9. 189 F.3d at 104 (*Jihad* is described as "the sense of struggle against the enemies of Islam"). Abdel–Rahman believed that the Koran mandated *jihad* against the U.S. and Egypt because of their support for Israel.

10. *See* Robert I. Friedman, *Sheik Abdel Rahman, the World Trade Center Bombing and the CIA,* Open Magazine (Pamphlet Series) Pamphlet 27, Oct. 1993, at 8–9 [originally appeared as *The CIA and the Sheik*, The Village Voice, Mar. 30, 1993]; Jill Smolowe et al., *Sheik Omar Abdel Rahman: A Voice of Holy War*, Time, Mar. 15, 1993, at 31–34, available at http://www.time.com/time/magazine/article/0,9171,977948,00.html

although he was acquitted of any criminal conduct in the matter, Abdel–Rahman was charged by Egyptian authorities with encouraging the 1981 assassination of President Anwar Sadat.[11] Before escaping Egypt, Abdel–Rahman was essentially on house arrest for his suspected part in instigating a Mosque riot.[12] One story claims that he slipped by Egyptian authorities by hiding inside a washing machine that was being moved from his house.[13] After leaving Egypt in 1990, he spent time in Saudi Arabia, Sudan, Iraq and finally Pakistan, where he became the spiritual leader of Afghan–Arabs and began working for the mujahedeen—the Afghan rebels who were fighting the Soviets.[14] He arrived in the United States in 1990 on a tourist visa, which one commentator claims was arranged by the U.S. Central Intelligence Agency.[15] The claim is not outlandish given that Abdel–Rahman was on a U.S. State Department terrorist watch list for participation in acts of terrorism in his native Egypt,[16] when he received the visa. While he delivered sermons at mosques in Brooklyn and New Jersey, his goals in America were not only to spread his fundamentalist ideology but also to raise funds and locate recruits for the mujahedeen.[17] It was his spreading of his religious beliefs to followers who coordinated violent anti-government actions that became the source of the charges against him. Ironically, however, when he was arrested in America, it was initially on immigration charges; when he was indicted for his suspected terrorist activities, he was in custody and scheduled to be deported on a charge of bigamy.[18]

   In the federal district court, prosecutor Robert Khuzami referred to Abdel–Rahman as the "spiritual guide" of the indicted terrorist cell;[19] moreover, the appellate opinion later characterized Abdel–Rahman's role in the conspiracy as "generally limited to overall supervision and direction of the membership, as he made efforts to remain a level above

---

   11.   Abdel–Rahman was charged with encouraging the 1981 assassination of Egyptian President, Anwar Sadat, but he was cleared of that offense. *See* Mary Tabor, *Sheik, In Court, Denies Terror Charges*, New York Times, Aug. 27, 1993, at A1; Friedman, *supra* note 10.

   12.   Richard Bernstein, *Out of the blue: The Story of September 11, 2001, from jihad to Ground Zero* 43 (2003).

   13.   *Id.* at 43–44.

   14.   *Id.* at 43–45.

   15.   Simon Reeve, *The New Jackals* 60 (1999) (indicating the visa was arranged to cultivate a relationship with Abdel–Rahman when the Agency feared Islamic fundamentalists might gain a stronghold in Egypt.).

   16.   *See* Keisha A. Gary, *Congressional Proposals to Revive Guilty by Association: An Ineffective Plan to Stop Terrorism*, 8 Geo. Immigr. L.J. 227, 250 (1994).

   17.   Friedman *supra* note 10, at 9.

   18.   Mylroie, *supra* note 7, at 185.

   19.   Peg Tyre, *Prosecutor Takes Defensive Stand*, Newsday, Jan. 31, 1995, at A04.

the details of individual operations."[20] While he was not directly involved in the individual planning or carrying out of acts in furtherance of the groups' terrorist agenda, he was charged on the basis of his use of religious teachings to encourage and sanction violence to achieve the group's goals. His guidance and supervision largely took the role of dispensing *"fatwas,"* religious missives to his followers. These messages were expressive of Abdel–Rahman's disdain for the U.S. and Egypt, and also condoned violent acts by his followers, if the acts were in furtherance of *jihad*.[21]

During the trial, the prosecution characterized Abdel–Rahman as a religious firebrand—in stark contrast to the image of the cleric displayed in the courtroom. One media source reporting on Abdel–Rahman's courtroom appearance and demeanor noted:

> "In the courtroom, the feeble appearance of the sheik—who has diabetes, a heart condition and, most recently, a case of tuberculosis.... belies the severity of the charges against him. In recent weeks ... he mostly has sat quiet. He mumbles prayers to himself each time a small pocket alarm softly sounds the traditional five-times-a-day Muslim call to worship. Sometimes, in the afternoons, he appears to doze off as the trial's tedious preliminaries continue."[22]

Abdel–Rahman's defense counsel also made references to his ailing health during the trial.[23]

Abdel–Rahman, for his part, claimed that the evidence in the case was insufficient to support a conviction against him on any charge.[24] Two days prior to the jury returning a verdict, he told an interviewer, " 'I am not the first and will not be the last to face prison for the Islamic cause.' "[25] Prior to his sentencing, "he delivered an angry 100–minute speech in which he castigated the United States as an 'enemy of Islam' and cast himself as a victim of an 'unlawful trial.' "[26] Relying on evidence of his religious guidance and encouragement, a jury found Abdel–Rah-

---

20. 189 F.3d at 104.

21. *Id.* (emphasis in the original).

22. Mike Dorning, *Trial on Urban Terrorism Begins: Egyptian Cleric Accused of Ties to N.Y. Bombing Plots*, Chicago Tribune, Jan. 30, 1995, at 5.

23. *See, e.g.*, Neil MacFarquhar, *Sheik Remains Defiant to the Bitter End: He Lashes Out at Egypt's Regime, U.S. Justice System*, New York Times, Oct. 2, 1995, at A3.

24. 189 F.3d at 123.

25. MacFarquhar, *supra* note 23.

26. Joseph P. Fried, *Sheik Sentenced to Life in Prison in Bombing Plot*, New York Times, Jan. 19, 1996, at A1.

man guilty of all charges, including seditious conspiracy, and sentenced him to life in prison.[27]

In an appeal of their convictions, Abdel–Rahman and all of his co-conspirators challenged the charge of seditious conspiracy, claiming it was illegal because it failed to satisfy the Treason Clause of the Constitution.[28] Abdel–Rahman also claimed that the seditious conspiracy statute was an unconstitutional burden on free speech and the free exercise of religion; that he was convicted not of conspiring but for his religious words and deeds;[29] and that his speeches, writings and preaching were improperly used as evidence of solicitation or conspiracy.[30]

Abdel–Rahman joined other defendants in claiming that the District Court's voir dire of prospective jurors was insufficient and deprived them of their Sixth Amendment right to an impartial jury.[31] Individually, Abdel–Rahman also argued that the Court violated his right to due process by denying him the opportunity to present a relevant defense, to call an expert witness, and to be represented by a law firm which represented other of his co-defendants (an ineffective assistance of counsel claim).[32] Finally, he offered the novel, if quixotic argument that violation of the Due Process Clause attached not due to one particular government action, but instead, from the "cumulative unfairness" of his trial.[33] While these are important procedural claims, this chapter will focus on the core substantive issue in the case.

Abdel–Rahman's case and story turn largely on his words and on the various acts/crimes undertaken by his followers, to give effect to the stated intent of the cleric's religious beliefs. In addition to the bombing of the World Trade Center and an attack on Rabbi Kahane, a former Israeli legislator, there were plans to attack then Egyptian president, Hosni Mubarak during a planned March 1993 visit to New York City and to bomb the United Nations, as well as such other New York locations as a federal building, the George Washington Bridge, and the Lincoln and Holland tunnels. Beyond his generalized words of encouragement for these plans, the government claimed that Abdel–Rahman also specifically directed his followers to target U.S. Army assets[34] and offered insights

---

27. 189 F.3d at 103–04.

28. *Id.* at 114.

29. *Id.* at 116.

30. *Id.* at 117–18.

31. *Id.* at 121.

32. *Id.* at 134.

33. *Id.* at 145.

34. *Id.* at 109. One source describes his encouragement to attack army assets as a preferred course of action in response to the question of whether the United Nations should be attacked. *See* Mylroie, *supra* note 7, at 189 (" 'It would not be forbidden, but it

on the training of followers in *jihad* tactics.[35] Further, the government argued, he intentionally discussed the plans of his followers in a circumspect manner to avoid self-incrimination.[36]

Constructing a cohesive narrative of all of the overlapping and disparate activities of the named defendant's followers is outside the scope of this chapter.[37] The significance of Abdel–Rahman's trial and story, however, turn not so much on these acts in furtherance of the conspiracy, but rather on whether Abdel–Rahman's support and encouragement for these activities was sufficient to hold him criminally liable. For that reason, the remainder of this chapter will only briefly discuss the various acts of Abdel–Rahman's followers and co-conspirators, in service to a conspiracy to commit multiple terrorist acts within the United States.

The greatest portion of this chapter will focus on Abdel–Rahman's role in the events, how his case more generally represents the government's approach to charging conspiracy and other inchoate offenses, the government's specific decision to charge his conduct as giving rise to a seditious conspiracy, and the way this particular charge raises questions for the U.S. Constitution's Treason Clause, free speech and free exercise doctrines.[38] Specifically, Abdel–Rahman's story and trial is remarkable for what it could have but apparently did not achieve: establishing a workable modern standard for seditious conspiracy and carefully marking when espousing anti-government religious beliefs crosses into the criminal incitement of violence.

The Brief Tale of the Charges of Abdel– Rahman's Co-Conspirators

The facts surrounding the *Rahman* case are not only centered on the actions of the cleric. To the contrary, much of the case focuses on the plans and actions of his followers, nine of whom were charged and convicted with him for carrying out a variety of activities in service to an overall terrorist scheme the government attributed to Abdel–Rahman.[39] As a number of the criminal actions of Abdel–Rahman's co-defendants

---

would muddy the waters for Muslims.' . . . '[F]ind a plan to inflict damage on the army, the American army, because the United Nations would harm Muslims, harm them tremendously.' ").

35. 189 F.3d at 107.

36. *Id.* at 109.

37. For a detailed description of all of the conspiratorial activities of Abdel–Rahman's followers, see *id.* at 105–111.

38. Relevant to this analysis, the First Amendment to the U.S. Constitution provides: "Congress shall make no law . . . prohibiting the free exercise thereof [religion]; or abridging freedom of speech. . . ." U.S. Const. amend. I.

39. *See* 189 F.3d at 105–11.

and other separately tried co-conspirators were charged as acts in furtherance of the bombing and seditious conspiracies at the heart of the *Rahman* case, they are briefly presented here.

In November 1990, El Sayyid Nosair, an Abdel–Rahman follower, was accused of shooting three people, including Rabbi Meir Kahane, a former member of the Israeli Parliament and founder of the Jewish Defense League.[40] During the course of their investigation, the police discovered a handwritten notebook, in which Nosair claimed that in order to create a Muslim state, enemies of Allah needed to be destroyed.[41] While he was incarcerated awaiting trial, he received a number of visitors, including his cousin and fellow co-conspirator, Ibrahim El–Gabrowny. From these visits the government learned that Nosair suggested terrorist acts El–Gabrowny and other followers could commit.[42] In June of 1992, Nosair criticized two visitors, one of whom, Emad Salem, was an FBI informant, for not advancing bombing plans.[43] He then instructed one of the visitors to seek a *fatwa* from Abdel–Rahman to approve the bombings.[44] For these and other actions, Nosair was convicted of seditious conspiracy, two counts of attempted murder, one count of murder in furtherance of a racketeering enterprise, attempted murder of a federal officer, three counts of use of a firearm in relation to a crime of violence, and possession of a firearm with an obligated serial number. Nosair was charged with but not convicted of participating in a bombing conspiracy.[45] He was sentenced to life in prison.

The World Trade Center was bombed on February 26, 1993. While not charged and convicted as a co-conspirator during Abdel–Rahman's trial, Ramzi Yousef was deemed to be most directly responsible for planning that bombing.[46] He was introduced to his fellow co-conspira-

---

40. Kahane was shot twice after he gave a speech at a NYC Marriott hotel encouraging American Jews to immigrate to Israel. Nosair, who was observed fleeing the Marriott with a gun in hand, shot two people, including a uniformed postal police officer as he left the building. *Id.* at 105. Nosair was acquitted of killing Rabbi Kahane, but found guilty of weapons charges and sentenced to 7 1/3 to 20 years in prison. *Id.* at 106 n.3.

41. *Id.* at 105.

42. Among his suggestions were that other Abdel–Rahman followers kill the judge who sentenced him and a New York City assemblyman. *Id.* at 105–06.

43. *Id.* at 106.

44. *Id.* at 107.

45. *Id.* at 103–04.

46. In a separate trial, in November 1997, Ramzi Yousef, who the court credits with actually assembling the team and planning the WTC bombing, and Eyad Ismoil, who drove the truck carrying the bomb to the WTC, were convicted of the bombing. Another person believed to be a member the conspiracy, Emad Salem, was actually an FBI informant, who befriended Abdel–Rahman's followers in order infiltrate the *Jihad* and testified against the co-conspirators. *Id.* at 106.

tors—Mohammad A. Salameh, Nidal Ayyad, Ahmad Mohammad Ajaj, and Mahmoud Abouhalima—by Abdel–Rahman, and he was substantially responsible for assembling and delivering the bomb. He escaped the U.S. and engaged in further acts of terrorism until, after an international manhunt, he was arrested in Pakistan and ultimately tried in a separate trial from that of his immediate co-conspirators and the group tried in the *Rahman* case. Of the nine co-conspirators tried with Abdel–Rahman for various crimes, Ibrahim El–Gabrowny was somewhat implicated as part of the World Training Center (WTC) bombing. A yellow van, rented on February 24, 1993, by Mohammed Salameh (a co-conspirator in the separate trial) and registered to El–Gabrowny's address, was used for the bombing.[47]

In support of charges related to Abdel–Rahman's conspiratorial bombing plans, FBI-informant testimony indicated that El–Gabrowny was also involved in planning to construct bombs—including locating detonators—and to secure a safe house for their creation.[48] When officers searched El–Gabrowny's house, they found stun guns as well as taped messages from Nosair encouraging *jihad*.[49] When El–Gabrowny was arrested he was in possession of five Nicaraguan passports and birth certificates bearing the pictures of Nosair, his wife and children.[50] El–Gabrowny was charged with seditious conspiracy, two counts of assault of a federal officer, assault impeding the execution of a search warrant, one count of possession with intent to transfer false identification documents, and five counts of possession of a fraudulent foreign passport. He was also charged with but not convicted of the bombing conspiracy.[51]

Amir Abdelgani, Faris Khallafalla, Clement Hampton–El, Fadel Abdelgani, Tarig Elhassan, Mohammad Saleh, and Victor Alvarez, by contrast, were involved with multiple moving parts of several different inchoate crimes. As part of the plot to bomb various New York City locations, Saleh was visited by another Abdel–Rahman follower, Siddig Ali, and FBI-informant Salem.[52] Saleh was a *jihad* supporter who owned a gas station and agreed to support the conspiracy by helping to purchase military equipment and supplying diesel fuel for bombs.[53]

---

47. *Id.* at 108.

48. *Id.* at 107.

49. *Id.* at 108.

50. *Id.*

51. *Id.* at 103–04.

52. The prosecutors admitted in court that Salem was paid over a million dollars by the FBI to infiltrate Abdel–Rahman's followers and that he had not always been truthful. *See* Peg Tyre, *Prosecutor Takes Defensive Stand*, Chicago Tribune, Jan. 31, 1995, at A04.

53. 189 F.3d at 110.

Siddig Ali was also charged with seditious conspiracy, conspiracy, solicitation of the murder of Hosni Mubarak, attempted bombing, and firearm charges. In perhaps the most surprising turn of events during the trial of the Abdel–Rahman co-conspirators, Ali—who was suspected of being the ring leader of this cell—became the only defendant to change his plea to guilty, a week into the trial.[54]

Hampton–El led paramilitary training for the group and claimed he could secure bomb detonators, ready-made bombs and weapons for the co-conspirators.[55] The Abdelganis participated in the paramilitary training, the purpose of which was to teach participants *jihad* tactics,[56] and were supposed to carry out the attack on Hosni Mubarak.[57] After the WTC bombing and in league with Siddig Ali, the Abdelganis, Elhassan and Khallafalla were substantially involved in planning the bombing of the United Nations, the Lincoln and Holland tunnels, the George Washington Bridge and the federal building in Manhattan.[58] The Abdelganis, Khallafalla, Hampton–El, Elhassan, and Saleh were charged with and convicted of seditious conspiracy, bombing conspiracy and attempted bombings.[59] As part of the planned bombings, Victor Alvarez attempted to secure stolen cars as delivery vehicles for the bombs and also provided Ali with a 9mm semi-automatic rifle.[60] He was charged and convicted of these bombing offenses and "facilitating the bombing conspiracy by shipping a firearm in interstate commerce and using and carrying a firearm in furtherance of a crime of violence."[61]

Taken together, the acts of Abdel–Rahman and his followers essentially supported five separate forms of inchoate crimes: assault; solicitation for murder and attacks on the military; attempted bombing and murder; conspiracy to commit murder and bombing; and seditious conspiracy. A number of these charges were for their immediate actions in service to attacking various targets, but each person was additionally convicted of seditious conspiracy for supporting what the government described as Abdel–Rahman's war of urban terrorism. While seditious conspiracy is the only charge that joined all of the defendants, one problem for the case and this story is that it is somewhat unclear

---

54. *See* Larry Neumeister, *Alleged Bomb–Plot Mastermind Implicates Sheik, He Pleads Guilty, Turns Against Other Terrorism Suspects*, Seattle Times, Feb. 6, 1995, at A1.

55. 189 F.3d at 107, 110.

56. *Id.*

57. *Id.* at 108.

58. *Id.* at 109–10. Amir and Fadil Abdelgani were specifically involved in making bombs out of diesel fuel and fertilizer. *Id.* at 110–11.

59. *Id.* at 103–04.

60. *Id.* at 110–11.

61. *Id.* at 104.

whether each defendant, including Abdel–Rahman, truly was aware of or committed to an overarching plan designed to effect the violent overthrow the government in the name of *jihad*.

This absence of a grand plan was not so for other defendants convicted of orchestrating the World Trade Center Bombing. When Nidal Ayyad was arrested, for example, Federal Bureau of Investigation agents found a letter on his computer which stated, "If our demands are not met, all of our functional groups in the [liberation] army will continue to execute our missions against military and civilian targets in and out of the United States."[62] No such smoking gun missive, and certainly not one issued from Abdel–Rahman to any of his co-defendants was introduced in the *Rahman* trial. Without such proof, the government was forced to rely heavily on the rhetoric in Abdel–Rahman's writings and sermons as creating a conspiratorial agreement. For this reason, the *Rahman* case could have been an opportunity for a federal court to carefully explore the nature of sedition and the difference between religiously motivated government criticism and treasonous/seditious activity. That the Second Circuit panel in *Rahman* neglected to do so in response to several appellate challenges to the co-defendants' seditious conspiracy convictions, is next considered.

Rahman *as a Tale of Conspiracy and the* Rebirth of Seditious Conspiracy

Looking back at the *Rahman* case, post–9/11, reveals that the United States was in a very different place with regard to questions of how to treat the actions of domestic terrorist cells in 1995. As the following quote evinces, at the time, there were no conflicts regarding how to treat unlawful enemy combatants or questions more generally about whether terrorist acts should be treated as acts of war or crimes.

> We know that, in the very recent past, when terrorists have struck, they have been apprehended under the criminal law in United States courts. Thus, the criminal law has been our primary tool in asserting the values of our society and protecting our citizens against the likes of Timothy McVeigh, who destroyed the federal building in Oklahoma City in a terrorist bombing, and Sheik Abdel Rahman and his followers, the terrorists who carried out the first attack against the World Trade Center in New York City in 1993.[63]

In fact, all the individuals suspected of the first World Trade Center bombing and planning other acts of terror in support of Abdel–Rahman's alleged *jihad* had their cases—*United States v. Rahman, United States v.*

---

62. Reeve, *supra* note 15, at 61.

63. David Harris, *Teaching Criminal Law in at Post–9/11 World: If Everything Has Changed, So Must We,* 48 St. Louis L.J. 1249, 1250 (2004).

Yousef,[64] and *United States v. Salameh*,[65]—tried and appealed in federal
courts. Unlike our more recent experiences with domestic terrorism in
the United States, these cases could not use forum as a basis to allege a
lack of due process.[66] In 1995, while the forum for prosecution was not
the issue, the scope and content of the charges were. Whether Abdel–
Rahman was engaged in appropriate exercises of freedom of speech and
religion or a member of a violent conspiracy was a central question to his
trial. As the quoted remarks that begin this chapter confirm, opposing
counsel in the trial court alternatively described his participation as the
intellectual leadership of a war of urban terrorism versus one who
merely engaged in constitutionally protected religious speech, which was
targeted for political reasons.[67] One of the significant legacies of *Rahman*
is that the case both revived then debunked a notion of religious speech
as sacrosanct (or nearly so), even as it failed to create precise guidelines
for discerning when religious messages will be deemed constitutionally
unprotected calls for violence. Another outcome from the case was that
where domestic terrorism was concerned, conspiracy, which had become
a lynch-pin for punishing group activities in the United States, would no
longer be deemed a sufficient charge for capturing the full breadth of
some wide-ranging criminal enterprises.

Rahman *and the Inadequacy of Mere Conspiracy?*

Were it not for the added charge of seditious conspiracy, the *Rahman* case could serve as a primer on the standard array of inchoate
crimes—assault, attempt, solicitation and conspiracy—one observes in
most U.S criminal jurisdictions. Without the added charge, much of the
criticism of the case would likely focus on the charging of the bombing
and murder conspiracies. Conspiracy law has been criticized as creating
significant charging advantages for the government.[68] Because in many
jurisdictions conspiracy does not "merge" with the target crime, a

---

64. 327 F.3d 56 (2d Cir. 2003).

65. 152 F.3d 88 (2d Cir. 1998).

66. Post 9/11 the question of military over civilian adjudication of terrorist activity
became a significant issue. *See* Note, *Responding to Terrorism: Crime, Punishment and
War*, 115 Harv. L. Rev. 1217, 1224, 1228 (2002) (moving away from the regime of crime to
the regime of war to adjudicate terrorism claims). Only recently, the Attorney General of
the United States announced that one of the lead architects of the 9/11 attacks, Khalid
Shaikh Mohammed, would be tried in military court rather than federal district court. *See*
Charlie Savage, *Sept. 11 Suspects to be Tried in Military Court*, New York Times, Apr. 4,
2011, at A1. *See also* Military Commissions Act of 2009, (Pub. L. 111–84, 123 Stat. 2190,
enacted October 28, 2009) (authorizing the use of military commissions to try unlawful
enemy combatants).

67. *See supra* notes 1–2; *see also* Dorning, *supra* note 22.

68. *See* Cynthia Lee & Angela Harris, Criminal Law: Cases and Materials 834–35
(2nd ed. 2009) (discussing conspiracy, which can be tried anywhere an overt act has been
committed, as being a favorite charge of federal prosecutors).

defendant can be charged both for the target offense or attempt to commit the target offense, as well as for the agreement to commit the offense, thus dramatically increasing his or her punishment for basically the same bad act.[69] Further, each party to the agreement becomes liable for the reasonably foreseeable crimes committed by co-conspirators.[70] The offense has several key aspects that raise concerns related to the propriety of constructing additional charges based upon the collective nature of crimes committed by two or more persons and the thinness of actions necessary to constitute said offense. First, conspiracy punishes anticipatory action that aims at, but does not necessarily ever reach, a criminal object.[71] The main focus of the crime of conspiracy is the

---

69. In a number of Common Law jurisdictions, conspiracy does not merge with the target offense. Hence, the Government can charge and convict a person of both conspiracy to commit and the actual commission/attempted commission of the object crime. Moreover, at Common Law, and to some extent still in federal law, the object of the conspiracy need not even be a crime per se, but can be some act declared illegal under noncriminal statutes. *See e.g.*, California Penal Code § 182 (creating an offense punishable by not more than 1 year in county jail or a $10,000.00 fine (or both), where "two or more persons conspire; . . . To commit any act injurious to the public health, to public morals, or to pervert or obstruct justice, or the due administration of the laws."); United States v. Oliver North, 708 F. Supp. 375 (D.D.C. 1988) (permitting trial of conspiracy to violate the Boland Amendment, inserted as a provision in the annual military appropriations bill to forbid transfer of any weapons to the rebel Contras, the rebel group trying to overthrow the government of Nicaragua).

70. An agreement to engage in a crime creates vicarious liability, where each co-conspirator becomes responsible for reasonably foreseeable acts done by his or her cohorts in furtherance of achieving the target offense. *See* Pinkerton v. United States, 328 U.S. 640 (1946) (defendant held liable for the substantive offenses committed by his brother pursuant to their agreement to commit a separate offense, even though the defendant was in prison when the offenses were committed). This rule operates along with a special exception to the hearsay rule, which allows an out-of-court statement made by one co-conspirator in furtherance of the conspiracy to be admissible against another co-conspira-tor, just as a defendant's own statements are admissible against her (whether formal confessions or unintentionally overheard inculpatory "admissions"). This exception helps to further explain the great prosecutorial advantages of trying to link as many potential co-conspirators into a single overarching conspiracy as possible. *See* United States v. Recio, 537 U.S. 270 (2003) (Person A can be guilty of conspiring with person B even if, unknown to A, B has already terminated her participation and begun cooperating with authorities). The prosecutor can also benefit from the possible guilt-by-association effects of placing many alleged conspirators before the same jury and the attendant possibilities of inducing cooperation of some defendants against others.

71. Ironically, conspiracy was initially directed neither at preparatory activity nor at group crime in general. Rather, it was a narrowly circumscribed statutory remedy designed to combat abuses against the administration of justice. According to Edward Coke, it consisted of "a consultation and agreement between two or more to appeal or indict an innocent man falsely and maliciously of felony, whom accordingly they cause to be indicted and appealed; and afterward the party is lawfully acquitted." A writ of conspiracy would lie only for this particular offense, and only when the offense (including acquittal of the falsely indicted party) had actually taken place. However, in 1611 the Court of Star Chamber

agreement itself, which both serves as an additional element to distinguish conspiracy from the attempt/completion of the target offense,[72] and creates a greater threat to society due to the policing challenges that such collective criminal actions create.[73] The actus reus of the crime is the agreement itself, although some jurisdictions also require an "overt act"—some step taken toward the fulfillment of the conspiratorial object. This act, however, can be very minimal, and well short of what is needed for crossing from mere preparation into the more significant steps necessary to actually attempt the object crime.[74]

Second, because it involves multiple parties in agreement to try to reach a goal, conspiracy often exists in close tension with organized political action and thus tests the boundary between, on the one hand, the legislature's authority to define and the prosecutor's power to charge crimes and, on the other, the First Amendment's protections of free speech and political assembly.[75] Conspiracy law, therefore, must finesse

---

extended the law by upholding a conspiracy conviction even though the falsely accused party was not indicted. Poulterers' Case, 77 Eng. Rep. 813 (KB. 1611) (Coke).

72. Based on the added element of an agreement, the conspiracy is not a lesser included offense of the completed crime, and so double punishment does not constitute double jeopardy. Callanan v. United States, 364 U.S. 587 (1961). The Model Penal Code's version of conspiracy, mirroring the law of many states, is much narrower than the federal version, in some ways. For example, it forbids double punishment for the conspiracy and the object crime or for conspiring toward and attempting the object crime. Additionally, unlike the common law, *see supra* note 69, it limits the conspiratorial object to substantive crimes defined by the penal code; and, it rejects the broad vicarious liability of co-conspirator crimes. *See* ALI Model Penal Code § 5.03. It, however, does make a conspiracy conviction available to persons, who with the purpose of promoting the achievement of the target offense, merely *agree* to aid others in planning the commission of said offense. *Id.*

73. As Justice Frankfurter noted:

... Concerted action both increases the likelihood that the criminal object will be successfully attained and decreases the probability that the individuals involved will depart from their path of criminality. Group association for criminal purposes often, if not normally, makes possible the attainment of ends more complex than those which one criminal could accomplish. Nor is the danger of a conspiratorial group limited to the particular end toward which it has embarked. Combination in crime makes more likely the commission of crimes unrelated to the original purpose for which the group was formed. In sum, the danger which a conspiracy generates is not confined to the substantive offense which is the immediate aim of the enterprise. Callanan v. United States, 364 U.S. 587, 593–94 (1961) (Frankfurter, J.). On whether the unique nature of group-based dangers supports the charging of conspiracy, see Paul Marcus, *Conspiracy: The Criminal Agreement, in Theory and in Practice*, 65 Geo. L.J. 925, 934–38 (1977).

74. Rollins Perkins, *Criminal Law*, 618 (2d ed. 1968).

75. For a broad review of the issues, *see* Eugene Volokh, *Crime–Facilitating Speech*, 57 Stan. L. Rev. 1095 (2005). This tension between law enforcement charging authority and First Amendment protections becomes clearer when one considers the expansive investigation and enforcement practices used to police "communities of interest" post-September 11, 2001. *See, e.g.* Eric Lichtblau, *FBI Data Mining Reached Beyond Initial Targets*, New York Times, Sept. 8, 2007, at A01 ("Federal Bureau of Investigation used

the elusive speech-conduct distinction, attending to the important Supreme Court pronouncement that government cannot forbid or proscribe advocacy, even of violation of the law or use of force or violence, except where that advocacy is directed to inciting or producing imminent lawless action and is likely to incite or produce such action.[76] It is for this reason that one would have imagined federal conspiracy charges (for bombing and murder) alone could have been used to discern whether Abdel–Rahman's activities were inciting of violence or protected speech.[77]

Finally, the federal prosecutor has great leeway in framing the number and scope of conspiracy charges. Often she will prefer to charge many disparate figures in a single conspiracy, either by linking them in a linear chain of conduct (as in a grower-to-wholesaler-to retailer-to customer drug conspiracy)[78] or as a large wheel conspiracy (as in *Rahman*) with a pivotal figure in the middle of a many-spoked wheel,[79] or she can

---

secret demands for records to obtain data not only on individuals it saw as targets but also details on their 'community of interest'—the network of people that the target was in contact with.") *available at* http://www.nytimes.com/2007/09/09/washington/09fbi.html

   76.   Brandenburg v. Ohio, 395 U.S. 444 (1969) (per curiam). Of course, this issue tends to arise at times of great political upheaval and controversy. *See* United States v. Spock, 416 F.2d 165 (1st Cir. 1969) (First Amendment victory for activists charged with conspiracy to promote resistance to military draft during Vietnam War, reversing convictions of famed pediatrician Benjamin Spock, along with antiwar leader Rev. William Sloane Coffin and others.).

   77.   It is not clear under what circumstances the government is most likely to charge seditious conspiracy, or whether the charge is typically successful. *See, e.g.*, Leonard Zeskind *The Hutaree Militia & the Charge of Seditious Conspiracy*, The Huffington Post, Mar. 30, 2010, *available at:* http://www.huffingtonpost.com/leonard-zeskind/strongthe-hutaree-militia_b_519066.html (reporting on the government charging the Hutaree Militia with seditious conspiracy for killings they planned to carry out and noting the government had "never won a sedition case against militia-types, white supremacists, or neo-Nazis"). In a recent case closer in context to the facts in *Rahman,* the imam for the oldest Mosque in Miami, Hafiz Muhammad Sher Ali Khan, and four of his family members have been federally indicted on four counts of conspiring to provide "material support" to terrorists in Pakistan by providing funds "for guns, training, schools and other resources to carry out violent attacks against U.S. forces and allies in that region." *See* Jay Weaver, Laura Edwins & Melissa Sanchez, *Feds Indict Miami Imam, Family Members on Charges of Supporting Taliban*, Miami Herald, May 14, 2011, *available at:* http://www.miamiherald.com/2011/05/14/2216850/miami-feds-indict-6-on-charges.html; Jay Weaver & Curtis Morgan, *Attorney says Imam Will Fight Terror Charges*, Miami Herald, May 17, 2011, *available at:* http://www.miamiherald.com/2011/05/16/2219657/attorney-muslim-accused-of-backing.html. It is not apparent yet in this case whether the defendants will claim First Amendment protections—freedom of association, in particular. It is clear, however, that the government has not additionally charged the defendants with seditious conspiracy.

   78.   *See* United States v. Blumenthal 332 U.S. 539 (1947) (illegal liquor distribution); United States v. Bruno, 105 F.2d 921 (2d Cir. 1939) (per curium) (88 individuals indicted as part of one conspiracy to import and sell drugs, even where smugglers only dealt with middlemen, not the drug retailers).

   79.   *See* Kotteakos v. United States, 328 U.S. 750 (1946) (single conspiracy chargeable when "spokes" of the wheel can be "rimmed" because the person at the end of each spoke

maximize the number of charges by, say charging each link in the chain only with the adjacent links, or tying the figure in the middle of the wheel with separate conspiracies along each spoke.[80]

Even though, Abdel–Rahman and a number of his conspirators were charged with murder and bombing conspiracies, these charges were not deemed to be sufficient to capture the breadth of the terrorist activities of Abdel–Rahman and his followers. In addition to the conspiracy and other inchoate charges, seditious conspiracy charges were added for each defendant to convey what the government perceived to be the purpose of the group's terrorist activities—the overthrow of the government.

Seditious Conspiracy and the Treason Clause of the U.S. Constitution

Challenging Seditious Conspiracy

On appeal, El Sayyid Nosair joined Abdel–Rahman and the other eight co-defendants in alleging that their seditious conspiracy charges should be overturned because the federal statute providing for the offense violated the Treason Clause, Art. III, Sect. 3 of the U.S. Constitution.[81] Abdel–Rahman, joined by his other co-defendants, raised a separate basis for overturning the conviction: his speeches were religious teachings and not intended to incite criminal conduct. For this basis of appeal to the charge, the dispositive legal question turned on whether his words constituted protected speech or the free exercise of religion under the First Amendment.[82]

In order to press their theory of the case to the jurors in the trial court, the Government read Sheik Abdel–Rahman's speeches to jurors, and claimed the sermons incited his followers' criminal activities.[83] For

---

knows his deal with the person at the hub depends on economies of scale with other spoke-hub agreements); United States v. Perez, et al., 489 F.2d 51 (5th Cir. 1973) (court criticizing the usefulness of spoke, rim, hub characterizations of conspiracies in a case involving a single insurance fraud scheme comprised of separate entities who recruited participants ("recruiters"), persons who intentionally caused the accidents ("hitters"), and those that occupied the target vehicle ("targets, drivers, and riders"). The metaphors multiply when each spoke of a rimmed wheel is itself a linear chain conspiracy. And the scope of the conspiracy expands even farther when each spoke represents a different kind of illegal business (drugs, loansharking. etc.) so that the larger scheme achieves both economies of scale and diversification of its portfolio.)

80. For a comprehensive analysis of the possibilities, see Jerome Campane, *Chains, Wheels, and The Single Conspiracy*, 50 FBI Law Enforcement Bulletin 24–31 (Aug./Sept. 1981).

81. 189 F.3d at 111.

82. *See* Brandenburg v. Ohio, 395 U.S. 444 (1969) (Court holding the First Amendment does not protect inflammatory speech directed to and likely to incite imminent lawless action).

83. *See* Nadia Abou el-Magd and David Kocieniewski, *Sheik Urged 'City Battles'*, Newsday, Mar. 1, 1995, at A21.

example, in January of 1993, Abdel–Rahman attended a conference in Brooklyn, where he expressed his views in favor of violent *jihad*, claiming that it was fine to be labeled a terrorist in light of the anti-Islamic actions of the United States.[84] On February 26, 1993, Abdel–Rahman's followers bombed the World Trade Center. In line with constitutional jurisprudence governing inciting speech, a critical question on appeal should have been whether he intended his comments to encourage what he understood to be the imminent criminal conduct of his followers. The competing claims and judicial decisions regarding these challenges to the seditious conspiracy charge, as well as historical and legal analyses of the same are considered next.[85]

Analyzing the Challenge: Construing the Statute and Framers' Intent

Recall that Abdel–Rahman and his followers were charged under a statute which provides: "If two or more persons in any State or Territory, or in any place subject to the jurisdiction of the United States, conspire to overthrow, put down or destroy by force the Government of the United States, or to levy war against them ... they shall each be fined under this title or imprisoned not more than 20 years, or both."[86] By contrast, Article III, Section 3 of the Constitution provides: "Treason against the United States Shall consist only in levying War against them, or in adhering to their Enemies, giving them Aid and Comfort. No person shall be convicted of Treason unless on the Testimony of two Witnesses to the same overt Act, or a confession in open court."[87] Abdel–Rahman and his co-conspirators claimed that "because the seditious conspiracy statute punishes conspiracy to 'levy war' against the United States without a conforming two-witness requirement, the statute is unconstitutional."[88]

The Second Circuit responded to this challenge by referencing both constitutional text and the intent of the framers. With regard to the text, the court claimed that the Treason Clause did not apply to the prosecution in this case because the clause *only* governed treason. According to the court, "seditious conspiracy differs from treason not only in name and associated stigma, but also in essential elements and punishment."[89] The difference in stigma and punishment were also germane to a framers' intent argument. The court surmised that since the late colo-

---

84. 189 F.3d at 107.

85. The appeal which confirmed all the convictions and eight of the nine sentences in the case, was presided over by circuit Judges Newman, Leval and Parker. *Id.* at 101.

86. 18 U.S.C. § 2384 (1994).

87. U.S. Const., Art. III, Sect. 3.

88. 189 F.3d at 112.

89. *Id.*

nial period, "treason [has] carried a 'peculiar intimidation and stigma.' "[90] Moreover, at the time of the drafting of the Constitution, treason was punishable by a particularly cruel form of death reserved for traitors: the male offender would be " 'hanged by the neck, then cut down alive,' that 'his entrails [are then] taken out, and burned, while he is yet alive,' that his 'head [is] cut off' and that his 'body [is then] divided into four parts.' "[91] Treason is still punishable by death, while the maximum penalty for seditious conspiracy is twenty years in prison.

The circuit judges reasoned that the Framers wished to limit the severest punishments to those who levied war against or adhered to the enemies of the United States, and as such, the Treason Clause was formulated as "a protection against promiscuous resort to this particularly stigmatizing label, which carries such harsh consequences."[92] As a consequence of this desire, the Treason Clause should be interpreted as only applying to charges of treason. The court further indicated that the Supreme Court had left open the question of how to treat offenses "that include all the elements of treason, but are not branded as such."[93] This panel, however, did not address the question further because it determined that while seditious conspiracy included the element of levying war, it differed significantly from treason. For one thing, unlike treason, the seditious conspiracy charge included no element of requiring allegiance to the United States.

While the appellate court's reasoning here was defensible,[94] this charge appeared odd for a number of reasons. First of all, there is the danger that will be discussed further below, that the statute has a significant tendency to punish based on a person's negative attitude toward the United States.[95] Second, at the time of the *Rahman* case, the offense of seditious conspiracy was rarely charged.[96] According to one

---

90. *Id. (quoting* William Hurst, *Treason in the United States (Pt. II), 58* Harv. L. Rev. 395, 424–25 (1945)).

91. *Id.* citing *Blackstone Commentaries.* Women by contrast would merely be " 'drawn to the gallows and . . . burned alive.' " *Id.*

92. *Id.*

93. *Id.* at 113.

94. *See* Susan Kelly Babb, *Fear and Loathing in America: Application of Treason Law in Times of National Crises and the Case of John Walker Lindh,* 54 Hastings L.J. 1721, 1741 (2003).

95. *See* Kevin Fedarko, *The Imaginary Apocalypse: A U.S. Court Finds a Blind Muslim Cleric and Nine of His Followers Guilty of "Seditious Conspiracy" to Conduct a Bombing Spree Throughout New York City,* Time, Oct. 16, 1995, at 46.

96. The charge was left over from the Civil War era, where it was mostly charged against secessionists. *See* Joseph Grinstein, *Jihad and the Constitution: The First Amendment Implications of Combating Religiously Motivated Speech,* 105 Yale L.J. 1347, 1351 (1996).

source, there had only been ten prosecutions under the sedition statute between 1950 and 1995.[97] Moreover, and more troubling, was the same author's claim that it was the outsider status of the defendants, based on race, ethnicity, religion, etc. which dictated the imposition of the charge.

A separate concern then becomes that defendants who are readily identifiable as minorities are more likely to be convicted of seditious conspiracy. For example, the defendants sentenced in the New York City terrorism case were religious, racial, ethnic and linguistic minorities and most, including Sheik Omar Abdel–Rahman, were also immigrants. In earlier seditious conspiracy prosecutions, the defendants' cultural identities varied, but, taken as a whole, the cases reflect a pattern of prejudice.[98]

Certainly, in the wake of 9/11 there have been numerous claims that the enforcement of anti-terrorism initiatives was often infused with migrant/Muslim backlash.[99] Still, American extremist groups have been recently charged using the statute,[100] and it is unlikely on the facts of this case that one could effectively claim that Abdel–Rahman and his followers were targeted and convicted *because of* their race, national origin, or religion.[101] In any event, when the *Rahman* case was tried the more prevalent critiques were doctrinal in nature.

First, unlike some other forms of conspiracy, seditious conspiracy requires no overt act in furtherance of the agreed upon plan in order to charge someone under the statute; the agreement is all that is necessary. This renders more salient the claims that defendants are being charged under the statute for thoughts rather than deeds. Second, there have been criticisms of the Second Circuit's comparison of treason and sedi-

---

97. *See* Bradley T. Winter, *Invidious Prosecution: The History of Seditious Conspiracy–Foreshadowing the Recent Convictions of Sheik Omar Abdel–Rahman and His Immigrant Followers*, 10 Geo. Immigr. L.J. 185, 188 (1996).

98. *Id.* at 187. The author further claimed that minority defendants were disproportionately convicted under the statute. *Id.* at 209–10.

99. *See, e.g.,* R. Richard Banks, *Racial Profiling and Antiterrorism Efforts*, 89 Cornell L. Rev. 1201, 1206–14 (2004); Leti Volpp, *The Citizen and the Terrorist*, 49 UCLA L. Rev. 1575, 1576–86 (2002); Mario L. Barnes and F. Greg Bowman, *Entering Unprecedented Terrain: Charting a Method to Reduce Madness in Post–9/11 Power and Rights Conflicts*, 62 U. Miami L. Rev. 365, 388–97 (2008); Asli U. Bali, *Scapegoating the Vulnerable: Preventive Detention of Immigrants in America's "War on Terror,"* 38 Studies in Law, Politics and Society 25 (2006) (detailing the Bush administration's post–9/11 indefinite detentions of immigrant men of predominantly of Middle Eastern background, under the pretext of civil immigration violations).

100. *See supra* note 77 and the FBI press release detailing the capture of the Hutaree militia, *available at*: http://detroit.fbi.gov/dojpressrel/pressrel10/de032910.htm

101. *See, e.g.*, McCleskey v. Kemp, 481 U.S. 279 (1987) (evidence of purposeful governmental discrimination is required to sustain a constitutional claim of race or national origin discrimination).

tious conspiracy. For instance, the court claimed that treason and seditious conspiracy should not be treated similarly because treason included the requirement of allegiance not found in the sedition statute. The Supreme Court and commentators, however, have noted that, historically, even those temporarily within a country have been deemed to owe allegiance to the sovereign.[102] Hence the allegiance analysis in *Rahman* may have represented a distinction without a difference.

The circuit judges' strong assertion of a distinction between treason and seditious conspiracy was somewhat further undermined by the court claiming that treason was the appropriate analogy crime for arriving at a sentence on the seditious conspiracy charge. Rather than point to the element of allegiance as signifying a distinct difference between seditious conspiracy and treason, one commentator has argued that sedition should be treated as a lesser included offense of treason.[103] Doing so would lead to a potentially different answer to the question of whether the requirements of the Treason Clause govern such cases. The more typical criticism of the seditious conspiracy charge, however, has turned on the Government using Abdel–Rahman's religious speeches and writings to support the existence of the plan to levy war against the United States.

Revisiting Dennis *and* Brandenburg: *Seditious Conspiracy and the First Amendment*

Abdel–Rahman's challenge to the statute claimed the government had violated his First Amendment rights to free speech and free exercise of religion. First, he claimed that the seditious conspiracy charge was facially invalid because "it criminalized protected expression and that it was overbroad and unconstitutionally vague."[104] Additionally, he claimed that he was being punished solely based on his political views and religious practices. There is at least some evidence that government officials were not uniform in their judgment that Abdel–Rahman should be charged for his involvement. According to writer Lauri Mylroie, FBI

---

102. *See* Carlton F.W. Larson, *The Forgotten Constitutional Law of Treason and the Enemy Combatant Problem*, 154 U. Pa. L. Rev. 863, 875 (2006) (noting the U.S. conception of allegiance was premised upon English law which provided: "All aliens that are within the realm of England, and whose sovereigns are in amity with the king of England, are within the protection of the king, and do owe a local obedience to the king ... and if they commit high treason against the king, they shall be punished as traitors"); Carlisle v. United States, 83 U.S. (16 Wall.) 147, 154 (1873) (Court relying on international law to claim, "temporary allegiance by an alien resident in a friendly country is everywhere recognized by publicists and statesmen.").

103. *See* John Alan Cohan, *Seditious Conspiracy, The Smith Act and Prosecution for Religious Speech Advocating the Violent Overthrow of the Government*, 17 St. John's J. Legal Comment 199, 226–27 (2003) (analyzing sedition as attempted treason).

104. *Id.* at 114.

Chief, Jim Fox, wanted to deport rather than prosecute Abdel–Rahman.[105] Before his indictment for seditious conspiracy, the U.S. and Egypt were attempting to work out extradition pursuant to an extradition treaty between the U.S. and the former Ottomon Empire.[106] It was apparently, Attorney General, Janet Reno, who strongly argued in favor of his prosecution.[107]

Facial Challenge

For the facial challenge, the critical question in the Abdel–Rahman case is when does speech move from being protected expression to punishable as incitement. Since at least World War I, the Supreme Court has interpreted certain forms of incitement of illegal activity to be unprotected by the First Amendment. In a series of cases applying the Espionage Act 1917,[108] as amended by the Sedition Act of 1918 (both repealed in 1921),[109] the Court articulated a "clear and present danger" standard to evaluate violations of the statutes which placed severe restrictions on anti-government, anti-war speech.[110] This standard was substantially modified, with the holdings in two cases, *Dennis v. United States*[111] and *Brandenburg v. Ohio*,[112] being most helpful for deciding modern questions of incitement.

Dennis involved a challenge to the Smith Act, which made it unlawful to advocate the violent overthrow of the government; or, while having the intent to cause the violent overthrow, to produce material's advocating the same; or to organize people to advocate the violent overthrow. Using an analysis that weighed the gravity of the evil (discounted by improbability) against the encroachment on the First Amendment, the Supreme Court held that the Act did not "inherently, or as construed or applied" violate the First Amendment.[113] Additionally, the Court indicated that the organizing activities of the Communist Party constituted a "clear and present danger" of an attempt to overthrow the government.[114]

---

105. Mylroie, *supra* note 7, at 187.

106. *Id.* at 185.

107. *Id.* at 187–88.

108. 18 USC § 792 et seq. (1917).

109. Pub. L. 65–150. Stat. 40.553. 16 May 1918.

110. *See* Schenk v. United States, 249 U.S. 47 (1919); Frohwerk v. United States, 249 U.S. 204 (1919); Debs v. United States, 249 U.S. 211 (1919); and Abrams v. United States 250 U.S. 616 (1919).

111. 343 U.S. 494 (1951).

112. 395 U.S. 444 (1965) (per curium).

113. 343 U.S. at 516.

114. *Id.* at 517.

A first blush, the *Rahman* case seems somewhat similar to *Dennis*, in that it involves limitations on speech pursuant to a statute designed to limit anti-government speech and activities. While *Dennis* also involved inciting behavior, the statute in that case and the seditious conspiracy statute in *Rahman* are very different. In *Dennis*, the Court held that the statute in question criminalized advocacy of the overthrow of the government,[115] and that restricting such speech did not violate the First Amendment. Post-*Dennis*, the Court made clear that criminalizing encouragement or inducement of violent action is not the same thing as criminalizing the expression of anti-government views.[116]

Brandenburg, by contrast, involved the activities of the Klu Klux Klan and the Klan's violation of an Ohio statute which criminalized advocating or teaching a duty or necessity for violence as a means of accomplishing industrial or political reform. Ultimately, the Court struck down the statute because it failed to distinguish advocacy from incitement.[117] Per *Brandenburg*, one cannot be convicted for incitement unless there is imminence of harm, a likelihood of producing illegal action, and an intent to cause imminent illegality.

Without much discussion, the Second Circuit in *Rahman* concluded that the seditious conspiracy statute satisfied the *Dennis* and *Brandenburg* standards. The court appeared to place some weight on the differences between the statutes in *Dennis* and *Rahman*. While the Smith Act specifically addressed advocating violent overthrow, 18 U.S.C. § 2384 does not. The *Rahman* appellate court asserted that the latter statute is further from the realm of speech because it criminalizes the use of force or conspiracy to commit the same.[118] There is no direct reference to speech. The court then cited support in the line of Supreme Court cases which distinguished between expressions of belief and threatening or using force.[119]

The decision to exempt Abdel–Rahman's sermons and advice from First Amendment protection may be the most significant decision in the *Rahman* case, especially since the U.S. Supreme Court refused to hear the appeal of the case.[120] The appellate decision, however, did not clearly establish precisely when religious advocacy of violence becomes punishable. For example, prosecutors described Abdel–Rahman's sermons as

---

115. Although, notably, the case actually punished the defendants for *conspiring* to advocate. *Id.* at 511.

116. *See, e.g.*, Yates v. United States, 354 U.S. 298 (1956); Burks v. United States, 437 U.S. 1 (1978).

117. 189 F.3d at 115.

118. *Id.*

119. *Id.*

120. Abdel–Rahman v. United States, 328 U.S. 1094 (2000) (cert. denied).

"frequently urging his followers to conduct guerilla wars, 'city battles' and assassinations in the name of Islam."[121] The defense, in contrast, characterized the speeches as "inspirational sermons" that were the Muslim equivalent of singing *Onward Christian Soldiers*.[122] While the meanings of Abdel–Rahman's speeches were in dispute, the case law has clearly indicated that people cannot be punished for merely expressing abstract, although unpopular, beliefs.[123]

Three criticisms of the Court's opinion deserve note. First, it can be alleged that most of Abdel–Rahman's expressions were abstract in nature, not specific admonitions of harm.[124] Second, some commentators have criticized the conspiracy-advocacy split that the appellate court relies upon.[125] Although Abdel–Rahman was convicted of conspiracy, the support for the charge was his advocating violence in his sermons and separately to individuals. Hence, it may have been ill-advised for the Second Circuit to suggest such a stark difference between the Smith Act and the seditious conspiracy statute. Third, other than to suggest that the relevant standard was met, the *Rahman* appellate court did not specifically apply the *Brandenburg* standard for incitement to the facts of the case. As one commentator surmised on the precipice of the *Rahman* appeal, one would have expected the court to engage in the following type of analysis: The B*randenburg* test distinguishes between protected speech and unprotected speech. Rahman's speech is not protected under *Brandenburg* if Rahman (1) expressly advocated violence, (2) called for imminent law violation, and (3) the imminent law violation was likely to occur. In this case, the limited evidence available to the public indicates that Rahman expressly advocated violence and that the violence was likely to occur. The problem, as is often the case in *Brandenburg*-type cases, lies in the interpretation of the word "imminent."[126]

Specific evidence suggested that Abdel–Rahman *advocated* for the assassination of Hosni Mubarak and attacks on U.S. military bases. It is not clear, however, that he *commanded* or *directed* these crimes. Additionally, Abdel–Rahman was convicted of solicitation and conspiracy to

---

121. Nadia Abou el-Magd & David Kocieniewski, *Sheik Urged City Battles*, Newsday, Mar. 1, 1995, at A21.

122. *Id.*

123. *See, e.g.*, Wisconsin v. Mitchell, 508 U.S. 476 (1993).

124. *See* Holly S. Hawkins, *A Sliding Scale Approach for Evaluating the Terrorist Threat Over the Internet*, 73 Geo. Wash. L. Rev. 633 (2005).

125. *See* Thomas Healy, *Brandenburg in a Time of Terror*, 84 Notre Dame L. Rev. 655 (2009).

126. Holly Coates Keehn, *Terroristic Religious Speech: Giving the Devil the Benefit of the First Amendment Free Exercise and Free Speech Clauses*, 28 Seton Hall L. Rev. 1230, 1251 (1998) (citation omitted).

commit these acts and conspiracy to bomb sites throughout New York City. There is some question as to whether Abdel–Rahman's actions should also have been alleged as proof of seditious conspiracy—an agreement to commit a wide-ranging plan of urban terrorism. Per *Brandenburg*, the Second Circuit should have inquired whether it was Rahman's intent to incite violence and whether violence was "imminent" as a result of his teachings. Although prosecutors read Abdel–Rahman's sermons to the jury, they did not articulate precisely how Abdel–Rahman commanded specific overt acts in support of an overarching seditious conspiracy.

To use Rahman's religious teachings to identify him as the leader of the multifaceted destructive plot seems odd for at least two reasons. First, as one of the World Trade Center bombers surmised, the plans of Abdel–Rahman's followers were modest until Ramzi Yousef took control of organizing the group.[127] Second, even if Abdel–Rahman engaged in the specific conduct the state alleged, one could argue that this evidence bore on solicitation or limited conspiracies to assassinate Mubarak and target U.S. military bases for which he was convicted, not necessarily a plan of urban terrorism. This was essentially the argument of Abdel–Rahman's co-defendant, Fadil Abdelgani, who conceded there was sufficient evidence to convict him of attempted bombing and conspiracy to bomb, but not seditious conspiracy.[128] At bottom, one would need to know whether Rahman's conviction was supported by more than evidence such as the videotaped image that was shown to the jury of him stating, " 'Jihad is . . . fighting the enemies for God's sake.' "[129] If this were all it took to create a seditious conspiracy, it would provide support for those who claim that the case involves "the criminalizing of the content of religious speech."[130]

Claims that neither Abdel–Rahman nor his co-defendants subscribed to a plan that was tantamount to levying war on the United States were rejected by the trial court and the Second Circuit. These decisions, however, did not indicate the amount or type of encouragement necessary to affect the charge. Furthermore, other than to assert that religious inciting speech was not protected speech, there was no discussion of a standard that would allow courts to know precisely when negative religious expressions are more than abstract, or are otherwise unprotected. If the answer to questions of this nature is merely that *Brandenburg*

---

127. Reeve *supra* note 15, at 145. Although Yousef was also described as more of a calculated killer than an Islamic fundamentalist. *Id*. at 249.

128. 189 F.3d at 127.

129. Joseph Grinstein, *Jihad and the Constitution: The First Amendment Implications of Combating Religiously Motivated Speech*, 105 Yale L.J. 1347, 1352 (1996).

130. *Id*. at 1353.

remains the standard, the Second Circuit should at least have inquired into whether it was Abdel–Rahman's intent for his actions to imminently result in harm. At the most, they could have answered the more intriguing question whether *Bradenburg* was the right standard to review religious speech,[131] or whether analysis under free exercise would have yielded a different result.

Other Bases of Appeal: Overbreadth, Vagueness, and Punishment Based on Political Views and Religious Practices

In addition to determining that prohibitions on speech contained in the statute did not violate the Constitution, the Second Circuit ruled that the seditious conspiracy statute was neither overbroad nor vague. Specifically, Abdel–Rahman claimed that Congress could have written the statute more narrowly, or achieved its goals without "chilling First Amendment rights."[132] The court acknowledged that the sedition charge "must be scrutinized with care to assure that the threat of prosecution will not deter expression of unpopular viewpoints," but it ultimately concluded that the statute prohibited only conspiratorial agreement and contained no issue of real and substantial overbreadth.[133]

The vagueness challenge questioned whether the statute defined the criminal offense with sufficient definiteness to give notice or fair warning of what conduct is unlawful. The court acknowledged that the word "seditious" may not adequately describe what conduct was prohibited, but the text of the statute—which prohibited conspiracies to levy war against the United States—was clear.[134] This basis of appeal was also rejected.

The Second Circuit also rejected Abdel–Rahman's claim that he was punished solely because of his political views and religious practices. The government answered this challenge by advancing two related points. First, it claimed that freedom of speech and religion do not bar prosecution of one who uses public or religious speech to commit crimes.[135] Second, the court determined that one is not immunized from being charged with speech-based crimes merely because one commits them through political speech or sermons.[136] The fact that Abdel–Rahman's

---

131. *See id.* at 1376 (questioning whether "clear and present danger" is an effective standard to review religious speech).

132. 189 F.3d at 116.

133. *Id.*

134. *Id.*

135. *Id.* at 116–17.

136. *Id.* at 117.

speeches were religious in nature did not prevent them from providing the basis for a conspiracy charge.[137]

Abdel–Rahman essentially crossed a line, in that his speeches were deemed more than expressions; they constituted a conspiracy and solicitation to wage war against the U.S.[138] As such, the court rejected his challenge to the admissions of his speeches, writings and preaching on a similar basis. The First Amendment protects his right to voice hostility toward the government, but does not place limits on the expressions being used as evidence, when they are relevant to a criminal prosecution.[139]

Abdel–Rahman either argued or joined several other bases for appeal, but those matters are not discussed here.[140] Specifically, a significant portion of the appeal deals with largely unsuccessful challenges to the defendants' sentences for sedition.[141] The lower court used the sentencing guidelines for treason to impose consecutive sentences for sedition. The appellate court found this acceptable. The Second Circuit also rejected a claim that the treason guidelines for sentencing should not be applied to any participant in the seditious conspiracy unless "the sentencing judge finds that the defendant agreed to wage war."[142]

Conclusion

In some ways *U.S. v. Rahman* presents a bit of a paradox. With regard to the then-uncontroversial decision to try multiple terrorist suspects in federal criminal trials, it represents a high-water mark for unchanging standards of due process, even in the face of devastating domestic terrorism. The substance of the trial, however, at least as it pertains to the intersection of inchoate crimes and religious speech, is a bit more vexing. There is no doubt that various attempt and conspiracy charges were germane to the activities of Abdel–Rahman and his co-defendants, as well as other followers who participated in the bombing of the World Trade Center. Ironically, basic conspiracy—which has historically been a source of significant debate within criminal law—was not the issue in this case. The sticking point was the separate seditious conspiracy charge, with which each defendant was charged. The offense is problematic for anyone charged because of the absence of an overt act requirement and the uneasy relationship between sedition and the

---

137. *Id.*

138. *Id.*

139. *Id.* at 118.

140. *See id.* 121–126, and 134–145.

141. *Id.* at 145–60. Of numerous sentencing-based challenges, only El–Gabrowny's was remanded for further consideration on mitigation of his sentence. *Id.* at 175.

142. *Id.* at 154.

Constitution's treatment of treason. These problems, however, do not represent the greatest challenges to the offense. At least since the *Rahman* case, the concern should be how we manage the potential restraints on speech that the sedition statute portends, especially for religious expressions, which vary between lawful abstract criticism and illegal specific encouragement to commit criminal acts.

Clearly, there was evidence in this case that Abdel–Rahman advocated violence against the U.S. and Egypt. That doesn't answer the question, however, about whether his religious speeches and sermons should have been determined to be unprotected speech. On the one hand, the appellate court did very little inquiry into whether Abdel–Rahman called for his followers to commit imminent unlawful actions that were likely to occur through his religious guidance. Second, it also did not carefully demarcate the parts of his expressions that were abstract and protected criticism versus those that appeared to command or direct specific acts of violence. For these reasons, the case is more valuable for its core precedential value—e.g., domestic terrorists' plots may be charged as sedition—rather than its analysis of the intersection of crime and First Amendment rights. Given that terrorism is no longer perceived as a set of isolated incidents and that since 2001 we have been fighting a "war" against the practice, that precedent looms quite large. Any group deemed to advocate extreme anti-government positions, religious or otherwise, is in danger of facing such a charge. At the end of Abdel–Rahman's trial, defense counsel, Lynne Stewart—who is now in prison for crimes of obstruction of justice and conspiring to provide material support to terrorists related to her representation of Abdel–Rahman[143] perhaps, accurately foreshadowed the place we are now in with defending charges in cases such as this: to prevail, it will be necessary "to defeat the government *and* the climate."[144]

---

143. *See* John Eligon, *Heftier Term for Lawyer in Terrorism Case*, New York Times, July 16, 2010, at A22.

144. Lisa Anderson, Sheik, *Nine Others Found Guilty in N.Y. Bomb Plot: U.S. Hails Verdict; Security Tightened Around Airports*, Chicago Tribune, Oct. 2, 1995, at 1.

12

Sara Sun Beale

The Story of *Ewing:* Three Strikes Laws and the Limits of the Eighth Amendment Proportionality Review

The Eighth Amendment prohibits "cruel and unusual punishments,"[1] and by long tradition it provided a mechanism for challenging particular methods of punishment, such as flogging. The more controversial question is whether the amendment also imposes limitations on the excessive use of permissible forms of punishment.

The Supreme Court first began to answer that question in death penalty litigation. In *Coker v. Georgia*,[2] decided in 1978, the Supreme Court established that it is cruel and unusual to impose a sentence of death when that penalty is disproportionate to the offender's crime. The Court concluded that the Eighth Amendment bars the imposition of the death penalty for the rape of an adult woman, because that crime, though heinous, does not warrant the state's imposition of death. *Coker* was the first in a line of decisions in which the Court has applied the proportionality standard in death penalty cases.[3] Although the death

---

1. "Excessive bail shall not be required, nor excessive fines imposed, nor cruel and unusual punishments inflicted." U.S. Const. Amend. VIII. The Amendment was modeled on a parallel provision in the English Declaration of Rights of 1689, which provided: "[E]xcessive Bail ought not to be required nor excessive Fines imposed; nor cruel and unusual Punishments inflicted." Roper v. Simmons, 543 U.S. 551, 577 (2005).

2. 433 U.S. 584 (1977). For an in depth discussion of *Coker*, see Sheri Lynn Johnson, Coker v. Georgia: *Of Rape, Race, and Burying the Past, in* Death Penalty Stories at 171–201 (John H. Blume & Jordan M. Steiker, eds., 2009).

3. The Supreme Court's most recent death penalty proportionality decision is *Kennedy v. Louisiana*, 544 U.S. 407 (2008) (holding that the Eighth Amendment prohibits the death penalty for the rape of a child where the crime did not result, and was not intended to result, in death of the victim).

penalty decisions based on proportionality have been difficult and controversial, they rest on a clear categorical distinction and apply to only a
relatively small and easily identifiable group of cases. Death is different
in kind from any other penalty in its severity and finality, and death
sentences are relatively rare.

Sentences of imprisonment, in contrast, are far more numerous, and
by their nature they fall all along a continuum ranging from probation to
incarceration for any number of days, weeks, months, or years. Fashion-
ing a constitutional proportionality standard for cases involving sentences of imprisonment is a much more difficult judicial task, with the
potential to affect a much larger number of cases. A constitutional
proportionality standard would restrict the options available to the
states, which prosecute the vast majority of crimes in the United States
and vary widely in their sentencing policies. For that reason, the
extension of the proportionality principle beyond capital cases necessarily raises hard questions of federalism and judicial competence.

In 1994 California enacted the nation's harshest "three strikes" law.
The name "three strikes" comes from a baseball analogy: after a third
qualifying conviction (or "strike"), an offender is "out" of civil society.
Under the California law, a third strike requires a mandatory prison
sentence of 25 years to life. In *Ewing v. California*[4] the Supreme Court
held that sending a drug addict who shoplifted three golf clubs to
imprisonment for 25 years to life under the three strikes law did not
violate the cruel and unusual punishment clause of the Eighth Amendment.

This chapter explores three questions. First, why did California
impose such a draconian sentence for such a minor offense? Second, why
wasn't such a sentence prohibited by the cruel and unusual punishment
clause? Finally, what limits—if any—does the Eighth Amendment impose on the state's authority to replace policies based on rehabilitation,
retribution, and individualized sentencing with a policy that seeks to
protect society by incapacitating recidivists?

The California Three Strikes Law

During the last quarter of the twentieth century most U.S. jurisdictions adopted major sentencing reforms. Before the adoption of the
various reforms, sentencing was generally individualized, discretionary,
and indeterminate. Sentences were individualized and discretionary because judges had largely unreviewable authority to set the sentence for
an individual offender at any point within a wide statutory range, from
probation to a maximum sentence of many years. Sentences were also
indeterminate because they were subject to a second phase of discretion-

---

4. 538 U.S. 11 (2003).

ary decision making by the parole authorities, who had discretion to release a defendant on parole before he finished serving his sentence if they deemed him sufficiently rehabilitated. Thus at the time a defendant was sentenced it was not ordinarily possible to know whether he would have to serve his full sentence.

Many factors contributed to the support for major changes in the discretionary sentencing regimes.[5] Lawmakers and policy makers came to agree that the current system, based on the goal of rehabilitating offenders, simply did not work.[6] Crime rates had increased dramatically since the post-war period, and during the 1990s media coverage of crime, especially violent crime, increased even more dramatically.[7] Conservatives argued that the excessive leniency of the system was a threat to public safety, and the public by a wide margin agreed that sentences were generally too low.[8] By the beginning of the 1990s, crime was an increasingly salient political issue, and there was wide support for a variety of tough on crime measures. Additionally, victims (and their families) were becoming an increasingly important political force.

To respond to all of these concerns, U.S. jurisdictions began adopting a variety of restrictions on judicial sentencing discretion, most notably sentencing guidelines and mandatory minimum sentencing laws.[9] These general developments set the stage for the adoption of the recidivist statutes popularly called three strikes laws. Although the three strikes terminology was new, habitual offender statutes, which provide enhanced sentences for an offender who had prior convictions for a specified number of felonies, had a long history. California was one of

---

5. Although some of the sentencing reforms, particularly the three strikes legislation and other mandatory minimum sentencing laws, had greater support among conservatives than liberals, both liberals and conservatives were concerned that discretionary sentencing was arbitrary. That agreement was the basis for the bipartisan support of the federal legislation authorizing the promulgation of federal sentencing guidelines. This legislation was co-sponsored by conservative Republican Senator Strom Thurmond and liberal Senator Edward (Ted) Kennedy. For a description of the events leading to the passage of the Sentencing Reform Act, see Kate Stith & José Cabranes, *Fear of Judging: Sentencing Guidelines and the Federal Courts* 38–48 (1998).

6. *See generally* Francis A. Allen, *The Decline of the Rehabilitative Ideal: Penal Policy and Social Purpose* (1981); *See also* Jennifer E. Walsh, *Three Strikes Laws* 4–9 (2007).

7. Sara Sun Beale, *The News Media's Influence on Criminal Justice Policy: How Market Driven News Promotes Punitiveness*, 48 Wm. & Mary L. Rev. 397, 422–36 (2006) (describing dramatic increase in crime coverage in network news, local television news, and newspapers).

8. *Id.* at 418–20 (noting that in every year from 1980 to 1998 more than 74% of respondents in a national poll said sentencing was not harsh enough, and in 2002, 67% said sentences were too lenient).

9. *See generally* Candace McCoy, *Sentencing: Mandatory and Mandatory Minimum Sentences, in* 4 Encyclopedia of Crime & Justice at 1443 (Joshua Dressler ed., 2nd ed. 2002).

the pioneers when a wave of new three strikes laws swept across the nation. Indeed, in just a two year period, from 1993 to 1994, twenty-four states enacted three strikes laws.[10]

The first three strikes law was adopted in the state of Washington in 1993 through the ballot initiative process. A victims' rights coalition drafted the measure in response to concerns that new sentencing reform legislation had weakened the sentencing laws applicable to recidivists. The ballot initiative required a mandatory life sentence without parole upon conviction of a third violent offense. With the financial backing of the National Rifle Association, which pledged up to $100,000, supporters mailed more than 400,000 forms within the state and collected more than twice the required number of signatures to place the initiative on the ballot. It was adopted by a 3–1 margin.[11]

A reform based on the Washington measure was proposed in California by Mike Reynolds, whose eighteen-year-old daughter, Kimber, had been shot and killed during an attempted purse snatching. Both of her assailants had long criminal records, and Reynolds was enraged when one of them received a nine-year sentence as part of a plea bargain. This meant, Reynolds said, that one of Kimber's attackers would get out of prison about the time the Reynolds family finished paying for her funeral.[12] At the sentencing, Reynolds also accused the state of California of being an "unindicted conspirator" in Kimber's murder, because it had not locked her killer up long ago.

Kimber's murder propelled Mike Reynolds on a crusade that ultimately led to the passage of the current California legislation. Reynolds took a harsh view of recidivist criminals:

> They're little more than animals. They look like people, but they're not. And the unfortunate thing is they're preying on us. And we have to get them out so the rest of us can go on living our lives.[13]

Reynolds vowed to go all out against recidivists. After a bill introduced by his local assemblymen failed to get out of committee, Reynolds drafted a similar initiative and began seeking the necessary signatures to

---

10. After California and Washington State adopted their three strikes laws in 1993 and 1994, twenty-two other states and the federal government adopted new laws enhancing punishments for repeat felony offenders. *See generally* John Clark et al., *"Three Strikes and You're Out" Legislation: A Review of State Legislation* 1997 Nat'l Inst. of Justice 1.

11. Walsh, *supra* note 6, at 37.

12. Joe Domanick, *Three Strikes and the Politics of Crime in America's Golden State* 24, 68 (2004). The state allowed Douglas Walker to plead guilty because he had not pulled the trigger and could plausibly have argued that he did not know what the triggerman, Joe Davis, intended. Davis had been killed in a shootout with police.

13. Sasha Abramsky, *Hard Time Blues* 112 (2002) (quoting an episode of the television news show *20/20* that aired after Polly Klaas was buried).

place it on the ballot as an initiative. But getting an initiative on the ballot requires collecting hundreds of thousands of signatures, and Reynolds initially had little success.[14]

Everything changed with the abduction and murder of twelve year old Polly Klaas on October 1, 1993. A stranger who had entered through an unlocked door took Polly from her own bedroom in Petaluma where she and two of her friends were having a sleepover party.[15] Polly's mother was asleep in a nearby room. A massive effort to find Polly was launched. Her photograph and the details of her abduction appeared in all of the state and national media, and she was featured in publications ranging from *People* magazine to *MTV News*. Actress Winona Ryder, a native of Petaluma, offered a $200,000 reward for information leading to Polly's safe release. Polly was the first famous missing child of the Internet age, and by the time her body was found over two billion images of Polly Klaas had been distributed worldwide.[16] Polly's father and grandfather, Marc and Joe Klaas, made a deliberate choice to use the media to keep her story on the front page and help to find her.[17]

The search for Polly went on for nine weeks. The case finally broke when police put together circumstantial evidence pointing to Richard Allen Davis and arrested him on other charges. After several days of interrogation, Davis confessed and led police to Polly's body. News of the December 4, 1993, discovery of Polly's body set off a wave of grief, fear, and anger.

Davis had a long criminal record beginning at age twelve, when he was arrested for stealing checks out of mailboxes.[18] He had shown a violent streak as a child, setting fire to cats and using dogs as targets for knife-throwing practice. His early offenses were mainly property crimes, including burglaries, and his first prison commitment was for a property crime. But weeks after his release, he kidnapped a woman and sexually

---

14. Walsh, *supra* note 6, at 38 (noting that Reynolds was using his own money for this effort and had only been able to obtain a fraction of the approximately 400,000 signatures he needed).

15. The intruder appeared suddenly, telling the terrified girls that he had come to commit robbery. He gagged the girls, tied their hands behind them, put pillow cases over their heads, and told them to lie down on the floor and count to 1,000. Then he carried Polly away. Domanick, *supra* note 12, at 94.

16. Polly Klaas Foundation, Polly's Story, at http://www.pollyklaas.org/about/pollys-story.html (last visited Feb. 14, 2010). This site includes Polly's photograph and the posters which included her photo, a police sketch of her abductor, and the $200,000 reward.

17. Joe Klaas had majored in public relations and worked as a disc jockey for a radio station, and he knew the media could help. Marc Klaas gave dozens of interviews to keep the story alive. Domanick, supra note 12, at 118–119.

18. The description of Davis's background is drawn from Domanick, *supra* note 12, at 97, and Walsh, *supra* note 6, at 39.

assaulted her, and in the years that followed, Davis was convicted of burglary, assault, robbery, and kidnapping. Within two years of his parole, he kidnapped and assaulted another victim. Davis was then sentenced to sixteen years in prison, but he earned good time credits and was released on parole after serving about half of his sentence. Less than three months later, he abducted and killed Polly Klaas.

As details about Davis's criminal history emerged, they created "a political firestorm."[19] Two days after the news of Polly's death was announced, Mike Reynolds appeared at a press conference with California's Attorney General, who endorsed the three strikes initiative and urged all Californians to support it. Fifteen hundred people attended Polly's memorial service, which was held in a church decorated for the event by famed filmmaker George Lucas. Governor Pete Wilson, who was facing a tough reelection campaign, spoke at Polly's memorial service and urged the legislature to take action against sex offenders and career criminals. Within a few weeks, Reynolds had collected more than double the signatures needed to get the initiative on the ballot in November of 1994.

With the Klaas family looking on, Governor Wilson gave a "State of the State" address that focused on crime issues, and he pressed the legislature to take action on three strikes legislation. The legislature took up the three strikes bill under the glare of intense publicity. For example, when the bill was introduced into the Public Safety Committee, the event was filmed by eleven television camera crews, including crews from CNN and the television news program *20/20*.[20]

Within fifty-nine days of its introduction, Reynolds's bill (AB 971) had been approved by four committees and passed by both houses of the California legislature by votes of 63–9 and 29–7.[21] When his bill reached the floor, Reynolds made it clear that he would accept no amendments (even one that would have included money for crime prevention).[22] Legislators faced overwhelming political pressure to support the bill exactly as written, and it passed rapidly despite various warning signs.

Reynolds's bill was significantly different from the three strikes laws adopted in Washington and later in other states, because it defined the

---

19. Unless otherwise noted, the description of the political response to Polly's abduction and Davis's arrest is drawn from Walsh, *supra* note 6, at 39–40, and Michael Vitiello, *Three Strikes: Can We Return to Rationality?*, 87 J. Crim. L. & Criminology 395, 410–22 (1997).

20. Domanick, *supra* note 12 at 136.

21. Vitiello, *supra* note 19, at 414 n.107.

22. Although spectators are rarely permitted to speak during legislative debates, Reynolds simply walked to an open microphone and addressed the Assembly. Domanick, *supra* note 12 at 136.

"strike zone" so much more broadly. All of the laws required first and second strikes to be serious or violent offenses, but the Reynolds bill defined a larger number of offenses as serious or violent for this purpose. (It included, for example, all robberies, not just the most serious robberies such as those involving a weapon.) Even more important, the Reynolds bill did not require the third strike to be a serious or violent offense. Any offense defined as a felony under the California code could serve as a third strike and trigger a mandatory sentence of twenty-five years to life. Finally, unlike other state laws that excluded prior offenses after a number of years, under the Reynolds bill even crimes or juvenile offenses committed many decades earlier could come back to haunt an offender convicted of a non-violent third felony. In addition, the Reynolds bill, unlike the Washington law, also imposed significantly enhanced penalties for the second strike.[23] Thus it affected a far larger number of cases.

These critical features did not go unnoticed as the Reynolds bill and other more narrowly tailored three strikes bills wended their way through the state legislature.[24] The Senate Judiciary Committee and many individual members were aware, for example, that the Reynolds bill would require the imposition of a sentence of twenty-five years to life in prison on a repeat felon who had never committed a violent felony, and a preliminary report from the Legislative Analyst's Office estimated that implementation of the bill could cost the state billions of dollars. The legislature nevertheless approved the Reynolds bill without amendment or a full fiscal analysis. Afraid of the charge that they were soft on crime, the legislative leaders announced they would pass whatever bill the governor backed. Governor Wilson supported the Reynolds bill rather than a narrower bill supported by the California District Attorneys Association.[25] At that point, nothing could stop the Reynolds bill, not even late opposition from the Klaas family. (Polly's father, who had initially supported the Reynolds bill, later withdrew his support because of the inclusion of non-violent offenses. As he explained, "I've had my car broken into and my radio stolen and I've had my daughter murdered, and I know the difference."[26])

Although Mike Reynolds had initially stated that he would drop his ballot initiative if the bill incorporating his three strikes proposal was passed by March 7, 1994, he changed his mind and continued to campaign for the initiative to be sure the new three strikes law could not

---

23. For this purpose, the Reynolds bill did not require the second strike to be a serious or violent felony; a conviction for *any* felony was sufficient to subject an offender to the higher penalties applicable to second strikes.

24. Vitiello, *supra* note 19, at 414–15 (footnotes omitted).

25. Franklin E. Zimring et al., *Three Strikes and You're Out in California*, 6 (2001).

26. Walsh, *supra* note 6, at 67.

be easily changed or dismantled.[27] His initiative provided that it could be amended or repealed only by another initiative or a two-thirds vote of the legislature.[28] On the same day that the governor signed his bill, AB 971, into law, Reynolds delivered 800,000 signatures—more than twice the number required—to put his initiative on the ballot.[29] His three strikes proposal had become the fastest qualifying initiative in state history, and in November 1994, it was passed by a vote of nearly three to one (72% in favor and 28% opposed).[30]

Implementation of the new three strikes law was left to the elected district attorneys, and early studies found that the law was being applied much more frequently in some counties than in others. For example, a 1999 study found that in Los Angeles County 3.6% of felonies were charged as third strikes, but in Alameda and San Francisco Counties, only .07 and .03% of felonies were charged as third strikes, respectively.[31] Densely populated Los Angeles County sent the greatest number of second and third strikers to prison, accounting for 40% of the state's third-strike population—well in excess of its proportion of the general population.[32] By March of 1996, the county was experiencing a backlog of three strikes cases that threatened to overwhelm the system.[33] The large number of three strikes cases in the county was due in part to the rigorous enforcement by District Attorney Gil Garcetti, who generally took a hard line on cases that fell within the statute. At one point, Garcetti delegated authority to his supervising deputies, and as a result the policy even began to vary from courthouse to courthouse within that one county. But Garcetti later issued a memo stating that "all county prosecutors were duty-bound to object every time a judge opted for leniency in sentencing under the Three Strikes law."[34] In the 2000 election, Garcetti was defeated by one of his deputies, Steve Cooley, who campaigned on a promise to use proportionality in deciding whether to

---

27. Dan Morain, *Three Strikes Clears State Legislature*, L.A. Times, Mar. 4, 1994, at A1.

28. Walsh, *supra* note 6 at 42.

29. *Id.*

30. *See* Vitiello, *supra* note 19, at 412 (rapid qualification for the ballot); Walsh, *supra* note 6, at 47 (final margin of victory).

31. Mike Males & Dan Macallair, Symposium, *Striking Out: The Failure of California's "Three Strikes and You're Out" Law,* 11 Stan. L. & Pol'y Rev 65, 71 tbl.6 (1999).

32. *See* Andy Furillo, *Begging Help for Swamped Courts, Jails*, Sacramento Bee, March 31, 1996; Douglas W. Kieso, *Unjust Sentencing and the California Three Strikes Law* 82 (Marilyn McShane & Frank P. Williams III eds., 2005) ("As of December 31, 2001, the county had ... 3,046 third strikers (40% of the state) in the prison population").

33. Furillo, *supra* note 32.

34. Kieso, *supra* note 32, at 118–20 (describing shifts in Garcetti's policies).

charge a third strike.[35]

Whatever the hopes of its supporters, the variation in charging policies among California's district attorneys reflects the fact that the adoption of the three strikes law did not eliminate all discretion in cases falling within its terms. To the contrary, prosecutorial discretion survived, and—perhaps more surprisingly—an important form of judicial discretion survived as well. Prosecutors normally have wide discretion not to prosecute an individual whose conduct violates the law. And just as they often declined to prosecute first offenders who entered drug treatment, California prosecutors exercised their discretion by not charging second or third strikes in some individual cases.[36] Once the prosecutor charged a second or third strike, however, the evident purpose of the three strikes law was to restrict judicial sentencing discretion. But another section of the state penal code that was not amended by the three strikes law gave state courts the authority to dismiss criminal charges when necessary in "furtherance of justice," and in *People v. Romero*[37] the California Supreme Court concluded that the three strikes law had not stripped the state courts of their authority to dismiss (or "strike") the allegations of prior felonies when necessary in "furtherance of justice." *Romero* rested on earlier decisions of the California Supreme Court holding that once a prosecution has been initiated, the power to dismiss in the interests of justice is "fundamentally judicial in nature" and qualifying that power would unacceptably compromise judicial independence.[38] A later decision established that prior convictions charged as second and third strikes should be dismissed "in furtherance of justice" when the court finds the defendant falls outside the spirit of the three strikes law in light of the nature of the offense and the defendant's background and character.[39]

The capital murder case against Richard Allen Davis was unaffected by the passage of the new legislation. He was convicted and sentenced to death in 1996,[40] and his conviction and sentence were affirmed by the California Supreme Court.[41]

---

35. *Id.* at 123–26.

36. This point might have been disputed, because the three strikes law provided that the prosecutor must "plead and prove" all prior felony convictions. Cal. Penal Code § 667(f)(1). Some critics of the law argued that this provision would violate the separation of powers if it were construed to strip the executive branch of its traditional broad discretion to determine whom, and for what offenses, to prosecute. *See* People v. Romero, 917 P.2d 628, 637 n.7 (Cal. 1996).

37. 917 P.2d at 628 (relying on Cal. Penal Code § 1385(a)).

38. The *Romero* court also relied on the principle that legislation should be construed, when possible, to be constitutional, as well as the principle of lenity. *Id.* at 647.

39. People v. Williams, 948 P.2d 429, 437 (Cal. 1998).

40. At his sentencing hearing, Davis suggested that Polly had been sexually abused by her father, Marc Klaas. Klaas lunged at Davis, and was forced out of the courtroom. The

The Supreme Court Considers Eighth Amendment Challenges to the Three Strikes Law

In 2000, the U.S. Supreme Court granted certiorari in two three strikes cases from Los Angeles. Neither defendant was a violent offender like Richard Allen Davis. Both were drug addicts with lengthy criminal records whose third strikes were nonviolent shoplifting offenses. For procedural reasons, only Gary Ewing's case squarely presented the constitutional issues.[42]

Gary Ewing was born October 11, 1962, and by 2000 he had a long criminal history. His first recorded criminal offense was theft, committed in Columbus, Ohio when he was twenty-two years old. The Ohio court suspended Ewing's six-month jail sentence, so he served no time on that offense. Four years later, in 1988, Ewing was again convicted of grand theft, this time in Los Angeles, California. Although he was sentenced to one year in jail, the sentencing court allowed him to withdraw his plea and then dismissed the case after Ewing completed his jail term and three years of probation. In the years that followed, Ewing racked up a series of convictions in California for petty theft, battery, possession of

---

judge then sentenced Davis to death, saying that sentencing someone to death is "always a traumatic and emotional decision for a judge. You made it very easy today by your conduct." Domanick, *supra* note 12, at 155.

41. People v. Davis, 208 P.3d 78 (2009), *cert. denied*, 130 S.Ct.1079 (2010). As of October 31, 2012, Davis had not been executed, and he was maintaining a website, hosted by the Canadian Coalition Against the Death Penalty, available at http://www.ccadp.org/richarddavis.htm (last visited October 31, 2012). It has photographs of Davis, some of his artwork, and a statement about his childhood.

42. Unless otherwise noted, the facts concerning Ewing's case are drawn from the Supreme Court's opinion in *Ewing v. California*, 538 U.S. 11 (2003), the Supreme Court docket, the joint appendix, the parties' briefs, and the unpublished opinion of the California Court of Appeals in *People v. Ewing*, 2001 WL 1840666 (Cal. App. 2d 2001). The other three strike case was *Lockyer v. Andrade*, 538 U.S. 63 (2003). Andrade received a 50 year to life sentence for two felony counts of petty theft with a prior conviction. He had stolen approximately $150 worth of children's videotapes from two different Kmart stores. Andrade, "a nine-year army veteran and father of three," was similar in many ways to Ewing. He too had a long criminal history and a problem with drug abuse. Andrade had been in and out of state and federal prisons since 1982. His various crimes included petty theft, multiple residential burglaries, transportation of marijuana, and a state parole violation for escape from federal prison. Unlike Ewing, Andrade did not use or display a weapon during the commission of any of those crimes. But whereas Ewing's case arose on direct appeal, Andrade could not win his case unless the Court ruled in favor of Ewing on the Eighth Amendment issue, and even then Andrade faced an additional hurdle. Under 28 U.S.C § 2254(d), because his conviction was final and his case was in federal court on a habeas petition, the question was whether the state court's action in upholding his sentence was contrary to, or involved an unreasonable application of, clearly established federal law.

drug paraphernalia, appropriation of lost property, burglary, and possession of a firearm. Some of these offenses occurred in Los Angeles, the
others in the nearby communities of Torrance, Seal Beach, and Long
Beach. Ewing was sentenced to jail terms ranging from ten days to six
months in jail, with various terms of probation.

Ewing's most serious offenses occurred in Long Beach in 1993, when
he went on a five-week crime spree, committing three residential burglaries and a robbery in which he brandished a knife. All of the burglaries
were committed in a single residential complex. On two occasions he
encountered a resident. One of the victims was asleep on her living room
sofa and awakened to find Ewing trying to disconnect her video recorder.
Ewing ran out the front door when the victim screamed. On the other
occasion, Ewing accosted a male victim in the mail room of the apartment, told him he had a gun, and ordered him to hand over his wallet.
When the victim resisted, Ewing threatened the victim with a knife and
forced him into his apartment, where Ewing took the victim's money and
credit cards. Ewing was arrested when he once again returned to the
apartment complex. The knife he had used in the robbery and a cocaine
pipe were found in the patrol car used to drive him to the police station.
Ewing was convicted, sentenced to nine years and eight months in
prison, and released on parole in 1999 after having served less than six
years.

On March 12, 2000, when he was just ten months out of prison and
still on parole for the burglaries and robbery, Ewing walked into the pro
shop of The Lakes of El Segundo golf course. Although the name
suggests an exclusive country club, The Lakes is a municipal golf course
run by the city of El Segundo.[43] El Segundo, one of many separate
municipalities in Los Angeles County, is a predominantly white town
just south of Los Angeles International Airport.[44]

Ewing entered The Lakes pro shop and looked at golf clubs for ten
to fifteen minutes before purchasing a token that could be retrieved for
golf balls on the driving range. He asked for directions to the driving
range and then walked back to the golf clubs. As Ewing left the pro shop,
the employee running the shop noticed that Ewing was noticeably
limping, that he was heading to the parking lot rather than the driving
range, and that he looked "totally out of place." The employee called
911. When the police arrived at the parking lot, they observed Ewing

---

43. Information about the golf course and the pro shop, including photos, is available
at http://www.golfthelakes.com (last visited Sept. 15, 2011).

44. In the 2000 census, it had a population of 16,033, of which 83.6% were white,
11% Hispanic or Latino, 4.5% Asian, and 1.2% Black or African American The median
household income of its residents was $61,341. *See* U.S. Census Bureau, Fact Sheet, El
Segundo city, California, http://www.census.gov/main/www/cen2000.html (follow "American FactFinder" hyperlink; then search for "El Segundo, California").

pulling three golf clubs from his pants leg. They arrested him on the spot.

A mug shot of Ewing provided by the El Segundo police department is reproduced below.[45]

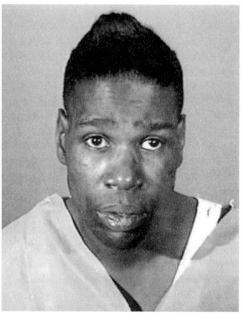

Gary Ewing's mugshot, taken by El Segundo, California police department, March 2000.

Ewing's Trial, Sentencing, and State Appeal

Ewing was charged with one count of felony grand theft in excess of $400 and one count of burglary. The case was tried to a jury, with Superior Court Judge Deanne Myers presiding. Myers, who had been on the bench for more than ten years, was a cum laude graduate of Loyola Law School with experience as both an Assistant U.S. Attorney and a

---

45. As his photo indicates, Ewing is a dark-skinned African American. There is no way to know whether his race had any effect on his case. Was he acting so oddly that anyone would have noticed him in the pro shop? Or was his race one of the reasons he looked "out of place" in El Segundo? Once he was arrested, did his race (and his appearance) influence the prosecutors in some subtle way? Or the sentencing judge? At a systemic level, one might also ask whether racial concerns affected the passage of the three strikes laws. There is some evidence that racial stereotypes, amplified by the news media's treatment of crime, played a role in the support for California's three strikes law and other harsh sentencing laws. *See generally* Beale, *supra* note 7 (describing media coverage of crime during the 1990s and its relationship to public support for punitive policies).

civil litigator. Ewing was represented by Los Angeles County Deputy Public Defender Gail Bristo, and the state was represented by Deputy District Attorney Jodi Link.

The state's main witness was the pro shop employee, who testified that the clubs found in Ewing's possession were Callaway golf clubs priced at $399 each, that they still had the shop's identification numbers on them, and that Ewing had neither paid for them nor had permission to remove them. The jury found Ewing guilty of grand theft but acquitted him of burglary (which required proof of intent to commit larceny or some other felony at the time of entry into the pro shop).

The jury's verdict set the stage for the sentencing phase. The prosecution charged that the grand theft conviction was Ewing's third strike. Although grand theft normally carries a maximum three-year sentence, if treated as a third strike it would require a prison sentence of twenty-five years to life. Ewing might not have been charged as a third striker if the theft had occurred in another county, but Los Angeles County District Attorney Gil Garcetti generally took a hard line on three strikes cases.[46] Ewing's timing was particularly bad because Garcetti was just then in a tough (and ultimately losing) reelection race against a challenger who campaigned on a policy that third strikes should be charged only when proportional to the crime.[47]

Judge Myers had discretion not to sentence Ewing as a third striker, and two options were open to her under state law. First, state law defined grand theft as a "wobbler" offense, which meant it could be treated as either a felony or a misdemeanor. If Judge Myers treated the wobbler as a misdemeanor, rather than a felony, it could not be Ewing's third strike. Alternatively, Judge Myers had the authority to "strike"— or dismiss—either of the prior offenses that the prosecution was counting as the first and second strikes "in furtherance of justice,"[48] meaning Ewing would not yet have reached his third strike even if the wobbler were treated as a felony.

Judge Myers held a sentencing hearing. Deputy District Attorney Link presented evidence that Ewing had previously been convicted of first degree robbery and three separate residential burglaries in 1993, all of which were classified as serious or violent felonies under the three strikes laws. Link urged Judge Myers to sentence Ewing as a third striker, emphasizing his long criminal record. "He has had 10 convictions in his lengthy criminal history for someone as young as he is. . . .

---

46. Garcetti's policy is discussed *supra* at 434.

47. Cooley's campaign to unseat Garcetti is discussed *supra* at 434–435. In 2010 Cooley announced a plan to run for Attorney General and Mike Reynolds attacked him as weak on crime. See infra at 455.

48. For a discussion of the judge's discretion in three strikes cases, see supra at 435.

He has repeatedly been placed on probation. He has repeatedly failed miserably at probation. He goes to state prison, he gets paroled. He fails miserably on parole."[49]

Ewing's lawyer, Bristo, asked Judge Myers to treat his current offense as a misdemeanor or to strike one of the first two offenses on which the prosecution was relying. She argued that all of Ewing's offenses were drug related, and that he had never received assistance for his drug problems. In addition to his drug addiction, Ewing was battling full blown AIDS. At the time of trial, complications from the disease had caused him to go blind in one eye (and he later began to lose vision in the other). Bristo portrayed Ewing as a terminally ill man who posed no threat of violence in the future.

Ewing himself addressed the court, stating, "I would just like to beg the mercy of the court asking that any sentence I be given be suspended and I'm given a chance in a drug rehab to get my life together. I don't have very long and the little time I do have left to live I want to do something, make myself better." Several people, including a jail chaplain, wrote letters on Ewing's behalf. One such letter suggested that Ewing could spend the remainder of his life acting as an AIDS advocate and warning others about the dangers of drug abuse. The judge took time during the hearing to read the letters.

At the conclusion of the hearing Judge Myers refused to strike any of Ewing's prior convictions and declined to treat the wobbler as a misdemeanor. She stated that the question was whether Ewing fell "outside the spirit and intent of the three strikes law." Noting Ewing's long record of "consistent criminal activity" and the fact that he was on parole when the grand theft offense occurred, she concluded:

> I think there is no way I could find, which is what I am required to find, you are outside the [three strike law's] spirit and the intent. I do have to consider threats to the community and although there isn't a real pattern of violent crimes that you pose a threat, you are clearly posing a threat for theft offenses.... And it's for that reason that I cannot consider and will not strike any of the strikes.

Finding that Ewing had committed a qualifying third strike, she sentenced him to imprisonment for twenty-five years to life. He would first become eligible for parole in the year 2025 at the age of sixty-three (if he were still living). After the trial and sentencing, defense attorney Bristo stated she was "really disturbed" by the life sentence for the theft of three golf clubs. When asked about Ewing's earlier crimes, including

---

49. The description of the sentencing hearing is drawn from the transcript included in the Joint Appendix, available at 2002 WL 32102970.

the residential burglaries, Bristo said that as far as she knew, "he scared [the victims] half to death but he didn't physically hurt them."[50]

Ewing appealed to the California Court of Appeal for the Second District, and Karyn Bucur, a solo practitioner, was appointed to represent him. In an unpublished opinion, the Court affirmed Ewing's conviction, rejecting both his arguments that the trial judge had erred under state law and his claim that the resulting sentence was cruel and unusual. Relying on numerous state precedents, the appeals court held that Ewing bore the burden of establishing that his sentence was unreasonable. In light of Judge Myers's conclusion that Ewing posed a threat to the community based on his recidivism and that his rehabilitative prospects were weak, she had not abused her discretion or acted arbitrarily in declining to reduce grand theft to a misdemeanor or to strike any of Ewing's priors. Nor was his sentence cruel and unusual punishment under either state or federal law. Rather, it was "reasonably proportional" to both the offense and offender, and the severity of the sentence was properly affected under the three strikes law by his prior offenses. The Court emphasized that the state's three strikes law served the legitimate goals of deterring repeat offenders and separating recidivists from the remainder of society.

Ewing Takes His Case to the Supreme Court: The Players and Their Preparation

After the California Supreme Court summarily denied Ewing's petition for review, Bucur filed a petition for a writ of certiorari to the U.S. Supreme Court which presented the following question:

> Does petitioner's twenty-five year to life prison sentence violate federal constitutional provisions against cruel and unusual punishment because his sentence is grossly disproportionate to the offense of "stealing golf clubs"?

The petition was granted on April 1, 2002,[51] and Ewing was optimistic that the Supreme Court would hold his sentence to be excessive and grant him relief.[52]

Quin Denvir was added to the Ewing defense team to brief and argue the case in the Supreme Court. Denvir, then sixty-two years old, was the Federal Public Defender in Sacramento. He had already argued two Supreme Court cases and had an impressive and varied professional background. After graduating from Notre Dame he obtained a master's

---

50. Carla Hall, *Thefts Were Petty, but Ruling Won't Be*, L.A. Times, Apr. 7, 2002, at 2:1.

51. Ewing v. California, 535 U.S. 969 (2002).

52. Jan Crawford Greenburg, *Court Upholds 3–Strikes Sentencing*, Chi. Trib., Mar. 6, 2003, at 1.

in Economics at American University and a law degree from University
of Chicago School of Law with honors. Although he had experience with
private firms in both Washington, D.C. and California, Denvir had also
spent nearly twenty years working for various federal and state organizations representing indigents. Before representing Ewing, Denvir had
been involved in several high profile cases. Most notably, he negotiated a
plea agreement that spared Unabomber Ted Kaczynski from the death
penalty.[53] Colleagues spoke of Denvir in glowing terms, calling him a
"complete lawyer," "a guy with a first-class academic pedigree," "smart
and even-tempered."[54] Judy Clark, Denvir's co-counsel in the Kaczynski
case, said that "Quin Denvir comes as close as anyone I know to walking
on water."[55] Speaking of his motivation and his role as federal defender,
Denvir said, "What I like the most, is [to] represent the nameless
defendants facing the might of the federal government. Helping the little
guys with no resources get through the federal criminal justice system is
what the office is all about."[56]

The state was represented in the Supreme Court by Deputy Attorney General Donald De Nicola. De Nicola was born in Brooklyn, New
York, in 1951. He received his bachelor's degree at Fordham University
and his law degree from Georgetown University Law Center.[57] De Nicola
joined the California Attorney General's Office directly from law school
and worked in the criminal division, specializing in state appellate and
federal habeas cases. At the time De Nicola took over the Ewing case, he
had been in the Attorney General's office for almost twenty-five years.
This was his first U.S. Supreme Court argument, but it would not be his
last.[58] De Nicola's first reaction was that it would be an uphill battle to
defend a twenty-five year to life sentence for stealing three golf clubs,
but as he immersed himself in the case he became convinced of the
state's argument of the importance of judicial deference to legislative

---

53. For more information about the Unabomber investigation, the prosecution of
Kaczynski, and a critical appraisal of Denvir's role in the case, see Michael Mello, *The
United States versus Theodore John Kaczynski: Ethics, Power, and the Invention of the
Unabomber* (1999). Many of the documents in the case are available online at http://
unazod.com/sacbee.pdf (last visited Feb. 10, 2010).

54. Howard Mintz, *Complete Lawyer in Kaczynski's Corner*, The Recorder, June 18,
1996, *available at* http://www.lectlaw.com/files/cur71.htm

55. Denny Walsh, *A "Lawyer's Lawyer": Quin Denvir Prepares to Retire After a
Decade of Defending the Poor*, Sacramento Bee, Oct. 12, 2005, at B1.

56. *Id.*

57. Email from Donald De Nicola to Sara Beale (Feb. 10, 2010), (on file with author).

58. In 2006, De Nicola was named Deputy State Solicitor General and given supervisory responsibility for all California criminal cases in U.S. Supreme Court and California
Supreme Court. He argued *Giles v. California*, 554 U.S. 353 (2008), a major confrontation
clause decision.

judgments as well as federal deference to the states.[59] The United States participated in the case as an amicus supporting the state, and De Nicola worked closely with an attorney from the Office of the Solicitor General who peppered him many times a day with emails as they prepared their briefs, requiring De Nicola to think through every possible issue and argument.

The United States was represented at the oral argument by Michael Chertoff, then Assistant Attorney General for the Criminal Division in the Department of Justice. Chertoff was an experienced prosecutor who had prosecuted mob and political corruption cases as an assistant U.S. attorney and later served as U.S. Attorney for New Jersey.[60]

The Earlier Eighth Amendment Cases

In three previous cases, the Supreme Court had considered the question whether an individual sentence for a term of years constituted cruel and unusual punishment under the Eighth Amendment. The cases had produced sharp divisions within the Court about the question whether the Eighth Amendment included a prohibition against disproportionate punishments in non-capital cases, and, if so, how robust the proportionality review should be.

Three views had emerged in the prior cases. One view, championed by Justice Antonin Scalia, was that the proportionality principle is limited to death penalty cases, and is not applicable to sentences of imprisonment.[61] Put simply, death is different, and the proportionality review that courts undertake in death penalty cases cannot be carried over into non-capital cases. Other members of the Court agreed on the principle that the Eighth Amendment prohibits both capital and non-capital sentences that are disproportionate to the crime committed, but they disagreed on the proper standard for proportionality. The second view, advanced by Justice Lewis Powell, held that the Eighth Amendment requires a proportionality analysis grounded on three "objective" factors that include a comparative review of sentences both within and between jurisdictions.[62] The third view, articulated by Justice Anthony Kennedy, was a stripped-down version of the three-factor test designed

---

59. Telephone Interview with Donald De Nicola, Deputy Attorney General, California Department of Justice (Feb. 11, 2009).

60. Chertoff subsequently served briefly as a judge on the Third Circuit, from which he resigned to take the post of Secretary of Homeland Security. He is credited as one of the co-authors of the USA PATRIOT Act. A brief biography of Chertoff is available on the website of the Chertoff Group, which he founded to advise on crisis management, global security, and risk identification. http://www.chertoffgroup.com/team.html.

61. *See* Harmelin v. Michigan, 501 U.S. 957, 984, 985 (1991).

62. *See* Solem v. Helm, 463 U.S. 277 (1983).

to be substantially more deferential to state legislative judgments.[63] Under this view, unless a court first finds that the penalty is "grossly disproportionate" to the gravity of the offense, it should not undertake any comparative review.

In the early 1980s, the Court decided two cases involving recidivist sentences by votes of 5–4. Although the results in the two decisions were difficult to reconcile, it seemed that by a bare majority the Court had adopted Justice Powell's three-factor test for proportionality.

The first case, *Rummel v. Estelle*,[64] upheld a life sentence for the offense of obtaining $120 by false pretenses in the case of a defendant whose only prior convictions were for two nonviolent property offenses. The majority rejected the three factor approach proposed by the dissenters, and suggested that proportionality review (if it existed) would apply only in an extreme (and presumably hypothetical) case "if a legislature made overtime parking a felony punishable by life imprisonment."[65]

Just three years later, in *Solem v. Helm*,[66] the Court reversed a life sentence for a recidivist convicted of a seventh non-violent felony, writing a $100 check on a nonexistent account. The dissenters in *Rummel* were now in the majority, joined by Justice Harry Blackmun, who provided the swing vote but did not write in either case.[67]

In an opinion written by Justice Powell, the new five-member majority in *Solem* held that the proportionality analysis under the Eighth Amendment should be guided by three objective factors:

> (i) the gravity of the offense and the harshness of the penalty; (ii) the sentences imposed on other criminals in the same jurisdiction; and (iii) the sentences imposed for commission of the same crime in other jurisdictions.

But surprisingly the majority opinion did not overrule *Rummel v. Estelle*; instead, it noted that defendant in *Rummel* had been eligible for parole, while the defendant in *Solem* was not.

---

63. *Harmelin*, 501 U.S. at 997–1001 (Kennedy, J., concurring).

64. 445 U.S. 263 (1980).

65. 445 U.S. at 274 n. 11.

66. 463 U.S. 277 (1983).

67. The case also involved some extenuating circumstances: the defendant, an alcoholic, went on a bender after getting paid and was surprised to awake and discover he had more money than when he began drinking. When he was charged with writing a check on a nonexistent account, he pled guilty without the assistance of counsel. It seems doubtful that he realized this would subject him to a mandatory life sentence without possibility of parole. Some or all of these features may have tipped the balance for Justice Blackmun. Legal historians may be able to shed light on the question of what factors motivated Justice Blackmun. At his death, Blackmun donated his papers to the Library of Congress, and the catalogue indicates that Box 385 contains material related to the *Solem* case.

The majority that came together briefly in *Solem* did not hold. Eight years later, in 1991, in *Harmelin v. Michigan*,[68] the Court upheld a first-time drug offender's life sentence for possession of 672 grams of cocaine. Although the amount suggested that the drugs were intended for distribution, the state had neither charged nor proved intent to distribute. The Michigan law, which was enacted in response to the crack epidemic, imposed a mandatory life sentence without possibility of parole for anyone found in possession of 650 grams or more of the drug. The case produced no majority opinion. Four members of the Court adhered to *Solem v. Helm*'s three-factor analysis and concluded that the sentence was cruel and unusual punishment for mere possession. Two members of the Court took the view that the Eighth Amendment included no proportionality principle in non-capital cases. Writing for the three swing votes, Justice Kennedy sought to define a middle position. While not overruling *Solem*, Justice Kennedy wrote that the focus on the first step of the analysis should be to determine whether the sentence in question is grossly disproportionate. Only if a sentence meets this threshold should the second and third factors of the *Solem* test, the comparative analysis, come into play. In Justice Kennedy's view, this version of the proportionality standard gives appropriate deference to the states' legislative policy judgments. But the Justices who advocated continued adherence to the three part *Solem* test saw the Kennedy reformulation as unworkable: how, they asked, can courts determine whether a penalty is grossly disproportionate without comparing it to other sentences?

When the Court granted certiorari in the California three strikes cases, more than ten years had passed since the decision in *Harmelin* and the Court's membership had changed. Justices Blackmun, Thurgood Marshall, and Byron White had retired, and Justices Stephen Breyer, Ruth Bader Ginsburg, and Clarence Thomas had taken their places. *Ewing* gave the Court an opportunity to revisit the debate about the Eighth Amendment and proportionality review in non-capital cases.

The Oral Argument[69]

At the beginning of the oral argument, one of the justices asked defense counsel Quin Denvir about Ewing's record and then commented that "the purpose of the three strikes law, as I understand it, is to take off the street that very small proportion of people who commit an enormously high proportion of crimes." Ewing, the justice suggested,

---

68. 501 U.S. 957 (1991).

69. A transcript of the oral arguments are available at *Ewing v. California*, 538 U.S. 11 (2003) (No. 01–6978), 2002 WL 31525401. The description that follows is drawn from that transcript. The transcript does not identify the individual justices, though occasionally the identity of a justice is clear from the context.

was "precisely the kind of person you want to get off the streets" because he's "obviously going to do it again."

Denvir responded that, under *Solem v. Helm*, the focus for determining whether Ewing's sentence was disproportionate must be on the offense for which he was sentenced, although his prior record could be "relevant" because it aggravated the crime for which he was being sentenced. The sentence for a recidivist can be a stiffened penalty for the instant crime, Denvir argued, but it may not be punishment for the prior offenses. Denvir struggled to explain and justify this distinction. He argued that any added punishment for prior offenses would offend the Double Jeopardy Clause. Accordingly, he asserted, the focus at sentencing must be on what the defendant did on this occasion.

One of the justices observed that Denvir's characterization of the case as one about a life sentence for stealing three golf clubs made it seem "like we're some judges out of Victor Hugo," but Denvir was really asking the Court to completely ignore recidivism. And recidivism, the justice said, was "the whole purpose of the California law." Denvir responded that California could impose a reasonable enhancement of the normal penalty for grand theft for a recidivist, but at some point that enhancement becomes unreasonable.

Under *Harmelin*, Denvir argued, the sentence in this case was grossly disproportionate. Regardless of his recidivism, a sentence of twenty-five years to life was disproportionate to the offense for which Ewing had been convicted.

Denvir was then asked about a hypothetical defendant who had committed a much longer series of offenses, such as 100 thefts of golf clubs; couldn't the state ever say enough is enough, and give him a life sentence? No, Denvir responded, the offense for which he has been convicted is still just stealing golf clubs, not a serious offense like robbery, rape, or murder. Otherwise, he argued, someone who had 100 jaywalking offenses could be given a life sentence. But, a justice responded, jaywalking does not hurt others as does theft, which may also lead to a physical confrontation. True, responded Denvir, but when California assessed the degree of harm from grand theft, it set the maximum penalty at three years in prison. Moreover, he noted, Ewing was certainly trying to avoid any physical confrontation. This led to a light hearted question by a member of the Court: "Was he a very tall man, or were these irons rather than wood[s]?" Denvir responded that Ewing was not a tall man, and he had no idea how he had managed to get the clubs out of the shop.

The respondent's argument was divided between California and the United States as amicus in support of the state. Donald De Nicola began his argument for the state by emphasizing that California had revised its sentencing laws to move away from a more lenient policy of rehabilitation to a tougher policy of incapacitation. The first question to him was whether he knew of any case anywhere in the U.S. within the past 100 years in which a person, even one with a serious prior record, had received as long a sentence as Ewing for stealing property worth $1,200. When De Nicola said he did not know, a member of the Court asked how they could determine proportionality without such empirical evidence. De Nicola responded that the major objective factor the Court should employ is the legislative definition of the offense as a felony, rather than a misdemeanor. That is the traditional line of demarcation by society of offenses that are deemed to be serious. In making these judgments, he said, the Legislature is subject to significant political and economic restraints, and courts should not second guess legislative decisions.

A member of the Court noted that the statute sounded mandatory for a third strike, but both prosecutors and judges have discretion under state law. Were there guidelines for prosecutors in exercising their discretion? De Nicola responded that there were no statewide guidelines. Each elected district attorney had the option to promulgate guidelines. Some had done so, and some of the guidelines differed. He noted that this was "rather unremarkable" because "prosecutorial discretion is always going to lead to some sort of different approach depending on local conditions."

Most of the remainder of De Nicola's argument was spent on the question whether the Eighth Amendment would bar a life sentence after a hypothetical defendant had been convicted of a long series of speeding offenses. De Nicola's first response was if the legislature classified the offenses as felonies, under *Harmelin* that would be a major objective factor suggesting the sentence was not grossly disproportionate. He was then asked whether the legislature could really provide the same penalty for speeding as for torture and murder. When De Nicola hesitated, Justice Scalia suggested a possible response: "[I]t might seem disproportionate insofar as the penal goal of punishment or retribution is concerned, but it depends on what you want your penal goals to be." If the goal is incapacitation, then the penalty would not be disproportionate. De Nicola agreed that the state had adopted and relied upon a theory of incapacitation.

Another justice followed up, asking whether allowing the state to change its penological theory would "read comparability analysis right out of the law?" How could the courts engage in comparisons, when they would have "apples and oranges instead of oranges and oranges?" De Nicola responded that under *Harmelin* the courts should defer to the state's choice of penological objectives. The Eighth Amendment should not be construed to disable the states from changing to deal with new conditions.

As amicus, Assistant Attorney General Michael Chertoff took the remainder of the respondent's time. He noted that the final questions to De Nicola had framed the issue in light of *Harmelin*, and that he read that case as establishing two principles. First, because the standard analysis is not close proportionality but rather gross proportionality, it provides an "extremely rare basis to invalidate a statute." Second, "states are entitled to adopt different penological theories, or a mix of theories." Accordingly, the Court has very limited review of comparability. Chertoff noted that the California three strikes regime was very different from the situation in *Solem*, "where you have a single judge who is apparently an outlier." In contrast, Chertoff noted, there were 200 to 300 individuals in California prisons whose third strike was a property-based crime. Ewing did not, therefore, represent a rare or exceptional case. The state of California had permissibly embraced an incapacitation theory, rather than deterrence or some other theory.

Chertoff agreed with the suggestion of a member of the Court that the proportionality analysis could be framed as the question whether the state had a reasonable basis for imposing the sentence under its statute given its theory of sentencing. He argued that even in the case of relatively minor felonies, the state could say that if someone is repeatedly unable to conform his conduct to the law, the state may incapacitate him. He paraphrased Blackstone, saying that "when you deal with habitual offenders, it would be cruel to the public simply to allow that person to get out again and commit their next crime." Chertoff concluded that where state law gives the sentencing judge the power to tailor the sentence to the offender and offense, for the federal courts to "come in under gross disproportionality analysis and recalibrate" would convert the federal courts "into a constitutional sentencing commission."

On rebuttal, Quin Denvir closed with a warning against allowing the state to defend Ewing's sentence as incapacitation. This "writes the Eighth Amendment protections against grossly disproportionate sentences out," because a state can "always say they want to incapacitate any criminal for any amount of time."

The Opinions

On March 5, 2003, exactly four months after the oral argument, the Supreme Court upheld Gary Ewing's conviction[70] (and also reversed the Ninth Circuit's decision granting habeas relief to three-striker Leandro Andrade).[71] The Court continued to be divided into three camps, and there was no majority opinion.

---

70. Ewing v. California, 538 U.S. 11 (2003).

71. In *Lockyer v. Andrade*, 538 U.S. 63, 77 (2003), a majority of the Court held that the gross disproportionality principle "reserves a constitutional violation for only the

Justice Sandra Day O'Connor announced the judgment of the Court in an opinion in which only Justice Kennedy and Chief Justice William Rehnquist concurred. After reviewing the Court's prior decisions, she announced that Justice Kennedy's earlier distillation of the proportionality principles in *Harmelin* would guide the plurality's application of the Eighth Amendment. She described those principles as follows:

> Justice Kennedy specifically recognized that "[t]he Eighth Amendment proportionality principle also applies to noncapital sentences." He then identified four principles of proportionality review "the primacy of the legislature, the variety of legitimate penological schemes, the nature of our federal system, and the requirement that proportionality review be guided by objective factors"—that "inform the final one: The Eighth Amendment does not require strict proportionality between crime and sentence. Rather, it forbids only extreme sentences that are 'grossly disproportionate' to the crime." Justice Kennedy's concurrence also stated that *Solem* "did not mandate" comparative analysis "within and between jurisdictions."[72]

Before turning to Ewing's sentence, Justice O'Connor reviewed the legislative history and purpose of California's three strikes laws, noting that the lawmakers responded to widespread public concern about crime by "targeting the class of offenders who pose the greatest threat to public safety: career criminals." The three strikes law in California and similar laws in other states represented a "deliberate policy choice that individuals who have repeatedly engaged in serious or violent criminal behavior, and whose conduct has not been deterred by more conventional approaches to punishment, must be isolated from society in order to protect the public safety." The Court's deference to legislative policy choices meant that sentencing policy is made by the state legislatures, not the courts. Recidivism is a serious concern, and states have a valid interest in deterring and segregating habitual criminals. Moreover, there was evidence that California's policy had been effective: four years after the passage of the three strikes law, the recidivism rate of parolees had dropped dramatically.

Against this backdrop, Justice O'Connor concluded that Ewing's sentence was not grossly disproportionate, because "[t]he gravity of his offense was not merely 'shoplifting three golf clubs.' Rather, Ewing was

---

extraordinary case," and that "it was not an unreasonable application of our clearly established law for the California Court of Appeal to affirm Andrade's sentence of two consecutive terms of twenty-five years to life in prison" for twice stealing a small number of videotapes. Justice O'Connor wrote the majority opinion for five members of the Court. Justice Souter wrote a dissenting opinion, in which Justices Stevens, Ginsburg, and Breyer concurred.

72. *Ewing*, 538 U.S. at 23.

convicted of felony grand theft for stealing nearly $1,200 worth of merchandise after previously having been convicted of at least two 'violent' or 'serious' felonies.' " If the Court did not consider Ewing's prior history in weighing the gravity of his offense, she reasoned, it would fail to accord the proper deference to the California legislature's policy judgments. Ewing's sentence was "justified by the State's public-safety interest in incapacitating and deterring recidivist felons, and amply supported by his own long, serious criminal record." It was "of no moment" that the grand theft offense was a "wobbler," since the trial judge had justifiably exercised her discretion not to reduce it to a misdemeanor.

Justice Scalia and Justice Thomas concurred in the judgment (but not O'Connor's opinion). Both took the view that the Eighth Amendment contains no proportionality principle, at least in non-capital cases. Writing separately, Justice Scalia argued that a review for proportionality cannot be squared with deference to the legislature's choice among different sentencing theories. Proportionality, he reasoned, compares the gravity of the offense to the sentence because it assumes that punishment is intended to serve a retributive function. But in enacting the three strikes law the California legislature could and did adopt a different sentencing goal: incapacitation.

The four dissenters—Justices Ginsburg, Breyer, Stevens and Souter—concluded that Ewing's sentence was disproportionate to his crime under either the original *Solem v. Helm* test or the stripped-down version first advanced by Justice Kennedy in *Harmelin*.

Writing for all of the dissenters, Justice Stevens argued that the full *Solem* three-factor proportionality review—not the very limited version advocated by Justice Kennedy—was both "capable of judicial application" and also "required by the Eighth Amendment." Stevens noted that courts already undertake Eighth Amendment proportionality reviews in the context of bail and fines, and it would be anomalous to refuse to undertake the same review in cases of imprisonment. The Eighth Amendment broadly prohibits excessive sanctions, and the absence of some bright line rule does not prevent courts from exercising their discretion in construing the outer limits of sentencing authority.

Justice Breyer dissented and took the unusual step of reading part of his dissenting opinion aloud from the bench to draw attention to it.[73] Breyer (whose opinion was joined by all of the dissenters) accepted Justice Kennedy's "gross disproportionality" test for purposes of the case and concluded that this was one of the rare cases that crossed even Kennedy's narrow gross disparity threshold. Considering the harm to society, the absolute magnitude of the crime and his culpability, he

---

73. Greenburg, *supra* note 52, at 1.

inferred that Ewing's offense ranked "well toward the bottom of the criminal conduct scale." The proper focus was on the offense that triggered the life sentence, "with recidivism playing a 'relevant', but not necessarily determinative, role." Applying these standards, the disparity between Ewing's offense and his sentence was sufficient to cross the gross disparity threshold.

Turning to an analysis of sentences within California and nationwide, Justice Breyer identified a number of points of comparison.

- Before the passage of the three strikes law, Ewing could have served no more than ten years in prison in California.

- Except for cases to which the three strikes law applies, California reserves sentences as severe as Ewing's for criminals convicted of far worse offenses, such as murder, and 90% of typical first degree murderers serve less than twenty years in prison.

- Under the Federal Sentencing Guidelines, Ewing's sentence as a recidivist would be no more than eighteen months; the Guidelines reserve a twenty-five year to life sentence for recidivists convicted of a triggering offense such as murder, air piracy, or an aggravated robbery involving the discharge of a firearm, serious bodily injury, and a loss of $1 million.

- It would be impossible for Ewing to serve more than ten years in prison in at least thirty-three jurisdictions.

- Exhaustive research had disclosed only one case from a state other than California in which an offender was serving or would serve a sentence as long as Ewing's for a similar offense.

In Justice Breyer's view, this comparative review confirmed that Ewing's sentence was grossly disproportionate, and no other considerations could justify it.

The Impact of the Decision

Although the Court could not agree on a single opinion or even a common rationale, the bottom line was clear: California's three strikes law had withstood constitutional challenge, and a majority of the Court was prepared to give substantial deference to state legislative judgments about sentencing. But the Court had not completely closed the door on constitutional challenges to sentences of imprisonment as cruel and unusual punishment. Seven members of the Court agreed that the Eighth Amendment includes a proportionality principle, and that it bars the rare punishment that is grossly disproportional to the offender's crime. But what would it take to meet that standard, if a twenty-five year to life sentence for shoplifting by a recidivist offender was not grossly disproportionate?

Ewing thus set in motion two developments. One was legislative. The Court's decision accorded deference to the state political process, thereby putting the ball back in the state legislature's court. In California, however, that political process also included both the legislature and voter initiatives. At a national level, Justice Anthony Kennedy emerged as a surprising advocate of legislative change, and, as noted below, his call to action spurred a major initiative by the American Bar Association. But *Ewing* also left open a role for the judiciary. Courts in California and elsewhere continued to review individual sentences, and in a few cases they granted relief as described more fully below.

Of course the case was also about an individual. Before his death on August 24, 2012, Gary Ewing, Inmate #J15228, was incarcerated in the California Medical Facility in Vacaville, California, and finally transferred to San Joaquin General Hospital where he died still guarded 24 hours a day by correctional officers.[74] Blind in one eye at the time of trial, he had lost the sight in his other eye due to complications of AIDS and what he regarded as substandard medical treatment in prison.[75]

Efforts to Amend the California Three Strikes Law

Because California law insulates voter initiatives from legislative change, Mike Reynolds's decision to continue his three strikes ballot initiative—even though the legislature had already enacted his proposal—made it very difficult in later years to amend the three strikes law. Under the California constitution, unless an initiative itself provides otherwise, a law enacted by the initiative process may be repealed or amended by legislation only when that legislative action is itself ultimately approved by the voters.[76] Reynolds's initiative included a specific provision governing subsequent amendment or repeal, providing that the three strikes law could be amended by two means only: a roll call vote in which two thirds of legislature concurred, or a statute passed by the normal legislative process and then approved by the voters.[77] Not surprisingly, interest groups seeking amendment or repeal of the three strikes law were unable to muster the necessary super majority in the California legislature, and a variety of reform bills introduced between 1997 and 2003 either died in committee or failed to get the necessary two-thirds approval.[78]

---

74. Email from Jane Bahnson, Reference Librarian and Senior Lecturing Fellow, Duke Law School, to Sara Beale (Sept. 18, 2012) (on file with author), based upon information provided by the California Department of Corrections. Ewing died of colon cancer and pneumonia, guarded 24 hours a day by correctional officers in the hospital. The Correctional Department reserved 25 beds at the hospital and assigned 30 officers to the ward, at a cost of $2.7 million per year. Dan Morain, *A case that proves the need to fix '3 strikes' law*, SACRAMENTO BEE, Oct. 17, 2012.

75. Telephone Interview with Quin Denvir (May 8, 2010).

76. Cal. Const. art. II, § 10(c).

77. Cal. Penal Code § 667(j).

78. Walsh, *supra* note 6, at 155, 167 n.12 (listing the proposed bills).

Accordingly, reformers sought to change the law with their own voter initiative, leading to a hotly contested campaign in which millions of dollars were spent on advertising and public opinion shifted dramatically in the days before the vote. The initiative campaign was launched in 2004 after polling found that more than 70% of respondents disapproved of applying the three strikes laws to offenses such as petty theft and other non-violent offenses.[79] Jerry Keenan, a wealthy insurance broker whose son was serving a long prison sentence, spent more than $1.5 million to finance an initiative campaign. The measure, Proposition 66, narrowed the strike zone for future cases and allowed resentencing for those convicted under the old law.[80] Unlike the original law, which allowed any felony to serve as the third strike, Proposition 66 limited third strikes (which require sentences of twenty-five years to life) to violent or serious felonies. Supporters argued that voters had been misled in 1994 to believe that the law targeted violent and serious offenders, and did not mean to sweep up persons convicted of minor property offenses. This argument seemed to resonate with voters. Less than a month before the election, a *Los Angeles Times* poll found 62% supported Proposition 66, and only 21% opposed it.[81]

The proposition, however, had numerous opponents. These included the California District Attorneys Association (which had ironically opposed the original Reynolds initiative), as well California's current governor, Arnold Schwarzenegger, and four former governors.[82] The powerful California prison guards union, which opposed the amendment, contributed $700,000 to the effort to defeat it.[83] The opponents argued that (1) the Three Strikes law was working well and had helped significantly reduce crime rates without raising prison costs, and (2) the prosecution and the courts already had discretion to exclude offenders who should not be subject to a mandatory sentence.[84] They emphasized the danger of narrowing the strike range and releasing violent offenders.

---

79. Kieso, *supra* note 32, at 233.

80. Walsh, *supra* note 6, at 154–55. The initiative (1) required that all first, second, and third strikes be serious or violent felonies, (2) excluded some felonies (including residential burglary, attempted burglary, non residential arson, and conspiracy to commit assault) from the definition of serious or violent felonies, (3) made these changes retroactive and allowed for resentencing of offenders whose crimes no longer fell within the law, (4) prohibited a defendant from earning more than one strike at a single trial, and (5) increased sentences for child molesters.

81. *Id.*

82. *Id.* at 156. Former Democratic Governors Gray Davis and Jerry Brown and former Republican Governors Pete Wilson and George Dukemejian opposed Proposition 66.

83. Kieso, *supra* note 32, at 233.

84. *Id.*

In the final two weeks before the election, wealthy individuals pumped millions into television advertising focusing on the three strikes initiative. An opposition advertising blitz was funded by Broadband founder Henry Nicolas, who provided at least $1.5 million (some news stories say he gave $3.5 million), and Governor Arnold Schwarzenegger's California Recovery Team, which contributed $1 million.[85] In response, George Soros and John Sperling both donated $500,000 for advertising to support the initiative.[86]

Fifteen-second ads featuring Governor Schwarzenegger blanketed the state in the last few days before the election. Walking among oversized mug shots of convicted felons, Schwarzenegger warned:

> Under Proposition 66, 26,000 dangerous criminals will be released from prison. Child molesters. Rapists. Murderers. Keep them off the streets and out of your neighborhood. Vote no on 66. Keep them behind bars.[87]

Was this number accurate? Although proponents and the state legislative analyst's office said that Proposition 66 would affect only about 4,000 prisoners whose prior strikes would not fall within the narrower strike zone, a study by the California District Attorneys Association (which opposed the initiative) supported the Governor's ad.[88] On the other hand, the inmates who were affected would be resentenced, not simply released.

Both sides sought to personalize the effects by focusing on individual stories. Supporters of the initiative created tombstone-shaped placards captioned "Buried Alive" with photos of inmates incarcerated for their third strikes, such as one stating that the inmate had received a sentence of twenty-five years to life for aiding in a shoplifting offense. Opponents responded with their own mug shots, such as one featuring a convicted murderer who had raped his own mother and was caught with a two foot machete etched with an anti-gay slur.[89]

Proposition 66 failed by a vote of 47.3% in favor and 52.7% opposed. Polling data suggested that 1.5 million voters changed their minds in the last ten days of the campaign, which was the fastest reversal of public opinion in decades.[90] Voters in liberal counties supported Proposition 66

---

85. Megan Garvey, *Big Money Pours in for 3–Strikes Ads*, L.A. Times, Oct. 28, 2004, at 1.

86. *Id.*

87. *Id.*

88. Megan Garvey, *Initiative Fight Puts Focus on Felons*, L.A. Times, Sept. 27, 2004, at 1.

89. *Id.*

90. Walsh, *supra* note 6, at 157–58.

regardless of relatively high crime rates, and more conservative counties with lower crime rates voted against it by wide margins.[91]

More than fifteen years after its adoption, the three strikes law continues to be a controversial issue in California politics, and Mike Reynolds remains a force to be reckoned with. In 2010, Reynolds tried to use his influence to thwart veteran Los Angeles County District Attorney Steve Cooley's run for state attorney general, denouncing Cooley as "liberal" and "pro criminal."[92] Cooley had been an advocate of introducing greater proportionality into the three strikes laws, making that his policy in Los Angeles County and backing an unsuccessful initiative effort in 2006 to narrow the statute.

Another initiative to modify the three strikes law qualified for the ballot in the November 2012 (also a presidential election). The 2012 initiative restricts third strikes to "serious or violent" felonies and authorizes resentencing for offenders currently serving life sentences if the third strike was not serious and the judge determines that a new sentence does not pose an unreasonable risk to public safety. The state estimated that it would save $70 to $90 million annually. Former LA district attorney Steve Cooley (who lost the race for the Attorney General's position to a Democrat) was one of the initiative's backers. Although polls in September showed very high levels of public support, the initiative was opposed by Mike Reynolds, the Republican party, and many law enforcement groups, including local police and state-wide associations representing California's district attorneys, police chiefs, and sheriffs.

Has California's three strikes law reduced crime? The answer depends on whom you ask. Although California government officials say the law has been a major success,[93] academic researchers are divided. The academics whose work has raised doubts about the law's effectiveness found no evidence it has had a major impact on crime. Their data show that crime was dropping in California before the passage of the three strikes law and continued to drop at the same rate after the law went into effect.[94] As for deterrence, they found only "weak evidence of a

---

91. *Id.*

92. Tim Ruttten, *GOP hard-liners take aim at Cooley*, L.A. Times, Feb. 3, 2010, at 19, *available at* 2010 WLNR 2233599.

93. *See, e.g.*, Emily Bazelon, *Arguing Three Strikes*, N.Y. Times Magazine, May 23, 2010, at 40 (noting that Governor Arnold Schwarzenegger opposed reforms of the three strikes law based on his belief that the law as originally devised was responsible for reducing crime); Bill Jones, *Why the Three Strikes Law is Working in California*, 11 Stan. L. & Pol'y Rev. 23, 23, 25 (1999) (declaring the law to be "a proven and effective tool to combat crime" because it ensures that after a certain point, "there will never again be a chance for repeat offenders to continue committing crimes").

94. Franklin E. Zimring et al., *Crime and Punishment in California: The Impact of Three Strikes and You're Out* 69 (1999).

detectible, marginal deterrence on the primary targets of the legislation," i.e., defendants eligible for treatment as second- or third strikers.[95]
Their final estimate of the short-term deterrent effect was between zero
and 2% of California crime.[96] But supporters of the law have challenged
the critics' methodology and analysis.[97] And one researcher concluded
that California's three strikes law had a significant deterrent effect on a
different group of potential offenders; after the three strikes law persons
who did not yet have a first or second strike committed fewer offenses
that would qualify as first or second strikes, but they committed more
offenses not covered by the law. According to this analysis, during the
first two years the law deterred approximately eight murders, 3,952
aggravated assaults, 10,672 robberies, and 384,488 burglaries (though
larcenies increased by 17,700).[98]

California's emphasis on incarceration—including the three strikes
law—has been costly in both financial and human terms. In 2010, the
Department of Corrections and Rehabilitation had a staff of more than
63,000, and its proposed budget for 2009 was $10.6 billion or $49,000 per
year for each inmate.[99] Despite these expenditures, the population of the
state's prisons grew to 188% of capacity.[100] After a decade of litigation, a
sharply divided Supreme Court held that the "[n]eedless suffering and
death" that had resulted from California's failure to provide medical and
mental health care in its overcrowded prisons constituted cruel and
unusual punishment.[101] Writing for the five-member majority, Justice

---

95. Franklin E. Zimring et al., *Punishment and Democracy: Three Strikes and You're
Out in California* 105 (2001) (finding arrest data showed no perceptible decline in the
percentage of offenses committed by second-strikers and only a .06% decline in the
percentage of crimes committed by third strikers).

96. *Id.* at 85.

97. Brian P. Janiskee & Edward J. Erler, *Crime, Punishment, and ROM: An Analysis
of the Case Against California's Three Strikes Law*, 39 Duq. L. Rev. 43, 43, 44, 46–47 (2000)
(arguing that Zimring et al. focused unduly on deterrence alone, ignoring incapacitation,
and they relied upon inexact sampling techniques, conflated arrests with crime rates, and
ignored anecdotal evidence of the law's deterrent effect).

98. Joanna M. Shepherd, *Fear of the First Strike: The Full Deterrent Effect of
California's Two- and Three–Strikes Legislation*, 31 J. Legal Stud. 159 (2002).

99. Cal. Dep't Corrections & Rehabilitation, Fourth Quarter 2008 Facts and Figures,
http://www.cdcr.ca.gov/Divisions_Boards/Adult_Operations/docs/Fourth_Quarter_2008_
Facts_and_Figures.pdf (last visited Feb. 8, 2010).

100. Cal. Dep't Corrections & Rehabilitation, Weekly Report of Population as of
January 27, 2010, *available at* http://www.cdcr.ca.gov/Reports_Research/Offender_
Information_Services_Branch/WeeklyWed/TPOP1A/TPOP1Ad100127.pdf (last visited Feb.
8, 2010).

101. Brown v. Plata, 131 S. Ct. 1910 (2011). The majority described a host of
disturbing conditions, including the practice of confining suicidal inmates in telephone-
booth sized cages and housing more than fifty sick inmates in a twelve-by-twenty foot room

Kennedy ordered California to reduce its prison population to no more than 137.5% of capacity within two years by prisoner releases or other means. Writing in dissent, Justice Scalia charged that the Court had approved "the most radical injunction ... in our nation's history," and he warned of the "the inevitable murders, robberies, and rapes to be committed by the released inmates."[102]

As of December, 2009, 41,009 California inmates were serving sentences for second or third strikes, including 8,570 third strikers.[103] More than 10,000 of the second and third strikers had been convicted of property crimes. The third strike offense for 479 of these inmates (including Gary Ewing) was grand theft or petty theft with a prior offense.

Justice Kennedy Calls for Reform

Recall that it was Justice Kennedy's concurring opinion in *Harmelin* which became the blueprint for the decisive votes that upheld Gary Ewing's sentence. Less than six months later, Justice Kennedy made a dramatic speech at the annual meeting of the American Bar Association in which he attacked mandatory minimum sentencing laws like the California three strikes statute and called on the legal profession to become advocates for reform.[104] He spoke of what he called the "inadequacies" and "injustices" of our prison system, drawing attention to the "remarkable scale" of incarceration in the United States and its enormous costs. He said that "[o]ur resources are misspent, our punishments too severe, our sentences too long." Finally, Kennedy called for the repeal of mandatory minimum sentences:

> Courts may conclude the legislature is permitted to choose long sentences, but that does not mean long sentences are wise or just. Few misconceptions about the government are more mischievous than the idea that a policy is sound simply because a court finds it permissible. A court decision does not excuse the political branches or the public from the responsibility for unjust laws.[105]

---

for hours on end. *Id.* At 1924. The opinion included several photographs to convey the full extent of the overcrowding. *Id.* at 1949–50.

102. *Id.* at 1950, 1957 (Scalia, J., dissenting).

103. The statistics from December 2009 are drawn from Dep't Corrections & Rehabilitation, *Second and Third Striker Felons in the Adult Institutional Population,* Dec. 31, 2009, Table 1, available at http://www.cdcr.ca.gov/Reports_Research/Offender_Information_Services_Branch/Quarterly/Strike1/STRIKE1d0912.pdf.

104. Justice Anthony M. Kennedy, Address at American Bar Association Annual Meeting (Aug. 9, 2003), *available at* http://www.supremecourtus.gov/publicinfo/speeches/sp_08-09-03.html.

105. *Id.* at 6.

The ABA responded by forming what it called the Justice Kennedy Commission, and the Commission prepared and presented a lengthy report including a large number of recommendations.[106] Most notably, the Commission recommended that all mandatory minimum sentences be repealed. The ABA House of Delegates adopted the Commission's recommendations in August 2004.

More recently, in a 2010 speech in California, Justice Kennedy criticized the state's sentencing policies and crowded prisons, and called the influence that unionized prison guards had in passing the three strikes law "sick."[107] He noted that U.S. sentences are eight times longer than those issued by European courts, and he urged voters to compare spending on prisons with spending on elementary education. Kennedy's speech provoked an editorial in the New York Times, which called for the courts to impose constitutional limits on state sentencing policy just as they had imposed such limits on punitive damages in state civil cases.[108]

Cruel and Unusual Punishment Cases After Ewing

Ewing did not shut the door completely on Eighth Amendment claims in cases involving sentences of imprisonment. Although the dissenters were unable to muster a majority for the full three-factor *Solem* test, seven members of the Court agreed that a sentence is cruel and unusual within the meaning of the Eighth Amendment if the court finds it to be grossly disproportionate to the crime and this disproportion is then confirmed by a comparative review. But *Ewing* also established that the threshold for establishing gross disproportionality is high indeed, and that proportionality must be assessed in the light of great deference to the state's legislative judgments and penal objectives.

Accordingly, successful post-*Ewing* challenges under the Eighth Amendment are rare. In the main, courts reject these charges without extended discussion, citing *Ewing* and *Harmelin*. The most difficult cases continue to arise under mandatory minimum sentencing laws. These statutes take no account of the degree of the individual defendant's involvement in the offense and allow no mitigation based on

---

106. Am. Bar Ass'n, Justice Kennedy Comm'n Reports with Recommendations to the ABA House of Delegates (Aug. 2004), *available at* http://www.abanet.org/crimjust/kennedy/JusticeKennedyCommissionReportsFinal.pdf.

107. Carol J. Williams, *Justice Kennedy Laments the State of Prisons in California, U.S.*, L.A. Times, Feb. 4, 2010, *available at* http://articles.latimes.com/2010/feb/04/local/la-me-kennedy4–2010feb04. One press report estimated that the union representing California's prison officers contributed $100,000 to the original three strikes initiative, and $1.29 million to defeat the 2004 ballot initiative. Morain, supra n. 74.

108. *See* Editorial, *Justice Kennedy on Prisons*, N.Y. Times, Feb. 16, 2010, at A26. For a discussion of the Supreme Court's decisions regarding punitive damages, see *infra* at 462.

individual offender characteristics. In some cases, these statutes require sentences even longer than Ewing's sentence of twenty-five years to life.

In cases involving mandatory minimum sentencing statutes, the courts in post-*Ewing* cases have generally upheld the sentences, deferring to the legislative judgments embodied in the statutes even when they disagree strongly with those policies. For example, in a case involving consecutive mandatory minimum sentences for federal gun offenses, a reviewing judge announced that he was bound to uphold the sentence under *Ewing* and *Harmelin* despite his sense that the sentence was profoundly unjust:

> [I]t is difficult to escape the conclusion that the current mandatory sentencing laws have imposed an immensely cruel, if not barbaric, 159–year sentence on a severely mentally disturbed person who played a limited and fairly passive role in several robberies in which no one was physically harmed.[109]

There have, however, been a few successful Eighth Amendment challenges in both the state and federal courts, including three cases involving mandatory minimum sentences for sexual offenses and sex offender registration offenses. In a Georgia case that garnered national publicity, the state supreme court held that a ten year prison sentence was grossly disproportionate to the offense committed by a seventeen year old high school honor student who received oral sex from a fifteen year old who initiated the act at a New Year's Eve party. At the time of the offense Georgia law treated consensual vaginal intercourse between teens as a misdemeanor offense, but oral sex, even if consensual, as a felony punishable by a mandatory term of ten years. A jury acquitted the teen, Genarlow Wilson, of rape but convicted him of the oral sex offense, and he was sentenced to ten years in prison. Wilson's conviction and sentence received wide negative coverage in the press,[110] and the state legislature responded by amending the law to bring down the penalties for oral sex. But because it did not make the changes retroactive, Wilson's sentence was unaffected. After Wilson had served two years of his sentence, the state supreme court voted 4–3 that his sentence constituted cruel and unusual punishment.[111] Emphasizing the "sea

---

109. United States v. Hungerford, 465 F.3d 1113, 1120 (9th Cir. 2006) (Reinhardt, J., concurring). *See also id.* at 1121 (noting that the principal who wielded the firearm during the robberies pled guilty and received a sentence one-fifth the length of that received by his mentally disturbed accomplice though the accomplice's conduct was relatively minimal and her mental illness prevented her from acknowledging her guilt).

110. *Wilson* was covered in not only the national press, but also in sports-related publications. *See, e.g.*, Wright Thompson, *Outrageous Injustice*, E–Ticket ESPN.com: The Magazine, http://sports.espn.go.com/espn/eticket/story?page'Wilson (last visited Feb. 17, 2010).

111. Humphrey v. Wilson, 652 S.E.2d 501 (Ga. 2007).

change" in the state legislature's view of the seriousness of oral sex among teens (which was now a misdemeanor) and the prevalence of oral sex among teens, the majority found Wilson's sentence to be grossly disproportionate, a view confirmed by its inter- and intra-jurisdictional comparisons.

Two California three strikes cases involving technical failures to comply with the sex offender notification laws have also been found to be cruel and unusual punishment. In the first case, the California Court of Appeal held that a sentence of twenty-five years to life was grossly disproportionate to the offense of failure to update a sex offender registration within five days of the offender's birthday.[112] The Court characterized the offense as "a passive, nonviolent, regulatory offense that posed no direct or immediate danger to society." Because there had been no change in the defendant's address since he had registered a few months before, he did not evade or intend to evade law enforcement officials, and his parole officer was aware of his residence at all times, the court found this "the most technical and harmless violation of the registration law we have ever seen." Moreover, the court's comparative review revealed that California was the only state that would require a twenty-five year to life sentence for non-compliance with an annual registration law. This state decision laid the foundation for a federal habeas decision setting aside a sentence of twenty-eight years to life for a similar technical violation of California's sex offender registration law.[113]

These cases are rare outliers, and it is clear that only a minuscule fraction of California three strikes offenders will be able to mount a successful Eighth Amendment challenge under *Ewing* and *Harmelin*. For that reason, advocates for three strikes prisoners have taken a new tack: seeking resentencing to lesser terms based upon additional information not presented at the time of sentencing. In 2009, law students from Stanford Law School convinced judges to reduce the sentences for four prisoners, and three were released after having completed reduced sentences ranging from six to ten years.[114]

---

112. People v. Carmony, 127 Cal. Rptr. 3d 365 (2005).

113. Gonzalez v. Duncan, 551 F.3d 875 (9th Cir. 2008). The state did not seek en banc review or certiorari in the U.S. Supreme Court, and Gonzalez was resentenced to nine years, which was the maximum two-strike sentence and equated roughly to the time he had already served. Email from Gia Kim, counsel for Gonzalez, to Sara Beale (March 4, 2009) (on file with author). The *Gonzalez* decision is of particular interest, because the defendant had to surmount two barriers: he had to show that his sentence was constitutionally excessive under the *Ewing/Harmelin* test, and also to show that habeas relief was warranted under *Lockyer v. Andrade*, discussed in *supra* note 42.

114. Jack Leonard, *Helping to Free 3–Strikes Inmates*, L.A. Times, May 13, 2009, at 1.

Defendants convicted of state offenses may also be able to turn to the state constitution for relief. Most state constitutions contain a provision similar to the Eighth Amendment's cruel and unusual punishment clause, and the state courts are the arbiters of those provisions. They are equally free to follow a U.S. Supreme Court decision they find persuasive, or to construe the state constitution as providing broader protection. One year after the Supreme Court upheld a mandatory life sentence for mere possession of cocaine under the Michigan statute in *Harmelin*, the Michigan Supreme Court concluded that the provision in question violated the state's provision banning cruel and unusual punishments.[115]

Conclusion

The *Ewing* decision let stand a sentence that many would find far too harsh, and it signals that the federal constitution provides only the most minimal limitations on state sentencing policy. Why did a majority of the Supreme Court decline to adopt a more exacting standard of proportionality under the Eighth Amendment? And were they right to do so?

The toughest question in *Ewing* may have been one that was not directly posed during the oral argument: if the Court had found that twenty-five years to life was disproportionate for Ewing's offense, what was the maximum sentence that the legislature could constitutionally impose? Twenty years? Fifteen? Ten? What qualifies the federal courts to override a state legislature if it chooses twenty years instead of fifteen? If there really is no good answer to this question, should courts be in the business of second-guessing the length of sentences? And if they do review such sentences, are they competent to do anything other than nullify the rarest of outliers?

Writing thirty-five years before the decision in *Ewing*, Justice Hugo Black articulated a deep skepticism of the limits of judicial competence to decide contested issues of criminal justice policy and a preference to leave issues to local decision making. He wrote:

> This Court, instead of recognizing that the experience of human beings is the best way to make laws, is asked to set itself up as a board of Platonic Guardians to establish rigid binding rules upon every small community in this large Nation.... It is always time to say that this Nation is too large, too complex and composed of too great a diversity of peoples for any one of us to have the wisdom to establish the rules by which local Americans must govern their local affairs. The constitutional rule we are urged to adopt is not merely revolutionary—it departs from the ancient faith based on the premise that experience in making local laws by local people themselves is

---

115. People v. Bullock, 485 N.W.2d 866 (Mich. 1992).

by far the safest guide for a nation like ours to follow. I suspect this is a most propitious time to remember the words of the late Judge Learned Hand, who so wisely said:

> 'For myself it would be most irksome to be ruled by a bevy of Platonic Guardians, even if I knew how to choose them, which I assuredly do not.'[116]

Ewing can be understood as a decision in which a majority of the Court avoided the temptation to usurp the role of Platonic Guardians, respecting the need for the federal courts to defer to legislative judgments and local policy making.

There are two problems with that characterization. First, to some degree the Constitution itself places the federal courts in the role of "Platonic Guardians." Creating a constitutional ban on cruel and unusual punishments necessarily makes courts the guardians of the individual's right to be free of such punishments. It forces upon courts the difficult task of determining when to set aside the sentences imposed in conformity with local law. Indeed, in holding the Cruel and Unusual Punishment Clause required California to reduce prison overcrowding, a majority of the Supreme Court stated that the "need for deference" to state judgments does not permit courts to "shrink from their obligation to 'enforce the constitutional rights of all persons.' "[117]

Second, in the decade since *Ewing* the Court has not always deferred to legislative policy choices and local decision making. In the criminal context, the Court employed proportionality analysis in *United States v. Bajakajian*[118] to strike down a forfeiture order that a majority of the Court found to be disproportionate to the crime in question and thus an "excessive fine" prohibited by the Eighth Amendment. The Court seemed to be willing to use proportionality analysis to protect a criminal defendant's property, but not his liberty. And in the civil context, the Court has been very active in policing the permissible scope of punitive damages. It has identified five factors that it will employ to determine whether a punitive damage award is reasonable, and employing those criteria it has overridden punitive damage verdicts authorized by state law and approved by local juries.[119] Are these decisions consistent with *Ewing*? Critics of the *Ewing* decision think they are not.[120] The Constitu-

---

116. Powell v. Texas, 392 U.S. 514, 547–48 (1968) (Black, J., concurring) (citation omitted).

117. Brown v. Plata, 131 S. Ct. 1910, 1928 (2011) (citation omitted).

118. 524 U.S. 321 (1998).

119. *See* Erwin Chemerinsky, *The Constitution and Punishment*, 56 Stan. L. Rev. 1049, 1071–78 (2004).

120. *See* Adam M. Gershowitz, Note, *The Supreme Court's Backwards Proportionality Jurisprudence: Comparing Judicial Review of Excessive Criminal Punishments and Excessive Punitive Damages Awards*, 86 Va. L. Rev. 1249 (2000).

tion includes an express provision banning cruel and unusual criminal punishments but includes no provision directly addressing punitive damages, and the corporate defendants in civil cases generally have more political influence and ability to protect their own interests than criminal defendants. Can judicial deference and principles of federalism justify providing criminal defendants facing long terms of imprisonment with less judicial protection than persons facing financial losses from forfeiture or punitive damages?

Biographies of Contributing Authors

Mario L. Barnes is a Professor of Law and Senior Associate Dean of Academic Affairs at the University of California, Irvine, School of Law. He also holds a joint appointment (by courtesy) in the U.C.I. Criminology, Law and Society department. He teaches and writes in the areas of criminal law, constitutional law, national security, anti-discrimination and critical theories. He previously taught at the University of Miami School of Law from 2004 to 2009 and visited at the University of Connecticut School of Law in the spring of 2009. He received his B.A. and J.D. from the University of California, Berkeley, and a Master of Laws from the University of Wisconsin, where he was a William H. Hastie Fellow from 2002–2004. Prior to entering academia, he spent twelve years on active duty in the United States Navy, including service on the commission that investigated the 2000 bombing of the USS COLE and worked as a prosecutor, defense counsel, Special Assistant U.S. Attorney, and associate admiralty counsel.

His recent work with Seattle Law School Professor Robert Chang on citation/search rates and police profiling appears in the *Seattle Law Review*. His work on race, class and equal protection (with UCI Law Dean Erwin Chemerinsky) has appeared in the *Connecticut Law Review, Georgetown Law Journal* (also with Duke Law Professor Trina Jones) and *Law and Contemporary Problems*. His work on anti-discrimination and workplace identity performance (with Iowa Law Professor Angela Onwuachi–Willig) is published in the *Indiana Law Journal* and *Wisconsin Law Review*.

He is a former trustee and active member of the Law and Society Association; he is also active in the Society of American Law Teachers and Latina/o Critical Legal Theory, Inc. (LATCRIT). In 2008, the Association of American Law Schools, Minority Groups Section, awarded him the Derrick A. Bell, Jr. Award, which is presented to a junior faculty member who, through activism, mentoring, teaching and scholarship, has made an extraordinary contribution to legal education, the legal system, or social justice.

Sara Sun Beale is a Charles L. B. Lowndes Professor of Law at Duke Law School, Duke University in North Carolina where she teaches first year criminal law and upper-class courses in criminal justice policy and federal criminal law. Her principal academic interests include the federal government's role in the criminal justice system, the laws defining federal crimes, and various issues of criminal procedure, including prosecutorial discretion. She is also interested in studying the factors that shape public attitudes regarding crime and how those attitudes ultimately translate into legislative changes in criminal laws and procedures.

Beale is the author of scores of articles, and the co-author of *Federal Criminal Law and Related Actions: Crimes, Forfeiture, the False Claims Act and RICO* (1998), *Grand Jury Law and Practice* (1986 & 2d ed. 1997), and *Federal Criminal Law and Its Enforcement* (5th ed. 2010) (with Norman Abrams and Susan Klein). Her work has been cited on many occasions by the United States Supreme Court and lower federal courts.

Beale has been active in law reform efforts related to the federal government's role in criminal justice matters. Since her appointment by Chief Justice Rehnquist in 2004, she has served as the Reporter for the Advisory Committee on Criminal Rules, which drafts the Federal Rules of Criminal Procedure. Beale previously served as an associate reporter for the Workload Subcommittee of the Federal Courts Study Committee (where much of her work focused on the Sentencing Guidelines) and as the reporter for a three branch federal-state working group convened by Attorney General Janet Reno to consider the principles that should govern the federalization of criminal law. Beale also served as a member of an American Bar Association task force studying the federalization of criminal law. She has argued before the Supreme Court on six occasions, representing the United States, and as appointed counsel for an indigent defendant.

A member of the board of the International Society for the Reform of Criminal Law, Beale has lectured or taught in Australia, Belgium, Canada, Ireland, Japan, New Zealand, the Philippines, Scotland, Spain, and Switzerland. Beale received her B.A. degree in English and her J.D. degree, *magna cum laude*, from the University of Michigan. She clerked for Judge Wade H. McCree Jr. on the 6th U.S. Circuit Court of Appeals, and served in the Office of Legal Counsel and the Office of the Solicitor General in the U.S. Department of Justice before coming to Duke in 1979.

Gabriel "Jack" Chin is a Professor of Law at the University of California, Davis School of Law where he is a teacher and scholar of Immigration Law, Criminal Procedure, and Race and Law. His writing has appeared in the *University of Pennsylvania, UCLA* and *Harvard Civil Rights—Civil Liberties* law reviews and the Duke and Georgetown law journals among others. In *Padilla v. Kentucky*, 130 S. Ct. 1473 (2010), the U.S. Supreme Court cited his *Cornell Law Review* article, *Effective Assistance of Counsel and the Consequences of Guilty Pleas*, five times in opinions agreeing that the Sixth Amendment required defense attorneys to advise clients about the possibility of deportation.

Professor Chin was Reporter for the *Uniform Collateral Consequences of Conviction Act* (2010), and the *American Bar Association Criminal Justice Standards on Collateral Sanctions and Discretionary Disqualification of Convicted Persons* (2003). Holder of a J.D. from the University of Michigan and an LL.M. from Yale Law School, he served as a defense attorney with the Legal Aid Society of New York and a prosecutor with the Arizona Attorney General's Office.

Donna Coker is a Professor of Law at the University of Miami School of Law where she teaches in the areas of criminal law, evidence, and domestic violence and the law. She has a J.D. (1991) from Stanford Law School, an M.S.W. (1982) from the University of Arkansas at Little Rock and a B.S.W. from Harding University (1978). She served as Academic Associate Dean at the University of Miami School of Law from 2005–2009. She worked as a social worker in the domestic violence field for 10 years prior to attending law school.

Professor Coker is a nationally recognized expert in domestic violence law and policy. Her research concerns three major areas: the connection between economic vulnerability and domestic violence; restorative justice and other alternative criminal justice interventions; and gender and criminal law doctrine. She is a leading critic of the disproportionate focus on the criminal justice response that characterizes U.S. domestic violence policy. Her empirical study of the adjudication of domestic violence cases in Navajo Peacemaking Courts has influenced work in the fields of restorative justice and domestic violence in the United States and abroad. Her work on the nature of "heat of passion" doctrine uncovered gender related assumptions imbedded in criminal law doctrine. She serves as co-editor, with Jonathan Simon, of the Criminal Law section of *Jotwell* (an online journal) and is an editorial board member for *New Criminal Law Review: An International and Interdisciplinary Journal*.

Markus D. Dubber is a Professor of Law at the University of Toronto. He was formerly Professor of Law and Director of the Buffalo Criminal Law Center, SUNY Buffalo. Professor Dubber's publications include *Handbook of Comparative Criminal Law* (ed. with Kevin Heller, Stanford 2010), *Police and the Liberal State* (ed. with Mariana Valverde,

Stanford 2008), *New York Criminal Law: Cases and Materials* (Aspen, 2008), *Modern Histories of Crime and Punishment* (ed. with Lindsay Farmer, Stanford 2007), *The New Police Science: The Police Power in Domestic and International Governance* (ed. with Mariana Valverde, Stanford 2006), *The Sense of Justice: Empathy in Law and Punishment* (NYU, 2006), *American Criminal Law: Cases, Statutes, and Comments* (with Mark Kelman, Foundation 2005, 2d ed. 2009), *The Police Power: Patriarchy and the Foundations of American Government* (Columbia, 2005), *Criminal Law: Model Penal Code* (Foundation, 2002), and *Victims in the War on Crime: The Use and Abuse of Victims' Rights* (NYU, 2002).

Lindsay C. Harrison is a Partner with Jenner and Block LLP in Washington D.C. She is a member of the Firm's Appellate and Supreme Court Practice, regularly participating in appellate litigation matters in a wide variety of subject matters. In 2009, she successfully argued on behalf of an asylum-seeker before the United States Supreme Court in *Nken v. Holder*. She also has an active pro bono practice which includes the ongoing representation of a death row inmate in Georgia and the submission of amicus briefs in numerous Supreme Court cases, including seminal cases involving domestic violence, voting rights, immigration law, and criminal sentencing. She holds a J.D. from Harvard Law School and a B.A. from the University of Southern California. Her articles have appeared in the *Harvard Civil Rights—Civil Liberties Law Review* and the *University of Miami Law Review*.

Leo Katz is a Frank Carano Professor at the University of Pennsylvania Law School where he focuses on criminal law and legal theory more generally. By connecting criminal law, moral philosophy and the theory of social choice, he tries to shed light on some of the most basic building block notions of the law—coercion, deception, consent, and the use and abuse of legal stratagems, among others. Katz is the author of several books: *Bad Acts and Guilty Minds: Conundrums of the Criminal Law* (University of Chicago, 1987); *Ill-Gotten Gains: Evasion, Blackmail, Fraud and Kindred Puzzles of the Law* (University of Chicago, 1996); and most recently *Why the Law Is So Perverse* (University of Chicago, 2011), which he researched with the support of a Guggenheim Fellowship. Together with Stephen Morse and Michael Moore, he edited *Foundations of the Criminal Law* (Oxford, 1999).

Joseph Kennedy is a Professor of Law at the University of North Carolina at Chapel Hill where he teaches in the areas of criminal law, computer crime law, criminal justice policy, constitutional law, and international and comparative criminal law. His research interests include the sociology and politics of mass incarceration, computer crime, and the Chinese Legal System.

Professor Kennedy's scholarly writings have been published in the *Georgetown Law Journal*, *Michigan Law Review*, *Harvard Civil Rights—Civil Liberties Law Review*, the *Journal of Law and Contemporary Problems*, *Emory Law Journal* and the *Hastings Law Review*. His article, *Monstrous Offenders and the Search for Solidarity Through Modern Punishment*, was recently selected for publication in *Criminal Law Conversations*, a collection of seminal criminal law articles published in 2009 by Oxford University Press.

Janine Young Kim is an Associate Professor of Law at Marquette University Law School where she teaches torts and courses in the area of criminal law and race. Her scholarship focuses on criminal law theory and race and the law, with recent articles appearing in such journals as the *Tulane Law Review*, *Nebraska Law Review*, and *Berkeley Journal of Criminal Law*. Prior to teaching, Professor Kim practiced for three years with Simpson Thacher & Bartlett in New York and served as a law clerk to the Honorable Alfred T. Goodwin of the United States Court of Appeals for the Ninth Circuit. Professor Kim received her J.D. from Yale Law School and both her M.A. and B.A. from Stanford University.

Erik Luna is the Sydney and Frances Lewis Professor of Law at Washington and Lee University, where he teaches and writes in the areas of criminal law and procedure. He graduated summa cum laude from the University of Southern California and received his J.D. with honors from Stanford Law School. Upon graduation, Luna was a prosecutor in the San Diego District Attorney's Office and a fellow and lecturer at the University of Chicago Law School. He has served as the senior Fulbright Scholar to New Zealand, where he taught at Victoria University Law School (Wellington, NZ) and conducted research on sentencing alternatives. Luna has also been a visiting scholar with the Max Planck Institute for Foreign and International Criminal Law (Freiburg, DE), a visiting professor with the Cuban Society of Penal Sciences (Havana, CU), and a visiting professional in the Office of the Prosecutor of the International Criminal Court (The Hague, NL). Prior to coming to Washington and Lee University, Luna was the Hugh B. Brown Professor of Law at the University of Utah and co-director of the Utah Criminal Justice Center. His recent scholarship includes *The Prosecutor in Transnational Perspective* (Oxford, 2012) and *The Law of Terrorism* (forthcoming 2013). Luna has testified before Congress and the U.S. Sentencing Commission, and his commentary has appeared in print and broadcast media (e.g., *The New York Times*, *The Economist*, and National Public Radio). He is an adjunct scholar with the Cato Institute and a project director with the Alexander von Humboldt Foundation.

Susan D. Rozelle is a Professor of Law at Stetson University College of Law, and past chair of the Association of American Law Schools Criminal Justice Section. Prior to joining the legal academy, Professor Rozelle clerked for the Massachusetts Appeals Court and the Supreme Judicial Court of Massachusetts. Her work with Nutter, McClennen & Fish, founded by former U.S. Supreme Court Justice Louis Brandeis, focused on appellate practice.

Professor Rozelle's primary research interests lie in the areas of criminal responsibility and death qualification. Her scholarship has been cited by the New York Governor's Council on Capital Punishment, and by the Law Commission for England and Wales in its Report to Parliament recommending reform to the law of murder and manslaughter. She has presented at scholarly conferences across the country, from Georgetown University Law Center to the University of California at Berkeley, and has appeared as a featured legal commentator on the ABC, CBS, NBC, and FOX evening news, as well as on NPR and FOX News Radio.

Jeannie Suk is Professor of Law at Harvard Law School where she has taught criminal law, criminal procedure, family law, and the law of art, fashion, and the performing arts. Before joining the faculty in 2006, she served as a law clerk to Justice David Souter on the United States Supreme Court, and to Judge Harry Edwards on the U.S. Court of Appeals for the D.C. Circuit. She was educated at Yale (B.A. 1995), Oxford (D.Phil. 1999) where she was a Marshall Scholar, and Harvard Law School (J.D. 2002). Her book, *At Home in the Law: How the Domestic Violence Revolution is Transforming Privacy*, was awarded the Law and Society Association's Herbert Jacob Prize. Her writing has also appeared in *Yale Law Journal*, *Stanford Law Review*, *Columbia Law Review*, *Wall Street Journal*, *Slate*, and the New York Times. She has been a Guggenheim Fellow and a MacDowell Colony Fellow. She is an Advisor for the American Law Institute's revision of the Model Penal Code's Sexual Assault and Related Offenses.

Robert Weisberg is an Edwin E. Huddleson, Jr. Professor of Law at the Stanford University Law School and works primarily in the field of criminal justice, writing and teaching in the areas of criminal law, criminal procedure, white collar crime, and sentencing policy. He also founded and now serves as faculty co-director of, the Stanford Criminal Justice Center (SCJC), which promotes and coordinates research and public policy programs on criminal law and the criminal justice system, including institutional examination of the police and correctional systems. Professor Weisberg was a consulting attorney for the NAACP Legal Defense Fund and the California Appellate Project, where he worked on death penalty litigation in the state and federal courts. In addition, he served as a law clerk to Justice Potter Stewart of the U.S. Supreme Court and Judge J. Skelly Wright of the U.S. Court of Appeals for the District of Columbia Circuit. In 1979, Professor Weisberg received his J.D. from Stanford Law School, where he served as President of the *Stanford Law Review*. Professor Weisberg is a two-time winner of the law school's John Bingham Hurlbut Award for Excellence in Teaching.

Before joining the Stanford Law School faculty in 1981, Professor Weisberg received a Ph.D. in English at Harvard and was a tenured English professor at Skidmore College. Drawing on that background, he is one of the nation's leading scholars on the intersection of law and literature and co-author of the highly praised book *Literary Criticisms of Law*.

†